1395-

Windows NT
Security Handbook

Tom Sheldon

Osborne **McGraw-Hill**

Berkeley   New York   St. Louis   San Francisco
Auckland   Bogotá   Hamburg   London   Madrid
Mexico City   Milan   Montreal   New Delhi   Panama City
Paris   São Paulo   Singapore   Sydney
Tokyo   Toronto

D1377238

Osborne **McGraw-Hill**
2600 Tenth Street
Berkeley, California 94710
U.S.A.

For information on translations or book distributors outside the U.S.A., or to arrange bulk purchase discounts for sales promotions, premiums, or fundraisers, please contact Osborne **McGraw-Hill** at the above address.

The Windows NT Security Handbook

1234567890 DOC 9987

ISBN 0-07-882240-8

Publisher
Brandon A. Nordin

Acquisitions Editor
Wendy Rinaldi

Project Editor
Nancy McLaughlin

Associate Editor
Cynthia Douglas

Editorial Assistant
Daniela Dell'Orco

Technical Reviewer
Dave Kosiur

Copy Editors
John Gildersleeve
Carl Wikander

Proofreader
Stefany Otis

Computer Designer
Jani P. Beckwith

Illustrator
Leslee Bassin

Series Design
Marcela Hancik

Cover Design
Ted Mader Associates

To my pals,
the Colgans, and of course, Becky and Alicia

About the Author...

Tom Sheldon is no stranger to the computer industry. A certified network engineer, he has worked since the late 1970s as a computer programmer, consultant, and network administrator. His articles have appeared in *BYTE, PC World*, and *PC* magazines, and he has written more than 20 books, including the *Windows NT Web Server Handbook, NetWare 4.1: The Complete Reference*, the *LAN Times Encyclopedia of Networking*, the best-selling *Windows 95 Made Easy*, and the upcoming *LAN Times Guide to Building Microsoft Networks*. Tom is a member of Microsoft's Developer Network, and he participates in the beta testing program for their network and Internet products. He is also familiar to thousands of computer users who have learned by watching his popular educational videotapes.

Table of Contents

III ▬▬ General Network Security Issues

12 ▬▬ Client/Workstation Security Issues 305

Acknowledgments

Thanks to Wendy Rinaldi, who pushed a hard schedule but kept me on track, and to Daniela Dell'Orco, Nancy McLaughlin, Cynthia Douglas, Heidi Poulin, Marcela Hancik and the whole hardworking Production staff, Scott Rogers, and everybody else at Osborne.

Introduction

In the early '80s, I spent a summer in Ireland at the home of my father-in-law. Much of that time was spent driving the countryside looking for castles. Upon seeing any pile of rocks, we stopped the car and crossed the cow pasture to see what remained of a once-mighty structure. Many castles and tower homes were broken down over the years by farmers who used the rock for fences and building materials. Some suffered the blows of cannons.

In a way, this book is a natural outcome of that summer. I completely immersed myself in Irish history and books about castle design, defensive systems, vulnerabilities, attacks, and warfare of the time. The computer systems we install today require "virtual castles" that can withstand attacks of a different kind—attackers that slip into your systems through unknown or unprotected holes and do damage for any number of reasons. Perhaps the attackers are competitors who want to shut down your systems or ex-employees with a grudge. Whatever the case, the threat is real and you need defensive systems to stop them. Indeed, the castle analogy aptly described the kinds of defenses you need to put in place. You might want to jump ahead to "Defensive Strategies" on page 462 for a continuation of this castle analogy. Figure 18-2 illustrates a medieval castle design that you might want to adapt for your information defense system!

In 16th century Ireland, castles that had stood for years were brought down by the cannon. I can't help but think that our computer systems might suffer a similar fate. Indeed, as this book was going to press, a new threat emerged for Internet-connected systems called the **SYN attack**. In such an attack, a malicious person floods a Web server with session-request packets. The Web server tries to establish a session for each of those requests, but the malicious user makes sure that a response is never sent to the server after the initial request. It's like someone reaching out to shake your hand, then pulling it away when you reach out with your hand. The server keeps waiting to "shake hands" with the hacker's system and eventually crashes when its runs out of resources to handle the load. The hacker has caused a **denial-of-service** attack in which legitimate users cannot access the system.

This type of attack was successfully staged against Panix, a New York Internet Service Provider in September of 1996. Thousands of people were denied Internet access at the time, and similar attacks took place elsewhere, apparently after the attack strategy was discussed openly on the Internet. While no data was destroyed, this incident points out how vulnerable our information systems and networks are. In many cases, we just don't know what all the vulnerabilities are.

About This Book

This book is about security for Microsoft Windows NT computers as stand-alone desktop systems or as network-connected workstations and servers. Some of the information presented here will scare you into taking action to protect your systems, and it will show you how to put together a defensive strategy.

Paranoia is good thing. The more paranoid you are, the more likely you are to protect your systems from attack. Reading this book and just concentrating on security is a good start. In fact, you need to start planning and managing your network with security as the number one goal. Many network administrators get so wrapped up in attaining performance or some other objective that they leave their systems wide open for attack. What good is the fastest server or faster network if some unknown user can bring your system down at any time and thus deny access to legitimate users?

Security has been a big concern in the last few years, primarily because more and more organizations are connecting their networks to the Internet. But security threats come from both the Internet and from internal sources. In fact, the internal threat is considered the biggest problem for a number of reasons. First, internal users know more about your systems and where valuable data is located. Internal users are also more likely to hijack some other user's account or access some system because improper security measures are in place. You probably trust many of your coworkers, but in an open internetworked environment, you need to reevaluate how much trust you want to extend.

People also have more knowledge about computers and networks and know how to access information. Often, a person gets curious and starts peeking into places where they don't belong. Before long, they discover all the areas of your network where security is weak. Many organizations have installed TCP/IP networks in the last few years, and this network technology only helps hackers because it allows them to extend their electronic reach to many interconnected networks. The Internet is one big TCP/IP network. If you connect your internal network to it, anyone anywhere in the world can access your systems. But only if you leave the door wide-open.

This book is about tightening the security on your Windows NT systems and networks to prevent malicious users from attacking your systems and valuable data. There are four main sections, as described below.

- ◆ **Part 1** provides a general description of security problems on networks in general and networks that are connected to the Internet. You'll learn the scary truth about hacker and cracker attacks. You'll also learn how to protect your systems and about the security features in Windows NT.

- ◆ **Part 2** gets into more detailed information about Windows NT security. You'll learn many interesting tips and tricks about security features for domains, user accounts, file systems, and management functions.

- ◆ **Part 3** covers security topics related to the general network environment in which Windows NT systems may be running, including mixed heterogeneous environments that include UNIX, Novell NetWare, and Apple Macintosh systems. You'll also learn about how clients on the network can affect Windows NT security. There are also chapters on securing remote connections and wide area networks.

- ◆ **Part 4** covers Internet- and TCP/IP -specific security threats and countermeasures. You'll find descriptions of how hackers use scanning and sniffing tools to get information about your networks, view transmitted information, and even hijack user sessions to make your servers think that they are legitimate users. You'll also learn about building firewalls between your networks and the Internet (or your own internal networks) and how to do business on the Internet in a safe and secure way.

- ◆ **The Appendixes** should certainly not be overlooked. If you want to learn about the Windows NT security architecture, the logon and authentication process, or how to protect vital system information, refer to the back of the book. You'll also find a discussion of valuable tools and techniques that can help you protect your system.

Keep in mind that this book points out known security problems and makes recommendations that can help you secure your systems and networks. Every environment is different and some of the suggestions provided here may not be appropriate in your case. Always test any changes or security recommendations mentioned in this book on a non-production test platform before you implement those changes on an actual system.

Visit Our Web Page!

Need more information? Want to get the latest news about Windows NT security problems and solutions? Need training materials or management guidelines? Then visit our page on the World Wide Web. Just point your Web browser at **www.ntresearch.com**. You'll see a page similar to the following and find information such as:

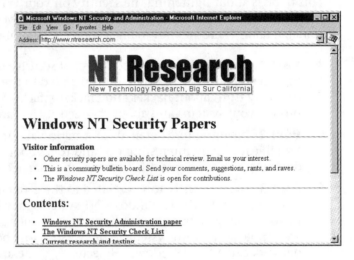

♦ The latest information about security in the Windows NT environment

♦ Security alerts and information about fixes and patches for Windows NT

♦ Security white papers

♦ The "Windows NT Security Checklist" to help you evaluate site security

♦ Links to important Web sites with security information

♦ Training material and security policy information

♦ Update news from Microsoft and elsewhere

If you're not connected to the World Wide Web, then call us at 1-800-280-9555 and ask for our Windows NT security information. We'll mail you information as soon as possible. You can also write us at:

NT Research
Big Sur Multimedia
PO Box 947
Cambria CA 93428

PART 1

Security Boot Camp

CHAPTER 1

The Network Landscape: LANs and Global Networks

Information systems have evolved in the last few decades from centralized and highly secure host-based systems to decentralized *enterprise computing systems,* in which computers and information resources are distributed throughout an organization. It is often said that in the enterprise model, "the network is the computer."

In the 1980s, users gained important ground in the information age with the personal computer. Suddenly they could store vast quantities of information at their own desktops, rather than on centralized computers controlled by "information czars." But of course the potential for data theft, corruption, and eavesdropping increased. The situation got worse as companies installed local area networks (LANs) to connect everything together, and in the process increased opportunities for security breaches. Ultimately, the systems became so large that they were hard to manage effectively.

To make things still worse, users of laptop computers and remote systems demanded connections into corporate offices from their homes, from hotel rooms, and from customer sites. Then the Internet became popular, and people inside the company wanted to connect out to it. To most administrators, the Internet is a nightmare that can potentially open the company's entire internal network to outsiders.

With all of these security risks, you need to maximize *your* system's security in every way possible. Just thinking about it is helpful. The more you concentrate on security, the more likely you'll be to recognize important things you can do to protect your company's assets—and your job.

That's what this book is about. While it can't possibly provide all the answers for your security needs, it will help you take advantage of the security features in Windows NT to build strong defenses. Keep in mind that no operating system can solve your security problems, because the solution involves much more than the operating system. It includes physical security, well-designed policies, user cooperation, and much more. Your job as the network administrator or security officer is to learn as much as you can about security and about your system, and then to use this information to create a secure environment.

From PCs to Enterprise Networks

In the last few decades, information systems have gone from large, centralized computers to decentralized desktop systems and departmental networks. Information is no longer stored in a safe location at a single site, but everywhere in the organization. This section discusses these systems and notes the weak points where security managers need to focus their attention. As you'll see by the end of this chapter, there is a subtle trend toward putting data back at centralized locations.

Personal Computers

The personal or desktop computer is the starting point for this discussion. It is the place where people store all sorts of information about themselves, the projects they are working on, and all the applications that they depend on for their jobs. Security, however, is basically non-existent:

♦ Most desktop operating systems provide no features for securing data. Anyone can walk up to a machine and copy files to a floppy disk unless the floppy is disabled or removed.

♦ Some systems have keys, but they are rarely used—or may even be thrown away by system administrators who fear that users will lose them. In some cases, the key for the computer in the next office will unlock your system.

♦ Screen savers may provide the appearance of security, but they are really designed to prevent people from disturbing a computer that is working on some important task while the user is out to lunch. Most experienced users know how to bypass a password-protected screen saver. Even the "hardened" screen savers in Windows 95 are bypassed by booting the system with a DOS disk. All the files are then available for access on the hard drive using DOS commands.

♦ Hard drive passwords are available on some systems so users can password-protect access to the drive. Sometimes these are effective, but you can't absolutely depend on them.

♦ Computers store their setup information in special CMOS memory chips. Some systems will store a password in the chip as well, providing a relatively effective way to prevent access to a PC. However, a dedicated hacker can simply remove the cover and disconnect the battery to erase the CMOS, then reprogram it and fully access the system. Obviously, you need to bolt components down if you're worried about these kinds of attacks.

♦ Encryption is good. It does a reliable job of preventing access to information stored on PCs that basically are freely available in an office environment for anyone to access. However, encryption does require that users remember a password to unencrypt data. Over time, passwords can be forgotten.

Local Area Networks (LANs)

The next step in the evolution of personal and desktop computers was to link them all together using network technologies. The name *local area network* (LAN) implies that the network is relatively small and within a specific area. Typically, a cable connects all the systems in a department of an organization. The electrical characteristics of the cable often define the limits of a LAN and the number of computers you can attach to it.

All the users in the department trust one another (in theory at least), making the network manager's job easy. Security is not a big issue, because all the users are known and work in the same department. Detecting the perpetrators of malicious activity is possible in most cases.

In the early days of LANs, few people concerned themselves with the thought that someone would tap their network cable and monitor transmissions: few people knew how to tap a cable. Besides, most information on LANs was easy to manage and secure because it was usually stored on a single server, and all the users connecting to it were known.

The file server is the central theme of the LAN. It provides a place to put critical and sensitive information where a manager can set access controls and protect data using security techniques and backup methods. However, users may copy sensitive files to the local hard drive or to a floppy disk, ruining any security scheme you might put in place.

Interconnected Networks

As soon as the CEO and other corporate managers became computer literate, a mandate usually trickled down to connect all the departmental LANs together and make information accessible throughout the company, at least to select people. A company-wide e-mail system was usually part of this plan as well.

Now the once secure (relatively speaking) departmental LANs were bridged across an unknown void to other departmental LANs. Network cables were thrown up in unusual and unsecured places such as the ceiling above hallways or outside the building. These interconnected networks contributed little to security.

Most companies are still fairly relaxed about the way they interconnect their information systems. I visited a site where the network cable was tacked above the front of a bar that separated two offices. Anyone could have tapped that cable in a matter of minutes during the night.

The end result of all this interconnected networking was a mesh of cable running in all directions. Managers and technicians had trouble keeping track of every cable run. If you ran cable through the ceiling, then you had to be wary of the air-conditioning service technician who might find some reason to tap your cable. If cable was concentrated in the telephone closets, the telephone repairer was suspect.

Growing companies typically install cable throughout the building and put connections in offices that are not yet occupied. Industrial spies who

1

manage to get into your building may "set up office," posing as temporary employees or people from a branch office. They connect into the network and monitor its traffic using devices called packet sniffers. Monitoring network traffic can provide vast amounts of information, such as logon names and passwords or information about the servers on your network and the types of services they provide. There are devices that let perpetrators of industrial espionage monitor computer network traffic by simply being near a cable that emanates a signal. To prevent this, use fiber-optic cable; it does not emanate an external signal.

There are some advantages to interconnected networks: they can be constructed in such a way that they're easily managed from a central location. Wiring systems are available that are hierarchical in nature. In a multistory office building, computers on each floor are connected to a hub, which is connected to a building hub, which in turn is connected to an enterprise hub. All the connections are easily controlled and managed. Once the network connections are under control, it is generally easier to provide security by controlling access to the network itself rather than to individual computers. Firewalls are isolation mechanisms that control traffic flow between parts of the internal network (or to and from the outside world if you have an Internet connection).

Distributed Client-Server Architectures

Client-server computing is an important aspect of network computing. In the client-server model, the processing load is distributed between desktop computers and network servers. This model takes advantage of the fact that desktop computers have quite a bit of processing power, unlike the terminals that connect to mainframe computer systems. With client-server applications, part of the code runs on the client, and part on the server. The client side interacts with users while the server side works with stored data and resources attached to servers. There is a request-and-response conversation that takes place between the client and server on a continuous basis.

Part of the client-server trend is to distribute data around the organization. Data replication is a method of duplicating information from one system to another in real time to make that information more available to people at different locations throughout the organization. While replication may provide safeguards against local disasters and equipment failures, it also introduces a level of complexity, i.e., care must be taken to ensure that information is constantly synchronized throughout the organization and that people in all locations are working with information that is up-to-date.

While the client-server model provides many advantages, it also has some drawbacks. Although security for the servers can be administered from a central location, the clients' security is difficult to manage. Clients often manage their own security. Since information is not centralized, but moves around the organization, it is vulnerable to a higher degree of risk and exposure at the distributed client locations. Sensitive information may end up on a local user's hard drive, where it might be copied to a diskette and carried out of the building. Because administering clients is a problem, users are typically given more responsibility for managing their own systems. In this situation, thorough staff training and strict security policies are vital for preventing mistakes and accidents.

Heterogeneous Networks

Interconnecting all your computer systems with a spaghetti-like complex of cables is hard enough to manage. Throw in a bunch of different types of computer systems and you compound the problem. Large organizations may have every conceivable type of computing system attached to their networks, including IBM host systems, UNIX workstations and servers, DEC minicomputers, Novell NetWare servers, and Windows NT workstations and servers, as well as DOS, Macintosh, Windows, and UNIX clients. This conglomeration is usually the result of interconnecting departments and divisions that have each set their own computing standards and policies for years.

Network administrators and technicians have spent the last few years trying to get these systems to communicate with one another and allow users to exchange information among systems. The TCP/IP (*transmission control protocol/Internet protocol*) network communication protocol has provided exactly what administrators need to get these systems operating together. It was designed by the Department of Defense and other government agencies as a protocol to integrate diverse computers working together.

However, making it easy for one computer system to communicate with another doesn't help your security. For instance, consider that passwords are well protected in Windows NT, but relatively easy to break in the UNIX environment. A user may use the same password to log in to both systems, thus weakening the security of the Windows NT system.

Managing security on heterogeneous networks is also difficult. Each different type of computer runs an operating system with its own security system. An administrator faces a formidable task in developing a security strategy that accommodates all these different systems.

Campus, Metropolitan, and Wide Area Networks

Large organizations are faced with the need to interconnect systems in different buildings on business and college campuses, in metropolitan areas, or around the globe. These networks are called *campus networks, metropolitan area networks* (MANs), and *wide area networks* (WANs). The main point is that the cabling system or other transmission medium is leased from a communication provider that you trust to provide some level of privacy for your transmissions.

Local and long-distance phone companies are the usual providers of metropolitan and wide area network links. A dedicated leased line is set up between your site and a local telephone switching office. Another connection is set up between your local switching office and the remote switching office, and from there a third connection is set up to your remote site. This arrangement is usually called a *private network* because you pay for exclusive use of the lines. However, can you be sure that the lines are private? There are too many places where industrial spies or *phreakers* (people who know how to break into phone systems) can monitor your traffic. Once again, data encryption is a good idea.

Private network connections can get quite expensive. The equipment costs are high and the lines carry a monthly lease charge that increases with distance and in some cases with the amount of traffic. Recently, many organizations have begun to build private networks across the Internet using a technique called *tunneling,* which I'll discuss later in this chapter.

In business park settings, the property managers may have restrictions against running cable between buildings. You may need to connect in with an existing cable that spans the park and that is used by everyone else who leases property. The question is, can you trust these transmission facilities?

Running your own cables in metropolitan areas is a little difficult, if not impossible. You can't just prop a cable up across the street in most towns, although the town I grew up in might allow it. You need special permits once you try to put anything on public properties. Then even if you do, the cables could be tapped by just about anybody who can get close to the cable runs. Service providers in many metropolitan areas now provide optical cable lines that restrict eavesdropping because the cables do not emanate a signal.

Dish-to-dish microwave transmission systems are useful if you have a clear line of site between facilities. Companies with offices in two downtown buildings, for instance, might set up a microwave system between the two buildings. However, signals that are transmitted through the air can be monitored. As with a flashlight, what starts out as a small-diameter beam ends up a large-diameter beam. Someone could place a receiver somewhere in the line of the beam to pick up your transmissions. Encryption is essential.

Remote Access and Mobile Computers

Telecommuting is the latest trend in corporate computing. Workers with laptop computers or systems at home connect into the office network to access resources, send and receive electronic mail, and check the company bulletin boards for news and information. Telecommuting is essential for mobile salespeople and employees who need to work in the field. It makes economic sense to let employees with home computers do their jobs at home. A home worker saves on commute time and costs and lowers the expense of maintaining an office at the corporate center. My brother, a professional programmer, drives into the office two days of the week. The rest of the time he sets his own schedules and works towards deadlines for completing projects.

As this trend increases, so do the vulnerabilities of your information systems. Someone might steal a mobile user's portable computer along with the sensitive information it contains, including logon scripts for accessing your corporate network. The same thing can happen to a home computer. You cannot be sure who is dialing into your network unless you take steps to properly authenticate these users, as I'll discuss further in Chapter 3.

Branch offices are another security problem. A typical branch office has a small LAN and a staff of people who log on to corporate systems. In many cases, these offices are understaffed and prone to break-ins. If salespeople and other staff are out in the field, the receptionist may be the only one in the office during long periods of the day. That's when industrial spies break in and access computer systems with connections to the corporate network. There are a number of interesting tales about hackers who, posing as managers or technicians from the corporate office, have been escorted into secure areas of the company.

The Internet-Connected Enterprise

The Internet and the TCP/IP network communication protocol suite have become a major component in the information infrastructure of almost every large company. The Internet lets people exchange e-mail with business partners, serves as a platform for electronic transactions, and provides a way to build private links to branch offices or remote sites.

TCP/IP has become the grand unifier for computer systems and networks everywhere. It is now the primary communication protocol suite for all Microsoft networks. The U.S. Defense Advanced Research Projects Agency (DARPA) originally created TCP/IP as a protocol for a communication system designed to ensure continuous connections during emergencies—even in the event of a nuclear war. A testament to the reliability of this system was the UN forces' inability to knock out Iraq's TCP/IP communication system during the Persian Gulf war.

While the Internet and the TCP/IP protocols have many advantages, there are security risks as well. Connecting to the Internet is like opening the

1

doors of your company to strangers. The connection is two-way, allowing traffic to flow in both directions. Without proper defenses, any computer on an internal TCP/IP network can be accessed by any user on the Internet. *Firewalls* are devices that, when built right, put up barriers that prevent intruder attacks.

Transmitting information over the Internet poses another security problem. The Internet is a web of telecommunication cables and other media that spans the globe. Anyone can tap into the system and monitor transmissions. Although it is unlikely that someone could glean any useful information by tapping a link just anywhere, well-placed monitoring equipment in the vicinity of your site might capture the transmissions that are funneling into your site. Monitoring is the least of your problems. Every Internet system has a unique address, and some very crafty people know how to spoof your system into sending data to the wrong address or receiving data from a phony computer. (These issues are covered more fully in Chapters 2 and 17.)

TCP/IP Networks

TCP/IP networks are shared communication systems, meaning that many different communication sessions can take place at the same time. The data transferred in each session is divided up and placed into individual *packets.* These packets are addressed to a destination computer and sent out over the Internet. As pictured in Figure 1-1, the Internet is a mesh of connections with many possible paths that packets can take through the network. Devices called *routers* interconnect transmission channels. When a packet reaches a router, it is forwarded along the best available path to its destination.

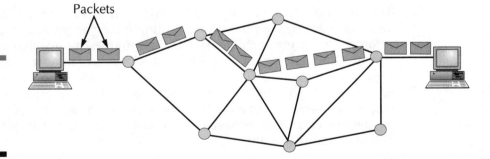

Packets

Packets of
information
traveling over
the Internet
Figure 1-1.

Freeway systems provide a good analogy for the way the Internet works. People get into cars and drive to their destination. Each car (packet) is an independent delivery system. At intersections (routers), cars can switch paths to get on a more direct route to a destination. An appropriate exit is taken for the final leg of the trip.

A typical communication session might involve hundreds or thousands of individual packets of information traveling along cables and routers on the Internet. Information is divided into packets by the sending computer and reassembled by the receiving computer. One advantage of using packets is that a small glitch on the network may affect only a few of the packets. When this happens, only the lost packets are retransmitted, not the entire message. The packet nature of the Internet makes it easy to avoid problem areas. If a transmission line is down, a router simply sends packets along another path.

TCP/IP-Based Information Services

The Internet has made system and network administrators rethink the way they provide information to users. In particular, the *World Wide Web* (or simply the *Web*) has provided a whole new model for client-server computing that many organizations are imitating for their own internal networks. An *intranet* is an internal network that uses the same protocols and programs that are used on the Internet.

The Web is built onto the Internet and uses TCP/IP protocols to transport information from place to place. Users (called *clients*) run software (called *browsers*) that connect to Web servers, which provide information to clients on "pages" displayed in a graphical interface. The pages have hyperlink buttons so users can quickly jump to other pages of cross-referenced information.

The Web should not be taken lightly. Web browsers have been called *universal clients* because they provide a unique way to get at all types of information on any computer system. Mainframes, minicomputers, UNIX systems, NetWare servers, and Windows NT servers can operate as Web servers. Only a few years ago, programmers, network administrators, and data managers were trying to figure out ways to make information on these systems available to anyone. When the Web's client-server model appeared, people immediately realized that it would be a significant tool for achieving this universal availability.

1

Providing information via Web pages is relatively easy to do, and new tools are emerging every day to make the job easier. Organizations are installing Web servers within their company to provide all kinds of information to employees, and are building public Web servers to disseminate information about products and services. Even information in databases can be queried by Web users. The results of the queries are dynamically placed on a Web page and returned to the user.

Web servers are changing the look of the client in a way that will interest security managers. So-called *thin clients* are inexpensive terminal-type computers for accessing Internet or intranet Web servers. The devices run Web browsers and are specifically designed for simple client activities. They don't have disk drives in most cases because users interact with and store information on central servers. This model is a lot like mainframe-terminal computing, and returns control of information to network administrators.

Thin clients are really a combination of hardware and software. A specification called the Network Computer (NC) Reference Profile defines these clients. They typically run sub-operating systems that rely heavily on server connections. Thin clients are designed to bring together the world of the Internet, client-server computing, and host-based connectivity. The systems will bring down the cost of corporate computing by creating inexpensive devices that can be used by a wide range of users who don't need all the processing power and peripherals of standard desktop computing systems.

Behind the Web are new Internet protocols, such as *Hypertext Transfer Protocol* (HTTP) that provide client-server services over TCP/IP networks. Secure versions of these protocols that encrypt transmissions are in the works. The operation of these protocols will be of interest to security managers; they are discussed further in Part 4 of this book.

Virtual Wide Area Networks

The Internet provides a whole new way to build private networks among your remote offices and reduce communication costs. Instead of leasing dedicated lines to interconnect your offices, you use special devices to build private transmission circuits through the Internet. These are often called *virtual WANs* and *tunnels*. Since the Internet is already in place as a global communication system, all you need to do is get a connection into it. With the right equipment, virtual WANs can provide a secure encrypted channel to transmit packets of information to other sites.

Point-to-Point Tunneling Protocol (PPTP) was developed by Microsoft, 3Com, Ascend, and several other companies. It supports secure, multiprotocol virtual private networks across the Internet. With PPTP, clients can access their corporate networks over secure Internet connections. Clients do not need to upgrade software. All that is required is that Internet service providers upgrade their access server to support PPTP. Secure communications are provided by the authentication and encryption built into Windows NT *remote-access service* (RAS).

So despite the Internet's own security problems, it has the potential to solve many of your existing network and security problems. Tunneling protocols can help make remote connections more secure and reduce the cost of building wide area networks to interconnect worldwide organizations.

CHAPTER 2

Security Threats

The conventional army loses if it does not win. The guerrilla wins if he does not lose.

—Henry Kissinger

The threats to your information systems and the battle to protect them are akin to guerrilla warfare. The guerrilla uses stealth tactics to undermine and sabotage your system. The enemy is usually unknown and is careful to cover his tracks so he can easily attack again. In some cases, the guerrilla gets information necessary to break into your system from your own trusted employees. In some cases, the guerrilla *is* the trusted employee.

No more Mr. Nice Guy.

—Unknown (but heard in an Alice Cooper song)

OK, now that I've diminished your trust, "no more Mr. Nice Guy," right? Really, that's the way it should be. If you're not the paranoid type, then hire a security manager: someone who can lay down the law and enforce the essential security you need to protect your business.

This chapter outlines some of the more common threats to the security of your computer systems and networks. Keep in mind that some of these threats have been documented in the UNIX environment, but not yet in the Windows NT environment. Specific Windows NT security threats are covered in more detail in Chapter 6. This chapter is meant to introduce you to "hacking," "cracking," "spoofing," and "sniffing"—activities performed by the underground community of pranksters, hardened criminals, industrial spies, and international terrorists who want to break into your systems for profit and pleasure. Have a nice day.

What Are the Threats?

The biggest problem with the hacker threat is that hacking is fun!

—John O'Leary, Computer Security Institute

Threats by floods and fires are easy to understand: the techniques for protecting against them are well known. But threats perpetrated by

2

malicious users, disgruntled employees, and unknown hackers are a true nightmare. Every day some new technique for attacking systems is developed.

You may not know you are being attacked or have been attacked. No site is an exception. Even small businesses like corner food stores are targets for local hackers who notice an online computer system while in the store. They break in using their computer and modem just for the fun or challenge. Often these systems are the least secure because the owners think that no one would care about their system or even know it exists. Professional hackers are quite busy as well. Recent reports indicate that unemployed Russian security experts are hacking into and looting American corporations of billions of dollars.

There is no doubt that we are entering an era of electronic crime. Software systems are vulnerable. It's that simple. Accept it and start dealing with the problem. Methods of encrypting data to hide it from prying eyes are breakable, given enough time and resources. A major developer of encryption algorithms announced that its encryption system would take years to break. Within a year of undertaking the challenge, some university students managed to break the code. They used hundreds of Internet-connected computers to break it simultaneously.

Natural Threats and Direct Assaults

Security threats are both natural and intended. The data on your systems are vulnerable to both natural disasters and corruption by malicious people. Floods, fires, competitors, foreign governments, revengeful—or just plain curious—persons, hate groups, and many others could be the source. A human-perpetrated attack is either active or passive:

♦ **Active attacks** involve actually changing transmitted or stored data. It may also include deleting, corrupting, delaying, or jamming transmissions. Active attacks may appear to be accidents.

♦ **Passive attacks** involve collecting information without anyone knowing about it. Electronic eavesdropping and wiretapping are examples. The information is often used to mount an attack on another, more desirable system.

Ex-employees, competitors, or foreign governments can disrupt your operations by using various techniques that slow down or crash your systems. These are called "denial-of-service" attacks because they deny authorized users access to a system. Internet sites are often swamped with useless messages generated by groups that are opposed to the products, services, or information at the site. This is a form of active boycotting.

An attacker can corrupt information for competitive reasons or for revenge. A typical target is the employee payroll information. Theft is another concern. A competitor may do just about anything to steal your valuable product information or research material. Hate groups or political adversaries attempt to access confidential information that can be used to discredit you or your organization.

You get the idea. There are millions of users on the Internet that use its global communication infrastructure to access systems around the world. While some systems are easy to break into, others are accessed by using accounts and passwords that have been stolen from your employees or obtained through techniques such as blackmail or payoffs. Eavesdropping on network transmissions is another way to obtain access information.

Don't be so naïve to think that this doesn't happen, or that no one would want to break into your computer. Never underestimate the potential for a break-in, and never underestimate a real break-in if it occurs. Remember, your system might provide a doorway to another system—or may simply present a challenge to someone looking for fun.

Areas of Security Weakness

How do hackers break in? What are the weak areas that they exploit? The following list describes some of the weakest areas on company-wide networks:

- ♦ Well-known (and easily guessed) passwords, or leaked passwords, that compromise user logon and authentication

- ♦ Poorly implemented logon settings, user account rights, and file access permissions

- ♦ Disks and electronic mail that carry viruses

- ♦ Open doors into internal networks, created by users that access the Internet or by poorly implemented Internet firewalls

- ♦ Dial-up mobile and remote computers that have been stolen along with logon information

- ♦ Inefficient and unsecured routing techniques that provide pathways for hackers into your systems

- ♦ Network cables that are susceptible to eavesdropping equipment

- ♦ Data replication strategies that duplicate viruses throughout the network

- ♦ Program bugs that hackers take advantage of to break into your systems

- ♦ Backdoors that have been left in applications by programmers

♦ Maintenance ports on network equipment and PBXs that are used by service personnel to locally or remotely access the devices

♦ Modems attached directly onto networks or attached to computers on a network and set to auto-answer mode

Who Are the Hackers?

2

You may not know any hackers personally. On the other hand, a hacker might be your next-door neighbor's son—someone with a computer and modem who is familiar with what you do, and who might guess your logon password because you use some derivative of your kids' names. Hacking is seen as an electronic sport by the people who do it. They will spend all of their free time breaking into systems just for the thrill of having done so. Don't try to understand why, just know that they are out there.

Dangerous hackers are very knowledgeable about computers and security techniques, and they use sophisticated techniques to break into computer systems. Your competitor may hire such a hacker. If hackers cover their tracks, you might never know that they have stolen your customer mailing list or trade secrets. The information that your competitors, foreign governments, and other hackers are after may include the following:

♦ Research information

♦ Product information

♦ Customer lists and proprietary customer information

♦ Information about your organization, such as employee records, financial data, or legal information

♦ Almost anything else of value

Hackers learn about hacking by sharing information with their fellow hackers. There is an incredible amount of information available. Bulletin boards and electronic newsletters exist for the purpose of spreading this information around. Hackers get online to brag about their techniques and exploits. Check out the Web site called "Hack Microsoft" at **www.c2.org/ hackmsoft**.

Hackers often intend to make a profit or want to obtain free services. A phone hacker (or phreaker) is intent on obtaining logon information to online services or on making long-distance phone calls through your phone system so that you pick up the charges. A hacker often uses information obtained during one break-in to access and break into another computer system. They might sell information obtained during a break-in, such as credit card numbers and access codes, to foreigners or competitors.

A new trend is code cracking by so-called *cypherpunks,* a loosely organized group of hackers who often work together to break encryption schemes. The idea is to pool resources and computing power in order to crack encryption keys that would normally take many years to break. Cypherpunks use the Internet as a communication platform to consolidate their efforts.

E.B. White said that "the most time-consuming thing is to have an enemy." Your company is on the right track if it has hired a security officer and provided funds for security. If your company is broken into, learn from the experience and tighten up your security. If the hackers didn't do any damage, try to track the path of their break-in and thank them in your mind for helping you discover a security weakness.

The Internal Threat

A recent online survey by *Network World* magazine (**www.nwfusion.com**) revealed that most security experts and readers felt that internal employees were the biggest threat to their information systems. Employees are familiar with the network, know which systems hold valuable information, and may have easy access to those systems through their own account or the account of another user. The American Society for Industrial Security estimates that 77 percent of information theft is perpetrated by insiders.

Revenge is a common theme: workers against co-workers, employees against personnel staff, subordinates against managers, and so on. Downsizing may put people in jobs where they are overworked and underpaid. They may break into company employee records or, to cover a trail of theft, alter inventory and asset records. An employee who is being laid off may plant a virus.

Janitors have become dangerous in the information age. They steal information that can be used to break into computer systems from the outside, such as user accounts and even passwords that users paste on their walls. The latest trend among hackers is to share information about how to get a job as a janitor!

Contractual partners are also a threat. Organizations involved in *electronic data interchange* (EDI) set up communication links with other companies for the purpose of exchanging business information. Hackers take advantage of these links. The hacker may be an employee of the other company, or an external hacker who has found a way into one company and uses the link to gain access to the other company. Any data-exchange agreement with other companies should be considered a potential threat in which your company's trade secrets and other vital information are at risk.

Trusted users are a constant security threat as well. They spread viruses from one system to another. They can inadvertently leak sensitive information or reveal their password to unauthorized users. They can be duped by a caller into giving out a password or some other vital information. These last two points describe what is often called "social engineering."

Hacker Lore

To be a hacker, your primary goal must be to learn for the sake of learning—just to find out what happens if you do a certain thing at a particular time under a specific condition.

2

—*Emmanuel Goldstein, Editor,* 2600 Magazine *(Spring, 1994)*

Some of the more "interesting" hacker exploits are described in the following list. I'm not trying to glorify these activities, just to increase your paranoia in hopes that you'll tighten up security.

♦ The infamous Internet "worm" of 1987 was developed by a Cornell student. The worm replicated itself throughout the Internet in a period of two days, filling computers with copies of itself until they were disabled.

♦ Hundreds or even thousands of unemployed Russian computer experts have begun to attack systems around the world for fun or profit. They are especially skilled at break-ins. In 1994 a Russian hacker cracked Citicorp's electronic funds transfer system more than 40 times and managed to transfer millions of dollars into other accounts. He was stopped only by being arrested, and they never figured out how he broke into the system.

♦ Kevin Mitnick is a "professional" hacker who was arrested for hacking telephone systems and corporate computers. His theft of 20,000 credit card numbers from an Internet service provider went undetected until the provider was informed of the theft by an outsider. Mitnick also broke through a firewall at the San Diego Supercomputer Center by spoofing a legitimate TCP/IP communication session.

♦ In 1977 Ron Rivest, one of the founders of RSA data systems, created the public key encryption system that is used in a variety of operating systems and Internet programs. His so-called RSA-129 challenge invited anyone to break a specific message he had encrypted with a 129-digit prime-number key. Rivest believed that it would take 40 quadrillion years to crack the message. In 1994 a team organized by MIT student Derek Atkins simultaneously used 1,600 computers connected to the Internet to break the code over a non-contiguous period of eight months. Note that the current RSA implementation uses much larger keys.

After the Mitnick attack and the inability of the Citicorp system to keep out the Russian hacker, most security experts agree that no form of security is entirely reliable. Your only defense is to implement multiple levels of security and constantly monitor for break-ins or potential break-ins. If your system is difficult to break into, hackers will most likely move on to another system.

Methods of Attack

Attackers will do just about anything to get a valuable piece of information that gives them access to a computer system. Account passwords are the usual target. It is not uncommon for hackers to plant bugs, tap into wires, set up hidden cameras, or dive into dumpsters to get the information they need. Once the information is obtained, your systems and possibly those of your business partners, customers, and employees are at risk.

Once intruders have access to an account, they will attempt to elevate their privilege level. The process is often like a journey for hackers: getting deeper and deeper into a system, with each level bringing greater excitement. Hackers may return every night as if playing some sort of video game. Primary targets are system files, so the hackers can execute management programs and gain greater privilege; and log files, so they can cover their tracks. Covering tracks allows the hacker to return again and again. Hackers may also create a "backdoor" into the system to use at another time in case their current entry point is no longer available.

One of the worst things that can happen to your system is for a hacker to gain access to administrative accounts or directories that contain administrator-only programs and files. A hacker may gain this access through a weak security scheme or by obtaining a password in an unscrupulous way. Once in, the hacker can change passwords for other accounts in order to access them later, or do some other nasty things such as mess around with the Windows NT Registry.

Site Invasions

Do not ever doubt that a potential computer hacker, industrial spy, or other unauthorized person will one day walk into your building looking for useful information to steal. An article called "Can You Social Engineer Your Way Into Your Network?" by Bill Hancock in the April 1996 issue of *Network Security* magazine (Oxford, UK, Tel: +44-(0) 1865-843848) describes some of his exploits as a security analyst. Companies pay him to break their security. Here are some of the finer points of the article:

> The main idea of social engineering is to put the human element in the network breaching loop and use it as a tool. For instance, showing up at the computer room with network hardware in hand and with an appropriate vendor ID usually results in someone helping you into the communications closet and even to the point of helping to "install" the hardware on the network.

Mr. Hancock's advice on breaching the physical location is to "look like you belong" and "have a good legend" (spyspeak for a fake ID and reason to be there).

In one case, he walked into a company's branch office, claimed to work for the corporate office, and asked for a space where he could get some work done before a plane flight. They gave him a spare office that had a live network connection. While he was there, he used the network analyzer on his laptop to capture traffic on the company's network.

In another case, he created a fake laminated badge using a company logo from a business card and some black electrician's tape to simulate a magnetic strip. Although the badge couldn't give him access to a sensitive area, he simply waited for someone to enter and hold the door for him. While in the room, he took the backups off-site and managed to crack about 50 percent of the passwords.

Mr. Hancock also notes methods for gaining access by posing as a vendor and demonstrating some new product, or by applying for a job at a company and gleaning information during the internal tour of the facilities. He has also obtained useful information about a company from its main vendor and managed to get a password from a third-party service technician by posing as an angry manager of the company. He ends his article by noting that paranoia is useful: "The more you have, the less the chance of being attacked."

2

Phone Attacks

A *phreaker* is a person who takes advantage of the telecommunications system to make free long-distance telephone calls, listen to private conversations, access internal systems, or hack into other systems via the system broken into. Phreakers are familiar with telephone switches, networks, and other equipment, and often have manuals from the manufacturers of telecom equipment that describe exactly how to operate and repair that equipment. Experienced phreakers can manipulate telephone billing, access codes, and call routing.

Phreakers can make free long-distance phone calls by gaining "dial-in/dial-out" capabilities. For example, a phreaker calls a number in your organization, then asks to be transferred back to the operator. He then poses as an important person within the company and asks for an outside line. His call is now looped through your company, and you pay the bill. Attacks on other systems may be perpetrated in this way. Worse, the targets of the attack may think your company is responsible.

Hackers and phreakers even pose as service technicians to gain access to phone closets and PBX systems, where they reprogram the systems, install bugs, or set up circuits that can be accessed later and used to attack your company or other companies.

War dialing is another technique that phreakers use to gain access to systems. Basically, they want to break into a computer but don't know any phone numbers to call. The war dialer discovers phone numbers of modem-connected computer systems by dialing one number after another until a modem answers. When a modem is found, the phone number is put into a log and the system continues to search. This may go on all day or all night. Once the list is complete, the phreaker calls each of the systems on the list and attempts to break in. Autodialing programs are commonly available on bulletin boards, along with phone number lists.

Hacking User Accounts and Passwords

As I mentioned earlier, an attacker's first priority is to obtain user account names and passwords since this provides easy access to a system. Once inside, the hacker will find a way to elevate his privileges. The attacker can often obtain a list of user account names from a number of likely sources. For example, the company e-mail system might provide such lists. In high-security environments, make sure these lists are not readily available. Internal users will usually have easy access to account names.

Once a user account list is obtained, the hacker will try to determine which account will give the most access if broken into. The PC support staff may inadvertently provide this information in the form of lists of users to contact in case of problems. In the DOS and Windows environment, a user may try the following:

♦ Using the NET USE command at a DOS prompt to connect with shared resources on remote systems.

♦ Using the NBTSTAT (NetBIOS Over TCP/IP Statistics) to display information about systems. If you type **NBTSTAT -A ip*address***, where ip*address* is the IP address of a server, you can get the domain name and computer name of the computer and the names of users logged in to it.

2

♦ On a Windows computer, viewing the logon name of the last person to use the logon dialog box.

♦ Using the FINGER command, which will provide user account information for systems that are running TCP/IP and domain name service (DNS).

Once a hacker obtains a legitimate user account name, cracking the password is the next step. Hackers take advantage of common passwords: if they know the user of an account, they may try various combinations of the user's kids' and pets' names. Many people use the same password to log on to other systems, such as ATM machines. A co-worker/hacker could obtain this password by watching you at the bank machine with a pair of binoculars (yes, it's done). A good reason to choose an obscure password is to make it difficult for people with good eyes to follow your keystrokes as you type it.

If a hacker obtains a user account name, but not a password, he can try brute force methods of breaking into the account. A program is set up to try thousands or millions of different passwords until the account opens. This methods is ineffective if logon restrictions that limit the number of attempted logons are set. Windows NT locks an account by default after three failed logon attempts.

Exhaustion attacks and dictionary attacks are methods for cracking password files and other encrypted information. In an *exhaustion attack*, thousands of password combinations are used until a password is guessed. In a *dictionary attack*, a complete dictionary of common passwords in multiple languages is tried until a password is guessed. Hackers often know the manufacturer's default passwords to equipment like routers and depend on the fact that the passwords are not changed.

Another method that hackers use to get passwords is to place a capture program or keystroke reader at the keyboard if they have access to a workstation. Such programs are put in the path of the workstation and run when the user starts the system.

Hacking Trusted Systems

Hackers love transitive trusts where they can log on to one machine and get access to another. These attacks are 25 percent effective.

—Captain Kevin J. Ziese, U.S. Air Force Information Warfare Center

Network computer systems maintain *trust relationships* with each other so that users on one system can access another, or so that a program on one computer can access information stored on another computer. Data is often replicated (copied) to trusted systems. Hackers use these trust relationships to their advantage. In fact, a hacker will often have less interest in the computer he is currently attacking than in the computers it has trust relationships with. He may be able to obtain access to a legitimate account that has access to another system. In addition, it may be possible to attack the trust relationship, which often acts like a secure user account and allows two systems to exchange information or to run processes on one another.

Trust relationships are transitive in some environments. If System A extends its trust to System B, and System B extends its trust to System C, then a trust relationship may be established between Systems A and C through System B. This may be good in some cases, but it opens up too many unknowns and discrepancies in most cases. Windows NT Server does not allow such transitive trust relationships. However, a critical problem in Windows NT Server domains is that the administrator in one domain can naively grant access to an "administrator" in another domain without knowing the true identity of that "administrator." In addition, a trust relationship may grant access to groups of users on other machines—even though some users in those groups may not be worthy of trust. This is discussed further in Chapter 7.

Electronic Eavesdropping and Cable Sniffing

A *packet sniffer* is a device or software that can read transmitted packets. Windows NT Server inclueds a packet sniffer (see Chapter 10). Network technicians usually have such devices in their toolkits to monitor network traffic and locate problems on the network. This is analogous to a postal worker reading letters that are in transit. While thousands or millions of packets may pass by during a sniffer session, the devices can filter out undesirable packets, allowing hackers to target a particular system or user.

Packet sniffing is a passive eavesdropping technique that is hard to detect. The packet-sniffing devices may be installed on internal or external networks. Although packet sniffing an Internet transmission line is not necessarily informative, sniffing a cable that runs into your facilities is. Overall, the biggest threat is from people inside or near your facilities who are armed with packet sniffers, or from hackers who have penetrated your building and planted listening devices.

Obtaining logon information is the usual goal of a hacker armed with a packet sniffer, although he might just as well monitor any kind of data transmission on the network. In the case of Internet supplier A2i Communications in San Jose, a hacker found his way into the company's facilities and installed a packet-sniffing device that was able to record session information for logons to the company's customers, including the Army, NASA, IBM, Intel, Microsoft, and Novell. The hacker was then able to replay this information and log on to the customer's computers as well. Fortunately, these replay attacks are difficult on Windows NT networks. Appendix A describes how passwords are implemented in the Windows NT environment.

2

In another scenario, hackers may disrupt a network by capturing large numbers of packets and playing them back. The target network becomes congested and may fail.

Other Vulnerable Areas

Hackers use various tools and techniques to break into your system. Usually, they take advantage of vulnerable areas that are known to provide good entry points. Some of these vulnerable areas are described here.

Files and Directories

Windows NT provides two file systems: the traditional File Allocation Table (FAT) file system and the NT File System (NTFS). FAT does not provide the file system security that NTFS does. With FAT, someone can boot a computer with DOS and access files in any directory. NTFS directories and files can be accessed only by properly authenticated users, which means that you must first boot a system and log on with a password.

Recently, however, a program called NTFSDOS.EXE has surfaced that exposes an NTFS volume to a user who boots a system with DOS. While this sounds like the end of Windows NT security, appropriate security measures can protect data. Basically, you must lock up servers and prevent booting from floppy drives.

Public-domain hacker utilities are a constant threat. A single program that circulated in the NetWare community is responsible for most of the hacker activities on NetWare. You never know when an extremely creative and talented hacker will discover some new hole in the NT environment that can be exploited.

A user may access your system through a guest account that provides access to various public files on your server, but gain further access due to improperly configured directory and file permissions.

Users who have access to directories with execute rights can run programs. A security problem exists if users also have the ability to copy files into the directory: they can copy a virus-infected program or a program to hack the system into the directory, then execute it. It's usually not a good idea to combine these rights in directories that are available to the public (i.e., on a Web server) or to non-administrative employees.

Mobile and Remote Users

Providing network logon services to mobile and remote users is another problem. The number of mobile users has greatly increased, causing heightened management problems. A typical mobile user travels with a portable computer and connects to a company's network, usually with full client rights and permissions. The mobile user exposes your system to potential security problems in a number of ways:

♦ Someone sitting next to a user in an airport or other public area can monitor the user's logon, either visually or by using devices that eavesdrop on devices in close proximity.

♦ Logons take place over public lines that can be monitored by hackers who are looking for ways to break into systems.

♦ Portable computers are often stolen. Any valuable company information on the system will be available to the thief, including user account names from e-mail address books, passwords that the user has stored on disk, and sensitive company information that the user has downloaded to his or her own computer.

♦ A remote system may be at a location where a hacker can physically sit at the computer and hack away at the system for hours without being disturbed by a user or a security officer.

There are a number of ways to protect portable systems, including encryption of data and using two-way authentication devices in which a user enters the password produced by the card and the memorized password to gain access to a network.

Backdoors and Program Bugs

A *backdoor* is a hole into a program, left there purposely by the original programmer or designer. I once attended a training session in which a

Novell instructor described a backdoor method for getting into the NetWare operating system. The instructions were meant to be used by certified NetWare representatives who needed to help their customer gain access to a system after losing a password; however, I'm sure that a number of hackers managed to attend the classes or get the information from other sources.

A backdoor (or *trapdoor*) is often put into a program by a developer as a way to bypass a particular system or process until the program is complete. Backdoors can simplify the program-testing process by bypassing certain steps or control procedures that might require a lot of time to complete and are not necessary when testing. However, programmers often forget to remove backdoors or are not aware of other holes that the backdoor might have created. A person who discovers a backdoor may find a way to use it to exploit a system.

2

When a backdoor is discovered, it usually doesn't take long for the hacker community to spread information about it onto bulletin boards and e-mail lists. This hole becomes a prime target for hackers who may already have access into your network. By using the newly discovered security hole, they may elevate their privileges to gain further access to your systems or find some technique for doing damage.

A bug in a program may also provide a weakness that a hacker can take advantage of. A custom application written by an in-house programmer, for example, might have a bug that allows a hacker to bypass directory and file-system security. In some cases, a bug or system defect may provide a similar path.

Network Applications

A typical program contains many different procedures. In a client-server environment, clients run programs on their own computers, on the server, or both. *Remote procedure calls* (RPCs) provide a way for a programmer to create procedures that can be stored on a server where they are readily available to many clients, easily updated, and kept in a safe place. RPCs provide a link between a program running in a client's computer and procedures designed to run with that program that are located on a remote server.

RPCs are used to create a number of services that run over networks, including administrative and monitoring programs. However, RPCs have been a source of security problems, most of which have been documented in the UNIX environment. Similar problems may arise in the Windows NT environment. For example, in the UNIX environment, it is possible for a hacker to spoof an RPC message and send a server message in place of another system. It is possible that a similar problem could be exploited in the Windows NT environment.

The RPC mechanisms in Windows NT 3.51 and above use a 40-bit encryption algorithm to provide secure data transmissions. This provides some assurance that the message contents are secure, but there is still potential for message spoofing and for breaking the encryption, although doing the latter in the time frame of the message is unlikely.

Electronic Mail Security Problems

There is little doubt that e-mail is beneficial to companies and to business in general. Using Internet e-mail is a popular trend because so many people and organizations are connected to the Internet and because proprietary e-mail systems have been difficult to integrate into enterprise-wide environments that use a variety of such systems. However, using the Internet for e-mail has its security problems, although solutions are in the works.

The identification of a sender can be forged, and users may receive bogus mail from what appears to be someone they trust. Users should trust only mail that they know is in transit, and then it is probably wise to verify messages with the sender. Encryption and digital signatures methods are available to validate messages, as discussed in Appendix B. The ability to deny having sent a message is another problem, especially when its comes to business transactions. For example, someone who purchases stocks using e-mail might attempt to deny having placed the order if the stock goes down in price. Digital signatures can prove the source, time, and authenticity of messages.

Spamming is another problem. In a spamming attack, the perpetrator sends hundreds or thousands of phony or useless e-mail messages to your site in an attempt to overload your systems and stop all communications.

Employees need to know the dangers of transmitting sensitive information in e-mail messages that could be captured or monitored by industrial spies. Alternatively, be aware that e-mail provides a convenient way to steal information. Any employee might circumvent security measures designed to prevent files from being carried out the front door by simply e-mailing the files to their home computer.

E-mail is also quick and direct. One of your employees in a fit of anxious rage may send a hateful, unethical, or illegal message to someone without pause for reflection, thus increasing the liability of your company.

One last subtle threat inherent in e-mail is its tendency to hang around for a long time. Messages may be held in a "deleted messages" folder for months, then make their way to tape backups where they may be stored permanently. This information may either benefit or incriminate your company. Courts have subpoenaed backup archives for the purpose of searching old e-mail. Just ask Oliver North: although he deleted the messages on his system, they were archived on a mainframe and used as evidence in the Iran-Contra affair. If you don't want the courts to subpoena your old e-mail, you must create a policy that defines how it is destroyed. Otherwise, the courts may accuse you of destroying evidence. On the other hand, saving e-mail may provide you with evidence to use in future cases against dishonest employees.

Communication Systems

Communication systems such as microwave and satellite links between your sites are vulnerable to monitoring and tapping. A microwave system may emit a signal the diameter of a nickel. That same signal will have a diameter of one mile when it reaches a receiving dish approximately 20 miles away. Anyone with the right equipment can monitor the signal if they are within the beam path. A communication satellite has a footprint that is as big as North America. Once again, the signal is easy to monitor. All of your sensitive transmissions must be protected with encryption.

The Internet and TCP/IP

Most organizations create links to the Internet and use the TCP/IP network communication protocol on their enterprise networks. An Internet connection is an open door into your organization that outside hackers can exploit to attack your systems. In addition, when your users use the Internet to transmit information, there is a possibility that those transmissions will be monitored.

A recent article in *Information Week* magazine* described how hackers continuously try to break into the systems of Rockwell International via its Internet connections. Roy Alzua, a manager at the company, was quoted as saying, "Someone may already be inside, because we're seeing unusual activity at the host level. But there's no way to tell; they cover their tracks." Rockwell reportedly uses the latest firewall and encryption technology.

TCP/IP and Internet Attacks

When you decide to use the Internet protocols and TCP/IP networking, you open your system to a variety of potential attacks that are well known in the hacker community. Fortunately, because these hacks are well known, Microsoft has done a good job of protecting Windows NT from many of them. In some cases, commands have been removed or given limited

---

* Information Week; February 19, 1996; p. 34.

functions. In other cases, bugs or backdoors that existed in the UNIX environment are irrelevant due to Windows NT Security features.

TCP/IP networks are vulnerable to attacks by hackers who utilize sniffer devices to monitor traffic (transmitted packets) on networks and use the information they obtain to mount an attack. If a single cable connects two systems, then it is fairly easy to read all the packets sent between those systems. If two systems communicate across the Internet and a sniffer is connected to the Internet, the sniffer might be able to capture some of the packets of the communication session, but it would be difficult to capture all of them. That is because the Internet is a mesh of many different paths that packets can travel between systems. However, the sniffer can be connected to the "last leg" of a route through which all the packets must travel to get to a destination system, or the sniffer can be attached to an internal network.

Any hacker who obtains only some of the packets transmitted between two computers might be able to discern enough information to launch an attack. Packets contain information such as addresses, IDs, and even non-encrypted passwords in some cases. Once the hacker has found a communication session of interest, he can use filtering options on the sniffer to display only packets for that session. The hacker might monitor a network connection for a long time to collect millions of bits of data that might hold just one vital piece of information. A sorting and searching routine makes it fairly easy to isolate useful information.

A hacker can also masquerade as another user/system by generating packets that appear to come from that system. The hacker "wedges" packets into the transmission that replace the original systems packets and the original system is bumped. This type of attack is difficult because the timing must be just right. However, it has been done.

NOTE: A more complete description of the TCP attack described here is available by requesting a document called "Simple Active Attack Against TCP" from Laurent Joncheray at Merit Networks, Inc. (e-mail: lpj@lmerit.edu). Another paper, "Security Problems with TCP/IP Protocol Suite," is available from S.M. Bellovin (e-mail: smb@lulysses.att.com).

A hacker who wishes to break into an existing communication session between a client and a server creates a state on the line in which the two systems desynchronize from one another. This is accomplished by sending null information to both the client and server. The null data is essentially "invisible" and does not cause the session to crash. The hacker then injects spoofed packets into the line and takes over the session. This scenario assumes that the hacker has been listening to the packet exchanges between the original client and server and is able to forge appropriate packets. Fortunately, there are fixes in various implementations of the TCP/IP protocol, and advanced techniques that can reduce the chances of these types of attacks. Packets can be encrypted to prevent modification and intrusion into the session. In addition, digital signatures also help reduce intrusions. Still, never say never. Clever hackers may find unique ways to overcome even the best security methods.

There are quite a few problems with the programs that run on the Internet, including TELNET, SENDMAIL, and others. The primary problems are the inability to authenticate users, hide data, or prevent backdoor attacks. Some of these utilities are available in various implementations on Windows systems. You can install them when you install Windows and the TCP/IP utilities during setup. Web servers and Web browsers also have their own unique problems and security risks.

2

NOTE: TCP/IP and Internet security problems are covered in Chapter 17.

Viruses and Trojan Horses

Viruses are small programs that mimic the activities of real-life viruses. They get into computer systems by being copied from contaminated disks or downloaded from online services by unsuspecting users. Once a system is contaminated, the virus executes some immediate action, or waits until a specified time or for a specific command executed by the user. Viruses may display harmless messages or destroy the information stored on entire hard disks. A *Trojan Horse* is similar to a virus, but contaminates a system by posing as some other type of program.

Viruses are especially dangerous on networks, because once they contaminate one system, they may spread to systems throughout the entire network. The biggest threat is that unsuspecting employees will pick up viruses through normal business transactions and spread them throughout an organization.

Virus contamination comes from a number of sources:

♦   Library computers or company kiosk computers that many different people use

♦   Service technicians who use disk-based utilities to check computers

♦ Computers infected by malicious users or by disgruntled employees who want to get even with the company or another employee

♦ Yes, even packages of off-the-shelf software

In fact, viruses were available for sale in a recent magazine advertisement for the purpose of testing your anti-virus software! Anyone not sure how to get a virus can now just buy one in order to infect someone else's system.

Viruses are created by authors who are fascinated by how quickly their virus may spread through computer systems. Terrorists and industrial spies create viruses that cause damage in order to seek revenge on an opponent or to damage the operations of a competitor. Some viruses are intended for a specific target, but get out of control and spread to unintended targets.

Fortunately, you can protect yourself against viruses by implementing appropriate security measures, training users, and using virus-protection programs. Some new strains of viruses are especially dangerous because they have the ability to change themselves in order to avoid detection by popular virus-protection programs. It is important to choose such programs from reputable vendors that provide continuous updates to their programs.

NOTE: Appendix C provides more information about viruses, Trojan Horses, and other such threats.

Natural Threats

Obviously, not all threats to the integrity of your network come from people. Power surges, failing components, and other problems may bring down systems and cost your organization thousands or millions of dollars in downtime. In some cases, continuous access to information is critical to the operation of the entire business. The following list covers most major natural threats:

♦ Electrical power may be lost during storms or for other reasons. Backup power supplies are essential.

♦ Hardware failures can cause loss of data availability. Redundant systems and backup are imperative.

♦ Fires, floods, earthquakes, and other disasters require backup systems, alternate data centers, and disaster-recovery plans.

In any of these situations, communication lines that are essential to the operation of your company may be cut. You need to establish alternate lines or backup methods to keep systems online in emergencies. These techniques are discussed in Chapter 11.

CHAPTER 3

Countermeasures

Two friends walking across the African plains notice a lion following them. One stops and pulls running shoes out of a pack. "Hey, you can't outrun a lion," says the other, to which the first replies, "All I need to do is outrun you."

—*As told by Len D'Alotto, GTE Laboratories, at NetSec '96*

The point is, if you are hard to catch, attackers may move on to other targets. That is the approach you need to take to security. While you may never achieve a totally secure environment, at least you can make things difficult for hackers. Don't let your guard down, and don't get tired of running from the lions!

Defining Security

Information security is the practice of protecting resources and data on computer systems and networks, including information on storage devices and in transmission. Make it your business to control and monitor the security of your systems and to implement security policies and procedures that people can follow.

The National Institute for Standards and Technology (NIST) has outlined the following security standards, which it refers to as the Minimal Security Functional Requirements for Multi-User Operational Systems. You can use these standards as a guideline for developing your own security policies and procedures:

- ♦ **Identification and authentication** Identification and verification of users through a logon process, and authorization to use other systems based on this security clearance

- ♦ **Access control** Rights and permissions that control how users can access network resources and files

- ♦ **Accountability and auditing** A system of tracking and logging activities on network systems and linking them to specific user accounts

- ♦ **Object reuse** Methods for providing multiple users with access to individual resources

- ♦ **Accuracy** Methods for protecting resources against errors, corruption, and unauthorized access

- ♦ **Reliability** Methods for ensuring that systems and resources are available and protected against failure or loss

♦ **Data exchange** Methods for securing data transmissions over internal or external communication channels

In addition to these standards, physical security measures are required to prevent valuable equipment and data from being stolen, damaged, or destroyed.

Security Costs

Consider how much your organization can afford to spend on security. At the physical level, power surges, failing components, and other problems may bring down systems and cost your organization thousands or millions of dollars in downtime. In some cases, continuous access to information is critical to the operation of the entire business.

There are also direct costs, such as equipment costs, as well as administrative expenses. Beyond the dollar costs, there are expenses related to the inconvenience of the security system. It may simply take more time to get things done when complex procedures are in place to provide security. Will users circumvent these security procedures? How much will it cost to make sure they don't?

3

It's wise to have a security manager for large organizations. This person should work with upper-level management, department managers, system administrators, and users to develop a workable security plan. Just having a person who concentrates solely on security is one of the biggest advantages in the battle against computer crime. As organizations connect their internal systems—and connect to the Internet—a security manager becomes even more important.

Protective Measures

There are a number of protective measures that help you "harden" your defenses, put up walls, and lessen the chances that someone is going to physically or electronically attack your systems. A few obvious steps are:

♦ Create security policies, plans, and job positions as appropriate.

♦ Set up a security-response team, experts who handle security problems. The team can provide a place for users to report security breaches or contacts by suspicious people who may be industrial spies.

- ♦ Perform background checks on personnel and keep tabs on employees who are disgruntled, who are working closely with other companies, and who are in the process of leaving the company.

- ♦ Classify your employees much the way the military classifies its personnel, giving some people higher clearance for access to sensitive information than others. Make sure to differentiate between part-time and temporary employees.

- ♦ Simulate attacks against your own company to check its vulnerability. The military does this on a regular basis. In one case, a system was thought so secure that it could not be broken into. Then someone decided to try breaking into a different system, which was discovered to have a "backdoor" trust connection with the target system.

This last point is of interest only if you know how to launch an attack. An alternative method is to use some of the security evaluation packages discussed in Appendix D to automatically detect the weaknesses in your systems.

Physical Security Measures

You need physical security measures to protect your systems and data from theft, corruption, and natural disasters. They start with securing your sites. Security guards, key-card access systems, and surveillance equipment are critical if your site is "open" to the public or if your information is extremely sensitive. If hackers can enter your building undetected, they will have free access to computers, wiring systems, phone systems, and other equipment, as well as files and useful information on desktops or bulletin boards.

These intruders may pose as service personnel to access critical areas of your business. With enough time, they can copy files to disk or remove an entire hard drive from a system. They can also install bugs or monitoring equipment such as hidden cameras that watch people enter their passwords.

Thieves who steal a computer or a hard disk from a computer can take their time cracking encrypted files at their own site. The obvious way to prevent theft is to lock down systems. You can put a locked protective cover over a computer case, place computers in a sealed office, or use the locks that are installed in most desktop computers.

TIP: Physical locking devices are available from Kensington at (415) 572-2700 or by accessing **www.kensington.com.** Another vendor is PC Guardian at (800) 288-8126.

If you lock a computer in an office, consider using key-card access methods along with physical keys and password systems. Most desktop computers include locks that can minimize break-ins. However, it's simple for locksmiths to pick the locks. In many cases, the key for another system will unlock a computer that is locked down. Worse, users who lock their computer often lose the key. If you plan to use the keys, make sure you know about their limitations.

Some other points related to physical security are outlined here and relate to both desktop computers and servers:

♦ If you configure a computer's startup settings in CMOS memory to ask for passwords or set special system configurations, lock the cover so no one can erase the CMOS by removing the battery.

♦ Enable boot passwords and other security features on desktop PCs.

3

♦ Disable or remove floppy drives to prevent files from being copied to disk and to prevent users from uploading files that might contain viruses.

♦ If users must have access to a floppy drive, set the CMOS so the system always boots from drive C. This prevents intruders from starting a system with their own operating system disk.

♦ Secure your network equipment and cable to prevent wire taps. Always monitor the activities of service personnel. Don't trust anyone who wants access to this equipment.

Record all serial numbers on systems and mark them to indicate your company's ownership. If systems are stolen and recovered, these records and markings can be used as evidence, improving your chances of getting your systems back after the case is closed. In addition, a thief might sell your system to a "good citizen," who may in turn report the equipment as possibly stolen.

Fault Tolerance and Redundant Systems

Fault-tolerant systems are designed to withstand hardware failures and software errors. A fault-tolerant feature called *disk mirroring* writes data to two disks at the same time. If one disk in the pair fails, the other remains accessible to users. Windows NT Server supports disk mirroring options as well as RAID (redundant arrays of inexpensive disks) systems.

A RAID system writes data to an array of drives and protects against the failure of any one drive in the array. Data is "striped" to the set of disks, meaning that it is divided up into pieces with each piece written to a separate disk. The information that is written across the disks is encoded in a special way so that if any one of the disks should fail, the information on the rest of the disks can be rebuilt and made immediately available to users.

Replication servers provide a way to automatically copy data to other servers on your network. You can install servers in branch offices, then replicate information to those offices. This puts information "closer" to users at the remote offices and reduces transmissions over long-distance lines. In addition, replicated data provides real-time backup to fully functioning systems that can be accessed in case the primary system fails.

For some companies it is not unreasonable to create redundant data centers located far from any disaster that might destroy the primary data center. The military uses this strategy. You can build a complete secondary site or a scaled-down site that can be brought into service at a moment's notice. At this site you can also store backups that can be restored quickly.

Windows NT Server also supports *uninterruptible power supplies* (UPSs). A UPS can provide battery power to a server in the event of a power failure. The UPS automatically begins supplying power as soon as normal power is lost. While the Windows NT Server is running on battery power, it automatically begins an orderly shutdown procedure that closes files and writes information to disk should the battery power run out as well.

Backups

Backups are essential. You already know that. If your systems are stolen, destroyed by fire, or corrupted by hackers, you'll need to go back to the last uncorrupted backup. The National Computer Security Association provides some interesting figures. It estimates a cost of around $17,000 to recreate 20 megabytes of sales and marketing information. That figures goes to $19,000 for the same amount of accounting data and $98,000 for engineering data.

The procedures you use to restore backups are critical in the case of virus attacks. Your backups may be corrupted, in which case you'll need to go back in the archive until you find a non-corrupted backup set. Back up as frequently as possible and place backup media into permanent archives as often as possible. Virus contamination can destroy a whole series of backups, and you may need to go into permanent archives for the last good set of data.

A user who backs up files must have Read privileges in the directories that require backup and Write privileges to restore files. You must give these rights to trustworthy people, since they could use them for unauthorized activities. Anyone restoring files must be knowledgeable of virus-contamination issues to prevent viruses from being written to disk. In the Windows NT environment, a backup operator with special rights is charged with handling backup and restoring operations.

Windows NT and Windows 95 computers store all initialization and configuration information in the Registry. Back up the Registry on a regular basis so that you can completely restore a system to its original state if need be.

 NOTE: The Registry is discussed further in Appendix F, and you can learn about backing it up in Chapter 11.

Encryption

You can use cryptographic techniques to protect files stored on disks and backups from prying eyes, or to conceal data transmissions and electronic mail. Encryption utilities scramble files and lock them with a password key. Using encryption may cause a drop in performance. A number of encryption methods are available, as discussed in Appendix B.

Encryption may give you the feeling that your files are private, when in fact someone might have cracked your encryption key and begun reading all your files. The stronger the encryption system, the better, but be sure to implement additional security measures as appropriate. Also be aware that someone who gains access to your system might replace your encryption program with a Trojan horse version of the program that steals your password. Make sure the encryption software is protected and secure. Then take actions to monitor for possible virus infections.

Virus Protection

Viruses are a real threat to your network. They are easily contracted from unknown disks or by downloading files from online services, bulletin boards, and the Internet. Any of your network users can contract a virus at any time and spread it to the network. A virus is often hard to detect. It may wait on your system before it executes. Vigilant users or network administrators may detect unusual activity or notice an increase in the size of files (indicating potential infection).

You can monitor your system for telltale signs of virus activity, such as increased file sizes, changes in file timestamps, unusual disk activity, or an abrupt decrease in disk space. A better way is to install virus-detection software that does this for you automatically. Administrators and users must be trained in techniques for avoiding and detecting viruses.

Even after detecting and cleaning up a virus infection, there is still a good chance that the virus is lurking somewhere in your organization, ready to reinfect systems. It may even have infected the backup sets. You may need to implement a plan to detect and remove the virus throughout your organization. Check all workstations, disks, and other data sources for infections.

If you need to rebuild systems from backup, carefully scan the backups to detect the virus. Start with the most recent set of backups and remove the virus if possible. Otherwise, go back through the archives until you find an uncontaminated set. If you do need to rebuild a system, back up the most recent data files only. Executable files may contain unknown viruses. You can restore program files from your original program disks, assuming they are uncontaminated.

 NOTE: Refer to Appendix C for more information on viruses.

Securing Electronic Mail

Electronic mail is one of the greatest tools available in the information age, but at the same time it has created some very dangerous security problems that must be dealt with. Some problems with e-mail can be solved by implementing physical systems and safeguards, but your best defense is to implement strong policies about what can and cannot be done with the organization's e-mail system. Techniques for securing e-mail systems include:

- ♦ Concentrate all mail activities on a single mail server so that you can better manage the flow of messages and implement programs that safeguard against viruses.

- ♦ Implement advanced e-mail gateways that can check and correct all headers on outgoing mail and monitor the sources of incoming mail.

- ♦ Use encryption methods to secure the contents of messages. Users can encrypt their own messages, but if messages are going outside the company, you may want to install an e-mail gateway that encrypts all messages on their way out.

- ♦ Use digital signature to electronically sign all messages.

Microsoft Exchange Server is an advanced e-mail system that provides high levels of security and many convenient options for administering e-mail. It takes full advantage of the security features in Windows NT Server and provides Internet e-mail capabilities, the ability to set up discussion databases and create forms, and many other features, as outlined in Chapter 13.

Users must read and sign an e-mail policy either when they are hired or when they get an e-mail account. Both the employee and the personnel office should have a copy of the signed policy. Your e-mail policy must state that any messages sent on the company's system are subject to monitoring. As the system administrator, you have the right to read other people's e-mail, but only if you state it in a policy. You also need to limit your company's liability by forcing users to put disclaimers in messages to indicate that the e-mail author—and not your company—is solely responsible for the content of the message.

Your e-mail policy should include a statement similar to the following:

> *<Company Name>* provides electronic mail for business communications. You may use it in performing your assigned job duties. Inappropriate use of e-mail may result in loss of privileges, or in dismissal. Your electronic mail may be monitored in transit or stored on disk by management personnel for later review. E-mail may be archived for future reference or destroyed at the discretion of management.

3

For more information, refer to a white paper called "CSI Manager's Guide to E-Mail Security," available from Computer Security Institute at (415) 905-2626, or by contacting their Web site at **www.gocsi.com**. This paper outlines e-mail threats and countermeasures, and walks you through the process of creating e-mail policies. It also includes example policies and legal documents, and provides important legal information that you need to know if you plan to monitor e-mail or implement other security controls.

Securing Printers and Print Queues

There are security risks with printers and print queues. If printers are shared by network users, you might need to secure the printer area to safeguard queued documents that are coming out of the printer. Users who send print jobs to queues may need to wait quite a bit before their job is printed. In the meantime, someone could wait at the queue and steal the print job just as it comes out of the printer. To avoid this threat, lock the printer in a special room or put a staff member in charge of distributing print jobs.

While print jobs are waiting in the queue, people could either rearrange the order of printing or stop a print job in order to get their job printed first. A hacker might be able to copy a print job out of the queue and read the document. Windows NT lets you set up operators to manage printers and print queues.

Securing Network Communication

Cable and wireless forms of data transmission are subject to monitoring by people with network sniffers or receiving devices. You can protect internal network cables from tampering by posting guards and securing the wiring closets as appropriate. Check the credentials and closely monitor the activities of all computer service technicians, telephone repairers, and other service personnel, including air-conditioning and heating technicians.

If you have long runs of outside cable between sites, consider using fiber-optic cable, which does not emanate a signal outside the cable and cannot be monitored with devices that read cable signals (like the way your radio receiver reads radio signals). In addition, it is relatively easy to detect taps into the cable with optical-cable analysis equipment.

Data encryption is your best bet to prevent eavesdroppers from easily viewing and transmitted data. There are a number of bridging and routing devices for building long-distance networks between your corporate site, branch offices, and other facilities. Encryption is available with some devices. Each packet is encrypted and put into a new packet with a new header for transmission over the lines. The only information that eavesdroppers can glean from these packets is the addresses of the sending and receiving devices.

NOTE: Virtual WANs are covered further in Chapter 15.

Securing Remote Connections and Mobile Users

Remote sites and mobile users pose some interesting security problems for network administrators. More and more, users have a need to connect with corporate LANs from their home, branch office, customers sites, or hotel rooms. However, remote and mobile systems are subject to theft or to intruders who manage to access your enterprise network through the accounts of authorized users at remote sites. You can't be sure who is on the other end of a remote connection.

Lax security at remote sites gives intruders a chance to break in and plant bugs, viruses, and monitoring devices on computers. There is little choice but to add more locks, hire a guard, and tighten up security policies. You can improve your ability to positively identify remote users by using two-way authentication devices such as smart cards. Refer to "Advanced Authentication" later in this chapter for more information.

Once you've improved the security on the side of the remote user, consider putting restrictions on the internal resources that remote users can access. Then if unauthorized users do manage to break in, they won't be able to get very far in your system. For example, you can limit all remote-user access to a single directory on a single server. News and postings of interest to remote users are placed in this directory along with any files they might need to access. Replication techniques discussed in Chapter 11 can be used to copy data to and from the isolated server and other servers in the organization.

Web servers are a unique and practical solution for disseminating information to your remote users. Think about a Web site you've recently visited, then consider using this same technique to provide information like price sheets and inventory reports to your remote sales staff. You can put this information up on your public Web server, but require a password logon so that only your staff can get to the private company information. The Microsoft Internet Information Server (included with Windows NT Server) supports secure challenge/response logons over network connections. See Chapter 20 for more details.

3

Some other ideas:

♦ Require that your staff use hard-to-guess passwords, and assign them logon account names that are also difficult to guess. For example, instead of an account name like *JohnJones,* try a less obvious name such as *turbosalesman.*

♦ Enable passwords on laptops to prevent thieves from easily accessing information on the systems. You enable passwords by setting options in the setup program for the system.

♦ Require that all remote users encrypt sensitive information stored on their portable computers. Then if the system is stolen, all but the most determined hackers will be unable to view the information.

♦ Use dial-back options that call remote users back as soon as they call in, or call them at a specific location at a specific time. Calling back users at a pre-designated, trusted phone number has the additional advantage of centralizing telephone charges.

Internet Security Measures

The words "secure" and "Internet" are rarely, if ever, used together. Connecting internal systems to the Internet is a foolish thing to do unless you build defenses. Internet connections are like two-way streets on which external users can access systems on your internal networks while you are accessing the Internet. You might not even know that packets from Internet users have infiltrated your system. Firewalls are therefore essential.

Firewalls

A *firewall* is a system that puts up a defensive wall to keep intruders out of your internal network. A firewall is often called a *choke point* because it restricts traffic flow to a well-defined, easily monitored channel. A toll booth is an example of a choke point. At the firewall, you can implement various filters and services to allow and deny packets, and you can monitor traffic to look for intruders.

A firewall uses a number of techniques to allow or deny network traffic. One technique is *packet filtering*, in which only packets that match specific address requirements are allowed to pass. Another technique is to block packets that are not responses to requests made by systems on your own network. Firewalls may also perform *proxy services*. A proxy service makes requests on the Internet for internal clients or handles requests by Internet clients for services provided by internal systems. In this way, no Internet user ever interacts directly with your systems, and no internal user ever interacts directly with an Internet-connected system. The proxy server can be programmed to handle only specific types of requests from specific users.

Firewalls may also run different protocols to separate internal and external networks. For example, the Web server pictured in Figure 3-1 is accessible by both internal and external users. Internal users access the system using the IPX protocol; Internet users access the server using TCP/IP protocols. Traffic cannot be routed between the two network interface cards, because they run different protocols. A problem with this configuration is that internal users can't access the Internet because they use the IPX protocol instead of TCP/IP, which is required for the Internet. Note that IPX does give administrators access to the server so that they can manage its features and update files.

Web sites have become popular as a way for companies to provide information on the Internet. The most secure Web server is a stand-alone computer connected to the Internet but not to the internal network. However, this setup is not practical if internal users need to access the Web server as well. There are a number of techniques for allowing both internal and external users to access the same server while blocking intruders. These techniques are covered in more detail in Part 4 of this book.

I recommend using Microsoft's Internet Information Server for your Web site, not only because it tightly integrates with the security features of Windows NT, but also because it comes with the operating system without additional charge. It also works with Microsoft's new proxy server, as discussed in Part 4 of this book.

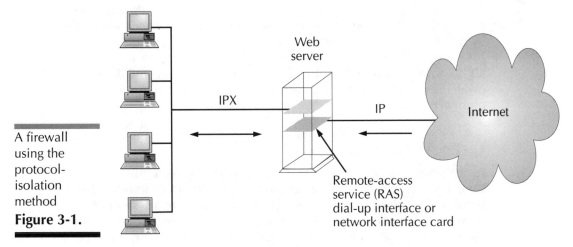

Web server

IPX

IP

Internet

A firewall
using the
protocol-
isolation
method

Figure 3-1.

Remote-access
service (RAS)
dial-up interface or
network interface card

3

There are a number of security protocols that can provide secure connections between Web servers and clients. For example, you can use security protocols such as SSL (secure sockets layer) and S-HTTP (secure hypertext transfer protocol) to strengthen the security of client-server Web connections. SSL can be used with any networking protocol, while S-HTTP is designed for HTTP use only. There are also secure protocols for business transactions, as covered in Chapter 21.

Security issues for Internet-connected networks can be quite complex. There is some question about whether systems are ever really secure, because hackers are learning new break-in techniques and discovering new security holes every day. All you can do is put up the best defenses possible and continuously monitor for break-ins.

Access Controls

The restraints that prevent authorized users and intruders from having free access to your information systems and data are called access controls. Some are logon controls that prevent users from logging on at certain times or from specific computers. There are also permission levels that determine exactly which directory and files a user can access. Access controls may be established by committees that include workgroup managers, department managers, division managers, system administrators, and security officers. Once the control policies are set, they are put into place by network administrators who grant access to individual user accounts or to groups of user accounts.

While access controls may restrict the activities of users, they also help protect a user's personal files from the prying eyes of other users. With Windows NT, each network user has a personal directory that he "owns" on a server. The owner's permissions in this personal directory include the ability to create new directories and files, change them, and delete them. No other users can access these directories and files, although the owner can grant access if necessary.

User Accounts

In the Windows NT environment, administrators create a user account for every person who needs access to the network. User accounts have a name and a password that users type to gain access to a system or to the network in general. A special guest account is available for temporary employees or visitors who don't require a special account but need limited access to the system.

Accounting systems and system logs can track the activities of users. Administrators can use this feature to track a user who is suspected of breaking into unauthorized systems on a network. However, a hacker might break into a system through a user account and masquerade as the real user, causing a trusted employee to be suspected of illegal activities. In one such instance, a nurse was accused of administering a fatal overdose to a patient who was due to testify in court against some mobsters. A look at the backup archives showed that a hacker had actually broken into the system and changed the prescription on the patient's medical records.

Logons and Passwords

The logon "event" has the greatest potential for compromising security on your systems. Users must make sure that no one sees them type in their password. Obviously, anyone who obtains a password for an account can access a computer system with all the rights and privileges of that account. It can be especially disastrous if someone obtains the password for the Administrator account. Two-way authentication schemes that use cards and passwords are recommended for maintaining secure environments.

Always use passwords that are not real words. Mix up characters to create passwords like "Qp&yTxT8e3." That's extremely difficult to guess or even crack, but also easy to forget. A more effective method is to create a phrase and use the first letter of each word as the password. For example, the password "Mbiot4oJ" is derived from "My birthday is on the 4th of July." (By the way, don't use this "my birthday" phrase. Now that its published here, someone might add it to the dictionary of a password-cracking program.)

Never write a password down or give it to another person for safekeeping: even a trusted person can have her wallet (containing the password) stolen. Change the password often, and don't use the same password that you use to access any other secure system, such as your bank machine.

On Windows NT computers, always press CTRL-ALT-DEL to activate logon. This resets the system and prevents Trojan horse logon programs from executing. Such programs are designed to look like a Logon dialog box, but they really run a hidden program or routine. For example, a program could capture your password as you type it, then make it available to someone else.

Users should always log off of a computer when leaving a system. A password-protected screen saver can be used to lock out the keyboard and screen and to protect programs that run while the user is away. These screen savers can also be set to engage if there is no keyboard activity for a period of time. It's a good idea to set these options just in case a user of a system walks away from the system unexpectedly without logging off.

3

Windows NT passwords can be up to fourteen characters long. If users take advantage of this full length, the possibility of passwords being guessed or cracked is greatly minimized. To further improve security, Windows NT never transmits passwords over the network in plain text.

When a user starts up a Windows 95 or Windows for Workgroups computer that is connected to a network, a logon screen appears. You must understand that this logon does not protect local files. It collects only logon information to be used to access shared resources on a network. All the files on the local system are accessible.

Windows NT is different. Files stored on NTFS volumes are hidden to anyone who does not log on with a proper password. This assumes that a DOS partition is not available on the hard drive and that the floppy drives are disabled to protect against hacker programs that read NTFS volumes by booting a system with DOS. Note that a truly secure system, as defined by the U.S. government, has its floppy drives disabled.

Protecting Directories and Files

Security for directories and file systems is your best tool for controlling post-logon access to a system. With it, you can control access on a granular level to directories and files, and put up restrictions that prevent intruders from gaining access to various systems and data areas. You can grant some users the ability to only read files while allowing others to both read and change files. You can also grant access to entire directories or just to specific files within directories. The NTFS file system in Windows NT is required to achieve this level of security. You can choose this disk-format option during setup, or upgrade an existing FAT drive at any time.

NTFS provides a variety of ways to protect files and directories. You can specify exactly which groups or individual users can access the resources on your systems. Inherited rights are used to simplify this task. A user or group that is granted rights in a directory has those same rights in the subdirectories of the directory unless they are specifically revoked.

There are two key things to remember when moving or copying files in Windows NT:

♦ Files that are moved retain all of the protections previously assigned to them.

♦ Files that are copied inherit the protections of the directory they are copied to.

Here's some information that's important to know when working with sensitive documents. Let's say that a user copies a file to her local drive or to a personal directory on the server. The file may now be unprotected, and subject to theft or unauthorized viewing. One way to retain the original rights of a file is to move it to one directory, then copy it back to the original, but this is an activity normally performed by an administrator.

Another safety measure is to keep files that are available to the public on a disk or disk partition that is separate from your operating system, application, or personal files. The public directories and the files in them should be marked as Read Only so that the files can't be changed or corrupted. If Internet users need to put files or other information on your server, create a "drop box" directory that has Write-Only permissions. This action allows users to put files in the directory but not to view, change, or execute any files in the directory. Be sure to check these files for virus contamination before using them.

Advanced Authentication

Passwords are the traditional method for providing a secure logon to a system, but it has been shown that passwords, even those that are encrypted, are relatively easy to capture in a network transmission and hackers are getting better at cracking encrypted passwords. Many vendors are providing a number of alternative methods for authenticating users, including the following devices:

Dial-Back Systems   These call a user back at a preset number to ensure that the originating call is not from an unauthorized location. However, dial-back does not work well for mobile users, and is rendered useless by such telephone features as call forwarding. Dial-back is best used for remote dial-in to remote-access servers, rather than as an authentication device over public networks like the Internet.

The Global Positioning System (GPS)   Certain devices use this system to verify the physical location of a user on the planet, thus ensuring that a call is not coming from an unauthorized location. For more information on the GPS, contact Peter MacDoran at International Series Research (303) 447-0300.

Biometric Devices   These scan eyes or fingerprints to verify the identity of a user for access to computer systems, data centers, and other facilities. However, biometric devices are costly, and it's unlikely that many people will like having their eyes scanned by a light-generating device every time they log onto a system.

Token Devices   Devices such as microprocessor-controlled *smartcards* are used to implement *two-factor authentication*. The smartcard generates *one-time passwords* that are good for only one logon session. Users enter this password along with a password they have memorized to gain access to a system.

3

This last technique has become the most practical for use with mobile and remote users. The technique is similar to using a bank card at an ATM machine. A typical smartcard such as the SecurID card from Security Dynamics (**www.securid.com**) contains a microprocessor that generates and displays a new, unpredictable password (card code) every 60 seconds. The card displays this unique password, which is different for each card, on a liquid-crystal display. Each card is programmed with a unique seed number and Security Dynamics' proprietary algorithm.

Here are several vendors of advanced authentication systems along with brief descriptions of their products:

♦ **Datakey Inc.** produces a line of security products called SignaSURE that can provide authentication and certification services. Call (800) 328-8828, or access **www.datakey.com**.

♦ **E-Systems** produces Authdisk, which provides authentication, discretionary access control, and powerful tamper protection for notebook computers and remote systems. Contact E-Systems at (813) 573-0330.

♦ **ActiveCard** makes token devices that work with computer security systems for all major computer and communication networks, including public switched telephone networks, cellular networks, LANs, WANs, intranets, and the Internet. Call (415) 654-1700, or access **www.activcard.com**.

♦ **Digital Pathways** makes a complete line of security devices including authentication systems based on smartcards and software. Call (415) 964-0707, or access **www.digpath.com**.

TIP: For a complete discussion of token authentication techniques, refer to an article in *Data Communication* magazine (May, 1995) by Johna Till Johnson entitled "The Safety Catch." The article describes dial-in access protection schemes and the products available from a number of vendors. You can get a copy by calling (212) 512-6615.

Auditing Systems

Accounting and auditing systems are designed to track the activities of users. When an auditing system is enabled, processes and activities are logged to files for later review. Users who access the system leave a trail that auditing administrators can follow to determine if the user is engaged in unauthorized activity.

Auditing a system tends to reduce that system's performance. Each event is written to disk, which can fill quickly with auditing information. In addition, sorting through auditing logs can be a chore. The Windows NT Server auditing system lets you audit specific events to help keep the auditing load minimized. For example, you can audit only the systems that are most vulnerable to hackers or only those that unauthorized employees might attempt to access. You should always audit failed logon attempts, attempts to access sensitive data, and changes to security settings. Monitor the audit logs on a regular basis to locate intrusions.

If you know that your system is under attack, you should enable appropriate auditing options to monitor the attacker. Keep in mind that an attacker who has gained access to administrative accounts may be able to change the audit logs and hide his activities. You'll need to monitor your system in real time if you suspect this type of activity. Be careful in this case. If a hacker knows he has been detected, he may lock you out or destroy information on the system before you manage to lock him out.

It's a good idea to select an auditor who can watch over the audit and system logs and maintain a somewhat neutral position with regard to your other system administrators. In addition to managing the auditing system, an auditor might also use various security diagnostics tools to evaluate the security settings of systems on your network and make necessary corrections. Security diagnostics tools, as discussed in Appendix D, can detect the following security weaknesses:

♦ New accounts that are unknown or unauthorized

♦ Weak user account settings and accounts without passwords

♦ Unusual account activities, such as access to unauthorized resources, logons at strange hours, or logons from unauthorized systems

♦ Missing file ownership information: this file may be a bomb by someone who doesn't want to leave any trace of where it came from

The auditing system can also be used to detect virus outbreaks. You can monitor unexpected attempts to access executable files (.EXE) and program libraries (.DLL), or attempts to modify these files or create new executable files. However, auditing these events may generate a lot of information, so do this only when actively monitoring a system.

NOTE: You'll find more information about auditing in Chapter 10.

3

Detecting and Dealing with Attacks

When you start to notice suspicious activity on your systems, or when your auditing logs show the telltale trails of hackers, you can either take immediate action to block these activities, or you can secretly monitor their activities and attempt to find out who they are and what they are doing.

The first option is dangerous because the hacker may take some immediate action if he knows he has been discovered, such as taking whatever information he needs before you completely lock him out. The second option is dangerous because you allow him to continue breaking into your system, but that might be essential if you are interested in apprehending him.

NOTE: Incredible as it sounds, you cannot legally monitor a hacker's activities unless you post logon notices that say all users must log on to valid accounts and that all activities may be monitored.

Set system alarms that alert you when a hacker has intruded into a system. This approach assumes that you are aware of a hacker's activities. Try creating false files that divert the hacker into an area of your system that is being monitored. If you suspect hacker activity, enable the auditing system in the areas where you suspect he is working. The hacker may follow the same pattern every time he breaks into your system.

While monitoring the hacker, keep your activities hidden. If the hacker finds out that he has been discovered, he may access your system through other unknown routes to lose you. He may also damage some part of the system or steal information in a last-ditch effort. You may prefer just to cover up the holes in your security and block out the intruder as soon as possible.

In addition to the auditing system, backups can provide a sort of "log" that helps you locate files that the hacker may have altered or changed. For example, you can check file sizes and dates; if they have been changed, try to determine unauthorized access.

If you suspect that the hacker is an inside operator, use the audit logs to determine which system is perpetrating the attacks, then set up hidden cameras or equipment to monitor keystrokes and catch the hacker red-handed, so to speak. To track a hacker outside your organization, get the help of local and/or long-distance telephone carriers, Internet service providers (ISPs), local police, and possibly the FBI. Keep in mind that computer-related crimes are still misunderstood by the law-enforcement community. Officials in most areas are not familiar with techniques for investigating these crimes and may not have the proper equipment or staff to do so. They may also have little experience in prosecuting a hacker they apprehend.

If you catch a hacker, never take him in as a "security consultant" unless you prevent him from using or accessing your systems. Try to meet off-site, and be sure not to give out vital information. Most hackers have criminal minds and will plan the next break-in while suggesting ways to strengthen your security.

Counterattack!

And if you wrong us shall we not revenge?

—William Shakespeare

To some people, revenge is a viable option. (Whatever makes you feel better.) If your system is under attack and you know the attackers, why not attack their system? Cyberwarfare! Some have even proposed that such attacks are justified. Some hackers think themselves so smart that they fail to put up defenses of their own. In that case you might be able to knock out the hacker's ability to attack your system, at least for a while.

Notorious hacker Kevin Mitnick made the mistake of breaking into the home computer system of Tsutomu Shimomura, a member of the security community. Shimomura launched a counterattack that traced Mitnick's location, where he was arrested by authorities.

In reality, counterattacks are probably not a good idea. First, your attacker might be able to hide all of his activities on your system but record yours, then press charges claiming that you are the attacker. You'd better know what you're doing before you annoy a hacker!

3

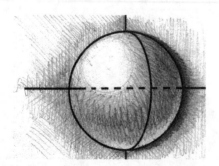

CHAPTER 4

Security Policies and Management

Despite all the countermeasures you can take to protect your systems, perhaps the most practical way to provide security is through a consistent set of policies and procedures. Policies must be implemented company-wide and adhered to by everyone. You can hire a security manager or create a security committee or task force to locate security weaknesses, develop policies, and enforce the rules. Good security also depends on a well-defined hierarchy of administrators, system operators, and users as well as a clearly defined policy defining user access to resources. Some of the other things you need to implement as part of your security plan are discussed in this chapter.

Planning for Security

To create a security policy, first determine problems with the existing systems and get some idea of your objectives. Look at your current systems and assess your needs:

♦   What are the current problems? Interview managers, users, technicians and anyone else who can provide information about security problems and requirements.

♦   Gather information about people, data, and resources, and how they are managed. Flow charts, personnel profiles, job descriptions, and other information should be available from personnel departments, division managers, and department managers.

♦   Based on job descriptions, determine who needs to access what and grant users the lowest level of access possible for the resources they need to access.

♦   What types of protection do you need? Look at your physical security requirements and the requirements of systems and software.

♦   Evaluate each component and grade its importance so you know which systems require the most immediate attention.

♦   Determine the cost of the system and work it into your budget without spending too much money on a security that is so difficult to use that users circumvent it.

♦   Consider your liabilities. If private information about employees or customers gets into public hands, you or your organization may end up in court. The United States has 6 percent of the world's population and 70 percent of its lawyers.

Each one of these areas may require the attention of a separate person on your security management team, or the attention of department, workgroup, or division managers, depending on the size of your organization. Specific items to develop in your security policy and plans include:

♦ Physical protection measures to prevent theft and guard against natural disasters

♦ Security measures for desktop systems that prevent theft of equipment or data

♦ Password policies that specify long, hard-to-guess (but easy to remember) passwords or coding scheme that creates hard-to-guess passwords from phrases and other information

♦ Security for local area network and wide area network communication to prevent line monitoring or transmissions by unauthorized areas

♦ Virus and Trojan Horse controls for the entire network

♦ Internet security such as firewalls, Web server access, and secure business transactions

♦ Electronic mail and business-transaction safeguards, including the use of digital signatures to validate messages

♦ Encryption techniques to protect stored files, backups, electronic mail, and data transmissions across private or public networks

♦ Encryption techniques to protect proprietary information on laptops and other portable computers

4

♦ Management structures that define administrators, local managers, users, information security officers (ISOs), and information security auditors (ISAs)

♦ Active monitoring to detect break-ins, hacker activities, or unauthorized access to resources by employees

♦ Data protection plans that define backup procedures, off-site storage, and data recovery methods

♦ Methods for securely distributing programs and information throughout the organization

♦ Intrusion detection/reporting and lockout policies that protect the company and its officers from accusations of cover-ups, misappropriations, and theft

♦ Employee training programs designed to reduce security exposures and to define your security policies for legal purposes

The controls you put in place should be consistent throughout the organization and enforced equally in all areas. A breakdown in one area will create security holes that may put the rest of the system in jeopardy.

Your objective is to discover and define all the threats that may exist for your organization. Constantly reevaluate your systems and your operating procedures to find new holes or problems that could lead to security exposure. If you have formed a security committee or security team, schedule regular meetings where everyone can discuss issues.

Implement the plan at an appropriate speed. You'll need to make a smooth transition to a security system that implements many new controls. Implement the plan in stages, tightening controls further at each stage.

Getting Help

There are a number of organizations that will help you build security into your information systems. Internet Security Corporation (ISC), a wholly-owned subsidiary of Software Developers Company, consults with organizations to identify and prevent security risks associated with using the Internet and intranets to conduct business. They assist in security audits and assessments, analyze security vulnerabilities, develop and review security policies, and plan and implement security for your organization. You can contact ISC at (617) 863-6400 or visit their Web page at **www.security.com**.

Of course, there are appropriate responses for dealing with hacker attacks, and there are many people and organizations that can help you. CERT (Computer Emergency Response Team) is a group that watches over security threats on the Internet. It provides advisories, security tips, and information about recovering from and preventing intrusions. You can contact CERT at **www.cert.org** or (412) 268-7090.

Another organization that can provide you with information about security is the Computer Security Institute (CSI). CSI is an international organization that trains security professionals and provides a wide variety of information to members and nonmembers. It publishes several newsletters and holds conferences and exhibitions. You can connect with CSI's Web page at **www.gocsi.com**, or call the institute at (415) 905-2626.

The Information Systems Security Association (ISSA) is an international organization of information security professionals that provides educational materials, publications, and general knowledge about security issues. ISSA's goal is to promote management practices that ensure the availability, integrity, and confidentiality of resources on computers and networks. ISSA's Web site is at **www.uhsa.uh.edu/issa/**, and its phone number is (708) 699-6369.

The National Computer Security Association provides information and material about security in general and can be contacted at **www.ncsa.com** or (717) 258-1816.

Finally, you can contact me for updates on Windows NT security. I provide periodic updates about Windows NT networking and Windows NT security in my "Windows NT Update Notes." These notes also provide information about training seminars and video tape training material. Send your name and address to the following address. This is a private mailing list.

Windows NT Security Update Notes
P.O. Box 947
Cambria, CA 93428

Information Management and Control Issues

Your organization no doubt owns the information it generates, but who controls this information and access rights to it? Where do you store information? Who handles backups and archives? Usually, individual departments, workgroups, or divisions claim ownership and control over the information they create. That makes it difficult to implement company-wide security plans and procedures. You need to work closely with these groups, but getting too many people involved can be chaotic. Upper-level management may need to dictate a centralized security plan to meet the information protection needs of the company. Information owners need to be made aware of their role and responsibilities in regards to information protection.

In client-server environments, these issues get complicated. Users have powerful desktop computers generating information that is stored on local drives. Can you keep this information secure from hackers, theft, or corruption? Managing information that is spread out all over the network can be a nightmare, but centralizing the data on servers at a data center may be a monumental task that creates other requirements, such as the need to protect against local disasters or to improve network response times due to increased traffic.

4

There are, of course, advantages to centralized operations: servers and other equipment can be kept in very secure rooms where a trained staff can manage systems under tight supervision. Backup systems are then easier to implement, and expenses are lower in most cases.

Access Issues

How do you decide who gets access to information and at what level? This process is simplified if users are assigned to groups such as "temporary employees," "clerks," "engineers," or "department managers." Workgroups are groups of people who work together on projects but may not work in the same department. For example, a workgroup that designs a new product may consist of people from engineering, marketing, sales, and administration. A hierarchy of managers who set security policies can decide how access is assigned to these groups.

Generally, a Windows network consists of the management and user-level groups outlined below. You should create a hierarchical structure on paper that defines access for these groups:

♦ **Top-level administrator** The person who controls the Administrator account for Windows NT Servers in local groups or domains.

♦ **Administrators** Managers from different departments, workgroups, or divisions who control and manage information resources for specific areas of the company.

♦ **Trusted users** Employees who have access to sensitive information.

♦ **Risky users** Employees who should have limited access to network resources. They are either temporary employees, new users, or users with limited job responsibilities.

♦ **Public users** As organizations connect to the Internet, users on the Internet may access resources on FTP servers and Web servers. These users have very limited access to information on specific servers. You may require system logon with a password so you can track who is accessing a system.

♦ **Anonymous users and guests** Public users or internal users who sign onto the network without a name or password. They use the generic anonymous or guest account to access limited resources.

♦ **Intruders** Anyone attempting non-authorized access to any resources on a network.

Administrators

The administrator on a Windows NT Server or network holds an incredible amount of power. He or she controls access to all system resources and information. This is no mindless position! It's a full-time job that requires a competent person. For security reasons, you need to run a thorough background check on any person hired for the job. Some organizations may choose to establish a committee of managers who execute the highest-level administrative tasks. As mentioned in the previous chapter, each person on the committee has a piece of a password that must be entered with the other members' pieces to gain access to the system.

 NOTE: A secondary group with a "backdoor" password may be essential in case one of the members of the primary committee is unavailable in an emergency.

The Windows NT environment is organized around domains, which are groups of computers that belong to individual departments, divisions, workgroups, or other structures. Trust relationships are set up between domains so that a user in one domain can access resources in other domains. Each domain may have its own administrator who either sets policies or answers to a higher-level administrator who sets policies for the entire organization.

Domain administrators decide how trust relationships are established between domains. However, there are some potential security problems with this scheme. If administrators freely grant access between domains, security holes can quickly develop. To improve security, it is recommended that a company-wide administrator review and set up trust relationships among domains. This is discussed further in Chapter 7.

Large organizations will have subadministrators who manage either various resources on the network or systems at branch offices. These administrators are not always familiar with the inner workings of the systems they manage; they may need detailed policies and procedures to help them perform more effectively. Make sure that all system managers are properly trained.

If the organization has a diversity of systems, security policies will be difficult to implement, because mainframes and network servers have different security implementations. The administrative staff should include people who are familiar with the security and management requirements of each system.

4

Information Security Officers

An information security officer (ISO) specializes in planning, implementing, and monitoring the security policies of the organization. The ISO must have a technical background to outwit wily hackers and attackers. He or she must know about the inner workings of operating systems, network communication, monitoring equipment (sniffers), software analysis tools, and techniques for detecting problems and catching intruders. At the same time, the ISO should have a good business sense and the ability to work with the rest of the organization.

ISOs are security police who look for and track potential security problems. They must ensure uniform levels of security to prevent weak spots. The ISO also collects information from employees about security incidents and contacts by suspicious people. Simply having a security officer helps improve security, because that means someone is concentrating solely on the problems of security.

Security Auditor

The security officer may also be the security auditor, but in large organizations separate auditors are used to spot suspicious activities, policy deviations, and other security problems. The auditor watches the activities of all employees, including administrators and managers. The auditor must operate in a way somewhat detached from the rest of the organization.

Security Standards

The National Security Agency has outlined the requirements for secure products in a document titled "Trusted Computer System Evaluation Criteria" (TCSEC). TCSEC is more commonly called "The Orange Book." This standard defines access-control methods for computer systems that computer vendors can follow to comply with Department of Defense security standards. Secure networking is defined in the "Red Book," or "Trusted Network Interpretation."

As of August, 1995, the National Security Agency (NSA) granted the C2 security rating for Windows NT Server and Workstation version 3.5. The C2 rating refers to a set of security policies that define how a secure system operates. As a result, Windows NT is on the NSA's Evaluated Products List (EPL). Being on the evaluation list implies that Windows NT is an operating system that can help you achieve C2 certification for your installation.

 NOTE: No operating system is ever C2 certified. Certification applies only to a complete installation that includes not only the operating system, but hardware, software, and the environment in which a system is installed.

The security policy defined in C2 is called *Discretionary Access Control* (DAC). It is implemented in Windows NT as a system in which users own objects. Objects such as files are easy to understand, while the Clipboard and a window are a little more esoteric. Users control protections over the objects they own and are accountable for all their actions related to object access. This system differs from the NSA's B-level security, which defines classified objects and a Mandatory Access Control (MAC) system in which objects have a security level defined independently from the owner's discretion. A user who receives a file marked "secret" cannot give other users permission to view the file unless they have a "secret" clearance.

To learn more about C2 security in Windows NT, refer to Appendix A. For information on operating-system security-certification specifications, contact the National Computer Security Conference (NCSC) at (202) 783-3238.

Educating Users

Education is the key to ensuring that employees take your security plan seriously. In large organizations, it is critical that everyone in the organization comply with security policies in a consistent way.

If your users are not aware of security risks or security policies, you will end up with security breaches, accidents, lost data, or other problems. You'll improve your confidence that your network is secure by educating users. It helps to make users aware of the following:

♦ The security policies of your organization

♦ The sensitivity of personal and corporate data

♦ The need to keep an organization's data private

♦ The need to keep logon information private

After educating users, it's a good idea to have them sign a statement to verify their understanding and agreement to the policies and procedures for your network. The document can be used for legal purposes in cases where employees are caught deliberately hacking your network.

4

Tell users what level of access they have to resources on the network so they don't attempt to access files or devices that they don't have access to. You can also tell them about how the auditing system tracks user activities!

You can educate users with training sessions, a newsletter (printed or sent over e-mail), brochures, and other techniques. You can even stage security intrusions and drills.

For more information about making people aware of the importance of security, get your hands on a copy of CSI's "Manager's Guide to Computer Security Awareness." It describes how to get a security-awareness program started and how to use various tools such as presentations, slides, posters, pamphlets, and newsletters to keep in touch with computer users. You can get the brochure by calling (415) 905-2626 or by visiting CSI's Web page at **www.gocsi.com**.

Recovering from Disasters

An essential part of your security policy is recovery from disasters. Consider how much of your business relies on your information systems. Loss from downtime could cost hundreds of thousands to millions of dollars, as well as your job once the smoke clears. Do people know how to do their job manually if systems are down for extended periods of time?

Identify the most critical applications and services in your organization, then identify the hardware systems these applications require and any dependencies on other systems. Also watch for shifts in what qualifies as the most critical system in your organization.

You may need to keep backup equipment nearby or build an alternate data center, depending on your budget and the critical nature of the information. Spare equipment can become a lifesaver in a disaster. All those old PCs that your company moved out during an upgrade can be stored in a warehouse away from the main site. Set up a small network with servers in the warehouse that can be quickly expanded in case of emergency. In an emergency, your most critical business functions can be handled from this site, if necessary.

Your backups are your most important recovery tools. Test your backups and the procedures you use to restore them. Store backups as permanent archives in off-site locations. You might need to go back through several sets of archived backups if information was corrupted by malicious users or a virus. Keep records of changes made to system settings, user accounts, and data files. You might need to redo these changes after you restore data.

Replication servers can protect against local disasters by copying information on a real-time basis to servers at other locations. Also consider creating multiple connections between sites to protect against failed links. Ideally, those links should follow different paths and connect with different service providers.

Finally, create an emergency response team and train the members to handle problems as they occur, such as virus incidents or failed equipment. Assign a team leader who will coordinate plans and activities in preparation for disasters as well as during disaster drills and actual disasters. A rehearsal can involve the following:

♦ The immediate response once a problem is discovered. For example, if a virus is discovered on a server, you might want to abort a planned backup or disable replication of information to other servers.

♦ Contacting the appropriate people to rebuild systems, reenter critical information that was lost, or manage the restoration of sensitive information

♦ Steps for getting systems back online or moving the operations to a backup site

♦ Rebuilding systems as appropriate

♦ Recovering backups from off-site storage and restoring them

You get the idea. There are many steps involved in this process, and your safest approach is to develop a well-conceived plan that can be tested and proven effective in an emergency situation.

Security Policies

A security policy is an organization's statement about how it will provide security, handle intrusions, and recover from damage caused by security breaches. It sets policies for employees and for how security is managed. Write security policies into employment contracts and include some level of "user accountability" to ensure that users comply with policies. Use auditing and other techniques to monitor policy compliance and track users who might be compromising the system. Post notices on bulletin boards and on computer logon screens that describe the policies of the organization.

Once a policy is in place, compliance is important to maintaining the same level of security throughout the organization. However, that does not mean that deviation is not allowed. In fact, the policy must be flexible enough to allow for changes in policy. But changes must be handled appropriately. Managers and users should not change policy on their own. Any changes must be authorized by management and written as an amendment to the policy.

4

Policies conjure up images of large unreadable documents and difficult rules that are sometimes ignored. Strive for a policy that is easy for you to implement and for users to understand and follow. In fact, the process of developing a policy is probably more important than the policy itself, because it forces you to look at all the things you must do to attain a level of security that is appropriate for your organization. You must also consider what actions you will take in the event of an intrusion or disaster before these events occur. A policy is a tool that prepares you for the worst.

Policy and Procedure Statements

This section discusses policy highlights for Windows NT networks. If you need to know more about the policy-writing process, including appropriate structure and wording, refer to books on the subject, or contact organizations such as CSI (**www.gocsi.com**) and NCSA (**www.ncsa.com**).

Logon Policies and Procedures   The logon process is a potential security risk. Warn users to protect their passwords and use caution when entering passwords during logon. Someone could be looking over their shoulder.

♦   Implement a password policy. Change passwords frequently and avoid using passwords that are easy to guess. Never write passwords down.

♦   Log off when leaving a computer, or use a password-protected screen saver.

♦ To avoid accidents, managers should avoid logging on as the Administrator.

♦ Do not log on to any administrative account from workstations in unfamiliar environments. Viruses could attack critical system files. Logons could be monitored with hidden cameras or other devices.

♦ Display information to users about the last time they logged on so they can detect if anyone else has been using their account.

User Accounts and Groups

♦ Administrative users need two accounts: one with extended privileges that is only used to manage the system, the other with limited privileges to use for all other activities.

♦ Rename the Administrator account with an obscure, hard-to-guess name.

♦ As an option, implement a fail-safe Administrator account logon in which two or more people have a piece of the logon username and password and must be present to sign on.

♦ Set logon-failure lockouts for user accounts to prevent security intrusions.

♦ Disable or delete user accounts when employees leave the company.

♦ All users should use an account with only the privileges necessary to perform their assigned tasks. Assign as few privileges to an account as possible.

♦ Disable the Guest account, or if you need to keep it, carefully review where it has privileges.

♦ Keep no unnecessary accounts on any system.

♦ Set up separate system-management roles for backup operators and printing-system operators.

Directory and File System

♦ Use NTFS (NT file system). It provides advanced security that can lock out unauthorized users.

♦ Make users aware of the permissions attached to files, and inform them that the permissions may be lost when files are copied.

♦ Do not grant mistrusted users with the ability to execute programs in a directory where they can copy files.

♦ Never copy sensitive files to directories that do not have adequate security settings.

♦ Create directory structures on servers to help you protect files.

♦ If you provide information to the public, restrict access to isolated directories on isolated systems if possible.

Data-Protection Policies

♦ Don't leave the backup media in the backup device where they can be stolen.

♦ Encrypt backups if the information is sensitive.

♦ Use tape-rotation methods and store permanent backups in safe off-site locations.

♦ Ensure the protection of backups during delivery to off-site locations.

♦ Document and catalog all backups to provide evidence of theft.

♦ Perform periodic data-recovery drills to test the integrity of backups as well as backup-and-restore procedures.

♦ Back up files on workstations as appropriate.

Policies for Secure Transmissions

♦ Take active measures to protect against eavesdroppers, wire tapping, and hijacked sessions.

♦ Physically secure all areas where cables run or terminate.

♦ Monitor the activities of outside service technicians and consultants who might put a tap on an internal network.

♦ Use fiber-optic cable for all cable runs that cross public areas, such as between buildings in campus settings.

♦ Require encryption to transmit sensitive information and to prevent packets captured by sniffers from being replayed on your network.

♦ If you use the Internet to connect remote sites, use link-encryption devices that automatically maintain links between sites and encrypt all transmitted information.

Policies for Remote and Mobile Users

♦ Establish strict policies for anyone who travels with company information on portable computers or who connects to the company's network from a remote site.

♦ Require and implement additional identification procedures for remote users, such as one-time logon devices.

♦ Use difficult-to-guess logon names and passwords and key card systems.

♦ Don't let users save their passwords on disk for the next logon. A hacker who steals a computer could break the passwords and log on to a network.

4

♦ Encrypt sensitive company files on portable computers to make it difficult, if not impossible, for hackers to view them.

♦ Use callback systems in which a computer calls a remote user back at a known and trusted telephone number.

♦ Change logon names and passwords often, as well as the phone numbers that users dial into. If you use callback options, change remote phone numbers often, if possible.

Virus-Control Policies

♦ Control how software is shared to prevent the spread of viruses.

♦ Control the use of public-domain software, such as shareware and freeware.

♦ Run anti-virus software on systems throughout the organization and get the latest updates.

♦ Check files from unknown sources with anti-virus software.

♦ Control how disks and mobile systems move in and out of the company.

♦ Make users aware of virus problems through training, education programs, and regular postings on company bulletin boards or e-mail.

♦ Lock down computers to prevent malicious people from directly copying viruses to them.

♦ Keep up with the latest virus information by reading weekly computer journals or joining organizations like the National Computer Security Association (**www.ncsa.com**).

♦ Set up a quarantine computer to test disks, programs, and other possible virus-carrying media until they can be cleared as virus free.

Electronic Mail Policies

♦ Write a strong, enforceable policy that outlines appropriate uses for e-mail and penalties for abuse.

♦ Reserve the right to monitor e-mail.

♦ Implement security controls and virus protections.

♦ Consider the use of encryption and digital signatures.

♦ Ensure the physical security of the post office server.

♦ Promote security awareness for users.

♦ Establish procedures for destruction and/or retention of archives.

♦ Have users read and sign e-mail policies, as outlined in the preceding chapter.

Post and Display Legal Notices   Your policies must specify the posting of legal notices. You can post these notices on bulletin boards throughout the company and on the logon screens of users' computers. A legal message should notify users that they can be held legally responsible for any activities on the computer that are outside their normal activities or that undermine the security of the information systems.

If legal notices do not exist, users may feel they can freely browse the network and access directories and files without restriction. Windows NT provides a way to display a legal notice upon logon, as described in Chapter 6. The following is an example of a legal notice that can appear on a user's screen at logon:

```
Authorized Users Only
The information on this computer and network is the property
of (company) and is protected by intellectual property rights.
You must be assigned an account on this computer to access
information and are only allowed to access information as
defined by the system administrators. Your activities may
be monitored.
```

4

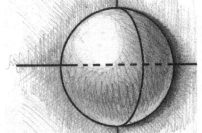

PART 2

Windows NT Security

CHAPTER 5

An Overview of
Windows NT Security

This chapter looks at Windows NT security through a microscope and from the vantage point of high-level administrators who need to maintain it. Windows NT security can be quite complex, especially when you look at how it works deep down in the operating system. Still, as complex as Windows NT security may seem, it accomplishes two very simple things:

♦ Restricting access to objects such as system resources, files, and devices

♦ Providing auditing services that generate an entry in a log for operations on an object

The rest of Windows NT security is built on these concepts. The idea is to verify that users are who they say they are during logon, then authorize their access to resources. This requires a user account that defines who users are and what they can do on the system. In a network environment, security is critical. Users place data on servers that are shared with other users and expect a high level of security.

You can't install Windows NT without its advanced security features. If you could, your system would be more like Windows 95 than Windows NT. However, the default security settings that are made during the initial setup are not necessarily optimized for tight security. You must evaluate and upgrade the security settings to fit your needs. That's what this book is about.

An interesting side point is that getting advanced security is practically impossible on operating systems like MS-DOS, Windows, the Macintosh, and OS/2. These operating systems are designed so that users can access system resources with few, if any, restrictions. The underlying operating system is too weak to allow the addition of strong security. Windows NT is an object-oriented operating system, and its security is built into the lowest levels of the object structure. That makes Windows NT easier to secure than almost every other operating system.

Windows NT takes advantage of features in the Intel 80386 (and above) processors to implement some of its security features. Protected-memory features prevent any program from accessing the code or data used by another program or by the operating system itself. Every program runs in its own protected memory. Unauthorized attempts by one program or process to access the memory of another program or process is denied by the operating system.

The user account is a central theme of the Windows NT operating system. Anyone who wants access to a computer or network types a username and a password to gain access. The information the user types is checked in a user account database that holds information to verify users. If the information matches, the user is "authenticated" onto the network.

You can compare user account security to the physical security you might put in place for your own home or business. You give your mother an extra set of keys to your house because you trust her (at least *most* people trust their mothers). If you own a business, you give some trusted employees keys so they can get into the office after hours. All the while, you lock areas such as the warehouse or the accounting department to all but the most trusted employees. An operating system should provide this same type of flexibility, allowing you to give some users greater access than others to a system or network.

This chapter will explain the underlying security controls and the elaborate security systems that have been built on top of it in Windows NT. First, I'll discuss the basic access controls as they apply to a Windows NT computer, whether it's a server or workstation. Then, under the section "Windows Network Models," I'll discuss how NT security applies to network users.

As you read through this chapter, keep in mind that operating systems don't make security problems go away. No operating system can provide you with a complete security solution. You must define a level of security that fits your needs and integrate Windows NT and its security features into your scheme. Your security plans must include both physical and logical security measures. Your objective is to build the best defense you can against intruders and accidents.

About C2 Security

5

Security in Windows NT is based on security guidelines developed by the U.S. Department of Defense. This level of security applies to stand-alone workstations but not to network security. The latter is a completely different and much more complex security level that requires a whole range of security considerations beyond what any computer operating system can supply (such as securing the transmissions lines).

However, following these guidelines for individual systems provides a high level of security and an incremental step toward what is needed to secure an entire network. C2 certification is discussed in Appendix A, along with a tool that helps you ensure that your Windows NT installation is C2 secure.

A Microscopic View of Windows NT Security

NT security provides a way to control user access to your system that can be compared to security clearances for a business or even a military facility. Windows NT uses *discretionary access controls* that let you control exactly which users get access to what. You may already use discretionary access controls in your own business: some employees get access to personnel records and some don't; some employees can pull stock from the warehouse and some can't.

The level of access may vary for different areas of the business. For example, you might give a group of employees permission to access the warehouse, but restrict their access to especially valuable items that are locked up in caged areas. You might create a security policy that categorizes employees into groups called "warehouse personnel" and "warehouse managers." Of course, warehouse managers will have a higher level of access in the warehouse. You might control entrance to the warehouse by employing a security guard, installing an electronic cardkey system, or both.

Metaphorically, the Windows NT security system is similar to this guard-and-cardkey system: a guard at the Windows NT door validates users and lets them in, then gives them a cardkey that grants them access to secured resources throughout the system.

At your warehouse, the guard identifies employees by sight or some other method, then lets them into the warehouse and gives them a special cardkey. The employee uses the cardkey to gain access to secure areas of the warehouse. However, the cardkey doesn't guarantee access to those secure areas. The cardkey reader, which is connected to the company's computer system, might disallow access to a secure area at the discretion of management, even though a user has a cardkey that normally permits access.

Likewise, Windows NT uses this "two-way" authorization. A user must first have the right to access some resource on the system, then the resource must allow it. The former is a "right" and the latter a "permission." Users may have rights to access resources, but the resources must have permissions to allow it. You can think of rights as a sort of job description for a user. Windows NT has rights that allow users to do some very interesting things, such as back up system files, shut down the system, load and unload drivers, and manage auditing logs. Permissions define how users can access such objects as directories, files, and printers. This is like letting a warehouse employee operate a forklift. Anyone allowed into the warehouse can sit in the driver's seat, but only employees that have been given permission in the form of a key can start it up and run it.

The "rights" side of the picture is controlled by user accounts. In the Windows NT environment, a user account can be compared to the personnel file of an employee. It contains information about the user and the rights she has on the system. The account is assigned a unique security identifier (SID). In the warehouse analogy, the SID is like an employee number. When employees arrive for work, the security guard may give them a cardkey based on their employee ID.

If the user has an account, the password is valid, and the user has permission to access the system, a security *access token* is generated when a user logs on to a Windows NT computer. The access token contains the user's SID in addition to IDs for groups the user belongs to. As the user accesses resources on the system, information in the access token is compared with information that resources hold about exactly who can have access. This is where two-way authorization comes into play. Every resource holds a list of users who can access it; the entries in this list are compared to the entries in the user's access token.

Windows NT Architecture

The components that provide security in Windows NT make up the security subsystem. Figure 5-1 shows how this system fits into the Windows NT architecture. Like most other models, it is layered with the computer hardware at the bottom and high-level applications at the top. Users interact with the highest-level components. All the layers in between provide services to upper layers and interact with lower layers.

Suppose you've decided to design a brand-new computer operating system. To ensure that it gains industry acceptance, your first objective is to make it

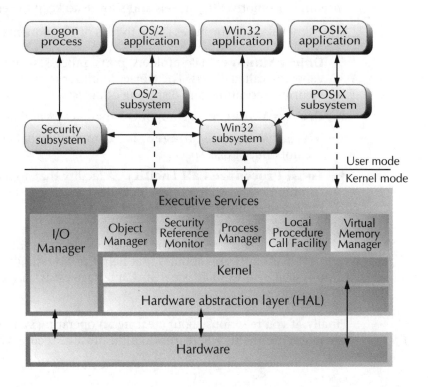

The Windows
NT architecture
Figure 5-1.

easy for hardware and software vendors to design products that work with it. Imagine that you are Bill Gates, with many millions of dollars to spend on this project. You decide to call the operating system Windows NT.

First, you realize that there are many different computer processors on the market, including the Intel, DEC Alpha, and PowerPC chips, so rather than choose one platform, you create a very small core software module (called a Kernel) that runs on each one of these chips. To make it easy for developers, you create a "hardware abstraction layer (HAL)" that hides (abstracts) differences in hardware from upper layers. With this approach, developers see different types of hardware in the same way, making it easier to write programs.

Next, you know that the operating system will be used in a variety of end-user environments, and that not everyone will need all the services that an operating system is expected to provide, so you create a modular system in which components can be added and removed. These modules conveniently attach to the Kernel.

The Kernel schedules activities for the processor to run. These processes are called threads, and the Kernel is in charge of keeping the processor busy running threads. It makes sure that higher-priority threads are pushed ahead of lower-priority threads. The Kernel is like the guy who shovels coal into a speeding locomotive: he shovels and shovels to keep the engine running hot.

The Kernel also synchronizes the activities of components attached to it:

♦ **Object Manager** Files, folders, ports, processes, and threads are generally called *objects*. The Object Manager is in charge of naming, security, allocating, and disposing of objects.

♦ **Process Manager** A component that creates and deletes processes.

♦ **Virtual Memory Manager** The component that creates simulated memory out of disk space.

♦ **Local Procedure Call Facility** A facility that applications use to communicate with lower levels of the operating system via a message-passing facility.

♦ **I/O Manager** A component that manages communication between the operating system and the outside world. It handles device drivers, which are software modules that help the operating system access physical devices such as network interface cards, disk drives, and cache memory.

Finally, if you're serious about creating an operating system that people will use in environments where information must be secure, you'll need a security system. That's discussed in the next sections. Windows NT provides all of these components in a system designed from the ground up to be portable among different processors, scaleable to multiprocessor systems, secure in a way that meets U.S. government standards, and extensible in a way that allows modules to be added as needed.

Object-Oriented Design

Almost everything in the Windows NT operating system is represented as an *object*: files, memory, devices, system processes, threads, and even windows that appear on the desktop. Objects are the key to providing a high level of security in the Windows NT operating system:

♦ An object is a self-contained entity that contains its own data and the functions needed to manipulate that data.

♦ There are many types of objects; what they can do is defined by the *object type*.

♦ All objects in Windows NT can be accessed only by the operating system itself through strict controls.

♦ The security system checks all access to objects, and the auditing system can log these events.

The concept of a self-contained object with its own data and functions is a little odd at first. Think of an object as a box that contains information and functions for manipulating that information. Perhaps the object contains information about your bank account. On the outside of the box are functions (think of buttons) for retrieving information such as your current balance. Any process outside the object must use the functions to get information from the object.

5

A typical application may be built from hundreds or thousands of objects. A good analogy is a car, which is built by assembling many small objects. For example, the steering wheel object controls the steering objects. It connects to those objects through a standard interface. The driver who is at the upper level of all this simply turns the wheel and doesn't need to be concerned about the underlying objects that make it work.

What does this have to do with security? First, objects hide their data from the outside and provide information only in certain ways, as defined by the functions of the objects. This prevents external processes from accessing internal data directly. That makes sense when you consider that a data file is an object that you restrict access to by controlling who gets to look inside. Just keep in mind that everything in the Windows NT operating system is an object.

Windows NT achieves high levels of security by never letting programs access objects directly. Any action on an object is authorized and performed by the operating system. It is relatively easy for Windows NT to perform these checks on objects since individual objects hold much of the information that is needed to do a security validation.

The Windows NT Security Subsystem

The Windows NT Security subsystem affects the entire Windows NT operating system. It provides a single system through which all access to objects, including files on disk, processes in memory, or ports to external devices are checked so that no application or user gets access without proper authorization. The security subsystem components described here are pictured in Figure 5-2.

Local Security Authority (LSA)   This is the central component of the security subsystem that generates access tokens, manages security policies on the local computer, and provides authentication for user logons. In the warehouse analogy, this system is comparable to a person or system that manages security for the entire site.

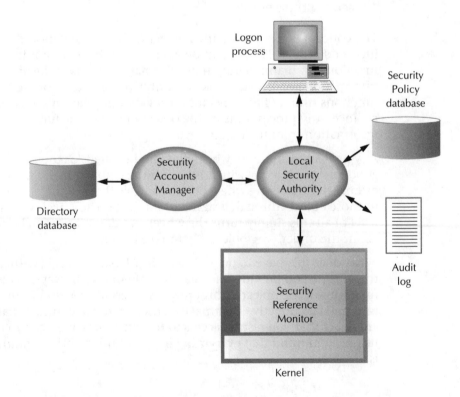

The Windows
NT security
subsystem
Figure 5-2.

Logon Process   This process logs on both local and remote users. In the warehouse analogy, this is what happens when an employee arrives at work and checks in with the security guard.

Security Accounts Manager (SAM)   This system maintains a database of users who are authorized to access the system and verifies users during the logon process. In the warehouse analogy, this can be compared to a computer that checks personnel records.

Security Reference Monitor (SRM)   This is a Kernel mode component that prevents direct access to objects by any user or process. It validates all access to objects. In the warehouse analogy, the SRM is like a security officer who enforces security policies. It also generates appropriate auditing messages.

The directory database is interesting because in a network environment it may exist on a number of machines. When a user logs on to a local machine, the SAM on that machine retrieves user IDs from the database. In a Windows NT domain network environment, user account information may be stored in a directory database on one or more servers called domain controllers, which share and update account information. This shared database allows users to log on once in order to access resources throughout the network.

The Logon Process

The process of gaining access to a Windows NT system starts by booting the operating system or by pressing CTRL-ALT-DEL to initiate a new logon. Pressing CTRL-ALT-DEL protects against Trojan Horse-type programs that masquerade as the operating system to trick users into typing their logon name and password. The CTRL-ALT-DEL key sequence assures you that a valid Windows NT logon sequence will initiate. This key sequence should always be pressed when logging on to a machine that is already running.

5

NOTE: Windows 95 computers and other non-Windows NT computers do not have this logon protection.

The logon process also allows users at desktop systems to have their own personal desktop configurations. When users log on, the settings they had in a previous session are fetched from a profile and restored.

A service called Netlogon provides a single access point for users to log on to a domain network. Netlogon is responsible for replicating changes in the security database to all domain controllers so that users can log on from any of the controllers. The Netlogon service runs on any Windows NT computer that is a member of a domain.

The Windows NT logon process is outlined here and pictured in Figure 5-3.

1. When the logon screen appears, users enter their username and password, and the name of the computer or domain to log on to. The username is used for identification and the password is used for validation.

2. The Local Security Authority (LSA) runs an authentication package to validate the user. The authentication package may be the built-in Windows NT authentication package or a custom package from another vendor.

3. If the user has specified logon to the local machine, the authentication package has the local Security Accounts Manager verify that the username and password are in the directory database. If domain logon is specified, then the authentication package forwards the credentials to a domain controller for authentication via the Netlogon service.

4. The local or domain Security Account Manager returns appropriate security IDs if the account is valid. The SAM also provides other information such as account privileges, home directory location, and logon scripts.

5. The LSA creates an *access token* that contains the user's security ID, the security IDs of groups that the user belongs to, and the rights that the user has in the local system.

   Windows NT uses subjects to track and manage permissions for the programs each user runs. A subject is the combination of the user's access token and a program that acts on the user's behalf. Programs or processes that run on the user's behalf are running in a security context for that user; the security context controls what access the subject has to objects or system services.

6. The last step is to create a subject and run programs.

   At this point, the user is identified in the system and can begin accessing objects based on the discretionary access controls on those objects.

More about the Logon Process

Users can either log on to a local computer using an account on that computer, or log on by being validated by another computer. In domain networks, the user is validated by a primary or backup domain controller that holds a copy of the directory database. The outcome depends on what the user types into the Domain field of the Logon dialog box.

♦ If the user types the local computer name in the Domain field, the local computer will log the user on to the local system.

♦ If the user types a domain name in the Domain field, a Remote logon takes place in which the logon request is sent to a local domain controller for verification. If the domain specified is not the local domain, the domain controller forwards the request to a domain controller in the trusted domain specified.

Domain controllers authenticate the user account name and password by comparing them to entries in the directory database. If the entries are valid, account identification information is sent back to the logon computer through the domain controller that originally tried to verify the user account. Note that if a normal logon fails, the user will be logged in to the Guest account, but only if the Guest account is enabled and passwords are not required.

Now assume the user is already logged on and attempts to access resources on other computers. In this case, the credentials that were used to verify the original logon are "passed through" to the new server and used to authenticate the user for access to those resources. This is called "pass through authentication" and it frees users from having to log on to every new resource they access.

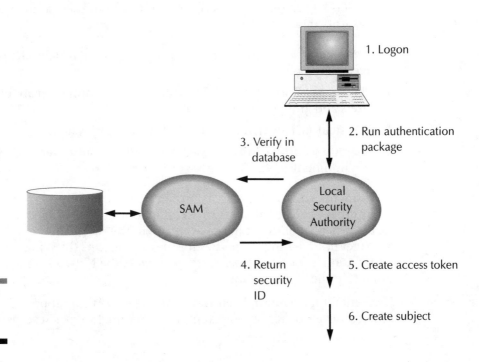

1. Logon

2. Run authentication package

3. Verify in database

SAM

Local Security Authority

4. Return security ID

5. Create access token

6. Create subject

The Windows NT logon

Figure 5-3.

5

NOTE: Refer to Appendix A for detailed information about the logon process.

Discretionary Access Controls

As mentioned previously, objects in Windows NT include everything from files to communication ports to threads of execution. Every object can be secured individually or as a group. Objects have different types of permissions that are used to grant or deny access to themselves. For example, directory and file objects can have Read, Write, and Execute permissions while print queues have permissions such as Manage Documents and Print. Also note that directories are "container" objects that hold files, so permissions granted to the container are *inherited* by the file objects in it.

Keep in mind that access controls and user-account rights are two different aspects of the Windows NT security system. User-account security identifies and validates users, while access controls restrict what users can do with objects.

All objects have a security descriptor that describes their security attributes. The security descriptor includes:

♦   The security ID of the user who owns the object, usually the one who created the object

♦   The Access Control list (ACL), which holds information about which users and groups can access the object

♦   A system ACL, which is related to the auditing system

♦   A group security ID that is used by the POSIX subsystem, a UNIX-like environment

ACLs are the crux of this discussion. An ACL is basically a list of users and groups that have permissions to access an object. Every object has its own ACL. Owners of objects can make entries in the ACL using tools like File Manager or by setting properties for files and folders (in Windows NT 4.0). Other utilities for setting permissions include the Network and Services utilities in the Control Panel.

Users might have multiple entries in an object's ACL that provide them different levels of access. For example, a user might have Read permission to a file based on her user account and Read/Write permission based on a group membership. Each of these permissions is listed in a separate entry in the Access Control list.

When a user attempts to access an object, she usually has a certain *desired access* such as Read or Read/Write. To grant (or deny) access, the Security Reference Monitor compares information in the user's access token with entries in the ACL. Remember that the access token contains security IDs and the list of groups that the user belongs to. The SRM will compare this information with one or more entries in the ACL until it finds sufficient permissions to grant the desired access. If it doesn't find sufficient permissions, access is denied.

If the SRM finds several entries for the user, it will look at each entry to see if that entry or a combination of the entries can grant the user the desired permission to use the object. For example, in Figure 5-4, user AColgan has requested Read/Write access to a file object. The Security Reference Monitor compares AColgan's access token to the file's ACL. Entry 1 is checked first, and the SRM finds that the Users group has Read permission and AColgan is a member of the Users group. However, AColgan has requested Read/Write access, so the SRM checks the next entry with similar results. Entry 3 provides a correct match because AColgan belongs to the Managers group and has requested Read/Write privileges.

5

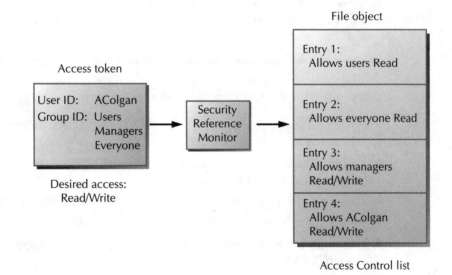

Comparing access tokens and ACLs to validate access to objects

Figure 5-4.

Entry 4 is not needed because Entry 3 has satisfied the security requirements. Note that some entries in an ACL may deny access rather than allow access to an object. For example, the No Access permission would revoke all access to an object even though a user might have access permissions through other entries in the ACL.

Windows NT Auditing System

Remember that the Windows NT security system does two primary things: it restricts access to objects and provides an auditing service that keeps track of operations on objects. The auditing system collects information about how objects are used, stores the information in log files, and lets you monitor events to identify security breaches. If a security breach is discovered, the audit logs help you determine the extent of damage so you can restore your system and lock out future intrusions.

You control the extent to which the auditing system tracks events on your systems. Too much auditing can slow a system down and use tremendous amounts of disk space. You'll need to carefully evaluate how much auditing you need. When you suspect unauthorized activities, probably the best approach is to audit these events:

♦   Failed logon attempts

♦   Attempts to access sensitive data

♦   Changes to security settings

NOTE: Chapter 10 provides more information on how the security system can help you detect intruders.

You can use the Event Viewer to view the following security events:

♦   User and group management events, such as creating a new user or changing the membership of a group

♦   Subject tracking, which tracks the activities of users, such as when they start a program or access objects

♦   Logon and logoff events on the local system or for the network

♦   Object access, both successful and unsuccessful

♦   Changes to security policies, such as changes to privileges and logon capabilities

♦   Attempts to use privileges

♦   System events that affect the security of the entire system or audit log

Here is a typical security log in the Event Viewer:

By double-clicking any event in the log, you can get detailed information about that event. In this example, a file was successfully opened and closed. You can imagine that tracking these types of events will require quite of bit of the system's time and disk space if many files are opened and closed on your system.

The auditing system tracks security events by two IDs: the user ID and the impersonation ID. This is to help identify users who might otherwise be impersonated by certain processes in the system. A process-tracking mechanism is also used to track new processes as they are created and provide information about both the user account that is performing an action and the program that was used to perform the action.

The auditing system has one drawback that is true of auditing systems on almost any operating system: it can tell you which account was used for an operation, but it can't be sure that it was the original owner who was using the account. Don't be quick to blame a user for unauthorized activities just because his user account is recorded for those activities.

Windows Network Models

While this book is primarily about Windows NT Server and its security model, a typical Windows network consists of Windows for Workgroups, Windows 95, and Windows NT Workstation computers. These computers can implement their own schemes for sharing resources that are somewhat independent of the security system in Windows NT.

5

First, consider that there are basically two networking models in the Windows environment: the workgroup model and the domain model.

Workgroup Model   A simple network model in which users at their own workstations participate with a group of other users to share resources. The local user can be responsible for granting access to resources on her computer to other users in the workgroup. All current versions of Windows support workgroup networking out of the box. The names of computers are important in this model.

Domain Model   In the domain model, access to resources is tightly controlled by a central administrator who manages a Windows NT Server computer that is running a domain-management service. This model implements valid user accounts which are required for permission to use shared resources.

The domain model is really an advanced form of the workgroup model. The collection of workgroup computers simply becomes a domain in which user account security is handled by a domain controller. However, even when the domain model is in use, any client can still choose to share a resource on her computer with another computer on the network.

The Workgroup Model

Workgroups are ideal for small department networks in which a few people need to share resources. Figure 5-5 illustrates a network that consists of three

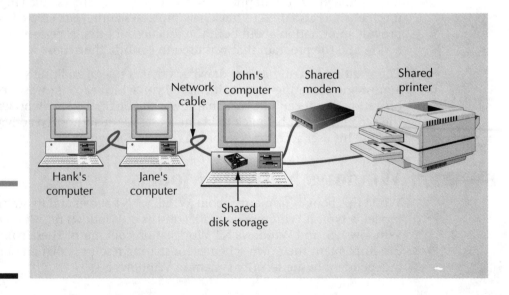

A Windows
workgroup
computing
model
Figure 5-5.

workstations that share the resources on one of the workstations. Larger networks might consist of linked workgroups in different departments, such as accounting, sales, manufacturing, and design.

The workgroup concept does not imply any sort of security. Its main benefit is to make it easy for a user to locate a computer when browsing the network. For example, if only one workgroup were used for a network of 100 or more computers, users would need to browse a long list of over 100 computers to find a system they want to access. If the computers are divided into workgroups, the user chooses a specific workgroup to open a window on a much smaller list of computers in that workgroup.

On Windows workstations, you can choose between two access control methods: *share-level* access control and *user-level* access control. The first is available on any Windows network, while the latter requires that a Windows NT computer or NetWare server be attached to the network to handle user accounts. Incidentally, if you want to set up a domain, you need a Windows NT Server computer.

To specify either share-level or user-level access control, you go to each workstation on the network and enable the option of choice in the Network utility. Shown here is the Network utility for a Windows 95 client:

5

You click the Access Control tab and choose one of the options. If you choose user-level access control, you must specify the name of a Windows NT computer (or NetWare computer) that holds a list of user accounts.

Share-Level Access Control

In the share-level model, a user chooses to share resources on his computer with other network users. Notice that I said "other network users," not "a specific network user." Take a look at the following dialog box:

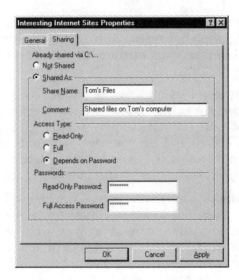

This is what you see when sharing folders on Windows 95 computers that have share-level access enabled.

Notice the Access Type and Passwords sections. You can't specify any particular user name. You choose to share the folder with everybody on a Read-Only basis, with Full access, or depending on password. If you choose Read-Only or Full, users can access the folder without typing a password. If you choose Depends on Password, then you specify a password in the Passwords field that users must type to access the folder for Read-Only access and for Full access. Then you give the Read-Only password to users who get Read-Only access and you give the Full access password to users who need full access. This is a flexible scheme, but not secure because passwords are often exchanged on a casual basis.

Sharing folders in this way gets interesting if you're concerned about security on your network. It gets really interesting if the user attaches to the Internet and does not disable sharing while online. In the latter case, any user on the Internet could connect with the computer and access the files! Fortunately, Windows 95 will disable file sharing when it sets up certain remote connections, but that doesn't mean that the options are guaranteed to be turned off whenever the user is online. You can manually change the options in Windows 95 by opening the Networks utility and turning the file-sharing options off.

User-Level Access Control

User-level access control is the second method for sharing resources on workstation computers attached to a network. Once again, settings are made at client workstations. With this method, access to resources is granted to individual users rather than just everybody. The user names come from the user account databases that are stored on a Windows NT computer or a NetWare server. You specify the name of the server on the Access Control page of the Network utility as pictured earlier.

When you share folders on your workstation using this method, a dialog box similar to this one appears:

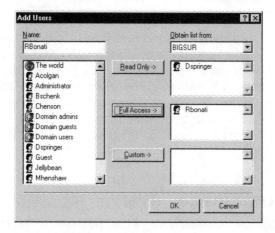

Here you can choose from a list of users who will be authenticated by the Windows NT or NetWare computer that manages user accounts. You don't need to have users type in a password, because they've already done so when logging on to the servers. In this way, passwords are kept private and not passed in the open like the share-level access method.

NOTE: To grant Read-Only access, you pick a user and click the Read-Only button; to grant Full access you click the Full access button.

Security Limitations of Workgroup Models

Share-level and user-level access controls restrict users on a network from freely accessing files on another network computer. But this only works over the network. Security on client computers running Windows 95, Windows 3.1, and DOS is basically non-existent because anyone can walk up to the computers and copy files to a diskette. There is no logon process or file permission system that prevents users from accessing files. Windows NT computers are secure in this respect because they have strong logon requirements and implement the security system discussed previously that includes Access Control lists, user IDs, and permissions.

With user-level security, users are already validated by typing their own personal password when logging on to the network. You don't need to share a password with the people who will access the shared resources on the workstation, so there's no proliferation of passwords throughout the workgroups. User-level access controls give administrators more centralized control of security on networks where individual users are sharing resources on their own computers.

Another option for small networks is to designate a single Windows NT Workstation computer or Windows NT Server as a shared computer that everybody on the network accesses. In this setup, no other computers share resources. A Windows NT Workstation can be accessed only by ten users at a time, while a Windows NT Server can be accessed by an unlimited number of users, depending on the licenses purchased. In this arrangement, an administrator needs to manage only user accounts on the servers.

Domains

Domains are collections of computers and computer users that are managed by a central authority. Domains may span departments, divisions, and/or workgroups, as well as other types of computer groups. You use them to make groups of computers more manageable and to apply a security policy to specific areas of your network.

Because domains are groups of computers, they share some of the features of workgroups. For example, you can use domains to logically split up large networks into groups of resources that make it easy for users to find those resources. Also, users can still share the resources on their own computers when a domain is established using the user-level model. What domain networking provides is a way for network administrators to create highly secure network servers with strict access controls based on user accounts.

A *distributed network* is one in which networks in different divisions, departments, or workgroups, all with different data sources, have been linked together to provide an enterprise-wide information system, as pictured in Figure 5-6. Domains provide a way to maintain a single directory of users in large distributed-network environments. Because a domain is an administrative entity that encompasses a collection of computers, those computers might be next to each other or separated by some distance.

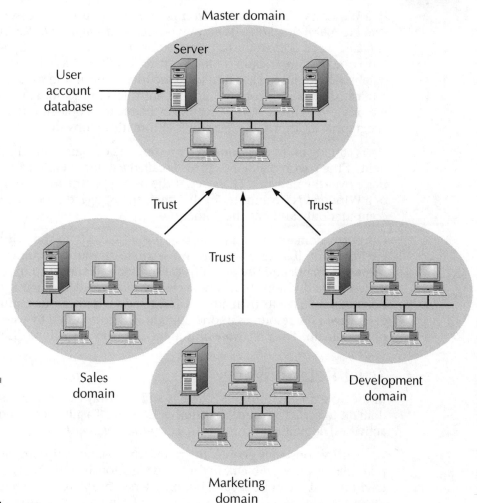

Master domain

Server

User
account
database

Trust

Trust

Trust

Sales
domain

Marketing
domain

Development
domain

Multiple
domains can
be centrally
managed or
individually
managed.

Figure 5-6.

5

Domains can provide:

♦ A single user account for any user, even though the network may consist of many different interconnected networks

♦ One-time logon for access to resources anywhere on the network

♦ Centralized network administration of users, groups, and resources

In a Windows NT domain environment, network users have user accounts that are maintained on a Windows NT Server *domain controller* in a *directory database*. Each domain has a primary domain controller (PDC) and may have one or more backup domain controllers (BDCs) as well. The directory database holds all the accounts and security information for a domain. It is replicated (copied) to other domain controllers in the domain for backup reasons and to make it more readily available to people in different geographic locations. Replication is automatic among domain controllers.

Users can log on to any domain by typing the domain name in the Domain field of the Logon dialog box. This is called a Remote logon, and it takes place over the network. However, if the user types the local computer name of a Windows NT computer in this field, she is logged on to the local computer only and not the domain.

Of course, domains are an important part of security in the Windows NT environment. If a company has two separate divisions, each may implement its own domain, and the domains can provide an administrative barrier between the divisions that can be closely monitored and managed. Each domain may have its own administrator, and together those administrators determine how resources in one domain will be accessed by users in the other domain. Trust relationships make this work, as will be discussed next.

Trust Relationships

In the domain environment, there is almost always a need for users in one domain to access resources in another domain. To allow cross-domain activities, domain administrators set up *trust relationships*.

To security-conscious people, the term "trust relationship" implies a potential security problem. In fact, trust relationships in the Windows NT environment are quite secure, but only when properly implemented. If you are not careful, there are many things that can go wrong, especially when administrators in one domain extend too much trust to another domain.

If an organization has only one domain, trust relationships are not required, but in large organizations many domains may exist, requiring trust relationships to allow information exchange. A single administrator can manage all the domains, or each domain can be managed separately with its own tight security. In the latter environment, the less that domain administrators trust one another, the better, since that mistrust will help maintain the autonomy of each domain. In organizations with lax security, administrators have been known to freely grant access to resources in their domain after a simple request made over the phone. Obviously, there are security risks involved in this if higher-level management thinks that domains are providing an adequate level of security.

There are one-way and two-way trust relationships. In a one-way relationship, one domain trusts the users in the other domain to use its resources, but not the other way around. In a two-way trust relationship, each domain trusts the other. Of course, after setting up trusts, the next step is to grant specific users and groups in one domain access to resources in another domain.

The best way to think of this is at the department level. For example, users in the accounting department often need a trust relationship with the sales department so that they can access daily sales information for accounting purposes. However, users in the sales department don't need a trust relationship with the accounting department, because the information on the servers in accounting is none of their business.

User Accounts and Groups

Any user who wants to access a secure Windows NT system must have a user account on that system. A username identifies the user and a password validates the user. Groups are collections of users. It is far easier for an administrator to assign rights and permissions to groups of users than to users one at a time. Groups can also be the focus of electronic mail lists and scheduling activities.

On stand-alone Windows NT Workstation computers, user accounts are for the workstation only and are managed with the User Manager utility that runs on the computer. In a domain network environment that consists of Windows NT Server computers, user accounts are managed for the entire domain, although Windows NT Workstation computers can still maintain local-only user accounts. In the domain environment, accounts are managed by the User Manager for Domains utility on the Windows NT Server computer.

5

T IP: You can install the Windows NT Server Tools package on a Windows 95 or Windows NT Workstation computer and run management packages like User Manager domains from an administrative workstation. The tools are included on the Windows NT CD-ROM.

User Accounts

User accounts contain information about users, such as their full name, their username, a password, the location of their home directory, information about when and how users can log on, and personal desktop settings if they are using Windows 95 or Windows NT Workstation.

When a new user account is created, Windows NT assigns it a unique security identifier (SID). All internal processes use the SID—rather than the username for the account—to identify a user account. This ID is unique for each account. If you create an account, delete it, then create a new account with the same name, the new account will have a different SID.

When you first install a Windows NT Server or Windows NT Workstation computer, two accounts are created:

Administrator   This is the highest-level account that provides full access to a system or domain. It is used to set up domains and alternate administrative accounts. The account cannot be deleted or disabled, but should be renamed and assigned a password to hide it from attacks.

Guest   This account allows very restricted access to a system for people who do not have an account. It is generally used for accessing information on "public" systems; it should not have the ability to write or delete information in most cases. By default, it is disabled in Windows NT Server 4.0. However, it is enabled in Windows NT Workstation 4.0 and Windows NT 3.1.

A system administrator is responsible for managing network and server equipment, system planning, user accounts, data storage, and a variety of other things. If other people will be managing a system by using the Administrator account, you should create alternate Administrator accounts for a very good reason: each account can be tracked individually in the audit log to detect malicious activities. If only one Administrator account were in use by several people, you would not be able to tell which user was doing what.

If the Guest account is enabled, unknown users can access any resource on a computer to which Guests and the Everyone group have access. In older versions of Windows NT, parts of the Registry can be accessed by a network client. The account is disabled by default on domain controllers, but enabled for other Windows NT systems. Carefully review the status of this account on all of your Windows NT computers. Keep in mind that users who log on as Guest don't need to specify a username, so you have no idea who is using the Guest account and you cannot audit a specific user's activities.

An Initial user built-in account is created on stand-alone Windows NT Workstation computers that are not connected to a network. During the setup procedure for the operating system, the user is asked to specify a username and password. If the computer is added to a domain during the setup process, the user is expected to log on using an account from the domain, so the Initial user account is not created.

Account Policies

The account policies control password restrictions and account lockouts.
You set account policies for all user accounts at the same time on individual
computers or in domains. The Account Policy dialog box is pictured here:

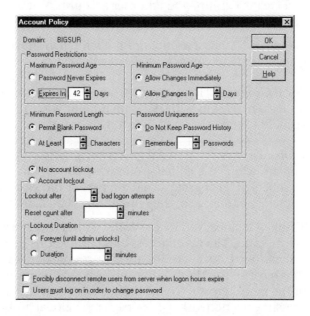

All of the settings on the Account Policy dialog box are critical if you want to
enable strong security. They ensure that passwords are not implemented
carelessly by users and are hard to guess. You can set the following options:

5

♦   Have passwords expire after a certain number of days.

♦   Force users to create passwords that have a minimum number of
     characters.

♦   Ensure that users don't reuse passwords that were recently used.

In addition, you can control intruder break-ins by setting the Account
Lockout options. If an intruder is attempting to break into a user account by
guessing passwords, you can lock that account out after a certain number of
unsuccessful logon attempts.

NOTE: Account policies are covered further in Chapter 8.

Groups

As previously mentioned, groups are collections of user accounts. It is far easier to grant rights and permissions to groups of users rather than to individual users, although you can still do the latter in special cases. After you create a group, you add user accounts to it and assign rights and permissions as appropriate.

Windows NT has a number of predefined groups. They fall into two categories: *local groups* and *global groups*.

Local Groups   This type of group defines permissions and rights for users on local machines within a domain, but you can add User and group accounts from other domains to this group.

Global Groups   A global group consists of user accounts only from the domain where the global group was created, but global groups can become members of local groups that are part of the same domain or belong to other domains. In doing so, they obtain the rights and permissions of those groups.

Think of a global group as a collection of users to whom you will need to assign various levels of access and permissions by making them members of other groups. Local groups are the groups that you add global groups to and that have all the rights and privileges that you want to grant to the members of the global group. Global groups exist only if a domain controller is present on a network. Of course, using global groups that span domains assumes that trust relationships exist among domains.

The following is a list of local groups for a domain. Note that except for Users and Guests, these groups are designed for management tasks; they have specific rights to administer devices or settings in the domain. Users added to these groups obtain the rights of the group:

♦ **Administrators** Users with rights to manage the system

♦ **Account Operators** Users with rights to manage user accounts

♦ **Server Operators** Users with rights to manage servers

♦ **Backup Operators** Users with rights to back up and restore files

♦ **Replicators** Users with rights to manage replication between servers

♦ **Print Operators** Users with rights to manage printers

♦ **Users** Normal users with accounts

♦ **Guests** Users without accounts who have very restricted rights

Local groups on Windows NT Workstation computers and Windows NT Server computers that are not domain controllers include Administrators,

Power Users, Backup Operators, Users, Guests, and Everyone. The Account Operators group is missing because these computers do not contain a copy of the directory database, nor do they participate in user and group management. Note that on stand-alone Windows NT computers that are not connected to a network, only local groups are created.

A typical scenario for granting access to resources in a domain, such as applications or devices (e.g., printers) is pictured in Figure 5-7. You use a local group (or create a new local group) that has permissions to access the resources, then add users or other groups to this group. If users in other domains need access as well, they are added to a global group in their domain; this global group is then added to the local group that has access to the resources.

For management purposes, a global group called Domain Admins is added to manage any Windows NT computer that becomes part of a domain. This group allows administrators working at Windows NT Server computers to remotely manage the computer's user environment and group accounts. This group also allows the administrator to perform any function that is allowed by the Administrator account on the computer.

User Rights

User rights define what users can do on the servers and workstations of a Windows NT network. Don't confuse them with permissions, which are the access controls that define which users can access objects (files, directories,

5

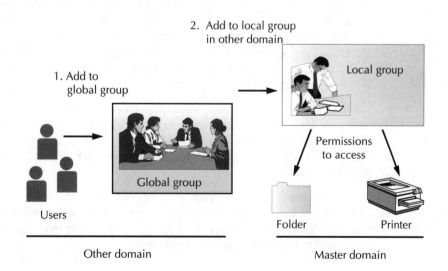

Managing global and local groups

Figure 5-7.

devices) and what they can do with them. User rights are granted directly to a user. Some of the more common rights are:

♦ The right to log on directly at a computer (local logon). Local logon at a server usually implies that the user will manage the server.

♦ The right to log on to a computer over the network (remote logon)

♦ Management rights, such as the ability to create new user accounts

Windows NT has some predefined groups that have specific sets of rights. You use these groups to make management easier. Users added to groups obtain all the rights and permissions of the group. For example, a Print Operators group has rights to log on locally, shut down the system, and share/stop sharing printers. A Backup Operators group has rights to log on locally, shut down the system, back up files and directories, and restore files and directories.

If the predefined groups don't fit your needs, you can create new groups with special rights. You can also grant a right to an individual user on a case-by-case basis, although this is not practical if you have a lot of users. Groups and rights are a critical aspect of maintaining a secure Windows NT environment. They are covered further in Chapter 8.

User Profiles

When a user logs on to a client computer running Windows, he can have various work environment settings loaded by the system. These settings include desktop layouts, color arrangements, network and printer connections, shortcuts, and other settings. Each user can have his own personal profile that is used no matter where he logs on, because profiles are stored on central servers. That means that a user can travel from one computer to another on the network and retrieve his personal Windows desktop settings.

All the administrator needs to do is specify a profile path into the user account. Then when a user logs on, their current profile is loaded. The first time a user logs on, the profile is empty, but any changes he makes to the desktop settings are stored in the profile when he logs off, to be reloaded the next time he logs on.

There are also mandatory user profiles set by administrators that cannot be changed by users. These mandatory user profiles are an important aspect of the security system, because they can prevent users from doing things on the system that might jeopardize security.

Windows NT File System (NTFS)

NTFS is a file system that provides more security than file systems such as the FAT system used in DOS. During Windows NT installation, you're given a choice of file systems, but if you're interested in security, you should always choose NTFS. NTFS provides a number of protections for files and directories that let you specify which users and groups get access to what information and exactly how they can access it.

There are some important distinctions between Windows NT and the NTFS file system as compared to other operating systems such as DOS. These features provide better security and higher performance:

◆ Windows NT does not rely upon DOS system services in any way. It boots on its own and uses its own services.

◆ All low-level disk access functions are performed by Windows NT-specific software drivers, not the disk drivers that are embedded in a computer's ROM BIOS.

◆ If you run a DOS program from within Windows NT, the operating system does not allow the program to directly write to hard drives.

While NTFS provides a high level of security, it is important to understand that this security is available only when Windows NT operating system is up and running. Someone who steals your system or hard drive could use a low-level byte editor to scan the drive and read or change its contents. NTFS provides a way to control access to files and directories with permissions, but those permissions do no good if the operating system is not available to control access. Your security must include physical security measures, and you might want to install encryption utilities to protect stored data.

5

Assuming that your physical security is in place, you can use the NTFS file system's special security features to restrict local and network user access to the drives. Keep in mind that permissions are the "other side" of security in Windows NT; they control access to all sorts of objects, not just file-system objects. The other parts of security are user logon, account management, and access rights.

Permissions determine the level of access that users and groups have to directories or files. You can set permissions on directories that are inherited by any files or subdirectories. You can also set individual permissions on files within directories.

Sharing Resources

There are two aspects to file-system security: the first is restricting access to information on a local computer to people who log on to that computer.

The second is restricting access to information that is shared over the network. When a directory is shared, users can access it from workstations attached to the network based on permissions.

To make information on a Windows system available to other users on a network, you share a folder. When you share a folder, all the files and all the subfolders in it are shared as well. You can then change the access permissions on any file or folder in the shared folder if you need to block access.

The name of a shared directory appears in the Network Neighborhood window for Windows 95 computers and Windows NT computers. MS-DOS users must use the Net View commands to see shared directories and files while Windows for Workgroups users can open shared folders in the File Manager.

Setting Permissions

Access to folders and files is controlled by permissions, and permissions are set by administrators or the owners of a resource. There are standard permissions and individual permissions. The individual permissions in the following list are used in combination to make up standard permissions, which will be described in a moment.

♦ **Read (R)** Open and view the contents of a file

♦ **Write (W)** Change the contents of a file or create a new file

♦ **Execute (X)** Run a program or executable file

♦ **Delete (D)** Delete files

♦ **Change Permission (P)** Alter the permissions of an existing file or directory

♦ **Take Ownership (O)** Make oneself the owner of a file or directory

The standard permissions are a combination of these individual permissions and are designed to provide a set of permissions appropriate for the most common user requirements. The standard permissions for folders are listed in Table 5-1. The second column lists the individual permissions that make up the standard permissions, and the third column indicates the permissions that new files obtain when they are added to the folder.

Table 5-2 lists the individual permissions that make up the standard permissions for files. Of course, you can create your own "special access permissions" at any time to fit a custom need.

Standard Folder Permission	Individual Permissions	Permissions for New Files
No Access	none	none
List	Read, Execute	not specified
Read	Read, Execute	Read, Execute
Add	Write, Execute	not specified
Add and Read	Read, Write, Execute	Read, Execute
Change	Read, Write, Execute, Delete	Read, Write, Execute, Delete
Full Control	All	All

Permissions for Folders
Table 5-1.

Users may get permission to access folders or files from a number of sources. For example, they might have Read permissions through their user account and Change permissions because they are members of a group. The highest-level permission applies, and the permissions are cumulative, so that permission assignments from different sources are combined. However, a No Access permission from any source denies access to the file or directory, no matter what other permissions are granted.

NOTE: Chapter 9 provides a more thorough explanation of permissions and the NTFS file system.

5

Standard File Permission	Individual Permissions
No Access	none
Read	Read, Execute
Change	Read, Write, Execute, Delete
Full Control	All

Permissions for Files
Table 5-2.

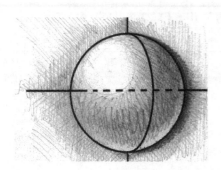

CHAPTER 6

Windows NT-Specific Threats and Solutions

This chapter provides an overview of security problems in the Windows NT environment and some of the solutions that are available to help you tighten security. While Windows NT implements strong security, it is not perfect. Here's just a small list of general problems.

♦ Users can log on as guests and gain access to resources available to the Everyone group.

♦ The Administrator account does not allow lockout (a good feature, but only if adequate precautions are taken).

♦ Administrative users can log on at insecure remote locations.

♦ Client systems may have weak security implementations.

♦ Unattended Windows desktops are doorways into the network for hackers.

♦ Malicious users might gain access to another user's logged on session.

♦ Network servers may not have been hardened against intruder attack.

♦ Network sniffers can capture traffic and hijack sessions.

♦ Electronic mail may contain viruses.

♦ Captured mail may contain sensitive information.

So with that, let's take a look at potential problem areas. Keep in mind that this section introduces many problems that are explained in more detail in later chapters.

About Holes and Backdoors

I read a line from an anonymous user in a chat room that asked "would you pay $5,000 for a completely bug-free version of Microsoft Word?" Good question. As large teams of programmers rush products to competitive markets, bugs and holes are inevitable. When putting program through test loops, programmers will bypass certain functions (like security checks) to make the tests run faster. But what if they leave the bypass mechanism in by mistake, and the program goes to production? Or what if the designers didn't fully understand the security requirements for running their program on Windows NT? Unfortunately, hackers may find and exploit these holes. Sometimes their discoveries become widely known. Sometimes the hacker guards them like trade secrets to prevent vendors from plugging the holes.

What holes and backdoors exist in Windows NT? They may exist in any running application or process. Consider the following advice given to programmers in a paper called "Windows NT Security in Theory and

Practice" by Ruediger R. Asche of Microsoft Developer Network Technology Group:

> When you write a secured server application, it is absolutely necessary that you design your application to be airtight; that is, you must protect *all* means by which clients may access your sensitive data. In the sample application, I show how remote access from a client to a server may be protected, but if the client and server happen to reside on the same machine, and the shared memory in which the database resides is not protected, the client can "sneak into" the database, thus violating security. One of the challenges of a secured system is to make the sensitive data airtight—this may be a fairly intricate task, as we saw in the case where protecting Registry entries alone is not good enough to protect a machine's device drivers.

What are the chances that any programmer can create a completely airtight program? You should carefully consider the implications of this question when installing any program or service on a computer system that holds sensitive information. Test all new programs on a quarantined system.

Windows NT has built-in services that are installed when you set up the operating system. It also has services that you can choose to install at any time, such as the networking components. You can also install services from third-party vendors. All this is done from utilities, such as Services, in the Control Panel.

If you open the Services utility, you see a dialog box similar to the following:

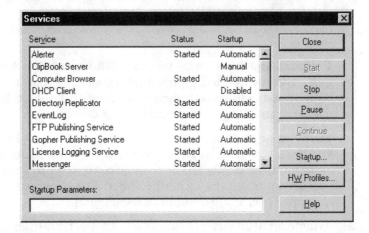

6

Notice that you can Start, Stop, or Pause services. You can also disable the Startup of options so they don't run at all. The basic strategy is to run as few services as possible so hackers can't exploit any bugs those services might have. Another strategy is to run services under less-privileged accounts, as you will learn in Chapter 10. Many services must run under the System account, which has privileges to the entire system. If you install a defective program that runs under this account, it could damage your system. Worse, a hacker might take advantage of a hole in the program to attack your system with the full privileges of the System account. Many attacks in the UNIX environment took place under similar conditions.

Logon Security

The logon process in any environment is prone to security breaches. If an intruder gains access to the Administrator account, you and your system are toast. Prepare to stand in an unemployment line. Some guidelines for protecting accounts are presented here.

Administrator Account Break-In Technique

How do intruders break in to your Windows NT system? The Administrator account is the first target for two good reasons: it has unlimited privileges, and it can't be locked out. If that doesn't work, they might enter through an authorized account, then find holes to gain more privileges.

 NOTE: The reason the Administrator account can't be locked out is to avoid complete loss of access to the server. If someone were to lock the Administrator account through failed logon, the server would become unavailable—essentially a denial-of-service attack.

The usual attack comes by someone who knows the Administrator account name and attempts to log on to that account. You did change the Administrator account name to something obscure, right? If not, an intruder will most likely try attacking Administrator right off the bat.

Your best protection is to change the name of the Administrator account and use a very hard-to-guess password, one that includes a long string of alpha-numeric characters and no discernible words. Set lockouts on all other user accounts. Set the lockout value to four to allow for mistakes in typing or improperly selecting domain or local logon.

Assume an inside user is attacking an NT Server. Internal attackers will collect user account names and periodically attempt logons over extended periods to prevent lockout. But the Administrator account is the best target. How do they learn its name if you renamed it? One technique is to type the

NBTSTAT command as shown here, replacing the *ipaddress* with the IP address of any computer that the Administor happens to be logged on to.

　　NBTSTAT -A *ipaddress*

Note that NBTSTAT also accepts NetBIOS names like those you see in the Network Neighborhood. The attacker can now attempt to crack the account. Because it has no lockout, he might be successful over a period of time if you use weak passwords and if you don't take some other measures, as we will discuss in a minute.

Try this. Go to a Windows workstation on your network and log on as Administrator, but assume you don't know the password. Type in the wrong password. When that fails, try another password. Keep trying as long as you like. Now consider how easy it would be to write a program that repeats those keystrokes and tries passwords from one of the password dictionaries available on the Internet.

Meanwhile, over on your server, the Event Log is filling up with failed log-on attempt messages, but only if you enable "Failure" for the auditing feature called "Logon and Logoff." To set this option, open the User Manager and choose Audit from the Policies menu. This technique is discussed further in Chapter 10. Now you just need to remember to look in the Event Viewer every so often to see if someone is trying to break in. You can also use the Performance Monitor to track logon failures as discussed in Chapter 10.

If the inability to lock out the Administrator account worries you, you can just have the system shut down. Technically, this is a denial-of-service attack, because it prevents legitimate users from accessing the system. That's the goal of some hackers, but you may prefer that your system shut down rather than allow the hacker to repeatedly attack your system.

6

Another intruder attack might come from a Windows NT user who attacks the administrative share accounts on your servers. Administrative shares are default accounts that cannot be permanently removed. They are created for the Windows NT root directory where the system files are kept and for the root of each disk partition. The shares have the dollar sign suffix (C$, D$, WINNT$) and are normally not visible to users. However, a malicious user on your network can open the Run dialog box and type something like \\*servername*\C$ in an attempt to connect with an administrative share. A logon dialog box, like the one in the following illustration, appears, and the hacker can type the administrator's name in the Connect As field and a guessed password in the Password field and keep guessing as long as she wants.

Enter Network Password   ☒

Incorrect password or unknown username for:

\\Ultra-2\C$

Connect As: [   ]

Password: [   ]

[OK]

[Cancel]

[Help]

There is actually an easy way to stop these attacks. I led you through this process just to give you an idea of what your system is up against. The easy solution is to prevent all administrative logons from the network. Think about it. Why allow any administrator to log on to a server from a remote location? There are too many ways that security could be compromised. Did someone install a camera to videotape the logon? It's been done. Is the logon computer trusted? Did someone install a Trojan Horse program to capture passwords? Not to mention that allowing remote logons allows anyone to attempt to log in to your Administrator accounts from an isolated location.

For security reasons, consider requiring that all server administration take place at the console of the server itself. This can be done by revoking network logon privileges for the Administrators and Everyone groups. Open the User Manager, click User Rights on the Policies menu, and remove the groups from the right called "Access this computer from the network." With that, you prevent all potential break-ins from the network to any Administrator account. Next, add back in special groups that can access the server from the network, making sure no Administrators are members of the group.

Once you've tightened the security of your servers and made them more difficult to break into, upper management might get a little concerned about what to do if you are suddenly unavailable. One technique is to create a backdoor, fail-safe password. The concept is to pick three trusted people in the company and give each of them one piece of a three-part password. Assume the password is "StudebakerHawk." The first person gets "Stude," the second person gets "baker," and the third person gets "Hawk." In the event of your absence and the need to access the server with administrative privileges, these three people must get together to enter the password. This scheme provides accountability among the password holders. You should also consider giving the entire password to the CEO of your company or a trusted third party. A bank safe deposit box also comes to mind.

Tip: "StudebakerHawk" is an example of a poor password choice. If the person holding "Hawk" is a car buff, he might guess the rest of the password. Create a password that is difficult for any one person to guess.

General Logon Cautions and Policies

While the Windows NT logon process is secure, there are many opportunities for compromise. Someone could videotape keystrokes and play them back in slow motion or use a sniffer on the line to capture an unencrypted password. While Windows NT passwords are encrypted, users might use the same password for a program that sends passwords over the line in unencrypted form. Users often divulge their passwords or allow unauthorized users to access their computer either intentionally or unintentionally. Here is a wrap-up list of threats and cautions.

Avoid "Open Door" Accounts Never create a logon account that does not have a password, and never create an administrative account with a simple name and predictable password. These are "open door" accounts to experienced intruders. Some administrators create temporary accounts to use for testing with names like Test or Temporary. Hackers target such accounts. These test accounts often have Administrator rights because administrators use them to test rights! If you create temporary accounts, set the accounts to expire automatically at a predetermined time. You can set account expirations on the Properties dialog box for accounts.

Watch for Unusual Activities Look for unusual activities on accounts, such as unauthorized attempts to start programs or open files, especially if they occur after hours when the normal user has left the office. These activities can be audited by setting the Failure option for File and Object Access, as discussed in Chapter 10.

6

Administrator Decoy Account To divert intruders, rename the Administrator account and create a "decoy" account called "Administrator," which has no rights. Intruders will spend all their time attacking a useless account, and you'll be able to track their failed logons in the Event log. If the person is an internal user, you'll know which workstation they are using. (Don't be quick to accuse the person at that workstation, though. Someone else might have used it to attempt break-ins.)

NOTE: Be aware that you can't legally monitor people's activities unless you've posted notices on the network or elsewhere that all activities may be monitored. Put this in employee contracts.

Administrators Need Two Accounts   All administrative users should have their own general user accounts for use when they are not performing administrative tasks to prevent someone from hijacking their account if they accidentally leave a system unattended.

Shut Down Intruders   One last thing. If you detect an intruder, use the Server Manager utility to lock the intruder out. Then rename the account and change its password to prevent further intrusions.

Weak Clients Compromise Security

The safety and strengths of passwords and the logon process are a major concern on non-Windows NT client systems. Systems that run DOS, Windows for Workgroups, and Windows 95 do not provide the strong logon and authentication protections that Windows NT computers provide. Logon screens on these systems log users on to a network, but they provide no local protection for files. Users might incorrectly believe that information stored on the computer is safe, when in fact anyone can sit down at the computer and access local files.

If users need to protect their files, have them store the files on more secure Windows NT Servers. Alternatively, if your budget allows, install the Windows NT Workstation operating system and format disks to the NT File System. Still, a hacker can use low-level disk scanning programs to view disk information if he can access a client computer without anyone seeing what he is doing. Physical security is essential, and you may need to lock up systems and post guards after hours.

A feature of Windows client workstations is that they cache passwords on local disk drives. This is both good and bad. By caching passwords, Windows will know the password for a resource that a user has previously accessed. These passwords are encrypted, but there have been reports of password cracking. Microsoft recently strengthened the encryption, but there is always the possibility that password files can be broken. If Administrators log on from a client workstation, the password is stored in a file called ADMINIST.PWD on the local hard drive.

A problem with clients in any networking environment is that they will use the same passwords for all the services they access. Some systems that users log on to may not provide a strong level of password encryption and protection. Someone sniffing the line could capture the password and use it to break into other systems that the user accesses.

Another problem with many network clients is that hackers can't be locked out when attempting to guess local passwords.

Still another problem with clients is that Trojan Horse programs can be installed or copied from disks that will capture user passwords. The user's passwords might get stored on disk for later retrieval by a potential intruder. In some cases, passwords are e-mailed back to the intruder. There have been cases where the co-workers set up the Microsoft Windows Recorder utility (available on all versions of Windows 3.x) to record passwords as they were typed by an unsuspecting user.

These issues are covered further in Chapter 12.

System Administration

Mismanagement is a big security concern. If you don't fully understand the security system and, as a result, set options inappropriately, intruders will take advantage of your system. Inappropriate file system permissions will allow intruders and legitimate users to access files they should not access.

As mentioned previously, administer all servers locally, but if that is not possible, use only Windows NT Workstation computers for your administrative activities, because the logon security is more secure than other operating systems. The CTRL-ALT-DEL logon process kills any Trojan Horse programs that might capture passwords and the NT File System protects information on disk better than other client operating systems.

The Windows NT Resource Kit (available in bookstores or directly from Microsoft) provides additional administration tools that managers of large network installations should not go without. Some of the tools are useful for evaluating security and the settings of user accounts and file permissions.

6

Administering a Windows NT Server from a remote workstation over dial-up lines is possible, but you should know all the risks of doing this before continuing. Your administrative passwords and programs may be at risk on remote workstations and the line between your system and the server could be monitored.

Setting Up Secure Systems

There are a number of things you can do to protect your system during the installation and setup phase. Use high-quality equipment to avoid downtime, and if you are upgrading an older system, check the hard drive for defects. Some not-so-obvious pointers are outlined here.

Do not create dual-boot systems for Windows NT Servers. A dual-boot system is one that contains two or more disk partitions, each with a different operating system. When you start the system, you can choose Windows NT or one of the other operating systems.

One problem with dual-boot systems is that an intruder who managed to gain physical access to your server may boot from the other partition and use it to launch programs that can scan the Windows NT disk partition. You should also remove the floppy disk drive and lock down the cover to prevent this same type of attack by someone who is armed with a bootable disk and a scanning program.

On a similar note, never start a system with an unknown floppy disk; it might contain a virus that could contaminate the hard drive.

Another reason for avoiding dual-boot partitions is that the non-Windows partition on the disk might become infected with a virus that corrupts the Windows NT partition of the disk. This is covered in Appendix C.

Someone who has access to your system might just reinstall Windows NT, sign on as the new administrator, and have full access to your existing data. Of course, this can be done only by an attacker who gains physical access to your computer or manages to steal its hard drive. Do you trust the janitors?

Administrative Hierarchy

If your network is small, you might be able to manage the entire network from a single management workstation or from a server such as the primary domain controller. If your network is large, you'll need to spread out the administrative tasks, allowing managers in other departments or divisions to control local user accounts and access to local resources.

You can divide networks into domains as described in Chapter 7, then assign an administrator to each domain. A single high-level administrator may be in charge of setting policies for all the domains of an organization, while individual domain administrators implement those policies within their own domains. Alternatively, domains can be set up that are individually managed.

Domain administrators can designate a "sub-administrator" to handle various management tasks. Windows NT includes built-in management groups that make it easy to create a management hierarchy. By adding users to these groups, you give those users rights and permissions to manage various parts of the domain. Chapter 7 covers this in more detail.

User Accounts

The out-of-the-box configurations for user accounts and file permissions may be inappropriate for many installations. Versions of Windows NT previous to version 4.0 have some default security settings that are risky, especially if systems are connected to the Internet. Windows NT 4.0 fixes some of these inadequacies, but you still need to take a close look at the default properties on files and directories and the rights of user accounts.

Be sure to differentiate between administrative and general user accounts and the activities associated with each. Administrative users should use non-administrative accounts for normal network activities. Windows NT includes some built-in groups such as Administrators, Account Managers, and Server Managers that are appropriate for most management activities. Predefined user groups are Users and Guests, but in most cases, you'll create your own groups to fit the requirements of your network.

The Guest account is available on Windows NT that allows people without accounts on local systems or in the domain access to log on. A password is not required by default, although you can require one. Guest users have access to all directories to which the Everyone group has been granted permissions. For security reasons, you can disable the Guest account.

The File System

To implement the highest levels of security, always format Windows NT partitions with the NT File System. The system provides extended permissions for controlling access to files and hides data on disk from easy access if someone manages to boot the system with another operating system.

For example, if you create FAT partitions on your Windows NT Server, someone who doesn't have rights to a directory but has physical access to the computer can simply reboot the computer with DOS and access the FAT directory. It is normally not possible to access an NTFS directory from DOS, but hacker utilities are available that allow it, as mentioned in Chapter 2, so you need to physically protect systems.

6

By default, the Everyone group, which includes all users, has full permission to almost every directory on a drive. You should evaluate these permissions for security, as discussed in Chapter 9.

Another thing to be careful of is that someone with physical access to your system could reinstall the Windows NT operating system, assign themselves Administrator status, and gain full access to your NTFS partitions.

Printers and Security

Printing is a relatively benign activity, but security in printing is an important issue for several reasons. In a network environment, users send print jobs to shared printers where the jobs wait in a print queue until they can be printed. Completed print jobs that contain confidential information may be exposed to theft if left in the printer tray. Physical security measures are necessary in the printer room. In addition, a malicious user might flood a print queue with jobs to deny service to others.

Windows NT allows administrators to designate exactly which printers a user can use and—to some extent—the priority those users have at the printer. Some users' print jobs may be more important than others and so require more immediate printing. Some low-priority print jobs may be postponed until later in the day when there are fewer jobs waiting at the printer.

The Registry

The *Registry* is a database that holds information about a computer's configuration, including hardware and software settings as well as environment settings. The Registry is similar to the .INI (initialization) files in previous versions of Windows, except that the Registry provides a single location where the operating system can store configuration data. Application and device driver information is also stored in the registry.

There are specific procedures for backing up and protecting the Registry information, and other important system information can be included in backups. Regular backups are an important part of your security plan for Windows NT computers and can help protect information in the event of accidents, viruses, or malicious activities. Techniques for backing up the Registry are covered in Chapter 11.

The configuration information in the Registry is not normally altered manually. You usually run a program or utility that makes the appropriate changes. However, in some cases, you need to make changes to the Registry that are recommended by various programs or manuals.

You can view or change information in the Registry by typing **REGEDT32** in the Run dialog box. Microsoft is careful to warn in all of its documentation that using the Registry Editor incorrectly can cause serious, system-wide problems that may require you to reinstall Windows NT. It does not guarantee that any problems resulting from the use of the Registry Editor can be solved. It is worthwhile to repeat this warning here: Use the Registry Editor at your own risk.

If you just need to view information in the Registry and you want to make sure you don't accidentally make changes to it, you can enable the Read

Only mode by choosing Read Only Mode from the Options menu in the Registry Editor.

Remote Registry Management

In most cases, Registry changes are safely made by applications and utilities, but malicious users could run the Registry Editor (REGEDT32.EXE) to edit it manually. The most serious security problem is that the Registry in Windows NT Server versions 3.51 and earlier can be changed by running REGEDT32 from a remote workstation. This feature was intended to allow for remote administration and troubleshooting. There are potential security problems in this arrangement, however, if the Registry is not properly protected. Appendix F covers this issue in more detail.

NOTE: Windows NT Server 4.0, by default, does not allow remote Registry editing.

Some of the keys in the Registry are secured so that only administrative users or a special System account can alter them. Other keys are alterable so that programs can make changes as appropriate. Administrators at high-security installations may want to set protections on certain keys in the Registry. However, these restrictions should be set with care because they can prevent authorized users from making needed changes to the Registry that are required by some applications they run.

One particular problem with versions of Windows NT previous to version 4.0 is that unknown users who log on as Guest (assuming the Guest account is enabled) can change the Registry from a remote location. As mentioned, not all the keys in the Registry can be changed by non-administrative users, but there is potential for damaging a system or causing a denial of service attack.

6

Some Registry Settings

You can make the following changes in the Registry to strengthen the security of your Windows NT systems or to post important messages. The Registry Editor is the tool you use to make changes. You can start it by accessing the Run dialog box (from the Start menu in Windows NT 4.0) and typing **REGEDT32**.

Hiding the User Name

When a user logs in to a Windows NT computer, he types his username in the Name field of the logon dialog box. The next time someone logs on to the system, the last name typed in the Name field is displayed. While this makes it easy to log on the next time, it is a potential security hole. To prevent Windows NT from displaying the username from the last logon, follow these steps:

1. Start the Registry Editor by typing **REGEDT32** in the Run dialog box.
2. When the Registry Editor appears, click the HKEY_LOCAL_MACHINE window.
3. Drill down to the following location in the hierarchical tree:

   SOFTWARE\Microsoft\Windows NT\CurrentVersion\Winlogon
4. In the right pane, double-click the DontDisplayLastUserName option.
5. Change the value to 1 to disable the display of the logon name.

Controlling Windows NT Shut Down

On Windows NT Workstation computers (not Windows NT Servers), a Shut Down button appears in the logon box. Any person who is physically at the computer can initiate a logon and click the button to shut the computer down in an orderly fashion. The Shut Down button is disabled on Windows NT Server computers because for security reasons you normally do not want just anyone shutting down the server.

Shutting down a computer using the Shut Down button may not be appropriate in some situations. For example, a Windows NT Workstation computer might be operating as a Web server in addition to being used as a local workstation. To prevent shut down, you can put a cover over the case to keep someone from turning off the power switch, then you can disable the Shut Down button as follows:

1. Start the Registry Editor by typing **REGEDT32** in the Run dialog box.
2. When the Registry Editor appears, click the HKEY_LOCAL_MACHINE window.
3. Drill down to the following location in the hierarchical tree:

   SOFTWARE\Microsoft\Windows NT\CurrentVersion\Winlogon
4. In the right pane, double-click the ShutdownWithoutLogon option.
5. Change the value to 0 to disable the Shut Down button.

You can change the same settings on Windows NT Servers if you want to enable the Shut Down button for some reason, although doing so is not recommended. Change the value to 1 if that is what you want to do.

NOTE: These changes will take effect the next time the computer is started. Update the Emergency Repair Disk after making these changes, as described in Chapter 11.

Legal Notices

If legal notices do not exist, users may feel they can freely browse the network and access directories and files without restriction. In fact, there are laws that prevent you from monitoring users even though they may be accessing your network without authorization. You must post legal notices that indicate that the network is only for authorized users and that all activities may be monitored. A sample notice is shown in Chapter 4, under "Post and Display Legal Notices."

You can put legal notices directly in the logon dialog box by following the procedures here. The basic idea is to insert a message that notifies potential users that they can be held legally liable if they attempt to use the computer without having been properly authorized to do so. The absence of such a notice could be construed as an invitation, without restriction, to enter and browse the system. Two message areas are available. LegalNoticeCaption is for a short title and LegalNoticeText is for extended text.

1. Start the Registry Editor by typing **REGEDT32** in the Run dialog box.
2. When the Registry Editor appears, click the HKEY_LOCAL_MACHINE window.
3. Drill down to the following location in the hierarchical tree:

   SOFTWARE\Microsoft\Windows NT\CurrentVersion\Winlogon
4. In the right pane, double-click the LegalNoticeCaption option.
5. Type the text for the *title* of the message box and click OK.
6. In the right pane, double-click the LegalNoticeText option.
7. Type the text for the *message* and click OK.

Remember that these changes will not take effect until the next time the computer is started. Update the Emergency Repair Disk, as described in Chapter 11.

6

Network Security Issues

Any network is a security risk. Eavesdroppers can listen in on your network by using packet sniffers that capture transmitted information for later analysis. To prevent eavesdroppers from reading signals that emanate from the cable itself, you can install fiber-optic cable across open areas. As mentioned in Chapter 2, someone could gain access to a branch office by posing as an executive or technician from the main office, then connect a sniffer to the network while working in a temporary office.

Some vendors have developed secure network hardware to protect against eavesdropping and sniffing. 3Com Networks (**www.3com.com**) for example, produces the Online Ethernet 10BASE-T security module, which provides a way to secure unshielded twisted-pair Ethernet networks against eavesdropping and unauthorized network intrusions. The module's ONguard security software allows ports to receive only transmitted data that has an authorized address. All other ports are jammed. In addition, the software can be configured to reject any data transmitted by an unauthorized source address and can automatically disable the port used by the intruder. Additional features can be implemented with an optional module, such as intruder alarm, view-only management access, and two-level password protection as well as the ability to use two modules for fault tolerance.

Chapter 12 covers LAN security issues in more detail. Securing remote logons and access by mobile users is another important security feature and is covered in Chapter 14. Chapter 15 covers methods for securing branch office connections over wide area network (WAN) links or over private and secure channels across the Internet (often called "tunnels"). In all cases, encryption techniques are essential to protecting your data transmissions across "unknown" networks.

Monitoring Utilities

You can monitor the activities of your servers using the Performance Monitor utility discussed in Chapter 10. The utility can track activities such as large bursts in traffic or unauthorized attempts to access resources. Unusual activities can be tracked by monitoring traffic patterns on your network and using the alarm system to warn you when these activities occur. For example, you can monitor bytes received to detect spamming attacks (someone is sending large amounts of e-mail in an attempt to deny service to legitimate users) on your server. You can also monitor for bytes sent during unusual hours of the day to detect if someone is stealing large files from your servers.

Sniffers and Network Monitors

The Windows NT Network Monitor is a software tool that can help you monitor data packet traffic on networks. The software runs on a Windows NT computer and lets you view traffic on the network to which the computer is attached. This is usually called *sniffing*. Network administrators use sniffers to troubleshoot networks and look for unusual activities or for packets being sent by hackers. Unfortunately, hackers can also use sniffers to gather information about your network by reading the contents of packets.

TIP: To learn the scary truth about the dangers of sniffers, refer to "Sniffing the Network" in Chapter 17.

Sniffers are designed to be diagnostic tools that let you look at selective traffic on the network to locate bottlenecks, downed servers, or the devices that are generating bad or excessive packets. Sniffers are also used to analyze network traffic, such as the type of traffic that is exchanged across routers. Programmers use sniffers to analyze network traffic when debugging drives. You can also use sniffers for security purposes.

Unfortunately, unscrupulous users can also use sniffers to look inside packets and glean useful information like passwords and company secrets. Telnet and FTP send plain text passwords that can be captured. If it's the same password you use to log on to more secure systems, that person will indirectly get a password they can use to break into your account. Use anonymous logon for such services so users don't need to transmit passwords.

Sniffer activities are hard to detect. The Windows NT Network Monitor is password-protected to prevent unauthorized logons. It also can detect the activities of another Network Monitor on the network. However, it cannot detect other types of network sniffers. In fact, network sniffing has become a major problem as software similar to the Windows NT Network Monitor becomes so cheap that just about any user can install it on his or her computer. You may need to implement a periodic inspection program to detect such programs.

6

The Network Monitor utility in Windows NT can monitor only one system, but a more advanced version is available in Microsoft's System Management Server (SMS). An administrator at an SMS system can take control of Network Monitor at a server to monitor its traffic. To prevent unauthorized use of this feature, you can require password authentication before anyone runs Network Monitor on a server from a remote system.

File Sharing Problems in the Windows Environment

The file and printer sharing system in the Windows environment is the Server Message Block (SMB) protocol. SMB is implemented as the Server and Workstation service (and indirectly as the NetBIOS service) on Windows NT computers and as "File and printer sharing for Microsoft Networks" on Windows client computers. However, SMB is generally considered a security problem if you are connected to an untrusted network. A session can be "hijacked" by someone who then masquerades as the real client. The sharing features of SMB are also prone to security violation, primarily due to inappropriate use.

NOTE: For security reasons, you can disable file and printer sharing on client workstations. Clients will still be able to access other servers, but won't be able to share information on their own systems. To disable sharing in Windows 95, open the Network utility in the Control Panel and remove the File and Printer Sharing option or the ability to crack a password easily.

Connecting an SMB file sharing system to the Internet is not a good idea unless you know what you are doing. To get enlightened on this subject, check out Winserve at **www.winserve.com**. It describes how to access SMB file sharing sites on the Internet and how to rent disk space on your SMB computer. You connect to an SMB site by typing NetBIOS names like the ones you use on your own internal network. For example, after making the appropriate settings, you can connect to Winserve's experimental Windows 95 shared directory by opening the Run dialog box and typing **\\winserver95\guest**.

I was curious about security, so I tried connecting to the administrative share at Microsoft's SMB share site, which is called \\ftp. I opened the Run dialog box and typed **\\ftp\C$**. Sure enough, a logon dialog box popped up. If the password were weak, I could have broken it with enough determination. Not only would that let me into the system, but it would also give me the Administrator password to use for other break-ins.

The reason I describe this is to make you aware of the potential for people on the Internet to break into your site if SMB file sharing is in use, especially if the Guest account is enabled. You also need to guard against internal users that might try to break into shared systems. If you are sharing folders, disable the Guest account and require logon with strong passwords, then check the permissions for the folders, especially the permissions of the Everyone group.

An interesting side point is that Windows 95 will disable SMB when you configure an Internet connection. At least it asks you if you want to disable it. You could choose No, but doing so makes your shared folders available to Internet users. This is not necessarily bad if you've adequately protected the folders, and the computer is a standalone system. However, if one of your network clients connects to the Internet with sharing enabled, he creates a potential backdoor into your TCP/IP network. Savvy administrators ban internal modems and provide Internet access only through a firewall-protected network connection.

If you are concerned that SMB may be insecure, you can implement other file sharing mechanisms (such as FTP or HTTP) or take the steps outlined in Part 4 of this book to protect your system from unwanted intruders.

Internet and Web Connections

The Windows NT Server has become a popular system to connect to the Internet. It comes with its own Web server software and can dish up information to users of Web browsers on the Internet or on *intranets* (internal Internets). However, you must use some form of firewall to connect internal networks to the Internet. Not taking this precaution will expose your internal resources to all sorts of malicious activity. Firewalls are discussed in Part 4 of this book.

Because Windows NT uses the TCP/IP protocol suite it is prone to some of the security problems that have been documented in the UNIX environment and on the Internet. With TCP/IP, every computer on the network is potentially "reachable" by any other computer on the network.

As an example, try "pinging" another computer on your own network or on the Internet with the PING command as follows,

    PING *ipaddress*

where *ipaddress* is the address of the computer. For example, you can ping Microsoft's Web site by typing **PING 198.105.232.4**. My favorite command is TRACERT because you can use it to get a listing of all the routes that are required to get to a particular computer system. For example, **TRACERT www.whitehouse.gov** produced the following output when executed from my location on the Internet. Notice that each router crossed to get to the White House is listed along with IP addresses. You can bet that hackers find this information useful.

6

```
TRACERT www.whitehouse.gov

Tracing route to www.whitehouse.gov [198.137.240.91]
over a maximum of 30 hops:

  1   181 ms    192 ms    196 ms  Max10.Los-Angeles.CA.MS.UU.NET [204.177.246.10]
  2   391 ms    408 ms    395 ms  Loopback0.Cisco2.San-Francisco.CA.MS.UU.NET
                                  [137.39.2.63]
```

```
3      495 ms    397 ms    457 ms    Hssi1/0.San-Jose3.CA.Alter.Net [137.39.100.17]
4      295 ms    496 ms    442 ms    Hssi2/0.CR1.SCL1.Alter.Net [137.39.100.2]
5      308 ms    296 ms    285 ms    107.Hssi4/0.CR1.DCA1.Alter.Net [137.39.30.17]
6      296 ms    271 ms    282 ms    Hssi2/0.Vienna6.VA.Alter.Net [137.39.100.78]
7      274 ms    277 ms    271 ms    Fddi0/0.Vienna1.VA.Alter.Net [137.39.11.1]
8      283 ms    336 ms    310 ms    mae-east.nsn.nasa.gov [192.41.177.125]
9      300 ms    363 ms    303 ms    GSFC8.NSN.NASA.GOV [128.161.166.1]
10     356 ms    317 ms    289 ms    198.116.87.2
11     708 ms    281 ms    343 ms    198.137.240.33
12       *         *         *       Request timed out.
13     368 ms    344 ms    337 ms    www.whitehouse.gov [198.137.240.91]

Trace complete.
```

Hackers have been known to divert network traffic from a designated route onto a route that lets them examine packets or that lets them infiltrate a network by appearing to be another system. At worst, they can disrupt router function to disable routers and cause "denial-of-service" attacks.

Obviously, the real danger is that a hacker will get past your routers and firewalls and into systems on your network. Part 4 of this book provides more information on routers, firewalls, and Internet connections.

CHAPTER 7

Domains, Domain Logons, and Security Controls

Domains are groups of computers that share the same security policy and user account database. All computers in a domain have a trust relationship so that one computer can authenticate a user for access to other systems in the domain. It's easy to assume that one domain is completely separate from another, an assumption that people new to the concept may make. In fact, when a single physical network is split into two separate domains, a user in one domain can still see systems in other domains using certain commands. Further, a person in one domain can access resources in another domain as a guest even if there are no trust relationships or accounts in common, assuming the Guest account is enabled.

As you'll see in this chapter, the *Guest account* provides a way to make public information in one domain available to users in other domains. The relationship is similar to what happens when you access a Web server on the Internet. You log on to a server without supplying a username and access information with Read Only privileges. This may be good or bad, depending on your environment.

Back to that description in the first sentence of this chapter—a domain provides the following very important functions:

Security Policy   The security policy for a domain consists of password policies (restrictions, expirations, length) and account lockout policies (which determine whether an account locks out if too many logon attempts occur). You set these policies in the User Manager for Domains by choosing Account from the Policies menu.

User Account Database   The user account database holds accounts for all the users that can log in to the domain. As you'll see, you can create a master database that holds the accounts of users who belong to other domains. Doing this simplifies management by keeping all the user accounts in a single database.

Since each domain can have its own security policies and user account database, domains can provide a logical separation of users and information systems that reflects the departments, divisions, or branch offices of your organization. Security policies are discussed under Security Policies near the end of this chapter. The next section describes domains in general, trust relationships, user accounts, and the user account database.

Keep in mind that a Windows NT Server computer is required on the network in order to create domains. If your network consists of Windows NT Workstation computers and other clients, like Windows 95 systems, you can create only a workgroup environment. If a Windows NT Workstation computer exists in the domain, it can hold a user account database that other computers on the network can use to authenticate users. Workgroups are generally used for small networks of Windows 95 and Windows NT Workstation computers. If a Windows NT Server computer is present, a domain network is in order.

Domains

To understand domains, it's important to understand how they are implemented in large and small companies and how they affect user logon and access to resources. Keep in mind that domains serve primarily all as a management tool that simplifies user account administration. Domains are not secure barriers between networks.

Let's evaluate the process of moving from a single domain to a multiple domain environment. In the following illustration, an organization has one domain, and a single user account database (UAD) in that domain holds all the accounts for all users. The folders represent shared folders on one or more server computers.

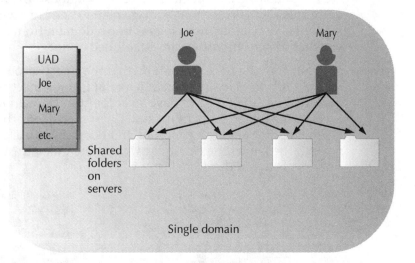

Now assume the company has expanded, created a branch office, or decided to let department or division managers administer part of the network and users on their own. In the next illustration, the single domain is split into two domains. Now Joe can access only shared folders in his domain, and Mary can access only shared folders in her domain.

7

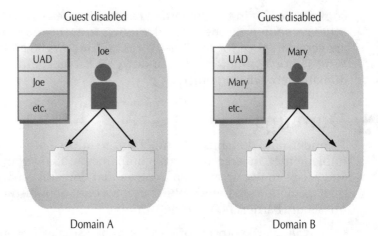

Here's a critical piece of information: If the Guest account is enabled, users in other domains can access shared folders to which the Everyone group has permissions (which is common) or to which the Guests group has permissions (which is normally a manual setting), even if trust relationships are not established. Remember that trust relationships are established to make cross-domain account management easier. However, the Guest account allows anonymous logons into a domain from any other domain, whether trust relationships are established or not.

So assume, in the next illustration, that the Guest account is enabled in Domain A, and Mary in Domain B attempts to connect with a folder in Domain A. She does not have an account in Domain A, but when she accesses the folder, it opens because Guest is enabled. This would occur if Guest does not require a password. If it does, she can access the folder as Guest if she knows the Guest password. Note that a trust relationship does not exist between the domains.

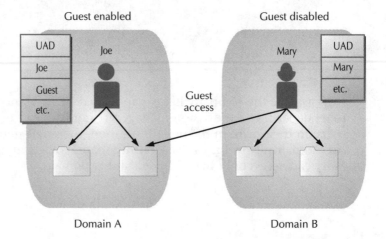

Now assume that, for security reasons, the manager of Domain A does not want to allow Guest logons to the domain. However, Mary still needs to access folders in the domain. (I'm building up to trust relationships, but for now let's assume that trust relationships don't exist between the domains.) To let Mary log in to Domain A, the manager of the domain can create an account for her, as shown in the following illustration.

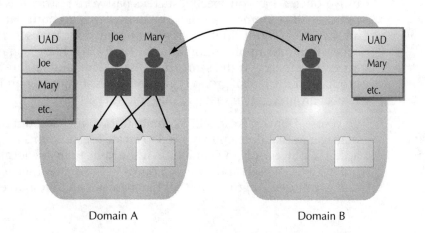

Domain A   Domain B

Now Mary can log in to Domain A because she has an account there. An interesting thing happens if the account name and password are the same for both accounts. After logging in to Domain B, Mary's credentials (username and password) are cached; when she attempts to access a resource in Domain A, the credentials are *passed through* to Domain A in the background and used to automatically log Mary in. She does not need to fill out a Logon dialog box.

But what if the manager of Domain A sets a security policy that requires a 7-character password while Domain B requires only a 5-character password? Mary can either synchronize her password in Domain B with Domain A, or she can log on and enter the appropriate password every time she accesses a folder in Domain A.

In the previous examples, the existence of an account for Mary in two different domains can lead to confusion and to discrepancies, such as the difference in passwords. What if you want to maintain a single user account database to simplify management, but still use separate domains to maintain a division of resources according to department, division, or branch office? This is where trust relationships come into play.

7

Trust Relationships

Assume that Domain A will become the *master domain* where the master user account database exists that holds all of the user accounts for all domains, as pictured in Figure 7-1. You set up a trust relationship so that Domain B "trusts" Domain A (refer to Figure 5-6 in Chapter 5). Also assume that you manage the database alone and that managers in other domains implement only policies that you specify, such as password restrictions and user account policies. Since Domain A holds the master user account database, you create all the user accounts in it, then grant permissions for users in the database to access resources in other domains. In Figure 7-1, Mary is granted direct access to a folder. At the same time, Mary, Tim, and Jan are added to a global group, and the global group is granted access to a folder and a printer. Global groups, which make management tasks easier, will be discussed later.

Of course, Domain B can still maintain its own user account database. A local manager in that domain may need to create user accounts for people who access resources only in Domain B. At the same time, the local manager can pull up a list of users and group accounts in the master user account database and grant users or groups in that database access to resources in domain B.

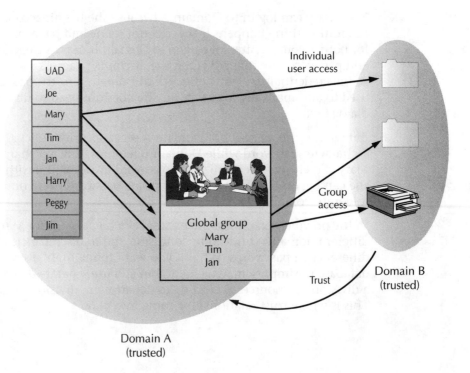

Now suppose that Jim is visiting the branch office and logs on to a computer in Domain B. He does not have an account in Domain B, so he logs on to the system as a Guest (assuming Guest is enabled). Once logged on, Jim can open the Network Neighborhood and search for shared folders in his home domain. When opening a folder, Jim is prompted with a Logon dialog box, and he can type his regular account name and password to access the folder. The account name and password are passed to the master domain and verified in the master user account database.

The trust relationship shown in Figure 7-1 is a one-way trust. Domain B is a *trusting* domain that trusts Domain A, the *trusted* domain. This relationship is what Microsoft calls the *master domain model*. It is most often used when a central MIS (management information system) department wants to maintain all user accounts in a central location. Notice the global group in the figure. This group could very well be called MIS and contain users who have administrative rights in other domains. In this way, it is easy to set up a management structure in which the specific users who manage systems are added to management groups, and the groups are granted rights and permissions in other domains.

A trust relationship can be explained by how an Administrator uses the User Manager utility to manage them. User Manager is an administrative tool you use to manage user accounts, trust relationships, policies, and other domain features. When a domain becomes a trusted domain for another domain, the manager in that domain can open the User Manager, choose the Select Domain option on the User menu, then pick a domain to manage.

This relationship is pictured in Figure 7-2. Note that the MIS domain is the master domain and that the domain manager can view the domain database for either the MIS domain or the department domain. She can also manipulate the user accounts in either domain.

More About Domains

A domain consists of one or more Windows NT Server computers that act as *domain controllers* to store and manage user account database information and other domain information. Other computers participate in domains and take advantage of the security provided by the domain controllers. These other computers include Windows NT Workstation computers, Windows desktop systems, LAN Manager 2.*x* servers, and DOS computers.

7

NOTE: Use the Server Manager to add a computer to provide pass-through authentication for users who log on to it.

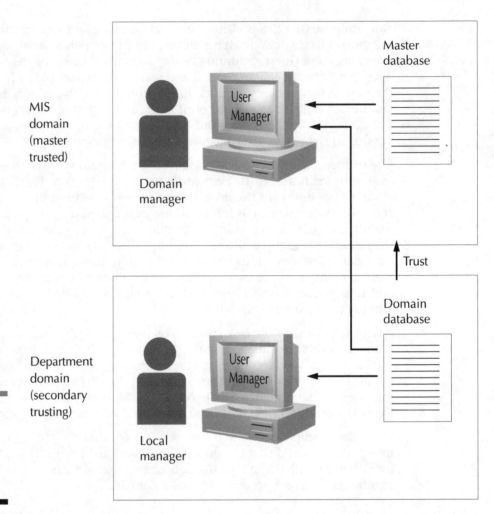

MIS
domain
(master
trusted)

Master
database

Domain
manager

User
Manager

Trust

Department
domain
(secondary
trusting)

Domain
database

Local
manager

User
Manager

Cross-domain
management
with User
Manager for
Domains
Figure 7-2.

Each domain can have its own administrator who manages policies and the account database, or a central administrator can manage all domains. One of the big issues with domains is that users in one domain need to access resources in other domains. Central administration often provides a better way to manage how resources are allocated to users outside of domains, but large networks are impractical to manage in this way, and individually managed domains are often necessary.

Domains can be organized in a variety of ways to fit your organizational needs. For example, you might include all the servers belonging to your company's accounting department, or to its Chicago division, in a single domain. Figure 5-6 illustrates how domains can be organized around the departments of a company.

Each domain consists of one server designated as the *primary domain controller* (PDC) and other servers that are designated as *backup domain controllers* (BDCs). You make choices about the type of domain controller when you install the Windows NT Server software on a computer.

Primary Domain Controller (PDC)   The PDC authenticates users and does most of the work of maintaining user accounts and security information. Changes made to accounts are recorded in the Directory database on the PDC.

Backup Domain Controllers (BDCs)   The BDCs authenticate users and maintain copies of the Directory database. The information in the database is periodically synchronized with the database on the PDC to include any changes. If the PDC fails, a BDC is promoted to the status of PDC.

A third designation, *member server*, applies to servers that use the services provided by the PDC and BDC domains but which are themselves in neither domain. Member servers do not hold a copy of the Directory database. You should run critical applications and other services on member servers that are not burdened with the tasks of managing the Directory Services database and handling logon requests.

If a BDC is physically closer to a user than a PDC, the BDC can log users on and help reduce network traffic in doing so. All changes on the PDC database are made to the replicas on the BDCs as soon as possible. Clock synchronization is part of this scheme. It ensures the proper ordering of updates and backups. One of the reasons for creating separate domains is to reduce the overhead caused by synchronization and other activities as well as to simplify management.

Single-user logon is beneficial to users who travel to branch offices and other remote sites. If the site is within the user's normal domain, a BDC at that site will have a record of the user's account and will log the user on. If the user travels to a site that is in another domain, the domain controller in that site can contact the user's home domain to authenticate the user if a trust relationship has been established.

7

The Directory Database

The official name for the user account database is the *Directory database*. It holds all the security and user account information for a domain. The database's main location is the primary domain controller in the domain, but the database is replicated to other domain controllers in the domain. The main function of domain controllers in Windows NT domain networks is to store and maintain the Directory database.

Keep in mind that the Directory database provides just one side of Windows NT security. The other side is the Access Control list that each object in the system has. This relationship is pictured in Figure 7-3. The Directory database describes what users can do, and an object's Access Control list describes which users have permissions to access the object.

The scope of a domain may be a small local area network, a group of computers that are spread out through an office building, or systems that are interconnected over public communication lines. Replication makes the Directory database more accessible to users at different sites. For example, a branch office that is connected to the main office by a telecommunication link should probably have its own domain controller. In this way, users at the branch office can log on to a local computer. This arrangement cuts down on traffic over the link and improves performance for low-throughput links.

One account is created for each user in the domain. This account is stored and maintained in the primary domain controller and replicated to backup domain controllers. Any changes to the account are made in the primary domain controller.

The maximum recommended size of the Directory database is about 40MB. The database contains information about objects in the environment, such as user accounts, group accounts, and computer accounts for Windows NT Workstation and Windows NT Server computers.

More About Trust Relationships

If you give someone the key to your house while you are on vacation, you are the trusting party and your friends are the trusted party. They may go

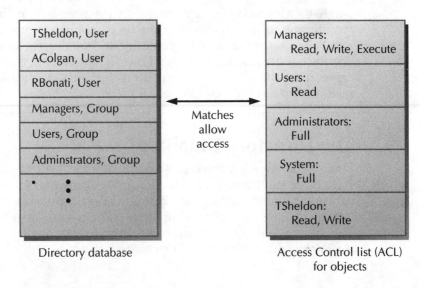

Differences between the Directory database and Access Control lists

Figure 7-3.

Directory database   Access Control list (ACL) for objects

into your house to take advantage of the pool table. In this case, your house is similar to a domain that has resources that people in the trusted domain want to use, that is, the pool table. So far, this is a *one-way trust relationship*. If your friends give you the keys to their house, then you have a *two-way trust relationship*. Here's the terminology for trust relationships:

◆ **Trusting domain** The domain allows another domain to access its resources.

◆ **Trusted domain** Users in the trusted domain can access resources in a trusting domain.

Technically, the trusting domain will accept from the trusted domain a list of global groups and other information about authenticated users. Figure 7-4 illustrates a trust relationship between the Main domain of an organization and its BranchOffice domain. In this case, BranchOffice is the trusting domain that trusts Main. Users in Main can access resources in BranchOffice.

If each domain has its own administrator, the administrators in each domain must agree to set up trust relationships and follow a specific procedure to ensure that security is maintained. If a single administrator manages all the domains, then setting up trust relationships is easy.

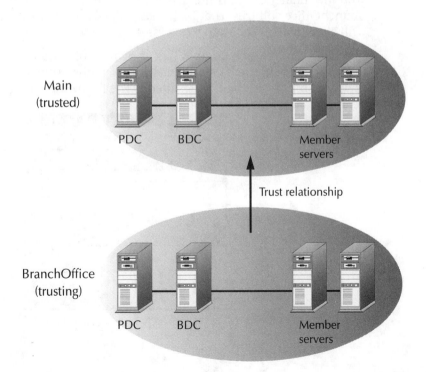

Main
(trusted)

PDC   BDC   Member servers

Trust relationship

7

A relationship between a trusted and a trusting domain

Figure 7-4.

BranchOffice
(trusting)

PDC   BDC   Member servers

When considering domains, keep these issues in mind:

♦ Trust relationships can be configured in only one direction at a time for security reasons. Remember that each domain might be managed by different administrators rather than by a single administrator.

♦ Administrators must explicitly create trust relationships. There are no transitive trust relationships. If Domain A trusts B and B trusts C, A does not automatically trust C.

♦ A user's access to resources is still limited by the rights and privileges granted by the administrator of a domain. A trust relationship in itself does not give users access to resources in another domain.

How Trust Is Established

When a trust relationship is set up, a secure channel exists between domain controllers. Only servers with proper access rights can send and receive information across this channel. For example, when a user from the trusted domain tries to log on to a system in the trusting domain, a trusting domain controller sends requests to validate users across the secure channel to a trusted domain controller.

Assume for this discussion that the Main domain is the trusted domain and that BranchOffice is the trusting domain, as pictured in Figure 7-4. BranchOffice will trust that Main has properly authenticated users and will allow users from Main to access its resources.

Assume also that each domain has its own administrator. The administrator in Main starts up the User Manager for Domains utility and chooses Trust Relationships from the Policies menu. The following dialog box appears:

There are two steps for setting up a one-way trust. First, the administrator in the trusted domain (Main, in this example) designates Branch Office as a trusting domain. This is done in the User Manager at the PDC for Main. Second, the administrator in BranchOffice completes the trust by designating that Main is a trusted domain. She does this at the PDC for her domain.

The administrator in the trusted domain sets up the trust by clicking the Add button next to the Trusting Domains field. The following dialog box appears:

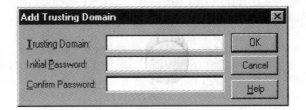

This is where the name of the trusting domain is typed, along with the password that the administrator of the trusting domain must type at her PDC to complete the relationship.

Here are some points of interest regarding trust relationships:

♦ The trusted domain *permits* a trust relationship, and the administrator in the trusting domain is *required* to enter a password to complete the trust.

♦ A hidden user account is created for the trust relationship.

♦ The password of the trust account is periodically changed by the primary domain controller in the trusting domain.

♦ Since all of the domain controllers in the trusting domain receive the trust account, any domain controller in the trusting domain can set up a secure channel to the trusted domain.

If you're not careful, trust relationships can get out of hand. For example, an administrator in one domain may call an administrator with another domain and "request trust." The latter sees no problem in this and allows the trust. However, the administrator in the trusted domain now has access to the trusting domain. He may allow groups of users in the trusted domain to access the trusting domain without considering whether access is appropriate for each member of the group. These groups are discussed next.

7

Domain Accounts

The Directory database (user accounts database) is the repository of account information for users. In order for any user to log on to a Windows NT computer, they must have an account in a local or domain user account database. Let's go over the difference between these databases.

A standalone Windows NT Workstation computer will have its own user account database that includes the names of users who log on at the physical computer itself. This scheme allows multiple people to use a single computer. If the Windows NT Workstation computer is attached to a network, it can participate in a workgroup, and other computers in the workgroup (such as a Windows 95 system) can even use its user account database to authenticate network users. This arrangement allows the Windows NT Workstation to share its advanced security features with less secure clients to provide a high level of security for access to network resources.

If a Windows NT Server computer exists on the network, you can create a domain. In such cases, a Directory database (global user account database) exists on the Windows NT Server that is used by all other computers in the domain to verify user account logons and access to resources. Each user has one account entry in the Directory database.

Basically, two types of user account databases may exist at the same time:

♦ **Local accounts** exist in the user account database on a Windows NT Workstation computer (or a Windows NT Server computer that is not a domain controller) for users who log on to the computer locally.

♦ **Domain accounts** exist in the Directory database on the primary domain controller and are replicated to backup domain controllers.

About Local and Global Groups

Groups are discussed in detail in Chapter 8, but some aspects of groups will be discussed here because of their importance to understanding how domains and domain security are managed. Users are put into groups to make it easier to grant rights and permissions to users. There are local groups and global groups, as described here.

As shown in Figure 7-1, some users in the master user account database need to have access to resources in other domains. The way to do this is to create a *global* group, put the users in the group, then give the global group access to the other domain.

In this strategy, the global group is just a group of users with no specific rights or permissions. However, by adding the global group to a local group in a domain, the users in the global group get all the rights and permissions that the local group has.

In Figure 7-1, three users in Domain A are part of the MIS team that will manage Domain B. The manager creates a global group called MIS group that includes the users. Remember that these users may physically work in Domain B, which could be a branch office; however, their user accounts are located in the master account database in Domain A. Domain B has a built-in local group called Administrators that has full administrative rights and permissions in Domain B. The MIS group global account from Domain A is added to this local group, thus giving members of the group administrative privileges in Domain B.

Use caution here. The Administrators local group has full access to the entire domain. It may not be appropriate to add the MIS global group to the Administrators local group in Domain B because doing this would give the administrators too much power. Instead, they can be added to some secondary management groups that have fewer rights and permissions. The default secondary management groups are Account Operators (users who maintain local user accounts), Server Operators (users who maintain servers and associated hardware), Printer Operators (users who manage printers and print queues), and Backup Operators (users who perform backups). Note that regular non-administrative local groups exist as well, such as Users and Guests. These non-administrative groups have limited rights and permissions in the domain.

The MIS group just discussed is a fictitious group that you can create on your own network if you need a central management structure. However, there are three built-in global groups that may be sufficient for your needs:

♦ **Domain Admins** is a global group of administrative accounts in the domain (which includes the Administrator user account, not to be confused with the Administrators local group).

♦ **Domain Users** is a global group of user accounts in the domain.

♦ **Domain Guests** is a global group of guest accounts in the domain that includes the Guest user account.

Global groups are significant in the multi-domain environments. You use them to create a hierarchical management structure or to give regular users access to resources in other domains. They are especially useful when the

7

user account database is managed in a single location—the master domain. You'll learn more about these groups in the next chapter, which deals specifically with users and groups.

Some confusion can result if a user has an account in a local user account database and an account in a Domain Account database, each with a different password. The local account can be used to access resources on the local machine, but if the user attempts to access resources in the domain, she is either prompted for a password or denied access. In the latter case, some applications deny access instead of prompting for a password. The solution is to make sure that users maintain one password that can be used throughout the network.

Workstation Administration

A standalone Windows NT system with local accounts that joins a domain (and becomes a member server) keeps its local account database for people who need to log on to the machine locally. In addition, an administrative group from the Domain Directory database called Domain Admins is added to this local database. This arrangement allows administrative users in the domain to access and manage the computer.

This system has security implications. The user/administrator/owner of the local Windows NT Workstation may not want administrators from the domain to control her system. If so, she can revoke the rights granted. To remove this right, the Domain Admins group can be removed from Administrators by the local user who logs on as Administrator.

Setting Up Domains

An organization can have a single domain or multiple domains with trust relationships. Those trust relationships can be either one way or two way, so there are quite a few choices you can make when choosing a domain model.

The potential domain models are

♦ **Single domain model**   One domain and one administrator

♦ **Single master domain model**   Clusters of domains with a single manager

♦ **Multiple master domain model**   Clusters of domains with managers in each cluster

Each of these models is described in the sections that follow, starting with the simplest model, the single domain. Each domain can have up to 26,000 users with individual workstations, although managing more than 15,000 users is not considered practical. In addition, you can have 250 groups per domain. While these numbers will allow most organizations to fit all of their users and resources into a single domain, you still need to consider the management and security advantages of using multiple domains.

The Windows NT Resource Kit available from Microsoft or in bookstores contains the Windows NT Domain Planner (OLPG.EXE), a Wizard that helps you plan and implement the most effective domain model for your networked organization. The Wizard prompts you for information about the resources on your network and how you want to manage them. It then recommends a domain model and provides a printed report with instructions on how to implement this model.

Domain Management with the Server Manager

The Server Manager is your primary tool for managing domains, while the User Manager for Domains is used to manage users and trust relationships. You start the Server Manager by opening the Administrative Tools group and choosing Server Manager. A window like the one in Figure 7-5 appears. The Server Manager can be run from an administrative workstation if you install the Windows NT Server Tools, which are included on the Windows NT Server CD-ROM.

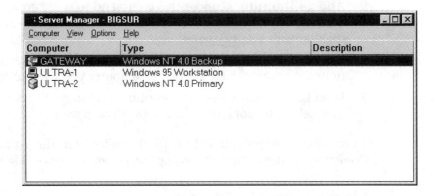

Use the Server Manager to manage domain controllers.
Figure 7-5.

7

You can perform the following management tasks in the Server Manager:

♦ Manage the roles of, and communication between, primary and backup domain controllers

♦ Manage the properties of individual servers in domains

♦ Manage the shared resources on individual servers in domains

You must be logged on as a member of the Administrators or Server Operators local group, or the Domain Admins global group, to manage domains with the Server Manager. If you just need to manage a Windows NT Workstation computer, whether it is connected to a domain or not, you must log on as a member of the Administrators or Power Users local group on that computer.

There are several options for configuring and managing domain-specific information and settings in the Server Manager. The following options are located on the Computer menu:

♦ **Promote to Primary Domain Controller** If the primary domain controller fails or needs to be taken down, select another Windows NT Server that is operating as a backup domain controller and choose this option to promote it to primary domain controller status. If the previous PDC is still running, it is automatically demoted to backup domain controller status.

♦ **Synchronize Entire Domain** This command replicates the Security database from the primary domain controller to all the backup domain controllers in the domain. You can choose it only after selecting the primary domain controller.

♦ **Add to Domain** Choose this command to add a computer to the domain. Computers that are added to a domain are given accounts in the domain's Security database.

♦ **Remove from Domain** Choose this command to remove a computer from the domain. First select the computer you want to remove.

♦ **Select Domain** Choose this option to manage a different domain, then select the domain from the list that appears.

To manage a computer in a domain, first select it in the list under the Computer heading, then choose options from the Server Manager menus.

Single Domain Model

The single domain model is a configuration of Windows NT Servers and workstations that, as its name implies, makes up one domain. Within this domain are a primary domain controller, one or more backup domain controllers, and member servers. The domain contains a single centrally managed user account database. This model is good for small- and medium-sized organizations that prefer to centralize management and use a simple domain model that is easy to administer. There are no trust relationships to configure because there is only one domain.

Single Master Domain Model

In the single master domain model, pictured in Figure 7-6, you designate a master domain from which to manage all other domains. This is done by creating trust relationships that designate the master domain as the trusted domain and all other domains as trusting domains. This model has very good security, because a single administrator or team of administrators at the central location manages the entire network. It's still possible to delegate management of resources in individual domains to local administrators, but the administrators in the master domain have the highest-level control in this arrangement.

Domains other than the master domain are called secondary domains in this model. All accounts are stored in a single user account database in the master domain and all users log on by being validated in this database. Secondary domains establish a one-way trust relationship with the master domain. At the same time, local system administrators can manage resources in their own departments or divisions based on administrative privileges that they have been assigned. One disadvantage of this model is that, as the network grows large, the single user database may become unwieldy.

Multiple Master Domain Model

The multiple master domain model consists of two or more single master domains and is appropriate for very large, international organizations. In the example shown in Figure 7-7, there are three master domains that are linked with two-way trust relationships. Each master domain has its own secondary

7

The single
master
domain model
Figure 7-6.

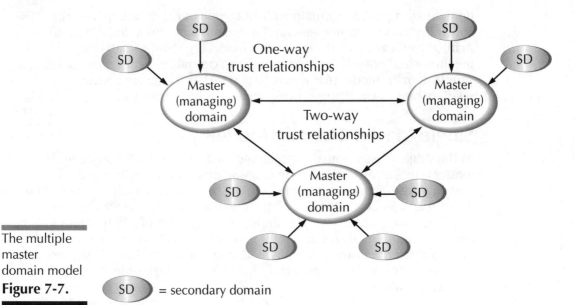

One-way
trust relationships

Two-way
trust relationships

The multiple
master
domain model
Figure 7-7.

SD   = secondary domain

domains that are linked with one-way trust relationships. User accounts are replicated among the master domains, so there is a web of trust relationships so Administrators can grant permission to users throughout the network. This model is especially appropriate for organizations of more than 40,000 users; it also accommodates mobile users, who can log on from anywhere in the network.

In any of these arrangements, it is important to consider the placement of BDCs. Recall that users can access a BDC for authentication. If users are located at a remote location, place a BDC at that location to log users in. The PDC and the BDC automatically perform replication to keep the user account database up-to-date at the remote location.

Choosing a Domain Model

Microsoft developed Table 7-1 to help you decide which domain model is appropriate for your network. You can use it to match the characteristics and benefits of each model to your needs.

As Table 7-1 shows, it is possible to have either centralized or decentralized account management under the multiple master domain model.

Domain Attribute	Single Domain	Single Master Domain	Multiple Master Domain	Independent Single Domains with Trust Relationships
Fewer than 40,000 users per domain	X	X		
More than 40,000 users per domain			X	
Centralized account management	X	X	X	
Centralized resource management	X			
Decentralized account management			X	X
Decentralized resource management		X	X	X
Central MIS	X	X	X	
No central MIS				X

Criteria for Choosing a Network Domain Model*

Table 7-1.

*Source: Microsoft Corporation

Logging On to Domains

You must log on to a Windows NT computer before you can use it (unless someone has made the mistake of not logging off and leaving the computer unattended!). A Windows NT computer may be in one of the following states at any time:

Logged Off State   In this state, access to local or network resources is not allowed until you log on to the computer. You press CTRL-ALT-DEL to initiate identification and the system's authentication process. After a successful logon, you can operate the shell program (Explorer or Program Manager) on the system.

Logged On State   In this state, the system is logged on, and you can either lock the workstation and leave all your work in place or log off. If you walk up to a computer that is logged on, press CTRL-ALT-DEL to initiate a new logon, thus avoiding the danger of Trojan Horse programs.

Workstation Locked State   In this state, the workstation is locked and a secure desktop is displayed. A valid password is required to unlock the

7

computer. When locked, a computer can still be logged on to the network, but an administrator can force its logoff using the Server Manager.

You press CTRL-ALT-DEL to execute the Secure Attention Sequence (SAS). The SAS provides a secure logon by forcing the system to switch to a secure environment that does not allow Trojan Horse programs to run. The logon screen appears:

Here you type your username and password in the appropriate fields.

In the Domain field, type the name of a local computer or a domain, depending on the type of logon you want to do. The steps for the logon process are outlined in the following list. These steps provide a very secure logon sequence that protects against "playback" attacks in which someone tries to replay captured information to gain access to or otherwise spoof a system. Actual clear text passwords are never sent over links. All passwords are encrypted before transmission.

NOTE: The following assumes you are logging on to a Windows NT Workstation. You will find more detailed information about the logon process in Appendix A.

1. Pressing CTRL-ALT-DEL displays the Logon dialog box. You fill it out, and a process called Winlogon passes your credentials to the Local Security Authority (LSA) on the same workstation.

2. The LSA forwards your credentials to an authentication package on the same workstation.

3. The Security Accounts Manager (SAM) on the local or domain computer is called to retrieve your SID (Security ID) and global SIDs. A process called Netlogon passes the credentials between network computers.

4. The LSA on your computer looks in the Policy database to retrieve user rights and other information associated with the SID and creates an access token.

5. Winlogon uses the access token to start up the local environment (a shell such as Program Manager or the desktop) so you can access the system and its resources.

Now you have an access token that you can use to run processes and access objects. If you access an object like a file, the SIDs in the token are compared to the SIDs in the Access Control list, as described in Chapter 5.

One of the following might happen during the logon:

♦ If the username is not valid, and if the Guest account is enabled, the user is logged on to the domain or trusted domain as a guest.

♦ If the Guest account is disabled, or if the username is valid but the password is not, an "access denied" message appears, and the logon fails.

♦ If a user attempts to log on to a domain and that logon fails, the client's computer (assuming it's a Windows NT Workstation) will check its own user account database for the username and password supplied. If those credentials are not valid on the local system, the client is logged on as a local guest if the Guest account is enabled on the local computer.

Discovery, Secure Channels, and Pass-Through Authentication

It may be necessary to look for a computer that can authenticate a user. This initiates a process called *discovery*. Somewhere in the domain is a domain controller that can log the user in. Netlogon finds this controller. Once a domain controller is discovered, it is used for subsequent user authentication.

Domain controllers will go through a discovery process when they are started up. The Netlogon service will try to discover domain controllers in all the trusted domains. If a trusted domain does not respond, the domain controller tries to recontact it in three 5-second intervals, then every 15 minutes until contact is made.

Once the Netlogon service has located a computer to use for authentication, it must first ensure that the computer at the other end of the connection is a valid system in the domain. The Netlogon services located on each system go through a challenge/response verification process. When the authentication is successful, a *secure channel* is established between the computers. Next, a communication session takes place between the two computers to log the user in. The channel is kept open so subsequent network calls can be passed between systems. It is also used to send the

7

username and encrypted password for pass-through validations, as will be discussed next.

Pass-through validation takes place when a user attempts to access a computer that does not know anything about the user. The MSV Authentication Package supports pass-through authentication of users in other domains by using the Netlogon service. For example, look at Figure 7-8: The user in the New York domain attempts to access the server in the Los Angeles domain. The Los Angeles server does not know anything about the New York user, so it asks the domain controllers in the user's home domain (New York) to authenticate the user. (This example assumes that a trust relationship exists in which the Los Angeles domain trusts the New York domain.)

Security Policies

Part of controlling the security on your domain is setting security policies. You start the User Manager for Domains and choose Account on the Policies menu. The dialog box in Figure 7-9 appears, in which you can set policies that affect all accounts in the domain. Keep in mind that you can set policies and properties for individuals by accessing the accounts themselves, as discussed in the next chapter. These individual user account properties include special profiles, logon times, logon workstations, account expirations, and others.

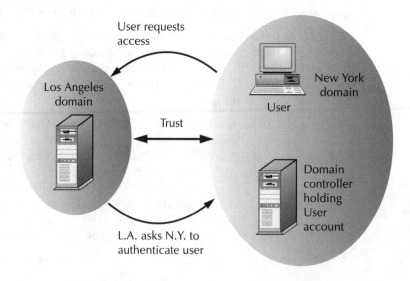

Pass-through
validation
Figure 7-8.

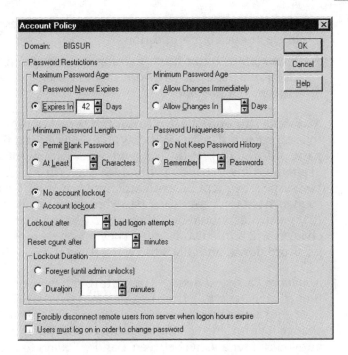

Setting
account
policies
Figure 7-9.

Password Restrictions

The Password Restrictions section of the Account Policy dialog box is where you set policies that control how passwords are handled in the domain. The settings you make here are critical to protecting passwords and your password security scheme. Each item is discussed in the following sections.

You should implement password policies that comply with the settings you make in the dialog box. Password policies protect the network from hacker attacks and define the responsibility of users who have been given access to the organization's information system. You should have users read and sign such policies as part of their employment contract. Here are some guidelines for a password policy:

7

♦   Always state that access to the network is granted only if conditions of other employment contracts are met and that all activities may be monitored. Legally, you can't monitor unless you let users know they are being monitored.

♦   Users should never write down passwords.

♦   Users should change passwords often and should use passwords that are difficult to guess and that include alphanumeric characters.

♦ Users should not communicate usernames or passwords using any form of electronic communication.

♦ If an administrator needs to inform a user of a new password via electronic mail, the password should be sent under separate cover and encrypted if possible.

Maximum Password Age   This is the period of time that a user is allowed to use a password before Windows NT requires that the user change the password. You can set this value to Never Expires, or you can set the expiration time to between 1 and 999 days. In a secure environment or if you suspect frequent break-in attempts, you might want to set this value to 7 so users need to change their passwords every week. However, keep in mind that passwords should be difficult to guess and that frequent password changes will burden your users. They may be tempted to write the latest password down, and that's the worst thing that can happen.

Minimum Password Age   This setting can be used to prevent a user from immediately reverting back to a previous password after a change. It specifies how long a user must wait after changing a password before the user can change it again. By default, users can change their passwords immediately, but you can set a value between 1 and 999 days to prevent users from changing their password during that period. If you are going to set a password uniqueness value, do not set Minimum Password Age to Allow Changes Immediately.

Minimum Password Length   This is a critical setting for security reasons. If users create short passwords, a cracker is more likely to discover a password. The default option is Permit Blank Passwords, which you should never set in a secure environment. Set this option to At Least *x* Characters, with *x* being between 1 and 14 characters. Choosing 14 characters will strain your users to come up with a password they can remember. They may be tempted to use familiar names or write the password down. An anonymous password cracker once said that passwords over 6 characters were hard to crack. However, if users are using easily guessed passwords such as their pet names, even 14-character passwords may be easy to crack.

Password Uniqueness   This option can prevent users from toggling among their favorite passwords and reduces the chances that a hacker/password cracker will discover passwords. If you set this option to Do Not Keep Password History, users can revert immediately back to a password that they previously used. Do not use this option in a secure environment. By setting the Remember option to a value of between 1 and 24, you can prevent users from using up to the last 24 passwords they used. This is also a critical security feature because it can prevent hackers from logging in to an account using a password that they previously discovered. To use this option effectively, do not set the Minimum Password Age parameter to Allow Changes Immediately.

 NOTE: Because of the way passwords are saved in a table, users cannot reuse a password until they have changed passwords $n+2$ times, where n is the number of passwords remembered. So if Password Uniqueness is set to 3, users cannot revert to the first password until they have changed their password five times (3+2).

Account Lockout

The Account lockout feature is your key to preventing brute-force password cracking/guessing attacks on your system. Consider this: The default setting is No account lockout, as you can see in Figure 7-9; if you retain this setting, someone could execute a dictionary attack against your server. Such an attack attempts, over an extended period of time, to log in to a user's account with different passwords with the expectation of actually guessing the correct password. In a dictionary attack, thousands of well-known passwords are tried. If your users don't create hard-to-guess passwords and you don't have Account lockout set, someone could use this method to break into a valid user account.

 NOTE: The Administrator account cannot be locked out. This prevents total lockout from the system in the event that an administrator forgets a password or some other similar situation. Be sure to use a difficult-to-guess password, as outlined in Chapter 6.

If an account becomes locked due to hacker attacks or other reasons, an administrator can reset it by opening the User Manager for Domains and opening the Properties box for the account that is locked out (by double-clicking the account name). The Account Locked Out option will be enabled. Disable the option to allow access to the locked out account.

7

You can track unauthorized attempts to access an account if failed logon attempts are audited. Each failure will then appear in the Security Event Log, which you can view with the Event Viewer. The account that is attempting to log on and the machine where the logons are occurring are listed in the log file. Chapter 10 provides information on the parameters and tools you can use to detect hackers and crackers. When you enable the Account Locked Out option in the Account Policy dialog box, you can set the following options:

♦ **Lockout after *x* bad logon attempts**   The value of *x* determines how many times a user can attempt to log in to an account before the account is locked. The time element for this value is set with the Reset count after *x* minutes option described next. A realistic value would be 2 or greater to allow for authentic users who might make typing mistakes or users who type in a previous password by mistake. The range for this setting is 1 to 999 logon attempts, but any setting above 5 would be ludicrous in a secure environment.

♦ **Reset count after *x* minutes**   Set this value to the maximum number of minutes that can occur between successive logon attempts before a lockout occurs. The range is 1 to 99999 minutes. This option counts the number of bad logon attempts within a set time interval. If no bad logon attempts occur within the specified time interval, then the bad logon attempts count is returned to zero. Keep in mind that an intruder could try a different password every half hour for days at a time to bypass lockout, so set this value appropriately.

♦ **Lockout Duration**   This setting lets you lock an account out forever—until an administrator unlocks it—or for a set period of time. The first option is best for security, but if users constantly forget their passwords and call you to reset their accounts, you might want to set the Duration option to an appropriate value. If you set the value low, valid users will be able to retry logging in to their accounts much more quickly and not hassle you to unlock them, but intruders will also be able to retry attempts more often to gain access to accounts.

♦ **Forcibly disconnect remote users from server when logon hours expire**   When this option is enabled, users are disconnected from the server when their logon hours expire. Logon hours can be set for each user individually using the User Manager, as described in the next chapter. If you don't enable this option, users are not disconnected when the logon hours expire, but they are not allowed to reconnect until a valid logon time occurs. In secure environments, you should enable this option to shut down accounts that have been accidentally left open by a user, so after-hours employees (or janitors) can't access the account.

♦ **Users must log on in order to change password**   This option basically prevents users from changing their passwords if the passwords expire. They won't be able to log on and will need to call the administrator to have that person change the password.

Tips for Domain Security

Domains can provide a barrier between different parts of your organization. If you indiscriminately create trust relationships and grant users and groups access to resources in other domains, your security plan will weaken. There is no guarantee that domain configurations can provide adequate security, no matter how well you set them up, but they provide a first step to controlling user access on your network.

Domains can be part of the barrier you build between your Internet-connected systems and your internal network. If you connect a Web server to the Internet, you should put it and other public servers in a separate domain so you can implement user and domain policies that are different than your other domains. You still need to set up hardware and software firewalls to protect your systems from hackers on the Internet, but a separate domain can provide another level of security that lets you control exactly who has access to the Internet servers and the internal network.

The general rule of providing the least amount of service applies to trust relationships. If you do need to set up trust between domains, make it one-way if possible. Consider also the critical nature of the services you have running in domains. If a service provides mission-critical information, don't establish any trust relationships that might allow someone to disrupt those services. Since some services are a security risk in themselves, you may want to avoid running them in all but the most secure domains, if possible—for example, in a domain to which only administrative users have access. A hacker who manages to log in to a low-level account in the domain might disrupt service or cause other damage by exploiting a weakness or administrative error.

Replication can be used in interesting ways. Just previously, I recommended running some services in domains that only administrative users have access to. These services might produce files or database information that other users need to access. You can extend this information outside the domain using replication. Then you have a safe and secure copy within the protected domain and duplicate copies on servers in other domains that are continuously updated and synchronized with the primary domain. Of course, the domains are separated at the network level as well, using some techniques such as protocol isolation, as described in Chapter 18.

7

Limit the number of user accounts in an isolated domain that runs mission-critical services so that you have better control over the actions of people who have access in the domain. Your log files will also be smaller if you need to track only a few user activities.

Once a trust relationship is established, the normal procedure is to grant global groups in one domain membership to local groups in another domain. This is actually risky, so you need to watch your step. Are you familiar with the users who have membership in the global groups of another domain? You will give them automatic access to your resources if you make the global group a member of one of your local groups. For example, if you add a remote global group to the Administrators local group, members in that group will have administrative rights and permissions on the servers in your domain! Keep in mind that while a user in another domain may be trusted in that domain, the same user might have malicious activities in mind when working in your domain. Domains often separate competing divisions of a company.

Be cautious when severing trust relationships. A severed trust relationship may not take effect immediately. You might sever a trust relationship and assume that users in other domains no longer have access to your domain, when in fact they still do for a short period of time. This situation could pose a problem if, after severing the relationship, you make sensitive information available. To resolve this problem, at least until the server can be rebooted, remove group permissions from the resources for the users in the other domain as appropriate.

CHAPTER 8

User and Group Security Management

A thorough understanding of user accounts and group accounts is critical for achieving a high level of security in Windows NT. In fact, the bulk of what is checked and evaluated by security-analysis tools, such as the Kane utilities discussed in Appendix D, is the proper setup of user and group accounts, excessive user rights, and user account policies. While some of the material in this chapter will be old hat to veteran Windows NT managers, it is presented with a slant toward security and should be of interest to everyone.

NOTE: Techniques for evaluating the current status of users, groups and permissions is discussed in Chapter 10.

Terminology

It's easy to get lost and confused in the terminology of local workstations, local domains, global groups, remote domains, and such. As you read this chapter, make sure to differentiate among these different systems and objects.

First, all of the references here are to Windows NT Server computers or Windows NT Workstation computers, because these computers maintain their own user account databases. Windows 95 and other versions of Windows do not maintain their own databases, but can participate in Windows NT workgroups or domains. This discussion is primarily concerned with domains rather than workgroups. Also note the following:

♦ A *Windows NT Server computer* operating as a domain controller maintains the domain's user account database.

♦ A *member server* is a Windows NT Server that is not a domain controller. It can maintain its own user account database and provide access to network users as well. It does not store the domain user account database and consequently cannot log users on to a domain.

♦ A *Windows NT Workstation computer* maintains its own user account database and can provide access to network users. It can also participate in a domain.

♦ *Workstation local accounts and groups* are located in the User database on Windows NT Workstation computers or member servers. Logging on to one of these accounts gives you access to resources on the local computer, not other computers.

♦ *Domain local accounts and groups* are defined on primary domain controllers and are replicated to backup domain controllers in the same domain. The group can only be used in the domain.

♦ *Global groups* are collections of user accounts and groups that can be made members of other groups.

The User Manager

You use the User Manager, as pictured in Figure 8-1, to create and manage user accounts, set user rights, set account policies for the domain, enable trust relationships, and set audit policies. If you're working at a Windows NT Workstation computer, the utility is simply called the User Manager, and you use it to manage local accounts on the workstation. If you're working at a Windows NT Server domain controller, the tool is called the User Manager for Domains, and you use it to manage accounts for the entire domain, or to enable access for accounts in other trusted domains. Throughout this chapter I will refer to either version as the User Manager.

Notice that individual user accounts are listed in the top pane, and groups are listed in the lower pane. In this figure, additional user accounts have already been added.

The name of the Administrator account has been changed to BTiaaanftAaitBSd to hide it from detection.

For security reasons, the owners of the administrative accounts also have their own personal accounts to use when they are accessing the network for non-administrative tasks. These accounts have fewer rights and privileges to guard against intrusions.

If you need to add an account, choose New User from the User menu. A dialog box appears, similar to the one shown in Figure 8-2.

Enter the properties for an account in the New User dialog box, then click the Add button to create another account, or Cancel to stop adding accounts. To change the properties of an existing account, double-click the account in the list. A dialog box with the same fields appears.

The User Manager for Domains (or simply the User Manager)

Figure 8-1.

: User Manager - BIGSUR		_ □ ×
User View Policies Options Help		
Username	**Full Name**	**Description**
AColgan	Anna Colgan	User account
BSchenk	Becky Schenk	User account
BTiaaanftAaitBSd	Administrator	Built-in account for administering the computer/domain
Guest		Built-in account for guest access to the computer/dom
HLewis	Hank Lewis	User account
hVXRssss060356bdt	Hank Lewis	Administrative account
IUSR_ULTRA-2	Internet Guest Account	Internet Server Anonymous Access
JBonati	John Bonati	User account
JFredricks	Jack Fredricks	User Account
n5u953THBSM5ddd	Jack Fredricks	Administrative account

Groups	**Description**
Account Operators	Members can administer domain user and group accounts
Administrators	Members can fully administer the computer/domain
Backup Operators	Members can bypass file security to back up files
Domain Admins	Designated administrators of the domain
Domain Guests	All domain guests

8

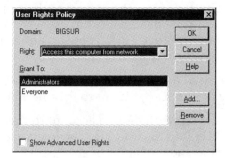

The New User
dialog box
Figure 8-2.

To set rights for users, choose User Rights from the Policies menu. A dialog box much like this one appears:

Here you can choose a right in the Right drop-down list box, then add or remove users and groups in the Grant To box.

A *right* is an authorization to perform some action on a system. These actions are often related to tasks that system administrators need to do, but there are some basic rights that all users need in order to access a system. Keep in mind that rights apply to a domain, whereas permissions determine how individual users or groups can access specific objects like files and directories. Refer to "Rights" later in this chapter for more information.

Network Client Administrator Tools

You can run the User Manager from a management workstation (rather than from the server console) by installing the Network Client Administrator options. When they're installed, you can run the Event Viewer, Server Manager, User Manager, Remote Access Administrator, User Profile Editor, Remoteboot Manager, DHCP Manager, and WINS Manager from the comfort of your office.

If you decide to run management tools from a computer other than the server, you must apply all the security precautions appropriate for servers to your administrative computer. If someone manages to access it and log on to your administrative account, he will be able to do whatever he wants on the server within the context of your Management account. All the while, the server may be locked up tightly in a secure location. Refer to the Windows NT Server CD-ROM for instructions on installing these utilities. They are located in the \Client\Srvtools directory.

CAUTION: A recommended security policy is to allow no administrators to log on from the network; instead, have them log on only at a server console.

User Accounts

All Windows NT computers provide access through user accounts, including Windows NT Server and Windows NT Workstation.

You create user accounts by choosing New User from the User menu in the User Manager. The procedure for creating accounts and granting access is to create an account for a user, then add the user account to a group that already has the rights and permissions you want to grant to the user. It is possible to grant rights and permissions to individual user accounts, but adding users to groups that already have permissions is the most efficient management practice. Keep in mind that there are two types of access:

♦ Normal user access to programs, data files, and other system resources for everyday tasks

♦ Administrative access to the system so selected users can manage user accounts, servers, peripherals, and other network resources

Windows NT has built-in administrative and user groups. By making a user a member of one of these groups, you automatically grant them the rights and permissions assigned to the groups for administering the system or for accessing it for everyday tasks.

You need to make sure that all accounts have appropriate security settings. First, specify a domain account policy as discussed in Chapter 7. Choose Account Policy from the Policies menu in the User Manager. After setting these policies, you can set individual restrictions for any user by double-clicking the name of the user in the User Manager. The New User dialog box appears, as you saw in Figure 8-2. In this dialog box, you can specify group memberships, profiles, hours that the user can log on, what computers the user can log on to, and other account information. These options are discussed in the next few sections.

8

Username and Password Properties

The New User dialog box holds the properties of an individual account. In the top fields, you can specify the username, full name, description, and password of the account.

When creating new accounts, make sure to follow a policy that makes usernames and passwords hard to guess. In minimum-security environments, you can create usernames that are the first letter of the first name plus the last name, such as TSheldon. In more secure environments where you want to hide usernames from potential intruders, you can set up naming schemes or use cryptic codes that have no logical meaning except to you. Here are some naming schemes; remember to make sure your scheme is not easy to figure out.

TSamBSM990	First letter of the following words	Tom Sheldon administrative manager Big Sur Multimedia 990 (start date)
am0001-990TFS	A coded username	am = administrative manager 0001 = employee number 990 = employee start date TFS = employee initials

The problem with using complex usernames and passwords is that users write them down in fear that they'll forget them, thereby compromising security. If the User Cannot Change Password option (described in the following list) is not set, users may simply change their password to something easy to remember. Here are the password options that you can set on the dialog box to enforce your password policies and improve security:

♦ **User Must Change Password at Next Logon** You must create an initial password for any account, but giving this password to a user may compromise security: someone could capture it in an e-mail transmission or overhear it on the phone. This option forces the user to change the initial password and avert any unauthorized logons with the initial password (unless of course the hacker who illegally obtains the password logs in to the account before the user).

♦ **User Cannot Change Password** You may prefer to create a hard-to-guess password for an account. By setting this option, you prevent the user from changing the password to something that is easy to remember or type.

♦ **Password Never Expires** The Accounts Policy dialog box, discussed in Chapter 7, lets you set a password expiration time for all user accounts in the domain. This option lets you override that expiration time for a specific account.

♦ **Account Disabled** You can set this option to disable accounts if a user goes on vacation or on temporary leave. It prevents anyone else from accessing the user account through illegal means.

♦ **Account Locked Out** This option appears if an account locks because there were too many failed logon attempts. Click it to free up the account so that the user can again gain access.

This last option is an indication that someone has attempted to break into an account unless the user simply forgot her password. The user obviously knows the account name, so the culprit may be someone who works near the original account owner. Set up auditing so you can track the activities of suspected users.

Hiding the Username

The username of the last user to log on to a Windows system appears in the Username field of the Logon dialog box. The feature is designed to make your next logon easier, but it can potentially compromise security. It exposes usernames and gives intruders the name of an account that they could potentially break into by cracking passwords. This is especially risky if you just signed on as the administrator and you previously renamed the Administrator account to some obscure name to hide it from detection.

You can prevent Windows NT from displaying the username from the last logon by using the Registry Editor to make the following changes in the Registry. For help using the Registry Editor, refer to your Windows NT manual or to online help.

Start the Registry Editor by typing REGEDT32 in the Run dialog box. When the Registry Editor opens, click the HKEY_LOCAL_MACHINE window. "Drill down" to the following key:

    SOFTWARE\Microsoft\Windows NT\Current Version\Winlogon

Next, double-click the name DontDisplayLastUserName and change its value to 1.

Properties of User Accounts

8

Look again at the New User dialog box (Figure 8-2) and notice the buttons at the bottom. This is where you set additional properties for a user's account. The Group button is where you specify the groups that the user belongs to. Groups are discussed later in this chapter. The other buttons and their dialog boxes are discussed in the following paragraphs.

Profile   This button opens the User Environment Profile dialog box:

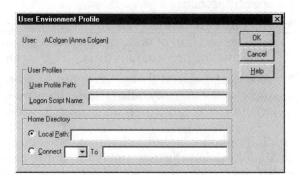

Here you can specify a logon script and home directory for the user as well as a profile, which includes the environment settings for the user. Profiles let users log on to a familiar environment from other computers in the domain. A user's home directory is where personal files and programs can be stored. If the directory should be located on the computer where the user logs on, click the Local Path button and type the path to the directory. If the directory is on a network server, click Connect and specify the drive letter and path for the directory. For more information about client profiles, refer to Chapter 12.

Hours   Click the Hours button to restrict the logon hours during which the user can log on to the domain and connect to a domain controller. "Hours" is an important security option, because it can prevent users from logging on to a system after hours when their activities are less likely to be monitored. This option can also prevent hackers from breaking into an account after the rightful user has logged off.

The Logon Hours dialog box pictured here has all hours enabled:

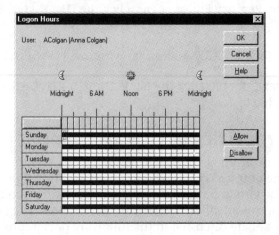

To change the hours, click and drag a box around a specific set of hours, then click Allow or Disallow. If a user doesn't have privileges for a particular time period, black bars do not appear in that period.

Logon To   Click the Logon To button to open the following dialog box:

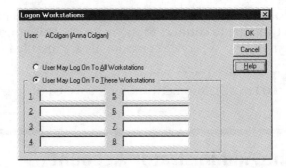

Here you specify the names of the computers that the user can log on to. This is an important security feature, because it forces users to log on to systems where their activities can be physically monitored. It also prevents hackers from logging on to an account from their base of operation, which might be outside your company. Click the lower button and type in the names of the computers that users can log on to.

Account   This button opens the Account Information dialog box:

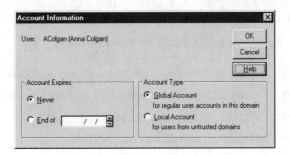

This box lets you specify when an account will become inactive if you set it up for a temporary user, a critical security option if you have consultants or other part-time workers accessing your systems. Expired accounts are not deleted, so you can reuse them if a temporary user returns. If a user is already logged on, the account expires after she logs off. Specify the type of account in the Account Type field, as described here:

8

♦   **Global accounts** are available over the entire domain and across trust relationships.

♦ **Local accounts** allow users from mistrusted domains to access local resources, but do not permit access to Windows NT Server domains. LAN Manager users use local accounts to access resources on a system over the network, because LAN Manager domains do not participate in trust relationships.

Dialup   The Dialup option is used to grant permission to use dial-up networking to connect to the network. This option is available only if the Remote Access Service components are installed.

NOTE: Dial-up networking is covered further in Chapter 14.

The Administrator Account

The Administrator account (not to be confused with the Administrators group) is a built-in account that is installed when a Windows NT system is set up. In a domain environment, the Administrator account is set up simultaneously with the primary domain controller in the domain. The person setting up the system specifies the initial password for the Administrator account. The Administrator account should be renamed, but it can never be disabled or deleted. This safeguard ensures that the Administrator can never be locked out of the system. You cannot even set lockout features for the account to prevent someone from trying multiple passwords in an attempt to illegally access the account.

The Administrator can do the following:

♦ Create and manage user and group accounts

♦ Create shared directories and connect to shared directories

♦ Establish trust relationships

♦ Manage all aspects of hard drives

♦ Manage all aspects of printers and printer sharing

♦ Manage security policies

♦ Manage auditing and security logs

♦ Modify the operating system and install new drivers

♦ Take ownership of files and other objects

♦ Lock, log on to, and shut down servers

In domain environments, the Administrator account for the domain permits you to manage servers and workstations in the domain, including domain controllers, member servers, and Windows NT Workstation computers. The Administrator account is a member of the built-in Administrators group, as well as of the Domain Admins and Domain Users groups. Through this membership, the Administrator account potentially has full access to every system in every domain on the network.

Here are some guidelines for the Administrator account:

♦ For security reasons, the Administrator account should be renamed something obscure.

♦ To enhance Administrator account security, create a two- or three-part password, with each part known only by one person, as discussed later in this chapter.

♦ Because the Administrator account has full access to the system, the administrator should log on to the account only when necessary and log off immediately.

♦ Create Subadministrators by adding users to the Account Operators and Server Operators groups.

♦ Convert the Administrator Account to an "Auditor" account, as described under "The Missing Auditor Account" in Chapter 10.

♦ Consider revoking all network access by Administrators, as discussed in Chapter 6. This means all administration must be done from the server console in a controlled environment.

♦ If there are multiple administrators, create a separate administrative account for each so you can audit their individual activities. If unauthorized activities are occurring, it will not be possible to ascertain which administrator is the perpetrator unless separate accounts are used.

♦ Avoid logging in to the Administrator account at mistrusted computers or at computers in unfamiliar settings. Your activities could be monitored electronically or photographically to capture passwords and other secure information.

♦ To audit attacks against the Administrator account, rename the original account, then create a "decoy" account called Administrator that has no privileges. Set auditing options to track failed logon attempts (as discussed in Chapter 10) to this decoy account so you can see if someone is trying to break into it. In Performance Monitor, you can set an alert for the Error Logon option to help warn you of repeated logon attempts, which may indicate that password-guessing programs are being used to crack the security on the server.

♦ If you forget the Administrator password, or if it is changed by a malicious user, pull out the emergency repair disk that you created

8

during Windows NT setup and reload the SAM database from it as a last resort. This restores the user accounts to what they were when you first set up the system. While resetting your accounts may not sound too appealing, it may be the only way to get back into your system short of reloading the operating system (unless you can locate a password-cracking program!).

♦ Any user who is a member of the local Administrators group on a Windows NT computer can take ownership of files and access the data in those files, no matter what the current permissions are on the files. Because of this, you need to closely monitor and audit the activities of users with administrative rights.

♦ Seriously consider whether you really can trust your administrators and subadministrators. For security's sake, be a pessimist. Your job and your company's assets may be at stake.

The System Account

The System account is not a user account, but an account that the operating system uses to run programs, utilities, and device drivers. The System account has unlimited power, and so rogue Trojan Horse services that manage to infiltrate your system and run under the System account have the ability do just about anything. They could also create and change user accounts or perform other activities that wreak havoc on your system.

System-type accounts are common in other operating systems, and one of the most famous UNIX security attacks was a worm that took advantage of a bug in TCP/IP services to take over the System account. The System account provides a way to run services without the need for an actual administrative user to be logged on. The System and Administrator accounts have similar, but the System account is used by the operating system and by services that run under Windows NT. The System account is an internal account that does not show up in the User Manager, cannot be added to any groups, and cannot have its rights changed.

Some services will only run under the System account, such as Server and Workstation. If you are installing a new service, especially if it is one that is untrusted, you should run that service under a special account that has the lowest level of access rights and permissions that the service requires. This will prevent an infected service from doing damage to your system. You create the account in the User Manager just as you create any user account. You then use the Services utility to configure a service to start up under the account. This procedure is described in more detail in Chapter 10.

The Guest Account

The Guest account allows people to access a Windows NT computer without logging in to a specific user account. The Guest account allows anonymous logon. A lot of people misinterpret the Guest account; they assume it is a security risk and that no one should log on without an account. However, recall the last time you accessed a Web site. You probably did so as an anonymous guest and were not required to enter a password. What would the Web be like if you had to enter a username and password every time you accessed a Web site? Tracking all those account would be a nightmare.

Be aware that the Guest account, like any other account, has access to every directory where the Everyone group has permissions, and Everyone has some risky permissions in the Windows NT System directories. This access is what makes people edgy about using the Guest account.

To use the Guest account safely, first set up a separate domain for systems that will allow guest access. That way, the systems in other domains are not prone to the potential security problems of having Guest enabled, assuming you disable Guest in those domains. Next, check the permissions that the Everyone group has in directories. *Do not* execute an across-the-board revocation of permissions for Everyone from the root directory, because that could lock up your system (the next time you reboot) and may prevent real users from making changes in some of the system directories that are necessary to run programs.

The permissions for directories in the *systemroot* tree (usually C:\WINNT) are of the most difficult to evaluate and change because some of them require that all users including guests have more than Read-only permissions. You can convert the Everyone group's access to Read Only or No Access permissions in all directories, but this will require that you add back in groups such as Domain Users with the same rights. The next chapter provides a little more insight on these techniques.

More About the Guest Account

The Guest account is disabled by default on Windows NT Server domain controller computers and enabled on Windows NT Workstation computers and member servers. In addition, on the latter, users can log on as Guest at the computer itself, but Guest has no built-in rights on a Windows NT Server computer acting as a domain controller. This distinction is important.

Technically, on Windows NT Workstation computers, the Guest account is a member of the Guests local group, which has log on locally rights. On Windows NT Server computers acting as domain controllers, the Guest account is a member of the Domain Guests group, which itself is a member of the Guests local group. However, none of these have log on locally rights.

8

Guests can only access the system over the network if the account is enabled. This is for security reasons. Only members of administrative groups such as Administrators and Server Operators can long on at the server itself.

When the Guest account is enabled, users can access computers in the domain where Guest is enabled as a guest, but you won't know exactly who the user is, because guest users don't type a logon name. If the Guest account is enabled, users can log on and view a list of resources, but access to those resources is limited by rights and permissions. If you decide to use the Guest account you could create a directory for public files and give guests Read Only access to the directory. Remember, each domain has its own Guest account.

There are security implications to enabling Guest. While you can restrict the Guest account's access, an administrator might inadvertently elevate the rights and/or privileges of the account and expose your system to attackers. Because the Guest account is well known, it is targeted by hackers.

Another security concern with the Guest account is that, if enabled, it gains any permissions that are granted to the Everyone group. That's why domain guests can delete files in the System32 directory, to which Everyone has Change permissions by default. Those permissions are granted so that users can make required changes to initialization files and the Registry. This is a potentially serious security problem since a hacker logging in as Guest on a domain could stage a denial-of-service attack by deleting files in the System32 directory.

Here's how a Guest logon works. A user who specifies an invalid username is logged in to the local Guest account on Windows NT Workstation computers or member server (not a domain). If a user specifies an invalid account name for a domain, the local computer that the user is at will check its own local user account database (assuming a Windows NT Workstation) and attempt to log the user in to the account. If a user account is not available, then the user is logged in as Guest, assuming Guest is enabled and no passwords are required.

Logon will fail in two cases: if a user tries to log on with an invalid username while the Guest account is disabled, and if the user types a valid username but an incorrect password. In the latter case, the system will start keeping track of failed logons to the valid user account because it assumes that someone is trying to break in, so it never grants the user Guest privileges.

Be aware that no one dialing in to a Windows NT Remote Access Service (RAS) gets automatic access to the Guest account if his username is invalid. However, it is possible to use RAS to log in to the Guest account by typing Guest in the Username field of the Logon dialog box, assuming Guest is enabled.

A feature of Windows NT, versions 3.5 and above, is that the Guest account has been removed as a member of the Domain Users group so that it does not default to this group. A new Domain Guest global group is now available, as discussed later in this chapter. This account contains the domain's built-in Guest user account. You can use the Domain Guests group to grant users rights and permissions in the domain that are more restricted than those of the Domain Users global group.

For security reasons, do not grant Guest write or delete permissions to any files and directories. Guests should only be allowed to read files in specific directories in most cases. If guests need to drop off files, create a "drop-box" directory in which guests have only Write privileges. They can copy files into the directory, but never read files in the directory, not even the one they just copied into it.

Tracking User Accounts

There are a number of tools that help you manage user accounts and monitor user activity on the system. The Performance Monitor includes a number of options for monitoring values that indicate the traffic generated by user logons and their access to resources. Performance Monitor can be invaluable in determining loads on a system. You can set alerts to inform you when various activities exceed their normal values.

For example, Performance Monitor can warn you when a system is under attack by someone trying to overload the server (a denial of service attack). You can set an alert for an option called Bytes Received/sec. This alert will warn you if the number of bytes received per second exceeds a predetermined value that is normal for your system. Such a jump might indicate that your server is being spammed.

Some other interesting alerts are discussed in Chapter 9. You can have the system alert you when somebody is randomly attempting to access files in hopes of getting at something that was not properly protected. You can also have the system alert you when someone attempts to access a file without proper access authorization. Another useful alert is Error Logon, which tracks failed logon attempts and alerts you when someone is guessing passwords in an attempt to log on.

The Server Manager in the Administrative Tools group lets you monitor and manage a number of user activities. After starting it, double-click a server in the domain you want to manage. This opens a Properties dialog box similar to this one:

8

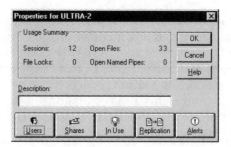

The Users, Shares, and In Use buttons are of interest if you are managing users, as outlined here:

♦ **Users** Click this button to view a list of all the users who are connected to the server over the network, and a list of resources opened by the users. This option is important, because you can use it to disconnect users who are intruding or performing malicious activities.

♦ **Shares** Click this button to view shared resources available on the computer as well as a list of users who are using the shared resources. You can stop users from sharing a resource with this option if you discover that they are inappropriately accessing a resource. After stopping access, review the permissions for the resource and reset them to prevent such access in the future.

♦ **In Use** Click this button to view a list of the computer's open shared resources. You can close any open resource using this option.

Groups

A group is a collection of user accounts that have rights and permissions to resources. When added to a group, the user obtains the rights and permissions that are already granted to the group. Windows NT has a set of default groups that are appropriate for the most common types of system access, but you can create and manage new groups by using the User Manager utility.

From a management perspective, it's much easier to manage the rights and permissions of groups than of individual users. It's easy to add users to a group, then remove them when you want to revoke their rights in that group. From a security perspective, it's not wise to assign rights and permissions to individual user accounts, because it's too difficult to keep track of them. For example, you can view the groups that have permissions on a directory by looking at the Permissions dialog box for the directory, as shown here:

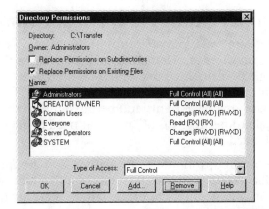

Keep in mind, however, that some users may have permissions that are inherited from parent directories.

TIP: The Somarsoft utilities discussed in Chapter 9 and Appendix D help you track down inappropriate and insecure permissions.

To find out which user accounts are members of a particular group, open the User Manager and double-click on the group. You will see a dialog box, similar to the one shown here, that describes the group and lists its current members:

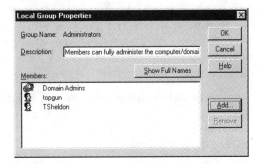

You can click the Add button to add a new member, or select any member and click the Remove button.

To create new groups, choose New Global Group or New Local Group from the User menu. The next section describes the differences between these kinds of groups.

8

Global Groups and Local Groups

There are two types of groups in the Windows NT environment: *local groups* and *global groups*. Domain local groups have rights and permissions in a single domain. Member servers (Windows NT Servers that are not domain controllers) and Windows NT Workstation computers have their own local groups that have rights and permissions on those computers only. Think of local groups in terms of tasks that need to get done or resources that users will need to access.

Global groups should be thought of as a grouping of people. You can add a global group (and thus its members) to a local group to give the former the rights and permissions of the latter. There are default local and global groups as discussed later.

New Windows NT users are often confused by global groups, because the name seems to imply a group that contains accounts from all over the network or possibly a group of users that can be assigned rights for the entire network, not just a computer or domain. In fact, a global group contains only members from a single domain, and you add the group to a local group or a local group in another domain. Microsoft likes to call global groups "export" groups and local groups "import" groups. Global groups are imported into local groups.

The procedure for setting up global groups is to add a user's account to a global group in the user's domain, then add the global group to a local group, either in the same domain or in another domain for which a trust relationship has been established. This procedure is illustrated in Figure 8-3. In step 1, a new user account is created. In step 2, the user account is added to appropriate global groups. In step 3, the global group is added to local groups in the same domain or other domains. Note that global groups may already belong to local groups when you add a new user to the group. The new user then gets all the rights and permissions already assigned to the global group.

Here are some other things to keep in mind:

♦ Local groups on domain controllers have rights only on the domain where they are created.

♦ Local groups on Windows NT Workstation computers and member servers have rights on the computer where they are created.

♦ Remember that groups on NT Workstation computers and member servers *are not* part of the security applicable to Domain groups.

♦ A local group cannot contain other local groups from the same domain. It can only contain user accounts or global groups from the same domain or other domains.

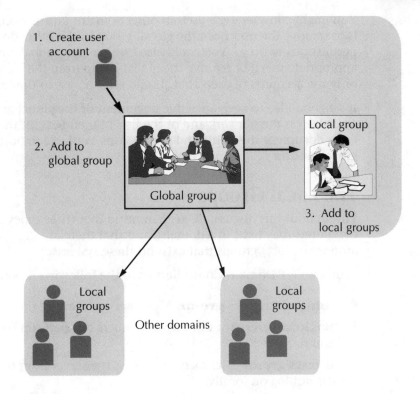

1. Create user
   account

2. Add to
   global group

Global group

Local group

3. Add to
   local groups

Local
groups

Other domains

Local
groups

♦   Trust relationships must exist before you can add a global group from a
    different domain to a local group in another domain.

♦   Global groups contain only user accounts from one domain. They
    cannot contain local groups or other global groups.

So how do you take advantage of these groups and use them to promote
security? You can start by creating very precise global groups that will hold
users with very specific job titles and tasks. Then it's easy to set rights and
permissions.

For security reasons, the members of global groups must be reviewed on a
regular basis. Because global groups can be added to local groups, thereby
obtaining the rights and privileges of the local groups, some members of
those groups may obtain inappropriate access rights. For example, assume a
former member of your management team moves to another department in
another domain. If that person is a member of a global group that is added
to your local Administrators group, she will gain administrative rights that
might be inappropriate in her new job, especially since she knows a lot
about your department.

8

You might consider some users in other domains untrustworthy. One approach is to remove the user from the global group in the other domain if you have permissions to do so. You could also create a new global group with only appropriate users, or remove the global group from the local group and add only the accounts of users that should have access to the local group.

It's a good idea to keep an active document of the global groups that are available on the network and of the lists of members for those global groups. Fully document the rights and permissions available to both local and global groups.

The Local Groups

Throughout this discussion, keep in mind that three types of Windows NT computers may exist in a domain, and that there are slight differences among the local groups that exist on these systems.

Windows NT Domain Controllers have the following groups:

◆ **Administrators group** Members can manage the entire domain.

◆ **Backup Operators group** Members can perform backups and restores.

◆ **Guests group** Members can access the server from the network but cannot log on locally.

◆ **Print Operators group** Members can manage printers.

◆ **Replicators group** Members can manage replication services.

◆ **Server Operators group** Members can manage servers.

◆ **Users group** Members can access the server from the network but cannot log on locally.

Windows NT Workstation computers and member servers (Windows NT Servers that are not Domain Controllers) have the following groups. Note the Power Users group and the absence of server-related groups.

◆ **Administrators group** Members can manage the local system.

◆ **Backup Operators group** Members can perform backups and restores on the local system.

◆ **Guests group** Members can access the local system but do little else.

◆ **Power Users group** Members can manage user accounts on the local system.

◆ **Replicators group** Members can manage replication services.

♦ **Users group** Members can log on to the local workstation and use it to access the network. They can also shut down the system and perform certain other tasks.

The rights assigned to each of the groups are discussed later in this chapter. First, each of the groups is discussed along with some security precautions for using the groups.

Administrators Group

The Administrators group, which exists on all Windows NT computers, has full control of the computer. No other group has such extensive abilities. The Administrator user account gains these rights by being a member of this group, and it can't be removed from the group (this prevents accidental lockouts). In domain environments, administrators manage the configuration of the entire domain.

Even though administrators have full control of a system, they only have access to every file on a server at first. As users start to create files, they become the owners of those files

Ownership of objects allows the owner to set all permissions and have complete access to the object. A user who creates a file or directory owns it. In contrast, if a member of the Administrators group creates a file or directory, all the members of the Administrators group own it.

Refer to Chapter 6 for detailed information about Administrator accounts and the security precautions related to them.

Backup Operators Group

Members of the Backup Operators group have the ability to back up and restore files on any directory in the system, even if they do not have permissions to access the files. Users who have both Backup and Restore rights can read, change, and write any file. The permissions of this group override other permissions. Normally, a user who creates a directory or file is the owner of that entity and can set permissions, but the Backup Operators group can override these permissions in order to back up the server to tape or other medium.

Obviously, membership in this group must be tightly controlled. A rogue user could steal information from the server, or an industrial spy could convince your backup operator to steal the files for her or grant her access to the account. A hacker who breaks into the account can also take advantage of the rights to steal valuable information, including files that contain passwords and user account information.

8

Designate only trusted people to this status, and make sure their rights are limited to only those files and directories they need to back up. In addition, log all backup operator activities in the Audit log. Remember that data on backup tapes is not encrypted. Someone with Restore privileges could restore the tape on another Windows NT system (such as her personal workstation). Chapter 11 discusses this topic in more detail.

Account Operators Group

Members of the Account Operators group have the ability to use the User Manager utility to create user accounts and groups. However, they can change and delete only the accounts and groups that they create. Account operators can also log on to servers, shut down servers, and add computers to the domain. This group has enough power to pose a serious security threat; its membership must be monitored. An unauthorized person who obtains Account Operator status can create and change user accounts.

Note that account operators cannot modify the Domain Admins global group, the Administrators group, the Account Operators group, the Backup Operators group, the Print Operators group, or the Server Operators group.

Guests Group

The Guests group is very similar to the Guest account with regard to its rights and permissions on the system. Since a Windows NT Workstation computer may be set up in an environment where multiple people log on to it at the keyboard, its Guest account has the right to log on locally. Keep in mind that member servers are set up the same way, which could pose a security problem if you store sensitive information on the server. Domain controllers do not allow the Guest account to log on locally, but allow guests to log on over the network if the Guest account is enabled.

Power Users Group

The Power Users group exists on Windows NT Workstation computers or member servers. Members of the group have a set of extended rights and privileges that can be considered subordinate to the Administrator rights. They can perform such system administration tasks as:

♦ Sharing directories over the network

♦ Installing printers and sharing them over the network

♦ Creating, modifying, and deleting user accounts (but not administrative accounts)

♦ Adding user accounts to the Power Users, Users, and Guests groups

♦ Performing other tasks such as setting the system's clock and monitoring performance

The typical management procedure for handling user accounts on Windows NT Workstations that participate in domains is to add the user's domain account to the Power Users group. Then users have their normal rights on the domain and the rights of the Power Users group on their workstation. Using this technique, domain administrators can decide which users should have Power User status on a particular workstation.

Print Operators Group

Members of the Print Operators group can manage printers. They have the ability to create, change, and delete how printers are shared in the domain. Print Operators can also log on to servers and shut them down.

Replicators Group

Windows NT servers on a network can replicate (copy) information among themselves. The contents of one directory can automatically be copied to a similar directory on another server automatically so that information is continually backed up in real time. This group should include domain user accounts that are allowed to log on to the Replicator services of the primary domain controller and the backup domain controllers in the domain.

 NOTE: See Chapter 11 for more information on replication.

Server Operators Group

Members of the Server Operators group have the ability to create, change, and delete shared printers, shared directories, and files. They can also back up and restore files, format hard disks, change the system time, lock the computer, and shut down the system. Note that the server operator does not have the ability to unlock a *workstation* that has been locked by another user. Only the administrator and the currently logged-on user can unlock a workstation.

To create sublevel administrators to manage domain servers, add users to the Server Operators group. As members of the group, they can shut down servers, share and stop sharing directories, and backup and restore files. However, they cannot change user attributes, add drivers, or take ownership of files.

Because of the extended rights and permissions of this group, you should follow all the security precautions that you follow for all other administrative accounts. Users who are members of this group should have a separate

8

personal account that they log in to for doing normal non-administrative work. Hackers who obtain access to accounts in this group can steal information and perform other malicious activities.

Users Group

Members of the Users group (not to be confused with domain users) do not have local or network access rights on servers, but can log on locally at Windows NT Workstation computers. The rights at workstations include the ability to log on locally, shut down the system, create local groups, and manage the groups that they create. Note that network users gain the ability to log on to servers by being members of the Everyone group, not members of the Users group. Everyone has the Access This Computer From Network right by default on servers. If you remove Everyone from this right, you need to assign a new group of network users to the right.

Other Groups

The following groups do not have members in the same sense as the groups discussed earlier. Instead, any account that uses the computer in a specific manner will automatically be a member of the group. Note that these groups reflect resource access but do not refer to the privilege level of the user.

- ◆ **Interactive Users** Any user who only logs on to the computer using an interactive logon.

- ◆ **Network Users** Any user who connects to the computer over the network.

- ◆ **Everyone** Any user who accesses the computer, including interactive and network users.

- ◆ **Creator/Owner** Any user who creates or takes ownership of a resource.

The Everyone Group

The Everyone group includes everyone who accesses a computer, including local and network users. Administrators must pay special attention to the Everyone group. By default it has permissions that may not be appropriate in secure environments. In particular, Guest users have access to all directories available to Everyone, as discussed previously.

For example, the Everyone group has the following permissions, which may be considered a security risk, depending on your environment. Note that change allows Read, Write, Execute, and Delete permissions.

- ◆ Full Control when you create or share a folder, although this is easily changed

♦ Change permissions on the Root directories of all NTFS volumes

♦ Change permissions in the System32 directory

♦ Change permissions in the Win32App directory

For security reasons, you may want to change permissions that Everyone has to directories throughout the file system. This is discussed further in Chapter 9.

Global Groups

When you add a Windows NT computer to a domain, several groups are automatically added to the local groups on those computers. These global groups are described in the following sections.

Domain Admins Global Group

How is it that Administrator can manage all the computers in a domain? Simple, due to the relationship among the built-in global groups. Understanding this relationship is critical to building a hierarchy of administrators who can manage various parts of your domain network. If you decide to create Subadministrator accounts to help manage your domain network, how do you grant those administrators the right to manage other Windows NT systems in the domain? The Domain Admins global group is the answer.

Throughout this discussion, be sure to differentiate among the *Administrator user account*, the *Administrators local group*, and the *Domain Admins global group*. Though quite different, they are used in concert to create a hierarchy of administrative control for local systems and domains, as shown in Figure 8-4.

1. When Windows NT is set up, the Administrator account is created and made a member of the Administrators local group. This is what gives Administrator full control of the local system. Administrator cannot be removed from this group.

2. When a Windows NT computer is designated as a primary domain controller, the Administrator user account is added to the Domain Admins global group.

3. The Domain Admins global group is automatically added to the Administrators local group on every Windows NT computer in the domain.

Consequently, anyone who logs in to the Administrator account has administrative rights on the local domain. If you want to give another user administrative rights in the domain, just add her user account to the Domain Admins global group. You can also put the Domain Admins group into the

8

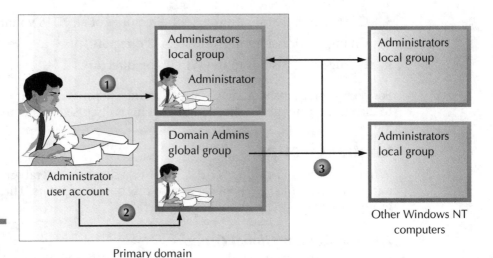

How Domain
Admins works
Figure 8-4.

Administrators local group on systems in other domains to grant the
members of the group administrative rights in those domains. However, a
trust relationship is required between those domains. To grant a user
administrative rights to a Windows NT computer that is not a domain
controller, add him to the Administrators local group.

Domain Users
The Administrator account and all new user accounts are automatically
added to the Domain Users global group. This group is a member of the
Users local group for the domain and the Users local group for every
Windows NT Workstation computer and member server in the domain.
Note that, by default, the Users group itself does not start out with any
permissions. Also, on Windows NT Workstation computers, the Users group
has the right to log on locally at the keyboard of the computer, shut down
the system, and create and manage local groups.

Domain Guests
The Domain Guest global group initially contains the Guest user account for
the domain.

Creating Groups
You can create your own local and global groups by choosing New Local
Group or New Global Group from the User menu in the User Manager.
When setting up accounts and groups, make sure to identify all of the

requirements that users have of the system and create accounts accordingly. The general procedure for creating groups is:

1. Create local groups with access to objects in the domain, such as directories that hold programs or devices (e.g., printers).
2. Grant rights to the group as described in the next section under "Rights."
3. Create one or more global groups that should have access to these objects.
4. Add users to the global groups.
5. Add the global groups to the local groups in any of the domains or computers where the users in the global group should have access to resources.
6. If you no longer want a user to have access to a resource, remove her account from the global group. If you no longer want all the members of a global group to have access to resources assigned to a local group, remove the global group from the local group.

When creating a group, you can copy an existing group and change its properties, or you can create a whole new group from scratch. Copying a group ensures that the new group will have the rights and permissions you have already assigned to the existing group. You can then upgrade or downgrade the rights and permissions of the new group.

When designing and creating your group hierarchy, think of global groups in terms of the departments, workgroups, and/or divisions of your company. This will help you create meaningful groups that correspond appropriately to the resources of the network. For example, you could create a management group that has access to directories that hold reporting information throughout the network. Since some of those directories might exist in other domains, you would want to create a global group for the managers.

Note the following:

♦ Create local groups with access to resources or management tasks in mind. The Print Operators group is a good example. It allows members to manage printers in the local domain.

To allow a user in a domain to administer a Windows NT Workstation computer but not servers, create a global group called something like WSADMINS; then on all the workstations in the domain add the new global group to the workstation's Administrators local group. To add additional workstation administrators, add their user account to the global group. On the other hand, if you don't want any domain users to manage Windows NT

8

Workstations, remove any domain global groups from the Administrators, Power Users, or Backup Operators group.

Rights

Rights are closely linked to groups. They give the members of a group the access they need to perform management tasks or simply to access a system as a normal user. You need to know about rights if you are trying to figure out the access levels of local groups and if you need to grant special rights to your own custom groups.

To change the rights of an existing group or grant a right to a group, choose User Rights on the Policies menu in the User Manager. The User Rights Policy dialog box appears. Choose a right in the Right field, then add or remove a group from the Grant To field.

Table 8-1 describes the standard user rights for Windows NT. Table 8-2 describes how these rights are implemented in Windows NT Server and Windows NT Workstation. Note that Windows NT Workstation computers have a Power Users group but do not have the Server Operators group, Account Operators group, nor the Print Operators group, which are server-oriented management groups.

If you study Table 8-2, you'll see that the rights assigned to groups make sense. If you need to grant a user a right, you should add her to a group that already has the right rather than grant her a right directly. There are also rights called "built-in abilities" that give certain groups their unique rights to manage the system. These abilities are defined in Table 8-3.

Keep in mind that rights and abilities are slightly different on Windows NT Workstation computers. A Power Users group exists in which users can create user accounts and modify or delete only the accounts that they create. Power users can also create local groups but modify or delete only the groups they create.

Also remember that rights apply to the whole system, for either the domain or a local computer. Permissions, on the other hand, apply to specific objects. Rights will often override the permissions set on objects. This is true in the case of the Backup Operator, which has the right to back up even files on which the owner has revoked access to all users.

In a secure environment, make sure that the Everyone group and the Guests group are not assigned the Log On Locally and Shut Down the System rights. The first option would allow anyone to log on at the computer, where he would have more resources available to perform malicious activities. The latter option would allow someone to shut down a server and deny service to others.

Rights	Description
Access this computer from network	Allows a user to access the computer from another account on the network
Add workstations and member servers to domain	Allows a user who is not a member of the domain's Administrators group to add computers running Windows NT Workstation or member servers to the domain
Back up files and directories	Allows users to manage data backups
Change the system time	Allows users to change time on the system
Force shutdown from a remote system	To be implemented in later versions of Windows NT
Load and unload device drivers	Allows users to manage device drivers on the system
Log on locally	Allows users to log on at the computer's keyboard, as opposed to logging on over the network
Manage auditing and security log	Allows users to manage the auditing system and logs
Restore files and directories	Allows users to manage data restores
Shut down the system	Allows users to stop the operating system
Take ownership of files or other objects	Allows users to change the name of the user who created or currently owns directories or files to their own name

Built-in
Rights for
Windows NT
Table 8-1.

Another right of interest is the advanced right called Bypass Traverse Checking. You access it on the User Rights Policy dialog box by clicking Show Advanced User Rights. This right, granted to Everyone by default, allows users to change directories through a directory tree even if they have no permission for those directories. In a secure environment, you can prevent users from browsing through the directory structure by revoking this right from the Everyone group and granting it only to groups where appropriate. Experiment with this option before setting it permanently. It is not appropriate to revoke the right in most cases.

8

Rights	Groups That Have This Right by Default
Access this computer from network	*Windows NT Server:* Administrators, Everyone *Windows NT Workstation:* Administrators, Power Users
Back up files and directories	*Windows NT Server:* Administrators, Backup Operators, Server Operators *Windows NT Workstation:* Administrators, Backup Operators
Change the system time	*Windows NT Server:* Administrators, Server Operators *Windows NT Workstation:* Administrators, Power Users
Force shutdown from a remote system	*Windows NT Server:* Administrators, Server Operators, Power Users in Windows NT Workstation *Windows NT Workstation:* Administrators, Power Users
Load and unload device drivers	*Windows NT Server and Workstation:* Administrators
Log on locally	*Windows NT Server:* Administrators, Backup Operators, Server Operators, Account Operators, Print Operators, Internet Guest Account *Windows NT Workstation:* Administrators, Power Users, Users, Guests, Everyone, Backup Operators
Manage auditing and security log	*Windows NT Server and Workstation:* Administrators
Restore files and directories	*Windows NT Server:* Administrators, Backup Operators, Server Operators *Windows NT Workstation:* Administrators, Backup Operators
Shut down the system	*Windows NT Server:* Administrators, Backup Operators, Server Operators, Account Operators, Print Operators *Windows NT Workstation:* Power Users, Users, Everyone, Backup Operators
Take ownership of files or other objects	*Windows NT Server and Workstation:* Administrators

Default
Rights in
Windows NT
Server
Table 8-2.

Built-in Abilities	Groups That Have This Right by Default
Add workstation to domain*	*Windows NT Server:* Administrators, Account Operators
Create and manage user accounts	*Windows NT Server:* Administrators, Account Operators *Windows NT Workstation:* Administrators, Power Users
Create and manage local groups	*Windows NT Server:* Administrators, Account Operators, Users *Windows NT Workstation:* Administrators, Power Users
Create and manage global groups*	*Windows NT Server:* Administrators, Account Operators
Assign user rights	*Windows NT Server and Workstation:* Administrators
Lock the server (or computer)	*Windows NT Server:* Administrators, Server Operators, Everyone *Windows NT Workstation:* Administrators, Power Users, Everyone
Manage auditing of system events	*Windows NT Server and Workstation:* Administrators
Lock the server (or workstation)	*Windows NT Server:* Administrators, Server Operators *Windows NT Workstation:* Administrators, Power Users, Everyone
Override the lock of the server (or workstation)	*Windows NT Server:* Administrators, Server Operators *Windows NT Workstation:* Administrators
Format server's (or workstation's) hard disk	*Windows NT Server:* Administrators, Server Operators *Windows NT Workstation:* Administrators
Create common groups	*Windows NT Server:* Administrators, Server Operators *Windows NT Workstation:* Administrators, Power Users
Share and stop sharing directories	*Windows NT Server:* Administrators, Server Operators *Windows NT Workstation:* Administrators, Power Users
Share and stop sharing printers	*Windows NT Server:* Administrators, Server Operators, Print Operators *Windows NT Workstation:* Administrators, Power Users

Built-In Abilities for Windows NT Server

Table 8-3.

8

*Ability not available on Windows NT Workstation

Managing User Environments

You can manage the environment of the user and establish a number of security features by using profiles and policies. User profiles are important when more than one person uses the same computer or when a user travels from one computer to another or from one site to another. Profiles contain user-definable settings for the work environment of Windows NT computers, including the following:

♦ The arrangement of the desktop that the user had the last time they were logged on.

♦ A custom desktop that is different than the desktop of another person who uses the same computer.

♦ Custom profiles that travel with the user to other computers. These are roaming profiles.

An important security feature of profiles is that you can make them mandatory to prevent users from changing their desktop settings. Profile settings are saved in files on the system.

You can control settings for each Windows NT and Windows 95 user with the System Policy Editor. Settings include the layout of the desktop, and most important, what features on the desktop that users can and cannot access. For example, you can restrict access to options in the Control Panel.

NOTE: For more information on managing user environments, refer to Chapter 12.

CHAPTER 9

File System Security and Resource Sharing

This chapter is about protecting files and resources on Windows NT computers and sharing those resources with users on Windows networks. If you're working at a Windows 95 computer, you can open the Network Neighborhood to browse for shared resources on Windows NT Server computers. A window similar to the following appears, listing the available domains and workgroups.

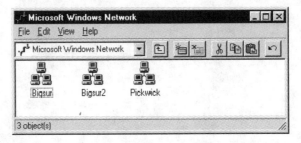

You can double-click any icon to see the computers or printers available in the domain or workgroup, then double-click a computer to see its list of shared folders.

T IP: Once you find a shared folder you want to use, you can click and drag it to your desktop so you won't need to browse for it again.

In the Microsoft networking scheme, just about any computer on the network can share its resources (directories, files, and printers), so other network users can access them over the network. This is called *peer networking*. In the peer networking model, users working at their own computers decide to share a folder with another user or group of users. The alternative is *dedicated server networking*, in which a computer running an operating system like Windows NT Server with advanced security is set up to provide shared resources to users.

Some network administrators may balk at peer networking, considering it a management and security nightmare. In that case, Windows NT Server domain networking is the only way to go. Each user must have a user account on a "security server" (i.e., Windows NT Server domain controller) and be authenticated by that server before they can access resources on the server or on personal computers that have shared resources.

To fully implement the highest level of protection when sharing files on Windows NT computers, you must format all drives with the NT File System (NTFS). This chapter is about NTFS and the security feature it provides.

Sharing and Permissions—What's the Difference?

Your network may consist of both workgroups and domains, as pictured in Figure 9-1. Workgroups provide a way to group computers, printers, and other resources, while Windows NT networking provides user account management.

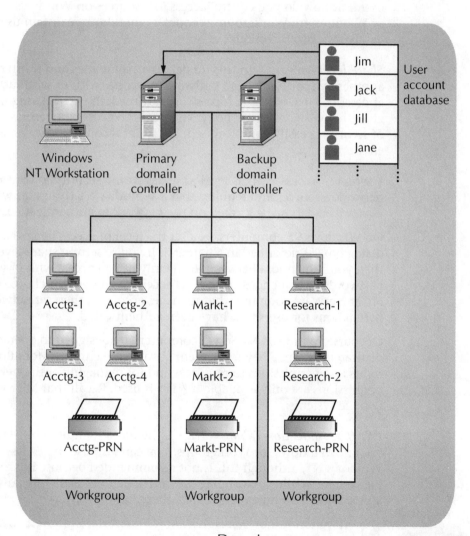

Workgroups within a domain

Figure 9-1.

Keep in mind that workgroup computing is really just a browsing tool. It puts computers and other resources into common groups so users can more easily locate a particular system. For example, if a user in the Marketing group wants to access information on a computer in the research group, she can open a window on a Research group and choose an appropriate computer located in that group.

On Windows NT computers, you can grant access to resources to a specific user. But how do you control access to resources on Windows 95 computers or Windows for Workgroups computers that don't maintain user account databases? Two techniques exist:

Share-level Access   In this model, users share files and printers with one another by specifying Read Only or Full access, with or without a password, as described in Chapter 5. If passwords are used, the user sharing the resource gives the password to anybody who needs to access the resource. This level of security is easily compromised and is not recommended for secure environments.

User-level Access   This level provides strong security to control access to network resources and requires that a Windows NT computer with a Security Accounts database be located on the network to authenticate users.

On Windows 95 computers, you set the level of access in the Networks dialog box, as described in Chapter 5. If you're setting share-level access, then you can choose between Read Only or Full access with or without passwords. If you choose user-level access, then you can choose a Windows NT or NetWare computer that manages accounts, then set network share permissions for users that have been authenticated.

Of course, Windows NT Server computers are designed to operate as dedicated servers. They implement advanced techniques for allocating user rights and permissions to resources and for managing entire networks. But permissions are only available if NTFS is used. Recall that Microsoft provides two file systems:

FAT (File Allocation Table)   This is the file system used in DOS, Windows 3.*x*, and Windows for Workgroups. You can also use the FAT system in Windows NT, although this is not recommended because it is an unsecured file system. While you can flag files as Hidden or Read Only, anyone with access to the computer can change these flags.

NOTE: Shared folders on FAT volumes are relatively secure because the operating system controls who can access files over the network.

NTFS (NT File System) NTFS is a highly secure file system that provides a reliable way to safeguard valuable information. NTFS works in concert with the Windows NT user account system to allow authenticated user access to files.

Security and performance mark the primary differences between these file systems, but it's helpful to take a look at the difference in the way access is granted to folders on each system. Take a close look at Figures 9-2 and 9-3. Figure 9-2 shows the Properties dialog box for a folder on a FAT volume, and Figure 9-3 shows the Properties dialog box for a folder on an NTFS volume. To display these boxes, you right-click a drive, folder, file, printer, or other resource and choose Properties. The boxes are very similar, but notice that the NTFS box has a Compress option (in the future, you may see an Encrypt option here as well) and a Security tab that the FAT folder doesn't have.

Both dialog boxes have a Sharing tab, where you set network share options. When you click Sharing, you see a dialog box for both FAT and NTFS volumes, similar to the one in Figure 9-4. However, the permissions for sharing FAT folders is quite a bit different from the permissions for sharing NTFS folders, as described next.

If you click the Permissions button in the Sharing dialog box for a *FAT volume*, you see the Add Users dialog box in Figure 9-5. This example is from a Windows 95 computer that is set up for user-level access. The list of users displayed in the box is from a Windows NT system. Notice that you can add a user to the Read Only, Full Access, or Custom list.

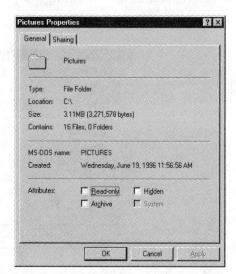

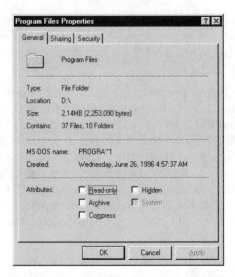

Properties for
a folder on an
NTFS volume
Figure 9-3.

Compare Figure 9-5 with Figure 9-6, which is what you see if you click the Permissions button in the Sharing dialog box for an *NTFS volume*. The Type of Access list box is dropped down so you can see the available permission. The main difference is the addition of the Change option, which allows users to read, write, and delete files in the folder but does not give them all the permissions of the Full Access option, which are excessive in most cases.

Now look again at the NTFS Properties dialog box in Figure 9-3; it has the Security tab. If you click Security, you see the dialog box in Figure 9-7. This is where you set permissions, auditing, and ownership of folders and files.

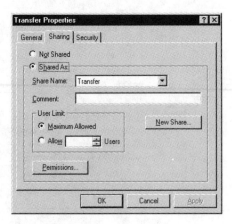

Sharing
options for
both FAT
and NTFS
resources
Figure 9-4.

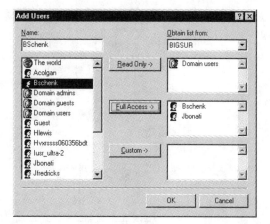

Share
permissions
for FAT
volumes

Figure 9-5.

If you click the Permissions button, you see the dialog box in Figure 9-8. This is where things get confusing if you're new to NTFS security. There are *share permissions* and *local permissions*. Figure 9-6 is where you set share permissions that control network access to folders and files. The Directory Permissions box in Figure 9-8 is where you set local permissions for user and group access to folders and files. The local permissions are more granular. Look at the difference between the permissions in the Type of Access drop-down list box.

The combination of local permissions and share permissions provides a high level of administrative control for folders and files. In addition, on NTFS volumes, you can control access to individual files (you can only share folders on FAT volumes).

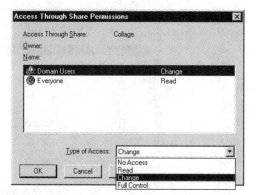

Share
permissions
for NTFS
volumes

Figure 9-6.

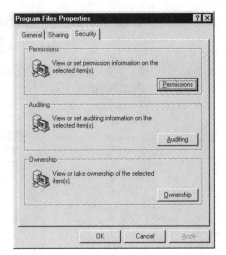

Security
options for
NTFS volumes
Figure 9-7.

NOTE: Normally, you share only folders and files, not drives. An exception is that you share an entire CD-ROM volume.

If you are a user on the network and you want to access a folder, your permissions are based on the intersection of the local permissions and the share permissions. Yes, local permissions determine your access to a folder over the network along with share permissions, as I will explain.

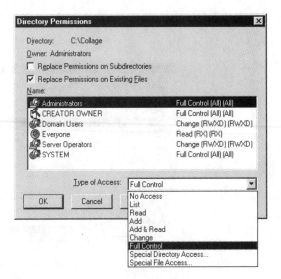

Directory
permissions
Figure 9-8.

Assume that you are a member of the Server Operators group, which has certain rights to manage the system. The group has been granted Full Access to a particular folder as a local permission but only the share permission of Read. If you are accessing the folder from the network, the intersection of these rights is Read, but if you access the folder while seated at the server, you have Full Access because share permissions are not used. In this case, people who gain access to your account from a workstation on the network cannot do much harm. They would need to gain physical access to the server itself in order to have Full Access permission.

Therein is the reason for having two different levels of permissions. With both share and local permissions, you can create varying degrees of access to the folder level and file level, each granting a unique combination of the available permissions.

Another thing to notice is that you can control the inheritance of local permissions for files in a folder or for subfolders. Take a look at the Replace Permissions options in Figure 9-8. If you mark one or both of these options when setting permissions, the permissions are also changed for all the existing files, for subdirectories, or both.

Once again, it's important to keep in mind as you read through the remainder of this chapter that you can set local permissions on individual files and folders. So while you might share an entire folder for users to access over the network, you can set local permissions on individual files in that folder to prevent network users from changing, deleting, or executing some of the files in the folder.

The remainder of this chapter discusses both types of permissions and how to manage them effectively to create a secure file system environment. Before going further, it is worthwhile to discuss just how secure NTFS is.

How Secure Is NTFS?

The security provided by NTFS is based on system controls that are managed by the Windows NT operating system. As long as the operating system is up and running, NTFS permissions and user access controls prevent anyone from accessing unauthorized files over the network. But if people manage to get physical access to your server and shut down the Windows NT operating system, they can use low-level byte-editing programs to scan NTFS volumes and read or change information on those volumes. This is not a remote possibility. Service technicians use such programs on a regular basis to recover data from defective drives.

In 1996, a program called ntfsdos.exe surfaced that is specifically designed to read files protected by Windows NT File System security. The program can be run after booting a server with a DOS disk. However, it is important to realize that this program does not compromise the security of the Windows NT operating system to protect files. A user of the program would need to shut down your server and have physical access to its disk drives to use the program. If you implement good physical security, this is unlikely to happen.

Microsoft's statement on NT security and the utility reads as follows:

> This utility [ntfsdos.exe] does not affect the ability of the Windows NT Server operating system to secure critical business data. The availability of this utility does, however, underscore one of the most important and fundamental necessities of network security—the need for physically securing server hardware. Using this utility violates this basic tenet of network security because it means access to the physical hardware is not controlled. Without physically securing server hardware, no operating system can protect against penetration. If the server hardware is physically protected, no other operating system offers the level of security that Windows NT Server offers.

Microsoft backs up its claim of file-system security by referring to the evaluation of the operating system done by the National Computer Security Council (NCSC), a division of the National Security Agency. The NCSC's C2 Trusted Products Evaluation Program provides a set of criteria for building and certifying C2-secure operating systems. The evaluation program found that Windows NT Server went beyond C2 security in certain processes and that its built-in security features for protecting objects at the lowest level provided a high level of security. Note that C2 does not address networking.

Microsoft does stress that Windows NT Server cannot protect critical business data if the operating system is not running, so administrators need to physically secure all server hardware. Use power-on passwords to protect servers from unauthorized booting. (Power-on passwords are part of a computer's hardware and are changed by accessing the programmable ROM on a computer as defined in the operator's manual.) Keep file servers locked in special rooms that only authorized users can access, and, to prevent the system from being booted with a different operating system, disable, remove, or lock floppy drives.

CAUTION: Anyone who manages to steal a hard drive that is formatted as an NTFS volume (the primary partition is NTFS) can place the drive in another Windows NT computer or reinstall the Windows NT operating system, then make themselves a member of the Administrators group and access files on the drive. Once again, physically securing the server (and controlling drives shipped off-site) is the key to averting this problem.

Compression and Encryption

You can use both compression and encryption techniques to protect files from being read by people who have stolen your drive. Compression was not designed for security, but it can provide a somewhat rudimentary form of protection from prying eyes by making it more difficult for someone to read your drive. The offender would need to boot the drive using Windows NT to uncompress the files, and then the full protection of the operating system would be in force.

To compress a drive, folder, or file, right-click it and choose Properties. A dialog box appears, similar to the one in Figure 9-3. Click the Compress option, then click OK. The following dialog box appears, where you can choose to compress subfolders as well.

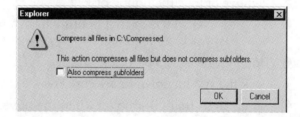

Encryption is not provided as a standard feature in Windows NT, but will be available in future releases. With encryption, you can provide high levels of security to protect files from snoopers or people who steal your systems. Brute-force methods would be necessary to view the contents of files, and with strong encryption, such methods might never be successful.

Encryption is provided in Microsoft Exchange Server, which runs on top of Windows NT Server and is part of Microsoft's BackOffice suite of products. It provides a unique public/private folder scheme that represents a new type of filing system that will more than likely be implemented in the next major release of Windows NT. Refer to Chapter 13 for more details.

NOTE: Encryption isn't always a good thing. A hacker who gains access to your server either locally or over the network might encrypt its files and lock you out. Also, what if you forget the password for the files you have encrypted?

Physical Protection

As I mentioned earlier in the book, paranoia is a good thing for security managers. The previous discussion is obviously not meant to give anyone ideas about how to break a file system, but it does imply that someone who has access to your system could do it. The bottom line is to lock everything up and take the steps listed next.

NTFS file protection is only good if someone can't boot the system from DOS or from another operating system such as LINUX. That protection involves taking the following precautions:

◆ Remove or lock the floppy disk.

◆ Set the server's BIOS so that booting from a floppy drive is disabled and boot passwords are required.

◆ Don't create a DOS partition on the server.

◆ Lock the system down in a secure area.

◆ Set up alerts that inform you when the server is shut down so you can catch a hacker in the process of doing this.

The first three steps are dependent on the last, because each can be circumvented if someone has access to the computer. For example, the disk could be removed from a server and put into another Windows NT system where a hacker might have free reign to crack passwords and encryption. The BIOS lock can be disabled by simply removing the battery in most cases.

Managing Permissions

You set permissions on drives, folders, and files to allow users to access those objects in a secure way. You can also grant permissions to use other objects like printers, but this chapter concentrates on the file system. Permissions can be granted to users or groups of users so that some users have only the ability to read a file while others can change it.

In most cases, you grant permissions to groups rather than to individual users. This provides simplicity and a more consistent way to manage the security of the file system.

There are issues of inheritance in NTFS. By default, the permissions on a folder apply to the files and subfolders contained by that folder. You can make specific changes to the permissions of files and subfolders, but if you don't, any user given permissions on the folder also has the same permissions on the subfolders.

If you grant a group of users access to a folder, you can also grant them access to any subdirectories of that folder, or you can restrict access to subdirectories, or you can even give them more rights in the subdirectory than they have in the parent folder.

Where and How to Set Permissions

In Windows NT 4.0, you set permissions for folders and files by right-clicking a folder or file to display its context menu. Then you choose Permissions to display the dialog box pictured in Figure 9-7. Click the Permissions button to change permissions. There are two ways to access folders and files in Windows NT 4.0.

My Computer or Network Neighborhood   From the Windows NT desktop, open My Computer to list drives and folders on the local system, or choose Network Neighborhood to list drives and folders on other systems. Right-click any object to open its context menu.

Windows NT Explorer   The Explorer shows a unique view of all the drives and folders for the local system and the network systems in a hierarchical tree format. You can right-click any folder in the tree to access its context menu.

If you are working in Windows NT 3.51, open the File Manager and select the folder or file you want to work with. Then choose Permissions from the Security menu.

Once you've opened the Permissions dialog box for a folder or file (similar to Figure 9-8), you can add or remove users or groups from the Permissions list or change the permissions of existing users. Here are the general procedures:

♦   To add a user or group to the Permissions list, click the Add button to display the Add Users and Groups dialog box as shown in Figure 9-9. In the List Names From box, you can choose to list users (click Show Users to show both groups and users) in a different domain. In the Names box, click a user or group, then click Add to add the name to the Add Names box. Finally, choose a permission in the Type of Access box and click OK.

♦   To remove a user or group, click the user or group, then click the Remove button.

♦   To change permissions, click a user or group, then choose a new permission in the Type of Access list box.

♦   To change permissions on all subdirectories or for all files, click one of the checkboxes at the top of the dialog box.

Notice that the Directory Permissions dialog box (similar to Figure 9-8) displays permissions that may have been inherited from parent directories. You can revoke an inherited permission by simply removing the user or group for which you want to revoke the permission. This allows you to grant different levels of access in parent folders and subfolders. Notice also that the Permissions dialog box shows the current owner of a folder.

The File Permissions dialog box looks very similar to the Directory Permissions dialog box, except that Type of Access permissions are No Access, Read, Change, and Full Control.

Individual Permissions

NTFS provides the following *individual permissions,* but keep in mind as you scan the list that you rarely grant these permissions by themselves. Instead,

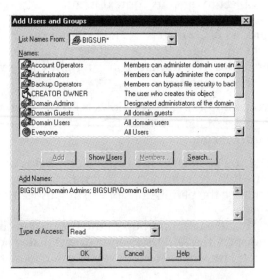

The Add Users and Groups dialog box

Figure 9-9.

you grant what are called *standard permissions* (see the next section), which are groups of the individual permissions that allow users to perform a specific task. The individual permissions are:

Read (R) View the contents of a folder or file.

Write (W) Change the contents of a file.

Execute (X) Run a program.

Delete (D) Delete a file or folder.

Change Permission (P) Change the permissions of an object.

Take Ownership (O) Become the owner of an object.

The last permission, Take Ownership, is interesting because it can define a new owner for a particular folder or file. The owner of an object controls the permissions of that object. When someone creates a folder or file, he automatically becomes its owner. By default, the Administrators group is the owner of folders and files on a newly installed system. The Administrators group can also take ownership of an object at any time.

Notice the letters following each permission. You'll see these letters when you display the permissions for folders and files, as shown in Figure 9-8. Each user and group is listed along with the permission it has. The permission shows the individual permissions to folders and files as two sets of parentheses. For example, in Figure 9-8, Domain Users has the permission Change (RWXD) (RWXD). The first set of parentheses indicates that members of this group have Read, Write, Execute, and Delete permissions on folders, and the second set of parentheses indicates Read, Write, Execute, and Delete permissions on files within the folder. In this case, the permissions are the same for folders and files, but that is not always the case.

Standard Permissions

Standard permissions are a combination of individual permissions. They are designed to allow a user or group to access a file in a fairly standard way. In most cases, standard permissions should provide the permissions you need for almost every NTFS security requirement. The standard permissions for folders are as follows:

No Access When this option is set, the folder cannot be accessed and the files in it cannot be listed. No Access overrides any other permission(s) users may have in a folder due to their membership in a group. The permission also overrides inheritance, and if a user is a member of a group that is

9

granted No Access, then she loses access no matter what other permissions have been granted.

List   List permission includes the Read and Execute individual permissions. It allows users to list the files and subfolders in a directory and to access the directory, but not to access new files created in the directory. This permission allows users to "climb through" a directory structure to get at a subfolder that they have permission to access.

Read   This permission has the Read and Execute individual permissions for the folder and for files in the folder. It allows users to display subfolder names and filenames, display the data and attributes of files, run program files, and switch to any subfolders of the folder.

Add   This permission provides Write and Execute individual permissions that allow users to add files to a folder but not read or change files that have been placed in the folder. Such a folder is often called a *drop box*.

Add & Read   This permission uses the Read, Write, and Execute individual permissions on the folder to allow all the rights of Add in addition to letting users read but not change the files in the folder. Individual files in the folder have the Read and Execute permissions.

Change   This permission has all the access of Read as well as the ability to create new subfolders, add files, change data in and append data to files, change file attributes, and delete subfolders and files. It includes the Read, Write, Execute, and Delete permissions for both the folder and the files it contains.

Full Control   Full Control permission includes all the individual permissions and allows users all the abilities of Change along with the ability to change permissions of the folder and its files. Take ownership can take place under certain conditions.

Table 9-1 shows the actions that are possible on directories for each of the permissions just described. Table 9-2 shows the actions that are possible on files for each of the permissions.

File Permissions

The standard permissions for files are very similar to the permissions for directories except that List, Add, and Add & Read are not included, because they are applicable only to folders. To set file permissions, right-click the file, choose Properties, and choose Permissions as outlined earlier. The standard permissions for files are:

No Access   This permission does not allow any access to a file by user, even if the user has been granted access through other means.

Read   The standard Read permission includes the individual permissions Read and Execute. If the file is a document, it can be opened. If the file is a program, it can be executed. Users can also list the file's attributes.

Change   Change has all the attributes of Read. In addition, it allows users to change data in and append data to the file, and to display the file's owner and permissions.

Full Control   This permission has all the attributes of Change, and also allows a user to take ownership of the file.

Special Access   Special Access lets you create custom permissions that include any combination of Read, Write, Execute, Delete, Change Permissions, and Take Ownership.

Comparison of NTFS to Other File Systems

If you are new to Windows NT but familiar with rights and permissions in other operating systems, Table 9-3 may provide some useful insight into the use of NTFS permissions. The following table was compiled by Dennis Martin of the Rocky Mountain Windows NT User Group in November, 1994. It compares NTFS permissions to the security controls used in other popular operating systems. As you can see, NTFS provides the widest range of controls for managing file access.

Cumulative Permissions, Inheritance, and Ownership

Permissions are cumulative, meaning that the permissions a user or group has to an object are based on the permissions granted to them from several sources, including the following:

♦   Permissions that have been granted to individual users

♦   Permissions based on group memberships (the user may get permissions from more than one group)

♦   Permissions based on inheritance from parent directories

Action	No Access	List	Read	Add	Add & Read	Change	Full Control
Display directory filenames		X	X		X	X	X
Display directory attributes		X	X	X	X	X	X
Change to subdirectories		X	X	X	X	X	X
Change directory's attributes				X	X	X	X
Create subdirectories and add files				X	X	X	X
Display directory's owner and permissions		X	X	X	X	X	X
Delete the directory and subdirectories						X	X
Change directory permissions							X
Take ownership of the directory							X

Actions Allowed by Each Permission on Folders
Table 9-1.

NOTE: If an object has No Access permission, all other permissions assigned to the user are overridden.

Action	No Access	List	Read	Add	Add & Read	Change	Full Control
Display file's owner and permissions			X		X	X	X
Display file's data			X		X	X	X
Display file's attributes			X		X	X	X
Run the file if it is a program			X		X	X	X
Change the file's attributes						X	X
Change data in and append data to the file						X	X
Delete the file						X	X
Change the file's permissions							X
Take ownership of the file							X

Actions Allowed by Each Permission on Files

Table 9-2.

Here's an example of how cumulative permissions work. Assume that an administrator has given you Read permission to a folder that contains information about the top secret *ProjectX*. Later, you become an active member of the project and the administrator adds you to the ProjectX group, which has Change permissions in the directory. Now you have these upgraded rights in addition to the original rights. Later, the administrator decides to close the project, so to deny access, she grants the No Access permission to the Everyone group.

Permission	NTFS	MS-DOS	MVS	OS/2	OS/400	UNIX	VAX	VM
No Access	X	-	X	-	X	X	X	X
List	X	-	-	-	-	-	X	-
Read	X	-	X	-	X	X	X	X
Add & Read	X	-	-	-	X	-	-	-
Change (Write)	X	X	X	X	X	X	X	X
Delete	X	-	X	-	X	-	X	X
Execute	X	-	X	-	X	X	X	-
Permissions	X	-	X	-	X	-	X	X
Take Ownership	X	-	-	-	-	*	-	-

Comparison of Permissions in Various Operating Systems

Table 9-3.

*Some variants of UNIX have limited versions of "Take Ownership."

CAUTION: Be particularly careful when granting No Access to the Everyone group. If you do so, the following dialog box appears, warning you of the consequences of this action. Make sure another user or group has full access permissions before continuing.

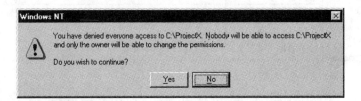

As new directories and files are added to folders, they *inherit* the permissions that are set on the parent directory. This simple feature makes it easy to manage large file systems, because you can create a folder structure with appropriate permissions at different levels in the structure. Then as you add new folders and files, they obtain the permissions that are set at the levels in the structure where they are added.

For example, assume you create a folder called Documents and grant the Temps group Change permissions to this folder. When you add a subfolder to Documents, the Temp group will automatically get Change permissions to it.

However, you can change the permissions for any file or subfolder to override the inherited permissions. In the example above, you could change the permissions of the subfolder to Read Only. You can change the permission on executable files or files that should not be changed to Read Only.

As mentioned earlier, ownership of an object gives a user the right to set permissions on the object and transfer ownership to someone else. By default, the Administrators group owns folders and files that were installed when Windows NT was installed. When you create new user accounts, you can create a personal directory that the user owns. Ownership allows the user to keep private information in the folder and set permissions so that no one else, not even administrators, can view the information. Of course, an administrator could take ownership of someone's private folder, but such actions are audited and open to scrutiny. An administrator might take ownership of a user's folder if that user is being let go or is under investigation. Otherwise, a user's folders should remain under the user's ownership if that is company policy.

NOTE: Owners can grant the Take Ownership permission to other users, allowing those users to take ownership at any time.

Subjects of Permissions

When discussing default permissions, you need to know about the *groups* or *special identities* that are granted these permissions. A group is a collection of user accounts that Administrators can manage by adding or removing users as necessary.

Several groups are important to this discussion. These groups are described here; they were covered more fully in Chapter 8.

Administrators   A group of users with administrative rights that usually include Full Control permissions to an entire file system.

Operators   Groups that have rights and permissions to maintain various aspects of a server's hardware, operating procedures, and User Account database. These groups include the Server Operators group, the Account Operators group, and the Print Operators group.

Special identities are groups that identify a particular set of users who have access to a server at a particular time, such as all the users who are currently logged on over the network. You don't add users to a special identity—the system adds them automatically.

Everyone   The Everyone group includes all the users who access a server while either sitting at its keyboard or accessing it from the network. If you want to give every person (including Guests) who accesses your server access to a folder such as a "public" folder, grant the Everyone group access to the folder.

Interactive   This group includes everyone who accesses the computer while working at the physical computer itself. It does not include network users. You can give members of this group access to resources that need to be managed while at the physical location of the server.

Network   Network users are all users who access a server from the network; this does not include users who are accessing the server at the server itself.

Creator Owner   This identity exists on folders and has a very interesting property: Any user who creates a folder or file in a directory becomes the "Creator Owner" of that folder or file. Of course, users must have permissions that allow them to create folders and files. The Creator Owner identity is interesting because you can use it to give users automatic control of the directories they create. For example, assume that you have a "Public" directory where users can create and share documents with other users, and that a user wants to create a new set of documents and share them only with selected users. If the Public directory grants Creator Owner the Full Control permission, then the user can create a new folder and have Full Control for that folder. Full Control allows the user to set permissions so he can control exactly who has access to the folder.

System   This is the identity of the operating system itself rather than a group of users. It provides the operating system with a way to execute processes or access resources in the same way that a user account is required for a user to execute processes or access resources. For example, the Server service that provides the means of sharing resources on a server is started under the System account, rather than a user account such as Administrator. The System service has a high level of access throughout the system, and any hacker who manages to take over some service that uses System will have that same level of access. Therefore, any service that uses System should be run only if absolutely necessary and only if it is a service that you can trust. There is a way to start some services under accounts that have very limited privileges for security reasons; this will be discussed more fully in Chapter 10.

Default Permissions

A number of default permissions are assigned to folders when the operating system is first installed. Some of these permissions are appropriate for most environments, but others are designed for environments where security is not a big concern, so you may want to change the permission settings to match your security requirements.

The default permissions for folders on Windows NT Server systems are listed in Table 9-4. Table 9-5 shows the default permissions on Windows NT Workstation computers. The folders listed are the ones created when you first install the operating system. You should study these tables carefully, because they provide vital information about the permissions that secure the Windows NT file system.

For example, notice that Everyone has the Change permission in the \System32 directory and the \temp directory. This setting allows any user to make updates to the Registry and initialization files. However, in a secure environment, you can alter the Change permission that Everyone has in the root directory to Read, then grant only specific groups such as Domain User the Change permission. Keep in mind that the Guest account is a member of the Everyone group, so if you allow for Guest access, you'll want to look at the permissions of Everyone very carefully. The Everyone group is discussed later in this chapter.

CAUTION: Do not use the Explorer or File Manager to examine the permissions on the *systemroot*\System32\repl\import folder. Doing so may result in a loss of the special permission that is set for the folder.

\ *root of NTFS volume*	Administrators, System	Full Control
	Server Operators	Change
	Everyone	Change
	CREATOR OWNER	Full Control
systemroot\System32	Administrators, System	Full Control
	Server Operators	Change

Default Permissions for Windows NT Server
Table 9-4.

	Everyone	Change
	CREATOR OWNER	Full Control
systemroot\System32\config	Administrators, System	Full Control
	Everyone	List
	CREATOR OWNER	Full Control
systemroot\System32\drivers	Administrators, System	Full Control
	Server Operators	Full Control
	Everyone	Read
	CREATOR OWNER	Full Control
systemroot\System32\spool	Administrators, System	Full Control
	Server Operators	Full Control
	Print Operators	Full Control
	Everyone	Read
	CREATOR OWNER	Full Control
systemroot\System32\repl	Administrators, System	Full Control
	Server Operators	Full Control
	Everyone	Read
	CREATOR OWNER	Full Control
systemroot\System32\repl\import	Administrators, System	Full Control
	Server Operators	Change
	Everyone	Read

Default Permissions for Windows NT Server (*continued*)

Table 9-4.

	CREATOR OWNER	Full Control
	Replicator	Change
	Network	No Access*
systemroot\System32\repl\export	Administrators, System	Full Control
	Server Operators	Change
	CREATOR OWNER	Full Control
	Replicator	Read
\users	Administrators	Read, Write, Execute, Delete
	Account Operators	Read, Write, Execute, Delete
	Everyone	List
\users\default	Everyone	Read, Write, Execute
	CREATOR OWNER	Full Control
\win32APP	Administrators, System	Full Control
	Server Operators	Full Control
	Everyone	Read
	CREATOR OWNER	Full Control
\temp	Administrators, System	Full Control
	Server Operators	Change
	Everyone	Change
	CREATOR OWNER	Full Control

Default Permissions for Windows NT Server (*continued*)

Table 9-4.

*Does not apply to the initial permissions granted to the Administrators, Server Operators, and Everyone groups.

\ *root of NTFS volume*	Administrators, System	Full Control
	Everyone	Change
	CREATOR OWNER	Full Control
systemroot\System32	Administrators, System	Full Control
	Everyone	Change
	CREATOR OWNER	Full Control
systemroot\System32\config	Administrators, System	Full Control
	Everyone	List
	CREATOR OWNER	Full Control
systemroot\System32\drivers	Administrators, System	Full Control
	Everyone	Read
	CREATOR OWNER	Full Control
systemroot\System32\spool	Administrators, System	Full Control
	Power Users	Change
	Everyone	Read
	CREATOR OWNER	Full Control
systemroot\System32\repl	Administrators, System	Full Control
	Everyone	Read
	CREATOR OWNER	Full Control

Default Permissions for Windows NT Workstation (*continued*)
Table 9-5.

systemroot\System32\repl\import	Administrators, System	Full Control
	Everyone	Read
	CREATOR OWNER	Full Control
	Replicator	Change
	Network	No Access*
\users	Administrators	Read, Write, Execute, Delete
	Everyone	List
\users\default	Everyone	Read, Write, Execute
	CREATOR OWNER	Full Control
\win32app	Administrators, System	Full Control
	Everyone	Read
	CREATOR OWNER	Full Control
\temp	Administrators	Read, Write, Execute, Delete
	Everyone	Read
	CREATOR OWNER	Read, Write, Execute, Delete

Default Permissions for Windows NT Workstation (*continued*)
Table 9-5.

*Does not apply to the initial permissions granted to the Administrators, Server Operators, and Everyone groups.

Suggested Permission

As you can see in Tables 9-4 and 9-5, you can quickly lose track of which permissions are set on the folders in your directory structure. It's also sometimes difficult to know which permissions you should set on folders to allow users and groups the type of access they need to access files or run programs. This situation is further complicated by inheritance. Consequently, you need to constantly monitor both how permissions are set and which permissions users inherit to ensure that no one has more rights than is needed.

The SomarSoft DumpAcl utility, which is discussed further in Appendix D, will produce a report on the permissions that are set on your file system. The report is organized into files and directories that have the same permissions, producing a relatively short list that is easy to scan through. Permissions are shown only for the root directory and for files and directories below the root where permissions differ from those of the root. The utility reports a single item if all files and directories have the same permissions. You can download this utility from the SomarSoft site at **www.somarsoft.com**.

The *systemroot* folder (usually called winnt) and all of its branching subfolders, starting with the *systemroot*\System32 folder, contain critical information such as the system databases and auditing logs. You should never share these directories.

In most cases, the Change permission is appropriate for folders that users access to store shared information or to access database information. Change allows users to create new files, change existing files, and delete files. If you don't want users deleting some of the files in the folder, change the file permissions to Read Only. If users need to change the contents of those files, they can copy them first and make their changes to the copy. Working with a copy keeps the original intact. You can use this technique in folders where you keep document templates, which are forms that users can change to fit their needs. If you maintain a public folder where you make files available to all users or to the general public (such as a Web server directory), grant the folder Read Only access so users cannot change the contents of the files.

Grant the Full Control permission only to trusted high-level administrators. Remember that Full Control allows a user to change the permissions and take ownership of a folder and its files. Recall that ownership of a folder allows a user to set permissions and revoke access to anyone, including the administrator. But administrators or users with the Take Ownership permission can take control of a folder that is owned by another user.

Permissions for Everyone

The Everyone group includes everybody that accesses a system. What makes system administrators uneasy is that Everyone, by default, has Full Access or Change rights in some important directories such as the *root* (Full Access), \winnt (Full Access), \winnt\System32 (Change). You might be wondering why Everyone has Full Access to the *root* by default. I, too, would like to know that. In the meantime, you can change the permissions manually to improve security, especially if you allow Guests to access your system. Recall that Guests don't need an account and can access any directory where Everyone has permissions.

Another thing to consider is that any new directories you create inherit the users, groups, and properties of the parent directory. That means when you create a new directory at the root, the Everyone group will inherit Full Access permissions to that new directory. If this is not what you want, you'll need to edit the permissions on the new directory. To avoid this hassle, you can change the permissions for Everyone at the root to Read Only, so any new directories you create will inherit this permission level.

But what about directories you have already created? Some people advocate changing the permissions of Everyone at the root to Read Only and then propagating that change to all subdirectories. Don't do this. The Everyone group has specific permission requirements in the *systemroot* tree (usually C:\winnt) that would be adversely affected by doing an across-the-board permission change for an entire drive. You might lock out the server or prevent users from running some applications.

One solution that I have found to work is outlined below, but note carefully that this may not work in every environment. Make sure that the Administrators group has full access in the affected directories before making any permission changes for the Everyone group. This is the default, but someone might have changed it on an existing system.

♦   Change the Everyone group's permission in the root directory and the *systemroot* directory (usually C:\winnt) to Read Only. Do not propagate these changes to subdirectories.

♦   Change the Everyone group's permission in *systemroot*\System32 to Read-only and propagate the changes to the subtree of this directory.

Note that the last step assumes a new server. If you have added a number of applications, you might need to manually revert some permissions. There are two directories where you will need to do this now. In the *systemroot*\System32\RAS and *systemroot*\System32\spool\Printers directory, grant the Everyone group the Change permission.

After making these changes, you need to test them to make sure that users can run the programs you need them to run. First set the Auditing option called "File and Object Access" to failure, then access the system as a user and try running programs. If some program don't run, log back in as an administrator and check the Event Log. Look for entries where the user failed to start a program or access a file in a specific directory. These are the directories that will require more than Read Only access. Change the permissions on those directories to allow the minimum amount of access required.

Permissions for Programs

You should separate executable program files from data files whenever possible. This way you can avoid giving users more than Read permissions in a directory that contains program files. This will prevent users from intentionally or accidentally introducing viruses and Trojan horse programs into the folder.

Another strategy to avoid infections from viruses is to grant managers of folders the Change Permission ("P") permission and revoke the Write permission. This way, even administrators don't have the Write permission. Having that permission would give them the ability to accidentally introduce a virus into a program folder. The trick is that administrators have the "P" permission, so they can change their own permissions to Write when they need to update folders with trusted programs. Of course, after the update, administrators need to revoke the Write permission to restore protection to the folder.

In some cases, you won't be able to grant Read Only permissions to a folder that contains programs. Some applications use initialization and/or setup files that require periodic changes as users run the program. Consequently, users will need Change permissions in the folder. In this case, change the permissions of each executable file in the folder to Read Only.

Write access can be a security problem, because it allows users to change the contents of files in a folder, or worse, to put corrupted files in a directory that other users might execute. This points out the fact that revoking Execute rights is not enough to avoid viruses and Trojan horses. If some people can write files into a folder and other people can execute those files, then you risk exposure to contamination. This is a problem, because some applications require users to have Write permissions on a directory so that configuration and initialization information can be updated.

If you're not sure which program requires users to have Write access in program folders, try changing the permissions on the folders to Read, then see if users can still run the programs. You can also enable auditing so that failed write attempts are tracked. The security log will then tell you which folders a program is trying to write to. It is also possible with some programs to designate a different directory where configuration/initialization information should be stored.

Permissions on Copied and Moved Files

Files can obtain inappropriate permissions if you copy them from one folder to another. Copying keeps a duplicate of the file in its original location, while moving deletes the file from its original location. Keep the following points in mind:

♦ When files are *copied*, they inherit the permissions of the directories into which they are moved.

♦ When files are *moved*, they retain the permissions they had in their original directory.

Now consider some problems that might occur when users copy or move files. It is possible to either upgrade or degrade permissions, depending on whether you move or copy files into a directory with greater or lesser permissions.

For example, if you copy sensitive files with strict permissions into a directory with lesser permissions, unauthorized users could gain access to the files. To remedy this, move the files into the directory, then copy them back to the original.

The reverse of this occurs when a user moves files into a directory with tighter permissions, hoping that the files will inherit the permissions of the directory. However, since the files were moved, they retain their original permissions, and the new directory does not provide any protection through inheritance. In this case, the user should copy the files so that they inherit the new permissions, then, if necessary, delete the source files from the original directory.

If users place files in "public" directories and then other users move those files out of the directory, you can set restrictive permissions on the directory so that if the files are moved, they retain the restricted permissions. Once users copy or move a file, they can change the permissions on it to fit their needs.

The SCOPY Command

If you have access to the Windows NT Resource kit, you can use the SCOPY command to copy files and directories to and from NTFS partitions and retain the permissions and ownership of those objects. The command takes the following form and is used in much the same way as the DOS COPY command.

```
SCOPY <source> <destination> [/o] [/a] [/s]
```

Replace source with the path of the folder and file(s) you want to copy and replace destination with the path of the location where you want to copy the files. The parameters for the command are described here:

- ♦ **/o** Copies the existing owner security information to the destination directory.

- ♦ **/a** Copies the existing auditing information to the destination directory. This option requires that the user have the Manage Auditing and Security Log user right, which can be assigned by accessing the User Right Policy menu in the User Manager.

- ♦ **/s** Copies all the subdirectories.

You can schedule the SCOPY command to run automatically with either the AT command or the WinAT scheduler (which is in the Windows NT Resource Kit). To do so, you must enable the Schedule service by opening Services in the Control Panel, then assign an administrative account to the service. See "Changing the Startup Account for Services" in Chapter 10 for more information.

Protecting Root Files

The root directory of the system partition on Intel-based server computers includes several files that must be protected from users who might have permissions that allow them to delete or alter the files. The files are listed in the following table, along with the permissions you should assign to them for security:

C:\boot.ini	Assign Full Control to Administrators and System
C:\ntdetect.com	Assign Full Control to Administrators and System
C:\ntldr	Assign Full Control to Administrators and System
C:\autoexec.bat	Assign Full Control to Administrators and System, and Read to Everybody
C:\config.sys	Assign Full Control to Administrators and System, and Read to Everybody

Getting Unauthorized Access Alerts

The Windows NT Performance Monitor utility can warn you when someone is attempting to access a file without proper authorization. You set the alerts described next as discussed in Chapter 10.

- ♦ **Errors Access Permissions** This alert can help you detect when someone is randomly attempting to access files in the hopes of getting at something that was not properly protected. It reports when a file opened was denied access.

♦ **Errors Granted Access**   This alert indicates attempts to access files without proper access authorization. It reports the number of times accesses to files opened successfully were denied.

Things to Know About Deleted Files

In a secure environment, you want to make sure that files are completely erased and cannot be recovered. When you erase a file at a Windows NT 4.0 system, that file goes into the Recycle Bin. The owner of that file can open the Recycle Bin and recover it if necessary. There are some interesting scenarios that can take place on a Windows NT computer that is physically accessed by more than one user (i.e., local users, not network users):

♦ If someone manages to log on to a Windows NT system under another user's account, he could recover files that the account owner may believe are safely deleted.

♦ If multiple users are accessing the same system, one user might intentionally or accidentally delete files that another user needs. The other user won't be able to recover the files since they are in another user's Recycle Bin.

♦ Intervention by the Administrator is necessary to recover files that were accidentally or intentionally deleted by another user. If those files are owned by another user, the Administrator may not be able to directly recover them.

Beyond the Recycle Bin is the threat of someone stealing a drive and recovering information that has supposedly been deleted. Such a person using byte editors can easily get at files in the Recycle Bin. Going further, even files that have been cleared from the Recycle Bin are probably not safe from a determined hacker. Residual information from deleted files will remain on the disk where it can be viewed.

You need to use wiping utilities to more effectively delete information on magnetic media. Wiping utilities write over deleted files with random information. Ideally, you'll want to wipe files a number of times, and U.S. Government standards suggest using three wipes in which 0's are first written to disk, then 1's, and finally the pattern 0101. The Norton Utilities from Symantec (800 441-7234) include a file wiping utility. Keep in mind that determined hackers with adequate financial and hardware resources may still be able to read deleted and wiped information from drives. For example, electron microscopes have been used to recover data from magnetic material, even after five or more wipings!

Sharing Directories and Files

This section describes folder and file sharing in the Windows NT environment and the techniques you use to make these resources available to network users.

Resource sharing in the Windows environment is largely handled by the Server Message Blocks (SMB) protocol. SMB is the native file-sharing protocol in the Windows 95, Windows NT, and OS/2 operating system environments. It is also used in pre-Windows 95 versions of the Windows operating system for file sharing across networks. In addition, the new Common Internet File System (CIFS), which allows file sharing across the Internet, is based on SMB. SMB is also widely available in the UNIX and VMS environments, and it has been an Open Group (formerly X/Open) standard for PC and UNIX interoperability since 1992.

SMB is implemented in the Server and Workstation components in Windows NT systems and as "File and Printer Sharing for Microsoft Networks" in Windows 95 clients. It provides redirector services that allow a client to locate files on other network computers running SMB and open, read, write to, and delete those files. As a side point, access to shared resources on NetWare servers is handled by the NetWare Core Protocol (NCP) file sharing protocol.

NetBIOS is used to establish logical connections, or sessions, between networked computers. NetBIOS also uses a unique logical name to identify workstations on the network. Once a session is established, a two-way conversation takes place in which the following types of SMB messages are exchanged:

♦ **Session control** Commands that start and end a redirector connection to shared resources at a server.

♦ **File** Messages to gain access to files at a server.

♦ **Printer** Messages to send print jobs to shared printers or get information about print queues.

♦ **Message** Provides a way to send messages to or receive messages from other network-attached workstations.

The major contention with resource sharing using SMB is the potential for unauthorized users to access resources on your network. Unless SMB and NetBIOS traffic is stopped at the connection to the Internet, someone at a Windows or DOS workstation—or someone using a compatible SMB service—may be able to access shared resources on your network. For example, a DOS user on the Internet could use NET VIEW and NET USE commands to view your shared resources and connect to them respectively.

Of course, their access to resources is restricted by the permissions on those resources and their ability to gain access to a user account that has rights on your network systems. Hackers often find that the Guest account or some similar loosely managed account gives them just such rights.

Closely monitor your user accounts and make sure that systems connected to the Internet do not provide a gateway that hackers can use to access your internal shared resources. This means disabling Server, Workstation, and NetBIOS services and using filtering to block unauthorized packets, as discussed in Chapter 10 and in Part 4 of this book.

Resource Sharing in Windows NT

Administrative users, operators, and power users can create shares on Windows NT computers. If you are running Windows NT Server as a domain controller, members of the Administrators and Server Operators local group can manage shared resources. If you are running a Windows NT Server that is operating as a member server (not a domain controller), then members of the Administrators and Power Users local group can manage shared resources. The owner of a folder (who is not necessarily a member of these groups) can also share the folder.

Finally, members of the domain Administrators local group can manage shares over the network by using the Server Manager utility, as we will discuss next.

 NOTE: If you share a folder, all of its subfolders are shared as well with the same permissions, unless you specifically change the permissions on a subfolder or stop sharing it.

To share a folder, printer, or other resource while working at the server, you right-click the object you want to share and choose Sharing. This opens a dialog box similar to what you see in Figure 9-4. Here's the general procedure for creating a share:

♦ Click Shared As and type the name for the share in the Share Name field. You can use the suggested name or type a different name.

♦ If a share already exists for this object, click the New Share button to create another share with a different name and with different sets of permissions.

♦ If there is no limit on the number of users that can access this share at any one time, click Maximum Allowed, otherwise, click Allow and specify the maximum number of users to limit access and prevent performance drops.

♦ Click the Permissions button to set permissions for the share. You'll see a dialog box similar to Figure 9-6. Click Add to add a new user or group, then choose a permission in the Type of Access field.

Keep in mind that shared resources only have the No Access, Read, Change, and Full Control permissions. You combine these with the permissions you set for folders as discussed earlier to come up with a combined set of permissions that users or groups have to the shared object.

For example, assume you want members of the Domain Users group to have the Change permission in a folder but not the ability to delete files in the folder. To revoke the delete permission on a file, change its Special Access permissions as described here:

1. Right-click a file (or group of files), then choose Properties

2. Click the Security tab on the Properties dialog box

3. Click the Permissions button, then choose a user or group account in the permissions list (such as Domain Users in this example)

4. In the Type of Access list, choose Special Access to display a dialog box similar to the following:

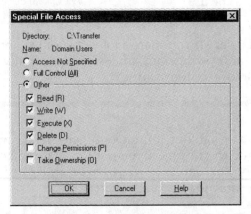

Now you can grant or revoke permissions as appropriate for this particular file. Be aware that you can choose groups of files and set permissions for the group, but you will only be able to set the basic four permissions (No Access, Read, Change, and Full Control) and not the Special Permissions.

This procedure underscores the importance of setting permissions in two places: on the folder or file itself, and on the share for a folder or file. It gives you great flexibility in manipulating permissions when many different users and groups are involved in sharing resources, and when you have managers who perform different levels of management activity directly at the physical server.

Once resources are shared, network users can access those resources. If a user is not authorized to access a resource, a dialog box appears that asks the user to enter a username and password that will give them access to the resource. Users browse for shared network resource in the Network Neighborhood window on Windows 95 and Windows NT 4.0 computers. MS-DOS users use the NET VIEW and NET USE command to view and access shared folders.

Hidden Shares

You can hide shared folders so they don't appear in listings of shared folders by typing a dollar sign ($) after the name in the Share Name field. For example, to hide a folder called Private, you would name it Private$. When a folder is hidden, clients running Windows 95 or Windows NT 4.0 will not see the folder in the Network Neighborhood. Other Windows clients will not see it when running commands like Net View.

Users who know the hidden folder's name can access it by creating a shared network drive. This is done by right-clicking either My Computer or Network Neighborhood and choosing Map Network Drive. A dialog box similar to the following appears:

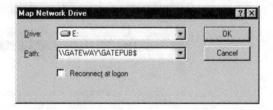

To connect to a folder, you type its name followed by a dollar sign in the Path field of this box as shown.

The usual procedure is for Administrators to create hidden shared folders and then distribute the name of the folder to authorized users. Keep in mind that this method does not guarantee any security. It simply provides a way to keep folders out of the general listings that appear in Network Neighborhood. It may prevent a hacker from attempting access on a folder if he doesn't know it exists. Even then, a savvy user can use the Find utility and search your server for folders using the following syntax:

```
*$*
```

If you think I've just divulged a big secret, don't worry. Most hackers already know about this. You use hidden shares to keep your "good network citizens" out of folders they shouldn't be in. By default, the Windows NT Server operating system automatically shares the root directory of each drive and the *systemroot* folder for Administrator access. Drives are shared as c$, d$, and so on, while the *systemroot* directory is shared as admin$. These shares are protected by an internal Access Control list (ACL) that allows only Administrators to connect to the shares. The ACL cannot be modified by any user, including an Administrator. Any attempt to change the shares results in a message that the folder has been shared for administrative purposes and that the permissions cannot be set.

Managing Shares with Server Manager

You can also use the Server Manager, either while working at a server or while working at a remote workstation to manage shares. The interface for doing so is slightly different and some Administrators may prefer it over the methods just described. You can run the Server Manager from a Windows 95 or Windows NT Workstation if the Client Administrator Tools are installed, as discussed at the beginning of Chapter 10.

Choose Server Manager from the Administrative Tools group at the Windows NT Server computer or from the Windows NT Server Tools group if you are working at a Windows Workstation. A dialog box similar to this one appears:

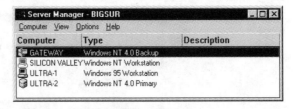

Creating a share with the Server Manager is a little more difficult than the methods just discussed. Earlier, you right-clicked the folder you wanted to share and set the share options. With the Server Manager, you click the New Share button on the Shared Directories dialog box and type a path to the shared folders. You need to know what the path is, and it can be confusing if the folder is buried several levels deep in the directory structure.

However, managing existing shared folders is easy with the Server Manager because the Shared Directories dialog box groups all the shared folders together. That is different than using the method described earlier, where you search for shared folders by browsing a hierarchical folder structure. Because of this, you might prefer to use the Server Manager when managing shares.

To change the permissions of an existing share, click the Properties button, or to stop sharing a folder, select it and click the Stop Sharing button.

Using SMB Services Over the Web

You can connect a Windows NT system to the Internet and share files using the SMB protocol, but doing so requires the same precautions necessary when connecting any other system to the Web. You should set up such a server as a stand-alone system (not connected to any internal network), then allow users to access it as Guests, or require that they log on to a user account that is defined in the server's local user account database. Because the system is connected to the Internet, do not store any sensitive information on the server, and be prepared to restore the system at any time should someone breach its security.

The basic trick to providing SMB services over the Internet is to have your remote clients create an LMHOSTS file on their computer that resolves the name of your server into its IP address on the Internet. For example, the LMHOSTS file might have the entry:

    200.1.1.1 SERVER1

which indicates that SERVER1 is at 200.1.1.1. Now when a user types **NET VIEW \\SERVER1** in the Run dialog box, a connection will be made to your server over the Internet.

Keep in mind that anyone on the Internet who discovers this IP address can connect to your server and access its information. Logons and directory permissions can provide file protection, but your system may need to withstand repeated hacker attacks. For more information on setting up SMB file sharing on the Internet, check out Winserve's Web site at **www.winserve.com**.

Using Web Servers for File Services

As mentioned previously, an internal network can fall prey to a hacker who manages to access SMB services through an Internet or other type of connection. These services can be disconnected on the Internet-connected side of a multihomed server. A multihomed server is a computer that has two network interface cards, each connected to a different network (one might be connected to the Internet). Normally, you would disconnect routing between the two network cards and remove Server, Workstation, and NetBIOS services on one side of the configuration to prevent anyone (including hackers) from browsing or using SMB services. However, if FTP, Gopher, and Web services are running, they will be able to access those services, which is what you want in this scenario.

You might create a similar configuration on an intranet to reduce the possibility of internal users hacking your servers through security holes or because they gained access to a user's account. The goal is to stop using any of the network sharing techniques discussed in the previous parts of this chapter. Instead, you can set up a server in which all public access to files can only take place through an HTTP Web server. This is discussed further under "Windows NT Home-Grown Filewalls" in Chapter 18.

Assume the Research department has a server that contains files that other departments need to access. For security reasons, you don't want to share files on this server using the standard Microsoft networking methods (i.e., SMB, NetBIOS, Network Neighborhood browsing, etc.). You can set up this system by disabling Server, Workstation, and NetBIOS and enabling Web services (or FTP or Gopher services).

Even though normal Microsoft networking is disabled, users can still connect to the server using their Web browsers and access information and files on the server. You can even enable a feature called "Allow Directory Browsing" on the Web server that allows users to see a list of files in directories (instead of fancy Web pages). This feature provides "file transfer protocol" capabilities from a Web page, allowing users to copy any of the files they see listed to their own system. The files are stored in Read Only directories for security reasons.

Unfortunately, this arrangement does not allow the normal open, save and change functionality that you might need in workgroup environments. Users copy a file to their system and use it as needed. If they need to change it, they might return it in an e-mail to the system administrator or another person who can then repost the file on the server. Inconvenient, yes, but secure. However, future products will allow more of these features.

New File Systems

Microsoft has new file systems or file system upgrades in the works. These are Common Internet File System (CIFS), which is an extension to the SMB protocol for use over the Internet; FAT32, which is a 32-bit version of the FAT file system with some added security features; and the object-oriented file system for the up and coming Cairo operating system.

FAT32

The File Allocation Table file system is of little interest to network administrators concerned with security, but a new version of this operating system is worth mentioning because some administrators may find it on their networks.

Microsoft is making a FAT32 service release for the Windows 95 operating system. The primary difference between FAT32 and previous versions of FAT is that it supports large hard drives of up to 2 terabytes (2,048 gigabytes). FAT only supports drives of 2 gigabytes in size. The number of clusters on hard drives is also expanded. The new FAT32 will have some problems with existing disk utilities such as Symantec's Norton Utilities because of the changes in the layout of the file structure. There could also be some problems with anti-virus software.

In general, the file system should become popular with users who need much more disk space than is supported by the traditional FAT. Users with multimedia and graphics requirements will benefit, but it provides no security benefits over the current FAT.

Common Internet File System

CIFS is a remote network file-sharing technology that allows collaborative work to be done over the Internet. It is an enhanced version of Server Messages Block technology that is already used in DOS, Windows, OS/2, and in the UNIX environments. The structure of CIFS files is the same as these environments; existing applications can be used to work with the files. It allows computer users attached to networks and the Internet to directly open and share remote files and provides a way to do interactive computing.

CIFS differs from file transfer protocols like FTP in that users can directly read and write files stored on remote computers without first downloading files to local systems. The objective is to improve performance, manage files in a single location, and improve security. The enhancements that CIFS adds to the existing SMB protocol are designed to make it suitable for use on the Internet. Some of these features are described here:

♦ The Domain Name Service (DNS) is used for address resolution

♦ It is designed to work well over slow dial-up lines

♦ Enables end users to work collaboratively across the Internet

♦ Provides authentication, file locking, data sharing, and file-level security

♦ Works well with so-called "network appliances" or Internet terminals

♦ Has options to support remote printer sharing as well

Windows NT Server Distributed File System

In the latter part of 1996, Microsoft announced its Distributed File System, or DFS. DFS is designed to make it easier to find and manage information on networks. It provides a hierarchical view of file servers and file server shares on an entire network. DFS lets users view this file system as a single directory structure that they can browse through, rather than a large collection of different servers.

At the time of this writing, DFS was in beta testing. You can obtain a copy of the beta by connecting with Microsoft's Web site at **www.microsoft.com.**

CHAPTER 10

Management,
Monitoring, and
Auditing

This chapter presents the Windows NT management tools that you can use to monitor the configurations, settings, performance, and activities of your servers and the network. Ultimately, you can use these tools to monitor the security of your systems, as described here. The following tools are discussed, as are some of the utilities that you can run at the command prompt, such as NET commands and TCP/IP commands.

Windows NT Diagnostics   This is a useful utility for configuring and troubleshooting system hardware and add-in components. It is covered in the next section of this chapter.

The Server Manager   You use this utility for managing individual servers in domains, user connections, and the properties of servers.

The Performance Monitor   This utility displays performance statistics about how well servers are operating under current loads. You can use this information to justify equipment upgrades or to account for the activity on Web servers.

The Network Monitor   This tool lets you capture and view packets (or, more appropriately, frames) on networks. You can use the utility not only to troubleshoot network problems but also to monitor the activities of hackers.

The Event Viewer   This is the tool you use to view the contents of the auditing logs.

There is one other important reason for learning about these commands and utilities: Hackers and rogue administrators might use them to view and change information on your systems, so it's a good idea to become familiar with their weapons. As always, use of these tools requires Administrator or Operator status to the *systemroot*\System32 directory.

Client Administrator Tools

The Client Administrator Tools were mentioned in Chapter 8. You can use them to run some of the utilities mentioned above from a Windows NT Workstation or Windows 95 computer. When they're installed, you can run the Event Viewer, Server Manager, User Manager, Remote Access Administrator, User Profile Editor, Remoteboot Manager, DHCP Manager, and WINS manager from the comfort of your office.

To install the tools, put the Windows NT Server CD-ROM in the CD-ROM drive of the administrative workstation and copy the utilities from the

CD-ROM to the local hard drive. The utilities are in one of two directories, depending on the operating system you intend to use. The directories are CLIENTS\SRVTOOLS\WIN95 and CLIENTS\SRVTOOLS\WINNT. You can also choose to install the utilities on a server's hard drive and run them from your administrative workstation. This option might provide a little more security. At the Windows NT Server, click the Start button, then choose Programs and Administrative tools, then Network Client Administrator.

Running administrative tools from a workstation requires extra precautions. The workstation you use could be under surveillance by a hacker. Also, if your workstation is a non-Windows NT computer, a hacker could easily install a Trojan horse program to capture the passwords you type. Windows NT computers are protected from this kind of attack when you press CTRL-ALT-DEL when you logon.

CAUTION: For security reasons, only run administrative programs from Windows NT computers, because of their built-in security.

Windows NT Diagnostics

The Windows NT Diagnostics utility is a powerful tool for evaluating and troubleshooting system hardware and environment settings. Windows NT 4.0 provides a new and improved utility that you can open by choosing Windows NT Diagnostics from the Administrative Tools group. A dialog box appears, similar to the one shown in Figure 10-1. Notice the tabs near the top of the dialog box. You click these tabs to display a particular page of information. In the figure, the Statistics information on the Network page is visible.

You can click each tab in the dialog box to view information about a server, its versions, and the hardware installed in the system. Click the Refresh button to get the latest statistical information on pages with values that require frequent updates. You can use the information to get a quick overall profile of the server for security auditing purposes, as follows:

♦   View the current version and build number of the operating system (Version page).

♦   View information about disk drivers, including whether they are NTFS volumes and whether security is preserved (Drives).

♦   See what services are running or stopped (Services).

♦   View the settings of hardware devices in the system (Resources).

♦   View critical information about the network, as discussed next.

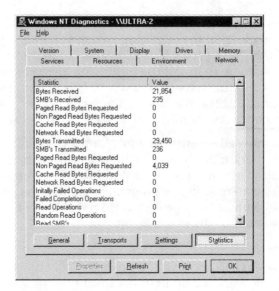

Windows NT
Diagnostics
Figure 10-1.

Click on the Network tab to get interesting and useful information about the network that the server is attached to. There are four buttons on the Network page:

♦ **General** Displays the current network settings, such as workgroup or domain, network version, logon domain, logon server, and name of the current user. Use this page to view your current logon account in case you forget whether you logged on as an administrator or regular user.

♦ **Transports** Displays a list of current network transport protocols and the addresses of the network adapters they are bound to.

♦ **Settings** Shows the current value of network parameters, such as session timeouts, buffers, caches, pipes, and encryption.

♦ **Statistics** Shows current statistics for the network, such as bytes received, requested, and transmitted, as well as many other parameters.

In particular, the Statistics page can indicate activities that are overloading a server (possibly an attempt to deny service) and break-in activities. If you think your system is under attack, watch the following statistics:

Server Password Errors This statistic tracks the number of failed logon attempts to the server. This value may indicate that someone is running a password-guessing program in an attempt to crack the security on the server.

Server Permission Errors   This is the number of times that clients have been denied access to files they were trying to open. This value may indicate that somebody is randomly attempting to access files in hopes of getting at something that was not properly protected.

10

Also watch for jumps in bytes received or other activities that are out of the ordinary. If you use the utility on a regular basis, and if your server has a relatively steady flow of traffic, you will notice an unusual spike that might indicate hacker activities. Denial of service attacks will be obvious if they are successful. By using the Windows NT Diagnostics utility along with the Performance Monitor and other Windows NT management utilities, you should be able to track a standard profile for your server and notice any deviations that might indicate unusual activities.

 NOTE: You can also use the Performance Monitor utility to alert you to illicit activities; this will be discussed later.

The Server Manager and Server Utility

The Server Manager and the Server utility provide similar functionality. They let you manage servers and the connections to those servers. The Server Manager, located in the Administrative Tools group, displays a list of servers in the current domain (or other selected domains) that you can manage. The Server utility is located in the Control Panel and provides the same functionality that the Server Manager does for managing the properties of a local server.

When you start the Server Manager, a dialog box similar to Figure 10-2 appears. It displays a list of servers in the current domain. Choose Select Domain from the Computer menu to choose a different domain to manage.

Server Manager - BIGSUR		_ □ X
Computer View Options Help		
Computer	**Type**	**Description**
GATEWAY	Windows NT 4.0 Backup	
ULTRA-1	Windows 95 Workstation	TOM SHELDON
ULTRA-2	Windows NT 4.0 Primary	

The Server
Manager
Figure 10-2.

Here are some of the management tasks you can perform in the Server Manager:

♦ Double-click a server to manage its properties. Refer to "Managing Server Properties" for more details.

♦ View and manage shared directories by first selecting a server and choosing Shared Directories from the Computer menu. The dialog box that appears lets you create new shares or stop sharing directories. (This topic was covered in Chapter 9.)

♦ Manage services by clicking a server and choosing Services from the Computer menu. This option, which lets you view and change the status of services that run on the server, is discussed later under "Managing Services."

♦ Manage domains by clicking a server and choosing one of the following options from the Computer menu:

Promote to primary domain controller Promotes a backup domain controller to the status of the primary domain controller (PDC). Choose this option if the PDC fails or if you want to replace it.

Synchronize Entire Domain Choose this option to force the primary domain controller to send updates to backup domain controllers.

Add to Domain/Remove from Domain Choose these options to add or remove computers from the selected domain.

Managing Server Properties

To manage the properties of a server, choose the server in the Computer list, then choose Properties from the Computer menu. You can also just double-click the computer name. A Properties dialog box similar to the following appears:

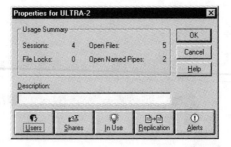

The Usage Summary field provides the following information:

♦ **Sessions** Number of users connected to the computer.

♦ **Open Files**   Number of files to be shared by the server.

♦ **File Locks**   Number of file locks in use. (A lock protects a file from being accessed by another person.)

♦ **Open Named Pipes**   Number of named pipes in use.

10

The buttons at the bottom of the dialog box are discussed in the following section, except for Replication, which is covered in Chapter 11.

Managing Users, Shares, and In Use Resources

The buttons at the bottom of the Properties dialog box open other dialog boxes that let you view both the users who are currently connected to the network and a list of resources in use by each user. For example:

♦ Click the Users button to display the User Sessions dialog box:

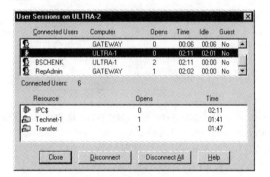

In this box, you can disconnect any user, or all users if you need to shut a system down. The Resource field shows the resources that are currently in use by the selected user. You might disconnect users if you suspect they are involved in unauthorized activities or if their accounts are being used by someone who gained unauthorized access.

♦ Click the Shares button to view a list of the shared resources available on the system and the users who are using them. You can then select any user who is sharing a resource and stop her from using it.

♦ Click the In Use button to view a list of resources currently in use, sorted by the user who is using the resources. You can disconnect any user from the resource he is accessing.

Managing Alerts

Alerts are a critical part of your security management strategy. You click the Alerts button to manage how server alerts are handled. Alerts are generated by a system when there are problems with security, access, sessions, power, and system processes. For example, you could be alerted when directory replication fails to occur or when a disk is near capacity.

 NOTE: The alerts in the User Sessions dialog box are predetermined by the operating system. Refer to the section "Monitoring Activities with the Performance Monitor" later in this chapter for information about additional alerts that you can set.

When you click the Alerts button, a dialog box similar to the following appears:

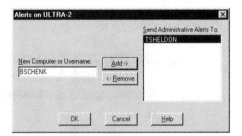

In the Alerts box, you specify which computers or users should be notified when an alert occurs. You can type either a username or a computer name in the text box and click the Add button to add it to the list of users or computers that will be alerted when events occur. If a user is logged on at several workstations, alerts appear at only one of the workstations, so the user may not see it. Do not have several people log on to the Administrator account, because alerts would be sent to only one of those people.

For alerts to be sent, the Alerter and Messenger services must be running on the computer originating the alert. For alerts to be received, the Messenger service must be running on the destination computer.

 NOTE: After assigning alerts, you must stop and restart the Server and Alerter services on the computer. Do this from the computer, not from a remote workstation where you are running the Server Manager. Services are discussed next.

Managing Services

Services are installed either during the Windows NT setup process or when you install components using Control Panel utilities or other methods. Managing services is critical in secure environments.

NOTE: Disabling services is a tricky business. The recommendations presented here may be inappropriate for the level of security you are trying to achieve. Try the security settings on test platforms in your own environment before enabling them on live production systems.

10

There are two ways to manage services: if you are working at the console of a server, you can choose Services in the Control Panel to view and manage the services running on that computer. A dialog box similar to Figure 10-3 appears. Alternatively, you can manage a remote server by opening the Server Manager and choosing a server in a domain, then choosing Services from the Computer menu.

Keep the following points in mind:

♦ You must log on to an account that has membership in the Administrators local group to configure services.

♦ You might want to pause or stop some non-essential services to improve the performance of the server.

♦ Run only the most essential services, because some services may pose security threats.

♦ Services can only be started under a logged-on account, just as users can only start programs if they are logged in to a user account. Many services start up in the System account which, by default, has full access to entire drives. This level of access is inappropriate for many services; you should choose to start them with a lower-level account as described later under "Changing the Startup Account for Services."

♦ If you *pause* a service, such as the Server service, it is still available to the Administrators and Server Operators group, but all other users are prevented from accessing it. If you *stop* a service, existing users are

Managing
Services
Figure 10-3.

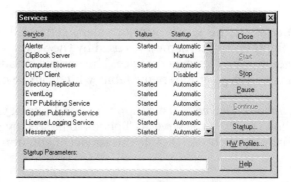

bumped off and no one can use the service until it is restarted. Pause a service before actually stopping it, then send a message to existing users so they can log off gracefully.

If you just need to provide information and file-download services to users, you could run only the Microsoft Internet Information Server (Web services) on a server. In this case, you could disable the Server, Workstation, and NetBIOS services if no one needs those services. I know it sounds strange to stop the Server service on a server, but if users only need Web services, why run it? This assumes users access the machine with a Web browser over the Internet or on intranets, and that administrators access the machine locally for maintenance, rather than over the network. Disabling these services removes some hacker opportunities. With Server disabled, users cannot execute commands like NET VIEW, NET SESSION, NET USER to look at the computer names and usernames on your servers.

NOTE: Disabling the Server service will improve security, but it will also prevent network users from accessing shared directories. Make sure that you want this configuration before disabling the service. Also, do not stop the Server service on existing domain controllers or systems that you need to perform replication.

The following services are installed by default. Your server may include additional services, depending either on your selections during setup or on the hardware and software you have installed. Carefully evaluate which of these services you need to run and which you can stop. Some services are dependent on others and can't be stopped without stopping those other services. If you're not sure whether you need a service in your particular environment, consult a qualified technician. A radical approach is to disable the service and see what effect that has on your system. This latter approach is appropriate only in test (pre-installation) environments.

Alerter   This service forwards alerts generated on local machines to remote computers or usernames. It's used by the Server service and other services; it requires the Messenger service. This service broadcasts the logged on user name in the Net Bios name table, which can be considered a security breach.

Clipbook Viewer   This supports the Clipbook viewer application, which allows pages in the server's Clipbook to be seen by users on other workstations that run Clipbook. Disable this service if you don't need it.

10

Computer Browser   The Browser service keeps very busy searching for and displaying lists of computers that provide services in a domain. For security reasons, you might want to disable browsing, but doing so removes the convenience of browsing. Users will need to type the computer name of computers they want to access or create shortcuts to those systems.

Directory Replicator   This service replicates directories and the files in the directories between designated servers. If you don't use replication, disable it.

Event Log   This service records activities on the server in the Event Log. You cannot pause or stop this service.

Messenger   This service sends and receives messages and alerts sent by administrators or by services that generate alerts, and displays them on the screen in the form of a message box. This service is stopped when the Workstation service is stopped.

Net Logon   On Windows NT Workstation computers, this service supports pass-through authentication of logon and is used for logon when the workstation participates in a domain. On Windows NT Server computers, this service authenticates user logon and keeps the server's security databases synchronized between the primary domain controller and the backup domain controllers. This service is required in most cases.

Network DDE   This service provides a network transport as well as security for DDE (Dynamic Data Exchange) conversations.

NT LM Security Support Provider   This service provides Windows NT Security to RPC (Remote Procedure Call) applications that use transports other than named pipes. This service is required in most cases.

Remote Procedure Call (RPC) Locator   This allows distributed applications to use the Microsoft RPC service and manages the RPC Name Service database. The server side of distributed applications registers its availability with this service. The client side of a distributed application queries this service to find available server applications. You can stop this service on isolated computers that provide minimal services, such as a Web server connected to the Internet, but servers connected to a domain or workgroup will need this service for most administrative and user applications.

Remote Procedure Call (RPC) Service   This is the RPC subsystem for Windows NT. It includes the endpoint mapper and other related services. Pausing or stopping this service on network-connected servers will result in unpredictable results and lock-ups.

Schedule   This service is required to run the AT command, which can be used to schedule commands and programs to run on a particular date and time. It is not started by default.

Server   This is the SMB service that enables a Windows NT computer to share its resources over the network. It does not attempt to connect with other computers, but allows other computers to connect to it. The message exchange between client and server is handled by the SMB (Server Message Block) protocol. If you stop Server services, other services such as Computer Browser, Directory Replicator, Net Logon, and Remote Access Services are also stopped. However, if you pause the service, these other services are not paused at the same time.

Spooler   This provides print spooler services.

TCP/IP NetBIOS Helper   This service provides NetBIOS over TCP/IP services and is only available if the TCP/IP protocol is installed. You can stop this service if you don't want to use NetBIOS for security reasons. Disabling this service also disables the Computer Browser and Net Logon service. Disabling this service on the Primary domain controller when TCP/IP is the only protocol in use will have unpredictable results. In most cases, leave this service running.

UPS   This provides services for the connection of power supplies that can't be interrupted.

Workstation   The Workstation service allows a Windows NT computer to access resources on a workgroup network and to log in to a domain. It is often called the *redirector*. All user requests for network service go through this component. Requests to connect, open, read, or write on a redirected drive (a drive that references a shared directory on another network computer) are forwarded to the redirector and packaged for delivery over the wire to a server. Windows NT Server computers running as primary domain controllers also run the workstation service so they can connect as clients with other domain controllers and exchange network information. You may need to run this service if you run Web services due to dependencies with other services.

There are of course many other services that you can optionally install or that must be manually started. For example, you can optionally install the FTP, Gopher, and Web services on Windows NT computers, as well as scheduling and spooling services. You also have the option of installing the Remote Access Service. Other unnecessary services may be installed when you set up new applications, so review the services list after reconfiguring your server.

There are several cases where you might want to disable these services for performance and security reasons. Assume you want to build an internally connected Web server that the users inside your company can access. You install the Microsoft Internet Information Server software on a Windows NT computer and stop the Server, Workstation, and Computer Browser services. Now your internal users can access Web pages, but that is it. Only directories that are made available in the Internet Service Manager can be accessed by Web browsers. Because the Browser service is disabled, users will not see the name of this computer in the browse list, nor can they type its NetBIOS name in their Web browser. They are required to type the IP address of the Web server they want to access. However, after connecting to the page for the first time, they can create a shortcut to it on their desktops to make future connections easy.

Changing the Startup Account for Services

As mentioned earlier, some services start only when you log in under the System account. This account has full access to an entire drive. Some consider this a potential security problem, because a hacker could exploit a bug in a service that runs under the System account to attack another part of your system. The general rule is to run services under an account that has the least privileges possible. You must create such an account and assign it appropriate rights, then follow the next procedure to enable accounts to log on under the service. Remember that someone might try to log on repeatedly to this account, locking it up and creating a "denial-of-service" for other users.

To assign a different logon account for a service, click the service in the Services dialog box pictured in Figure 10-3, then click the Startup button. A dialog box similar to the following appears:

Here you can click the This Account button and specify the new user account name and password.

Most of the services listed earlier cannot be configured to start under any other service except System. The following services can be configured to start up with an account other than the System account:

♦ Clipbook service

♦ Directory Replicator service

♦ Microsoft DNS (Domain Name Service) service

♦ Remote Access Server service

♦ Remote Procedure Call Locator service

♦ Remote Procedure Call service

♦ Schedule service

♦ Spooler service

♦ Telephony service

♦ UPS service

♦ Windows Internet Name service

Binding and Unbinding Services in Multihomed Systems

A server that has two network interface cards is called a multihomed server. You can take advantage of the two cards to configure a rudimentary firewall for your intranet or Internet-connected servers, as pictured in Figure 10-4. Multihomed systems provide router services that help you control the flow of packets between networks. Chapter 18 provides additional information under "Windows NT Home-Grown Firewalls."

On any computer connected to a network, software components provide an interface between the operating system and the network interface card. The

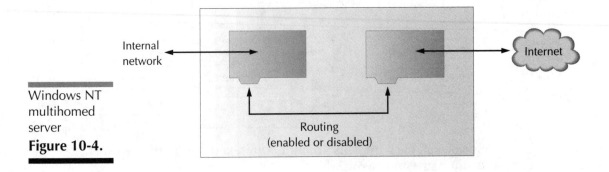

Windows NT multihomed server

Figure 10-4.

relationships between software components and the network interface cards are called *bindings*. For security reasons, you may want to remove some of these bindings. For example, in Figure 10-4, you could remove the Server, Workstation, and NetBIOS bindings from the network interface card that is connected to the Internet, so that Internet users can access Web services but not file- and print-sharing services.

To remove bindings, open the Network utility in the Control Panel and click the Bindings option. A dialog box resembling this one will appear:

The list in the Network dialog box shows the services that are bound to a network card. You click the appropriate plus sign to open up a particular service and see which network cards it is bound to. Notice in this example that two different NE2000 network cards have the Server service bound to them. Click the network card that you want to unbind the service from and click the Disable button. Do this for each service you want to unbind and make sure you unbind services from the correct card.

The NET Commands

NET is a command that administrators can execute in the Command Prompt window to display information about networks, servers, session connections, and shared directories. In addition, it has a number of command options that you can use to add user account and groups, change domain settings, and work with shared resources. The NET commands are described in the following section.

The NET commands provide a way to manage or access a server from the DOS prompt. You can do many of the same things you can do in the User

Manager and Server Manager by executing NET commands from a command line. You can even create batch files that include commands to create multiple user accounts and groups. However, some things must still be done from the User Manager, such as granting rights.

NOTE: If the Server service is disabled on a server, you can't use NET commands against it.

The following batch file illustrates an interesting way to use NET commands. It produces a security analysis report that displays important and useful information about a Windows NT computer. You can use this information to evaluate your security profiles and take action in the event that your system comes under attack by an intruder. Enter the following lines into a text editor, and save the file with a name like SEC_RPT.BAT.

TIP: Additional parameters that might be useful in your environment are available for most of these commands. To get help, type **NET HELP** at the command prompt.

```
echo ACCOUNTS > report.txt
net accounts >> report.txt
echo SERVER CONFIGURATION >> report.txt
net config server >> report.txt
echo WORKSTATION CONFIGURATION >> report.txt
net config workstation >> report.txt
echo GROUPS >> report.txt
net group >> report.txt
echo LOCAL GROUPS >> report.txt
net localgroup >> report.txt
echo NAMES >> report.txt
net name >> report.txt
echo SESSIONS >> report.txt
net session >> report.txt
echo SHARES >> report.txt
net share >> report.txt
echo SERVER STATISTICS >> report.txt
net statistics server >> report.txt
echo WORKSTATION STATISTICS >> report.txt
net statistics workstation >> report.txt
echo SHARED RESOURCES IN USE >> report.txt
net use >> report.txt
```

```
echo USER INFORMATION >> report.txt
net user >> report.txt
echo SHARED RESOURCES >> report.txt
net view >> report.txt
```

10

NOTE: The NET commands in this batch file append their output to a text file called REPORT.TXT, which you can view with any text editor. The ECHO commands simply place a header before each report. The single ">" in the first command causes any existing file to be overwritten. The ">>" in subsequent lines appends information to the new file.

The Windows NT batch command set includes a unique command called *AT*, which lets you schedule a time at which to run a command. An administrator could schedule a batch file like the previous example to run at a particular time every day and print the results for evaluation. This report could be used to detect unusual changes that might indicate intruders. Another example is to schedule a batch file that runs commands like NET SESSION at regular intervals throughout the night if you suspect that intruders are operating during evening hours. These examples can supplement the information that you obtain in your Audit Logs and with the tools discussed in Appendix D.

Be aware that hackers who gain remote access to your server might be able to use NET commands to list information about your server and change critical information, such as the status of user accounts, assuming they gain appropriate rights. With access to the Windows NT Server's version of the NET command, hackers can issue NET commands on servers in the domain or in trusted domains. Members of the Administrators and Server Operators groups have the ability to log on locally to a server and execute the NET command at that server. A rogue member of these groups could use the command to obtain information about other servers for malicious use. Of course, such a user would have access to other commands and utilities as well. The next section describes these commands so you can know what weapons your enemy can use against you.

NET Commands for Windows NT

Following is a list of NET commands for Windows NT. An additional list following this list displays commands available on DOS and Windows client workstations. Commands of special interest to security managers are NET ACCOUNTS, which tells you about the current settings for password and logon restrictions; NET FILE, which tells you what files are in use if you are tracking a hacker; NET PAUSE and NET STOP, which provide a quick way to pause or stop a service in an emergency (e.g., your system is under attack); and NET SESSION, which lists the current sessions and lets you delete an intruder's session. In fact, you could create a batch file that runs some of these commands in an emergency situation. Remember that these commands do not run against computers that have Server services disabled.

NOTE: Use the MORE option to page help information on the screen. For example, type **NET ACCOUNTS | MORE** to page account help information.

- ◆ **NET ACCOUNTS**   This command will display the current settings for password, logon limitations, and domain information. It also has options for updating the User Accounts database and modifying password and logon requirements for all accounts.

- ◆ **NET COMPUTER**   This command adds or deletes computers from a domain database and is available only on Windows NT Servers.

- ◆ **NET CONFIG SERVER** (or **NET CONFIG WORKSTATION**)   Displays configuration information about the Server service (or the Workstation service). When used without the SERVER or WORKSTATION switch, the command displays a list of configurable services. Users of Windows client computers can type **NET CONFIG** to view the computer name, logged username, workgroup or domain name, and other information.

- ◆ **NET CONTINUE**   Reactivates a Windows NT service that has been suspended by NET PAUSE. See NET PAUSE later in this list for more information.

- ◆ **NET FILE**   This command lists the open files on a server and has options for closing shared files and removing file locks. Listings include the identification number assigned to an open file, the pathname of the file, the username, and the number of locks on the file. This command works only on computers running Server service.

- ◆ **NET GROUP**   This command displays information about group names and has options you can use to add or modify global groups on servers. You can use this command in a batch file to add or modify groups as a whole.

- ◆ **NET HELP**   To get help with NET commands, type either **NET HELP** *command* or **NET** *command***/HELP.**

- ◆ **NET HELPMSG** *message#*   To get help with network messages, type this command, replacing *message#* with the number you have seen in an error message.

♦ **NET LOCALGROUP** Use this command to list local groups on servers. It also has options for modifying groups.

♦ **NET NAME** This Windows NT-only command displays the names of computers and users to which messages are sent on the computer. It also has options for adding and deleting a messaging name (alias).

♦ **NET PAUSE** Use this command to suspend the Windows NT services and resources described next. Pausing a service puts it on hold until the NET CONTINUE command is used to resume it. You can create a batch file to abruptly halt service in the event of a hacker attack or some other problem.

♦ **NET PRINT** This command displays print jobs and shared queues.

♦ **NET SEND** Use this command to send messages to other users, computers, or messaging names on the network. For messages to be received, the Messenger service must be running.

♦ **NET SESSION** This command lists information about current sessions and has options for deleting sessions between computers. You can use this command to disconnect an undesirable connection.

♦ **NET SHARE** Use this command to list information about all resources being shared on a computer. The command is also used to create network shares.

♦ **NET STATISTICS SERVER** (or **WORKSTATION**) Displays the statistics log for the local Workstation or Server service.

♦ **NET STOP** Stops Windows NT services, canceling any connections the service is using. Be aware that stopping one service may stop another dependent service. Administrative rights are required to stop a server. For security reasons, you might want to use the NET STOP command to quickly stop a service. The Event log service cannot be stopped.

♦ **NET TIME** Use this command to display or set the time for a computer or domain.

♦ **NET USE** This command displays a list of connected computers, and has options for connecting to and disconnecting from shared resources on other network computers.

♦ **NET USER** This command will display a list of user accounts for the computer, and has options for creating and modifying those accounts. It is used with Windows servers only. There are extensive options for creating user accounts; you can place multiple instances of the command in a batch file to create a group of user accounts.

♦ **NET VIEW** This command displays a list of resources being shared on a computer. You can specify options to display resources in other domains or on NetWare servers.

NET Commands for DOS and Windows Clients

The following commands can be executed on DOS and Windows client computers at the command prompt, in batch files, and in the AUTOEXEC.BAT file. As mentioned, one of the reasons for reviewing these commands is that they are available on network-connected workstations. Authorized (and possibly unauthorized) users can use them to get information about or manipulate systems on your network. Some of the commands display valuable information about your network and its resources that you might not want anyone to see. In particular, try out the NET VIEW command at a workstation and consider whether the information it displays is information you want any user to see.

- ◆ **NET CONFIG** Displays the controllable services that are running.

- ◆ **NET DIAG** Runs the Microsoft Network Diagnostic program to display diagnostic information about your network.

- ◆ **NET HELP** or **NET /?** Provides a list of network commands and topics you can get help with, or provides help with a specific command or topic.

- ◆ **NET INIT** Loads protocol and network adapter drivers without binding them. This may be necessary for network adapter drivers from other vendors. You can bind them using NET START BIND.

- ◆ **NET LOGOFF** Breaks the connection between your computer and the network resources to which it is connected.

- ◆ **NET LOGON** Identifies you as a member of a workgroup.

- ◆ **NET PASSWORD** Changes your logon password.

- ◆ **NET PRINT** Displays or controls print jobs.

- ◆ **NET START** Starts a service or displays a list of started services.

- ◆ **NET STOP** Stops a network service.

- ◆ **NET TIME** Synchronizes the computer's clock with that of a server or domain, or displays the time for a server or domain.

- ◆ **NET USE** Connects a computer to or disconnects it from a shared resource, or displays information about computer connections.

- ◆ **NET VER** Displays the type and version number of the network redirector you are using.

- ◆ **NET VIEW** Displays a list of servers or displays resources being shared by a server.

NOTE: Some of these commands can only be used in real mode (before you start Windows 95).

TCP/IP Commands

There are a number of tools you can use to monitor, troubleshoot, and maintain TCP/IP networks. In most cases, these tools are designed for internal networks, but you can use some of them over the Internet. The NBTSTAT utility is covered here because it can be used to look at information available on networks running NetBIOS over TCP/IP. For information about the other commands listed next, refer to Windows NT help, or a good book on TCP/IP, such as Sidnie Feit's *TCP/IP: Architecture, Protocols, and Implementation* (McGraw-Hill, 1996).

♦   **ARP**   Lets you view and manage the mapping between IP addresses and physical network addresses.

♦   **IPCONFIG**   Displays diagnostic information about TCP/IP networks and current TCP/IP network configuration values.

♦   **NBTSTAT**   Reports information about NetBIOS over TCP/IP connections.

♦   **NETSTAT**   Displays current TCP/IP connections and protocol statistics.

♦   **PING**   Tests connections on TCP/IP networks.

♦   **TRACERT**   Traces how packets hop around your network or the Internet.

The NBTSTAT command displays information and statistics about the current TCP/IP connections using NetBIOS over TCP/IP. You can type the remote name or IP address of another system on a network to get information about it, such as local user names. This command is a hacker's dream, and it gives you very good reason to set up TCP/IP firewalls as discussed in Part 4 of this book. The command takes the following form:

NBTSTAT [-a *remotename*] [-A *IPaddress*] [-c] [-n] [-R] [-r] [-S] [-s] [*interval*] [-?]

where

-a *remotename*	Lists the name table of a remote computer. Replace *remotename* with the computer's name.

-A *IPaddress*	Lists the name table of a remote computer. Replace *IPaddress* with the computer's IP address.
-c	Lists the contents of the NetBIOS name cache, giving the IP address of each name.
-n	Lists local NetBIOS names.
-R	Reloads the LMHOSTS file after purging all names from the NetBIOS name cache.
-r	Lists name resolution statistics for Windows networking. On a Windows NT computer configured to use WINS, this option returns the number of names resolved and registered via broadcast or via WINS.
-S	Displays both workstation and server sessions, listing the remote hosts by IP address only.
-s	Displays both workstation and server sessions. It attempts to convert the remote host IP address to a name using the HOSTS file.
interval	Sets the refresh rate for statistics. Replace *interval* with the time in seconds between redisplays. Press CTRL-C to stop redisplaying statistics. If omitted, configuration information is displayed once.
-?	Displays help information.

A typical display from the NBTSTAT command appears in the following listing (note that the Administrator's name is listed!):

```
C:\>NBTSTAT -s
NetBIOS Connection Table

Local Name          State      In/Out  Remote Host        Input   Output
---------------------------------------------------------------------------
BSM            <00>  Connected  Out     GATEWAY     <20>   1MB     16KB
BSM            <03>  Listening
BSM            <03>  Listening
ADMINISTRATOR  <03>  Listening
ADMINISTRATOR  <03>  Listening
REPADMIN       <03>  Listening
REPADMIN       <03>  Listening
```

The column headings that are generated by the NBTSTAT utility have the following meanings. (Not all headings will appear with each command option.)

10

Input	Number of bytes received.
Output	Number of bytes sent.
In/Out	Whether the connection is from the computer (outbound) or from another system to the local computer (inbound).
Life	The remaining time that a name table cache entry will live before it is purged.
Local Name	The local NetBIOS name associated with the connection.
Remote Host	The name or IP address associated with the remote host.
Type	The type of name. A name can be either a unique name or a group name.
<03>	Each NetBIOS name is 16 characters long. The last byte often has special significance, because the same name can be present several times on a computer. This notation is simply the last byte converted to hexadecimal. For example, *<20>* is a space in ASCII.
State	The state of NetBIOS connections.

Monitoring Activities with the Performance Monitor

The Performance Monitor is a graphical charting and statistics-gathering tool that you can use to display performance information about your servers. You can have it alert you when certain events occur. (The alerts are based on preset values that exceed or fall below a critical limit.) You can use the monitoring, charting, and logging features of the Performance Monitor to help with initial performance troubleshooting and capacity planning for the local server or for other servers on the network.

The Performance Monitor is pictured in Figure 10-5. You can start it by double-clicking the Performance Monitor option in the Administrative Tools group. Notice that four processes are being tracked in this chart; they are labeled at the bottom of the window. You can choose what to track and then store the collected information in files for later analysis.

Here is a partial list of what you can do with the Performance Monitor:

♦ Set alerts to warn you about intruder activities or attempted access to unauthorized files.

◆ View information about multiple computers at the same time. You can open multiple copies of the Performance Monitor and track multiple events on each copy.

◆ Collect information in the form of charts, logs, alert logs, and reports. View the charts and dynamically change settings to fit your needs.

◆ Export the information you collect to spreadsheet or database programs for further analysis and printing.

◆ Set up alerts to track and compare counter values against preset thresholds.

◆ Create long-term archives by appending information to log files.

◆ Save current settings and values for future charting sessions.

The Performance Monitor tracks *objects*, which are processes and services running in Windows NT server computers. Every object has counters that keep track of specific events or activities. Here's a partial list of the objects that you can monitor:

◆ Browser

◆ Cache

◆ FTP (File Transfer Protocol) Server

◆ Gopher Service

◆ HTTP Service

◆ Memory

◆ NetBEUI and NetBEUI Resource

◆ Network Interface and Network Segment

◆ NWLink IPX, NWLink NetBIOS, and NWLink SPX

◆ Physical Disk

◆ Processor

◆ Remote Access Services

◆ Server

◆ System

◆ TCP/IP

The counters for objects are tracked and charted in the Performance Monitor window. You can view a complete list of objects to track and get a description of what they are by clicking the Explain button. The explanation window then opens at the bottom of the dialog box.

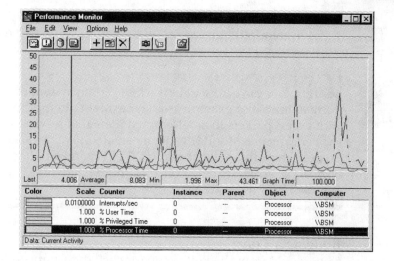

You can choose among four different viewing windows in the Performance Monitor. From the View menu, choose Chart, Alert, Log, or Report. Each window is quite different from the others, although all the windows share the menu bar, status bar, and toolbar of the Performance Monitor main window. The basic activities for the Performance Monitor are described here with reference to charting only. Alerts, logs, and reports are set up using similar procedures. For a complete description of how to use this utility, refer to Help.

Security Alerts

In particular, pay attention to the following security options. It's probably best to have the Performance Monitor alert you when these events occur. Choose Alert from the View menu and add these options to an alert list as described under "Alerts" later in this chapter.

♦   **Errors Access Permissions**   The number of times that a client attempts, but fails, to open a file and receives a STATUS_ACCESS_DENIED message. This alert can indicate whether somebody is randomly attempting to access files in hopes of getting at something that was not properly protected.

♦   **Errors Granted Access**   The number of times accesses to files opened successfully were denied. This can indicate attempts to access files without proper access authorization.

♦ **Errors Logon**   The number of failed logon attempts to the server. Can indicate whether password-guessing programs are being used to crack the security on the server.

TIP: You can also set alerts when certain system events exceed their normal limits. For example, someone might attempt to flood your server with excess packets in an attempted "denial of service" attack. You can have the Performance Monitor generate an alert if values such as "Bytes Rec/sec." You can track this value for an HTTP, FTP, and Gopher server, as well as a normal file server installed on an in-house network. The following section describes how to locate these options.

Building a Chart

Choose Add from the Edit menu (or click the + button) to add events that you want to track. The following dialog box appears if you are setting up to chart events.

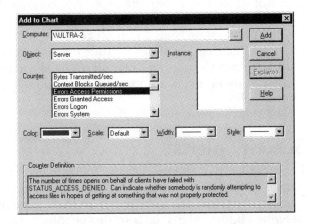

Be sure to click the Explain button to display the lower description field; then you can click on each counter to get a description of what it does and determine whether you want to add it to your chart.

Set the options in the Add to Chart dialog box as described here:

♦ **Computer**   Choose a computer to track in the Computer field.

♦ **Object**   Choose an object to track.

♦ **Counter**   Choose the events or processes that you want to track for the object. To get a description of each counter, click the Explain button, and then click the counter in question.

10

In the lower field, you can change the color, width, and style of the lines used to chart the event. The Scale field is where you change the vertical height of the chart. Click Add to start tracking the event on the chart. You can continue to add other events or click Cancel to close the box.

At any time you can change chart options by choosing Edit Chart Line from the Edit menu. You can also clear the current information by choosing Clear Display, or select a charted option in the lower field and remove it by choosing Delete from Chart.

Saving Charts and Exporting Information

You can save the chart setup you create for future use. This lets you create an array of charting options to track your system under various conditions. For example, you might want to set up charting options to track CGI events, then save the chart with the name CGI. The File menu has the following options that let you save Performance Monitor information:

♦ **New Chart** Select this option to create a new chart and clear any existing settings. You might also consider editing an existing file rather than creating all new settings.

♦ **Save Chart Settings As** Select this option from the File menu to save the current settings. After naming the chart, you can choose Save Chart Settings to save any future changes.

♦ **Save Workspace** Use this option to save chart, log, alert, and reports options in the same file.

♦ **Export to Chart** Select option to save information as comma- or tab-delimited; the information can then be read into spreadsheet or database programs for further analysis.

Logging Options

Choose Log from the View menu to switch to the logging mode. Logging lets you record information to a file for later viewing. The information you capture can be from the same objects and counters used in the Chart mode. You can capture information from multiple systems and create files that extend over long periods of time by appending new data to the files.

♦ To open an existing log settings file, choose Open from the File menu and specify the file you want to view. To create a new log file, choose New Log Settings from the File menu.

♦ To add objects to a log, choose Add To Log from the Edit menu or click the + button. In the dialog box that appears, follow a procedure similar to the one described earlier in this chapter to add options to the log file. Choose Save Log Settings As from the File menu to save the log options.

♦ To start logging, choose Log from the Options menu and type a name for the log file. If you use an existing file, data is appended to it. Choose either Manual Update or Periodic Update in the Update Time box. If you choose Periodic Update, you can set the interval for the updates. Click the Start button to start logging.

♦ If you want to stop logging, choose Log from the Options menu and click Stop Log.

Alerts

When alerts are set, you can let the Performance Monitor do all the work of tracking events on your servers. The procedure for adding alerts is similar to adding chart or log options, except that you need to set high and low threshold values. Choose Add to Alert from the Edit menu to display the following dialog box:

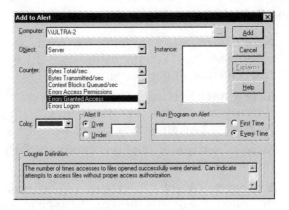

Once again, be sure to click the Explain button to view a description of the events that are selected in the Counter field.

Follow these steps to set alerts:

1. Choose a computer, object, and counter in the appropriate fields.

2. In the Alert If field, choose Over or Under, then enter a threshold value in the field.

3. In the Run Program on Alert, enter the name of a custom program that will run when the threshold value is met. Also click First Time or Every Time, depending on whether the program should run only once or every time the threshold is met.

   You can continue adding other alerts or click the Done button to exit the dialog box. A list of selected counters appears in the Alert Legend box at the bottom of the Performance Monitor window; alerts (if any) appear in the Alert Log area.

10

When counters exceed the threshold values you set, the date and time of the event are recorded in the Alert window. One thousand events are recorded before the oldest events are discarded. If you are monitoring a remote computer and the computer shuts down, an alert occurs and a comment is added to the alert log. You can save alert log selections by choosing Save Alert Settings As from the File menu.

Reports

The Report view lets you set up a reporting format for values that change constantly. The information is displayed in a columnar format; you can adjust reporting intervals, print a snapshot of the information at any time, or export the data to another file. You can access and edit your reports using the Open and Save options on the File menu, as discussed earlier.

1. To build a report, choose Add to Report from the Edit menu.
2. Specify a computer, object, and counter as described previously.
3. Click Add to add more counters, or click Cancel to close the box.
4. A list of selected objects appears in the reporting area; the values are updated as the system changes. You can save your report for future use by choosing Save Report Settings As from the File menu.

What to Do with the Data

Once you've collected data (probably more than you could ever assimilate), you can use it to track illicit activities, or activities that might be degrading the performance of your system. You can also use the data to justify the need for new equipment to budget directors.

Print the information that you have logged, or upload it into appropriate applications that can help you sift through the information and come up with meaningful numbers. You can choose the Export option from the File menu to export the data to comma- (*.CSV) or tab- (*.TSV) delimited files. These files separate data with commas or tabs; they can be read by the majority of spreadsheet and database programs on the market, including Microsoft Excel and Microsoft Access.

Network Monitoring

The Network Monitor utility lets you monitor network traffic on a computer. The utility can only be used to track packets of information that are sent from or received by the computer where you are running the program.

The Network Monitor is a diagnostic tool for monitoring local area networks, locating a downed server, or locating bottlenecks on the network. It provides a graphical display of network statistics. The Network Monitor is pictured in Figure 10-6.

The layout of the Network Monitor may look confusing, but notice that it contains four separate windows that each hold information:

◆ Information about the host that sent a frame onto the network

◆ Information about the host that received the frame

◆ The protocols used to send the frame

◆ The data, or a portion of the message being sent

The address is a unique hexadecimal (or base-16) number that identifies a computer on the network; it's the "built-in" hardware address assigned to every network interface card. To discover the hexadecimal address of a system, type one of the commands shown next, replacing *IPaddress* with the IP address of the computer in question, or *computername* with the NetBIOS name of the computer.

NBTSTAT -A *IPaddress*

NBTSTAT -a *computername*

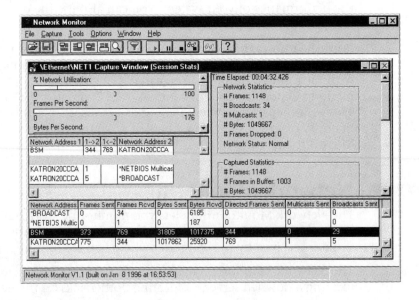

The Network
Monitor
Figure 10-6.

The Network Monitor uses a "capture" process to gather information about the network for a period of time. During this time period, information about all the frames transmitted over the network is recorded and made available in the Network Monitor display. You can view information in the graphical display as it occurs, and you can save the captured information to files for later viewing.

When capturing information, you can set filters to view only the information that is essential for detecting intrusions or other problems. For example, you can filter by protocol to view frames related to a particular command that a hacker might be using. You can also filter by network address to capture frames from specific computers on your network. That lets you track the activities of a known hacker. Up to four specific address pairs can be monitored. An address pair includes the addresses of two computers that are communicating with one another. You can also filter by data patterns, which lets you capture only frames that have a specific pattern of ASCII or hexadecimal data. You can also specify how many bytes of data into the frame that the pattern must occur.

You can also set *triggers*, which are conditions that must be met before an action occurs. For example, you can set a trigger that starts capturing if a pattern (such as a code or sequence used by a hacker) is found, or you can set a trigger to stop the capture of data.

Note that display filters are also available. You can use them to view information that has already been captured.

Because the Network Monitor captures a large amount of information that you may not need, you can create filters that prevent it from capturing specific types of frames. You can also set triggers that start a predesignated action when an event occurs on the network, such as when the buffer space is close to being full or when frames might be corrupted.

The Network Monitor requires a network adapter that supports what is usually called "promiscuous mode." In this mode, a network adapter passes all the frames that it detects on the network to the network software, regardless of the frame's destination address.

You can use Network Monitor Agent services on other Windows NT computers to capture statistics on those computers and have them sent to your Network Monitor computer. You can install the Network Monitor Agent by opening the Networks utility in the Control Panel and clicking the Services tab.

See the Network Monitor's help system for more information on how to set up and use its information-gathering tools. With proper use, you can monitor the traffic of intruders or users engaged in unauthorized activities.

Network Monitor Security

You should be aware that the Windows NT Network Monitor only captures the frames sent to or from the computer where you are running the utility. It will also display statistics for the network segment that the computer is attached to, such as broadcast frames, network utilization, and total bytes received.

To protect a network from unauthorized use of Network Monitor installation, the Network Monitor provides password protections and the ability to detect other installations of Network Monitor on the local segment of the network. The passwords can prevent someone at a Windows NT Server computer that is running System Management Server from connecting with the computer and running the Network Monitor on that computer.

You use the Monitoring Agent icon in the Control Panel to change the passwords for Network Monitor or Network Monitor Agent.

If other users run a copy of Network Monitor on their computers, they could use it to watch packets on the network and capture valuable information. Network monitor will detect other Network Monitor installations and display the information about them, such as the name of the computer, user, adapter address, and whether the utility is running, capturing, or transmitting information.

NOTE: Unfortunately, Network Monitor can only detect the existence of another version of Network Monitor. It cannot detect third-party monitoring software and/or equipment.

Auditing

Auditing is critical to maintaining the security of your servers and networks. The Windows NT Auditing system lets you track events that occur on individual servers related to security policies, system events, and application events. The auditing system produces logs that you can view with the Event Viewer. With this system, you can track activities performed by authorized users as well as by users who have gained unauthorized access through another user's account.

NOTE: Auditing is a practice that requires strict controls and procedures. This section shows you the tools you can use for auditing. If you are interested in developing proper guidelines, policies, and procedures for auditing, refer to the classic book *Windows NT 3.5, Guidelines for Security, Audit, and Control*, a Microsoft Press publication developed as a joint research project by Citibank N.A., Coopers & Lybrand, the Institute of Internal Auditors, and Microsoft Corporation. Copyright 1994.

There are two types of auditing that you can track with the auditing tools included in Windows NT:

♦ **User Account Auditing** Tracks security events and places entries in the server's security log. You enable this option in the User Manager for Domains utility.

♦ **File System Auditing** Tracks file system events. You enable this option in the File Manager (Windows NT 3.51) or in the Properties sheet for a drive (Windows NT 4.0).

Both of these options are discussed at greater length at the end of this chapter. Also see the section called "The Missing Auditor Account" if you are interested in designating a specific person or group as an auditor.

You must have Administrator rights to set auditing features. Once auditing is enabled, you use the Event Viewer to view the events that have been audited. The Event Viewer is accessible in the Administrative Tools group.

CAUTION: Auditing can consume a large amount of processor time and disk space. The more users you track, the more your hard disk will crank away, recording those events. To keep overhead down, enable auditing only when you suspect that malicious activities are occurring or you need to track system usage for marketing purposes. Make sure that unauthorized users don't have access to the *servername*\System32 directory where auditing information is stored.

Setting Up User Account Auditing

To enable user account auditing, choose Audit from the Policies menu in the User Manager for Domains utility. The Audit Policy dialog box appears, as shown in Figure 10-7. Click the Audit These Events button to enable the auditing system to track the success or failure of the following events. Suggested settings are shown in Figure 10-7 and described in the following list, but keep in mind that tracking all the events will consume quite a lot of resources. You must determine the best settings for your system. Also, you don't need to continuously track events; you should enable them when you think your system is under attack.

♦ **Logon and Logoff** A user has logged on or off, or made a network connection. Track failures to record possible unauthorized attempts to log on. (Tracking a successful logon may be unnecessary for your environment and will rapidly fill the security log.)

♦ **File and Object Access** A user has accessed a directory, file, or printer that was set for auditing. Once again, track failures only to detect attempted unauthorized access.

Windows NT Security Handbook

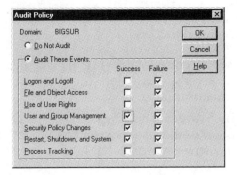

The Audit
Policy dialog
box
Figure 10-7.

♦ **Use of User Rights** A user has exercised a user right. Track failures for best results.

♦ **User and Group Management** A user account has been created or changed in some way. Track both success and failure to properly log when new accounts are created, changed, and deleted.

♦ **Security Policy Changes** A change has been made to the User Rights, Audit, or Trust Relationships policies. Once again, track both success and failure to properly log all security policy changes.

♦ **Restart, Shutdown, and System** A user has restarted or shut down the computer, or an event has occurred affecting system security or the security log. These events will probably not rapidly fill your Audit logs, so you can enable both success and failure.

♦ **Process Tracking** Records detailed tracking information for such events as program activation and exits. Enable these options when you need to track events in detail if you believe your system is under attack.

Be sure to choose only the events that you really need to track. If you track too many events, the security log file will fill up rapidly and your hard disk will work overtime to keep up with event logging. You can set the maximum size of these logs in the Event Viewer, as described later.

NOTE: The auditing system only tells you what user accounts were used for the audited events. If someone has misappropriated an account, you might wrongly think the owner of that account is responsible for unauthorized activities. In addition, only files and directories in NTFS partitions can be audited.

Setting Up File System Auditing

To enable file system auditing in Windows NT 3.5, open the File Manager and choose Auditing from the Security menu. In Windows NT 4.0, you right-click a drive or folder object to open its Context menu, then choose Properties. When the Properties dialog box appears, choose Security and then click the Auditing button. In either case, a Directory Auditing dialog box similar to this one appears:

```
Directory Auditing                                           ×
 Directory:    C:\Transfer                              OK
 ☐ Replace Auditing on Subdirectories
 ☑ Replace Auditing on Existing Files                  Cancel
 Name:
 ▓ Administrators                                       Add...
                                                        Remove
                                                        Help

 ┌ Events to Audit ─────────────────────┐
                            Success   Failure
 Read                         ☐        ☐
 Write                        ☐        ☐
 Execute                      ☐        ☐
 Delete                       ☐        ☐
 Change Permissions           ☑        ☑
 Take Ownership               ☑        ☑
```

NOTE: To audit files you must set the option called File and Object Access in the Audit Policy dialog box, as shown in Figure 10-7.

File System Auditing is granular in that you can choose to track a specific user's use of a specific directory or file. This helps minimize the events that are tracked and cuts down on the use of system resources such as the disk space required to store the auditing events.

You first add a user account or group account that you want to edit by clicking the Add button. Then you click the events you want to audit for that user or group in the lower box. Auditing changes are applied to directories, subdirectories, and files in the following ways:

♦ **Directory only** Clear both the Replace Auditing on Subdirectories and the Replace Auditing on Existing Files options.

♦ **Directory and its files only** Enable Replace Auditing on Existing Files.

♦ **Directory and subdirectories only, not files** Enable Replace Auditing on Subdirectories.

♦ **Directories, subdirectories, and all files** Enable both the Replace Auditing on Subdirectories and the Replace Auditing on Existing Files options.

To view file system events, open the Event Viewer and select the Security page. To save events to external files if you need to archive them or open them in another application, choose Save As from the Log menu.

Using the Event Viewer

The Event Viewer is the tool you use to look at system events and security auditing events. You start the Event Viewer by choosing its option in the Administrative Tools group. Then choose System, Security, or Application from the Log menu to view three different sets of events. The Event Viewer security log is pictured here:

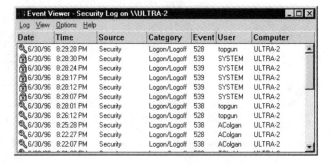

You can also choose the following options from the View menu:

♦ **All Events** View all the events.

♦ **Filter Events** Choose the events you want to look at based on dates, times, type of event, categories, and other information.

♦ **Newest First** View the newest events at the top of the list.

♦ **Oldest First** View the oldest events at the top of the list.

♦ **Find** Find a specific event.

To look at detailed information on any event, double-click the event. You can save events to external files if you need to archive them or open them in another application by choosing Save As from the Log menu.

There is an option for clearing the Event Log. Before doing so, be sure to save the logs for future reference.

Periodically view the Event Log, because it can indicate intrusions or other unauthorized activities. The Performance Monitor can alert you of possible intrusions, as discussed earlier, but the Event Log can provide you with details of events related to intrusions. You can sort the list in the Event Viewer based on the date and time of the event, its source, category, event number, user, or computer. Simply click the header name above a column to sort on that column. This can help you group events according to the user or the computer that is the source of those events.

The Event Record

If you double-click on any event in the Security Log, you'll see a dialog box similar to this one:

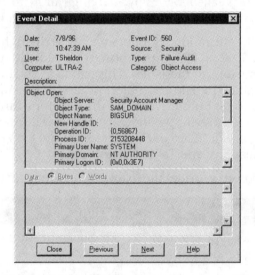

The Event Detail dialog box provides such information as the time of the event, the ID of the subject that caused the event, the name of the component or module that submitted the event, the ID of the event itself, the success or failure of the event, and the category of the event.

♦ **System Event**   An event that affects the entire system or the Audit Log

♦ **Logon/Logoff**   Successful or unsuccessful logons and logoffs, and the type of logon requested (e.g., interactive, network, service)

♦ **Object Access**   Successful and unsuccessful accesses to protected objects

♦ **Privilege Use**   Successful and unsuccessful attempts to use privileges, including a special case when privileges are assigned

♦ **Account Management**   Events describing high-level changes to the Security Account database (creating a new user or changing a user account)

♦ **Policy Change** Events that describe high-level changes in security policy, such as the assignment of privileges or changes in the audit policy

♦ **Detailed Tracking** Events providing detailed tracking of subject (user or process) activities

Techniques for Auditing

There are a number of tricks you can use in the auditing system. One was mentioned in Chapter 8: renaming the Administrator account to a name that is hard to guess, then creating a fake Administrator account with the name "Administrator." Make sure the latter account has no rights. Intruders will attempt to break into this account since it has an obvious name. You can track failed logons by enabling Failure for the Logon and Logoff option from the Audit Policy menu, as shown in Figure 10-7.

Another technique is to remove the Write right from executable files (files with .EXE or .DLL extensions); then audit attempts to write or change the permissions to these files. This will help you detect virus attacks. You need to set Failure for File and Object Access on the Audit Policy menu, then you need to set Failure events for the directories and files you want to track as described previously under "Setting up File System Auditing." Choose a directory or file to track, then set Failure for Write, Delete, Change Permissions, and Take Ownership.

Microsoft* provides the following recommendations for auditing various events:

Threat	Action
Hacker-type break-in using random passwords	Enable failure auditing for logon and logoff events.
Break-in using stolen password	Enable success auditing for logon and logoff events. The log entries will not distinguish between the real users and the phony ones. What you are looking for here is unusual activity on user accounts, such as logons at odd hours or on days when you would not expect any activity.
Misuse of administrative privileges by authorized users	Enable success auditing for use of user rights; for user and group management; for security policy changes; and for restart, shutdown, and system events. (Keep in mind that Windows NT does not normally audit the use of the Backup Files And Directories and the Restore Files And Directories rights, due to the great number of events that would be recorded.)

Threat	Action
Virus outbreak	Enable success and failure write access auditing for program files such as files with .EXE and .DLL extensions. Enable success and failure process tracking auditing. Run suspect programs and examine the security log for unexpected attempts to modify program files or creation of unexpected processes. (Be aware that these auditing settings generate a large number of event records during routine system use. You should use them only when you are actively monitoring the system log.)
Improper access to sensitive files	Enable success and failure auditing for file- and object-access events, and then enable success and failure auditing of read and write access by suspect users or groups for sensitive files.
Improper access to printers	Enable success and failure auditing for file- and object-access events, and then enable success and failure auditing of print access by suspect users or groups for the particular printers you want to audit.

Source: Microsoft Windows NT Resource Kit, Version 3.51 Update, page 36.

Securing the Audit System

You should take care to protect the Audit Log files that are stored in the *systemroot*\System32\CONFIG directory; their names are shown next. A rogue administrator might perform some activity, then delete the files to cover his tracks. It is also possible, but very difficult, to change entries in the files. A more likely scenario is that someone would just delete them.

- ♦ APPEVENT.EVT   Application events log
- ♦ SECEVENT.EVT   Security events log
- ♦ SYSEVENT.EVT   System events log

One thing you can do to ensure that only authorized users access the auditing system is to designate an auditor described later under "The Missing Auditor Account." Normally, on Windows NT Server, the Everyone group has Read rights to these files, the Server Operators group has Change rights, and the Administrators group has Full Access rights. In addition, the System account has Full Access rights. By following the procedure described in the later section, you can ensure that only an auditor has access to the files.

Managing the Audit Logs

If you choose to audit too many events, the Audit Logs will fill rapidly and you will find it difficult to review the information in them. This eventuality might lead you to clear the security log more often than is practical and cause you to miss important security events. Even if you archive the logs before clearing them, you won't be able to correlate events that take place over extended periods of time. For example, if you were tracking the activities of a particular user, you would normally sort the Event Log by user. If you had recently archived and cleared the Event Log, you might not be able to group and correlate the important events generated by this user (unless you upload them to another file).

Choose Log Settings from the Log menu to access the Event Log Settings dialog box:

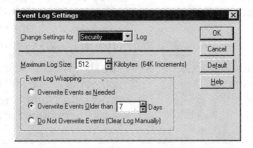

You need to carefully evaluate the options in this dialog box. First, select the log you want to work with in the top field, then change settings in the lower fields. You can increase the size of the file to log more events before the file fills up, then you can set options that determine what happens when it does fill up.

These options are:

♦ **Overwrite Events as Needed** This option simply pushes the older events out of the log and writes in new events; it assumes you are continually monitoring and saving the log.

♦ **Overwrite Events Older than [ ] Days** This option lets you set which events will be overwritten, based on their age in days.

♦ **Do Not Overwrite Events (Clear Log Manually)** If you choose this option, the system stops when log files are full so that no new activities can take place without an auditing record.

To recover a system that stops because the security logs are full, first make sure you are on the list of users who are alerted to such events, as I mentioned earlier in this chapter. Restart the computer and log on as the user who has access to the auditing system. Use Event View to clear the events; it will give you a chance to save the existing information.

Exception Management

Surrenden Systems Solutions (**www.surrenss.co.uk**) produces exception management tools that provide unique monitoring and alerting for Windows NT auditing. The first package, NTWatch, provides real-time monitoring of user-definable events occurring in either the Security, System, or Application logs. The second NTPager takes the output from NTWatch and notifies people or groups of people about critical events via paging service messaging or digital SMS phone service. Both utilities are highly configurable. If a program can post an event to any three of the NT logs, then you can be notified within seconds of its happening.

The Missing Auditor Account

In some operating systems such as Novell NetWare, an Auditor account exists that is separate from the Administrator account. Once an auditor is assigned, that person can track all activities of the Administrator and has full control of the auditing logs. The Administrator cannot touch the auditor account or the auditing logs. Therefore, all activities of the Administrator can be tracked by an independent Auditor.

Windows NT does not have such an Auditor account, and to create one, you will need to treat the Administrator account as an Auditor account. All other administrators must then be assigned to lower-level administrative groups, such as Account Operators and Print Operators. Do not use the Administrators or Server Operators groups because anyone that is a member of these groups can change or delete the auditing logs. Only the Administrator, who will now be the Auditor, will have the rights and permissions allowed by these groups. Also, do not give any user or group the "Manage Auditing and Security Logs" right. The basic steps for creating an auditor are as follows:

1. Designate two or three people as Auditors.
2. Rename the Administrator account to "Auditor" or some obscure name to prevent detection.
3. Remove all members of the Administrators and Sever Operators group and reassign them to custom management groups that do not have the right to change and delete the Audit Logs.
4. Gather the three new Auditors at the server and open the Properties dialog box for the Administrator account.

5. In the Password field, have Auditor 1 enter her password, then write that password on a card marked 1 and slip it into an envelope. The envelope will eventually go to a trusted party.

6. Have Auditors 2 and 3 do the same thing as Auditor 1.

7. Once the new password is entered, log on under the new account and test your setup.

As a test, go through this procedure using some low level account to make sure that everyone understands the procedure and that you can reopen the account by combining the parts of the password. In particular, don't use spaces in the password. If everything works, follow the procedure again with the real Auditor account and the real passwords.

Seal the envelope and give it to a trusted third party, such as the CEO of your company, or put it in a safe deposit box. If you're really paranoid, you could put each part of the password in separate safety deposit boxes with specific instructions about how they should be retrieved. From this point on, all high-level administration and monitoring of the auditing logs can only be done by the Auditors who must all be present to access the system. Granted, this procedure may seem a bit complex and may be unnecessary in your environment, but the basic procedure should give you an idea of what you need to do to set up an Auditor.

Keep in mind that the password you gave to the trusted party might be compromised or one of the Auditors may manage to obtain the other parts of the password. To prevent unauthorized access to the account, make sure that no one can log on to it from the network (i.e., a private workstation). This is good practice anyway, because it means that all administration must take place at the console of the server where other people are presumably present to monitor the activities of that person. To revoke network access for Auditors (and Administrators), open the User Manager and choose Rights from the Policies menu, then remove Administrators and Everyone from the "Access this Computer from the Network" right.

Note that removing Everyone will mean that no one can access your servers from the network. You will need to reassign the "Access this Computer from the Network" right to the custom groups that should have network access.

CHAPTER 11

Fault Tolerance and Data Protection

Your job as a system and network administrator is to make sure that information is both available to users and protected from corruption or loss. Attacks on your system by hackers, unauthorized users, or viruses can destroy your well-laid plans. Just as harmful is a system failure due to natural causes or overburdened systems. A downed system costs you more than frustration: it may cost your business hundreds or thousands of dollars in lost revenue and create a lot of customer dissatisfaction. It may also cost you your job. This chapter covers five topics that directly or indirectly deal with protecting the data on your servers:

♦ Protecting operating system files

♦ Providing fault tolerance with disk mirroring and disk striping

♦ Providing fault tolerance and data availability by replicating data to other systems

♦ Backing up data to tapes with the Windows NT Backup utility

♦ Addressing and solving power problems

Protecting the Operating System

A server may crash because of a hardware problem or because a malicious user or hacker has managed to corrupt or destroy files. A virus or Trojan horse program may also have attacked the system. The information presented here can help you quickly recover a system from such a disaster.

The Emergency Repair Disk

A critical part of the recovery process is the *Emergency Repair Disk* (ERD), which helps you recover from corrupted operating system files and systems that won't properly boot. You can create the disk when you first install Windows NT Server or at any time after the installation by typing RDISK in the Run dialog box. The following menu appears:

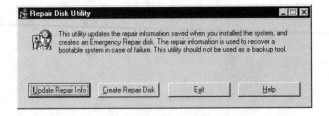

Notice that you can choose to create a new repair disk or update an existing one.

Here is what the Emergency Repair Disk can do:

- Repair bad Registry data

- Restore corrupted or missing files on the system partition

- Replace a corrupt *Kernel*, which is the core of the Windows NT operating system

- Replace a bad boot sector for a FAT partition

However, the repair disk is not a complete solution for protecting your system. It cannot repair any unmountable partitions except for the system partition, which is always the C drive on *x*86-based computers. It also does not replace a damaged NTFS boot sector or fully restore the Registry. You must use the Backup utility to create fully recoverable backup sets for your systems.

11

Fatal Errors and System Shutdowns

The System option on the Control Panel displays options for controlling how Windows NT starts and for managing its behavior in the event of a fatal system error. Fatal system errors can occur due to virus infections or because a Trojan horse halts the system. You may see the dreaded "blue screen of death" in this event. For example, a Trojan horse program might either cause some damage or ship information to an unknown e-mail address, then crash the system to hide its tracks. You might incorrectly assume that the system has crashed due to a hardware problem or because a cosmic particle crashed into a critical memory location.

When a fatal system error occurs, the system does the following:

- Writes an event to the system log

- Sends an administrative alert

- Writes debug information to the file *systemroot*\MEMORY.DMP

- Automatically reboots the system

You can enable or disable any of these options from within the System dialog box. Because the MEMORY.DMP file is overwritten by default, you should copy it to another location after restarting your system. The file contains information that helps you determine the cause of the problem, but it requires evaluation by a qualified technical representative. Contact Microsoft or a certified representative for such an evaluation.

If the system fails to boot after a fatal error, choose Last Known Good Configuration during startup. This option will help you recover after you've installed defective drivers or set options that lock up the operating system.

Protecting the Registry

The Windows NT Server operating system stores critical operating information in the Registry. Security databases and system information are stored in files that are located in the *systemroot*\System32\CONFIG directory. This information is also automatically backed up to the *systemroot*\REPAIR directory; you can manually update some of it to the Emergency Repair Disk.

CAUTION: The Registry must be protected from network users who could change its contents in malicious ways. See Appendix F for details.

However, using the repair information is not a replacement for backing up the Registry using the Backup utility, which I'll discuss later. You must use Backup to save all of the latest Registry information. During the backup operation, select the Backup Local Registry option in the Backup Information dialog box to automatically include a copy of the local Registry files in the backup set. You must use a tape drive attached to the primary domain controller to back up the Registry.

Because parts of the Registry are always in use, a completely accurate backup of the Registry is hard to obtain. Two programs that do a good job of backing up are Registry Backup (REGBACK.EXE) and Registry Restore (REGREST.EXE). They are available in the Windows NT Resource Kit (sold separately by Microsoft). REGBACK, for example, will back up parts of the Registry even if they are opened by the operating system.

Another method for backing up the Registry is to use the Save Key command in the Registry Editor. This is essentially a manual backup method that must be performed for each key in the Registry. Refer to Registry Help for more information on this method.

Recovering a Damaged Operating System

Your operating system may become damaged because of a disk failure or malicious activity by a hacker or virus. To recover a damaged system, you can either reinstall the operating system or use a recovery process that includes restoring system configuration information from an Emergency Repair Disk (ERD). The second option requires some advance preparation to get your system back up and running as soon as possible. Options that will help you prepare for a system failure include the following:

- Use two separate drives in your server, one for the operating system and one for data. Then if the operating system is corrupted, you can quickly get it back online without needing to restore all the data as well.

- Use the Backup utility to keep separate backup sets for the operating system and the data. In the event of a system failure, you might need to restore only the operating system information.

- Any time you make a change to the system configuration, run the **RDISK** command both before and after making the changes to update your Emergency Repair Disk. You might want to keep two disks with "before" and "after" information.

- In the event that you need to recover a failed system, restart it and use the Emergency Repair Disk to recover part of the operating system. Then reboot and use Backup to restore system partition information.

11

Keep in mind that the ERD does not contain a full backup of the Registry, nor can it fully restore the system partition information. Use the ERD to get the system back to a point where you can reboot it and restore the remainder of your operating system from backups. The backups include hardware-specific driver information. To recover the rest of the Registry, choose the Restore Local Registry option in the Backup program.

One thing you can do in advance to ensure a speedy recovery from a system failure is to set up a "recovery drive," an extra disk that has the Windows NT operating system installed on it. It can be attached to the server, but should be powered off during normal operations to prevent accidental or intentional modification by hackers. You can also use drives with removable disks as portable drives that you move from one server to the next.

On the recovery drive, install Windows NT Server and configure a local paging file and tape driver. Create an Emergency Repair Disk for this configuration and make sure the BOOT.INI file contains a pointer to the recovery disk drive. In the event of a system failure, connect and/or start up the drive, and restart the computer using the Emergency Repair Disk you created for it. Then restore the latest system configuration and Registry information to this disk from your backup sets.

Procedures exist for repairing individual components of the operating system that may be corrupt. These procedures should be used with caution but, in some cases, may provide quick-fix solutions to specific problems. These procedures are available from Microsoft or certified Microsoft representatives. You can also search Microsoft's Knowledge Base, a collection of information about problems and solutions. Knowledge Base is available online at CompuServe or by visiting **www.microsoft.com/KB/**.

Fault Tolerance in Windows NT Server

Fault tolerance refers to the protection of systems against potential hardware failures, disasters, virus infections, hacker attacks, and other risks. You protect data by creating redundant copies, usually in real time, as well as backing it up to magnetic tape and/or optical disk systems.

You can use the following methods to protect your data.

Mirrored Disks In this configuration, two hard disks (or sets of hard disks) are used, and data is simultaneously written to and read from each disk, as pictured on the left in Figure 11-1. If one of the disks fails, the other can provide data to users until the mirrored set is restored. Notice on the right in Figure 11-1 that the disk controller can be duplicated to guard against failure of this component as well.

Stripe Sets with Parity In this scheme, as pictured in Figure 11-2, data is written evenly over an array of disks rather than to one disk. Parity information is also written to the disks. The parity information is used to rebuild the data should one of the disks in the set fail.

A typical disk configuration for a data striping set is pictured in Figure 11-3.

Tape Backup with Off-site Archiving Here data is copied to multiple sets of tapes (or optical disks) and carried to safe remote sites for archiving. Backup methods are covered later in this chapter.

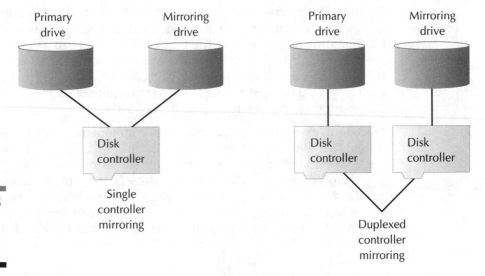

Disk mirroring and disk duplication
Figure 11-1.

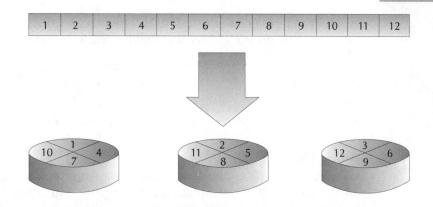

Data striping spreads data evenly across multiple drives to improve performance and reliability.
Figure 11-2.

11

Backup Power   Windows NT also supports uninterruptible power supplies and includes a program that can detect power failures and provide advance warning before the UPS runs out of backup power. Power issues are covered under "Power Problems and Solutions" at the end of this chapter.

TIP: After creating or changing any disk configuration, choose the Configuration/Save command from the Partition menu to save the disk configuration information to a floppy disk.

Disk Mirroring

Disk mirroring, as pictured in Figure 11-1, is a continuous backup method. Data is written to two disks at the same time. Because either disk in the set can continue providing data to users if the other fails, you can avoid the downtime and expense of recovering data from backup sets. Disk duplexing is a disk-mirroring technique that also duplicates the hardware channel to avoid downtime caused by the need to replace a disk controller.

Keep in mind that disk mirroring is a hardware backup technique that you use to recover from disk failures. You still need to back up data to protect

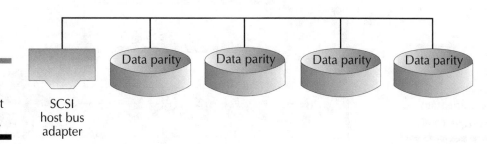

Disk configuration for a stripe set
Figure 11-3.

information from corruption. If information is corrupted, it is stored in that corrupted state on both disks, and you'll need to restore from backup sets.

TIP: A mirrored set improves disk read performance because data can be read from either disk in the set.

Setting Up Disk Mirroring

You use the Disk Administrator in the Administrative Tools group to set up disk mirroring. The Disk Administrator is pictured in Figure 11-4. Notice that Disk 1 and Disk 2 are two separate drives of the same size that are mirrored. In the Disk Administrator, a purple band indicates mirrored drives, but in this picture you can see that both drives also have the same drive letter (E), which indicates that they are mirrored.

To create a mirrored disk set, you need to have two disks; each must have a free partition that is roughly the same size as the other one. Excess space on one of the disks is not used. You can mirror any existing partition, including the system and boot partitions, onto an available partition of another disk. The disks can use the same or different controllers. Follow these steps to build the mirrored disk set:

1. Install any new disks in your system that are required to create the mirrored disk set.

2. In the Disk Administrator, create partitions on the disk using the Create or Create Extended options from the Partition menu.

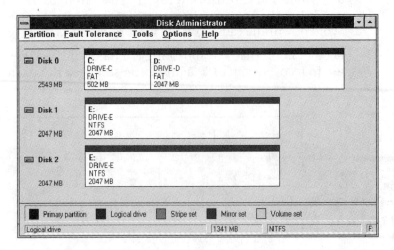

Mirrored disk
sets in the
Disk
Administrator
Figure 11-4.

3. Select a partition to duplicate, then hold down the CTRL key and click the partition on the second disk that will mirror the original.

4. Choose Establish Mirror from the Fault Tolerance menu.

A partition is created from the free space on each partition. If one disk is larger than another, its extra free space will go unused. Once the set is created, a single drive letter is assigned to all of the partitions and they are viewed as one drive by the operating system.

If an error occurs on one of the disks in the mirrored set, you need to first break the mirror, then replace the defective disk. While you are replacing the disk, the other disk can handle requests from users.

11

To break a mirrored set, first select one of the disks in the set, then choose the Break Mirror Set option from the Fault Tolerance menu. Confirm that you want to break the set. The remaining partition becomes a separate volume with its own drive letter. You then replace the defective disk and follow the preceding numbered steps to create a new mirrored set. The disk with existing data is automatically copied to the new disk to synchronize the new mirrored set.

Disk Striping

Disk striping in Windows NT lets you spread data over an array of up to 32 disks. The disks appear as a single volume to users. Striping divides the data at the byte level and interleaves the bytes over each disk. Parity information is also written to each disk partition in the volume to give a level of data protection that is equivalent to disk mirroring but requires less disk space and provides faster read performance.

Disk striping provides high performance, especially when users read data more than they write it. Writing to striped sets is slower than writing to mirrored sets, but if high-performance servers and drives are used, you won't notice.

Disk striping with parity for Windows NT Server requires a minimum of three disks to accommodate the way that parity information is striped across the disk set. Disks should be roughly the same size. Any extra space on partitions is not used.

How to Create Stripe Sets

To create a stripe set with parity, you must have three or more disks in the server. Follow these steps to create the stripe sets:

1. Install disks in your system for the stripe set. SCSI host adapters and drives are preferable.

2. Open the Disk Administrator, select the first free space for the stripe set, and then hold down the CTRL key and select free space on other disks.

3. Choose Create Stripe Set With Parity from the Fault Tolerance menu. The minimum and maximum sizes for the stripe set are displayed. Type a size and click OK.

The size you select is divided by the number of disks to create equal-sized unformatted partitions. The entire set is assigned a single drive letter, and you can then format the stripe set as a single disk. If you want to remove a stripe set, select it in the Disk Administrator, then choose Delete from the Partition menu.

Security Through Directory Replication

Directory replication is a fault-tolerant strategy for duplicating data in real time from a Windows NT Server computer to another computer. You can replicate data for backup purposes or to make it more easily accessible to people at remote locations. In Figure 11-5, the Windows NT Server computer that holds the master data is called the export server; it replicates data to import servers.

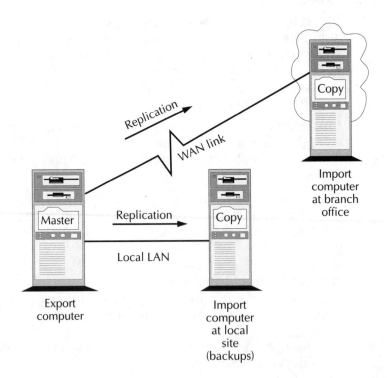

Windows NT
Server
replication
strategies
Figure 11-5.

In this setup, replication is used as follows:

♦ The master data on the export server is on the same LAN as administrators or users who update the information. The LAN provides a high-throughput link to the data.

♦ An import server on the local LAN acts as a backup device. It imports the data and stores it at a different location to protect it from local disasters that might bring down the export computer.

♦ Import servers can also be located at remote sites and branch offices to provide data to users at those sites. Users can access data locally rather than accessing the master data over the WAN link.

11

In the second case, users on the local LAN can access either the computer holding the master data or the import computer that holds a copy. This provides *load balancing*. In the third case, replicating data to the branch office on a periodic basis uses much less bandwidth than if multiple users access the master database over the WAN link.

Replication takes place automatically as files are added to the master directory or as information changes. It is necessary to maintain only the master copy of the information. The master copy can be exported to multiple import computers; you can change these exported copies by changing the master. In addition, information can be exported across Windows NT domains.

Keep the following points in mind:

♦ Export servers have a default export path called C:*systemroot*\\System32\\REPL\\EXPORT that looks like this:

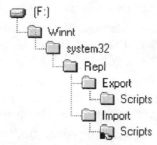

Files placed in this directory are automatically exported. You can also attach subdirectories to the path.

♦ The Import directory is where imported files are automatically placed on import servers.

♦ Any number of subdirectories can be replicated, with available memory being the only limit; up to 32 subdirectory levels can exist in the replicated directory.

♦ The Replicator local group on the export server should have Full Control permissions on any directories that are exported.

♦ Any computer running Windows NT Server can be set up as an export server. Windows NT Workstation computers cannot export but can import.

Setting Up Replication

The steps for setting up replication services involve creating a special user account, assigning that account to the replicator service, creating the subdirectories you want to export, and designating the directories for export.

Creating a Replication Account

1. You must create a user account that the replicator services can log on with. You create this account by following these steps: Start the User Manager for Domains and create a domain user with a name like RepAdmin. Make the new user a member of the Domain Users, Backup Operators, and Replicator groups, and set the following values:

   ♦ Select "Password Never Expires."

   ♦ Clear "User Must Change Password At Next Logon."

   ♦ Clear "User Can Not Change Password."

   ♦ Clear "Account Disabled."

   ♦ Allow all hours for logon.

   ♦ Do not define a user profile or logon script.

2. In the User Manager for Domains, choose User Rights from the Policies menu. Select Show Advanced User Rights and grant the Replicator group the Logon as a Service right.

3. Start the Server Manager utility, then select the server and choose Services from the Computer menu. A list appears of all services running on the server. Select the Directory Replicator service and choose Startup.

4. Specify the startup type to be Automatic and mark the default logon as This Account, then type in the name of the user account you created, such as RepAdmin. Also type in the password you specified when creating the account.

If you've set everything up correctly, you'll see a dialog box similar to this one:

Setting Up the Export Computer

11

This section describes the steps for setting up master directory replication on an export server. To set up replication, follow these steps:

1. Start the Server Manager and double-click the icon of the computer that will be the replication export server. The Properties dialog box appears for that server.

2. Click the Replication button to open a Directory Replication dialog box similar to this one:

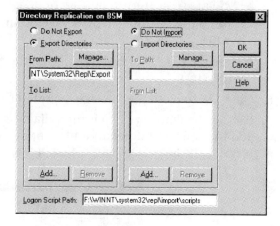

3. Click Export Directories to enable export replication on this server.

4. In the From Path field, use the default path, only changing it if absolutely necessary.

5. Click the Manage button to display the Manage Exported Directories dialog box:

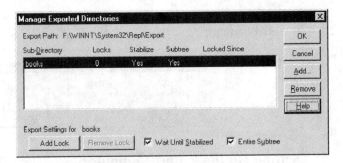

You can set the following options in this box:

♦ Click Add to add a directory. You must have previously created the directory as a subdirectory of *systemroot*\System32\REPL\EXPORT. This is because Add does not create directories; it only adds them to the list so you can set options.

♦ Click Add Lock or Remove Lock to add or remove a lock on the selected subdirectory. (A lock prevents the subdirectory from being replicated, either temporarily or permanently.)

♦ Enable Wait Until Stabilized to prevent replication until at least two minutes after any changes have occurred in a subdirectory or to a file.

♦ Enable Entire Subtree to replicate the entire subtree of the selected directory.

6. Click OK to close the Manage Exported Directories dialog box.

7. Back at the Directory Replication dialog box, click the Add button to add to the To List domains and computers that will serve as import servers. The Select Domain dialog box appears as shown here:

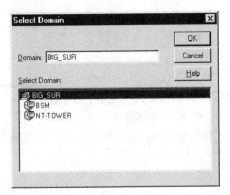

The To List is initially blank; exported directories are automatically replicated to the local domain. Adding a computer to the To List removes the automatic import status from the local domain.

8. Double-click a domain name to open its list of available computers, then click a computer and click OK.

9. Back at the Directory Replication box, click OK, then click OK again to close the Properties dialog box.

The Directory Replicator service is started if this is the first directory replication set up on the server. Now you are ready to set up importing on another computer, as I'll describe next.

11

Setting Up an Import Computer

You can import files to either Windows NT Server computers or Windows NT Workstation computers. You can also set up importing on a Windows NT Server computer that is already set up to export. A Windows NT Server computer can also import subdirectories from itself. This importing provides a sort of local backup and set of replicated files that users can access instead of accessing the master files.

Setting up import directories is simple. You do not need to create import subdirectories, because they are automatically created the first time the subdirectory is imported. Follow these steps to set up importing:

1. On the import server, make sure that the Directory Replicator service is assigned to the logon account that you created under the section "Creating a Replication Account" earlier in this chapter. Since the account is already created, you need to follow only steps 2 through 4 in that section.

2. In the Server Manager window, double-click the name of the computer that will operate as the import computer, then click the Replication button in the Properties dialog box that appears. A Directory Replication dialog box appears.

3. Click Import Directories, then type a new path in the To Path box if necessary. The default path list is appropriate in most cases.

4. To import subdirectories from a domain or computer, choose the Add button under Import Directories, then complete the Select Domain dialog box that appears.

5. Click the Manage button if you need to set a temporary or permanent lock on an import directory to prevent it from importing.

6. Click OK to exit the Directory Replication and Properties dialog boxes.

The From List is initially blank because the computer imports from the local domain. If you add a computer to the list, it no longer imports from the local domain, but from the computer you listed. Once you've set up the import computers, replication should begin; any changes to files in the export computer are replicated to the import computer at regular intervals.

Backing Up Data

It's essential to back up the data on your server's hard drives. There are a number of ways you can perform backups, including copying data to magnetic tape or optical disks, or by copying or replicating information to other systems.

However, the traditional method for backing up data is tape backup. Tapes are relatively inexpensive, which makes it economical to devise an archiving scheme where you store tapes permanently at safe locations, rather than reusing the tapes.

Before you can use the Backup utility included with Windows NT, you must install a tape drive and tape driver in your system. To load a tape driver, open the Tape Devices utility on the Control Panel and click the Drivers tab. Then click the Add button and choose a driver to install.

Here are some points to keep in mind:

♦ Back up the entire system regularly or whenever you make major changes to its software, directory structure, or configuration.

♦ Perform incremental backups to the files that have changed since you last made a major backup. If the information on your server changes constantly, you'll need to back up constantly.

♦ Store a duplicate backup set at an off-site location to protect the backups from local disasters such as fires, earthquakes, and floods.

♦ Schedule all of your backups during hours when fewer files are likely to be opened by users.

♦ Before you put your server into service, back it up, then try restoring the information to make sure everything works and that you are familiar with the process.

Locate the tape backup system on the server you need to back up if possible, rather than on a device connected elsewhere on the network. This will keep backup traffic off the network. However, you should still schedule backups after hours to keep them from affecting the speed at which the server is processing other tasks.

Choose your backup hardware wisely. Speed is an important consideration. If you need to restore your system, you'll want to get it up and running as soon as possible. The best performance is obtained if the device is directly attached to the apparatus you want to back up and restore. The primary tape-drive types used for server backup include quarter-inch cartridge (QIC), digital audio tape (DAT), and 8-mm cassette. High-capacity, high-performance tape drives generally use Small Computer System Interface (SCSI) controllers.

To make backups and restores easier, put your Windows NT Server operating system and data on separate partitions or physical disks. Then if one partition or disk gets corrupted or fails, you'll need to restore only that partition.

11

Backup Operators

By default, the Administrator and Backup Operators groups have the right to back up files, even though members of the group may not own the files they are backing up. Other users can back up any files that they own or that they are authorized to read. However, they cannot restore a file to a directory if they lack access to the directory or Write access to the file.

Since the Backup Operators group needs access to files that must be backed up and restored, members of this group have both Backup and Restore rights to read, change, and write any file. A hacker or intruder who gains access to the account could take advantage of these rights to steal files or gain further access into a system. Designate only trusted people as backup operators, and make sure their rights are limited to only those files and directories they need to back up. As an added precaution, you can log all backup operator activities in the Audit log.

Tape Security Issues

When you back up files on NTFS drives with the Backup utility, all the permissions, ownership rights, and audit flags associated with files can be written with files to tape. Files restored in an existing directory inherit the permissions of the directory, but if the directory has no special permissions, the file retains its previous permissions.

When a new tape backup set is created using the Windows NT Backup utility, the user making the backup can restrict access to the tape by choosing an option called Restrict Access to Owner or Administrator. This designates the tape as *secure* and allows only the system administrator, the tape creator, and a person with the Back Up Files And Directories right to access the tape. If you are the tape creator, you must be logged on to the computer where the tape was originally created.

However, you should keep in mind that this security method is a relatively low level of access restriction. Anyone who gets hold of the tapes and really wants to look at the information on them can use various utilities that are designed for that purpose.

When the tape is restored, the permissions are copied back with the files. The permissions do not restrict access to files on the tape, but keep in mind that the username and computer name are stored in the headers of the tape. A tape cannot be read by a person who has either a different username from the person who created the tapes or a different computer name from the computer that the tapes were created on.

Keep the following points in mind with regard to "securing" backup tapes:

♦ System administrators, tape creators, and users with the Back Up Files And Directories right are allowed to read, write, and erase the tape. Other users cannot modify or delete the tapes using the Backup utility; this restriction provides a level of security that prevents accidental deletion.

♦ If you need to transfer files between computers, do not set the Restrict Access to Owner or Administrator option. However, anyone can read, write, or erase such tapes.

♦ Tapes made with the Backup utility are not encrypted, do not provide a high level of security, and should be locked up to prevent theft by someone who would attempt to read tape data using non-Windows NT utilities.

Types of Backup

There are three types of backup: *normal*, *incremental*, and *differential*. The type of backup you choose depends on how many tapes you use, how often you want to back up, whether you are archiving tapes at a permanent storage location, and whether you rotate copies of your tapes off-site.

Normal Backup

A normal backup copies all the files selected for backup to a backup device and marks the files with a flag to indicate that they have been backed up. This method is the easiest to use and understand, because the most recent tape has the most recent backup. However, you'll need more tapes and more time for backup since all the selected files are backed up.

Incremental Backup

Incremental backup backs up only files that have been created or changed since the last normal or incremental backup. Files are marked with an archive flag so that they don't get backed up in the next backup unless they have been changed. This method requires that you create a normal backup set on a regular basis. If you need to restore from backup, you first restore the normal backup, then restore each incremental backup in order.

Differential Backup

With differential backup, you back up only files that were created or changed since the last normal (or incremental) backup. This method does not mark files with an archive flag to indicate that they have been backed up; consequently, they are included in a normal backup. If you implement this method, you should still create a normal backup on a regular basis. If you need to restore, first restore the normal backup, then restore the last differential backup tape.

Tape Rotation Methods

The number of backups you perform depends on the number of copies you want to keep, whether you want to keep on-site and off-site copies, and the age of the last backup (hours, days, weeks). You should consider a backup rotation method, which keeps incremental copies of backup data available.

The backup rotation method discussed here stores current and older data on a set of media that you can store in other locations, thus reducing the risk of losing your only backup set. If you have a five-day work week, you need 20 tapes. Increase the number of tapes if you have six- or seven-day work weeks. Here are the key points of this rotation method:

♦ Four tapes are labeled Monday, Tuesday, Wednesday, and Thursday. Use these tapes for incremental or differential backup.

♦ Four tapes are labeled Week 1, Week 2, Week 3, and Week 4. Create a complete backup to these tapes every Friday.

♦ Twelve tapes are labeled for each month of the year; back up to these tapes at the end of each month. These tapes are stored off-site.

♦ To create a duplicate backup set that you can carry to an off-site location, double the number of tapes.

 NOTE: This is only one example of a rotation method. You may need to alter this technique to fit your own needs.

With any backup system, you need to run a restoration test to ensure that your backup and restore procedures work. You might want to set aside spare servers and then run restoration tests using these servers on a regular basis.

Before dismissing the concept of spare servers as an unjustifiable expense, consider how much a downed server could cost you in dollars and in customer dissatisfaction.

The Windows NT Backup Utility

The Windows NT Backup utility can back up servers attached to the network from the central location where the tape drive is installed. You can back up and recover files on NTFS, HPFS, or FAT volumes, place multiple backup sets on a tape, span multiple tapes for a backup set or file, and create batch files to automate the backup process.

 NOTE: You can run the Backup program only on the system where the tape drive is installed, but you can back up almost any other type of computer on the network once you get the program running. You can back up the Registry and Event log files only on the local machine where the tape drive is located.

During a backup, you may be given the choice to back up local configuration information in the Registry. If you do back up the information, use care when restoring it. After restoring the Registry, you must reboot the computer; you will lose any configuration changes made since the last Registry backup.

If Backup encounters an open file, it normally backs up the last saved version of the file. During a restore, if a file on disk is newer than the file on tape, Backup asks for a confirmation to replace it.

To help you manage tapes in a backup set, each tape has the following information associated with it:

♦ A user-specified tape name

♦ An original tape-creation date plus the date and time that each backup set was created

♦ The computer name and the username of the user who created the tape

♦ A tape sequence number in the case of tape sets

The basic steps for using the Backup utility are described in the following sections. For detailed steps, refer to Backup's Help menus. To start the Backup utility, choose Backup in the Administrative Tools group. A Backup dialog box similar to this one appears:

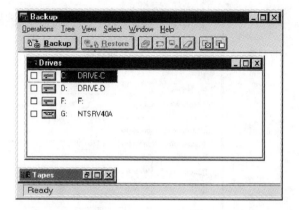

Backup and Restore Modes

There are two basic modes of operation: Backup and Restore. In Backup mode, you can select the drives, directories, and files you want to back up. In Restore mode, you can choose a previously created backup set to restore to your system. Remember the following:

♦ Choose Backup on the Operations menu to perform a backup, or choose Restore to restore previously backed up files.

♦ The Drive window shows a tree view of your hard drives. You can double-click on any drive to expand its view.

♦ Checkboxes appear in front of each drive, directory, or folder in the expanded view. When you check a box next to a drive, directory, or file, that entity is included in the backup or restore.

♦ If you click the checkbox for a drive, all the folders and files on the drive are included in the backup. However, you can open the drive and exclude any folders and files by disabling the corresponding checkbox.

♦ The Erase Tape, Re-tension Tape, and Format Tape options on the Operations menu are used to prepare physical tapes for use. Choose the Eject Tape option to remove a tape from the device. The tape is rewound in most cases. You might need to manually eject tapes with some drives.

♦ The Tree, View, and Window menus provide commands for manipulating windows and options, such as the status bar and toolbar in the Backup utility.

Once you've selected files to back up, you can choose the Backup command on the Operations menu. The following dialog box will appear:

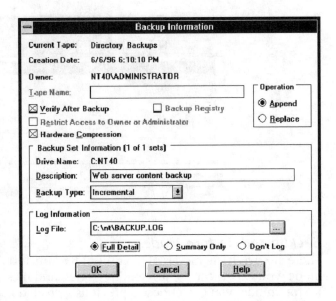

From the Backup Information box, you can do the following:

♦ In the Operation field, choose to append to existing backups or replace an older set with a new one.

♦ Secure the tape to limit access by checking the Restrict Access to Owner or Administrator box.

♦ Confirm backup accuracy by selecting the Verify After Backup checkbox.

♦ Back up the Windows NT Server Registry by selecting the Backup Registry checkbox.

♦ Compress the data on the tape media by selecting the Hardware Compression checkbox.

Logging Options   The log information field is where you specify that you want to create a log file for your backup. You type a log filename in the Log File field, then set one of the following options:

♦ **Full Detail** Log all operations information, including the names of all the files and directories that are backed up.

♦ **Summary Only** Log only the major operations, such as loading a tape, starting the backup, and failing to open a file.

♦ **Don't Log** Log no information.

After setting options in the dialog box, click the OK button. The Backup Status dialog box appears, and you can click OK again to begin the backup.

Restoring from Backups

To restore tapes, select a tape to restore from, then choose to restore either the current tape, one or more backup sets, or individual files on one of the tapes. To choose a tape, open the Tapes window. You'll see a selection of previous backup sets. Backup tapes contain catalog information about the contents of the tape. For sets of tapes, the catalog information is located on the last tape.

The information in the Tapes window describes the following for each tape:

♦ Drive backed up

♦ Backup set number

♦ Tape number, and what number it is in a set of tapes

♦ Backup type

♦ Date and time of backup

♦ Backup description

11

If you need to restore an entire tape, or if you need to get other backup sets on a tape, you must load the tapes catalog. From the Tapes window, select the tape whose catalog you want to load, then choose Catalog from the Operations menu. After searching the tapes, Backup displays a list of backup sets on the tapes. You then choose the backup set for which you want to view a catalog.

Now you can choose the files you want to restore by simply selecting them in the window. Check the box of the backup sets and files to restore. The Backup help files describe various techniques for selecting sets or groups of files.

After selecting tapes, backup sets, or files to restore, choose the Restore command from the Operations menu. The Restore Information dialog box appears:

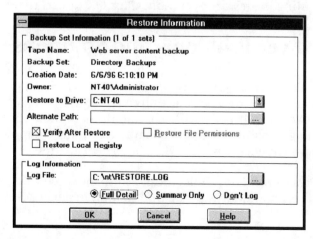

Set the following options in this dialog box:

- In the Restore to Drive field, specify the drive where you want to restore the information on the tapes.

- In the Alternate Path field, specify a different directory in which to restore a backup set's files instead of the directory where the files were originally stored.

- Click the Verify After Restore checkbox to verify that the files were copied correctly during the restore operation.

- Click the Restore File Permissions checkbox to restore permissions information along with the file. If this box is left disabled, files inherit the permissions of the directory into which they are restored.

- Click Restore Local Registry to restore the Registry files. (This option requires that you restart the computer for the restored information to take effect.)

Restore permissions only if you are restoring files to computers in the same domain as the original owner's account. Do not restore file permission if you are restoring to another computer outside the domain or to a computer that has not been completely restored following corruption of the operating system.

To create a log of the restore operation, type a filename in the Log File box or choose an existing file by clicking the browse button (to the right of the Log File field). Choose the Full Detail option to log all information about the restore, including the names of files and directories that are restored. Choose Summary Only to log only major operations, such as restore failures. Choose the Don't Log option if you want to skip the logging.

When you have set all the options for restoring files, click the OK button. The Restore Status dialog box appears so you can make one last check before starting the restore operation. Click OK to start the restore.

Power Problems and Solutions

Electrical power is rarely supplied as a smooth wave of steady energy, as is evident when lights flicker or when the television picture flickers off and back on. Electrical connections are polluted with surges and spikes (collectively called *noise*). You can think of these surges and spikes as shotgun blasts of energy. The way electronic equipment handles this transient energy is unpredictable. There are three likely scenarios:

Data Corruption   Electrical disturbances can cause memory to change states and can disrupt the information in data packets traversing a wire.

These glitches can alter a program in memory and cause it to fail. Such errors are frequently mistaken for program bugs.

Equipment Failure   If transient energy is high, it will cause permanent damage to equipment. Small microprocessor circuitry is especially susceptible to damage. Surge suppressors should be used to protect equipment, but if the energy is high enough, the surge suppressor can burn out. You'll see later in this chapter that some surge suppressors do not provide the right kind of protection against surges.

11

Slow Death   Equipment that is repeatedly subjected to low-energy surges will fail over time. The delicate circuits in a chip break down, and the equipment eventually fails for no apparent reason. *Transients* that cause this type of problem "sneak" through surge suppressors that are not designed to protect against them. After a period of abuse, the chips themselves weaken and energy is released in unknown patterns that ultimately destroy the chip.

Noise

The electrical environment is noisy. Equipment such as air conditioners, elevators, refrigerators, and even laser printers cause transients when they are switched on and off. The electric company causes transients when it switches grids to balance the system. In fact, any device that uses electricity in a nonlinear way can cause transients that affect other devices.

Noise problems cause slow or immediate damage to sensitive electronic equipment. Most computer power supplies include built-in protection against low-level noise, but surge suppressors can protect against transients that are stronger than normal, such as those caused by lightning. In fact, cheap devices often block such surges by simply burning out and preventing any further flow of electricity.

Improperly Grounded Equipment

Improper grounding can also cause problems. In fact, surge suppressors are often the cause of grounding problems, because it is in their design to route surges to ground. The surges then find their way back into the electrical system, where they wreak more havoc.

Buildings contain a low-resistance ground connection to the earth to protect people from electric shock. A good ground basically drains electrical charges into the earth. If equipment is not properly grounded and a person touches the equipment, a charge will pass into the earth through that person. Many commonly used grounding practices actually send noise from one system to another through the ground!

Grounding problems are especially prevalent in a network environment, because the cabling system can provide a path for ground loops. Consider that devices on networks are usually connected to different sources of power, which are grounded. When these networks are interconnected, bursts of energy on one system can flow to the other system. To solve ground-loop problems, you need to isolate equipment using one power source from equipment using other power sources.

On a large network, the creation of a single-point ground is usually impossible to achieve. Interconnected networks form links between close or distant points, any one of which can produce electrical problems due to poor wiring. These separate power sources might be in separate buildings or in a multistory office building that has separate power transformers on every floor or every other floor. Each transformer has its own electrical characteristics and should not be connected to equipment that is connected to other transformers.

Sag

When the power drops below the required level, a *sag* or "brownout" occurs, usually because the circuit is overloaded. A sag might continue for a period of time if the building is incorrectly wired or the utility company is having a problem. A long sag can cause damage to power supplies.

Swell

A swell is the opposite of a sag and can also cause damage to power supplies. It is often called an "over-voltage."

Hum

Hum is caused by neutral-to-ground connection problems. Such problems indicate a defect in one of the electrical wires to ground. Hum can cause transmission errors in data communication lines. As errors occur, the communication software must check and re-send incorrect packets, which causes a decrease in throughput.

Power Solutions

If your server is connected to a network, you can protect systems from ground loops, line noise, and surges by connecting the entire network to one central power source and ground. However, this is usually impractical and defeats the purpose of a network, which is to spread computing resources to users at outlying locations. Two solutions are outlined next.

Use a Power Conditioner and a UPS

Place a power conditioner (to smooth out surges) and an uninterruptible power supply at the server. The power conditioner provides a clean source of power and a solid reference ground. Ground any network cables to the power conditioner ground. Surge suppression equipment should be placed at the feed (outside) to electrical panels. If the surge suppressors are placed on the branch circuits (inside), they will divert surges to ground and back into the circuits of other systems through the ground connection.

Use a Nonconductive Fiber-Optic Cable

If you need to interconnect networks that are using different power supplies, use a nonconductive fiber-optic cable between the systems to eliminate ground loops. The primary reason for ensuring the separation of the power sources is that they will most likely have different ground potentials, which can cause problems in sensitive electrical equipment if they are linked together.

Ensure that a single LAN segment is connected to circuits that branch from a single power source, and that no point in the segment shares a ground with other power sources. An electrical contractor can perform this service.

Using Uninterruptible Power Supplies

Your basic power and grounding system can be augmented by an uninterruptible power supply (UPS). A UPS provides electrical power to computers or other devices during a power outage. A UPS can be any of the following:

♦ A battery system

♦ A rotary device that uses the inertia of a large flywheel to carry the computer system through brief outages

♦ Internal combustion motors that run AC generators

UPS devices come in two forms: online and standby. A standby device kicks in only when the power goes down. Therefore, it must contain special circuitry that can switch to backup power in less than five milliseconds. An online device constantly provides the source of power to the computer. Because of this, it doesn't need to kick in. If the outside source of power dies, the batteries within the unit continue to supply the computer with power. Although online units are the better choice, they are more expensive than standby units. But because online units supply all the power to a computer, that power is always clean and smooth.

When purchasing a battery backup system, be aware of the following:

♦ The amount of time the UPS battery supplies power

◆ Whether the UPS provides a warning system to the server when the UPS is operating on standby power

◆ Whether the UPS includes power-conditioning features that can clip incoming transient noise

◆ The life span of the battery and how it degrades over time

◆ Whether the device warns you when the batteries can no longer provide backup power

◆ Whether the batteries are replaceable

Purchase a UPS that the server can monitor to detect power drains. A monitoring cable usually attaches to the serial port. Make sure the UPS is compatible with Windows NT.

You also need to know the power requirements of the devices you'll hook to the UPS. For a server installation, this might include the CPU, the monitor, external routers, concentrator units, and wiring centers. You can determine the power requirements of these devices by looking at the backs of the equipment. Labels on the equipment list the power drawn by the unit in watts. Simply add the values of all the devices to come up with the requirements you'll need from the UPS.

Attaching a UPS to the File Server

Installing a UPS is fairly simple: Attach it to your computer according to the manufacturer's instructions. You should use a UPS that Windows can monitor for power loss; when power loss does occur, Windows can perform an orderly shutdown before the power is gone. An interface between the UPS and Windows NT sends signals about the state of the UPS so the server knows to warn users that it might be going down.

After installing the UPS, you need to configure how Windows NT will interact with the UPS. Log in as the system administrator and start the UPS utility in the Control Panel. The UPS installation dialog box appears:

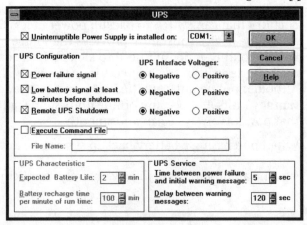

Click the top field to enable UPS support, then specify the COM port on which your server will communicate with the UPS. Next, fill out the options in the UPS Configuration field based on voltage levels sent by the UPS. Refer to the manual for this information.

The Execute Command File field lets you specify the name of a program to execute if the power starts to get low. Fill out the lower fields as appropriate for your UPS. You should probably test the UPS yourself to learn its actual battery life and recharge time, rather that relying on the information supplied by the vendor.

11

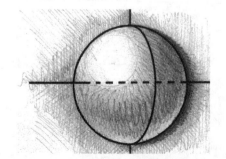

PART 3

General Network Security Issues

CHAPTER 12

Client/Workstation
Security Issues

305

This chapter is about client computers on Windows NT networks. It discusses potential security problems and how you can protect information from eavesdroppers and hackers. Client desktop operating systems—including DOS, Windows, UNIX, and Macintosh systems—can participate in Windows networks, exchange files, share folders, and share printers. In most cases, this sharing can also take place over wide area networks and the Internet. You'll find information about wide area network connections in Chapter 15 and information about interoperability with other operating systems in Chapter 16.

This chapter primarily covers security issues related to Microsoft's Windows 95 desktop operating system. Of course, the Windows NT Workstation can also participate as a client operating system, and it provides a much higher level of security than Windows 95. Those security features are outlined in previous chapters of this book.

Windows 95 is the natural upgrade to Windows 3.1 and Windows for Workgroups. It can serve as a platform for access to multiple network operating systems and host systems. Microsoft has gone to great lengths to support interoperability and connectivity to other systems in its products. Support is either built in or available as optional products.

Still, Windows NT Workstation, with its strong logon and authentication, is a clearly better choice for secure environments. I could spend the rest of this chapter convincing you to upgrade all your clients to Windows NT, but obviously that is not a clear path for budget-strapped IS managers. So, this chapter will provide information on working with what you a have and tightening the security in ways that are practical from a budgetary and management point of view.

User profiles and policies, which are discussed at the end of this chapter, are particularly useful in putting restrictions on what users can do at their workstations and in generally securing client systems. Windows 95 and Windows NT systems support profiles and policies, but a Windows NT computer or NetWare server must be on the network to use policies.

Clients in the Network Sharing Environment

Recall from Chapters 5 and 9 that Windows for Workgroups and Windows 95 computers can participate in *share-level* and *user-level* access control. The first is available on any Windows network, while the latter requires that a Windows NT computer or NetWare server be attached to the network to handle user accounts. The differences between these security controls was thoroughly explored at the beginning of Chapter 9.

With share-level security, the focus is on sharing a folder with everyone on the network while controlling access to that resource with a password. If you share a folder on your computer, you grant other people access to it by giving them the password. You can set Read Only or Full Access security with a separate password for each. Therefore, if you want Joe to only read files in the folder, you give him the Read Only password. If Jan needs to create and edit files in the directory, you give her the Full Access password. Keep the following points in mind:

♦ There is no granularity of access permissions: either you grant Read-Only or you grant Full Control. User-level security provides better access controls.

♦ Password control is practically impossible. People tend to look at the shared resource as a public entity. Jan may give her Full Access password to Joe without even thinking about the security implications.

12

With user-level security, you can take advantage of the logon and authentication features of a Windows NT system or computer (Server or Workstation) or a NetWare server. These systems can become "security servers" in the peer network. When you share a resource, you access a list of valid user accounts from the security server, then select the users that can access the resource. Users must then log on to the Windows NT computer or NetWare server and be fully authenticated before they can access any resources on the network. With these servers on the network, you can also take advantage of user policies as discussed later.

Implementing Client File and Printer Sharing

If you plan to implement file and printer sharing on individual client workstations, there are a number of things to keep in mind:

♦ Use user-level access controls, not share-level access controls. This will require that at least one system on the network be a Windows NT computer or a NetWare server with user accounts.

♦ Users might download sensitive files from servers into shared directories. Unauthorized users who normally don't have access to the sensitive files on secure servers might be able to access those files in shared directories where they have been downloaded to client workstations.

♦ If users are in charge of creating shares and specifying who has access, things are bound to go wrong. A user might grant everyone access to folders that contain sensitive information; then, anyone on any interconnected network can potentially access the information.

♦ In addition, if a user is in charge of sharing resources, he may be duped by someone who calls on the phone and convinces him to share a directory.

TIP: Remember that you can lock down Windows 95 computers and put them in physically secure areas, but when users share directories, anyone on the network can potentially access the system.

Make sure that users share only individual folders. If they share drives, then every folder on the drive will be accessible over the network. This is OK for CD-ROM drives, but sharing an entire hard drive would allow other network users to access valuable information, including encrypted password files in the Windows directory that might normally be inaccessible if systems are locked down and secured.

Disabling Client File and Printer Sharing

For security reasons, you may prefer to disable a client's ability to share files and printers. The file and printer sharing services are implemented as an installable service on Windows 95 computers that is easily removed. You can uninstall this service on all of your client workstations or on selected client workstations to prevent users from sharing resources on their hard disks with other users. To remove the sharing option, open the Network utility in the Control Panel and remove either "File and printer sharing for Microsoft networks" or "File and printer sharing for NetWare networks" from the dialog box.

With file and printer sharing removed, users can still access shared resources on other network computers. Network access to shared resources is provided by the client components, such as the client for Microsoft networks component, not by the file and printer sharing services.

Common Internet File System (CIFS)

Microsoft is extending the file and printer sharing features of Windows systems over the Internet by implementing the CIFS protocols. CIFS is a new file sharing technology based on SMB (Server Message Block) that will allow individuals and organizations to run file systems over the Internet. In the past, most Internet file exchanges have been one-way transfers. CIFS goes beyond this by allowing groups of users to work together and share documents over the Internet in the same way they share documents when running peer networking services on Windows clients. Users can collaborate over the Internet by defining shared folders and files on systems that are connected to the Internet.

CIFS has features that allow it to

♦ Use the same multi-user read and write operations, locking, and file sharing semantics that are used on most networks.

♦ Run over TCP/IP and utilize the Internet's global Domain Naming Service (DNS).

♦ Support slower speed dial-up connections common on the Internet.

CIFS is also widely available on UNIX, VMS, and other platforms.

CIFS is basically an enhanced version of Microsoft's open, cross-platform SMB protocol, the native file sharing protocol in the Windows 95, Windows NT, and OS/2 operating systems. CIFS complements standard Web protocols such as HTTP by providing a more sophisticated file sharing protocol. Users do not need to rely solely on their Web browsers to access Internet information, because with CIFS most existing applications can access that data directly by using the standard open and save dialog boxes that users are already familiar with.

The security features in CIFS include support both for anonymous transfers and for secure, authenticated access to named files. File and directory security policies are easy to administer, and use the same paradigm as share-level and user-level security policies in Windows environments. Most major operating system and application developers support CIFS.

Client Workstation Security Problems

As mentioned, this chapter will outline security "problems" primarily in Windows 95, although many of these problems date back to previous versions of Windows. Keep in mind that a problem in this context is not a bug. Instead, I am referring to shortcomings in the operating system that can compromise the security of your networks. They are either design limitations that Microsoft has no intention of upgrading, or weaknesses that Microsoft has no intention of fixing.

Security Updates to Know About

You should be aware of the following updates that Microsoft has made available to correct some security problems in the initial release of Windows 95. You can obtain the service pack by connecting with Microsoft's Web site at **www.microsoft.com** or by contacting a Microsoft Solution Provider in your area. Before going further, you should install these updates or obtain any further updates that may have been made available since the release of this book. The following information is based on material from Microsoft press releases.

Samba Update   There was a problem with file sharing when Samba SMBCLIENT existed on the network. The client could gain unauthorized access to a shared drive. The update prevents Windows 95 from accepting commands from SMBCLIENT that would allow unauthorized access.

NW Server Update   This update fixes a problem with file and printer sharing for netWare networks that might affect data security for corporate users. If your computer is configured for file and printer sharing and Remote Administration is enabled, another user on the network might gain Read Only access to your computer after the administrator has logged off the computer and before you have restarted your computer. The updated driver ensures that only valid administrators have access to the computer's drive.

Vredir Update   The Vredir update fixes a problem that affects only Windows 95 users who use Samba UNIX servers. The problem arises from the basic Windows 95 and UNIX filename formats. UNIX allows filenames that include the backslash (\) and asterisk (*) characters, but in Windows 95 these are wildcard characters. There is a potential that users might accidentally delete all the files in a directory by using commands with these characters. The updated version of Vredir prevents this from happening by rejecting filenames that contain the \ or * characters.

Windows 95 Password List Update   The Windows 95 Password List, which is stored as an encrypted file on the local disk, was shown to be crackable. Various postings on the Internet provided information and an algorithm for cracking the password. If someone gains access to your system, she could use the algorithm to crack the password file and gain access to the password-protected resources. The update provides vastly improved encryption that is 2^{96} (2 to the 96th power) harder to decrypt than the previous encryption method.

OLE 32 Update   The Windows 95 OLE 32 update fixes a file storage problem in Microsoft Word, Microsoft Excel, and Microsoft PowerPoint that could expose previously deleted data. Because of the way these applications use OLE for file storage, files created by these applications might contain extraneous data from previously deleted files. This data is not visible while you use the applications. However, when such a document file is viewed by using Windows Notepad, for example, it might be possible to see pieces of information from the previously deleted files. This possibility poses information security and privacy concerns if you distribute electronic versions of files that were created using these applications. The OLE 32 update is designed to prevent any application from potentially causing the same problem. (This is not a problem on Windows NT computers.)

Windows 95 Logon

The logon process for Windows NT computers is fairly secure. Appendix A provides details of the process. Passwords are double-encrypted and checked against a user database on a secure system using the Challenge/Response protocol. In contrast, the Windows 95 logon process has the potential to compromise security. It can also give you a false sense of security. Here are some points to keep in mind:

♦ If networking options are not installed on a Windows 95 computer, then the logon dialog box appears for a simple reason: to get the name of the user and display a customized desktop for that user. Multiple users can log on to the same system and have their own customized desktops.

♦ If networking options are installed for workgroup computing (not domain computing), the logon dialog box gets the user's name and password and passes it to computers that require user logon to access shared resources. If user-level or domain security is in use on the network, the information authenticates the user.

When a Windows NT or NetWare server is available to authenticate a Windows 95 client logon, a surprisingly high level of security is possible. First, if the user bypasses the logon (by clicking Cancel), then networking is not enabled. An intruder that can't log on legitimately at the computer won't be able to access the network where she could try to break in to shared folders. If the user does log on as a legitimate client, the username she logs on with is the only username she can use while accessing network resources. The intruder cannot change it to say "Administrator" and attempt to log on to administrative shares (such as *servername*\C$) by guessing the Administrator's password.

Continuing along these lines, if someone tries to access a shared folder without valid credentials, a logon dialog box appears, but this only asks for the password, not the username, so an intruder can't change from the original logon name to "Administrator." Unfortunately, this does not seem to be the case in Windows NT Workstation computers, where users can specify a different logon name when accessing shared folders and attempt to break in to the Administrator account. Administrators still need to implement complex passwords for Administrator.

With all this in mind, be aware that the Windows 95 logon does not protect local resources on Windows 95 computers. The FAT file system is used and

12

anybody can boot the system with DOS to access FAT file systems. If you want to protect a system from unauthorized booting, you need to implement physical security measures such as locking down the keyboard and case and disabling internal floppy drives.

You should also set BIOS-based passwords, but be aware that these can be disabled by someone who changes a jumper on the system or removes the battery in order to discharge the memory. You can also implement policies on Windows desktops, as described later in this chapter.

Another solution is to use a product that employs encryption to secure data on PCs, such as PC/DACS from Mergent Technologies or RSA Secure from RSA Data Systems (described later in this chapter).

Password Insecurities

The logon process on Windows 95 computers is susceptible to Trojan Horses. You already know that Windows NT computers require that you press CTRL-ALT-DEL to log on. This prevents Trojan Horse programs from capturing your password as you type it, because the CTRL-ALT-DEL process basically removes all running programs except the basic Kernel components, which are secure in their own right.

However, on Windows 95 clients (and almost all other clients), Trojan Horse programs can be made to start when the system boots. A co-worker, intruder, or even the janitor might install such a program on your computer to capture passwords the next time you log on. A hacker can even have the captured password sent to an e-mail address, as described later.

There have also been cases where the Windows Recorder (available in Windows 3.*x*) was set up by a co-worker to record keystrokes. When the user returned from lunch and logged in, the utility recorded the logon information to disk. The co-worker then retrieved it the next day during lunch.

Another problem with Windows 95 is that someone can attempt to log on indefinitely by trying different passwords. Unlike Windows NT, which lets you set lockout options that effectively lock an account after several unsuccessful logon attempts, Windows 95 allows repeated attempts at logging on. A co-worker who knows something about a fellow worker might be able to guess her password if it's based on a kid's name, license plate number, or other known information. The co-worker may already know the user's logon name if she sends that person e-mail, or if it is displayed in the name field of the logon dialog box from the last logon.

Be aware that repeated attempts to log in to a domain can be locked out and if domain logon is set as the logon procedure, then intruders will have a difficult time logging in. However, passwords are stored on local computers in encrypted form and it is these files that intruders try to crack, as described next. The previous applies to local logons; the danger is that someone might easily guess a local password that a user also uses to log in to a domain.

Information found at the Hack Microsoft Web site gives you some idea of what hackers might be up to and the techniques that can be used to capture passwords. You can access the site by pointing your Web browser at **www.c2.org/hackmsoft**. While most information at the site applies to Windows for Workgroups, it gives you some concept of what hackers can do.

Microsoft has released a fix to the password security problem as outlined earlier under "Windows 95 Password List Update." For your information, the next section describes the password caching scheme in the initial release of Windows 95 and how it was fixed.

Password Caching on Windows Clients

Windows clients such as Windows 95 and Windows for Workgroups store passwords for network logons in password files with the PWL extension. These files are stored in the Windows directory on the local machine. Password caching makes it convenient to log on to a network resource at a later time if you've logged on to the resource previously. The password is stored in a separate encrypted file for each user. When the user successfully logs on to a computer, the password file is opened, so the cached passwords in it can be used during the logon session.

 NOTE: In Windows for Workgroups, password list files are listed in the **[Password Lists]** section of SYSTEM.INI. You can disable password-list files by setting **PasswordCaching=No** in the **[network]** section of SYSTEM.INI.

In Windows 95, passwords are stored in .PWL files located in the Windows directory. Interestingly, a password file is even created if you log on to a Windows NT server as Administrator. Therefore, a file called ADMINIST.PWL is created on disk that someone might try to crack.

There are password cracking algorithms that attempt to generate an unencrypted password from the encrypted password file. These require physical access to the system. However, if a user has made the mistake of sharing his entire hard drive, then a network user could connect to the directory over the network and copy the password cache files.

You can disable password caching by editing the Registry on the computer as follows:

1. Type **REGEDIT** in the Run dialog box.

2. Drill down to the following location in the hierarchical file:

   HKEY_LOCAL_MACHINE\SOFTWARE\Microsoft\Windows \CurrentVersion\Policies\Network

3. Right-click in the right pane and choose New, then choose DWORD Value.

4. When the new value appears, rename it DisablePwdCaching and press ENTER.

5. Double-click the new entry and type **1** in the Value data field.

The password update described earlier strengthens the encryption used for Windows 95 password caching. It uses a 128-bit key as opposed to the 32-bit key used in the initial release of Windows 95. In addition, the fix provided by Microsoft no longer uses password caching for NET.EXE, which would allow users to log on to remote resources from the command line, making it possible to spoof another user. Users will be prompted for passwords when using NET.EXE to connect to resources on the network.

Synchronizing Passwords

You can synchronize the passwords that are used to log on to Windows 95 with the passwords that are used to access resources on networks by using the Passwords utility on the Control Panel. Open the utility, then click Change Windows Password. You see a dialog box similar to the following:

This feature could be a security problem if you consider that one of the passwords might be less protected than another. A person who cracks this password would then have access to other systems that use the same password.

Securing and Managing Network Clients

The following topics are directed at network managers and administrators. The first topic discusses a third-party option for securing Windows 95 desktops using encryption technology to provide many of the same features that are available in Windows NT. Additional topics include tools to manage clients and security features.

PC/DACS for Windows 95

With a little investment, you can upgrade your Windows 95 desktops to a higher level of security. PC/DACS is an access control product that allows administrators to gain precise control over information on hard drives and prevent intruders from using a floppy disk to "boot around" security. It also provides several levels of encryption to protect critical information. The product lets you implement organizational security policies at the PC level and close up doorways to hackers on the unsecured PC.

12

PC/DACS provides transparent security with C2-like functionality. That means it provides boot protection, encryption, time out (computer locks if the user walks away), and object reuse prevention (other processes cannot randomly use objects such as memory locations and files). To prevent anyone from booting a PC and accessing its hard drive, encryption can be implemented in the following ways:

♦ **Encrypt the boot record** This option hides the disk partitions so anyone booting from a floppy never sees drive C.

♦ **Encrypt the system area** This option hides both the boot record and the FAT (file allocation table).

♦ **Partition** This option hides the boot record, the FAT, and all the files on a partition of a drive.

♦ **Entire drive** This option hides the entire drive using encryption.

These levels of encryption can protect a system in a number of ways. End users can be prevented from tampering with system files such as the Registry, CONFIG.SYS, and AUTOEXEC.BAT. Accidental hard disk formatting is also blocked. The product also allows discrete access rights at directory, subdirectory, or file level for each user and auditing of all user and administrator activities, file and program activities, and attempts to breach security. Additional features include:

♦ Identification and authentication of users.

♦ Anti-hacking features that can disable the system after failed logon attempts and force the system to shut down.

- ♦ Control of access to serial and parallel ports and of floppy disk reading or writing.

- ♦ Plug and play support for Windows 95 ensures boot protection for multiple physical drives.

- ♦ Transparent boot protection encryption limits BIOS-level access by unauthorized users.

- ♦ Integration with SecurID Card available from Security Dynamics, providing dual authentication capabilities.

For more information on this product, contact Mergent International at (800) 688-1199, or connect with their Web site at **www.mergent.com**.

RSA Secure for Windows and Macintosh

RSA Secure is an encryption package for Windows and Macintosh computers available from RSA Data Security, Inc. It encrypts files on a user's computer or local area network. The key features of RSA Secure include ease of use, strong encryption, emergency access with key splitting, and file sharing.

On a Windows system, the software integrates with the desktop and provides a "set it and forget it" utility that automatically encrypts files when you exit Windows or shut down a Macintosh. You can also choose an "encrypt now" function to encrypt preselected files or files that you want to encrypt on an ad hoc basis.

The system uses RSA's RC4 stream cipher as described in Appendix B. A 128-bit encryption is used for versions sold in the U.S., and a 40-bit encryption is used for versions sold overseas. A corporate-based key escrow system is included whereby every file that is encrypted has the random RC4 key for that file, in turn encrypted by both the user's secret key and the organization's public key. The organization's private key might then be used to decrypt a single user's files. However, to prevent potential abuse, RSA Secure implements *Bloom-Shamir secret splitting*, which divides the private key into discrete "shares" that are held by a number of trustees.

You can also encrypt files and transfer them to another RSA Secure user for decryption. If the second user does not have RSA Secure, the encrypted file can be made a self-extracting executable file, in which case the second user runs the file, enters the password, and thus decrypts the file.

A free evaluation copy of RSA Secure can be downloaded from RSA Data Security at **www.rsa.com**.

Remote Administration

The management tools discussed here can help you manage the configuration of client workstations and maintain a reasonable level of security. While these tools can also help you troubleshoot problems, this section covers mainly security issues.

12

The System Monitor   Use this tool to monitor the performance of systems on the network. With it, you can monitor information about client activities and file systems.

The Net Watcher   If file and printer sharing is enabled on computers, you can use this tool to monitor and manage shared resources on remote computers.

The System Policy Editor   Use this tool to manage system policies and control system settings for computers on the network. (Policy management is discussed later in this chapter.)

The Registry Editor   Use this tool to edit the Registry on local or network computers.

These tools let you administer Windows 95 computers remotely from a Windows 95 workstation. There are some steps you must take to perform remote management, including enabling remote administration, enabling user-level security, and installing the Remote Registry service on every computer that you want to manage remotely. You can also set up SNMP (*Simple Network Management Protocol*) agents to allow the system to be managed by third-party management programs.

NOTE: Keep in mind that all the managed systems must run the same network protocol (TCP/IP for example).

For security reasons, the Registry Editor allows you to access the entire Registry of a remote computer while the System Policy Editor allows you to access a subset of keys on the remote Registry. When remote administration is enabled, two shared and hidden directories are created: ADMIN$ gives administrators access to the file system on the remote computer, and IPC$ provides an interprocess communication (IPC) channel between the two computers.

Setting Up Remote Registry Administration

To enable remote administration of Windows 95 computers, open the Passwords utility from the Control Panel of each computer, click the Remote Administration tab, and check the Enable Remote Administration of this server option, as shown here:

This procedure assumes that user-level security is already enabled. Be aware that when you enable user-level security, the Windows NT Domain Admins group or the NetWare Supervisor/Admin account can remotely administer clients. You can click the Add button to add other administrators.

Next, install the Remote Registry service on all the computers that will be managed, including the administrative workstation. Open the Network utility from the Control Panel and click the Add button. Double-click Service and then the Have Disk button. Put the Windows 95 compact disk in a drive and type **ADMIN\NETTOOLS\REMOTREG** as the path to the directory. Click OK, choose Microsoft Remote Registry, and then click OK again.

Once remote administration is enabled as just described, you can edit the Registry of other computers with the Registry Editor. Type **REGEDIT** in the Run dialog box to start the utility. When it appears, choose Connect Network Registry on the Registry menu and type the name of the computer to connect to. The contents of the computer's Registry are added to the window. Now you can make changes, as outlined in the Registry Editor's help system.

System Monitor

System Monitor lets you display information about the real-time performance of computers on the network in graphs and charts. You can use this tool for troubleshooting purposes or to track unusual activity on client systems. Multiple instances of System Monitor can run at the same time in case you need to track related activities (such as hacker activities) between two computers.

To connect to a remote computer in System Monitor, choose Connect from the File menu, type the name of the computer to connect to, and then click OK. You can also right-click a computer in the Network Neighborhood and choose System Monitor.

Net Watcher

You can create, manage, and monitor shared resources on remote computers with Net Watcher, assuming that the remote computer is running file and printer sharing services. With this utility, you can view information about shared resources, add or stop sharing a resource, close open files, or disconnect users.

12

To start the utility, type **NETWATCH** in the Run dialog box, choose Select Server from the Administer menu, and then type the name of the computer to connect to. Type the password for remote administration to gain access to the computer. You can also right-click a computer in the Network Neighborhood and choose Net Watcher.

Keep the following in mind:

♦ To create a shared resource on another computer, choose Add Shared Folder from the Administer menu and then type the drive and path of the resource to share.

♦ You can prevent a user from sharing files by enabling the Disable File Sharing Controls and Disable Print Sharing Controls system policies.

Microsoft's System Management Server

If you run Microsoft's System Management Server (SMS) on your network, you can use it to perform remote troubleshooting and performance analysis on client workstations running DOS, Windows, Windows for Workgroups, or Windows NT. You can also use the Network Monitor included with SMS to monitor network traffic. SMS provides tools that can help network administrators monitor security and control systems from an administrative workstation, but there is also the possibility that the product could be misused by a rogue administrator or by an unauthorized user who manages to gain access to the administrative system. If you use SMS, use it with care.

With SMS tools, administrators can provide "help desk" functions by connecting to a user's desktop over the network and taking control of the screen, keyboard, and mouse. The administrator can view real-time information on the remote system, such as memory maps and loaded device drivers, in order to troubleshoot problems that users are having. Systems can even be rebooted. At no time do administrators need to go to a user's physical workstation. At the same time, an unauthorized user could use this system to access workstations in "stealth" mode from the comfort of her own office to view and change sensitive information on client workstations. SMS tools can also be directed at Windows NT Server computers, which potentially have much more valuable information.

SMS also includes the network protocol analyzer called Network Monitor, which runs on any Windows NT computer and can remotely capture, filter, and replay any network traffic. Captured information can be sent to the SMS administrator console for decoding and analysis. From this information, administrators can troubleshoot networks. But, once again, in the hands of an unauthorized user, this tool could be very dangerous. It allows users to capture information that might contain passwords or other valuable information.

Profile and Policy Management

User *profiles* hold configuration preferences for each user's desktop settings and work environment. Profiles restore the settings of the desktop from the last logon session for a user. This feature allows several people to use the same computer, each customizing it for his or her own use. Profiles also have security implications. A manager can create profiles for users that are appropriate for the tasks they are doing and keep them within the bounds of those tasks. If the profiles are mandatory, they cannot be changed by a user, but mandatory profiles must be stored on a server away from the user's computer to prevent him from deleting or changing them.

Policies are network-wide profile settings controlled by a central authority that provide more control over what users can do. With policies, you can avoid having to go to each computer and enable user profiles. Instead, you have a system policy downloaded automatically from a server when a Windows 95 installation completes. The advantage of policies is that they combine with the user's own profiles to provide a custom configuration that is partly controlled by network managers.

So what is the difference between profiles and policies? First, profiles start out as a method to control the desktop of individual users. They hold basic user preferences. To gain control of the user's desktop, you can copy the profiles to a server and prevent the user from changing the profiles. The profile then becomes a *mandatory profile*. A Windows 95 computer automatically looks on a server at boot time for profiles. If profiles don't exist on the server, local profiles are used.

When mandatory user profiles are set, a user can change the desktop during any logon session, but those changes are not saved for the next session. This has implications for administrators: if a user messes up his desktop and then calls for support, you can simply have him restart his computer or logon session to restore previous settings.

System policies are comparable to mandatory profiles, except that they provide much more control for managing personal settings, restrictions, and security settings on client systems. You manage policies with the System Policy Editor, which as described next, gives a wide range of control over desktop and user settings. You can implement one set of standard settings for all users and computers, or you can customize settings for groups of users or individual users. In most cases, you will customize settings for groups of users.

Keep the following points in mind:

12

◆ For security reasons, consider only mandatory profiles or system policies, not profiles that users can manage themselves.

◆ For maximum control, use system policies rather than mandatory profiles. Both require a server on the network, so profile or policy files can be stored away from the user's computer, which prevents the user from deleting or changing them.

◆ Whether you decide to use system policies or profiles, you must still set an option on Windows 95 computers that enables profiles, as covered in a moment.

◆ A home directory must exist for each user on a server when using either system policies or mandatory profiles.

◆ A savvy user can override profiles and policies, so don't consider them a total security solution. They are designed to keep good network "citizens" from going astray or causing accidents.

Profiles

By default, user profiles are stored in a file called USER.DAT on Windows 95 computers and NTUSER.DAT on Windows NT computers. These files contain the initial, default profile information. The settings that are saved in a user profile include those for Windows Explorer, Taskbar, printer, Control Panel, Accessories, Online help bookmark, and Windows applications.

As mentioned, if you want to gain control of the user's environment, you need to copy profiles to a user home directory on a Windows NT or NetWare server. On a Windows NT network, the network directory is the user's home directory; on a NetWare 3.*x* network, the home directory is the user's mail directory. Once you copy the files, you rename USER.DAT to USER.MAN to create mandatory profiles, then hide the files and make them Read Only.

Roaming user profiles are profiles that are stored on a server and that follow a user who moves from one computer to another. These allow the user to maintain the same consistent desktop wherever he works. A home directory is required for the user on the Windows NT logon server.

In Windows NT, different customizable profiles are automatically created for each user who logs on to the computer. In Windows 95, you must enable individual user profiles; otherwise, everybody that logs on to the same computer sees the same desktop. Each of the profile types are discussed in the next sections.

Windows 95 Profiles

You must enable individual profiles in Windows 95 before users of a system can create their own custom desktops, or before you can implement network-wide policies. Open the Passwords utility from the Control Panel and click the User Profiles tab. Then enable the "Users can customize their preferences and desktop settings" option. Next, reboot the system. A profile is created for a user the next time she logs on. Windows 95 users can use profiles stored on Windows NT Server computers if Client for Microsoft Networks is the primary logon client. If Client for NetWare Networks is the primary network logon client, then profiles can be on a NetWare server.

Profiles and policies are tied to the Windows 95 Registry, which is a hierarchically structured storage file that holds system, user, and policy information. The Registry exists on a Windows 95 computer as two files:

♦ **SYSTEM.DAT** holds PC-specific information such as network, hardware, and security parameters.

♦ **USER.DAT** holds user-specific information such as desktop settings, application preferences, screen colors, and security access permissions.

If you want to manage a user or workgroup's PC environment remotely, you can move USER.DAT and SYSTEM.DAT to a server. To create mandatory profiles for Windows 95 users, log on to the system and create the customized settings you want. Next, copy the required files for the user profile to the user's home directory on a Windows NT logon server and rename the USER.DAT file to USER.MAN. Next, hide the file and make it Read Only. When the user logs on, the settings in this file are used rather than those in the USER.DAT file on his computer.

NOTE: Windows 95 profiles do not provide some of the features of Windows NT profiles. For example, Windows 95 does not support common groups, a centrally stored Default User profile, and some desktop settings. Also, Windows 95 clients do not use the Windows NT Server profile path to obtain roaming user profiles. These profiles are retrieved from the user's home directory. If mandatory user profiles are required, the network administrator must create a custom user profile for each user and copy the profile to the user's home directory.

Windows NT Profiles

For Windows NT Workstation clients, you can specify custom profiles for individual users in the User Manager. Double-click a user account, click the Profiles button, and in the User Profile Path field type the name of the path where profiles exist. The location can be a folder on the local computer or a server, but for *roaming users* specify a folder on a server that the users can connect with when they travel to other locations.

12

After specifying the folder for a profile, you must also copy a profile and grant permissions to use it. Open the System utility from the Control Panel, click the User Profiles tab, select a profile, and click Copy To. You can then specify the location where you want to copy the profile. Click the Change button in the dialog box to add the user or group to the permissions list.

The basic procedure for creating a custom profile is to log on to a Windows NT computer and create a custom user profile. After making the appropriate settings, you log off, then log back on as Administrator, open the System utility from the Control Panel, and click the User Profiles tab. Choose the new profile in the dialog box, then click the Copy To button, and specify in the "Copy profile to" field the *systemroot*\Netlogon folder on the primary domain controller. Also click the Change button and specify that Everyone is permitted to use the profile.

To create a mandatory profile, log on to a computer as the user who will use the profile, make the required changes to the desktop and other settings, then log off. Log back on as Administrator, open the System utility from the Control Panel, click the User Profiles tab as just described, and then copy the user profile to the profile path that you previously specified for the user account. Next, rename the profile so that it has the MAN extension instead of the DAT extension. When a user logs on, the mandatory profile is downloaded to her local computer.

Policy Management

System policies help you control and manage computers on networks by defining what users can and cannot do on their computers. For example, you can restrict access to the Control Panel, prevent users from changing the desktop, customize the desktop, and configure network settings. Providing effective security in several ways, system policies require user-level access, so users log on by having their usernames and passwords verified by a security server. The policy settings are stored on that server and combined with their user profiles.

Keep in mind that profiles and policies control the user environment of legitimate users who work with the user interface. They do not affect hackers who bypass logon by booting a system with a DOS floppy disk, or by someone who boots Windows in Safe Mode. Use policies with the notion that you are controlling "trusted users" or "good citizens," and with the understanding that policies can prevent them from compromising security or accessing unauthorized features from the Windows interface itself.

The System Policy Editor is the utility you use to manage policies. Windows NT includes a System Policy Editor that can manage policies for the entire network. Windows 95 includes a System Policy Editor (in the ADMIN\APPTOOLS\POLEDIT directory on the CD-ROM) that you can choose to install on a workstation where you want to manage policies. This section discusses the security settings you can make using policies while working at a Windows NT Domain Controller. Refer to the Windows help systems for a complete instruction on using policies and the System Policy Editor. This topic is too large for this book.

The System Policy Editor creates a policy file called CONFIG.POL that overwrites a user's default USER.DAT and SYSTEM.DAT settings in the Registry when the user logs on. By default, Windows 95 automatically attempts to download computer and user policies from the NETLOGON directory on a Windows NT Server or the PUBLIC directory on a NetWare server. This default location can be overridden in a policy file setting. If no server is present, Windows 95 uses the settings currently on the local computer.

NOTE: System policies are different from mandatory user profiles in that policies give you much more control over user and computer settings. Policies can also allow administrators to control some of the settings while users control the others.

You open the System Policy Editor (for Windows NT or for Windows 95) to edit policies. Simply choose New Policy or Edit Policy from the File menu. A window similar to the following appears:

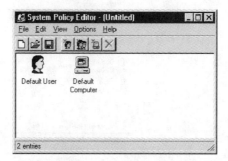

You edit user policies by double-clicking Default User, and you edit computer policies by double-clicking Default Computer.

When you create policies, a file called NTCONFIG.POL (on Windows NT) that contains user and computer settings is created. You can save this file in the Netlogon folder to create uniform policies for all network computer users. When a user logs on to a Windows NT computer, the contents of the file are copied to the user's local computer Registry where it overwrites the current user and local machine portions of the Registry. When a user logs on to the domain, the contents of the NTCONFIG.POL file on the server are merged with the NTUSER.DAT file found in the user profile location for the user logging on. Settings in NTUSER.DAT that do not match NTCONFIG.POL are overwritten, while settings that do not conflict are retained.

A similar process takes place when a Windows 95 user logs in, except that the CONFIG.POL created by the Windows 95 System Policy Editor is used. This file should be stored in the NETLOGON Windows NT directory on a Windows NT Server or the PUBLIC directory on a NetWare server, as mentioned earlier.

Changing Policies

You change policies in the System Policy Editor by creating a new policy or loading up an existing policy and then double-clicking on either Default User or Default Computer. A window similar to the following appears for Windows 95 policies:

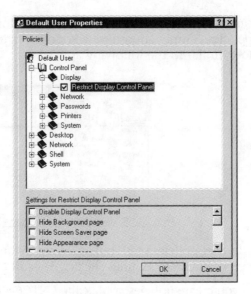

In this case, some of the options have been opened up so you can see how settings are made.

The basic procedure is to locate the options you want to change, click the + sign to open the tree under the option, then enable or disable options as appropriate. There are too many options to outline here on an individual basis. You should browse through the settings to see which are most appropriate for your systems.

The Microsoft Windows 95 Resource Kit includes two system policy files: STANDARD.POL provides basic policy settings, while MAXIMUM.POL provides high-level security settings for strict control of the user's environment. You should obtain a copy of these files if you want to see what a set of standard or maximum setting look like.

CHAPTER 13

Microsoft BackOffice
Security Issues

Microsoft BackOffice is a suite of server-based applications that run on Windows NT Server systems. These applications, described next, take full advantage of the security features of Windows NT, including directory services, user account logon, Access Control lists, auditing, and more.

The Microsoft SQL Server   This is the relational database component for managing and storing data.

The Microsoft SNA Server   This is the host connectivity component that provides Windows, Macintosh, DOS, and OS/2 clients with access to AS/400 and IBM mainframes.

The Microsoft Systems Management Server   This is the network management component that reduces support and administrative costs by providing a central location for managing network hardware and software, software distribution, troubleshooting, and application management.

The Microsoft Exchange Server   These are the electronic mail and messaging components that provide a messaging infrastructure for electronic mail and collaborative computing applications. Microsoft Mail is the predecessor of Microsoft Exchange Server.

The Microsoft Internet Information Server   This is the Web server component that is included with Windows NT itself without additional charge. It is covered in Chapter 18.

An installed Windows NT Server system is required before you can install the BackOffice components. These components take full advantage of the performance-enhancing features of the Windows NT Server as well as the administrative and client support features. The Windows NT Server and the entire BackOffice suite are modular products. You can add components and build custom applications on the BackOffice platform as your needs grow. Microsoft views BackOffice as the hub of an "information network." Some advantages of this hub approach:

♦ The Windows NT Server provides authentication services and secure data transfers, and meets C2-level security guidelines.

♦ Users log on once to gain access to shared resources on the SQL Server, the SNA Server, the Exchange Server, and the System Management Server. Administrators don't need to maintain separate Account databases on each system.

♦ BackOffice products make use of the networking support built into the Windows NT Server, including support for popular networks such as Ethernet, token ring, and Arcnet, as well as popular protocols such as TCP/IP, IPX/SPX, and NetBEUI.

♦ Support is provided for different hardware platforms, including Intel-based PCs and servers, DEC Alpha, MIPS, and PowerPC systems. Symmetric multiprocessing systems are also supported.

The Windows Open Services Architecture (WOSA) provides much of the glue that integrates Windows-based applications in the heterogeneous enterprise-wide computing environment. WOSA provides a consistent architecture and a set of development APIs through which Windows-based applications can access services on a variety of platforms. Standards in the WOSA architecture include the following:

Open Database Connectivity (ODBC)   ODBC is an open-standard way of accessing back-end data from front-end Windows (and Macintosh) clients.

Messaging API (MAPI)   MAPI defines a common interface that lets Windows-based applications access a variety of back-end messaging services.

13

The WOSA also includes some interesting extensions for various vertical markets, including extensions for financial services (branch banking), real-time market data (stock quotes and news), and extensions for engineering and manufacturing.

The following sections describe each of the BackOffice products and security-related issues.

BackOffice Internet Connections

In general, any Windows NT Server that is running BackOffice products or that connects to another server running BackOffice will need to have various safeguards put into place to prevent external Internet users from attacking internal systems. A firewall is a line of defense to protect systems. It can restrict both inbound and outbound access and can filter traffic based either on address information in packets or on the programs or applications that generated the packets.

A firewall may consist of a third-party router such as those provided by Cisco Systems or Bay Networks; a firewall can also be built within multihomed Windows NT Server computers (computers with two or more network interface cards). You connect one interface card to the Internet and the other to your internal network. You then disable routing between the cards to prevent Internet traffic from crossing over into your internal network. You then install special firewall applications that control traffic the way you want.

Microsoft has developed the "Catapult" proxy server, which runs as an add-on product for Windows NT Server. Proxy servers work on behalf of the client to provide access to the Internet. Basically, all Internet requests generated by internal clients are sent to the proxy server, which then screens these requests and submits them on the Internet for the client. The client never makes a direct connection to the Internet. The advantage of proxy servers is that they let internal users access the Internet while stopping Internet traffic on the internal network. At the same time, an NT Server might be set up to provide services to the Web as a stand-alone system.

These topics are covered in more detail in Part 4 of this book.

The Microsoft SQL Server

The Microsoft SQL Server is the distributed client-server relational database management system (RDBMS) component of the BackOffice suite. It's a foundation for an integrated set of data-management products that includes development tools, system-management tools, data-replication processes, and open-development interfaces.

SQL (Structured Query Language) was originally developed by IBM as a database query language in the mid-1970s to operate on the VM/370 and MVS/370 operating systems. It was later commercialized by Oracle Corporation, after which many other companies jumped on the bandwagon. The original intent of using SQL as a database query tool was never realized because it was too impractical to expect most users to learn and use it. It went through several repackaging phases in an attempt to make the language easier to use. Today, SQL is viewed as an interface to access data on many different types of database systems, including mainframes, midrange systems, UNIX systems, and network servers. SQL is currently undergoing standardization by the International Organization for Standardization and the American National Standards Institute (ANSI). Microsoft and several other vendors and groups are also involved in this process.

In the client-server environment, the user's front-end application interfaces to a relational database management system (RDBMS) "engine" running on a back-end server. In the past, the variety of available client operating systems made it difficult to create a consistent interface to back-end data. Each type of client required its own front-end application and interface. Now the trend is to provide so-called "middleware" products between the clients and servers to allow users to access any back-end server using a variety of front-end applications. Microsoft's Open Database Connectivity (ODBC) hides the differences between access languages and database APIs.

A recent development is to use Web browsers to access SQL data. Internet or intranet Web clients access a Web server that is integrated with an SQL Server. The client accesses SQL data by accessing a Web page and filling out a form. The information on the form is returned to the Web server, which in turn submits it as a query to an SQL Server. The SQL Server fulfills the request and returns it to the Web server, which builds a Web page on the spot that gets returned to the Web client. This is a fully dynamic process that allows Webmasters to provide the latest information at their Web sites without the need to build static Web pages.

SQL Server Security

Microsoft SQL Server can take advantage of the security features of the Windows NT Server, including password encryption, password aging, minimum length restrictions on passwords, and user account management features. When integrated security is put into place, the Windows NT user accounts are copied to the SQL Server; any user who logs in to Windows NT will also be logged on to the SQL Server. Logons to the SQL Server can be logged in to a file that indicates the time, date, and user who successfully or unsuccessfully attempted to log in.

13

Integrated security relies on the use of trusted connections, which are only available with both the named pipes protocol and Microsoft's new RPC-based Multi-Protocol Net Library. The SQL Server can implement a "mixed security" model that allows for its installation in environments that have a mix of trusted and untrusted connections. With this model, the server will first try to use integrated security; if that fails, it will then use the standard SQL Server logon security.

Administrators can monitor the logon success or failure of users so that both successful and unsuccessful logon attempts to the SQL Server can be tracked. Logon information, written to the Windows NT Event Log, includes the time, date, and user who successfully or unsuccessfully logged on.

The SQL Server provides mainframe-level security to protect sensitive data. User-level permissions can be implemented on tables, views, stored procedures, and SQL commands. Those permissions can be applied to groups as well, making security management easier. Field-level security is also supported. Security is handled centrally by the SQL Server, so it's not necessary to code elaborate user validation logic into client applications. In addition, the data streams that are generated during distributed transactions can be encrypted to provide high levels of security for over-the-wire transmissions.

Database Access and Integrity

The SQL Server provides database integrity within the database itself rather than in the front-end applications. All of the data-integrity rules, business policies, security permissions, and constraints are centrally managed and enforced. This centralization allows any client to access the database within the integrity constraints that have been applied at the server. Some examples of SQL Server integrity features are described below:

◆ Comprehensive user-level security protections can be implemented for database objects and commands. Special restrictions allow the system administrator to restrict particular columns, tables, and procedures to specific users.

◆ Users can be restricted to entering specific kinds of information, such as numbers only or dates only.

◆ Default values can be inserted in fields if no value is entered.

◆ Rules can be applied to fields to keep values within a specific range, to make them match a particular pattern, or to match another entry.

◆ Database administrators can grant users and groups of users specific Access permissions such as select, insert, update, and delete these permissions on specific database objects, such as tables, rows, columns, and views. (See Figure 13-1.)

◆ Stored procedures (described next) are simple or complex "programs" that users run to obtain information from a database. The procedures maintain database integrity by controlling how users access the database.

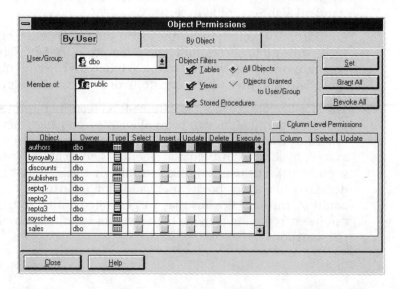

Managing
permissions
on objects in
the SQL Server
Figure 13-1.

Stored procedures are collections of individual SQL statements that are stored within an SQL Server database. They are coded by application developers in order to optimize access to a database, improve performance, and provide security by enforcing rules about how a database is accessed. Since the stored procedure is located at the database server, users need to execute only one command to invoke it, thus reducing network traffic. Procedures can be used by many different users, but access to a procedure can be denied to control access to the database in a very precise way.

Triggers are similar to stored procedures, but are automatically executed when an attempt is made to modify data. Triggers may operate like rules, forcing users to enter specific values. However, triggers invoke procedures that can enforce much more elaborate rules, and those procedures can be written with the SQL language. A triggered procedure might reference another table in the database to verify that some data can be changed or deleted. Alternatively, a trigger might duplicate changes made in one table to appropriate items in related tables.

Data Protection

13

With the Microsoft SQL Server, you can distribute a database among a number of servers to provide protection and make information more available to users at different locations. Servers communicate with one another using remote procedure calls. Information stored on two or more servers is kept updated using transaction processing and replication techniques.

The Microsoft SQL Server includes built-in replication services so that administrators can arrange to completely duplicate an entire database on another server. Replication services then ensure that the duplicate data is kept in sync with the original. Users can access data on either the original or the replicated database, whichever is closer to them. For example, an administrator might arrange to replicate a database in the New York office to the Los Angeles office to make that database more accessible to users in the Los Angeles office. Users in either location can change the database; those changes are synchronized whenever possible to ensure that both databases are the same.

To ensure that data is always available, the SQL Server implements an automatic backup system that can perform online backups even while users are querying and updating the database. Administrators can use a scheduling component to implement automatic backups. The backup scheduler will alert administrators via e-mail or pagers of the success or failure of the backups.

Management Features

The Microsoft SQL Server is a sophisticated data-management system that provides distributed information to use in both small and large organizations. To manage such a system, administrators need tools that help them monitor and maintain the system, often automatically and from a central location. Microsoft has designed the SQL Server's management tools on the Distributed Management Framework (DMF). DMF defines the following architectural tiers:

The SQL Server Enterprise Manager   This is a graphical interface that lets administrators manage, monitor, and control distributed SQL Servers from a central location, including the management of topology, security, events, alerts, scheduling, backup, server configuration, tuning, and replication.

SQL Executive   This runs as a Windows NT-based service and manages the replication, event handling, alerts, and scheduling components.

Distributed Management Objects (DMO)   This is the layer where OLE objects expose OLE Automation to SQL Server administrative functions. Developers can use Visual Basic to build custom administration scripts that can be scheduled with the SQL Executive.

The Windows NT Performance Monitor can be used to monitor statistics about the SQL Server, including memory usage, number of users, transactions per second, and CPU utilization. Alerts can be set to warn administrators or run commands when various operating thresholds have been met.

Other Security Options for the SQL Server

Security in the SQL Server environment goes beyond protecting the data. It also requires protecting the way data is manipulated. Microsoft recommends integrating the SQL Server with Windows NT security features in all cases. A Windows NT domain is required to allow users to log on to the network and access the SQL Server database with one password. Logon to Guest accounts should not be used.

The SQL Executive Logon Account

Windows NT services must run in the security context of an account in the same way that a user runs an application or accesses a resource in the security context of his personal user account. The default account for most Windows NT services is System account. Many Windows NT services can only be run under the System account. By default, this account has permissions to the entire local computer, but no rights on the network.

Like other services, the SQL Executive needs an account to log on as a service. However, since the System account has no network rights, you need to create a separate user account that will allow it to accomplish network tasks such as replication and scheduling that involve other servers. By default, SQL Executive is assigned to the System account. After installation, you should create a new account using the User Manager, then use the Services utility in the Control Panel to assign an appropriate user account to the SQL Executive as described in Chapter 10.

To create the new user account, start the Windows NT User Manager application and create a domain user account or a user account on the local server. Make the user account a member of the Administrators local group and set the following options:

♦ Enable the Password Never Expires option.

♦ Grant it the Log On As A Service right on the server.

♦ Allow all logon hours permitted if the account is a domain account.

Security Through Stored Procedures

The *stored procedure* is the other key to security in the SQL Server environment. A stored procedure provides a single point of entry to SQL Server objects for end users, as shown in Figure 13-2. In this respect, stored procedures are like a "database firewall." They can be designed to fit the different functions of a business. Access can be granted to appropriate User groups.

For example, you can prevent a user from directly updating tables, creating instead a stored procedure that updates the table. You then grant the user the ability to execute the stored procedure to ensure that all updates take

13

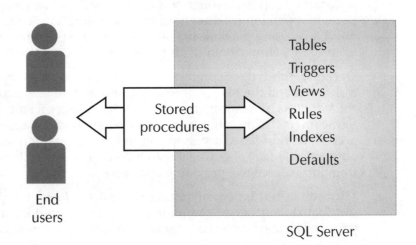

Access to the
SQL Server
through stored
procedures
Figure 13-2.

End
users

Tables
Triggers
Views
Rules
Indexes
Defaults

SQL Server

place in the controlled manner provided by the stored procedure. The stored procedure can write related updates to other tables as well and eliminate the possibility of integrity problems. Stored procedures can enforce data integrity in mixed-application environments as well. Users can be prevented from doing operations such as UPDATE, INSERT, and DELETE directly on tables, but only as part of redefined stored procedures. Administrators can use these techniques to control exactly which user or group can change data and how the data can be changed.

Microsoft outlines the following advantages of using stored procedures:

♦ Users who know how to code procedures or use database tools are not able to access any additional database functionality beyond the procedures they can normally run.

♦ Administrators need to manage only stored procedures, not client-side code or other database objects.

♦ Administrators will have complete, centralized control of all code that runs on the SQL Server. Business logic is "locked up" on the server.

♦ Developers will not have to "hard code" security checks into applications. When security administration changes, client-side code will not need to be recompiled.

You can use the Microsoft Open Data Services (ODS) component in the Microsoft SQL Server to write extended stored procedures and add audit and security extensions to the SQL Server.

The SQL Server and the Internet

The Microsoft SQL Server is tightly integrated with the Microsoft Internet Information Server. Through this integration, you can create dynamic Web pages that pull information from your back-end SQL Server databases. This is possible by using the built-in ISAPI gateway and the Internet Database Connector technology in the Internet Information Server.

Of course, this type of connection requires advanced security. The Microsoft SQL Server and the Microsoft Internet Information Server are integrated with the Windows NT security model to provide security features that are specific to the Internet. You can gain control over anonymous access, network access, and host-based access to your system. Encryption and secure Internet authentication are also available to protect your internal systems and data from intrusions while providing open access.

Microsoft calls this new environment the *Active Internet*. It provides distributed client-server computing beyond the traditional boundaries of your organization over the Internet. A major requirement is a secure platform to store information. Microsoft's efforts are designed to make the SQL Server that platform. By integrating the Microsoft SQL Server with the Internet (and/or intranet), you can expand your business beyond its normal boundaries.

Microsoft Exchange

Microsoft Exchange provides enterprise-wide information exchange by integrating electronic mail, scheduling, electronic forms, and document sharing. It also provides a basis for creating special applications that can take advantage of an enterprise-wide messaging system. With Microsoft Exchange, organizations can eliminate the barriers that have existed among different computers and different message systems, creating a network-based system that gives everyone in the organization quick access to information. Exchange also connects with the Internet and other networks outside the organization to provide global messaging. Exchange reflects Microsoft's vision of easily accessing, organizing, and managing information, and enabling people to use that information more effectively.

CAUTION: Obviously, installing such a system to your network and using it for Internet mail exchanges pose a number of security risks. These are discussed more fully later in this chapter, under "Security for Microsoft Exchange."

13

Exchange is a client-server product that is provided in the form of Exchange Server and Exchange clients:

Exchange Server   The Exchange Server is the "engine" for exchanging information, both throughout the enterprise and outside the enterprise. It runs on top of the Windows NT Server operating system and takes full advantage of the features that the Windows NT Server provides.

Exchange Clients   Exchange clients run on Windows 3.1, Windows for Workgroups 3.11, Windows NT, Windows 95, Microsoft DOS, Macintosh, and UNIX computers. A client provides an environment where users can create, send, receive, view, and store messages or other types of information, as pictured in Figure 13-3. Clients support features like file and object attachments (objects may be sound, video, text, or other data), address-book management, and information exchange with other services like CompuServe and the Internet.

Microsoft Exchange supports *electronic forms* so that workgroups can exchange "structured information" that can be distributed throughout the

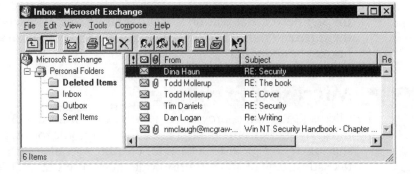

Microsoft
Exchange
client on
Windows 95
Figure 13-3.

enterprise. In addition, *public folders* serve as repositories for shared messages, forms, documents, applications, and databases. These folders can be replicated to other locations, placing information closer to users who need it and reducing network traffic. Exchange synchronizes replicated folders to ensure that users are working with the latest information. Shared *discussion databases*, similar to bulletin board chat sessions, are also supported in Exchange so that people can have a place to field and discuss ideas.

An example of how shared folders and information exchange can benefit an organization is best seen in the example of a customer-support organization. Problems that have been tackled by one support person can be documented in a shared database. Other support people can check this database before working on similar problems. Similarly, ideas can be shared and discussed company-wide. Shared discussion databases provide a perfect place to exchange ideas. People can read a history of a conversation and reply at any time. This eliminates the constraints of one-time meetings and phone conversations that are not documented for others to review.

Exchange provides messaging services, information services, directory services, connectivity services, and these additional features:

♦   Exchange supports standard network protocols such as IPX/SPX, NetBIOS, TCP/IP, and AppleTalk.

♦   Exchange also supports the Point-to-Point Protocol (PPP) for remote access.

♦   Exchange supports X.400 messaging standards and can run alongside existing X.400 messaging systems. Users on either system can exchange messages.

♦   An optional Simple Messaging Transport Protocol (SMTP) option provides connection to the Internet or to SMTP messaging systems.

♦   IBM PROFS/OfficeVision and SNADS gateways are supported.

♦ An organization can add a Microsoft Exchange Server and Exchange clients at any time into an existing Microsoft Mail environment. Microsoft Mail can coexist with Microsoft Exchange Server, and users can seamlessly exchange messages and information.

♦ Exchange supports MAPI (Messaging Application Programming Interface) so you can create custom message-enabled applications, and ODBC (Open Database Connectivity) so you can access stored information in a variety of data formats.

Exchange Server Components

The Microsoft Exchange Server consists of both client and server components. The client components run on each user's desktop computer; the server components run on each of the Microsoft Exchange Server computers. Client and server components work together to provide e-mail and groupware functionality across networks. The client makes a request of the server, such as sending an e-mail message or obtaining a mailbox address, and the server carries out those requests or provides the requested information.

Components of the server are:

13

♦ **Message Transfer Agent (MTA)**   The MTA delivers messages among Exchange servers and communicates with foreign MTAs. The MTA conforms to the 1988 CCITT X.400 specification.

♦ **Information store**   The information store, which applications can access, is a structured repository for mailboxes, messages, and public folders.

♦ **Directory**   The directory is an X.500-like directory service that contains information about Microsoft Exchange users throughout the enterprise, as well as users and resources outside the enterprise.

♦ **System attendant**   The system attendant builds routing tables, keeps track of messages, and monitors server performance.

♦ **Microsoft Mail Connector**   Provides Microsoft Mail network connectivity.

On the client side, Exchange is a "universal inbox" that works with many e-mail services. It is not necessary to have the Microsoft Exchange Server running to use an Exchange client. Message exchange can still take place with a number of different systems, including Internet mail systems. Messages can include special fonts, colors, and formatting as well as a variety of attachments, including text, sound, and video objects. Mobile users can dial in to send and receive their e-mail. They can also use filters to transfer only selected messages over the remote link. Users can also delegate access to the mailbox to another person. The delegated user can open other mailboxes as appropriate and manage the mail in those boxes as the original owner would. To enhance security of messages in transit, digital signatures and encryption are available.

On the server side, Microsoft Exchange provides a directory service that provides X.500 features and builds on Windows NT Server user account information. Mailboxes are associated with user accounts. The directory contains many extended attributes that hold information about users, such as their phone number and location. Each user mailbox can have alternate e-mail addresses to use when communicating with other messaging systems. Exchange folders can be used to store files and documents as well as messages to fit in with the requirements of the workgroups they belong to. Users can simply drag and drop files into public folders for others to view. Microsoft Office products have integrated Exchange features. A "Post to Exchange Folder" option appears on all Microsoft Office for Windows 95 applications. Exchange also includes a complete forms designer package for creating applications that hold structured information.

Exchange Server provides a centralized graphical program for administering all the aspects of Exchange throughout the enterprise. From a single console, you can manage users, servers, directories, and gateways. An administrator can create sites for organizing users, servers, gateways and other Exchange components into logical collections. Administrators can monitor the status of any service running on any server and take appropriate action. They can also monitor links between servers or sites, monitor system performance, and make necessary adjustments to optimize performance.

System Management

The Microsoft Exchange Server is a centrally managed enterprise messaging system. All key administrative operations can be done over a LAN connection or over a remote dial-up connection. Setup is almost completely automatic:

♦ Directory information, routing tables, and replication are automatically set up without administrator intervention.

♦ Mailboxes are created automatically from Windows NT user accounts or when a new account is created.

♦ Users can handle some of the distribution-list management by adding or deleting mailboxes.

Organizations that are moving from existing platforms to the Exchange Server can take advantage of the migration tools built into Exchange. These tools automate the process of moving from legacy e-mail systems such as Microsoft Mail for PC Networks, Microsoft Mail for AppleTalk Networks, IBM PROFS, Lotus cc:Mail, Verimation MEMO, and DEC All-in-1.

Exchange includes a replication engine that can perform all of its activities in the background without intervention. Exchange tracks all servers and reacts automatically to any changes, such as when a server goes down and comes back up, or when a server is added or deleted. If the network topology over which replication takes place changes, the replication engine recalculates routes. Replication can take place over direct, dial-up, or public e-mail systems like the Internet or X.400.

Exchange Server has a number of tools for managing reported system problems and for monitoring potential problems. In some cases, corrective actions are automatic. A server monitor makes sure that all messaging systems are up and running, and a link monitor tracks the status of links between points. In addition, Performance Monitor can be used to monitor and analyze system performance, and Event Log can be used to view error messages and warnings.

Exchange provides data protection with transaction logs. If the power fails, information in the transaction log is used during power-up to restore data that was being changed during the power failure to its original state. The backup system allows incremental backups of the information stores so that hard disk failures can be restored with the most recent data.

13

Exchange Connections

Exchange supports many different electronic mail systems and messaging standards, including the X.400 messaging protocol. You can plug Exchange directly into existing X.400 backbones or use it as an X.400 backbone. (Be aware, however, that with X.400 authentication, passwords are sent in the clear. The following support is also available:

♦   Exchange includes built-in support for Internet and SMTP/MIME mail. Exchange users are automatically assigned an SMTP e-mail address to send and receive mail on the Internet.

♦   Exchange Server fully supports Microsoft Mail 3.*x* post offices.

♦   Attachmate Corp. and IMI, Inc. have announced Microsoft Exchange Server-hosted gateways to IBM PROFS and IBM SNADS.

The Internet Mail Connector is a Microsoft Exchange Server component that provides built-in support for Internet and SMTP/MIME mail. The IMC provides Internet connection services that allow users to securely exchange messages over the Internet as though they were connected directly to it.

In this respect, it acts as a proxy service. Administrators can configure a number of security options. For example, specific TCP/IP addresses can be rejected, and only selected users can be allowed to send mail to the Internet. Administrators can also control the types of MIME attachments on messages and specify a default format that messages will be sent in. Digital encryption and digital signatures ensure message security.

Security for Microsoft Exchange

Any system that is connected to the Internet is subject to attempts by hackers and attackers to infiltrate the system's security and attack internal systems. The general rule is to run as few services as possible on Internet-connected systems. That's what scares administrators about electronic mail, which allows users to freely exchange information with people both inside and outside of the organization. Electronic mail is a hacker's dream come true. Here are some threats from electronic mail:

♦ Trojan Horses and viruses may be attached to messages. Unsuspecting users may execute the attachments and launch a program that infects their system, deletes files, or does other damage.

♦ Hackers attempt to sniff packets, intercept messages that are in transit, and read or tamper with those messages.

♦ Hackers may flood your Internet connection and e-mail systems with messages in an attempt to create a "denial of service" attack.

♦ Messages may be forged and made to appear as if they came from someone else in the organization. These messages may come into the organization from the outside or may be made to appear as if they are coming from your organization.

♦ Users may accidentally release sensitive information in a message or post a message to a bulletin board that infuriates other users, who then flood your system with messages or attempt to break your security out of anger.

Exchange Advanced Security

Windows NT and the Exchange Server together can help reduce the risk of electronic mail security problems. Windows NT protects your systems with all of its security features, including centralized user account administration, access controls, and auditing. The Challenge/Response security system authenticates users. Passwords are never sent in the clear. All communication between client and server uses the Remote Procedure Call (RPC) protocol, which provides the functions for authentication as well as encryption of the client-server conversion, even across the Internet. Windows NT RPC uses the RC4 Algorithm from RSA Data Security, Inc. with a 40-bit key, although this value may increase to provide more security due to recent U.S. government loosening of encryption controls.

Users of Windows and Macintosh computers can protect and verify messages by using message encryption and certification features. These combined features are known as *Advanced Security*, and they must be enabled on client machines before they can be used. Advanced Security is not available for DOS and UNIX clients. There are two primary features to Advanced Security:

Signing This technique lets the user put a digital signature on a message to certify the message's origin. Signing is important because it can guarantee that a message is from an authentic source and that no one has sent it under the guise of another person. Signing can also indicate that the contents of a message have been altered. Digital signatures are covered in more detail in Appendix B.

Sealing (Encryption) This process scrambles the contents of a message to make it difficult for anyone without a decryption key to read it. Sealing provides confidentiality. Message recipients unseal messages to decrypt and read their contents.

Message signing and sealing in the Microsoft Exchange Server follow industry standards and use public/private key technology. Each mailbox has its own public and private key; the public keys are maintained by a certification server. These technologies are discussed in Appendix B as well.

13

You can configure advanced security settings for clients by opening the Options menu and clicking the Security tab. A dialog box similar to this one appears:

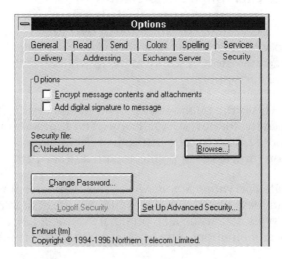

The Security Options dialog box contains the following elements:

♦ **Encrypt message contents and attachments** Seals the contents of your messages and attachments so that they can be read only by you and the recipients.

♦ **Add digital signature to message** Signs all of your messages so that recipients can be assured that the message is from you.

♦ **Security file** Displays the name and location of the file containing your advanced security information. Specify this name and location when you set up advanced security. This information is stored in your profile.

♦ **Change Password** Click this to change the password when advanced security is set.

♦ **Logoff Security** Turns off the Don't Prompt For Password Again Until Next Exchange Logon option for convenience. If you plan to leave your office for a while, enable this option to prevent someone else from sending a signed or sealed message from your mailbox.

♦ **Set Up Advanced Security** Opens the Set Up Advanced Security dialog box, where advanced security options are set.

NOTE: This discussion is not a comprehensive tutorial; however, it is designed to familiarize you with some of the security options available in Microsoft Exchange.

Message Encryption and Signatures

Microsoft Exchange users can digitally sign or seal messages that they send to other users in their organization or over the Internet. Encryption provides a way to scramble messages, rendering them impossible to read. Microsoft Exchange uses the RSA security system while specifically using DES or CAST for actual encryption.

RSA   This is the public-key encryption and certification "framework" developed by Ron Rivest, Adi Shamir, and Leonard Adleman (thus RSA) in 1977 at the Massachusetts Institute of Technology. RSA provides the definitions and usage of public and private key pairs.

DES (Data Encryption Standard)   This is an encoding and encryption algorithm designed by the U.S. National Bureau of Standards. DES encrypts and decrypts data using a 56-bit binary number key with 72 quadrillion possible combinations. The key is randomly generated for each session to create an encryption pattern. DES is generally considered impossible to crack without the decryption key.

CAST   This proprietary encryption method was created by Northern Telecom and is named after its creators, Carlisle Adams and Stafford Tavares. CAST is a "drop-in" replacement for DES that uses variable input key values between 40 and 128 bits in length to encrypt data. The longer the key value, the more secure the encryption. Microsoft Exchange uses 40-bit and 64-bit input keys for CAST.

Messages that have been encrypted (sealed) in the Microsoft Exchange Server can only be decrypted by a recipient on the Microsoft Exchange Server who has the proper private encryption key. The keys themselves are exchanged using a 512-bit public-key encryption from RSA Data Security, Inc. Digital signatures are also created using this public-key encryption.

NOTE: If a signed message is sent to a recipient who is not on the Microsoft Exchange Server or is outside of the organization, the recipient can read the message, but the signature cannot be verified.

13

The United States government and other governments impose import/export laws on cryptographic functions that require licensing. Currently, it is not possible to obtain an export license to a country for the CAST 64 or DES algorithm. Therefore, Microsoft ships the 40-bit version of CAST outside the U.S.

As mentioned, Microsoft Exchange clients use the Remote Procedure Calls (RPCs) to communicate with the Exchange server. Only clients that are logged on and authenticated to a Windows NT user account can access mailboxes. You can enable RPC encryption for clients to improve the security of the client-server communication. This encryption can be used for network connections and for dial-up connections. To configure Exchange Server clients to encrypt all RPC traffic, go to the Advanced page of the Properties for Microsoft Exchange Server and enable encryption for the network and/or for dial-up networking.

CAUTION: When you allow clients on the Internet to access their mailboxes using RPCs, you are exposing your internal network to hackers who might gain access to mailboxes and public folders. Refer to the Microsoft Exchange documentation to make sure you configure these services properly. A mistake in the configuration could be disastrous.

The TCP/IP port numbers used for RPCs are dynamically assigned to the Microsoft Exchange Server directory or information store. Clients always connect to port 135, which is the Windows NT RPC End point Mapper service. When clients connect to this port, they get information about which port numbers have been dynamically assigned to the Microsoft Exchange Server directory or information stores. If you use packet filtering, you can force Microsoft Exchange Server to use a fixed port for RPC by editing the Registry. This is covered in the Microsoft Exchange documentation.

Security Features and the Internet Mail Connector

Firewalls and proxy services protect your internal network from Internet attackers. They consist of hardware and software techniques that can block external users by filtering packets and by preventing the packets generated by various services and applications from entering your internal network. As mentioned previously, a proxy service fulfills Internet requests for internal clients, removing any open channels between internal clients and the Internet that hackers might take advantage of.

NOTE: The Microsoft Exchange Server, like many other e-mail systems, uses a store-and-forward messaging design, which inherently makes use of proxying. Clients connect to servers that reside on the local network. Servers in turn communicate with each other to transfer e-mail messages. Depending on how the Microsoft Exchange Server is configured, you may not need separate proxy software.

Recall that the Internet Mail Connector (IMC) provides a way to connect the Microsoft Exchange Server to the Internet. However, doing so requires advanced levels of security, especially in an electronic mail environment. Following are some powerful security tools provided by Exchange:

Accept/Reject by IP Address   With this feature, you can configure the IMC to communicate with specific SMTP hosts by rejecting connection attempts from any other IP address. This makes it difficult for someone to mount an attack on your system. By default, the Internet Mail Connector (IMC) accepts incoming connections from any IP address.

Message Size Limit   People who want to stage a denial-of-service attack on your message server can repeatedly send very large messages. The Message Size Limit feature lets you establish size limits for both incoming and outgoing mail. If an incoming message from another SMTP host exceeds the size limit, the IMC will stop writing data to disk and will throw away any remaining data. This feature also prevents large messages from filling up disk space.

Disabling Auto-Replies to the Internet   It is common for users who leave the office for a time to generate auto-reply messages that inform message senders that they will be gone. However, good security precludes sharing this information outside the organization. The IMC can disable outbound delivery of automated replies on a global or per-domain basis.

Delivery Restrictions   The IMC lets you configure exactly which users have permission to send mail outside the organization. This is useful if you want to prevent part-time employees from sending messages over the Internet.

The Microsoft Exchange Server can be set up to provide secure Internet access without additional software beyond the Internet Mail Connector, which should be configured to forward all mail to the host running the firewall software.

If you use the Internet Mail Connector to route mail between your organization and SMTP hosts on the Internet, you can minimize security risks by making the server a dedicated system that has no user mailboxes and that routes only Internet mail. Intruders who manage to gain access to this server (which is essentially a firewall) will not have access to data that would normally be stored in the users' mailboxes or public folders. If you are using a packet filter, you must configure it to allow TCP connections to and from port 25 on the Microsoft Exchange Server.

13

Domain Name System (DNS) Considerations

DNS is a naming system for the Internet that stores a link between host names and IP addresses in a distributed database. The database exists on various servers throughout the Internet; when you want to connect with an Internet site, you type in its DNS name and the nearest DNS server translates this name into an IP address. You are then directly connected with the site by means of the IP address. Many organizations have their own DNS servers to use internally or to provide information about internal systems to Internet users.

DNS also carries information about hosts, such as Mail eXchange (MX) records that specify one or more hosts that will accept mail for a domain. You can build your own DNS servers, or you can use the DNS services provided by your Internet service provider. In either case, Microsoft Exchange Server must be configured to use either internal or external DNS services.

However, if you choose to set up internal DNS services, you should be aware that Internet users can query your DNS server to get information about computers on your internal network. To prevent this, configure the DNS servers so that external hosts can query for information about your Internet server(s), but not about any other hosts on your internal network. This requires a pair of DNS servers. The first, which satisfies external DNS requests, must be registered with your parent domain and configured with the address and MX records for your firewall system. Do not create records for internal systems on this DNS server. The second DNS server will satisfy internal DNS requests and forward queries it cannot resolve to the external DNS server. In this way, clients on your internal network can get information about hosts on the Internet. This configuration works because the external DNS server has incomplete information about internal systems, and the internal DNS server cannot be reached by Internet users.

The System Management Server

The Microsoft System Management Server is a tool for managing small networks or enterprise-wide networks. It runs on the Windows NT Server and provides a central point of control where administrators can troubleshoot problems, eliminate downtime, and control administrative costs. The primary focus of the SMS is the central management of networked PCs.

Managing Hardware and Software Assets from a Central Location   The SMS lets you gather inventory-related information about resources attached to the network and software running on the network. You can determine how many copies of a software package are installed and which PCs need hardware upgrades.

Distribute New Software from the Central Site   You can upgrade software on individual PCs by distributing software to them from the SMS server. This eliminates the need to travel to PCs to perform software installations. The SMS can also install patches and perform virus checks on software before installation.

Analyzing Network Protocols and Traffic   The SMS lets you look at bottlenecks on the network and manage network traffic where needed. You can capture packets on the network and gather statistics about PCs or groups of PCs. Most importantly, you can monitor unauthorized activities by viewing packets.

Remote Troubleshooting   The SMS lets you analyze the configuration settings, hardware, and software of individual computers so you can troubleshoot problems over the phone with either the system's user or a technician.

Remote Control of Individual PCs   The SMS lets you control a remote PC with the mouse and keyboard of the management workstation. This provides a way to troubleshoot problems or help a remote user through a specific task.

The SMS Systems Manager is the console you use to perform all of these tasks. The underlying Sites window provides a map of the network sites where servers and client computers are located. You can click on a site to view information about systems located there. This mapping of systems provides administrators with a centralized global view of the network. The upper window shows the details for a software update job.

The SMS supports popular desktop operating systems including MS-DOS, Windows, OS/2, and Apple Macintosh. You can also take advantage of the many products from third parties that build on and extend the Systems Management Server. These products include DEC extensions that support VAX and OSF/1, Arcadia Systems' enterprise storage-management system, or Tally Systems' advanced software-recognition capabilities. You can also integrate the SMS with such traditional network management tools as Digital PolyCenter Manager on NetView, Hewlett-Packard OpenView, IBM NetView/6000, and Network Managers NMC Vision.

13

The SMS is compatible with the Desktop Management Interface (DMI), which is an emerging standard that makes it easier to manage software and hardware components on PCs and other devices such as fax machines. The SMS also takes advantage of the Simple Network Management Protocol (SNMP) support, built into Windows NT, and NetView support (supplied with SNA Server), which enables it to work with a variety of SNMP-based management systems.

While all of this sounds good, consider what could happen if a rogue manager or hacker gained access to your administrative workstation and ran the SMS Systems Manager! Obviously, a system that provides these types of services from a remote administrative workstation requires extra security precautions (physically securing the system and making sure no one captures the logon password). Still, the SMS provides some interesting tools that can help you monitor the security of your network.

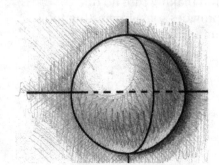

CHAPTER 14

Remote Access Issues

Every day, more and more people take to the road with portable computers, or move out of their corporate offices to work at home or at remote sites. Every day, you need to grant more and more users access to internal network resources. Increasingly, the office is just about anywhere a user happens to be, and that can open a can of security worms if those users want to connect to your internal network or carry sensitive and valuable information that could get lost.

The basic idea is to let users dial in to your network and access electronic mail, sales reports, inventories, company bulletins, and other information that is vital to their job on the road or at remote locations. There are two ways to do this, based on the level of access you want to give to users and the response time you want to achieve:

Remote Control Method   With this method, a user who dials in with a remote control system (such as pcANYWHERE) connects to a computer at the dial-in site. That computer executes all commands for the user while she is logged on. Only keyboard and screen update information is transferred across the line.

Remote Access Method   With this method, a user who connects with a remote access system interacts directly with systems on the dial-in server and/or network. Processing takes place on the user's computer. In most cases, network protocols are used across the line.

The remote control method provides somewhat better performance since less information is transmitted across the lines, but the remote access method provides more flexibility for users because it mimics an actual connection to the Internet. In addition, remote access connections do not require dedicated computers at the dial-in site to execute commands for users.

In some respects, Web services provide a unique alternative to dial-up connections. Picture a private Web page that includes company news and bulletins, plus pages where remote users can access files on internal servers or query corporate databases. Web technology has advanced enough to make building such pages as easy as using a word processor.

Most people think of Web pages as public postings on the Internet, but you can secure your Web pages for private access by using the same logon authentication that your internal users use to log on to a Windows NT Server. Remote users will need a browser such as Microsoft Internet Explorer to run the Microsoft authentication protocol. If users need information from databases or other sources, you can build dynamic Web sites that interact with SQL Server databases and Microsoft Exchange, as discussed in Chapter 13.

NOTE: The Microsoft Exchange Server discussed in the previous chapter can provide unique new solutions for servicing the information requirements of remote users. This chapter concentrates on traditional remote access methods.

Web protocols are very efficient at delivering information over dial-up connections; many users are already familiar with using Web browsers to access information. Web browsers have become a sort of "universal client," so taking advantage of this technology will likely reduce your training costs.

Not all remote and mobile user requirements fit into the Web server paradigm, and that is where services like RAS come into play. With RAS, users can gain access to your network and work as if they were using a computer directly connected to that network. Sound like an incredible security risk? You bet. If you leave a door unlocked, somebody is bound to come in. Fortunately, Microsoft has built security into RAS, as you'll see.

Here are the types of threats you can expect if you set up a dial-in connection on your network:

♦ Hackers armed with "war dialers" make hundreds or thousands of calls per day looking for modem connect signals. Once your remote access lines are located, a hacker will focus on breaking into your site. One solution to this problem is to have your modem answer calls after several rings, not on the first ring. If there's no speedy connection, a war dialer will likely proceed to a new number (and leave yours alone). You can also change the phone numbers often.

♦ A hacker who obtains a valid user's logon name and password can gain access to the system and steal valuable information from the comfort of his own office.

♦ A hacker who has physical access to a remote system that dials in to your network could crack the logon sequence to gain access. Callback security would be ineffective, since the user is at the site that is called back.

14

Once an unauthorized user gains access to a system, she may be greeted with a welcome message! With such a message, the courts may uphold the user's attack on your system, since you welcomed it. Post "authorized users only" messages on your systems wherever possible. In fact, the Electronics Communication Privacy Act (ECPA) prevents you from eavesdropping on the activities of an intruder—even if you own the system—unless you post a message to indicate that all activities are subject to being monitored.

Windows NT Remote Access Service (RAS)

Remote Access Service (RAS) is a dial-up networking service included in Windows NT and optionally in Windows 95. This discussion deals only with the Windows NT version of RAS, assuming that your Windows 95 client will be dialing into a Windows NT RAS server.

RAS consists of clients and servers. Clients dial in to RAS servers, and RAS servers authenticate clients and provide them with access to resources on the local server or network. Users of Windows, DOS, and OS/2 operating systems can dial in to Windows NT RAS servers via local modems, X.25 packet-switching services, and ISDN (Integrated Services Digital Network) to access resources on that computer or on the network that is attached to it. You can even set up a direct connection using an RS232C null modem cable. This last connection type is useful for connecting a local administrative system to a server so that an operator can access it if the network fails.

 NOTE: The Point-to-Point Tunneling Protocol (PPTP) can provide secure encrypted sessions between remote clients and servers, as discussed in Chapter 15.

Once connected and logged on, users can access files and databases on servers or shared resources as they normally would if working at a local workstation. You can allow users either to access only the server that they dialed in to or to access the network attached to the server. Users can also access NetWare servers and printers on an internal network, or they can exchange e-mail and access IBM host systems if Microsoft's SNA Server is running on the network. Administrators can even use RAS to manage systems remotely, although the security consequences of that must be considered.

Figure 14-1 illustrates the different remote connection methods that are possible with RAS. Most home and mobile users will connect with standard phone lines or ISDN. X.25 connections are useful when dedicated connections or frequent dial-up connections are required between branch offices or other sites. Many large companies have their own X.25 networks or make use of public X.25 network services. Direct connections can provide a fault-tolerant link to a server so that network administrators can access it if the network fails.

Most important for this discussion are the security options available with RAS. Because RAS can run on a Windows NT Server, it takes full advantage

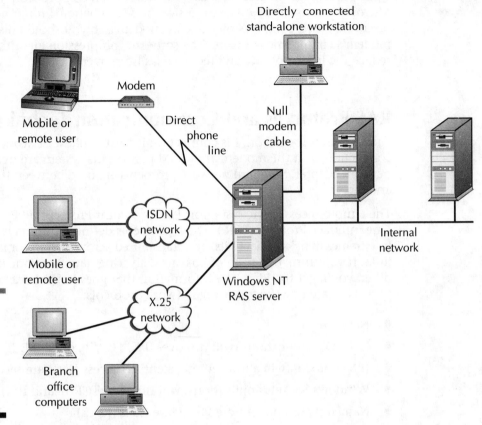

Types of
remote access
connections
available with
Windows
NT RAS
Figure 14-1.

14

of Windows NT security features, including user logon and authentication, domain security, support for security hosts, data encryption, and call back features.

Remote and mobile users dial in to a pool of modems that are automatically made available to them by the server. Security options include logon and domain security, data encryption, and callback (which can verify the caller's phone number and/or reverse the charges).

NOTE: With the PPTP protocol, you no longer need to maintain banks of modems at your site. Instead, your remote users dial in to the Internet to connect to your site, and all you need is a single line between your network and a local Internet service provider (ISP).

To improve performance, RAS uses software-based compression. In Microsoft's tests, software compression provided better throughput than hardware-based compression done by modems, so you should disable your modem's compression feature. The software compression algorithms also reduce the interrupt rate and reduce risks from overruns.

RAS Protocols and Communication Techniques

Once a user is logged on, his connection is treated like a network connection, and the modem and COM port on his system are treated like a network adapter. Standard network protocols are used between the client and server.

The remote access services support Point-to-Point Protocol (PPP) and Serial Line Interface Protocol (SLIP). These protocols define how data is divided up into frames (blocks of data bits) and transmitted across dial-up communication links. If you think of a train of boxcars delivering data from one place to the other, you'll get the idea. The information that goes in the boxcars include packets created by the following network protocols:

♦   NetBEUI

♦   NetBIOS applications (will run over IPX, TCP/IP, or NetBEUI)

♦   IPX protocol (will allow remote clients to access NetWare services)

♦   Windows Sockets applications (will run over TCP/IP and IPX)

♦   Named pipes and Remote Procedure Calls (RPCs)

Windows NT Server 4.0 includes enhanced IP and IPX routing capabilities. As pictured in Figure 14-2, Windows NT Workstation and Windows 95 clients can run TCP/IP and IPX locally and run Windows Sockets applications or NetBIOS applications over their local TCP/IP and IPX protocols. Prior versions of the RAS server required that administrators install a NetBIOS gateway on the RAS server to handle these applications for remote users.

The client-server connection will use all the protocols that are mutually available on both systems, so if TCP/IP and IPX are running on the server and on the client, both of those protocols are available for use.

RAS uses remote access protocols to transport network packets over dial-up links. Packets are put into frames and delivered across the link. The primary support in Windows NT RAS is the Point-to-Point Protocol (PPP), but several others are supported as well. All are discussed next.

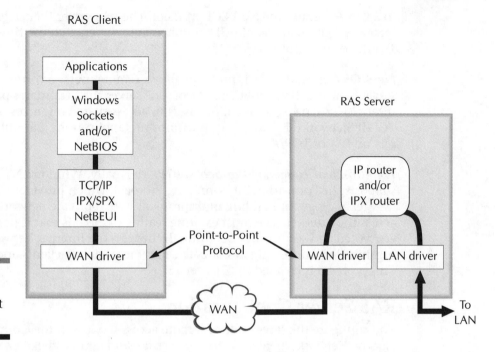

RAS Client

Applications

Windows
Sockets
and/or
NetBIOS

RAS Server

TCP/IP
IPX/SPX
NetBEUI

IP router
and/or
IPX router

Point-to-Point
Protocol

WAN driver

WAN driver

LAN driver

WAN

To
LAN

Remote
multiprotocol
router support
Figure 14-2.

NOTE: Which protocols are used depends on the operating system and
LAN protocols in use.

14

Point-to-Point Protocol   This is a wide area-linking protocol that puts IPX,
TCP/IP, and NetBEUI packets into *frames* for delivery across dial-up links.
All Windows computers now support PPP and can dial in to any server that
complies with the PPP standard. PPP resides at the WAN driver level just
below the TCP/IP, IPX, and NetBEUI protocols, as shown in Figure 14-2.

SLIP Protocol   This protocol is often used for connecting to UNIX systems.
It supports the TCP/IP protocol only. PPP has largely replaced SLIP in the
general environment because PPP supports the IPX and NetBEUI protocols
as well as the TCP/IP protocol.

Microsoft RAS Protocol   This is Microsoft's original remote access protocol
for supporting NetBIOS. It was implemented in Windows NT version 3.1,
Windows for Workgroups, and DOS and requires that a RAS client dialing in

to a RAS server use the NetBEUI protocol. The RAS server then acts as a "gateway," giving the NetBEUI client access to servers that use the NetBEUI, TCP/IP, or IPX protocol.

NetBIOS Gateway   This protocol allows remote users to connect with a server by using the NetBEUI protocol. The server then translates packets into IPX or TCP/IP packets that allow users to access shared resources on IPX or TCP/IP networks. However, users cannot run applications and utilities that rely on IPX or TCP/IP.

Point-to-Point Tunneling Protocol (PPTP)   Finally, Windows NT RAS supports the Point-to-Point Tunneling Protocol, which provides a unique new technology for building multiprotocol virtual private networks (VPNs) across the Internet. The most exciting feature of PPTP is that it provides an encrypted and secure channel (tunnel) through the Internet between your organization's different sites or between remote/mobile clients and servers. This protocol is covered in Chapter 15.

RAS Server Configuration

You configure the server side of remote access services in the Control Panel. Choose Network, then click the Services tab and double-click Remote Access Service to display the dialog box shown here. (This assumes that RAS is installed. If not, click the Add button to install it.)

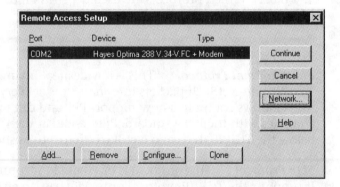

The Remote Access Setup dialog box shows a list of ports and dial-in devices that users call in to. You can select a port/device and click the Configure button to set the following options:

◆ **Dial out only**   Indicates that this device will only be used by internal users to dial out.

◆ **Receive calls only**   Indicates that this device will only be used to receive incoming calls.

♦ **Dial out and receive calls** Indicates that this port will receive incoming calls and allow internal users to dial out.

If you choose a port/device and click the Network button, the Network Configuration dialog box appears, as shown in Figure 14-3. This is where you choose the protocols you want to use on the port and set security options, which are discussed later.

The Network Configuration dialog box has the following options:

♦ **Dial out Protocols** Select the protocol to enable for internal users when they are dialing out through the RAS server. The protocol selections will influence the level of security at the server, as discussed later.

♦ **Server Settings** In this field, choose the protocol that external users will use when dialing in to the RAS server. As with the Dial out Protocols option, the selection you make here affects the level of security for your internal networks. You can also choose the level of logon encryption, as discussed later in this chapter under "RAS Logon and Authentication Methods."

♦ **Enable Multilink** If you enable this option, dial-in users can combine multiple dial-up lines to act as a single channel to improve transmissions speeds. When ISDN is used, this feature lets users combine the two available dial-up lines to achieve twice the throughput.

14

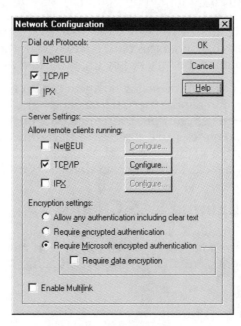

Network
Configuration
for a
port/device
on a remote
access server
Figure 14-3.

When you select a protocol in the Server Settings field, the Configure button next to it becomes available. Click this button to open a Configuration dialog box similar to the following. This is the Configuration dialog box for the TCP/IP protocol:

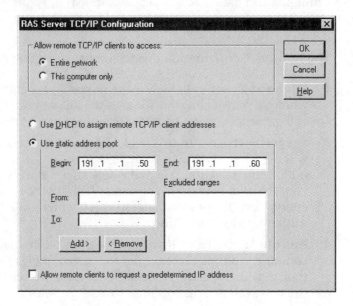

Here, the most important option for security purposes is at the top of the dialog box. You can allow external users to access only the server that is running RAS, or you can allow them to access the network attached to the RAS server. Choose this option wisely with the knowledge that a remote session might be hijacked by unauthorized users.

Lower down in the dialog box, you can set how you want IP addresses allocated to remote users. If you choose the Use DHCP option, IP addresses are assigned from a pre-configured pool on a DHCP server. Obviously, this option requires a DHCP server to exist somewhere on your network. If you don't have a DHCP server, choose the "Use static address pool" option and specify a range of IP addresses that you want to assign to dial-in users.

Configuring RAS Clients

You configure a dial-up network for Windows NT Workstation 4.0 and Windows 95 clients by opening the Start menu and choosing Program, Accessories, and then Dial-up Networking. You can choose Make New

Connection to create a new dial-up connection. A Wizard guides you through the steps of selecting a modem or other dial-up device, entering the phone number for the dial-up server, and naming the new connection. When the Wizard completes, the new dial-up object appears in the Dial-up Networking folder. You can click and drag this object to the desktop to make it more accessible.

CAUTION: Keep in mind that the phone numbers for your dial-up sites are stored on the client's computer, and are thus easy to view by someone who might want to target your site for attack.

To configure settings for the new dial-up object, right-click it and choose Properties to display the following dialog box:

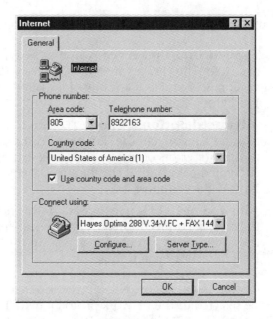

14

You can click the Configure button to change the configuration of the modem or dial-up device if necessary.

Click the Server Type button to configure the dial-up network settings. The following dialog box appears:

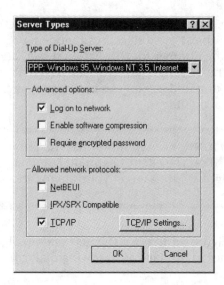

In the Server Types dialog box, you can set the following options:

♦ **Type of Dial-Up Server**   Choose the type of server you want to dial in to. The choices are NRN (NetWare Connect), PPP (Windows NT version 3.51 and 4.0) and the older Windows 3.1 and Windows for Workgroup RAS.

♦ **Advanced options**   Choose "Log on to network" if the remote server requires a logon, choose "Enable software compression" whenever possible (if errors occur, try disabling this option), and enable "Require encrypted password" if the dial-up server supports the option (Windows NT RAS does support it).

♦ **Allowed network protocols**   In this field, choose the protocols of the remote connection you want to use. Your choices here depend on the applications you need to access on the dial-up system and on the level of security you want.

Notice that if you choose NRN in the top field, only the IPX/SPX protocol can be selected in the network protocol field. If you choose the older Windows 3.1 and Windows for Workgroup option, only the NetBEUI protocol is available. If you choose PPP, all the protocols can be selected.

If you've selected the PPP server type and the TCP/IP protocol, the TCP/IP Settings button is available. If you click the button, you can set the IP address for the client or choose to have the remote server automatically assign an IP address, assuming a DHCP server is available on that network.

Managing RAS Services and Security Options

RAS security depends on user accounts and user logon, data encryption, and callback security. All of the user-account security and file-system permissions that apply to local users also apply to RAS users once they are authenticated and have access to the network. If you set up RAS in a Windows NT domain, you can grant any user in the domain the right to log on to the RAS server from a remote location. Of course, you can create new accounts using the User Manager for Domains for users who only log on from remote locations.

You manage RAS servers by opening the Remote Access Admin utility, which is part of the Program/Administrative Tools group on the Start menu in Windows NT 4.0. The Remote Access Admin dialog box appears:

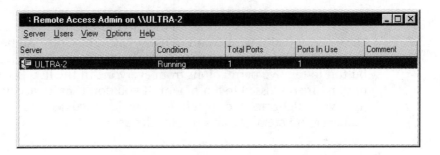

This box lists each of the ports that have dial-up devices, and provides status information such as whether the device is running, how many ports it supports, and how many ports are currently in use.

There are several options on the Server menu that let you start, stop, pause, and continue a remote device. You can also choose Communication Port to view the status of any port and disconnect users from it.

Managing User Permissions

From this menu, you can set up permissions for users to dial in to or dial out from the RAS server. Even if users are already authorized to access resources on an internal network, they still need permission to dial in to the network from a remote location. To set up permissions for users, choose Permissions from the Users menu. A Remote Access Permissions dialog box appears, similar to the one shown in Figure 14-4.

14

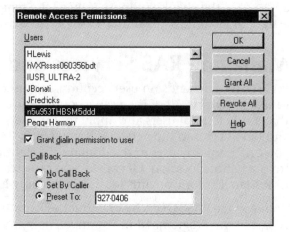

The basic procedure is to select a user-account name in the Users list, then click "Grant dialin permission to user." Click the Grant All button to grant everyone in the list permissions to access the server, or click the Revoke All button to remove permissions from everyone in the list. The Call Back options are discussed in a moment. If you don't see an account name for a user, you might need to switch domains (as discussed next) or open the User Manager and create an account for the user.

CAUTION: Do not grant members of the Administrators group RAS permissions. Their accounts could be hijacked, with devastating results. For security reasons, administer all servers locally. If members of that group need to dial in, create a non-administrative account for that purpose.

To grant RAS permissions for users in another domain, you need to switch to the domain so you can see a list of its user accounts in the Remote Access Permissions dialog box. Choose Select Domain or Server from the Server menu of the Remote Access Admin utility. A dialog box much like this one will appear:

Here you'll see a list of domains. You can select the domain that contains
the user accounts that you want to grant RAS permissions to. After selecting
domains, go back to the Permissions dialog box by choosing Permissions
from the Users menu. A list of users in the selected domain will appear in the
list so that you can grant them permissions.

NOTE: If you revoke RAS permissions for a user, it may take up to 15
minutes for the change to take place, because replication of user-database
information does not take place immediately in a domain. A user whose
permissions you have revoked may still be able to log on during that period.
To prevent this from happening, you can force re-synchronization in the
Server Manager.

14

Restricting Network Access

If you need to restrict users' access to only the RAS server that they dial in to,
you must enable the This Computer Only option for Remote Access Services
in the Network utility. Open the Network utility and double-click Remote
Access Services on the Services page. Choose the port to configure, then click
the Network button to open the dialog box pictured in Figure 14-3. Click the
Configure button next to the protocol you are using, either NetBEUI, TCP/IP,
or IPX; then, on the dialog box that appears, choose the option called This
Computer Only.

As mentioned, it is wise not to grant any user accounts that have Administrator privileges access to the RAS server. Anyone who hijacks the account will gain all the access rights and privileges granted to that account and wreak havoc on your network. Even if you have restricted access to the local RAS server only and not to the entire network, the user (now having Administrator access) could change this option, following the procedure just described, and gain access to the rest of the network.

When you grant any remote users access to your internal network, you need to control access to individual systems using access rights and permissions. Since the user's dial-in account is the same as his internal user account, it's easy to assign permissions on resources for remote users. Simply go to each resource and enable appropriate permissions as you would for any user.

One thing to consider is security measures that will protect your internal system from remote access accounts that have been hijacked by an unauthorized user. Let's say someone has stolen one of your employee's hand-held computers and has cracked the password. In such a case, the owner of the computer might call you to let you know the machine has been stolen. You could then revoke the RAS dial-in permissions for the user account or remove the user's account entirely from the directory database, then create an entirely new account for the authorized user. You should also enable the dial-back feature to ensure that the user calling in is at the location you expect.

T **IP:** Two-factor authentication can provide an added level of security for dial-up connections as discussed under "Two-Factor User Authentication" later in this chapter.

As an added precaution, you might want to set various settings on your RAS server in advance to protect against unauthorized access. After all, a mobile user who loses a laptop computer will not inform you until she discovers the loss. By then, a malicious user may have already broken into your system. To protect yourself against break-ins, make sure that remote users neither make their passwords publicly available nor store them on their systems in a way that is easy to discover.

On the server side, you can allow remote users access to only the RAS server by setting the This Computer Only option described earlier. This will prevent intruders from accessing other servers on your internal network. Then, store only non-sensitive files on the RAS server.

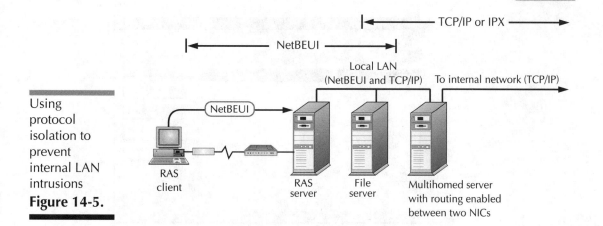

Figure 14-5.

But in many cases, both RAS users and internal users need to access the same server. For the RAS user, this server is attached to the internal network, so they need internal network access beyond the RAS server. What is a safe way to give both internal users and dial-up users access to the same resources? One technique, called protocol isolation, is pictured in Figure 14-5.

In this case, the RAS server is attached to a local LAN that includes three data servers. One of the servers is a multihomed system (one having two network interface cards). The internal network is attached to one of those cards, and the local LAN is attached to the other. The local LAN runs both NetBEUI and TCP/IP while the internal LAN runs TCP/IP or IPX/SPX. The key is that NetBEUI is not routable, so dial-up users are restricted to accessing only servers on the local LAN. Internal network users can access the servers using TCP/IP protocols, because routing is enabled in the multihomed system.

14

Sending Messages and Disconnecting Users

You might need to disconnect users if you determine that they have gained unauthorized access, or if they have simply locked up their system or left a connection open that is not in use. To disconnect a user, open the Remote Access Admin utility and double-click the server that the user is logged in to. The Communication Ports dialog box appears.

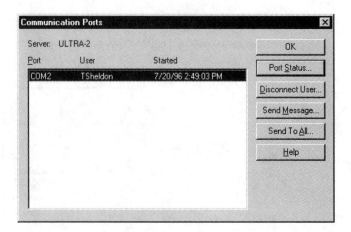

Click the name of the user you want to disconnect, then click the Disconnect User button. Before disconnecting a trusted user, click the Send Message button and send the user a message that you are about to disconnect her session. Perhaps the user has forgotten that the connection is still alive, and is working on something else. Disconnecting a session will free it for other users to dial in to. You can also send a message to all dial-up users by clicking the Send To All button.

TIP: You can view the status of a port by clicking the Port Status button on the Communication Ports dialog box.

Callback Options

Callback options provide an important service in secure environments: they call a user back at a predefined number and prevent intruders who have obtained valid logon information from dialing in at an unauthorized location. They also provide an additional bonus for remote and mobile users by reversing the charges on calls. When a client calls in, the RAS server authenticates the user, then hangs up the call and calls back. Thus, the call is charged to the account of the RAS server.

You configure callback options on the Remote Access Permissions dialog box, pictured in Figure 14-4. You access this box by choosing from the Start menu Programs, then Administrative Tools, and finally Remote Access Admin. When the Remote Access Admin utility appears, choose Permissions on the Users menu.

There are three types of callback options, described next. You set a callback option for each individual user.

♦ **No Call Back**   This disables callback options.

♦ **Set By Caller**   This option is primarily used to reverse toll charges for users. When a user calls in, RAS authenticates him, and a dialog box appears asking for the callback telephone number. The RAS server then disconnects the call and calls the client back. Note that this option provides no additional security.

♦ **Preset To**   This callback option does provide security, because you can specify in advance the telephone number where a user should be called back.

Select a user account in the Users list, then choose "Grant dialin permission to user" and select a call back option. Each user obviously has his own preset telephone number. When a user calls in, the RAS server authenticates him, then disconnects the call and calls him back at the preset number.

RAS Logon and Authentication Methods

RAS uses authentication protocols and encryption to provide security and ensure that remote access transmissions are protected from eavesdroppers. What are the logon procedures for a RAS connection? Here are the basic steps for Challenge/Response authentication:

14

1. A RAS-enabled client dials the Windows NT Remote Access Server.

2. The server challenges the client. It sends a *nonce*, which is a one-time value that is not known by anyone in advance, to the client. It also remembers this value for later comparison (in Step 4).

3. The client packages his encrypted password with the nonce and encrypts this bundle again, then sends it back to the server. Thus, the user password is double-encrypted during transmission.

4. The server already has a copy of the user's encrypted password in the User Account database. It gets this password and encrypts it with the session nonce (this is the same thing the client did with the nonce). This information is then compared to the logon information returned as the response by the client.

5. If the values match, the server checks to see if the client has RAS logon permissions.

6. If the account has RAS permissions, the client is authenticated and allowed access to the RAS server or network.

NOTE: The purpose of the nonce is to create a one-time session that cannot be "replayed" by a hacker who has sniffed the transmission.

If callback is enabled, the server hangs up the connection and calls the client back. The server again challenges the client, and the client returns its logon information to the server in encrypted form. Once again, the server checks all this information, and then connects the client if everything is valid.

RAS uses a number of authentication and encryption protocols to negotiate secure authentication and to protect logon information during transmission. The type of encryption protocols allowed depends on whether you are talking about the server or the client. Windows NT RAS services are discussed first, then Windows RAS clients in general.

While most of these techniques provide strong security, some organizations may prefer keycard devices or security techniques available from third-party vendors. Windows NT RAS fully supports these devices, as discussed later in this chapter under "Two-Factor User Authentication."

Where to Set Encryption

To manage authentication and encryption settings on Windows NT RAS servers, open the Network Configuration dialog box, as you saw in Figure 14-3, by opening the Network utility in the Control Panel and double-clicking Remote Access Services on the Services page. You then click the Network button. The options you can set for authentication and encryption are:

♦ **Allow any authentication including clear text**   When this option is selected, clients can connect to the RAS server using any supported authentication method, including CHAP, SPAP, and PAP (discussed in the next section, "Encryption Protocols"). Use this option if non-Windows RAS clients dial in to your RAS server.

♦ **Require encrypted authentication**   This option allows any supported authentication method except for PAP, which is not secure because it sends passwords in the clear.

♦ **Require Microsoft encrypted authentication**   This option specifies that only the Challenge-Handshake Authentication Protocol (CHAP) can be used by the RAS server.

In Figure 14-3, notice the "Require data encryption" checkbox. If this checkbox is enabled, all data sent over the wire is encrypted.

To manage authentication and encryption settings for Windows 95 and
Windows NT clients, open My Computer on the desktop, then the Dial-up
Networking folder. If you haven't already created a dial-up object, choose
Make New Connection and follow the instructions provided by the Wizard,
as described earlier under "Configuring RAS Clients." When the new object
appears in the Window, right-click it, choose Properties, then click the Server
Type button. On the menu that appears, choose "Require encrypted
password" for the highest level of security.

Encryption Protocols

The authentication and encryption methods provided in Windows NT 4.0
Remote Access Services are described here. The method used depends upon
the clients that dial in and the level of encryption that they can support.

The *Challenge-Handshake Authentication Protocol* (CHAP) is an encrypted
authentication mechanism that challenges the remote client for logon
information as described in the 6 steps presented earlier under "RAS Logon
and Authentication Methods." If both the client and server are using RAS, as is
the case with Windows NT, Windows for Workgroups, and Windows 95
computers, CHAP is implemented. CHAP uses DES-encrypted authentication,
which is an encoding and encryption algorithm designed by the U.S.
National Bureau of Standards. It encrypts using a 56-bit binary number key
with 72 quadrillion possible combinations. The key is randomly generated
for each session to create an encryption pattern that is generally considered
impossible to crack without the decryption key.

14

Keep the following points in mind:

♦ If the "Require Microsoft encrypted authentication" option is set on the
   Network Configuration dialog box pictured in Figure 14-3, only CHAP
   may be used.

♦ If the "Allow any authentication including clear text" or the "Require
   encrypted authentication" option is set, then the server attempts to use
   CHAP first but will negotiate with the client to use other protocols.

♦ If "Allow any authentication including clear text" is set, the server
   will negotiate down to the lowest-level encryption protocol available,
   including PAP (Password Authentication Protocol). PAP is only used
   if the client and the server cannot negotiate a more secure form
   of validation.

PAP provides authentication by sending weakly encrypted information.
It's not considered secure because eavesdroppers could capture logon
information and easily check it. Windows NT RAS server supports PAP

for interoperability with third-party PPP clients, such as NetManage Chameleon and Trumpet Winsock.

If a Windows NT Workstation connects to devices created by Shiva, Inc., the Shiva Password Authentication Protocol (SPAP) is used. Likewise, if a Shiva client connects to a Windows NT Server, it will use SPAP. Unlike PAP, SPAP encrypts passwords over the wire instead of sending clear-text passwords.

NOTE: Windows clients (but not RAS servers) can negotiate to use RSA's MD5 encryption standard when connecting with other vendors' remote access servers.

Two-Factor User Authentication

You can use third-party security devices to improve security for dial-up users beyond the security that is available with Windows NT RAS services. Security devices are typically keycards: credit card-size devices that display a different number every minute. The keycard is synchronized with a similar device at the server that generates the same number. When a user logs on, the number on the user's keycard is sent to the dial-up server as a supplement to the normal logon procedure.

This technique ensures that only authorized users with valid passwords *and* keycard numbers can log on to the system. The two factors in the scheme are the password that the user knows and the keycard value that they get at the time of logon. If a user loses her portable computer, a person who manages to crack its cached password won't be able to log on to the network without the keycard value. Likewise, the keycard is useless without the user's password.

Security devices exist in both hardware and software form. The hardware devices are typically about the size of credit cards and have a small LCD display to show the access number. Software devices are programs that run on a user's computer and perform the same functions as the hardware devices. In general, the software devices are more convenient, because they automate the process and do not require that users key in the access number. However, software devices are less secure, because hackers have a better chance to crack information that might be in memory or on disk.

Supplementing RAS in this way provides a high level of security. There are a number of third-party options available from the vendors listed below. The RAS server uses an open architecture that makes it easy for developers to create add-on security devices. There are a number of configuration options that are required to make these devices work. Refer to the manuals supplied with the devices as well as the Windows NT operating system manuals for more information.

Many vendors are working on these products, and some have not yet announced products specifically designed for Windows NT. Here is a fairly complete list of vendors that you can contact on your own:

ActiveCard, Redwood City, CA	800-529-9499
Communication Devices, Clifton, NJ	201-772-6997
Cryptocard Inc., Buffalo Grove, IL	708-459-6500
Datakey Inc., Burnsville, MN	800-328-8828
Digital Pathways Inc., Mountain View, CA	415-964-0707
E-Systems, Clearwater, FL	813-573-0330
Leemah Datacom Security Corp., Hayward, CA	510-786-0790
Microframe Inc., Edison, NJ	908-494-4440
Optimum Electronics Inc., North Haven, CT	203-239-6098
Racal Guardata, Herndon, VA	703-471-0892
Security Dynamics Inc., Cambridge, MA	617-547-7820

Auditing for the Remote Access Server

14

You can use the Windows NT Event Viewer to view activities on each of the remote access servers on your network, but to do so you must first enable auditing by setting a parameter in the Registry. Once auditing is enabled, you can view events that might indicate attempts to break into your system through a dial-up connection.

To enable Remote Access auditing, follow these steps:

1. Open the Registry Editor by choosing Run from the Start menu and typing **REGEDT32** in the text field.
2. Select the HKEY_LOCAL_MACHINE window.
3. In the hierarchical tree, "drill down" to the following location:

   SYSTEM\CurrentControlSet\Services\RemoteAccess\Parameters
4. Highlight Parameters and double-click Enable Audit in the right pane.
5. Make sure the value in "Data field" is 1, then click OK.

Performing these steps will generate records in the audit logs that indicate a number of activities, including normal connections, successful disconnection, successful callbacks, disconnects due to idle lines, timed-out authentication, and line errors. Pay particular attention to messages that indicate failed connections due to incorrect authentication. Excessive failed connections may indicate that someone is trying to break into an account. If you're sure of the source of the break-ins, remove the dial-up logon permissions for the account and set callback options.

CHAPTER 15

Securing Private WANs and Virtual WANs

This chapter is about securing networks that are connected over wide areas using data communication links such as leased lines, private microwave systems, and the Internet. Whatever the type of connection you use, high risk is involved, because your communication links are outside of the controlled and protected environment of your own facilities. Your data transmissions are vulnerable to eavesdroppers, hackers, and others who want to steal information for competitive or malicious reasons. You are dependent on the security of public facilities or the strength of your encryption systems.

While Chapter 14 described methods for securing dial-up connections for individual users, this chapter discusses how to secure entire networks that are located in different places but linked over public facilities. However, there is some overlap, because wide area networks often involve dial-up access similar to the type of dial-up connections that mobile users make into your corporate networks.

Building Enterprise Networks

If you've ever used the term *enterprise network* to describe your network, then part of it is probably at another location that requires long-distance communication. An enterprise network typically includes all types of computers that share leased lines or public networks. An enterprise network lets all users share information, exchange electronic mail, and access resources anywhere. (At least that's the theory.)

This chapter focuses on building wide area network connections that are both economical and secure. The Internet provides a relatively inexpensive solution for building wide area networks. It is basically a ready-made WAN. To interconnect remote sites, you connect them to an Internet access point in your local area and set up private transmission links to your other sites over the Internet.

But wait one minute! What about security? How is it possible to connect your private networks to the public Internet and use it to transmit sensitive information? That's where new protocols come into play that let you build so-called *tunnels* through the Internet for transmitting information in a very secure way. It's like having your own private lane on the freeway (at least it will appear that way).

 CAUTION: Depending on what you are connecting and the type of information you are transmitting, you may need full-featured firewalls to protect your internal system when connecting to the Internet. See Part 4 of this book for more information.

Take a look at Figure 15-1. Here we see the old way to build a private network and the new way to build a *virtual private network* (VPN) over the Internet (or other public packet-switched facilities). The network on the left requires a total of six dedicated leased lines to interconnect four sites! If those sites are quite a distance from one another, you're going to have a very large monthly telephone bill, since charges are based on distance. The virtual network on the right requires only one line from each site into a local Internet service provider.

Of course, the Internet is not the only public network available for building virtual private networks. There are many other services available from local and long-distance providers. Frame Relay is a packet-switching service offered by many service providers for building VPNs. Check with your local public network service providers and Internet service providers to find out which options are best for your needs. One thing to consider is access points. Mobile users will need access wherever they travel, so a contract with a nationwide service provider is a good idea for those users. If you're just connecting a stationary branch office, check with local service providers.

Keep in mind that VPNs over the Internet may impose delays on your data traffic that might not be acceptable for some data transmissions. Expect delays during the latter part of 1996 and early 1997 due to increased traffic and insufficient network capacity. These delays should clear up later in 1997 as the carriers and Internet service providers (ISPs) beef up their routers and transmission facilities.

15

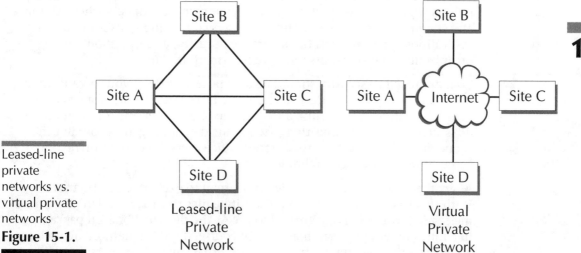

Leased-line private networks vs. virtual private networks

Figure 15-1.

Along with all the issues of interconnecting remote networks are the issues of providing reliable and efficient communication for everybody involved. What do you want to transmit over the lines? files? replicated databases? electronic mail? What is the best strategy for improving the communication among all your network users? One solution always seems to float to the surface: *electronic messaging*. Not only does it furnish the basis for intraoffice and interoffice communication, it also provides a foundation for building workgroup applications. Microsoft Schedule+ is a scheduling package that can schedule an entire organization. It is built on a messaging system.

Microsoft's new messaging platform, Microsoft Exchange, is the newest standard for creating a secure, enterprise-wide communication system. Exchange is designed for use with the Internet and you can use the Internet as a WAN to connect the Microsoft Exchange server to Microsoft Exchange clients or other Microsoft Exchange servers. Messages can include hot links to sites on the World Wide Web, and messages can use advanced security features such as encryption and digital signatures.

The point is that Exchange can add its own level of security, in the form of signed and encrypted messages, that exists above the network-level security provided by WAN hardware and software protocols.

Security for WANs and Remote Access

If you're concerned about security, why even consider extending your networks outside of your trusted facilities? It does seem crazy, but with the right protection, it is possible. Consider that banks use armored vehicles to move money and information from one location to another. That strategy reflects what you need to do to protect your own networks. Authentication and encryption are the keys. They are essential requirements for financial institutions, governments, the insurance industry, and just about any organization that transmits sensitive information.

Your approach to security should be to expose as little of your organization's information as possible. Do you really need to share files and folders over your WAN links? If you think about it, one of the riskiest things you can do is share folders on links that extend outside your organization. But that is one of the primary ways that branch office users have traditionally accessed resources at central offices.

As an alternative, you can use electronic mail to exchange information. With this technique, users request sensitive files from a "librarian" via e-mail messages. If the user is authorized to access the file, the librarian packages it in a fully encrypted e-mail message. Of course, digital signatures are used for all of these message transactions to ensure that message senders are valid and that information has not been tampered with.

Another method is to post company information and files on a secured Web server. This low-maintenance approach uses a well-understood user interface. Web servers can eliminate the need for file-sharing protocols altogether in some cases; that will improve your security. The Web server technique is discussed in Chapter 20; digital signatures are discussed in Appendix B.

Is it an extreme measure to hire a "data librarian"? Consider that one security slip-up may cost your company thousands or millions of dollars if sensitive information gets into the wrong hands. If you have trade secrets or work under military contracts, I can practically guarantee you that some unauthorized person would like to access your data files and transmissions.

Branch Office Issues

When an organization expands to multiple sites, the use of domain networking becomes even more important. While a single domain can encompass branch offices, you use domains to provide just one more level of security to your network, especially when wide area network links are used.

While the WAN may provide a physical separation between your different offices, the domain can provide a logical separation. Recall that domains require trust relationships before users in one domain can be granted access to resources in another domain. That in itself provides a level of protection. Then an Administrator must grant them access, usually after thoroughly reviewing the users' need for access. If a user account is compromised in one domain, the hacker won't be able to attack other domains where that account has no rights.

On the other hand, you may prefer to use a single domain for your entire network, because it provides centralized user account management. However, this might burden your WAN links. Assume your company has a main office, and a branch office; a primary domain controller (PDC) exists at the main office, but no domain controller exists at the branch office. When users log on at the branch office, their logon requests must go over the WAN link to the PDC at the main office. If many people log on at the same time and check their e-mail (as might happen when everybody arrives for work at the same time), a lot of traffic will be generated over the WAN link.

15

To avert this, you'll need to set up a backup domain controller (BDC) that can authenticate users at the remote site. User account information is then replicated from the main office to the branch office on a regular basis.

User account administration is affected somewhat by this strategy, because user accounts can only be created or modified at the primary domain controller. If you have a manager at the branch office who creates and modifies accounts, she will generate traffic over the WAN link as changes are sent to the primary domain controller. Of course, if the branch office is small, this traffic will be minimal, but if it is large and growing, you might have a traffic problem. Another consideration is that the branch office administrator has administrative access over the WAN link to the primary domain controller. If her account is compromised, the intruder can gain access to the main office.

By creating separate domains at each remote site and employing an administrator at each site, you may be able to create a domain structure that fits your security requirements. If users in one domain need access to resources in another domain, set up trust relationships, add the users to global groups, and grant the groups access in other domains. Managers in trusting domains should review the membership of trusted domain global groups fully to ensure that the groups do not contain members that are untrusted or should not have rights in the trusting domain.

WANs in the Windows NT Environment

As organizations grow, there is a need to interconnect networks over large geographic areas using WANs. You build a WAN by linking a LAN at one location to LANs at other locations. You can do this over the Internet or by setting up private leased lines (ISDN, for example) from public carriers such as the phone company. If you use the Internet, you'll need to implement a much higher level of security in the form of firewalls to keep intruders out of your system. Remember that the Internet is an open network that is accessible by anyone. Your Internet connection has an address that anyone can access, so security barriers are important. In contrast, a private leased line between your sites carries only your traffic, so encrypting routers (or bridges) can provide a reasonable security solution. This section is about using private leased lines.

A typical external ISDN router is pictured in Figure 15-2. Notice that it has connectors for an internal Ethernet LAN and for an ISDN WAN link. Internally, the box forwards and filters packets between the Ethernet and ISDN connections, which are seen as two separate networks. You can set up similar routing in Windows NT by installing two separate network interface cards, or by installing one network interface card and a WAN adapter (ISDN, X.25, etc.).

The typical scenario is to connect a branch office with a network at a central or home office. Figures 15-3 and 15-4 show two different configurations. In Figure 15-3, you'll need an internetworking protocol like TCP/IP to allow users at the branch office to communicate across the routers and the WAN link to the home office network. In Figure 15-4, users don't communicate across the WAN link. Instead, Windows NT servers are set up to replicate

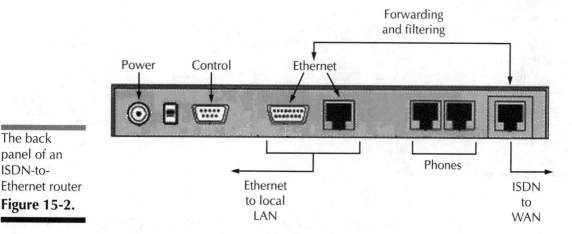

The back
panel of an
ISDN-to-
Ethernet router
Figure 15-2.

information such as the user account database, bulk e-mail, and data files
between sites; users access only local servers.

With the link in Figure 15-3, it is possible that someone could monitor or
tap the link, but encrypting WAN devices minimize this risk. It is also
possible that a system or account in the branch office might get hijacked by an
intruder who could then gain access to the home office network.

In Figure 15-4, users cannot directly access resources on other networks.
Instead, Windows NT replication is used to deliver that information to their
local network. Only replication traffic is allowed over the WAN link (and
possibly some administrative traffic), so the link remains secure. True, someone
might be able to tap it and capture transmitted information, but encryption
can be used to hide the information.

The connection in Figure 15-4 is basically a firewall technique called *protocol
isolation.* The two "outer" networks are separated by a network that uses a

15

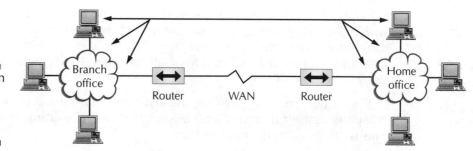

Communication
over a WAN
link
Figure 15-3.

Information replicated over the WAN link, with actual communication handled internally
Figure 15-4.

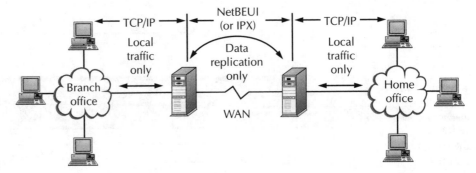

different protocol. In this case, the internal LANs run TCP/IP and the WAN runs NetBEUI. A TCP/IP user (or hacker) at the branch office can't extend a TCP/IP session over the NetBEUI network to the home office. This deterrent is good for security reasons in some environments, but might defeat the purposes of setting up a WAN in other environments. You need to evaluate your own security requirements.

NOTE: NetBEUI is a non-routable, non-internetworking protocol. All traffic on a NetBEUI network stays local and does not cross routers. Because of that, you can use it to create some interesting network configurations that enhance security.

In Figure 15-4, the WAN is viewed as a stand-alone network used only for replication between connected servers. Of course, this is only one solution. You could also use a setup like that in Figure 15-3 and implement TCP/IP across the link, as long as you use appropriate techniques to block, filter, and otherwise restrict network traffic across the link, as I'll discuss shortly.

Windows NT can support the internetworking needs of many organizations with its built-in routing, Remote Access Service (RAS) services, e-mail, and security features. You can even encrypt data transfers for added security. Later in this chapter I'll discuss in detail how to build secure wide area links using Windows NT.

In some cases, you may prefer to use dedicated routing and security equipment rather than rely on built-in Windows NT routing over the WAN. This is discussed in the next section.

Internetwork Models

The primary protocol for WANs in the Windows NT environment is TCP/IP (and IPX/SPX to some extent). TCP/IP is preferred, because it is designed for internetworking, is fully routable, and is widely supported. As mentioned, the NetBEUI protocol can't be used for LAN-to-LAN internetworks (at least not without using special techniques beyond the scope of this book).

The IP addressing scheme in the TCP/IP protocol provides a way to assign unique addresses to each subnetwork (LAN) in an internetworked environment and to each computer connected to those LANs. Routers join subnetworks. As packets arrive at routers, the routers look at the destination addresses in the packets to determine where to send them. Routers have tables that describe which router (also called a gateway) to send a packet to.

For example, if three networks (A, B, and C) are connected by routers AB and BC, as shown in Figure 15-5, then a computer on network A that communicates with a computer on network C sends packets to AB. Router AB has a table entry that indicates the destination computer is available on a network attached to router BC, so it forwards the packet to that router. Router BC then forwards the packet to the destination. Each computer has a gateway entry that defines the IP address of a router where it should send packets that need to be sent to other networks.

Router tables can be created by hand on small networks. For example, if you install two network interface cards in a Windows NT computer and set up routing (thus creating a multihomed system), you can use the ROUTE command to put an entry in the routing table that indicates what networks

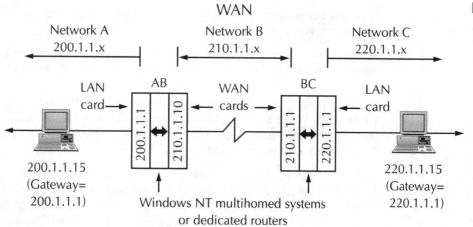

15

TCP/IP
internetworking
Figure 15-5.

are on the other side of the route. If your network is large, you run a *dynamic* routing protocol such as RIP (Routing Information Protocol) that automatically builds routing tables based on information the router receives about the network from other routers. For WAN links, you're usually better off manually configuring routing tables, since RIP can generate a lot of excess traffic across slow WAN links.

WAN links can transport TCP/IP, IPX/SPX, or NetBEUI protocols. These protocol packets are packaged into the lower-level Point-to-Point Protocol (PPP) frames and then transported over the WAN.

If you want to perform LAN-to-LAN routing over a WAN link by using Windows NT computers, at least one of the cards in the multihomed system must be a special WAN card. A number of companies offer WAN solutions for direct LAN-to-LAN connections or dial-up remote access solutions, including the companies listed here:

3Com	www.3com.com
Ascend	**www.ascend.com**
Bay Networks	www.baynetworks.com
Cisco Systems	www.cisco.com
Eicon Technology	**www.eicon.com**
Gandalf Technologies	**www.gandalf.ca (not com)**
Racal	**www.racal.com**
U.S. Robotics	**www.usrobotics.com**

You can connect with these sites to obtain product information and white papers on WAN security.

A typical solution provided by Ascend and other router manufacturers is pictured in Figure 15-6. These devices connect directly to internal Ethernet or Token Ring networks. (A typical back panel for one of these devices can be seen in Figure 15-2.) Several authentication methods are supported, including PAP (Password Authentication Protocol), CHAP (Challenge-Handshake Authentication Protocol), Calling Line ID (CLID) and token-based security. These methods are described in the next section.

Users at the branch office can access the central office or the Internet through the Frame Relay network connection. An additional connection provides links through an ISDN network. This extra line is important for two reasons: first, you might need to connect with another line in the event that the primary line fails. This ensures that your users stay connected. Second,

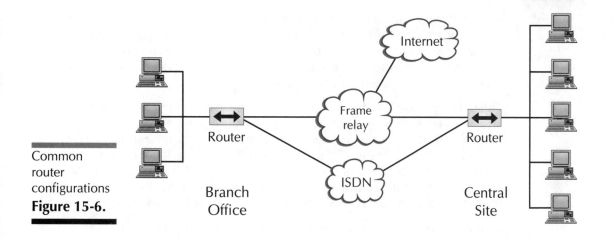

Common
router
configurations
Figure 15-6.

the extra port can provide supplemental bandwidth during times of peak demand. In environments where video conferencing is used, the extra line can supplement the bandwidth when needed.

WAN Security Protocols and Encryption

This section discusses methods for setting up WAN links in a secure way. It presents the security features in Ascend MAX and Pipeline routers, but these features are similar to what other vendors provide in their WAN devices. The MAX is a family of WAN access switch products for the central site that integrate routing, terminal server, bandwidth multiplexing, and remote access server functions. The Pipeline products are remote access bridges/routers for homes and offices.

Ascend provides security for these products through a combination of security standards and Ascend security extensions. Ascend supports both server-based authentication security standards (PAP and CHAP) and the centralized security administration standards (XTACACS and RADIUS). Ascend also supports multilevel password access, restricted address, callback, caller ID, and third-party dynamic password authentication products, including security cards.

PAP (Password Authentication Protocol) and CHAP (Challenge-Handshake Authentication Protocol) are standards-based security protocols commonly used to verify remote access logons by mobile and remote users, or automatic (scripted) logons by dial-up router devices. Both protocols will authenticate users.

The PAP protocol transmits both the user ID and the password in the clear, making it possible for an eavesdropper to capture logon credentials. This information is sent to the target device upon initiation of the call. The target then validates the information in a central PAP database. Keep in mind that the database is encrypted, but the transmitted passwords are not. The only reason for ever considering the use of this protocol is the need to provide interoperability between unlike devices.

The CHAP protocol validates users or systems with a challenge that requires an appropriate response. The challenge/response sequence starts when the remote user or system dials in to connect with a target system. The target requests credentials using a "Who goes there?" challenge. If the caller supplies proper credentials, the logon is validated and the WAN link is established. The most important feature of CHAP is that passwords are encrypted in the transmission. It is widely used and works well in multivendor environments.

Remote access security can also be handled by security administration systems such as TACACS (Terminal Access Concentrator Access Control Server) and RADIUS (Remote Authentication Dial-In User Service). These systems may be necessary in heterogeneous environments where Windows NT systems are not the dominant servers or where NT domain servers are not used (i.e., NT servers operate as stand-alone devices). They perform logon authentication services for remote users and systems by maintaining a central security database in much the same way that the Windows NT Server maintains a single user account database for an entire domain.

TACACS is a query/response protocol standard in which an authentication server validates a user's password based on security requests from remote access servers. Cleartext transmissions are used in some systems, so use caution. There are several extensions to TACACS, including Cisco's TACACS+, which provides additional authentication, authorization, and accounting for Cisco access servers.

RADIUS provides a central security administration system for managing authentication servers. It stores authentication information about all network users in individual profiles, which can include access restrictions, destination-specific routing, packet filtering, and billing information. RADIUS is used in conjunction with CHAP or third-party authentication servers, and can administer multiple security systems across complex networks.

The following Ascend security extensions operate in a stand-alone mode in both the MAX and the Pipeline products or in conjunction with a RADIUS security server:

Multilevel Access Password Security   The Ascend MAX and Pipeline provides multilevel password-based security to permit different levels of access for different users. Access permissions are defined in security profiles maintained on the MAX and the Pipeline. With multilevel security, fairly open access can be granted to "public" resources, using a firewall to secure all other non-public, network-attached resources.

Restricted Address A MAX or Pipeline may be configured with a list of IP network addresses that are permitted dial-in access. The MAX or Pipeline rejects incoming calls from any unrecognized network address. Destinations and routes can also be restricted on a per-user basis. Restricting network access provides high-level, front-line security.

Packet Filtering The MAX or Pipeline can be configured to check each packet's type, protocol, source and destination addresses, and port number for unauthorized access. Using the RADIUS user profiles, the filter profiles can be triggered on a call-by-call basis. Packet filtering is covered further in Chapter 18.

Callback The MAX or Pipeline can be configured to force a callback for any dial-in session. Each authorized user's callback number is registered in the MAX or Pipeline. The remote Pipeline system cooperates with the MAX or Pipeline transparently to the user (except for a small time delay). Callback provides a very high level of security.

Caller ID Caller ID validates the user's phone number, which is provided by the telephone company when the call is placed to the MAX or Pipeline. Caller ID works with both digital (ISDN or Switched 56) and analog WAN services.

Security Cards and Dynamic Password Authentication Servers Ascend's MAX or Pipeline products support security card and/or Dynamic Password Authentication Server solutions from the following vendors:

♦ CryptoCARD, Inc.—Buffalo Grove, IL

♦ Digital Pathways, Inc.—Mountain View, CA

♦ Enigma Logic, Inc.—Concord, CA

♦ Lee Mah DataCom Security Corporation—Hayward, CA

♦ Security Dynamics, Inc.—Cambridge, MA

♦ SmartDISK Security Corporation—Naples, FL

15

Encryption for WAN Links

Communication security is essential on networks that provide *end-to-end* data transmissions across any link outside of the organization. Encryption is the key to providing security for these links. A number of products that perform automatic encryption and decryption are available from Cisco, Digi, Racal, and other vendors.

The typical setup is to install encryption/decryption devices on both sides of an end-to-end WAN connection. Information is automatically encrypted before it is sent and is decrypted by the receiving device. The Data Encryption Standard (DES) is used in most cases. Recall that DES is an encoding and encryption algorithm designed by the U.S. National Bureau of Standards. It encrypts using a 56-bit binary number key with 72 quadrillion possible combinations. The key is randomly generated for each session to create an encryption pattern generally considered impossible to crack without the decryption key. Control information is left unencrypted and in the clear so that data can be properly routed over packet-switched networks.

The Racal-Datacom Datacryptor 64F is an example of an encryptor for Frame Relay networks. It is designed to provide an economical alternative to T1/E1 encryptors when used for the lower-speed 56/64K bits/sec circuits that constitute the vast majority of Frame Relay connections. The unit protects virtual circuits by using a unique crypto-key for optimum security. At the discretion of the administrator, some virtual circuits are encrypted, while others are not. This saves the cost of installing encryption at sites that don't need it. The encryption keys for entire networks of Datacryptor units can be managed from a single Racal Datacryptor Key Management Center.

The Datacryptor 64F is a stand-alone unit that attaches near the WAN connection. It has a front panel display with an LCD screen and controls for configuring the unit. Managers can control key management, unit configuration, and operating modes from the front panel, as well as perform diagnostics. Alarms can be set to warn managers of unit failure, encryption failure, expiration of keys, and loss of memory from tampering. Alerts are sent through local devices or network management systems.

Physical security is provided by a wraparound metal enclosure that restricts unauthorized access. An anti-tamper switch is activated if the cover is removed by an unauthorized person. If the anti-tamper switch is activated, all internally stored cryptographic keys are erased. The unit sells for under $3,500; one device is required on each side of the end-to-end connection.

Another vendor working in this area is Gandalf Technologies, which has developed a data-compression algorithm called Gandalf LZAplus that incorporates both high-performance data compression and strong encryption. Gandalf LZAplus is unique in that it can simultaneously encrypt and compress the data stream, using a strong *stream cipher*. (A stream cipher encrypts data byte by byte, as opposed to a block cipher, which encrypts several kilobytes of data at a time.) Gandalf LZAplus allows network managers to use strongly encrypted and highly compressed links to interconnect their Gandalf systems, maintaining privacy without sacrificing performance. Because Gandalf LZAplus is still a compressor, it can be readily applied to any Point-to-Point Protocol (PPP) data stream and is, in fact, negotiated by the Compression Control Protocol (CCP) to ensure interoperability with non-Gandalf equipment. Gandalf LZAplus can be deployed in all of Gandalf's PPP-compliant remote access products.

Other Security Techniques

A number of companies have developed products that can help you build secure WANs over the Internet or other networks without tying up Windows NT resources. For example, Bay Networks has developed a strategy that uses routers as the first line of defense in controlling external access to an enterprise network as well as securely routing traffic over public and private network paths. Bay has integrated CheckPoint's FireWall-1 security software into its BaySecure router operating systems to enable network managers to implement security without deploying additional hardware and software.

BaySecure FireWall-1 provides secure, bi-directional, anti-spoofing communication for all Internet applications and services. With BaySecure FireWall-1, network managers can specify logging and alerting for any communication attempt, whether it is accepted or rejected. Every single communication attempt and every valid connection can be tracked and recorded in Event Logs.

Bay Network's BaySecure LAN Access enables network operators to bring control and data privacy to common 10BASE-T departmental LANs by changing Ethernet from a party line to a private line and employing per-port filtering in hardware at every port. Normally, Ethernet networks broadcast data packets so that every transmitted packet can be read by all users on the broadcast segment, even if they are not intended recipients. In addition, Ethernet is relatively easy to access because of the proliferation of 10BASE-T. Hackers can easily connect a protocol analyzer to a network segment and monitor all traffic on that segment.

15

BaySecure LAN Access uses a feature called Eavesdrop Prevention to allow only users within the environment to receive packets addressed to their end station; it prohibits LAN monitors from reading network traffic unless allowed by the network manager. Another feature called Intrusion Control enables the network manager to maintain a list of authorized stations. If an unauthorized user attempts access, the intruder can be instantly segmented from the network. The system also can monitor additions, moves, and changes common in 10BASE-T networks, allowing network managers to establish and enforce the location of stations on a per-port basis.

WAN Support in RAS

A WAN connection using RAS can be a relatively inexpensive solution for transferring information between home office and branch sites. For example,

Connecting
an internal
network to a
home office
with a RAS
client and a
third-party
server
Figure 15-7.

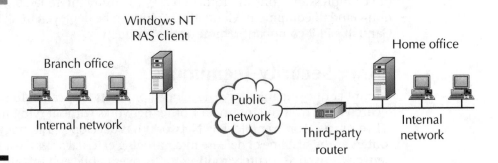

you can use it to do bulk e-mail exchanges or to replicate databases. You can even encrypt the transmissions.

The Windows NT Remote Access Server (RAS) can be used to function as a router between two networks. By routing between networks, resources on other networks across a WAN link can be accessed by users and system processes, although the speed of the WAN links should be factored in when considering what type of traffic you want to have on the link. The line can be a dial-up line or dedicated (i.e., never-to-be-disconnected) connection using standard modems, X.25 networks, or ISDN, with ISDN providing the best performance.

The methods described here involve setting up a Windows NT computer (server or workstation) at a branch office as a RAS client to dial in to a RAS server at another location or to connect to an Internet service provider (ISP). As previously mentioned, you can use the connection to do bulk e-mail transfers or database replications to branch offices. This involves connecting and disconnecting at preset intervals to make the transfers, as I'll discuss shortly.

There are three possible configurations. In Figure 15-7, a Windows NT RAS client connected to an internal network is set up to route to the home office network over a leased line. A third-party router is set up on that network. In Figure 15-8, a RAS client and a RAS server are connected over a leased line. At

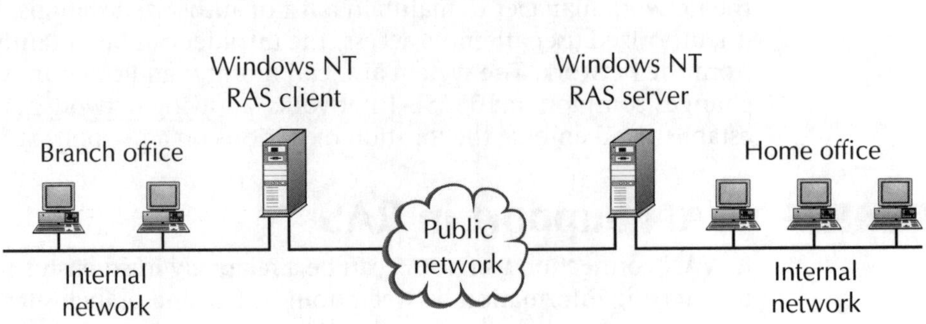

Connecting
an internal
network to a
home office
with a RAS
client and a
RAS server
Figure 15-8.

Windows NT
RAS client

Windows NT
RAS server

Branch office

Home office

Internal
network

Public
network

Internal
network

Connecting an internal network to the Internet with a RAS client and a local Internet service provider **Figure 15-9.**

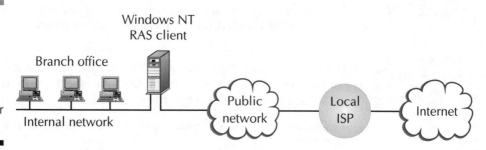

the time of this writing, Windows NT-to-Windows NT routing was not fully supported, but Microsoft had reported success with the configuration. In Figure 15-9, the RAS client connects to an Internet service provider to create a link to the Internet for internal users. (This last configuration is discussed in detail in the the following section.)

NOTE: You can obtain full instructions for setting up these links by visiting Microsoft Knowledge Base on the World Wide Web at **www.microsoft.com/kb/**. Search for document number Q121877.

The document just mentioned does not tell you about setting up a RAS session or about setting security options; I'll address these procedures now.

To create a dial-up object on the RAS client systems, open the My Computer object and double-click on Dial-Up Networking. If the software is not installed, you can choose to install it. When the Dial-Up Networking box appears, click the New button to configure a new phone entry. You'll see the following dialog box:

15

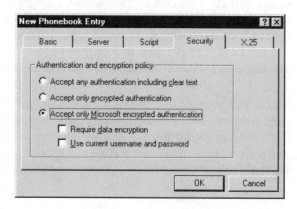

I've clicked the Security tab here, because those are the options of interest. Be sure to fill out the options on the Basic and Server pages as well.

CAUTION: You can set up a script on the Script page that automatically logs you on to non-Windows NT servers. Use caution, because the username and password are stored in the script file in clear text.

Next, go to the Security page. (Recall that these security options were discussed in Chapter 14.) If you are dialing into a non-Windows NT Server that supports some other form of encrypted password authentication (as in Figure 15-7), choose the "Accept only encrypted authentication" option. If you are connecting to a Windows NT RAS server (the LAN-to-LAN configuration in Figure 15-8), enable "Accept only Microsoft encrypted authentication" and the two options under it for maximum security. If the system you are dialing into does not support encrypted password authentication (more than likely your Internet connection, as shown in Figure 15-9), choose the top option, but be aware that your logon password is susceptible to detection by eavesdroppers.

The "Require data encryption" option is important, because it will force the RAS client and server to encrypt all data streams sent over the communication link. This protects your data transmissions from eavesdroppers.

Internet Connections with RAS

Now let's look more closely at Figure 15-9, which connects an internal network to the Internet.

CAUTION: This connection allows routing on the RAS client between the Internet and the internal network. Internet hackers will have an open door to your internal network. Firewalls and other security measures are required in most cases, as discussed in Chapter 18.

For the purposes of this discussion, let's assume that we are willing to take some risks and set up this configuration without any sort of firewall. As you'll see, the Windows NT RAS server becomes a sort of firewall when configured properly. Because Internet users might find their way into the internal network, we need to protect systems from attack. Assume that only user workstations are attached to the network and that all sharing is disabled on those workstations. Our intent is to give internal network users an easily accessible doorway to the Internet. If an attacker does get into the internal network, their activities on this network would be limited. You can connect internal servers to this network using IPX or NetBEUI, but not TCP/IP. This provides protocol isolation.

Consider the RAS system a dedicated connection machine. Write off any plans you had of running any other services on it. You should disable all unnecessary services and, using special filtering routers, allow only certain types of traffic if possible, such as HTTP. That will allow users to use their Web browsers to access Web servers on the Internet and receive responses from those servers. Internet hackers won't be able to access your network using any other protocols except HTTP, which would be quite restrictive. Here are the steps you can take to protect the server.

Open the Network utility on the Control Panel and disable unnecessary services on the Internet-connected side of the RAS router. Here you can see how NetBIOS, Server, and Workstation bindings are disabled from the Remote Access WAN adapter:

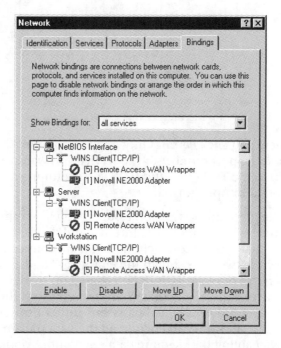

You select an adapter under each heading and click the Disable button, then restart the system.

15

The previous strategy will prevent Internet users from running Server Message Block (SMB) commands and NetBIOS utilities on the RAS server. However, since routing is enabled on the server, they can still get past it into your internal network and use a command like NBTSTAT or UNIX utilities to view information about your internal network. To prevent the use of these commands on individual servers, you can set TCP/IP security options to block the port address of all utilities except the services you want to run, such as HTTP. In the Networks utility, click the Protocols tab, then double-click TCP/IP Protocol. When the Microsoft TCP/IP Properties dialog box appears, click the Advanced button. Next, mark the Enable Security option, then click the Configure button. The TCP/IP Security dialog box appears:

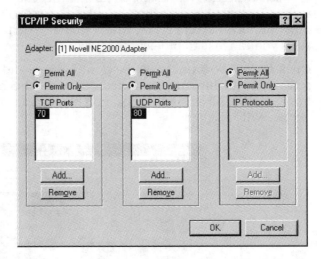

Here you click Permit Only on each column, then click the Add button and add the port number of the service you want to allow. For HTTP services, add 80 to the TCP Ports and UDP Ports columns. Other port numbers can be found in Appendix G.

The preceding discussion assumes you are connecting a RAS client with attached network to the Internet and describes security settings appropriate for that type of connection. If you are connecting over leased lines to your own network, as shown in Figures 15-7 and 15-8, you can remove the services or block TCP/IP ports based on the level of security you need between these networks. Your best option is the one in Figure 15-8, because you get fully encrypted password authentication between the systems upon logon, and you can encrypt all the data transmissions over the connection by enabling the "Require data encryption" option.

Automatic Dialing

Many WAN connections don't need to be connected 24 hours a day, especially if you just need to replicate information from one site to another or exchange electronic mail. Windows NT Servers in a domain need to exchange their user account information, and services like Microsoft Exchange need to exchange e-mail and public/private folder information. You can set up RAS to handle these periodic connections and save toll charges. It is more economical to have RAS make periodic connections than to stay connected full time.

Scheduling automatic dial-up involves running the Schedule service, which you can activate in the Setting utility of the Control Panel. You then create two separate batch files at the dial-up RAS system that runs the RASDIAL.EXE utility to connect to and disconnect from the home office. The *connect batch file* might contain the command RASDIAL HOMEOFFICE and the *disconnect batch file* might contain the command RASDIAL HOMEOFFICE /DISCONNECT. You then use the AT scheduling utility to schedule these batch files to run at regular intervals. Make sure to stay connected long enough to transfer all the information that needs to get transmitted between sites. You can find more information on the Schedule service, the RASDIAL command, and the AT utility in the Windows NT help system or in operator's manuals.

Virtual Private Networks Over the Internet

Virtual private networks (VPNs) are encrypted tunnels through the Internet for transmitting private information between your network sites. They provide a way to build a wide area backbone network on a global scale with a cost much lower than building private networks.

Basically, tunneling technology sets up a secure encrypted communication channel through the Internet for your remote offices, mobile users, and business partners. Instead of leasing a dedicated line (circuit) between two sites, it is far better to create a virtual circuit through the public switched network. Everybody who uses the network shares its cost, as opposed to a dedicated leased line, for which your organization pays the entire cost of a line that you might not use 100 percent of the time.

15

 CAUTION: If you transmit time-sensitive information, VPNs over the Internet may not be a good idea, because you may encounter performance problems.

Leased-line costs increase with distance, as illustrated here:

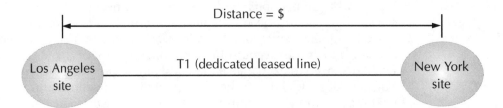

However, the Internet can be used to provide the long-distance part of the connection and dramatically reduce the cost of your WAN links, as shown here:

Notice that this configuration still uses a T1 line to get to a local Internet service provider on either side of the link, but the distance is much less. Charges can drop from thousands of dollars to hundreds of dollars per month.

You must consider security when building WANs over the Internet. Your transmissions are no longer confined to the private leased-line circuit; they travel across a web of circuits and routers in unfamiliar territory. While it is unlikely that someone monitoring a line in Tulsa will manage to capture part of your transmission and make sense of it, the possibility exists. That's why encryption is important.

When information is encrypted, a key is required to decrypt it. Devices on either side of a tunnel must have the appropriate keys to encrypt and decrypt the same data stream. If you're setting up a link between a branch office, it's easy to manage this key exchange. However, if remote users access your network, you need a way to verify who they are and a way to exchange keys for encryption. Public keys and digital signatures are used for this purpose; these devices are discussed further in Chapter 21 and Appendix B.

Due to a lack of interoperability standards, it has been necessary to buy routers and firewalls from the same vendor to implement VPNs. But standards are being developed to provide authentication, encryption, and key exchange among different vendors' products. The IETF's (Internet Engineering Task Force) IP Security (IPsec) working group has proposed a set of authentication and encryption standards that work with the IP protocols at the network layer.

The IPsec proposal defines an IP packet header for authentication and data integrity (Authentication Header, or AH) and an encryption header (Encapsulation Security Payload, or ESP). The AH provides assurance that the packet is from the intended party and that it has not been altered. A *security association* holds mutually agreed upon information that is required for authentication and encryption. A method for managing keys called ISAKMP (Internet Security Association and Key Management Protocol) is in the works, and it allows for a variety of key exchange methods.

From this work, the Secure Wide Area Network (S/WAN) initiative has developed. In addition, Microsoft and other vendors have developed a similar protocol called the Point-to-Point Tunneling Protocol (PPTP). These protocols are discussed in the following sections.

Secure Wide Area Network (S/WAN)

S/WAN is an initiative put together by RSA Data Security, Inc. to implement the IETF's proposed IPsec standard. S/WAN is supported by a number of vendors, including Bay Networks; CheckPoint Software Technologies, Ltd.; Digital Pathways; Frontier Technologies; FTP Software; Gemini Computers, Inc.; IBM Corporation; Netrend Corporation; Raptor Systems, Inc.; Secure Computing Corporation; Sun Microsystems; TGV, Inc.; TimeStep Corporation; Trusted Information Systems, Inc.; V-ONE; VeriSign, Inc.; VPNet; and Attachmate/Wollongong.

With S/WAN, companies will be able to use IPsec to mix and match the best firewall and TCP/IP stack products to build Internet-based virtual private networks. In the past, it has been difficult if not impossible to implement secure VPNs using mixed equipment, because vendors were unable to agree upon the details of a secure IP implementation. S/WAN provides a unique solution that puts data encryption at the IP level, where it can easily be handled by firewalls. In this way, organizations can implement one security solution rather than several. Higher-level security specifications such as Secure Sockets Layer (SSL) and Secure Hypertext Transfer Protocol (S/HTTP) can still be layered on top of S/WAN to provide an all-encompassing security solution.

15

S/WAN provides a common set of algorithms, modes, and options to guarantee IPsec interoperability. RC5 Symmetric Block Cipher, RSA's most advanced block encryption cipher, is used to provide encryption key sizes that range from 40 bits to 128 bits for exportability. The largest key size can withstand trillions of MIPS-years of computer attack. Older DES algorithms can also be used. S/WAN can be implemented using RSA's BSAFE cryptography engine, which provides software developers with multiple algorithms and modules for adding encryption and authentication features to any application.

BSAFE includes modules for popular encryption techniques, such as RSA, Triple DES, RC2, RC4, and RC5; it also supports digital signatures and certificates.

Point-to-Point Tunneling Protocol (PPTP)

Point-to-Point Tunneling Protocol is a communication protocol that supports the creation of virtual private networks across the Internet to Microsoft Windows NT Servers. Specifically, PPTP uses analog or ISDN communication lines to create a tunnel directly to a specific NT Server on a network, even if hundreds of NT Servers exists on that network. It is supported by Microsoft, Ascend Communications, ECI Telematics, 3Com, and U.S. Robotics.

Remote users and remote systems at branch offices connect to the Internet from wherever they are located and establish a connection to a designated Internet service provider (ISP) that handles your PPTP traffic. The ISP installs PPTP-capable dial platforms or *front-end processors* (FEPs) at their site. Any PPP client, not just ones that understand PPTP, can establish an encrypted PPTP connection back to a PPTP-capable server at the central office.

NOTE: An ISP doesn't need to be part of the PPTP equation. Many organizations will want to connect directly to the Internet through their own software and hardware. PPTP works in this model as well and provides security equal to that provided by ISP connections. Users of Microsoft Windows 95 and Windows NT Workstation operating systems can take advantage of this technology immediately. Be aware, however, that the initial PPTP release with Windows NT Server 4.0 will support dial-up users only (or single systems such as replication servers). Future releases of PPTP in Windows NT will support LAN-to-LAN connections.

In order for ISPs to provide PPTP technology, they must add or upgrade software in their existing remote access servers. These upgrades are already available from the previously listed vendors who support PPTP. Once the upgrades are in place, your clients/customers can start using PPTP's VPN without the need to change any client or server features.

Here are some of the benefits of using PPTP:

♦   Users and branch office LANs make a normal connection to the Internet. This removes the long-distance and toll charges incurred when calling the central site.

♦ Many organizations already use their Internet service provider for their electronic mail services, and remote users are already set up to dial in to the Internet in the first place.

♦ PPTP supports multiple protocols, Windows computers, and non-Windows computers. All that is required is that remote computers have a Point-to-Point Protocol (PPP) connection to the Internet. With PPTP, businesses can let their remote users access heterogeneous corporate networks that use TCP/IP, IPX/SPX, or NetBEUI.

♦ Users can connect to service providers using a variety of methods, including standard V.34 dial-up modems, ISDN, Frame Relay, and other services, based on their throughput requirements.

♦ Microsoft BackOffice applications like Systems Management Server (SMS) and Microsoft Exchange server can take advantage of PPTP to keep software distributions (an SMS feature) and message exchanges safe from unauthorized access or tampering while data passes between sites in an organization.

♦ By supporting virtual WANs over the Internet with PPTP, you can remove a lot of the headaches and hassles of maintaining dial-up services at your own central site.

One of the downsides of tunneling network protocols through the Internet is that some are time sensitive and may dramatically reduce the performance of such links. In addition, traffic on the Internet may not make it suitable for some operations that require immediate response between the client and server. Still, the protocol will have enormous benefits in many situations, especially if offices are situated at remote locations around the globe.

PPTP Implementation

Basically, with PPTP, an organization can move its remote access dial-up services from its own site to an ISP's site. Figure 15-10 illustrates the old method of implementing remote access. You set up a Windows NT RAS server and a bank of modems to receive incoming calls. You need enough incoming phone lines for each modem; you pay the toll charges for all of the lines if your remote users dial in from distant locations.

Figure 15-11 shows how shifting remote access services to the ISP changes things. Now you have one line from your site to the ISP, and your remote users dial in to the Internet to access your site in a secure way.

Of course, logon authentication is a critical aspect of remote access. If you use the non-PPTP method for remote access, in which users dial directly in

15

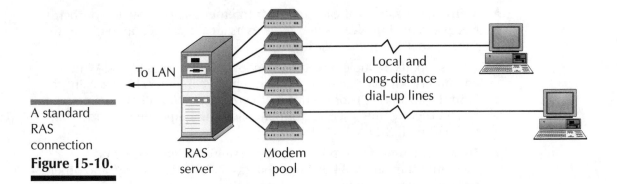

A standard
RAS
connection
Figure 15-10.

to your site, you can authenticate them using Microsoft CHAP, assuming the
clients run Windows. But if you move your remote access services to an off-site
ISP for the reasons just described, how do you properly authenticate users?
That is what PPTP is all about. It provides the security features you need to
encrypt data transmissions and securely authenticate users.

Many Internet service providers are starting to provide PPTP as an added-value
service for their customers, but general acceptance of PPTP will rely on the
number of ISPs that support it. By working with an Internet service provider
that provides PPTP, companies can let the ISP maintain all the equipment
required to support dial-up users. You can separate your modem banks
and ISDN cards from your server and locate those connections at an ISP's
modem bank or front-end processor (FEP). This reduces in-house hardware,
management, and maintenance costs. Your central site only needs one
connection with sufficient bandwidth to the Internet service provider to
handle all the traffic generated by remote users.

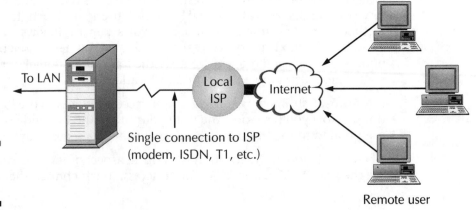

A PPTP
connection
Figure 15-11.

Any connection charges that a user incurs are based on the distance to the ISP's connection. If you go with a national service provider, users can travel to most major cities and connect to a local number. For example, if you are a member of the Microsoft Network (MSN), you can connect to MSN and the Internet in just about any major city. To avoid toll charges, it is critical that mobile users have accounts with service providers that have access points wherever they travel.

PPTP Authentication and Encryption

The existing Windows NT Remote Access Service (RAS) authentication protocols are used to validate user logons. These protocols include PAP, CHAP, and MS-CHAP, as discussed in Chapter 14. The Internet service provider can also perform additional authentication if appropriate. The same RC4 encryption protocols used by RAS are used to encrypt PPTP data streams.

The Microsoft form of CHAP is used to validate the user's credentials in a Windows NT domain. The resulting session key is then used to encrypt data in the transmission. Both the RAS client and the RAS server can be set to allow only encrypted sessions. Microsoft has leveraged the encryption support already available in RAS to provide secure access across the Internet. Distribution of security keys is not a problem, because credentials are available at both ends of the connection. This is accomplished through a "shared secret," as follows:

♦ A user-supplied password at the client is used to generate a hash value (a hash function is a computation that takes some input and returns an output, or hash value). RSA MD4 encryption is used to perform this hash.

♦ A similarly derived hash value is stored in the Windows NT Security database.

15

This shared secret solves the problem of distributing keys that are used to encrypt and decrypt information. Currently, a 40-bit session key (derived from the earlier hash) is used to encrypt data, but future versions of RAS will support 128-bit encryption.

PPTP can be used in conjunction with firewalls. While a firewall regulates data coming into the corporate network from the Internet, PPTP is designed to secure communication sessions between authenticated remote users and the corporate network. If both a firewall and a Windows NT RAS server are deployed, the RAS server sits outside the firewall and sends all packets that it receives from remote users to the firewall. The firewall simply provides the same security that it would if PPTP were not used.

DEC's Internet Tunnel

An alternative to PPTP and S/WAN is DEC's AltaVista Tunnels, which uses the Internet as the infrastructure for creating a virtual enterprise. AltaVista Tunnels supports direct LAN-to-LAN tunneling so that you can securely connect multiple users in your branch offices with your central office.

AltaVista Tunnels is available in Workgroup and Personal Editions. The Workgroup Edition creates a secure connection between remote networks. The Personal Edition allows a single remote user to link to a group to do business with the members of that group. Each edition has the security features and capabilities described here, but differs in the hardware on which it is installed:

◆ The AltaVista Workgroup Edition, which includes the Workgroup Tunnel server and management software, can be installed on any digital UNIX-based server. A variety of clients can connect with the server, including Windows 95 and Windows NT computers.

◆ The AltaVista Personal Edition can be installed on any PC that uses Intel technology and operates under Windows 95 or Windows NT. It works in conjunction with a server running AltaVista Tunnels Workgroup Edition. The package includes the PC Tunnel client software, administration programs, and appropriate drivers.

Additional information is available at **www.digital.com**.

CHAPTER 16

Enterprise-Wide Security

The Windows NT Server provides a high level of integration into many existing network environments, including Macintosh, IBM mainframe and midrange systems, UNIX, and Novell NetWare. Along with this integration comes the associated headaches of monitoring and managing additional levels of security. This chapter discusses security considerations for integrating Windows NT into heterogeneous environments of mixed computer systems and networks.

Windows NT already provides a high level of integration for environments that include Microsoft LAN Manager and Novell NetWare. LAN Manager user accounts are easily integrated into the Windows NT account model. If NetWare clients and NetWare servers exist on the network, you can give NetWare clients access to Windows systems and Windows clients access to NetWare systems. There is even software that allows a Windows NT system to emulate a NetWare system for organizations that are making the transition from NetWare to Windows NT.

Macintosh support in Windows NT includes Services for Macintosh, a feature that allows PC and Macintosh clients to share files and printers. These services are completely integrated into the Windows NT Server. Macintosh users do not need additional software to act as clients to Windows NT Server computers, although an optional user authentication module is available to provide secure logons.

Microsoft's plans for Windows NT include full support for TCP/IP networks and the Internet as well as UNIX interoperability. Windows NT has a full TCP/IP protocol stack; applications such as an FTP, Gopher, and a World Wide Web server; and utilities that allow Windows NT users to access UNIX systems.

Windows and UNIX users can exchange files in interesting ways. FTP servers can be set up on either platform to provide exchange. At a higher level, you can install NFS (Network File Systems) clients on Windows computers to allow users to access files on UNIX-based NFS servers, or you can install SMB (Server Message Block) clients on UNIX systems to allow those users to access files on Windows shares. In the latter case, Windows NT authentication may be possible, depending on the implementation.

Finally, Windows NT supports connectivity with IBM Mainframe and AS/400 host systems through the optional Microsoft BackOffice SNA Server product.

These topics are discussed throughout this chapter. At the end of the chapter, you will find a discussion of enterprise security management and several schemes that have been cooked up by vendors.

NetWare in the Windows NT Environment

The security environments of Windows NT and Novell NetWare are quite different. As you know, the Windows NT Server uses the domain security model, in which users gain access to network resources by first logging on with the username and password. The Windows NT Server checks these credentials with the Windows NT Security Accounts Manager (SAM), which maintains a database of users authorized to access the system and which verifies users. Security credentials are sent using the SMB or RPC protocols over the existing network protocols (TCP/IP, IPX, or NetBEUI).

The Novell NetWare environment uses one of two different security models, described as follows. Security credentials are sent by the NetWare client using the NCP (NetWare Core Protocols) over existing network protocols (usually IPX).

Bindery   NetWare 2.*x* and 3.*x* servers store all the information about users, groups, passwords, and rights in a database on the server called the *bindery*. Each NetWare server has its own bindery. Clients that need access to NetWare server resources log on with a username and password, and those credentials are checked in the local bindery to determine if the user can access the resources.

NetWare Directory Services (NDS)   NDS is implemented on NetWare 4.*x* servers. It consists of a tree-structured directory that defines organizations, departments, users, and resources in a hierarchical tree. NetWare users can log in to appropriate branches of the tree that represent the department or workgroup that holds their user account. NetWare 4.*x* servers can appear to have a bindery through bindery emulation, a feature that is enabled by default.

Client and Gateway Services for NetWare

Microsoft makes Client Services for NetWare (CSNW) available for Windows clients so they can access files and printers on NetWare servers. CSNW users can run NetWare user and management utilities such as SYSCON, PCONSOLE, and RCONSOLE. CSNW supports NetWare 4.*x* servers running either NetWare Directory Services (NDS) or bindery emulation. Logon scripts are also supported.

Gateway Services for NetWare (GSNW) is included on the Windows NT Server CD-ROM and can be installed at any time. It includes all of the features of CSNW, so that a Windows NT Server can connect with a NetWare

16

server. It also provides gateway services that allow the Windows NT Server to translate NetWare services for non-NetWare clients, with the advantage that clients don't need to run extra software. They simply connect with the Windows NT Server running GSNW to access resources on NetWare servers, as shown in Figure 16-1.

GSNW translates native Microsoft SMB packets to Novell NCP packets. The translation is dependent on the Microsoft NWLink protocol and NWLink NetBIOS. NWLink is Microsoft implementation of the IPX/SPX protocol, and NWLink NetBIOS is a Microsoft-enhanced implementation of Novell NetBIOS, which transmits Novell NetBIOS packets between a NetWare server running Novell NetBIOS and a Windows NT computer.

With GSNW, the Windows NT Server computer connects to the NetWare file server's directory and then shares it. The directory then becomes available to Microsoft network clients who access it by connecting with the Windows NT Server computer.

NOTE: Access through the gateway will be slower than direct access to NetWare resources. For this reason, you may want to install Client for NetWare Networks option on Windows clients so they can get direct access to NetWare resources.

File and Printer Sharing for NetWare (FPNW)

File and Printer Sharing for NetWare (FPNW) is a Microsoft Windows NT Server service that enables a Windows NT Server computer to function like a Novell NetWare 3.*x* file and print server. Novell NetWare clients can then access shared resources on a Windows NT Server computer without having

Microsoft
Gateway
Service for
NetWare
(GSNW)
Figure 16-1.

Microsoft
client

SMBs

Windows NT
Server running
gateway services
for NetWare

NCPs

NetWare
server

to change their client software. When you install FPNW, a Windows NT Server can provide both Server Message Block (SMB) and NetWare Core Protocol (NCP) services. When users log on to the Windows NT Server running FPNW, they log on to a bindery emulated by FPNW, not a Windows NT domain.

With FPNW it is easier for organizations with NetWare servers to make the transition to the Windows NT Server. Both Windows and NetWare clients can access file and print and application services off the same server computer without changing client software.

Windows 95 computers can also run a program called Windows 95 NCP that provides NetWare Core Protocol (NCP) services, but only if a NetWare server is on the network to authenticate a user's request to connect to shared resources. The Windows 95 NCP Server is designed to use the Novell NetWare server's user database and authentication authority to validate user access to resources. This feature is not a weakness but an advantage, because it allows administrators to manage a central account list while providing NetWare clients with access to resources on a large number of Windows 95 computers. It also prevents an unscrupulous Windows 95 user from acting like a NetWare server and capturing logon information from unsuspecting users.

While the Windows 95 NCP Server can process NCP-based requests for file I/O and printer output, it cannot run NLMs (NetWare loadable modules), perform client logons on its own, do internal IPX or IP routings, or other tasks that a NetWare server can perform.

Administrators can manage FPNW systems remotely by using tools such as Net Watcher and System Monitor. Right-click the appropriate FPNW server in the Network Neighborhood to display the context menu for the system. Click Properties, then choose one of the following options:

♦ **Net Watcher** enables you to see what folders are shared and who is using them over the network.

♦ **System Monitor** enables you to see disk access and network usage information.

♦ **Administer** enables you to change the settings on the selected computer.

Directory Service Manager for NetWare (DSMN)

Microsoft's Directory Service Manager for NetWare (DSMN) is a Windows NT Server utility that synchronizes user accounts between Windows NT Server domains and Novell NetWare servers. The advantage of DSMN is that you

16

can centrally manage user and group accounts for both systems using the Windows NT User Manager for Domains. Because the servers are synchronized, users need only a single account and password to access both types of servers and do not have to remember or use different passwords.

DSMN copies NetWare user and group account information to Windows NT Server and then incrementally propagates any changes to the accounts back to the NetWare servers. There is no need to install software on the NetWare servers to run DSMN. DSMN has these features:

♦ The guarantee that end users will have one user account name and password over both types of networks because they are managed in a single location

♦ The capability for backing up and replicating the account database to any location on the network

♦ Options for setting up initial passwords and selecting which user accounts to propagate each way

♦ User and group accounts from NetWare 2.*x* and 3.*x* (and 4.*x* in bindery emulation mode) that can be propagated to Windows NT Server

Users must use the CHGPASS utility provided by DSMN to keep their account passwords synchronized. CHGPASS changes the password on the Windows NT primary domain controller, which then replicates the new password to all the participating NetWare servers.

Browsing and Working with NetWare Systems

You can browse Novell NetWare servers using the Windows 95 or Windows NT user interface. Network Neighborhood is the primary way to browse the entire network, including NetWare servers. When you open the Entire Network window, a collection of computer objects appears with NetWare servers at the top, as shown here:

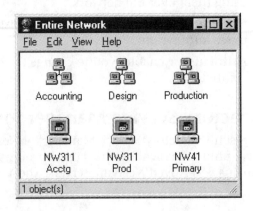

A major benefit is that users can browse the directory of a NetWare server without having to map a network drive. Users can even use drag and drop techniques to move and copy files to and from the NetWare servers. This has security implications, because you need to make sure that file permissions are set properly on NetWare servers.

When you right-click a NetWare server, volume, or directory in the Network Neighborhood window, a context menu appears with options to explore the drive, attach to and log out from a server, and do a number of other things, as described here:

♦ Right-click a NetWare server in the Network Neighborhood, then choose Attach As from the context menu to connect to the server. A Logon dialog box may appear if passwords are not synchronized.

♦ Map a directory on the NetWare server by double-clicking the server in the Network Neighborhood and right-clicking the directory to map. Choose Map Network Drive from the context menu.

♦ Create a shortcut by right-clicking and dragging a NetWare server directory to the Windows desktop.

♦ Administrators can create root mappings for users to directories on NetWare servers. A root mapping prevents the user from going further up in the directory tree than the mapped directory. Follow the preceding instructions to map a directory and enable Connect As Root Of The Drive.

The following **net** commands can be executed from a command prompt at a Windows client to view and work with information on NetWare systems. They can also be placed in logon scripts. These commands work in exactly the same way as their Novell counterparts. Administrators in NetWare environments should be familiar with these commands and realize that clients can use them to connect to and manipulate NetWare resources. Hackers might also use these same commands to gain unauthorized access to systems.

♦ **To view NetWare Servers** Type **net view** at a command prompt or in a logon script. A list of available NetWare servers appears.

♦ **To view volumes on a specific server** Type **net view** *servername* where *servername* is the name of a NetWare server. This command attaches to a server without actually logging on.

♦ **To create a drive connection** Type **net use** *drive*: *servername* *volume* where drive is the *drive* letter to map, *servername* is the name of the server, and *volume* is the name of the volume on the server.

16

These are the primary net command options, but you can view additional options and commands by typing **net /?** at the command prompt.

User-Level Security in NetWare Environments

In a NetWare network environment, a NetWare file server can provide all the resource sharing that network clients need. However, if Windows clients are on the network, they can provide their own peer-level resource sharing. Some administrators may prefer to disable peer-level resource sharing while others may find it beneficial. In the latter case, a NetWare server can be used to provide security for accessing resources.

As was discussed in Chapters 5 and 12, Microsoft networks can provide security for sharing network resources through share-level or user-level security:

Share-level security   Resources on network clients are shared using individually assigned passwords. The user who shares the resource gives the password to people who are allowed to access it.

User-level security   This is a "pass-through" security method in which a user's ability to access a shared resource is authenticated by a security provider, such as a Windows NT Domain controller or NetWare server.

User-level security is important to this discussion because a NetWare server can grant access to shared resources by verifying that a username and password are the same as those in its user account list. Because the NetWare security provider maintains a network-wide list of user accounts and passwords, each computer running Windows does not have to store a list of accounts. Of course, if Windows NT is available on the network, you may prefer to use those systems for authentication instead.

Access to shared resources can be granted on a full-access, Read Only, or custom level. Custom level options function like volume-level NetWare trustee assignments. Users can be granted read, write, create, delete, change attribute, directory search, and access control rights to shared resources.

Here's how the procedure works. Jim sets up his computer for user-level security and specifies a NetWare server called Green Acres as the security provider. When Jill attempts to access files on Jim's shared directory, Jim's computer will ask the NetWare security provider to authenticate Jill. If authenticated, Jill is given access to the files in the directory. For this to work, a network administrator must create a user account with no password and no trustee assignments on the NetWare server called WINDOWS_PASSTHROUGH. This is necessary because Windows clients need to log on to a NetWare server in order to get user authentication information.

Sharing resources on NetWare servers requires that the following service be installed:

♦ File and printer sharing for NetWare networks

You can install this option by opening the Network utility in the Control Panel on Windows workstations. Also in the Network utility, specify the security provider on the Access Control page by typing the name of the security provider in the user-level access control field. After these options are set, you can share directories, as discussed in Chapter 9.

A problem can crop up when you want to share Windows resources by choosing users from a NetWare server's list of user accounts. You can specify only one security provider in the Network utility. However, in the NetWare 3.*x* bindery environment, each NetWare server has its own list of user accounts. On the Windows computer, you will be able to specify only one NetWare server and access only the user accounts on that server. In addition, if you use a NetWare 4.*x* server, which has the global NDS database, you can still access only the list of users that are in the context of the particular server you specify. A way around this is to make sure that the server you specify has accounts for all the users you may want to specify for user-level security on Microsoft networks.

NOTE: User-level security in Windows 95 does not support the NDS global naming service in NetWare 4.*x*, but does support bindery emulation to obtain user lists.

You can manage user accounts on NetWare servers by running SYSCON for NetWare 3.*x* and NETADMIN for NetWare 4.*x*. These tools can be run on a Windows 95 administrative workstation by obtaining the proper utilities from Novell. Administrators can use Windows 95 system policies to control how Windows 95 systems access the network. Policies can restrict the actions of specific users, groups, or even individual workstations (regardless of who logs in). System policies are discussed in Chapter 12.

16

Profiles and Policies

The Windows 95 *user profiles* feature allows customized desktop settings (wallpaper, color scheme, and so on) to "follow" users when they move to different systems on the network. If they log in to a different Windows 95 computer, they see their specific user settings. This feature requires that user profiles be enabled on any computer that users travel to.

If users log in to NetWare servers, user profiles can be stored in the user's preferred server, on the SYS volume, in the MAIL directory, and in a subdirectory of the MAIL directory corresponding to an 8-digit hexadecimal bindery object ID assigned the user when the account is created. A directory under SYS:\MAIL corresponding to this user ID may also be created. This directory stores user logon scripts and user print job configurations in NetWare 2.*x* and 3.*x*.

Profiles are configured in the Password option of the Control Panel. Once a profile is configured, copies of the files containing the user profile (such as USER.DAT, the user-specific portion of the Windows 95 Registry) are placed in the appropriate server directory. The next time the user logs in, the user profiles are automatically copied down to the local system and the user's custom desktop appears.

System policies are an administrative feature of Windows 95 and Windows NT that lets administrators create standard desktop configurations for clients, control how clients access network resources, prevent users from modifying pre-set applications or desktop settings, and generally provide a more secure environment. Clients can, for example, be prevented from accessing Control Panel utilities to change settings on their own computer. System policies are merged into the Registry of a client computer during the logon process.

System policies are stored in a file called CONFIG.POL at a central location on the network and are created and edited with a utility called Policy Editor. Workstations download system policies after downloading user profiles, so it is important to remember that system policies can override user profiles.

On NetWare networks CONFIG.POL is copied to the PUBLIC directory on the SYS volume of the Preferred Server. When a Windows 95 user logs on to a NetWare server, the \PUBLIC directory is checked to see if the CONFIG.POL file exists. If it does, the settings in the file are copied across the network and implemented on the local computer's Registry.

Logon and Password Issues

To avoid the hassles of having to remember multiple passwords when accessing resources on mixed networks, Windows 95 provides a *password caching* feature that stores passwords on local systems in encrypted form. Users can type just one password to access resources on Windows NT and NetWare servers.

Alternatively, you can disable password caching if you feel this feature exposes your passwords to hackers who might try to crack them. This decision will be determined by your environment and whether hackers can gain access to the system to obtain the encrypted passwords.

The Windows logon consists of user credentials that are stored in a Password List File or Password Cache. Whenever a Windows 95 or Windows NT user connects with a network resource, the user credentials (username and password) specified to access that resource are stored in the Password List File for future use. Of course, this procedure requires that the user log on with a proper username and password to unlock the Password List File so it can be used to log on to network resources during the logon session.

The credentials stored in the cache include a ServerName-UserName-Password combination. Only the ServerName-Password is required on Windows networks since the UserName is always the Windows logon name. However, on NetWare networks, the additional UserName field is necessary because users can log on to different NetWare servers with different usernames while retaining their Windows logon name. The actual logon procedure for Windows 95 goes like this:

1. The logon username and password that the user specified when logging on to Windows 95 are tried. A connection is made if these credentials are valid.

2. If this attempt to log on fails because of an invalid username or password, Windows 95 searches the Password Cache for an entry that corresponds to the server that the user is attempting to access. If an entry is found, a logon is attempted with the credentials.

3. If the logon fails, Windows 95 prompts the user to enter a username and password with an option to connect as GUEST and a further option to save the username and password in the Password Cache.

In some cases, you might be logged on to a system with an inappropriate user account that has fewer rights on a system than you should have. For example, if you get to step 3 above, an entry to log on to a server with the Guest account is placed in your password cache. In the future when you get a real account on the server, the logon process may still connect you as a guest (use the WHOAMI command to check the account you are logged in to). To get around this, select Attach As from the context menu of the specific NCP server (you can right-click the icon for the server in the Network Neighborhood to see this menu), enter the new UserName-Password for the server, and then check the "Save this password in your password list" box.

An inconvenience can occur if the password for a resource expires or needs to be changed. A user must first enter the original password, which may have been forgotten. Another problem can occur when a user logs on to a system, unlocking the password file, and then leaves the system for awhile. A malicious user could walk up to the system and use it to access resources on

16

the network that are accessible with passwords stored in the Password Cache. Users must remember to log off whenever they leave their terminals.

You can set a primary logon to specify whether a user logs on to Windows 95 first or to a NetWare server first. To do this, open Network from the Control Panel and set the Primary Network Logon option. If the older NETX or VLM client is being used, clients must log on to the NetWare server before starting Windows 95. You can accomplish this by loading the client software and LOGIN command from the AUTOEXEC.BAT file. Once the logon is complete, Windows 95 can be started. In this configuration, passwords cannot be synchronized across Windows and NetWare environments.

Security in Windows NT and UNIX Environments

Windows NT is well-equipped to interoperate with the UNIX environment and accommodates most of the UNIX variants that are on the market. It has built-in TCP/IP protocols and utilities, the foundation for UNIX networking. It also supports other features that interoperate well with UNIX systems, including terminal emulation, file transfers, data sharing, and distributed processing support.

The Windows NT Server includes DHCP (Dynamic Host Configuration Protocol) services, which automatically assign IP addresses to TCP/IP hosts on Windows network, and WINS (Windows Internet Naming Service) services, which provide naming support in the Windows environment by translating network names to IP addresses. Windows NT 4.0 includes the DNS (Domain Name System) services, which is the hierarchical naming system for identifying hosts on the Internet. With DNS, organizations can set up their own internal DNS systems that connect with the Internet.

The TCP/IP protocol allows Windows computers to communicate directly with UNIX systems. In addition, the Windows TCP/IP protocol stack can be used in conjunction with NetBEUI Frame (NBF). It also includes an Internet Protocol (IP) router and supports the Serial Line Internet Protocol (SLIP) and the Point-to-Point Protocol (PPP).

Windows computers can be attached to the Internet to provide common Internet services, such as File Transfer Protocol (FTP) services, Gopher services, and World Wide Web services. In addition, Windows NT includes more than a dozen TCP/IP utilities that allow users to access UNIX systems from Windows NT and to administer TCP/IP networks. The Windows NT Resource Kit includes additional tools

Along with all these choices and tools are the security problems inherent in the UNIX environment. Perhaps the biggest problem with the TCP/IP protocol is that it is commonly used to interconnect with trusted and untrusted networks. The Internet is an untrusted network. Once connected, users on those networks can use a number of utilities and tools to view and access information on other interconnected networks unless proper measures are taken to protect against intrusions.

One of the problems with implementing TCP/IP protocols and UNIX support in Windows NT is the increased opportunity for hackers to access systems with tools that they are already familiar with. There are hundreds if not thousands of tools and utilities available in the public domain or from various vendors that can be used both for legitimate and for unscrupulous activities. Many of these utilities have been ported to the Windows NT environment to take advantage of TCP/IP and UNIX support.

Because TCP/IP and UNIX interoperability issues are so important in today's Internet-connected world, these topics are covered in more detail in Chapters 17 through 21.

UNIX/Windows NT File Sharing

There are a number of ways that UNIX and Windows clients can share files. The question is, which way do you want to go? Do you want Windows users to be clients of UNIX servers or do you want UNIX users to be clients of Windows servers? Both methods are possible, and it all depends on where the files are. The four most common file exchange/sharing systems are described here. Of course, there are many others in the UNIX environment, but you will need to investigate those on your own.

FTP (File Transfer Protocol)　　File Transfer Protocol is the most common way to exchange files in the UNIX environment. The Windows environment supports FTP as part of the TCP/IP protocol implementation. An FTP server comes on the Windows NT CD-ROM. When properly implemented, a Windows NT-based FTP server provides a safe way to make files available to any user. For example, you should only implement anonymous logons because passwords are sent in the clear. This means that you can't store sensitive files on FTP servers.

16

Web (HTTP) Services　　You can set up a Web server on a Windows computer or a UNIX system and use it as a way to make files (and information in general) available to any client. Clients run Web browsers to access servers. Windows NT comes with the Internet Information Server, a full-featured Web server. Refer to Chapter 20 for more information on this technology.

SMB (Server Message Block)   This is the native Windows file sharing system that you are familiar with from reading previous chapters in this book. It allows you to "share" files on any Windows system, even Windows desktop computers. UNIX clients running SMB clients such as Samba can access SMB shared directories on Windows systems.

NFS (Network File Systems)   This is the traditional file sharing system in UNIX (and other) environments. With NFS, you "publish" or "export" a directory. Clients then connect with the directory to access its files. NFS clients and servers are available from third-party vendors that run on Windows computers.

I will cover these last two file systems in the following sections. Whereas FTP and HTTP are basically file transfer systems, SMB and NFS allow users to open, edit, and close files at their current location. However, there are security concerns in doing this, some well-known and some that are, no doubt, unknown.

NFS (Network File Systems)

NFS was originally developed by Sun Microsystems and is now publicly available. It provides a way to make a file system accessible across a network. Clients can access the files as if they were local to their system. Exporting and mounting of drives is handled with text commands or through a graphical user interface, depending on the implementation. Obviously, exporting any file system from any server requires that you carefully evaluate any security problems that might arise. All the same rules apply for sharing folders on Windows systems.

A number of vendors provide NFS client support for Windows computers, which allows them to access NFS shares on UNIX systems or other systems. In this arrangement, the security of the Windows systems is no more a concern than when the system operates as a native SMB client. You still need to take all the precautions for avoiding virus and Trojan Horse attacks.

Installing an NFS Server on a Windows system is another matter. You open the system up to all of the potential attacks that have been documented for the UNIX-based version of NFS, as well as other potential undocumented attacks. Some of these problems are outlined here:

◆   Many NFS implementations are ported from UNIX systems and not designed to take advantage of NT security features such as logon authentication.

◆   If NFS is not set up properly, an attacker could gain access to the entire file system or spoof another user.

♦ Some NFS implementations do not provide adequate auditing.

♦ Some NFS implementations do not take advantage of Windows NT File System (NTFS) and its highly secure permission system.

When evaluating an NFS server to run on Windows NT, you should look carefully at its support for Windows NT security, its ability to map UNIX users and groups to Windows NT users and groups, its support for the NT File System, and support for Windows NT file naming conventions.

NFS clients and servers are available for Windows from Intergraph Corporation. You can contact their web site at **www.intergraph.com**. Their products are called DiskAccess (the client) and DiskShare (the server). These products are actually based on code that was originally developed by Microsoft when it had plans to develop a universal redirector for Windows NT 4.0. However, Microsoft dropped the plans and provided the code to Intergraph.

SMB (Server Message Block)

SMB is the native file-sharing protocol in the Windows 95, Windows NT, and OS/2 operating system environments. It is also used in pre-Windows 95 versions of the Windows operating system for file sharing across networks. In addition, the new Common Internet File System (CIFS) that provides file sharing across the Internet is based on SMB. Chapter 9 describes how SMB works and how to set up a share over the Internet.

SMB goes beyond the Windows environment and is a key to interoperability among different operating systems. The protocol is widely available in the UNIX and VMS environments, and it has been an Open Group (formerly X/Open) standard for PC and UNIX interoperability since 1992. A number of vendors support SMB in this context, including AT&T, Digital, Hewlett-Packard, IBM, Novell, and others. SMB is also the file and print sharing protocol used in Samba, a freeware network file system available for LINUX and many UNIX platforms. If you are interested in providing SMB support on UNIX systems, you should look into the Samba products, which provide both SMB clients and servers.

Samba is an implementation of SMB that runs over TCP/IP. It was written by Andrew Tridgell and is available in the public domain. When Samba is installed as a server on a UNIX system, Windows clients can access files and printers on the UNIX system natively. UNIX users can install the Samba client to access SMB shared directories on Windows computers.

Samba is available via anonymous FTP from **nimbus.anu.edu.au** in the directory called /PUB/TRIDGE/SAMBA/.

16

When choosing between the NFS or SMB options, your best bet may be to install Samba clients on UNIX systems and allow those users to access SMB shared directories on Windows NT systems. You have much more control over security on NT, and you can require user authentication to protect the file system.

CAUTION: There were problems with Samba in Windows systems; Microsoft cleared these up with bug fixes. For more information, access the Microsoft Knowledge Base at **www.microsoft.com/kb** and search on "Samba."

Security for Macintosh Services

Services for Macintosh makes it possible for PC clients and Macintosh clients to share files and printers. The feature is integrated into the Microsoft Windows NT Server. You can choose to set up the services at any time. Besides providing file and printer sharing, the services can function as an AppleTalk router. Macintosh clients do not need additional software to access the services, except that an optional authentication module can be installed to provide secure logons to the Windows NT Server.

File sharing is important in the PC and Macintosh environment because users often have similar applications designed for different platforms that access the same files. For example, Microsoft makes versions of its Excel spreadsheet package for Microsoft and Windows. Users of these applications can access the same files, and they can work together if they can easily share those files. A Windows user sees files in the familiar Explorer format, while Macintosh users see files in the familiar Macintosh folder structure.

A Windows NT Server provides a centralized platform for allowing this file sharing without the need to install Macintosh servers. The NT Server can also provide centralized and consistent file security by maintaining a single list of user accounts for both PC and Macintosh environments. File permissions are translated in the following way, providing an additional level of security:

♦ Macintosh access privileges are translated into the Windows NT permissions scheme.

♦ Windows NT permissions are translated into the Macintosh-style privileges scheme.

The interesting thing about this scheme is that files appear in the way that users would normally expect them to, no matter which platform they were created on. Of course, access to those files depends on the application in use.

Many vendor's applications support full interchange of file formats between the PC and Macintosh versions of those applications, retaining all formatting and document information.

Macintosh and PC users share files by placing them in shared directories. Each shared directory has a specific share name. In order for Macintosh users to access a shared directory on a Windows NT system, an administrator must designate the directory as a *Macintosh-accessible volume*. In this case, a volume refers to a directory that has been designated as both a shared directory and a Macintosh-accessible volume that both PC and Macintosh users can access. This is slightly different from the concept of volumes that PC users are familiar with, which refers to an entire hard disk partition.

There is some translation that takes place with filenames. Characters in Macintosh files and folders that are illegal in the NT File System are replaced. Names that are too long for MS-DOS users are truncated to six characters, a tilde (~), and a unique number. Long NTFS filenames are automatically translated to short names for MS-DOS users, and if NTFS names are longer than 31 characters, Macintosh users see the short name.

Services for Macintosh Security

The Windows NT Server and Services for Macintosh enforce security for both PC users and Macintosh users. The Windows NT User Account database is used for both types of users. You only need to create new accounts.

Logons

Macintosh users are logged on to a computer running Windows NT Server as either a guest, a user with a clear text password, or a user with an encrypted password.

With guest logons, Macintosh users without accounts can log on to the server without a password and can access resources at the discretion of the server administrator. Administrators typically grant restricted permissions to guest users.

The clear text passwords option sends unencrypted passwords over the line that could be detected by network sniffers. Clear text passwords are part of the AppleShare client software or System 7 File Sharing that limits passwords to no more than eight characters.

16

Encrypted passwords are designed to provide secure logons. Macintosh clients can take advantage of encrypted passwords of up to 14 characters in length when accessing Services for Macintosh systems.

Permissions

Control through permissions is the other side of security with Services for Macintosh. The Windows NT security system lets you control access to shared directories and files; the Macintosh permissions feature provides control only for folders, not files. While permissions are different for PC and Macintosh users, Services for Macintosh automatically translates permissions so that they are properly enforced on each system. The Windows NT Server Administrators account is the account that has full permissions to the Services for Macintosh volume.

NOTE: Windows NT permissions can be set for files in the folders, and those permissions will apply to Macintosh users even though file permissions are normally not part of the Macintosh system. Services for Macintosh enforces the Windows NT permissions for Macintosh clients, even though Macintosh clients can't see any indication of the permissions.

There are four types of permissions for Macintosh folders, and these permissions are inherited by the files in the folders:

♦ **See Files** Users can see files in folders and read the files.

♦ **See Folders** Users can see folders within folders.

♦ **Make Changes** Users can create, modify, rename, move, and delete files in folders.

♦ **Cannot Move, Rename, Or Delete** Users cannot perform these actions on folders.

There are three categories of users to whom Macintosh users can give these permissions, as shown in the following dialog box:

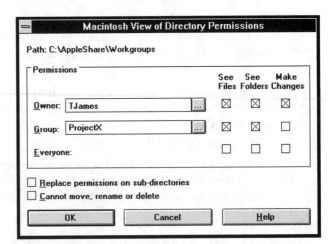

Notice that this dialog box contains a matrix in which you specify permissions for the owner of a folder, a group, or everyone, as described here:

◆ **Owner** The user that created the folder is the owner. The folder is assumed to contain private information that should be accessible only to the owner.

◆ **Group** The folder is accessible by a group of users. This is a workgroup option that assumes the folder is accessible by a specially designated group.

◆ **Everyone** The folder is accessible by all the users of a server.

This scheme provides a number of variations. For example, to create a special workgroup that can access files in a folder, select a workgroup in the Group box, then enable See Folders and See Files. Enable Make Changes only if you want the members of the workgroup to change the contents of files. Otherwise, the owner changes the contents, assuming the owner has the Make Changes permission. This configuration is shown in the previous illustration.

As mentioned, PC users can set permissions for files within a directory. Macintosh users cannot do this. The following outlines how permissions are translated in this environment:

PC file or directory set to Read	Macintosh permissions set as See Files and See Folders
PC file or directory set to Write and Delete	Macintosh permissions set to Make Changes
Macintosh folder set to See Files and See Folder	PC permissions set to Read
Macintosh folder set to Make Changes	PC permissions set to Write and Delete

Here are some other things to keep in mind:

◆ A Macintosh permission assigned to everyone overrides any more restrictive rights set for the owner or group. In Windows NT, permissions assigned to everyone do not override permissions set for the owner or group.

◆ A folder's owner can set permissions for directories from a PC because the owner has Change Permission (P) for that folder.

16

♦ An extra level of security is provided with volume passwords in Services for Macintosh. These passwords must be types used by Macintosh users who want to access the volume, but not by PC users.

Logon Security

You can set logon security for Macintosh users to Services for Macintosh by opening the MacFile utility in the Control Panel. From here, choose Attributes. You can then set the following options:

♦ **Allow Guests to Logon** permits Macintosh users to access the server without a password.

♦ **Allow Workstations to Save Password** permits Macintosh users to save their passwords on their own workstations so they won't be prompted every time they sign on to the Windows NT Server. This is not a good idea for security reasons.

♦ **Require Microsoft Authentication** specifies that Macintosh users must use Microsoft Authentication instead of the Apple authentication.

Microsoft SNA Server

Systems Network Architecture (SNA), first introduced in 1974, is IBM's scheme for connecting its 3270 family of products. SNA includes a suite of networking protocols. Included in this architecture are mainframe computer systems (hosts), midrange computer systems, 3270 terminals and desktop computers, and a strategy that lets these systems communicate with host systems, or with each other in a peer-to-peer arrangement.

Despite the proliferation of networked PCs, host systems are still widely used and will be for some time in the future. It has been estimated that more than 80 percent of all information is available on IBM SNA networks. Many organizations will continue to run their mission-critical applications on IBM hosts while migrating to network-based systems. With the widespread use of networks, the role of the host system has changed from a centralized processing system to a system that resides as a node on those networks. The host is now considered an application server and data repository that desktop PC users can access over network connections.

The Microsoft SNA Server is a gateway product that is designed to let users of desktop computers access host information over existing network links. The SNA Server provides complete support for industry standard network protocols and offers centralized or remotely controlled management features. It also takes full advantage of the security, fault-tolerant, and administrative features of the Windows NT Server.

PC users use standard LAN protocols to connect with one or more SNA Servers, and the SNA Servers provide shared links to host systems using SNA protocols. The SNA Server provides all the tools that administrators need to centrally manage and control the host environment.

Microsoft SNA Server Features

The Microsoft SNA Server runs on the Windows NT Server operating system and uses its native network communication protocols (TCP/IP and IPX) and IBM SNA protocols to provide a gateway to IBM networks. Clients on Windows, DOS, OS/2, UNIX, and Macintosh computers can run terminal emulation, printer emulation, file transfers, and program-to-program communications. These options are described here. The SNA Server acts as a server node to the IBM host and allows PCs to access data and applications on IBM host systems.

The type of connections that are possible with the SNA Server are pictured in Figure 16-2. Keep in mind that PCs on local and branch office networks connect to one or more SNA Servers using their native protocols (TCP/IP, NetBEUI, IPX, or others). The SNA Servers then provide the links to the host systems using SNA protocols. Remote Access Service connections can also be made into the Windows NT Server that runs the SNA Server.

One of Microsoft's objectives in designing the SNA Server was to eliminate some of the problems that have been associated with direct SNA connections and SNA gateways. Direct connections of PCs to hosts is expensive and difficult to manage, so in the past, SNA gateways were used to provide a connection for multiple PCs to the host. However, gateways were often slow and unreliable. The Microsoft SNA Server solves these problems in a number of ways:

◆ You can configure two or more SNA Servers to handle the load of multiple user connections to the host.

◆ Multiple SNA Servers work in concert to balance the load between network PCs and the host systems.

◆ Multiple SNA Servers eliminate any single point of failure.

Gateway performance problems can be reduced by using multiprocessor systems or high-end RISC platforms. The Windows NT Server also adds a level of security to host access. Administration is simplified because desktop systems do not need to be individually configured to connect with the host. They simply go through the SNA Server to access the host. This eliminates the need to load the DLC protocol that is required for direct connects. In addition, since all traffic is concentrated through the SNA Server,

16

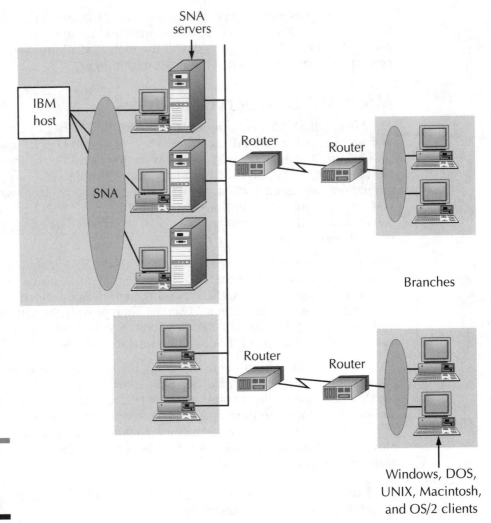

SNA Server
network
connections
Figure 16-2.

administrators can monitor and log it for security, performance
optimization, and troubleshooting purposes.

The SNA Server reduces the load on the host by off-loading communications
processes. In addition, a single Physical Unit (PU) can be defined to support
hundreds of users instead of defining a PU for each user. Normally, the host
would poll (try to contact) every desktop individually to maintain
connections. The SNA Server saves network bandwidth by eliminating the
need for the host to poll these systems. By improving performance and
simplifying administration, Microsoft has made the SNA Server a viable

alternative to direct-connect emulators. The cost per gateway client is typically less than $50.

The features and enhancements of the SNA Server are listed here:

♦ Uses graphical administration tools and the diagnostic tools that are integrated with Windows NT.

♦ Supports up to 10,000 LU host sessions per server and up to 2,000 clients per server. Supports up to 250 host or DSPU connections per server, and up to 50 SNA Servers can be used together in one or more domains.

♦ Supports native TCP/IP, IPX/SPX, Banyan VINES IP, AppleTalk, RAS (Remote Access Service) for clients, and DLC 802.2 (for DSPU connections).

♦ Runs on DEC Alpha, Intel, and PowerPC platforms.

♦ Includes Open Database Connectivity (ODBC) and Distributed Relational Database Architecture (DRDA) drivers to support connectivity to host databases. Users can run applications such as Microsoft Excel or Access to connect to DB2 on MVS, SQL/DL on VM, and DB2/400 on OS/400.

♦ Allows clients running 3270 emulators to connect through the SNA Server to host systems.

♦ Affords clients compatibility with IBM's CA/400 router so clients can connect to an AS/400 via SNA Server.

♦ Provides that applications written to IBM's APPC API will work unchanged with the SNA Server.

♦ Includes utilities that enable high speed file transfers between Windows systems and IBM hosts, eliminating the need for other file transfer protocols.

Administration and Security

The SNA Server provides a central point of administration for host connectivity and security. With the SNA Server, clients are easily configured in one place to accommodate any changes in the host configuration. Normally, direct connections would require that each desktop be reconfigured individually if the host's network address or other parameters change.

16

All users can benefit from the integrated security provided by the SNA Server. Administrators can control host access by using the combined security features of the Windows NT Server and the SNA Server. This provides a security benefit over direct connections, which allow each desktop user to access the host by simply knowing the parameters of the host.

Since all host-bound traffic is concentrated through the SNA Server, administrators can use performance monitoring, event logging, and tracing/sniffing tools of the server platform to monitor performance and security. The centralized platform provides stability and such features as hot backup and load balancing. *Hot backup* reroutes sessions over alternate paths when a communication failure occurs, assuming multiple connections have been set up. *Load balancing* dynamically routes traffic across multiple servers and minimizes response time between the desktop and the host. The SNA Server also takes advantage of the fault-tolerant recovery features built into Windows NT Server, such as UPS, tape backup, registration database, disk duplexing, disk mirroring, and disk striping with parity, as discussed in Chapter 11.

The SNA Server takes advantage of the C2-level security features implemented in Windows NT, which controls logons to Windows NT Server domains. A user must successfully log on to the Windows NT Server running the SNA Server before access is granted to any services provided by the SNA Server. This provides a level of security that MIS managers are used to having with their mainframe security programs.

Remote Access Server connections are equally as secure because the Windows NT User Account database is used to authenticate users. Administrators can create user and group accounts that can be used on both the Windows NT and the SNA Servers. A simple dialog box in SNA Server Admin allows you to specify which users and groups defined in the domain will be granted access to SNA sessions.

Here are additional security features available with the Windows NT Server and SNA Server combination:

♦ The administrative permissions control access to SNA Server tools as well as to the configuration files. They are Read Only, Read-Write, Full Control, and No Access.

♦ The Windows NT Event Viewer provides full audit tracking that is comparable to auditing capabilities common on hosts.

♦ A single logon is possible, making it convenient for users to access the system and for administrators to centrally manage user accounts.

♦ All communications between the client computer and the SNA Server can be encrypted.

Synchronization of passwords and automated logon to a number of environments is possible with an optional host component available from

Proginet (**www.proginet.com**). The company's SecurPass product synchronizes LAN passwords with host system security products so that users don't need to sign on to host systems separately. The product synchronizes NT passwords with IBM AS/400, IBM RACF (Resource Access Control Facility), Computer Associate's Top Secret, and Computer Associate's ACF2 host-security systems. It also provides a single logon for NetWare 4.1 and NetWare Directory Services (NDS).

SecurPass uses the host communication features in the SNA Server to provide password synchronization. Changes to passwords are also synchronized. If a user changes her password on the Windows NT domain, passwords are also changed on the host system. Alternatively, if the host password is changed by an administrator, the password is also changed on the Windows NT domain.

Enterprise Security Management

Enterprise-wide management of security and systems has become increasingly important as organizations connect all their computing resources. A typical enterprise network consists of Windows NT Servers, IBM mainframe and midrange systems, UNIX systems, Novell NetWare servers, OS/2 servers, DEC systems, and more. A number of vendors have produced products that are designed to manage the entire enterprise, including Axent (**www.axent.com**) and Technologic (**www.technologic.com**).

In the multiplatform enterprise network environment, it is difficult to obtain a consistent management structure. Centralized tools for managing systems and security are necessary to prevent problems that can occur through mismanagement of resources. Two enterprise management products are outlined in the following sections. I am not advocating the use of either product. I am simply trying to give you some sense of what enterprise management products do.

NOTE: The products discussed here work over a range of platforms. Windows NT-specific security tools are discussed in Appendix D.

16

Axent Enterprise Security Manager (ESM)

ESM is designed to provide security services for enterprise systems in the same way that a security firm provides security for your physical facilities. Policies and procedures are set and then checked for compliance. Recommendations are made to protect areas against security breaches, and those areas are regularly checked.

Conceptually, ESM works much like a security firm hired to secure physical facilities. The security firm makes sure that policies and procedures are set up to ensure that only authorized personnel are allowed in secure areas. It then checks the facility's compliance with these procedures and makes recommendations regarding potential breaches in security. Once the breaches are closed, these areas are regularly checked and reported upon. In a similar fashion, ESM provides the following services:

♦ Manages and ensures conformance with security policies

♦ Checks all systems for vulnerabilities, such as trap doors, logic bombs, or unauthorized privileges

♦ Provides integrity checks, including anti-viral protection

♦ Detects changes to security settings or files

Security is managed through a graphical interface that makes it easy for non-technical users to set policies under the supervision of appropriate managers. ESM gives you a choice of management platforms, including Microsoft Windows and UNIX systems.

ESM uses a manager/agent architecture. Functions that are common to all managed platforms are implemented on the Management Workstation and are accessed from the GUI. Functions that are specific to a particular platform are implemented as Agents that execute on the managed nodes. The user interface and manager and agent software can reside on different platforms. For example, the user interface can be placed on a Windows or UNIX workstation. The manager may be on a NetWare server, a UNIX server, or an OpenVMS server.

ESM agents run on a wide range of personal computers (PC), on UNIX, and on mid-range platforms including Windows NT, Novell NetWare (3.*x* or 4.*x*), HP-UX, IBM AIX, SunOS, Solaris, Digital Ultrix, OpenVMS (on VAX or AXP), and others.

ESM is intended to be the binding foundation of a suite of products that provide a total security solution. These modules can include Access Control, Intruder Alert, Single Sign On, Enterprise Backup Manager, and others. Additional modules can be plugged into ESM as required, a benefit derived from the open architecture of ESM. Each of these products sends a report of its activities to ESM, which ESM then rolls up into a management report that is delivered to you in a format suitable for importation into a spreadsheet or some other analysis tool.

Technologic Software's RAS Enterprise

RAS is a multiplatform security program that uses a unique electronic forms-based architecture to automate the entire access request/termination, approval, and administration workflow. RAS advances security administration from a manual or semi-automated process to a fully automated solution. It eliminates paper processing and automates the security administration function for operating systems, electronic mail programs, database managers, and applications. All of this is done securely without compromising the system.

Users in your enterprise-wide network can request, from their desktop, access to resources on any RAS-managed platform and be granted access to those resources within minutes of approval. Adds, changes, suspends, and deletes are accomplished dynamically through secure pathways that cover your entire enterprise resources. All security-controlled resources are managed by RAS agents resident on each system.

RAS provides auditability and control to enterprise security. For any resource, you can report on who has access to it. For users, you can see what access they have and who authorized it. RAS provides a repository of all accesses for instant query and reporting across all the computing resources in your enterprise. The RAS Auditor reduces the amount of time the organization spends preparing for and performing computing resource audits, thereby reducing their cost to the enterprise.

Requesters select access request forms from the RAS repository and point-and-click to add, change, suspend, or delete resources. The request is then automatically edited and routed to the access approver. With RAS you create a hierarchy of approvers and authorizers. If someone is unavailable, RAS can notify the next higher approver/authorizer in the hierarchy—that approver's supervisor, for example. If there are multiple approvers for resources on different platforms or systems, RAS will route the request to all appropriate approvers in the proper sequence.

Approvers and authorizers can approve or deny requests in seconds. They may delegate their authority to others by resource and time period to accommodate travel, meetings, illness, and so on. After access is authorized, the request is routed to the RAS intelligent agent for the platform for which access is requested. The RAS intelligent agent implements the approved request automatically and sends a notice to the requester.

16

Transferring authorization from one person to another (temporary or permanent) is done by simply clicking an icon and entering the delegate's name. Resource access terminations are also easily accomplished.

For additional information, visit Technologic Software's Web site at **www.technologic.com**.

PART 4

Defense Strategies for Public Networks

CHAPTER 17

Internet and TCP/IP Security Issues

This chapter describes potential security problems and threats that may be encountered when connecting networks to untrusted networks such as the Internet. Traditionally, administrators have hoped for "security through obscurity." Intrusions were not considered a serious threat because the administrator assumed that no one would know about the site, have reason to attack it, or be able to detect the connections that the site had to the Internet or other networks. This strategy is no longer viable because hackers are armed with automated tools that scan for holes and locate potential weaknesses and vulnerabilities in the network connection in a very short time.

This chapter discusses common threats and vulnerabilities in the TCP/IP and Internet environment and also touches on UNIX systems as well. Even though this book is about Windows NT security, you may find that a UNIX system is necessary to build a strong defense for your own network. Your requirements will determine the appropriateness of building defensive systems with Windows NT, as discussed in the next section and in more detail in Chapter 18.

This chapter provides an introduction to security problems associated with the Internet and TCP/IP environments. For additional information, I encourage you to contact the following Web sites:

♦ The National Security Institute (NSI) provides a variety of professional information and security awareness services to defense contractors and industrial security executives throughout the United States. NSI accomplishes this task through publishing newsletters and special reports, holding seminars, and disseminating information electronically via its World Wide Web site. NSI's Web site at **nsi.org/compsec.html** provides an incredible amount of information on TCP/IP-related security issues and references to other sites.

♦ The Computer Security Institute at **www.gocsi.com** has a collection of documents and information on security. In particular, a document called "CSI Manager's Guide to Internet Security" provides valuable information about protecting systems and networks that are connected to the Internet.

♦ Raptor Systems at **www.raptor.com** has a large and interesting library of white papers and other material on Internet security issues.

Connecting to the Internet

These days, no one in their right mind would connect an information system or network to the Internet without considering the security implications of doing so. Part 1 of this book described the most common security threats and problems. This chapter and the next chapter will touch on firewalls and other defensive systems and the types of attacks that they can protect against.

Firewalls are systems that stand between your internal network and untrusted networks like the Internet. When properly implemented, a firewall can keep intruders out by restricting inbound traffic. At the same time, it can let internal users access the Internet. The simplest firewall is a router that provides packet filtering, although the security options with routers is limited, as described in Chapter 18. The most advanced firewalls cost thousands of dollars and can provide you with a high level of security for protecting internal resources.

One of the basic problems with defensive systems is that we can never know if a system is completely secure. There are some very solid products on the market, but would you be willing to bet your job on the vendor's word that the firewall is secure? Readers may want to implement multilevel firewall systems that use different vendors' products. Then, if an intruder breaks through one system, he won't be able to use the same techniques to break through the next level.

Many vendors have so much confidence in the strength of their products that they have put sites on the Web and challenged anyone to break into them. What they are really doing is letting the Internet community test their products. As people try to break in, the vendors log all activities and learn how to strengthen their products from the break-in attempts. They also learn about holes that hackers have secret knowledge of.

One vendor that does this is Secure Computing Corporation, makers of the Sidewinder firewall. In recent tests by independent organizations that are in the business of breaking into systems, the Sidewinder was shown to be virtually impenetrable. There have been no break-ins. You can visit their site at **www.sctc.com**.

But here's a consideration. The Sidewinder runs on a UNIX platform. This book is about Windows NT security. Shouldn't I recommend a Windows NT firewall solution? Is UNIX a better operating system than Windows NT when it comes to security? In one very important respect, UNIX is better than Windows NT: it is a mature operating system that has been thoroughly explored for security weaknesses and vulnerabilities over the course of many years. In contrast, Windows NT is a relatively new operating system; we just don't know all of its weaknesses.

This is not to say that new holes won't appear in UNIX or that Windows NT does have holes. However, most of the weaknesses of UNIX are well known, so it is much easier to determine the weaknesses in new versions of the operating system or applications that run on it. In addition, vendors of

17

security products like firewalls know how to build systems that protect against known weaknesses in security. So which platform do you want to use? One that may have undiscovered security problems or one that has been fully tested for years?

The basic architecture of Windows NT is sound and may prove to be the most secure platform around, but perhaps we need a few more years of testing, break-in attempts, and hacking to determine this. So far, no one has publicly announced that Windows NT cannot be compromised, not even Microsoft. To be fair, I don't think anyone has said that about UNIX or any other operating system.

All of this said, the general consensus is that Windows NT makes a good firewall when implemented properly. Vendors such as Raptor Systems make firewall products that can protect internal networks; however, as you will see in the next chapter, part of this security is obtained by strictly prohibiting the use of many applications.

If you plan to use Windows NT for a firewall system, then make it only one part of your defense. Add additional firewall components and build strong security policies, then test and scan and retest. The security of your internal assets depends on it.

With this in mind, we can consider three different ways to connect your systems to the Internet:

The Home-Grown Windows NT Solution   A Windows NT dual-homed system in the proper configuration makes a good firewall in some specific cases. Even if you don't take this approach, its interesting to see how such a system is configured. I describe how to do this in Chapter 18.

Windows NT Platform with Proxy Services   The Microsoft Proxy Server provides an interesting solution to the problem of allowing internal users to access the Internet while maintaining a solid wall against any kind of internal access by Internet users. This solution assumes that no Internet users need to access your internal network. Refer to Chapter 19 for more information.

Industrial Strength Firewall and Proxy Server   Firewalls in this category are designed to let Internet users access your network, under very controlled conditions, and to let your internal users access the Internet. The systems work all the way up to the top of the network protocol stack to provide a high level of control over traffic that reaches the firewall.

Whether you need an inbound/outbound connection to the Internet depends on your requirements. For example, if you need to provide Web services to the Internet, does the Web server need to be attached to your internal network as well? Probably not. Figure 17-1 shows one method for

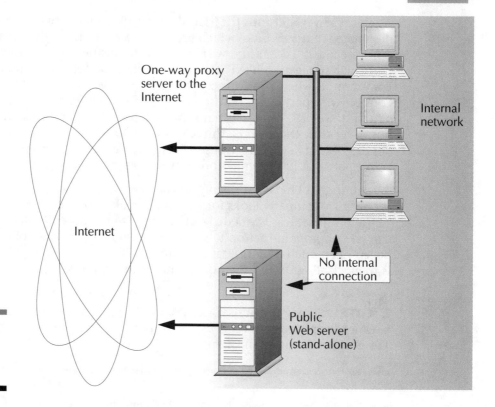

One method
of connecting
to the Internet
Figure 17-1.

allowing internal users to access the Internet through a proxy server (no Internet users can get into the internal network through this proxy server). A public Web server is set up as a stand-alone system with no internal connection in order to prevent security breaches.

One of the interesting things about this configuration is that internal users can access their own company's Web site by accessing the Internet and backtracking to it. This is only one possible configuration. Others are discussed in Chapter 18.

Scanning Tools

Scanning tools are legitimate programs that were designed to help network administrators find security holes and other problems in their networks. A typical scanning tool connects with a designated system and starts a scanning process. You can imagine the analogous situation of a security company coming out to your business and checking all the doors and windows to make sure they are locked and secured.

17

A typical server that runs the TCP/IP protocol stack has over a thousand designated "entry points," which are called *ports*. In the previous analogy, ports are like the doors and windows of your business. A port is where a particular application like FTP or HTTP makes connection with outside users. For example, when you connect with a Web server over the Internet, you connect with port 80 on that server. FTP servers use port 20. Appendix G has a full list of ports. Be aware that some applications open ports on their own, but never close those ports, thus exposing your system to security breaches. For example, a hacker might use TELNET to penetrate a firewall through an active port that has been left open by some previous process.

A scanning tool looks for open ports on your systems in the same way that the security company looks for potential break-in points at your business. The administrator is warned about open ports and other vulnerabilities and can take appropriate action to secure the system. Of course, some ports must be left open, such as port 80 if you run an HTTP server. The typical strategy is to block all ports and then open only required ports.

 NOTE: Some ports must be left open. To protect your system, you need advanced application-level gateways to precisely monitor and control ports. This topic is discussed in Chapter 18.

Administrators can use scanning tools to check for unauthorized services running on their own internal networks. For example, it's now relatively easy for network clients to install their own Web servers and provide information in this manner to internal and external users. To detect unauthorized services, a scan can be done on every system on the network.

Unfortunately, hackers can use these same scanning tools from the comfort of their personal workstations to look at all of the hundreds of ports on your systems and locate computers that are easy targets. Once an appropriate port is found, the attacker will try to connect to it and set up a session with the process running at that port. Hackers can even use scanning for denial-of-service attacks in some cases.

Scanner detectors are now available to detect when your system is being scanned by an unauthorized user. The idea is to alert administrators that their systems are under attack so they can take appropriate action. However, according to Christopher Klaus of Internet Security Systems (ISS), these detectors may give a false sense of security. He reports that, normally, a scanner must make a complete connection to a port before it warns an administrator who is checking a system. A scanner detector looks for numerous attempts by an external system to make these types of connections. However, intruders can use a technique called "half-open" scanning to detect an active port without actually making a connection. Therefore, scanner detectors cannot always detect the activities of a hacker who uses a scanner.

The next two sections discuss two common scanning tools. *SATAN* (Security Administrator Tool for Analyzing Networks) is a public domain utility that is the biggest threat to corporate networks simply because it is so easy to obtain and use. *Internet Scanner SAFEsuite* from Internet Security Systems (ISS) is available for purchase only. ISS claims that it only sells its program to reputable organizations, and, before shipping the package, it implements safeguards that allow the package to run only on designated systems.

 NOTE: The Internet Scanner SAFEsuite is covered in detail in this chapter because of the comprehensive checks that it performs.

SATAN (Security Administrator Tool for Analyzing Networks)

SATAN is the most well-known scanning tool, possibly because it was the first, is in the public domain, and has a catchy name. The program was originally designed to help administrators locate security holes in their interconnected networks, but the program made its way into the hacker community. It runs on UNIX systems and requires a Web browser to connect with the target system. Fortunately, detectors have also been developed, such as Courtney, that can detect a SATAN scan and other types of scans.

To check the security of your network, you go outside the network and scan from the same location that a hacker would use to break into your system. SATAN is available at the following site:

ftp://ciac.llnl.gov/pub/ciac/sectools/unix/satan/

The program is relatively easy to use because it uses the Web browser interface. It can also be run from the command line, but you'll still need a Web browser to view the results of a scan. The results are informative and can help you determine the vulnerability of network services running on your system. The "intrusions" made by the system leave traces in the auditing logs, which can be examined to see what an actual attack looks like.

In a paper called "Improving the Security of Your Site by Breaking Into It," the creators of SATAN describe the techniques they use to examine a system for holes. The paper may be obtained at the following Web site:

17

http://www.mcg.gla.ac.uk/staff/rory/admin_guide.html

According to the paper, "SATAN examines a remote host or set of hosts and gathers as much information as possible by remotely probing NIS, finger, NFS, FTP and tftp, rexd, and other services. This information includes the presence of various network information services as well as potential security flaws—usually in the form of incorrectly set up or configured network services, well-known bugs in system or network utilities, or poor or ignorant policy decisions."

Internet Security Systems' SAFEsuite

Internet Security Systems (**www.iss.net**) develops programs that can help managers experience the hacker attack from the other side of the firewall. SAFEsuite is an "attack simulator" that automatically scans each networked machine, searching for weaknesses and misconfigurations. Their Internet scanner, shown in Figure 17-2, works over a variety of platforms, and is designed to look specifically for holes that Internet hackers commonly take advantage of. It runs on UNIX and Windows NT platforms.

According to ISS, there are over 135 known holes on TCP/IP-based networks that hackers can take advantage of. Many of these holes are common problems that are easily fixed if you can detect them. These are the very holes that intruders look for when attacking your systems. SAFEsuite detects holes before intruders can find them.

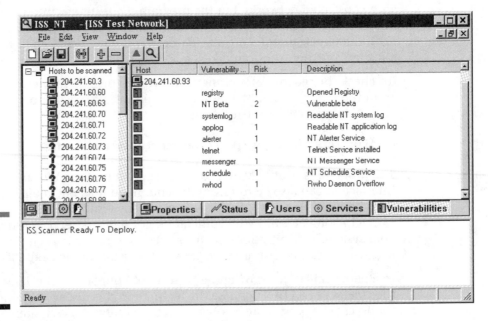

Internet Security Systems scanner

Figure 17-2.

The Internet Scanner SAFEsuite helps you measure the effectiveness of your security policy by assessing your network security. It can evaluate UNIX, Windows 95, and Windows NT systems. SAFEsuite consists of the following components.

NOTE: The following material describe vulnerabilities and known problems in both UNIX, Windows, and other systems that the SAFEsuite products can scan. Some of these are not applicable to Windows NT.

Web Security Scanner   The Web Security Scanner audits internal and external Web sites by testing the configuration of the Web server, evaluating the security of the underlying file system, and searching for CGI scripts with known vulnerabilities. It also attempts to exploit custom CGI scripts. CGI is commonly used to write programs that run on Web servers.

Firewall Scanner   The Firewall Scanner audits the security of firewalls by evaluating the underlying operating system, the firewall application, and the services enabled through the firewall. It also tests packet filtering and application proxy services.

Intranet Scanner   The Intranet Scanner assesses the security configuration of systems on internal networks by learning the topology of the network and the devices attached to it (UNIX, Windows, and X terminals) and probing each of those devices for known vulnerabilities. Intranet Scanner makes scheduled rounds to scour systems for security holes. When it spots a hole, Intranet Scanner can send you an alert and interpret the data, diagnose the hole, and present information on how to correct it.

System Security Scanner   The System Security Scanner provides real-time monitoring of computer security profiles and continuous checks for file ownerships and permissions, OS configurations, Trojan Horse programs, and hacker activities. Administrators can perform corrective actions or have the system automatically correct security vulnerabilities.

Vulnerability Tests Performed by SAFEsuite
Here are just of few of the vulnerabilities that are checked by the SAFEsuite components. Keep in mind that this is only a partial list. ISS uses a number of proprietary techniques, which it does not reveal for competitive and security reasons, to scan systems. Also, because each module is sold individually, there is some overlap in what each product does.

17

♦ Known vulnerabilities of CGI scripts, which are used by Web servers to pass data between databases and files, are checked.

♦ Password-protected private HTML is located and tested to identify easily guessed or default passwords.

♦ Well-known bugs are checked, including the .bat and .cmd bug in Microsoft Internet Information Server, and the cd.. bug that lets everyone access outside of a shared directory.

♦ Brute-force attacks are performed to find easily guessed logon passwords and passwords for shared SMB directories. Information provided by systat/netstat is used to aid in brute-force attacks.

♦ Other vulnerabilities are checked, such as broken local links, root dot dot, and anonymous FTP configurations.

♦ Attempts are made to force the server into a failure (denial-of-service) using udp bomb, finger bomb, chargen, echo, NetBIOS SMB dot dot bug in Windows NT, Nuke, Open/Close ports repetitively, and DNS attack.

♦ Attempts are made to exploit TCP sequence prediction by inserting TCP packets into a known stream of trusted packets by guessing the next packet number.

♦ Attempts are made to spoof the Routing Information Protocol (RIP) by sending out forged RIP packets. This attack would include sniffing, spoofing, hijacking, and dropping of packets on a connection not originally going through a network.

♦ PWL (password) files that can be cracked to allow access to Windows 95 computers are located.

♦ Searches are made to find vulnerabilities and problems in RPC services, sendmail, rlogin, rexd, admind, Network Information System (NIS), and others.

In addition to most of the checks outlined here, the Firewall Scanner performs the following vulnerability checks. These checks are specific to firewall products and may not apply to all the systems that can be checked by SAFEsuite:

♦ Does a SOCKs Scan to determine if unauthorized packets can be passed through the firewall.

♦ Verifies that WWW.FTP and e-mail proxies are present, and attempts to obtain information from these proxies that could be used to bypass the firewall.

♦ Attempts to bypass packet filtering using source porting and source routing methods. Source porting can be exploited if a firewall allows connections to be made to inside machines on ports greater than 1,024. When source routing is enabled, packet filtering rules can be bypassed.

♦ Attempts to repeatedly log on to the target using brute-force techniques that are specific to various firewalls and routers.

Sniffing the Network

Networks were designed to make sharing information easy. The most common LAN protocol is Ethernet, and by design, any computer on an Ethernet LAN broadcasts information on the open wire that all other computers can hear—much as a radio station broadcasts within a specific area. This is shown in Figure 17-3. If a computer detects a packet that is addressed to it, it receives the packet. All other packets are ignored.

However, most LAN adapters can be switched into what is called "promiscuous" mode, a setting that allows the adapter to receive all packets broadcast on the network. These packets can then be captured and saved for analysis. A *packet-sniffing* program makes this task a lot easier. It has all the controls an administrator (or hacker) needs to filter and sort through the transmissions to find and evaluate specific network traffic. Network technicians typically use sniffers to detect and correct network problems. Keep in mind that because broadcasts are limited to one network, only the traffic on that network can be monitored, including all traffic that passes through it on the way to other networks.

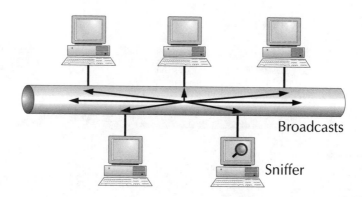

A basic
Ethernet LAN
Figure 17-3.

17

To prevent the threat of unauthorized sniffing, networks can be segmented to reduce the range of broadcasts, as shown in Figure 17-4. In a segmented network, the router prevents broadcasts on one network from propagating to the other network. The sniffer on the right-hand network can capture packets only on that network. However, any packets forwarded by the router between the networks can be viewed, which means that potentially any transmission on an internetwork can be monitored.

Taking this a step further, network switching techniques can introduce high levels of segmentation up to the point where each workstation has its own segment. This reduces congestion on the network and limits the amount of traffic that a network sniffer can capture. In Figure 17-5, you can see that the sniffer is located on one LAN segment, and can monitor the traffic only on that segment. However, notice that all WAN traffic must funnel through a single connection. A sniffer on this connection could glean quite a bit of information.

The solution is encryption. Figures 17-3, 17-4 and 17-5 show networks in which you could encrypt all data streams on local area networks and on the WAN connections. Depending on the devices and software, information may be encrypted at the point where it enters the WAN, or a tunnel may provide end-to-end encryption between a workstation on one side of the WAN and another workstation on the other side. This prevents both internal and external sniffing of the data stream. Basically, encrypted tunnels prevent "man in the middle" and "man at the end" sniffing attacks.

The chances of someone being able to sniff and glean valuable information from a data stream at some random location on the Internet is remote. On

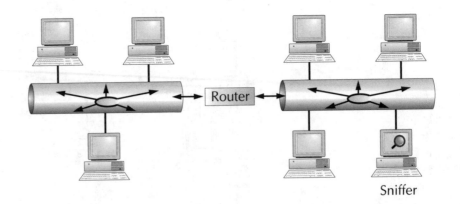

A segmented
network
Figure 17-4.

Sniffer

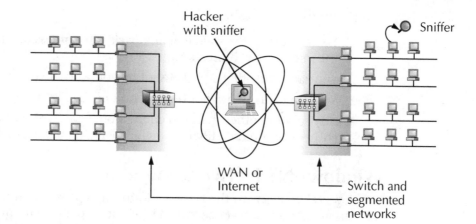

A network with very detailed segmentation

Figure 17-5.

the other hand, can you trust the phone companies and ISPs to keep their systems secure? In many foreign countries, the government controls the communication system and may actively monitor traffic for competitive or security reasons.

Recently, several large ISPs were broken into, but only one, BARRNet, publicly reported that its systems had been compromised. A sniffer program was installed on a computer attached to its backbone network and passwords were stolen. An insidious aspect of this break-in was that the captured information was encrypted on disk, so when the sniffer was discovered, BARRNet could not tell which of its customer's accounts had been compromised. All it could do was report the break-in to all of its customers, making the matter worse for BARRNet.

IP-Watcher, which is discussed later, gives you a sobering glimpse at just what hackers can glean from network transmissions. Mike Neuman of En Garde Systems, creators of IP-Watcher, wrote the following in a message posted on the Internet:

[Here are] the inescapable facts

1. IP can be monitored.
2. TCP connections can be hijacked (REGARDLESS of where the attacker is).
3. UDP pseudo-connections can have data inserted midstream.
4. IP source addresses are meaningless.

17

This means:

1. You can't trust the source of any packet, regardless of whether it's in the middle of a connection.
2. You can't trust that a packet sent by you will arrive at the destination.
3. You can't trust that your traffic won't be seen by a third party.
4. Any solution other than full encryption, or at least packet-level authentication (i.e., IPv6), is merely delaying the inevitable.

Windows NT Network Monitor

Windows NT comes with the Network Monitor, a packet sniffing program that lets authorized users (a password is required to use it) monitor all the traffic specific to a local computer or network segment. However, Network Monitor is somewhat limited in functionality as compared to the IP-Watcher from En Garde systems, which is discussed in the next section. The version that comes with Windows NT lets you monitor traffic to and from the computer running the software. An advanced version, available if you purchase Microsoft System Management Server, lets you capture frames sent to or from any computer on the network, edit and transmit frames on the network, and remotely capture frames from other computers on the network that run Network Monitor Agent (included in Windows 95 and Windows NT).

In contrast, IP-Watcher provides active monitoring that lets users view information, stop sessions, and even hijack (take over) sessions. It provides a much better illustration of the tools that administrators might use to monitor and stop hacker attacks. At the same time, it illustrates the types of tools that hackers might use against your network.

En Garde Systems IP-Watcher

IP-Watcher is a network monitoring tool that gives you control of any logon session on a network. En Garde recommends it as a tool for investigating suspicious activity, obtaining evidence of misuse, and even for stopping malicious users before they do any damage. Administrators are able to see exactly what is happening on the network, to collect data in real time, and to control misuse using active countermeasures. At the same time, En Garde warns, there are dangers if IP-Watcher is in the wrong hands.

 NOTE: I present this material not only to describe a tool that you might find of use, but to make you aware of tools that hackers can use against your network.

IP-Watcher has the following features:

- ◆ Data being transferred between two hosts is inspected, and all connections on a network are monitored.

- ◆ Administrators can display an exact copy of a session in real-time and see the session just as the user sees it.

- ◆ A user interface makes it easy to use the product, select sessions to monitor, and filter sessions.

A typical session window is shown in Figure 17-6.

IP-Watcher is basically a packet sniffer with an interface that makes it easy to view specific types of network traffic. As shown in Figure 17-7, you can select the protocol to view in the Input Configuration window. Any IP port can be selected.

IP-Watcher uses a technique called *active sniffing* (as opposed to *passive sniffing*) that allows it to interact with connections on the network. This interaction allows users of IP-Watcher to terminate and even take over active connections. This technique, which EnGarde calls "IP-Hijacking," involves intercepting and "spoofing" packets at the IP level. IP-Hijacking can be

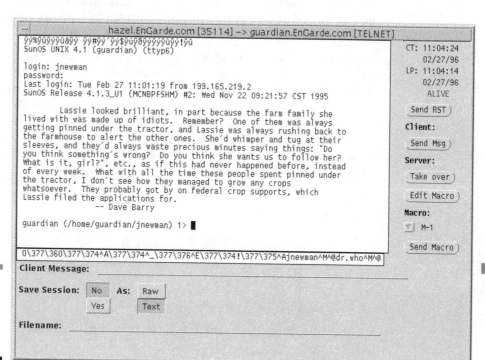

A typical
IP-Watcher
session
window
Figure 17-6.

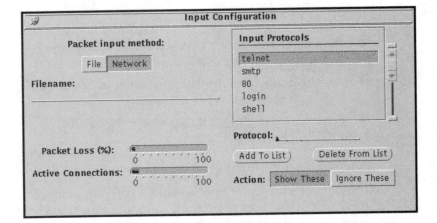

Choosing
protocols
to view in
IP-Watcher
Figure 17-7.

performed from any machine on a network. To the client, the hijacked connection appears to run slower, while the server sees no difference. All traffic that is broadcast on the subnet running IP-Watcher is visible, including all local traffic and traffic that is sent to the subnet or passes through it from other subnets.

Denial-of-service attacks can be staged by an attacker running IP-Watcher by simply disconnecting a session. This attack can get more specific. Because the software can be configured to track patterns in network traffic, all traffic from a specific host into a given subnet can be terminated.

IP-Watcher goes beyond traditional network sniffers in its ability to make sense of large amounts of captured data. A user can select individual connections that are interesting and log them either as pure text or as raw packet data. A raw log records all information that is passed over the network, including the packet headers and a time stamp. These raw logs can then be played back using IP-Watcher. En Garde assumes that administrators will use this feature to log a trail of evidence for later investigations, potentially involving even criminal or civil prosecution.

To play back a raw log file, you open the file and use the playback window pictured here:

You can control playback speed, pause playback, and log the playback files to a text file for offline analysis.

En Garde warns that the use of active sniffing by products like IP-Watcher opens up many new types of attacks that are difficult to defend against. These attacks range from simple denial-of-service on a host or network-wide basis, to information compromise. Here are some examples of these hazards:

♦ Many applications send clear text passwords that can be easily stolen by a packet sniffer. To get the password from a currently logged on user, the attacker can kill the connection and wait for the user to log back on.

♦ Active sniffing allows attackers to terminate or take over the session of a legitimate user. According to En Garde, it is no longer sufficient to authenticate users at the beginning of a session. They must be continuously authenticated during the session.

♦ Smartcards and other one-time or challenge/response systems are useful because of active sniffing. Any session is vulnerable to an attack after the real user has been authenticated.

♦ Many firewalls control access by looking at the address of incoming connections. After the firewall has allowed a connection, an active sniffer can take it over, thus bypassing the security provided by the filtering mechanism.

The solution to these problems is encryption of sessions and the use of firewalls that examine every packet for authenticity. Some firewalls now implement encryption between clients and servers. Indeed, most Web browsers and servers now support encryption. En Garde estimates that 99 percent of the hosts currently connected to the Internet are vulnerable to sniffing. The way to avoid packet sniffing attacks is with encryption.

Netcat: A Sniffer/Scanner

Netcat is another sniffer utility that has been available in the UNIX environment but was recently ported to the Windows environment. It is available as shareware at **ftp.avian.org/src/hacks**. I mention this program to warn you of the potential problems this program may produce. At the same time, you might find it makes a useful addition to your administrative toolkit. The program was created by "Hobbit," who prefers to remain anonymous.

17

Netcat reads and writes data across network connections using TCP or UDP protocols. You can use it for debugging or for exploring your network.

It can create almost any kind of connection. Here is a list of major features as provided by the designer:

◆ Outbound or inbound connections, TCP or UDP, to or from any ports

◆ Full DNS forward/reverse checking, with appropriate warnings

◆ Ability to use any local source port

◆ Ability to use any locally-configured network source address

◆ Built-in port-scanning capabilities, with randomizer

◆ Built-in loose source-routing capability

◆ Can read command line arguments from standard input

◆ Slow-send mode, one line every *N* seconds

◆ Hex dump of transmitted and received data

◆ Optional ability to let another program service establish connections

◆ Optional telnet-options responder

"Hobbit" recommends that you use the program to automate probes, scan ports, and create an inventory of services running on a system. It can also be used to test firewalls, test address spoofing, check network performance, and "1,001 other uses you'll likely come up with."

Other Attacks

Hackers will look for weaknesses in systems. Many of the weaknesses of UNIX systems are well known, and hackers take a systematic approach to finding those weaknesses. There are many levels of expertise within the hacker community. In the past, teenagers sitting at home computers simply looked for unprotected systems. Today, hackers find it more difficult to do their dastardly deeds, but the tools they use are much more efficient and automated. Most of these tools are readily available on the Internet.

The intruder begins his attack by looking for information about systems. While some hackers have a specific target in mind and concentrate all their efforts on breaking through that target, other hackers search for systems that might be susceptible to break-in and gather as much information as possible about them.

Routers interconnect networks and can provide a lot of information about network topologies. Hackers may target routers and glean information from them using common management tools. DNS servers also provide information about internal systems and addresses. Another method is to monitor traffic transmitted from your internal network to the Internet and note the IP addresses of internal systems. Once routes, routers, IP addresses, system names, and other information are known, the hacker can begin exploring the territory he has mapped out.

The most successful break-ins are against systems that are improperly configured. The bottom line is that you need to get very well acquainted with your systems and their configurations. If you are installing firewalls, the simpler the configuration, the better in most cases.

When an intruder successfully breaks in, one of her first activities may be to create some avenue for future access into the system since the current intrusion may be detected. The intruder may install packet sniffing software and gain valuable information about network traffic.

Spoofing

Spoofing is a way for someone located at some node on the Internet or an internal network to make itself appear as if it is a trusted node on some other network. This is done by "forging" false addresses in IP packets and sending those packets to the target network.

The most basic definition of an IP packet is a package of bits with a source and destination address. If you put the packet on the Internet, it gets transmitted and forwarded through a series of routers and is delivered to the system that has the IP address found in the packet. In most cases, all the routers along the path will happily forward the packet to the next hop without scrutinizing the source of the packet.

A hacker can use commonly available tools to forge packets and launch an attack against your computers. Assume the hacker has learned the IP address of your internal systems by monitoring traffic that emanates from your network. Basically, a packet is created that has the destination address of a computer on your system and a forged source address of some other computer on your network, as shown in Figure 17-8. Notice that the forged address on the outside network has the source address 200.1.1.2, which is the IP address of an internal "trusted" computer. When the packet arrives at your router, the router thinks the packet is from the internal computer and forwards it to the destination.

Of course, all this assumes that your network is wide open and is not doing any sort of packet inspection, filtering, and other technique to prevent such intrusions. Packet forgery is used for a number of other things besides attempting to break through your defensive systems. By changing the source address, attackers can do any of the following:

17

♦ Hide their identity in order to stage a denial-of-service attack or to gain insight about your network and what you do when you are under attack.

♦ Perform competitive activities. Competitors who want to look at subscription information on your public Web sites may not want you to know who they are. If they sign up with a different name and forge a different source IP address, you won't reject their subscription application (which you would do for competitors).

♦ Make you think you are communicating with some other person when, in fact, the attacker is convincing you to divulge private information by forging someone else's address.

♦ Make an attack appear to be from someone else so you accuse that innocent party of the attack and create all sorts of bad relations.

♦ Bombard your public Web servers or electronic mail system with packets that have many different source addresses, but that in reality are all from a single source. The idea is to make you think you are being attacked from many locations.

♦ Launch a multifaceted attack to cause confusion that might benefit the attacker's campaign to penetrate your defenses. While you are busy defending an attack from one direction, the attacker slips in through a hole you are not watching.

The most basic defense against forged packets is to use routers and firewalls that reject packets coming from the outside networks that have source addresses of an internal network. These techniques are discussed in Chapter 18. Routers and firewalls are programmed with rules that define exactly what type of packets can traverse the internetwork connections. These rules can become quite complex and may be prone to mistakes that can cause security

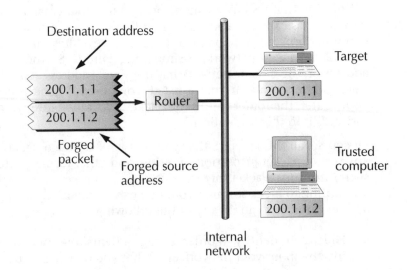

Packet spoofing: a packet from the outside has an inside source address!

Figure 17-8.

breaches. Many high-end firewall products simplify the process and base routing decisions on the requirement that users log on and authenticate themselves.

One way to avoid problems with any type of defensive system is to implement several layers of defense supplied from different vendors. Then, if one layer succumbs to an attack, the next layer will require a different plan of attack that will stall the attacker while you rebuild your defenses.

Router Attacks

Routers contain information about private networks, and hackers can use utilities based on the Simple Network Management Protocol (SNMP) to view information about routers. Normally, a network administrator uses an SNMP-compliant management utility to monitor and configure SNMP-compliant devices like routers. Unfortunately, hackers may have these same tools, and, if they can break through the security of a router, they can examine its routing tables. Routing tables contain valuable information about the location of systems on a network and the path to those systems through a routed network.

Another router-related option that has been exploited by hackers is the Routing Information Protocol (RIP). RIP defines how routers exchange routing tables. Tables are periodically exchanged among routers so that, over time, all routers know the best paths through the network to a particular system. Problems can occur when routers accept routing information that has been spoofed by a hacker, who may add entries that redirect traffic in a way that is beneficial to his attack.

Disrupting routing tables is also a way to create a denial-of-service attack. Another way is to send packets to the router that it normally cannot handle. In some tests, the router simply crashed and stopped providing service.

A command such as TraceRoute (TRACERT in the Windows NT environment) can provide quite a bit of information about the routes to a particular system and all the routers along that path. Internal hackers can use this command to view the layout of the network. The TRACERT command was mentioned under "Internet and Web Connections" in Chapter 6.

Source routing has been used for attacks. Source routing is normally a legitimate technique of routing packets through networks. The packet itself contains information about how the packet should be routed through the network, and this information is determined through a previous route discovery process. When source routing is used, a router that receives a source routing packet will use the routing information in the packet rather than in its routing tables information to determine how a packet should be routed. Source routing was originally implemented to provide a work-around

17

in case a router was unable to supply a suitable route. Obviously, hackers might use this mechanism to circumvent a router-defined route in order to access a particular system or bypass security systems.

A hacker can use commonly available tools to create source-routed packets that are routed to some target system. Reply packets from the target are created that have the inverse route, so the attacker can use this technique for a two-way conversation. On many systems, disabling IP forwarding doesn't block source route packets because they use their own routing mechanism. What you need is a router or firewall that drops any packets that specify source routing.

Internet Application Protocol Problems

The following protocols and utilities have been available on UNIX systems and TCP/IP networks for some time. Their problems are well known and most application-level firewalls can protect against them, as discussed in the next chapter. These utilities are also available in various incarnations on Windows systems. Some are available as freeware on the Internet or from third party vendors. The Windows NT setup program installs many of these utilities if the TCP/IP protocols are installed.

 NOTE: Because these utilities may be present in your own Windows network environment, this section discusses some of the more significant security problems.

Telnet   This is a terminal program. A logon procedure is used to provide access. One problem is that you cannot trust any system that initiates a telnet session since packets may be spoofed. Telnet is often used as a means of attack. When used for legitimate reasons, other problems exist. For example, all information is sent as clear text, including usernames and passwords, so that anyone monitoring or sniffing the session can see it. For security reasons, do not run telnet services on any Windows NT Server.

Finger   This command displays information about users on a system. Hackers have used it to gather information about potential targets or to crack passwords. It provides information about user accounts that become targets of password guessing programs. Untrusted users should not be allowed to run this command.

Berkeley "r" Commands   These commands provide various remote access functionality and include rlogin (remote login), rsh (remote command execution), rcp and rdist (remote file copy). The main problem with these utilities is that passwords and other information are transmitted in the clear. Using these commands could weaken your security, so use them at your own risk. Windows NT Remote Access Service is preferred.

NFS (Network File System)   NFS has been around for many years as a system for accessing files on network-connected computers. It was originally developed by Sun Microsystems and used in the UNIX environment, although versions of it have appeared in almost every operating system environment. The popularity of the Internet has boosted interest in NFS on all platforms, including Windows NT. But NFS comes with a history of security problems. Traditional NFS requires separate authentication for each operation. That is because the system is *stateless*—NFS servers don't store any information about client requests from one operation to the next. Basically, the server disconnects clients after satisfying a request, rather than holding the connection open in anticipation of another request. Actually, HTTP works much the same way, but a stateful design that has better performance and improves the authentication process is available. For more information about NFS, see "Security in Windows NT and UNIX Environments" in Chapter 16.

Electronic Mail Protocols   Simple Mail Transport Protocol (SMTP) is an electronic mail protocol and Sendmail is an e-mail program that uses SMTP. Sendmail has been a notorious security breach. Older versions of e-mail allow all sorts of unscrupulous activity, such as access to the root-level of a system. It is also hard to verify the authenticity and sender of a message. In addition, the e-mail server and gateway may contain the e-mail addresses of everyone in an organization. Also, a mail gateway is susceptible to e-mail attacks in which large numbers of useless messages are sent in an attempt to overwhelm it. Microsoft Exchange provides a relatively safe SMTP implementation.

MIME (Multipurpose Internet Mail Extensions)   MIME provides a way to insert a variety of different media formats into messages. It is a potential problem since messages may contain executables that carry viruses or Trojan Horse programs. Messages that appear legitimate may actually be sent by someone who has altered message header information. MIME messages can also carry Postscript files that may cause problems.

17

TFTP (Trivial File Transfer Protocol)   This is a simple file transfer program that does not require any sort of authentication. On UNIX machines, hackers could use it to directly download the encrypted password file and use a crack program to access the passwords in it. The program is available as a TCP/IP utility in Windows NT, but it is recommended that you not install it for security reasons.

FTP (File Transfer Protocol)   This utility allows file transfers on TCP/IP networks and the Internet. There is an anonymous FTP logon facility that lets anyone access files in a specific directory or subdirectories. The directories should implement Read Only rights, otherwise hackers might copy viruses or Trojan Horse programs into the directory. Since logon is often to an anonymous account, you will not know who is accessing the system. In Windows NT, you can create drop boxes, which might better be called "black hole" directories. Files can go in, but the user cannot see or do anything with files in the directory once they have been put in. Only authorized users can get
at the files.

DNS (Domain Name System)   If you run a DNS server, it will contain information about your site, such as computer names and IP addresses, from which an intruder can glean details about the structure of your organization. A hacker can use this information to spoof packets and attack specific systems. Never place critical information about internal systems on DNS servers connected to the Internet. Instead, create a pair of DNS servers. An external DNS server is set up so Internet users can query it about public servers on your network, but not about any internal systems. The external DNS server must be registered with your domain and configured with the addresses and MX records of your public Web servers and firewall (bastion host). The Internal DNS server is used by internal clients to find systems on the internal network. It should also be configured to forward queries that it cannot resolve to the external DNS server.

World Wide Web Protocols   Web servers running on Windows NT take advantage of NT Security and what has been learned about security over the last few years. However, Web servers typically execute scripts, which are programs that automate various processes. Scripts run in directories that have executable privileges, so a hacker who manages to get a program into the directory could do some damage. The scripts directory must have limited permissions to prevent this.

CAUTION: New and dangerous security problems are cropping up with the new breed of application technologies available on the Web, such as Sun Microsystem's Java and Microsoft's ActiveX.

Another vulnerable target area are the chat rooms at Internet sites. A hacker might use a technique to replicate a message continuously until the server is overwhelmed and must eventually be shut down and cleaned up. Hackers have been known to break into a system by filling up the buffer of a CGI script on a Web server, then inserting commands after the buffer that can take over the system.

You may have noted that many of these utilities are not considered secure because they send passwords in the clear that could be vulnerable to sniffing. However, you might be better off setting up services like FTP and HTTP with anonymous user access. That way, users don't even need to enter a password to access the system and risk the possibility of exposing some password that they use to access more sensitive systems. Obviously, this is useful only on public servers that do not have sensitive information, but at least users don't need to use passwords that might be the same password they used to access more secure systems.

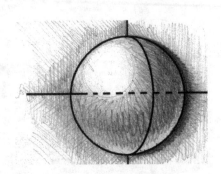

CHAPTER 18

Firewalls and Proxy Servers

A *firewall*, as shown in Figure 18-1, puts up a barrier that controls the flow of traffic between networks. The safest firewall would block all traffic, but that defeats the purpose of making the connection, so you need to strictly control selected traffic in a secure way. The highest level of protection today is provided by application-level proxy servers. In Figure 18-1, proxy services run at the application level of the network protocol stack for each different type of service (FTP, HTTP, etc.).

A *proxy server* is a component of a firewall that controls how internal users access the outside world (the Internet) and how Internet users access the Internal network. In some cases, the proxy blocks all outside connections and only allows internal users to access the Internet. The only packets allowed back through the proxy are those that return responses to requests from inside the firewall. In other cases, both inbound and outbound traffic are allowed under strictly controlled conditions. Note that a virtual "air-gap" exists in the firewall between the inside and outside networks and that the proxies bridge this gap by working as agents for internal or external users.

This chapter covers firewalls and proxy servers in general, and Chapter 19

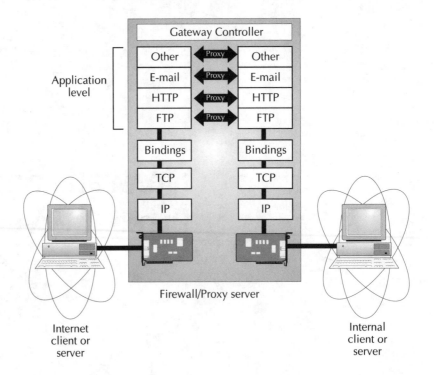

A firewall/
proxy server
Figure 18-1.

covers Microsoft's Proxy Server. If you're interested in building a homegrown firewall with Windows NT, refer to "Windows NT Home-Grown Firewalls" later in this chapter.

Readers who want to explore firewall concepts and architecture in more detail should refer to the following books:

♦ *Firewalls and Internet Security: Repelling the Wily Hacker.* William R. Cheswick and Steven M. Bellovin. Addison-Wesley, Reading, MA. 1994.

♦ *Building Internet Firewalls.* D. Brent Chapman and Elizabeth D. Zwicky. O'Reilly & Associates, Sebastopol, CA. 1995.

The books and their authors are the usual sources of reference in just about any article or book you're likely to read on modern network security. Although the authors are UNIX experts, the books deal primarily with TCP/IP networks and the Internet—the focus for almost any discussion of firewalls.

Defensive Strategies

Discussions about protecting networks usually focus on threats from the Internet, but internal users are also a threat. Indeed, surveys indicate that most unauthorized activities are perpetrated by internal users. In addition, organizations that connect with business partners over private networks create a potential avenue for attack. Users on the business partner's network may take advantage of the inter-company link to steal valuable information.

The current trend is to implement data encryption on all network transmissions. Encryption can take place right at the source of the transmission for the highest security, whether it is the client on the LAN or the router that connects wide area networks.

Firewalls are often described in terms of perimeter defense systems, with a so-called "choke point" through which all internal and external traffic is controlled. The usual metaphor is the medieval castle and its perimeter defense systems, as pictured in Figure 18-2. The moats and walls provide the perimeter defense, while the gatehouses and drawbridges provide "choke points" through which everyone must travel to enter or leave the castle. You can monitor and block access at these choke points.

Dr. William Hancock, a well-known firewall expert with Network-1 Software and Technology in Grand Prairie, TX, describes firewalls this way:

> The concept [of security barriers] is much like that of the strong castle being protected by a series of moats around the castle. As the storming hoards gets close to the castle, they must traverse the series of moats. It is

possible to traverse some moats with pole vault activities, but eventually the leaper of the moat is bound to fall into one of the moats and is caught. If there is only one moat and the leaper is good, there is not much protection. If there are moats, concertina wire, razor wire, tall fences with broken glass on them, land mines, cans full of pennies suspended by trip wires, Doberman pinschers and other such traps in the path from the intruder to the "jewels," one or more of the obstacles is going to alert the keepers of the castle that someone is trying to infiltrate the castle and something must be done to protect the assets and destroy the intruder. Firewall products provide a "moat-like" barrier control method for network assets which varies dramatically with the product selection. The typical use of a firewall product in a network is to isolate corporate assets from each other and from the outside world in a secure and manageable manner.

While the storming hoard analogy might be appropriate in some cases, the real threat is often the stealthy spy who slips over walls in the dark of night and scales every barrier undetected to reach his target of attack.

If a firewall is like a castle, how far do you let people into it, and what do you allow them to do once inside? Local townspeople and traders were usually allowed to enter the market yard of the castle with relative ease so

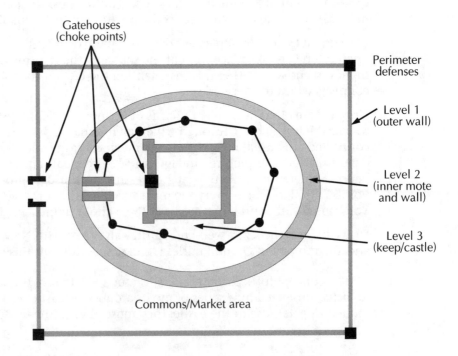

Firewalls provide perimeter defenses with choke points, much like medieval castle designs.
Figure 18-2.

Gatehouses
(choke points)

Perimeter
defenses

Level 1
(outer wall)

Level 2
(inner mote
and wall)

Level 3
(keep/castle)

Commons/Market area

they could deliver or pick up goods. At night, the gates were closed, and goods were brought into the castle—usually after close inspection. Following this analogy, the market yard could be compared to the public Web and FTP servers that you connect to the Internet for general availability.

While just about anybody could enter the market yard, only trusted people and people with special credentials were allowed into the inner perimeters of the castle. Within these walls is the *keep*, a heavily fortified structure that provides the last defense against attackers.

NOTE: Interestingly, the castle proved quite capable of withstanding attacks until the cannon came along. In the 16th century, Essex and Cromwell overran many castles in Ireland with little artillery. They simply blew the parapets off the top of castle walls to make them indefensible, then scaled the walls. What similar weapons will our network defenses face?

In Europe, there were many different types of strongholds. Tower homes were relatively simple defensive structures designed to protect residents from marauding bands of looters and neighboring clans. Still larger castles with massive walls and bastions were built by the wealthiest of clans. Similarly, businesses with the biggest budgets or the most valuable information to protect build the strongest defenses.

Like the multiple perimeter defenses of the castles, multiple firewall devices can be installed to keep wily hackers out of your networks. The spies or assassins vaulted moats and scaled walls to reach their targets. Of course, it helped if the castle guards were sleeping, so don't slack off on your own defense. You can build a "trip wire" defense by putting "relatively weak" devices on the outer edge of your defense that sound alarms when attacked.

In times of peace, the rulers of a castle would meet with local townspeople, tradesmen, and dignitaries from other areas. Any direct meeting with the king or queen was usually preceded by a strip search. But if the political situation was tense, the ruler might prefer to avoid direct contact with visitors. In this case, the protocol was for all visitors to meet with the agent of the king or queen, who would then relay messages between parties. The agent provided proxy services.

Firewalls have been designed around these two approaches. A *packet filtering firewall* uses the strip-search method. Packets are first checked and then either dropped or allowed to enter based on various rules and specified criteria. A *proxy service* acts as an agent for a user who needs to access a system on the other side of the firewall. A third method, called *stateful inspection*, is also coming into use. This method would be analogous to a gatekeeper remembering some defining characteristics of anyone leaving the castle and only allowing people back in with those characteristics.

Once in place, a firewall, just as a castle, requires constant vigilance. If someone can climb your fence at night when no one is looking, what good is the fence? Security policies and procedures must be put into place. In defending a castle, the archers and boiling oil men need a defensive strategy, and they need regular drills to ensure that the strategy works. If your internal systems are hit by flaming arrows, you'll need a disaster recovery plan to quench the flames and get the system back online.

Castle parapets and towers protect the soldiers who defend the castles. Without defenders, the castle is vulnerable to attackers that scale walls or knock down doors. Likewise, your firewall is not a stand-alone device. You need to manage and monitor it on a regular basis and to take action in the event of an attack. It is also only one part of your defense. If the attackers do get inside, you need to keep them from looting your systems by implementing security measures at each domain and server.

This brings up another point. While firewalls are keeping Internet intruders out, your internal users might be looting your systems. You may need to separate departments, workgroups, divisions, or business partners using the same firewall technology, and you may need to implement encryption throughout your organization. Firewalls also do not protect against leaks, such as users connecting to the outside with a desktop modem. In addition, if some new threat comes along, your firewall might not be able to protect against it. Viruses and misuse of security devices are also a threat.

NOTE: This entire discussion avoids the problems of packet sniffing as discussed in Chapter 17 in order to concentrate on firewall features. Session hijacking is a serious problem and you will need to implement encryption to protect against it.

Classifying Firewalls

Any device that controls network traffic for security reasons can be called a firewall, and in fact the term "firewall" is used in a generic way. However, there are three major types of firewalls that use different strategies for protecting network resources. The most basic firewall devices are built on routers and work in the lower layers of the network protocol stack. They provide packet filtering and are often called *screening routers*. High-end *proxy server gateways* operate at the upper levels of the protocol stack (i.e., all the way up to the application layer). They provide proxy services on external networks for internal clients and perform advanced monitoring and traffic control by looking at certain information inside packets. The third type of firewall uses stateful inspection techniques.

Routers are often used in conjunction with gateways to build a multitiered defense system, although many commercial firewall products may provide all the functionality you need.

Figure 18-3 and Figure 18-4 illustrate the differences between screening routers and proxy servers, both of which are described in the next few sections.

Screening Router (Packet Filters)

Screening routers can look at information related to the hard-wired address of a computer, its IP address (Network layer), and even the types of connections (Transport layer) and then provide filtering based on that information. A screening router may be a stand-alone routing device or a computer that contains two network interface cards (dual-homed system). The router connects two networks and performs packet filtering to control traffic between the networks.

Administrators program the device with a set of rules that define how packet filtering is done. Ports can also be blocked; for example, you can block all applications except HTTP (Web) services. However, the rules that you can define for routers may not be sufficient to protect your network resources, especially if the Internet is connected to one side of the router. Those rules may also be difficult to implement and error-prone, which could potentially open up holes in your defenses.

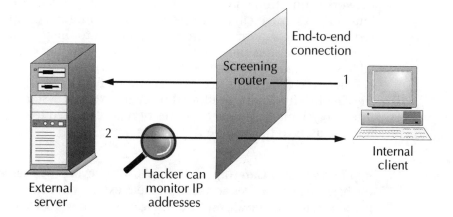

Screening
routers
Figure 18-3.

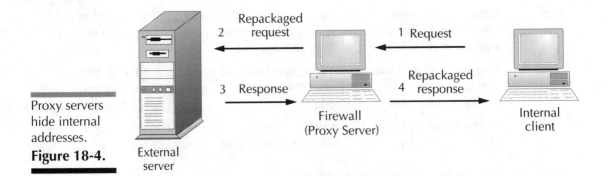

2   Repackaged request

1   Request

3   Response

4   Repackaged response

External server

Firewall (Proxy Server)

Internal client

Proxy servers hide internal addresses.

Figure 18-4.

Proxy Server Gateways

Gateways work at a higher level in the protocol stack to provide more opportunities for monitoring and controlling access between networks. A gateway is like a middle-man, relaying messages from internal clients to external services. The proxy service changes the IP address of the client packets to essentially hide the internal client to the Internet, then it acts as a proxy agent for the client on the Internet.

Using proxies reduces the threat from hackers who monitor network traffic to glean information about computers on internal networks. The proxy hides the addresses of all internal computers. Traditionally, using proxies has reduced performance and transparency of access to other networks. However, current firewall products solve some of these problems.

There are two types of proxy servers:

Circuit-Level Gateway   This type of proxy server provides a controlled network connection between internal and external systems (i.e., there is no "air-gap"). A virtual "circuit" exists between the internal client and the proxy server. Internet requests go through this circuit to the proxy server, and the proxy server delivers those requests to the Internet after changing the IP address. External users only see the IP address of the proxy server. Responses are then received by the proxy server and sent back through the circuit to the client. While traffic is allowed through, external systems never see the internal systems. This type of connection is often used to connect "trusted" internal users to the Internet.

Application-Level Gateway   An application-level proxy server provides all the basic proxy features and also provides extensive packet analysis. When packets from the outside arrive at the gateway, they are examined and evaluated to determine if the security policy allows the packet to enter into the internal network. Not only does the server evaluate IP addresses, it also looks at the data in the packets to stop hackers from hiding information in the packets.

A typical application-level gateway can provide proxy services for applications and protocols like Telnet, FTP (file transfers), HTTP (Web services), and SMTP (e-mail). Note that a separate proxy must be installed for each application-level service (some vendors achieve security by simply not providing proxies for some services, so be careful in your evaluation). With proxies, security policies can be much more powerful and flexible because all of the information in packets can be used by administrators to write the rules that determine how packets are handled by the gateway. It is easy to audit just about everything that happens on the gateway. You can also strip computer names to hide internal systems, and you can evaluate the contents of packets for appropriateness and security.

NOTE: Appropriateness is an interesting option. You might set up a filter that discards any e-mail messages that contain "dirty" words.

Stateful Inspection Techniques

One of the problems with proxies is that they must evaluate a lot of information in a lot of packets. In addition, you need to install a separate proxy for each application you want to support. This affects performance and increases costs. A new class of firewall product is emerging that uses stateful inspection techniques. Instead of examining the contents of each packet, the bit patterns of the packets are compared to packets that are already known to be trusted.

For example, if you access some outside service, the server remembers things about your original request like port number, and source and destination address. This "remembering" is called *saving the state*. When the outside system responds to your request, the firewall server compares the received packets with the saved state to determine if they are allowed in.

While stateful inspection provides speed and transparency, one of its biggest disadvantages is that inside packets make their way to the outside network, thus exposing internal IP addresses to potential hackers. Some firewall vendors are using stateful inspection and proxies together for added security.

The debate over whether proxies or stateful inspection techniques are better rages on. If you are choosing a firewall, talk to vendors and read the product reviews. In the meantime, some router vendors such as Bay Networks and

Ascend are starting to implement firewalls in their router products, closing the gap between inexpensive hardware-based devices and high-end application-level servers.

Firewall Policies

If an intruder can find a hole in your firewall, then the firewall has failed. There are no in-between states. Once a hacker is in, your internal network is at her mercy. If she hijacks an administrative account, you're in big trouble. If she hijacks an account with lesser privileges, all the resources available to that account are at risk.

No firewall can protect against inadequate or mismanaged policies. If a password gets out because a user did not properly protect it, your security is at risk. If an internal user dials out through an unauthorized connection, an attacker could subvert your network through this backdoor. Therefore, you must implement a firewall policy.

Obviously, the firewall and the firewall policy are two distinct things that require their own planning and implementation. A weakness in the policy or the inability to enforce the policy will weaken any protection provided by even the best firewalls. If internal users find your policies too restrictive, they may go around them by connecting to the Internet through a personal modem. The firewall in this case is useless. You may not even know your systems are under attack because the firewall is guarding the wrong entrance.

The most basic firewall policy is as follows:

♦   Block all traffic, then allow specific services on a case-by-case basis.

This policy is restrictive but secure. However, it may be so restrictive that users circumvent it. In addition, the more restrictive your policy, the harder it will be to manage connections that are to be allowed. On screening routers, you'll need to implement complicated sets of rules—a difficult task. Most of the firewall products described later (and the Microsoft Proxy Server described in Chapter 19) simplify this process by using graphical interfaces and a more efficient set of rules (packet filtering is not even employed in most cases).

Security policies must be outlined in advance so administrators and users know what type of activities are allowed on the network. Your policy statement should address internal and external access, remote user access, virus protection and avoidance, encryption requirements, program usage, and a number of other considerations, as outlined here:

♦   Network traffic to and from outside networks such as the Internet must pass through the firewall. The traffic must be filtered to allow only authorized packets to pass.

♦ Never use a firewall for general-purpose file storage or to run programs, except for those required by the firewall. Do not run any services on the firewall except those specifically required to provide firewall services. Consider the firewall expendable in case of an attack.

♦ Do not allow any passwords or internal addresses to cross the firewall.

♦ If you need to provide services to the public, put them on the outside of the firewall and implement internal settings that protect the server from attacks that would deny service.

♦ Accept the fact that you might need to completely restore public systems from backup in the event of an attack. You can implement a replication scheme that automatically copies information to a public server over a secure channel, as discussed at the end of this chapter.

For outbound connections, implement any number of encryption schemes to hide transmitted information. If users are accessing the Web with Web browsers, you can implement the security features discussed in Chapter 20, which discusses Web client-server security protocols.

You also need to evaluate what kind of traffic you want to allow in from the external side of the network. Electronic mail is the usual requirement. Be sure to evaluate Microsoft Exchange Server for this purpose. Not only does it provide a feature-rich platform for information exchange, it also provides a secure platform for electronic mail exchange between the Internet and your internal network.

More About Screening Routers

Routers are used to join individual network segments that have different network addresses as shown here:

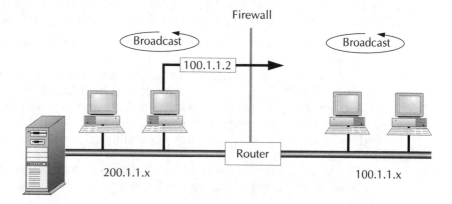

You can purchase stand-alone routers from vendors like Cisco, 3Com, and Bay Networks, or you can build a router in a Windows NT Server computer by installing two network interface cards and enabling the routing option. The latter is a dual-homed system.

Broadcasting is an important concept. Packets that are broadcast on one network do not cross over the router to the other network. Only packets that are specifically addressed to the other network can cross the router. Picture a radio station in Los Angeles. It broadcasts over a certain range—the Los Angeles basin. Someone in San Francisco cannot hear these broadcasts because they are out of range. However, occasionally the San Francisco station might want to broadcast some program that is aired in Los Angeles. To accomplish this, the radio station might set up a telephone link to receive the program and then broadcast it in its area. In this analogy, the telephone link is like a router that joins two networks to allow some, but not all information to propagate between the networks.

A router actually looks inside packets to see what the target IP address is and determines whether it should forward the packet across the link. In the previous illustration, a packet in network 200.1.1.x is addressed to a workstation on network 100.1.1.x, so the router forwards it across the link. In the absence of any security provisions, the router has served its purpose by doing this simple task.

In terms of a network protocol stack, routing information is found at the Network layer. However, routers that use this information provide only the most basic firewall services. They simply stop broadcasts on one network from crossing over to other networks. Any packet addressed to another network is forwarded without question. If I wanted to access a system across the router, I could simply address a packet to it and the router would forward the packet. In fact, most routers on the Internet are designed to forward all traffic. For example, you can PING the White House or use the TRACERT command to view all the routers between your location and the White House. See the TRACERT listing under "Internet and Web Connections" in Chapter 6.

Screening routers have the additional capability of filtering packets based on the source and/or destination IP address of the packet. If a packet is from an undesirable source, the router can be programmed to drop it. The basic filtering rule is "all that is not expressly permitted is denied." That means that all packets are dropped except for packets that the router has been specifically programmed to allow onto the network. The router looks inside each packet and evaluates any of the following, depending on the type of router:

♦ The *source address* of the IP packet can be evaluated to determine whether the person sending it is someone you want to access the network. For example, you could block all IP packets that have your competitors' IP address.

♦ The *destination address* of the IP packet can be evaluated to restrict packets from reaching a particular system. For example, you could block all packets from the Internet that are destined for an internal system that is supposed to be secure and should be accessed only by internal systems.

♦ Specific *service ports* can be evaluated to prevent someone from using an application such as Telnet, FTP, SMTP, or various other Internet services. This process is discussed in the next section.

One reason for blocking IP addresses is to prevent *spoofing* attacks. A spoofed packet originates from an unknown/unauthorized source and contains a fake source address. The fake address makes the packet appear to be from a computer on your own internal network. Your router will send this packet to the destination system without question unless appropriate security options are set. A screening router can be programmed to drop packets that are spoofed. How does it know a packet is spoofed? It's actually simple: if the packet arrives on the external port with an internal source address, it is fake.

Ports and Port Filtering

In addition to the filtering based on IP addresses, screening routers can look at information available at the Transport layer of the protocol stack and make forwarding decisions based on that information. The Transport layer is responsible for delivering packets in a reliable way between systems and for managing multiple sessions over the same network connection. Each session has its own channel. For example, if you use FTP to request a file from a server, the requests are sent over one channel and the file is transmitted back to you over another channel. The endpoint of the channel is called a *port*. FTP normally uses ports 20 and 21. A list of TCP/IP ports can be found in Appendix G.

The basic idea is to block a port if you don't want someone to use it in some inappropriate way. For example, if you don't run FTP services, you can configure your screening router to block ports 20 and 21. Looking at this a different way, if you want to provide only World Wide Web services on a server that is directly connected to the Internet, you can block all other ports except port 80, which is the HTTP port.

In conjunction with port filtering, a screening router also looks at the TCP flags in a packet header. Each packet has a flag that defines its purpose in the "conversation" that is taking place over the channel between the client and server. These are the most important flags:

- ◆ **ACK** If this flag is set, the packet is part of an ongoing conversation. A packet that does not have this flag set is part of a request to establish a connection.

- ◆ **FIN** A packet with this flag set is a request to close the connection.

- ◆ **RST** A packet with this flag set causes the channel to be reset because of some error.

- ◆ **SYN** A packet with this flag set indicates a request to open a connection.

Flags are used in conjunction with port filtering to provide a more extensive rule base. For example, you can set a rule that says something like, "let our internal users initiate a session with an outside host and accept only replies from the outside host." This rule prevents outside hosts from initiating their own sessions. The ACK and SYN flags are the keys to doing this. Keep in mind that the first packet to initiate a conversation will *not* have the ACK flag set but will have the SYN flag set. Subsequent packets related to that conversation have the ACK flag set, as shown here:

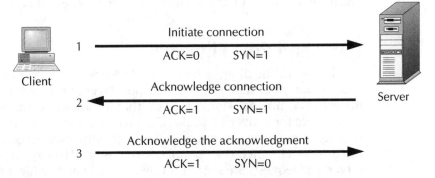

Using this procedure, we can let internal users initiate connections and reject any attempts by outside users to initiate connections. Looking at step 1, ACK is 0. If the IP address of the client is an internal address, the packet is allowed, but if the IP address is an outside client, it is discarded because we don't want outside systems to initiate their own connections.

Now assume that in step 1 the client makes a request through our firewall to an external server. In this case, step 2 is a response from an external system. However, we accept this packet because it is a response to an internal request. We can tell this because the ACK flag is 1, indicating that the packet is an ongoing conversation and that an internal host must have started the conversation.

There are many other ways to implement filtering, and I recommend that you refer to the texts referenced at the beginning of this chapter for more details. Another place to find useful information about security routers is to connect with the Web pages of major router vendors, such as Cisco (**www.cisco.com**), 3Com (**www.3com.com**), and Bay Networks (**www.baynetworks.com**).

How Secure Are Screening Routers?

While screening routers have their place, they are not likely to provide the protection you need when connecting internal networks to the Internet. First, they directly expose your internal network to the Internet as a route that can possibly be traversed by a wily hacker. Someone can monitor the packet stream that emerges from your organization and glean valuable information, such as internal IP addresses of systems to attack! The more advanced proxy servers discussed later hide your internal network addresses from the Internet.

Screening routers may be an easy target for experienced hackers. A single port left open may provide all that the hacker needs to breach your security. Screening routers are usually configured by using a difficult and error-prone process. For example, you must first define a set of rules based on your security policy that specifies exactly which packets are allowed. You then translate this set of rules into the syntax required to program the router, often writing several hundred lines of scripting code. Put simply, there are a lot of chances to make dangerous mistakes. In contrast, many firewalls let you set similar rules with just a few commands.

However, despite their shortcomings, screening routers may be useful in some network configurations where you are connecting internal networks to other internal networks, assuming there is some level of trust involved. It all depends on your security requirements and the level of protection you can get from the router.

On internal networks, it is easier to identify users since they are probably using a known computer whose address or name appears in system logs. In addition, the user must log on and access systems through an account. Even if the internal hacker is not using her own account or computer, you may still be able to track her down through investigative techniques. However, this still doesn't account for any damage she might do in the meantime. You need to evaluate your own security requirements. If they are high, you will need to set aside a budget for advanced firewalls.

Some other disadvantages or problems with screening routers are as follows:

◆ Most commercial routers do not run higher-level applications that can detect suspicious activities.

◆ Some routers do not generate alerts that can warn you of attacks on your system.

♦ Some devices do not even know how to detect and log an actual break-in.

If you plan to implement a routing solution with Windows NT Server 4.0, keep in mind that it does not have built-in filtering capabilities like those you will find on some third-party products. You can block ports, but you cannot create advanced rule sets like the ones described earlier. However, you can install the Microsoft Proxy Server to obtain advanced proxy firewall services, as discussed in Chapter 19.

High-End Firewalls

A router-based Internet connection allows point-to-point connections between clients on internal networks and Internet servers. Because such connections are generally considered unsafe, network administrators have been turning to gateways in cases where traffic is passing through the gateway from both internal and external sources.

You can use port filters on routers to block traffic from applications that external hackers might use to subvert your internal systems, but this policy is not discretionary. Some users may need to use those applications for legitimate reasons. When you try to make exceptions, the rules can become so complex that mistakes are bound to occur.

Application-level gateways provide proxies that control access through the firewall in a unique way. They fully understand the protocols of the applications that are allowed to interoperate through the gateway and fully manage both inbound and outbound traffic at a level that is not possible with screening routers.

According to Cheswick and Bellovin (in their book cited earlier):

> An application-level gateway represents the opposite extreme in firewall design. Rather than using a general-purpose mechanism to allow many different kinds of traffic to flow, special-purpose code can be used for each desired application. Although this seems wasteful, it is likely to be far more secure than any of the alternatives. One need not worry about interactions among different sets of filter rules, nor about holes in thousands of hosts offering nominally secure services to the outside. Only a chosen few programs need to be scrutinized.

The FTP service provides a good example of how an application-level proxy server can provide advanced filtering. The application-level server can allow users from the outside to access an FTP server, but it will look in each packet and block any packets with the PUT command for specific users. This prevents just anyone from writing files to the server.

Another important feature of application-level servers is authentication. You can allow only specific users through the firewall on the basis of their credentials. Doing this is useful for trusted mobile users or people from affiliated organizations who need to access specific systems on your networks.

Also keep in mind that firewalls can hide your internal network addresses from the Internet for security reasons and so that you can implement any IP addressing scheme you need without having to register with Internet authorities. This feature is increasingly important as registered IP addresses become scarce.

Proxy services can provide additional functions of interest to network administrators:

♦ Tracking all the sites that users access on the Internet, and keeping records, can help reduce Internet activities. Mailing these records to users on a periodic basis will let them know they are being monitored.

♦ Screening of specific hosts and URLs can be used to restrict the sites that internal users access.

♦ Caching often-accessed Web pages can reduce requests and responses to the Internet (discussed under "Proxy Server Caching").

Firewall Implementations

The Cheswick/Bellovin and Chapman/Zwicky books mentioned at the beginning of this chapter provide the material that most firewall vendors use when describing their firewall implementations. This section outlines the basic architectures that are described in Chapter 4 of Chapman and Zwicky's *Building Internet Firewalls*.

Note that these texts refer to the firewall as the *bastion hosts*. According to Chapman and Zwicky, a bastion host is

>...a computer system that must be highly secured because it is vulnerable to attack, usually because it is exposed to the Internet and is a main point of contact for users of internal networks. It gets its name from the highly fortified projections on the outer walls of medieval castles.

Of course, a firewall installation must consist of several devices, including the packet filtering routers discussed previously. Often these routers are used for "perimeter defense," providing the first wall that attackers must scale in order to reach the bastion host. They may also be used for other lines of defense inside the network, as you'll see.

Dual-Homed System

The dual-homed system is a computer that includes at least two network interface cards, as pictured here. Windows NT supports this configuration, and you can enable or disable routing between the cards, depending on your requirements. Routing is disabled between the network interface cards in the dual-homed system so that the application-level software can control how traffic is handled between networks.

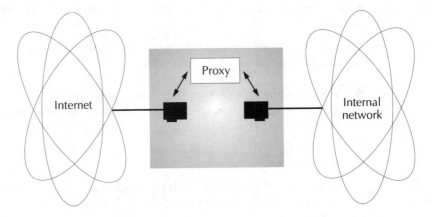

There is one other use for this type of configuration. Assume that the dual-homed host runs an HTTP (Web) service. If routing is disabled, then the host on either network can still access the Web services but packets cannot travel past the server. For example, if several departments in an organization need to share the same Web server but you don't want to create a routable link between the departments, you could use this configuration.

Screening Host Architecture

In this scenario, pictured in Figure 18-5, the screening router only allows Internet users to connect with a specific system on the internal network—the application-level gateway (bastion host). The gateway then provides inbound and outbound control as described earlier under the discussion about such devices.

The packet filtering router does a lot of work in this configuration. Not only does it direct packets to a designated internal system, it may also allow internal systems to open connections to Internet systems or disallow these connections. You set these options based on your security requirements. Chapman and Zwicky note that this architecture may be risky because it allows packets to move from the Internet to the internal network, unlike the dual-homed architecture, which blocks all packet movement from the external network to the internal network.

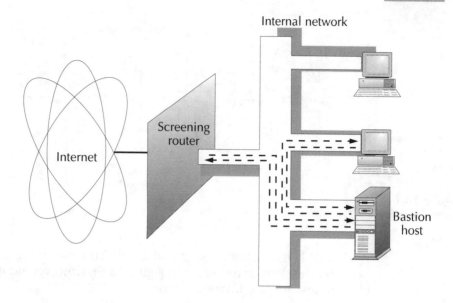

Screened Subnet Architecture

This architecture, pictured in Figure 18-6, is similar to the screening host architecture described in the previous section, except that an extra layer of security is added by putting up a perimeter network that further separates the internal network from the Internet.

A reason for doing this is to protect the internal network if the bastion host succumbs to an attack. Since the bastion host is basically connected to the Internet, hackers will target it. According to Chapman and Zwicky,

> By isolating the bastion host on a perimeter network, you can reduce the impact of a break-in on the bastion host. It is no longer an instantaneous jackpot: it gives an intruder some access, but not all.

Variations

Chapman and Zwicky offer some variations on the designs described in the previous section, along with some warnings. For example, they mention that using multiple bastion hosts attached to the perimeter network is OK. You might run different services in each of these hosts, such as HTTP (Web) services, e-mail services, or an external DNS service. Of course, each system must be hardened against attacks.

Another option is to combine the interior and exterior routers (see Figure 18-6) if you use a router that has more than two ports, although this configuration

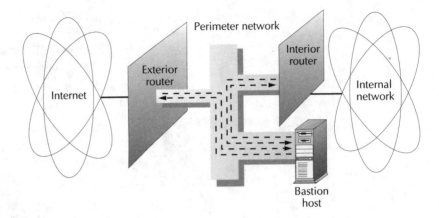

is vulnerable if the single router is attacked. You can also merge the bastion host and the exterior router (as in Figure 18-6). However, do not merge the bastion host and the interior router.

If multiple interior routers are used, a situation could occur in which the internal router decides that the fastest way to another internal system is via the perimeter network, thus exposing internal network packets on the perimeter network.

For more information about these configurations and others, refer to the previously mentioned books. In a later section, I look at the way various firewall vendors have implemented some of the architectures.

Proxy Server Caching

A proxy server usually manages a disk cache that holds frequently accessed Web pages that other people in your company are likely to access. If someone requests a page, the proxy server intercepts the request and returns the appropriate page in the cache. This procedure reduces traffic on your Internet connection. Bottlenecks are reduced and people who need to get real work done on the Internet are not held up.

A perfect example of the need for a proxy server is "Dilbert." Yes, the cartoon. People in your company may access the Dilbert site every morning to get the latest cartoon. With a proxy server, the comic of the day is cached by the first person to access the site (or by an automatic process at night) and all other people access the comic in the local cache. Many companies will find that half of their Internet traffic can be handled by a proxy cache.

A similar process takes place when users need to download the latest version of Netscape Navigator or Microsoft Internet Explorer. It gets cached at the proxy server and internal users get the latest version from the cache, rather than directly from the Netscape or Microsoft site.

Socks

Socks is an IETF (Internet Engineering Task Force) standard that defines how to develop proxy mechanisms that control traffic between networks. Socks essentially defines how to implement firewalls. A Socks server is installed between the internal and external networks (the Internet). It allows internal users to access the external network but blocks all attempts by external users to access the Internal network. In this way, it provides one-way firewall services.

One of the key elements of Socks is the ability to "fool" the internal client and the external server into believing that they are talking directly to one another. In fact, the client talks to the socks server and the socks server talks to the target server on the external network.

The Microsoft Proxy Server implements Socks, as discussed in Chapter 19. In addition, the NEC PrivateNet system implements Socks. In fact, NEC maintains the original implementation of Socks developed by Dave Koblas and has developed its own advanced versions.

The three important operations performed by Socks are:

♦ Providing a way for clients to request an outside connection from a proxy server. This request contains the address of the target server and other pertinent information.

♦ Setting up a circuit between the client and the proxy server. Once the circuit is in place, the client thinks that he is directly accessing the Internet.

♦ Relaying data between the outside and inside network.

In order for a client application to use Socks, it was once necessary to build the support directly into the application. Companies such as Aventail and Hummingbird have developed programs that make any application Socks-aware.

A new version of Socks (version 5) that was finalized in 1996 includes interesting features such as authentication, the ability to go through multiple firewalls, improved security policies, and more flexible filtering methods.

Commercial Firewalls

As mentioned, firewalls that provide circuit-level proxy services, application-level proxy services, and stateful inspection techniques are available. You can refer to Chapter 19 for more information about the Microsoft Proxy Server.

If you need to allow some access to internal systems, then you'll need to look beyond screening routers to application-level gateways and other high-end firewall products like those discussed in this section, although routers might still be included in our defensive system. There are a number of important features to look for in such products:

Address Translation/Privacy Prevents internal network addresses from appearing on the Internet. The firewall itself appears to be the originator of all traffic as it makes the Internet available to internal users.

Alarms/Alerts Warns administrators when an attacker is attempting to breach the system. Threshold settings must be available and properly tuned to warn of attacks without triggering unnecessary alarms. Notification of attacks should be done with real-time messages, pagers, electronic mail, and other means.

Logs and Reports Provides valuable information that helps you evaluate and detect potential security problems.

Transparency Allows internal users who need to access the Internet without facing hurdles or delays that make access difficult.

Virus Checking Checks for viruses and looks for Trojan Horse executable programs (available in some commercial firewall products). However, this feature can affect performance and is not yet widely available.

For more information about what to look for in firewalls, consult the many reviews and lab reports presented in industry journals and magazines. You should also obtain a document called "CSI's 1996 Firewall Product Matrix" from the Computer Security Institute (**www.gocsi.com**) at (415) 905-2626.

Some firewalls are beginning to appear that provide interesting and advanced features. For example, the Sidewinder from Secure Computing (**www.sctc.com**) will spoof potential intruders into thinking that they have broken into a secure area. It basically detects the attack and takes it over, leading the attacker along using a "hall-of-mirrors" approach. If the attacker believes that he has entered a part of the system that may provide further access, his activities can be tracked and he can possibly be traced.

If you can keep a hacker involved online for some time, you might be able to track the hacker down. For example, you could use the FINGER command to trace him or set up a large "decoy" file that requires a long time to transmit, then track the file transfer backwards over Internet connections to the hacker's site.

The following sections present several firewall examples. I mention these not because they are particularly better than other products on the market, but because they represent different categories of firewalls. The Milkyway product is a UNIX-based application server while the Raptor system is a Windows NT-based application server. The Network-1 product implements stateful inspection techniques.

Milkyway Networks' Black Hole

Milkyway Networks calls its Black Hole firewall a second-generation application-level firewall that is designed to address the problems of transparency and performance usually inherent in application-level firewalls. It is both an application- and circuit-level gateway. Users don't need to make a request to proxies—the proxies intercept the traffic, verify authorization, and retransmit the data to the final destination. In this respect, the firewall is transparent, and performance is close to real-world Ethernet speeds, so the firewall is suitable for intranets. It runs on Sun-OS and UNIX (BSDI) operating systems and is designed around the "that which is not explicitly permitted is prohibited" philosophy.

The Black Hole can connect with other Black Holes at branch offices via an encrypted tunnel through the Internet. The resulting virtual private network (VPN) provides a secure channel for transmitting data between sites in a way that provides integrity, confidentiality, authentication, and non-repudiation. Milkyway has adopted Nortel's Entrust technology to offer central X.500 directory public and private key management and certification.

The important features of the Black Hole are:

User-Level Authentication   All traffic flowing through the Black Hole, including e-mail, Web services, Gopher services, and others, must receive authentication based on a user ID, password, source/destination network addresses, type of applications, and time of access.

Bi-directionality   Traffic can flow in both directions through the firewall. However, all traffic must be authenticated as specified by the network administrator.

18

Logging, Auditing, and Alarms   The Black Hole will track all critical events and log information about those events, including source/destination network addresses, the application involved, user ID, time of the event, and bytes of transmitted information.

No other services should be run on the firewall to improve security. The more complex the firewall, the more likely that an attacker could exploit some hole to subvert the system.

The Black Hole supports future applications with either generic proxies or through custom proxies. Multiple Black Holes can be installed in a parallel configuration for performance benefits or to provide multiple walls of security. However, if an organization plans to use firewalls in a multitiered configuration, it may be wise to get those firewalls from different vendors. Then, if a hacker manages to break one, she will not be able to use the same procedure to break the other.

Common Black Hole configurations are pictured in Figure 18-7 and Figure 18-8. Milkyway likes to refer to the connection between the Internet and the internal network as an "event horizon," because the internal network is unknown to Internet users. Notice that an organization's network is divided into an *outside network* and an *inside network* in all cases.

The basic setup is pictured in Figure 18-7. The Black Hole separates the outside network from the inside network. Only public servers are attached

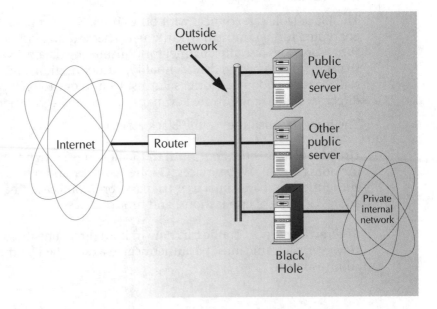

Basic
configuration
for Milkyway
Black Hole
firewall

Figure 18-7.

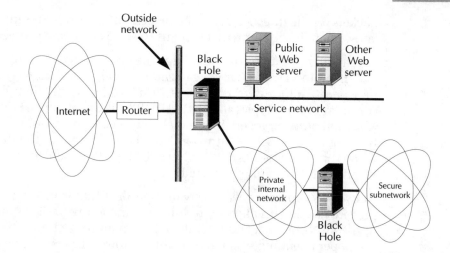

A more complex Milkyway Black Hole firewall
Figure 18-8.

to the outside network, and they must be protected using whatever means available, such as removing unnecessary services and bindings on network cards or using port filters (for example, activating only port 80 on an HTTP Web server).

Some administrators are uncomfortable with putting public servers on an Internet-connected network without any sort of firewall protection. In Figure 18-8, the public servers are attached to a third "service" network, and access to these servers by external users is controlled by the Black Hole. This configuration requires three network interface cards in the Black Hole: one for the Internet connection, one for the service network, and one for the private network. Notice that Internet users can directly access the service network, but authentication is required. Notice also that an additional internal subnetwork is separated from the main network by another Black Hole firewall to provide additional security for that subnetwork.

Because the Black Hole hides the private network from the Internet, it is not necessary to register the addresses of internal machines. You can use any IP addressing scheme you like. Since internal host addresses are unknown to the Internet, all outside users must go through the Black Hole proxy service to get a session with an internal host.

Network-1's FireWall/Plus

Network-1 Software and Technology (**www.network-1.com**) took a unique approach with its stateful inspection firewall product called FireWall/Plus. It assumed that most threats to data security are on the internal network. While an Internet-connected firewall is necessary to guard against unknown hackers on the Internet, often the biggest threat is from internal users who know enough about internal systems to stage an effective attack.

On internal networks, the threat goes beyond the usual problems with the TCP/IP protocol suite. Many organizations run multiple protocols on internal networks to allow users to connect with a variety of different systems. It is common to find AppleTalk, NetBEUI, IPX, IP, StreetTalk, DECnet, SNA, OSI, XNS, and other protocols on internal networks. If you concentrate on building firewalls against TCP/IP intrusion, you'll do nothing to stop the internal user who is on the same IPX/SPX or NetBEUI LAN to which your NetWare or Windows NT server is connected.

Network-1's approach was to create a product that works at all levels of the protocol stack. This allows it to intercept incoming traffic at the lowest levels of the protocol stack and filter it so that unauthorized packets never reach the upper operating system layers. At the lowest layers, it is possible to easily filter just about any network protocol. Of course, the product also works at the application layer to provide normal firewall and proxy server support.

Network-1 notes that FireWall/Plus is capable of supporting filter rules at any level in the network protocol stack, including the frame, routing, transport, and on up to the application layer. The stateful nature of the product allows it to work with current protocols or future protocols. FireWall/Plus was designed from the start to be used on every node of an organization's network. That lets you control incoming and outgoing transactions on an end-to-end basis, not just at the Internet-connected firewall, and it lets you control any protocol, not just IP.

Raptor Systems Eagle NT

Raptor Systems was the first commercial firewall vendor to provide a firewall product for the Windows NT platform. Its Internet firewall is called Eagle NT, but the company also has two secondary products called EagleLAN NT and EagleRemote NT. EagleLAN NT secures transactions between different internal LANs or intranets. The configuration of this product with the Eagle NT is shown in Figure 18-9. EagleRemote NT is basically the same firewall as Eagle NT without the management interface. It allows organizations with remote sites to manage firewalls at those sites from a central location.

The Eagle NT provides most of the functions of the application-level firewalls discussed earlier. It hides IP addresses from external users. The Eagle NT installs with reverse DNS lookups enabled, so that it attempts to resolve the IP address of each packet it receives before proxying it to its destination. The Eagle does this by looking up the host name that should be associated with a given IP address. There is a slight performance degradation in doing this, but

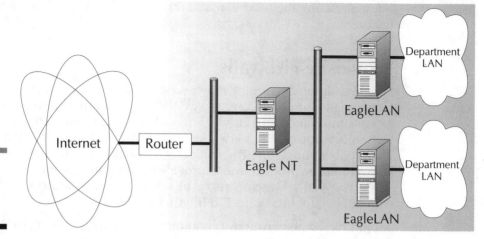

The Eagle NT
and EagleLAN
firewalls
Figure 18-9.

there is an assurance that the packets sent by authorized IP address actually originated at the known (and authorized) hosts associated with them.

The product uses strong user authentication that works with Digital Pathways and Bellcore's S/Key authentication method. S/Key is a one-time password authentication system. Alarms warn of suspicious activities based on threshold levels set by administrators. Notification can be made through pagers, e-mail, audio, video, or SNMP (Simple Network Management Protocol) alerts.

The Eagle NT uses a dual-level DNS configuration to resolve the names of external hosts without exposing the structure of your internal network in the process. Clients that connect from the outside are only aware of the outside IP address of the Eagle NT firewall. This requires two DNS servers. One DNS server runs on the Eagle NT firewall and only knows about and keeps information about external hosts. Another DNS server, running inside the firewall maintains information on internal systems. Note that the Eagle NT comes with its own DNS software for the internal DNS server.

EagleLAN NT is basically an internal firewall that can provide a wall of security between departments, workgroups, or divisions of your organization. It allows only authorized users to access protected resources and acts as an outbound gateway to ensure that only authorized connections are made to destinations beyond the workgroup.

EagleRemote NT is for organizations that want to allow their remote NT sites to access the Internet while still maintaining the same security requirements as the main office. This product is designed for use at remote sites that have an inexperienced or limited staff. It uses the authorization tables of the Eagle

NT, eliminating the need to maintain an authorization database at each remote site.

Would-Be Firewalls

Several traditional screening router vendors have begun to implement firewall technologies into their routers. Bay Networks (**www.baynetworks.com**) recently announced that it was imbedding CheckPoint Software's FireWall-1 technology into all Bay Networks routers. FireWall-1 uses the stateful inspection architecture. The company is also implementing encryption across its entire product line to provide secure transmissions across the WAN. FireWall-1, which is also available to run on Windows NT Server computers, supports up to 120 Internet services.

Ascend (**www.ascend.com**) is another company that is "firewalling" its router products. The Secure Access Firewall is an inexpensive upgrade (approximately $500) for Ascend's Pipeline and MAX series. The dynamic firewall technology opens specific ports for authorized users only when required and closes those ports at the end of the session. All unused ports are automatically kept closed to block intruders. Applications can also be controlled. Security is provided at various levels including network addresses, hostnames, protocols (UDP, TCP, ICMP), source/destination ports, either send or receive, time by day and by hours, and application level (TFTP, FTP, WWW, SMTP, POP Mail, SATAN probe, Source Routing, Anti-Spoofing, Telnet, NNTP, Talk/chat, archie, finger, whois, UNIX utilities, RealAudio, Time Services, Ping, and more).

Ascend Secure Access Firewall extends the standard security features of the routers with Calling Line ID (CLID), RADIUS authentication, Local authentication, UNIX password authentication, PAP/CHAP, Token-card authentication, Data/Call/Generic filtering, and the Ascend Password Protocol.

Windows NT Home-Grown Firewalls

It is entirely possible to connect a Windows NT computer to the Internet as a gateway for your internal clients, or to provide Web, FTP, and other services to Internet users. However, you must carefully evaluate your goals and the security implications. Here are some of things you might be trying to accomplish:

◆ Provide FTP, Web, and other services to the Internet

◆ Provide FTP and Web services to both the Internet and to internal users on the same server

◆ Provide a gateway for internal users to the Internet

♦ Provide Internet users with access to internal network services

The last option is a little risky unless you take steps to protect internal systems. In most cases, the internal network is a not your full corporate network, but what some industry people call the "dirty net." That means that untrusted packets flow on it. However, done right, a Windows NT connection to the Internet may work quite well for you.

Consider that there are two types of networking services available on a Windows NT computer system:

♦ Microsoft's SMB (Sever Message Block) native network and file services. These services are usually installed by default.

♦ TCP/IP and Internet services such as Web servers and FTP servers. You install these as optional services.

One consideration when connecting any Windows system to the Internet is the potential security risk of the SMB protocols. This section describes how to disable those services where appropriate. If SMB shared folders are available on a network that you connect with the Internet, potentially anyone on the Internet can access folders or hijack sessions. In addition, there are security problems with the protocols themselves.

However, completely disabling SMB may not be practical. Assume you set up the Web server to publish information about your company on the Internet. For security reasons, you set it up as a stand-alone system that is not connected to any internal network. Now suppose the marketing people in your company need to frequently update information on that Web server. If the Web server is isolated and locked up in some closet, they are going to have a tough time making those updates. If the content is complex, transferring it to the Web server via floppy disk, tape, or other media will be difficult and they will probably rely on you, the system administrator, to handle those updates. Here are two possible solutions to this problem and others are presented later:

♦ Use a temporary internal network connection that is disconnected after updates are in place.

♦ Connect the internal side of the Web server to a non-TCP/IP network that runs either NetBEUI or IPX/SPX. TCP/IP users cannot access networks running other protocols, at least without great difficulty.

If your internal network runs only TCP/IP, installing another protocol may be difficult or go against your security policies. For example, you might have internal firewalls and security configurations that can protect against internal TCP/IP attacks, but not against attacks using other protocols. However, using multiple protocols is a reasonable solution when implemented properly.

Now for another consideration. Suppose you want to allow internal network users to access the Internet over your Windows NT Internet connection. This will open a doorway to the Internet for internal network users, but Internet users can find their way into your network as well. This may or may not be a problem, depending on what you are trying to accomplish. The internal network might have additional servers you want to make available to the public. On the other hand, if you want to give internal users access to the Internet and block access by Internet users, install Microsoft's Proxy Server as discussed in Chapter 19.

Let's look at a configuration that allows Internet users to access an internal network. This is actually a common scenario. For example, Figure 18-10 illustrates a network for the Marketing department of some company. All the systems on the network are set up to provide some type of Internet service. Employees can surf the Internet by using the kiosk system and Internet users can access the public Web server and other public servers on the internal network. A firewall protects the corporate network.

There are two possible ways to connect this network to the Internet. One is to use a dial-up RAS (Remote Access Server) connection in which Windows NT provides the routing of packets between the networks. Another method is to install a stand-alone screening router and just attach your internal servers to the LAN that is connected to the inside port on the router. A commercial router will provide advanced security options, such as the ability

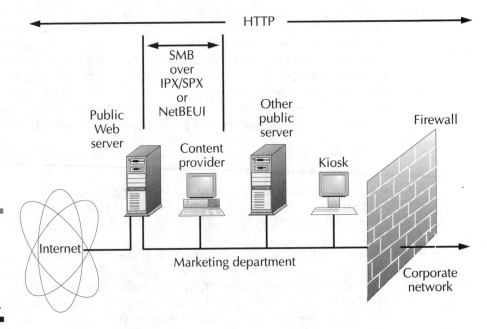

One example of an Internet-connected Web server and LAN
Figure 18-10.

to block specific protocols from the Internet. For example, you could allow only HTTP traffic. A commercial router will also provide better performance then a Windows NT router. However, I discuss the RAS method here for readers who might want to try this connection using existing equipment.

Figure 18-11 shows the protocol configuration for this server. Refer to "WAN Support in RAS" in Chapter 15 for more information about routing with RAS. Note the following:

◆ IP forwarding is enabled between the dial-up adapter and the LAN adapter to allow the free flow of IP packets in either direction.

◆ The server runs both Web services and SMB services. However, SMB services can only be accessed in this configuration through the NetBEUI or IPX/SPX protocol stack by internal clients. This allows content providers to update the server (i.e., write files to it using SMB Server services).

◆ All SMB bindings are disabled on the TCP/IP protocol stacks to prevent potential security breaches. To disable bindings, you open Network on the Control Panel and click the Bindings tab. Next, expand the TCP/IP options under the NetBIOS, Server, and Workstation headings, then select the adapter to disable and click the Disable button. The dialog box should then look similar to the following. Note that both the dial-up adapter and network adapter are disabled for TCP/IP, but NetBEUI bindings are left intact.

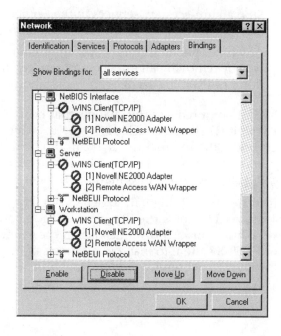

♦ Only port 80 (HTTP) is enabled on both the internal and external TCP/IP stacks to prevent attacks. You configure ports in the Network utility by opening the Properties box for TCP/IP protocols. Click the Advanced button, mark Enable Security, then click Configure to display the following dialog box. On a multihomed system, choose an adapter in the Adapter field. In each column, click Permit Only, then click Add to add the value 80 to the list. You can add other ports as necessary. See Appendix G for a listing of ports. Configure all the servers on the internal network in this same way.

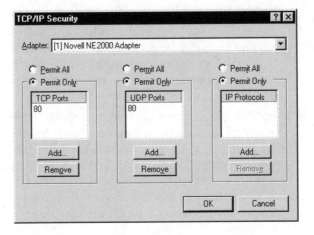

♦ Stop all unnecessary services in the Services utility. See "Managing Services" in Chapter 10 for information on configuring services.

♦ Any other public servers on the internal network are secured in the same way by removing all unnecessary services and protocol bindings. Also, don't run sharing services on workstations.

This last point reduces the chances that hackers might find some technique to exploit HTTP and attack those systems which are exposed on the internal network to the Internet through this protocol. You should consider these systems "expendable" (i.e., keep backup and be prepared to restore systems). Do not store sensitive information on them.

There are other configuration details not covered here. For example, internal clients need to know the IP address of the gateway so packets targeted for external systems are forwarded across the gateway. In addition, you may need a DNS system to map out addresses of internal systems (or you can rely on your Internet service provider for this).

NOTE: This same configuration could be used to connect two internal networks. You would create a dual-homed system with two network interface cards, then configure one adapter as if it were the Internet connection described previously.

Variations

The previous configuration assumes you want to connect an internal LAN to the Internet and allow a free flow of packets across the link. There are a number of variations on this theme. One is to install a third network interface card for the non-TCP/IP protocol. That way, TCP/IP and NetBEUI (or IPX/SPX) are not transported over the same network.

The most obvious variation is to take the configuration in Figure 18-11 and simply turn off IP forwarding so that no routing takes place between the internal and external networks. This prevents internal users from accessing the Internet and prevents Internet users from accessing internal systems.

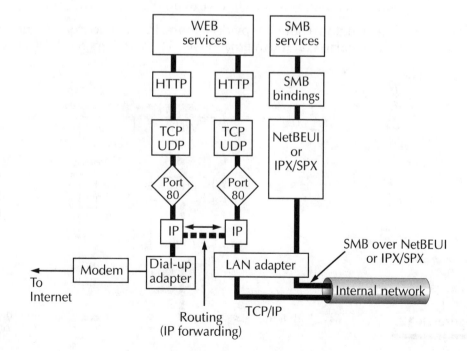

Protocol configuration for an Internet-connected Web server
Figure 18-11.

18

However, both groups of users can still access Web services on the server and content providers can still update files using SMB services. If internal users need to access the Internet, you can set up another server and run Microsoft Proxy Server as described in Chapter 19.

This configuration is safe as long as routing is not turned on. If routing is enabled by accident, the internal network is exposed. Also, it's possible that a hacker might devise some way to "jump over the air gap" that separates the inner and outer networks using some hole in higher-level services.

Figure 18-12 illustrates the *protocol isolation model.* You use it to set up a Web server for Internet access. There is no internal TCP/IP connection to the server, however, content providers can connect to the server using NetBEUI or IPX/SPX and update files using SMB. This connection method is safe as long as no one devises some way to translate TCP/IP packets on your server into IPX/SPX packets (for example) and target some system on your internal network.

Finally, we get to the *replication model,* which Microsoft has used for its own Internet-connected servers. This model is pictured in Figure 18-13 and is a variation of the protocol isolation model. There is an internal and external server. Internal users access Web services running on the internal system and Internet users access Web services on the external system.

In addition, content providers on the internal network put new information and updates on the internal server. The Windows NT Replication Service

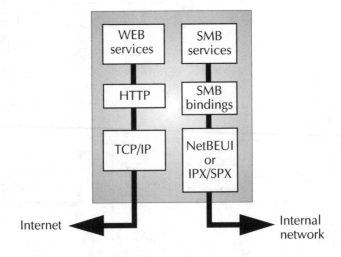

Protocol
isolation
model

Figure 18-12.

Internet

Internal
network

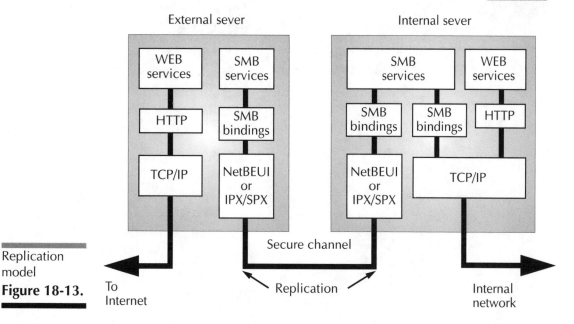

External sever | Internal sever

Replication
model
Figure 18-13.

Secure channel

To
Internet

Replication

Internal
network

then copies all the information placed on this server to the external server
where Internet users can access it. If Internet users fill out forms or use other
methods that write data to the external server, that information is replicated
back to the internal server using the same process where content providers
can pick it up for processing.

NOTE: Server replication sets up a secure channel between servers that is
difficult to hack. In addition, the protocols for the replication channel are
not TCP/IP, but NetBEUI or IPX/SPX, so protocol isolation is enforced. Also
note that the internal TCP/IP stack has SMB bindings so network users can
access SMB services on the internal server using the same TCP/IP protocols
they use to access Web services.

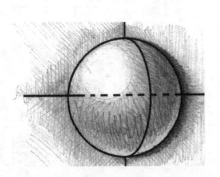

CHAPTER 19

Microsoft Proxy Server

Microsoft's Proxy Server provides a way to control how individual users access the Internet using protocols such as FTP, Gopher, and Web services. As discussed in the previous chapter, the Microsoft Proxy Server provides inside users with access to outside resources and blocks attempts by outsiders to access the internal network. In most cases, the outside network is the Internet, but an outside network could also be another "untrusted" internal network. All further references to the Microsoft Proxy Server are made as "Proxy Server."

NOTE: The information in this chapter is based on pre-release software and is presented here as an overview for anyone who does not yet have the software. At the time of this writing, Microsoft had not implemented some security features, such as "Server Protection." If you are installing the product, refer to your Proxy Server documentation for more details.

When an organization connects to the Internet, it often faces the dilemma of how to provide security for internal networks while providing information to the public. One method is to put up public Web servers as stand-alone devices, as illustrated here. Internet users who access these servers cannot access internal resources, because there is no internal connection. But what if internal users need to access the Web server as well? One method is to let them access the Internet through a proxy server and backtrack to the Web site as shown. I present this example just to show how the Proxy Server might be used.

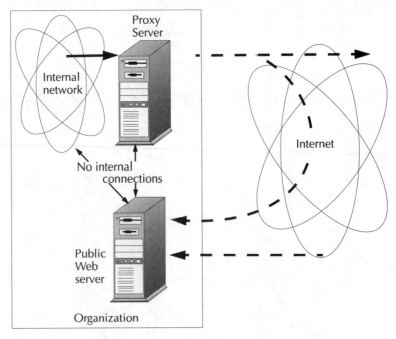

When internal network (intranet) clients attempt to connect with an Internet site, Proxy Server intercepts the request, repackages it, and forwards the request to the target server. When the server on the Internet responds, Proxy Server receives the response, makes sure that it is indeed an authentic response, and forwards the response to the internal client. This is the normal procedure that any proxy server uses to hide internal network addresses from hackers who want to learn the addresses of internal systems and attempt to spoof packets in order to access the network illegally. No unrequested packets from the Internet are allowed to pass into the internal network.

Proxy Server supports most Internet protocols, including Web (HTTP), FTP, RealAudio (streaming audio), VDOLive (streaming video), IRC (real-time chat), and mail and news protocols. Most importantly, Novell's IPX/SPX transport can be used on the internal network so organizations don't need to switch to TCP/IP. IPX/SPX traffic can be routed to both Internet server and internal intranet servers. Proxy Server can also provide a secure channel over the Internet to branch offices so organizations don't need to set up expensive dedicated leased lines.

Proxy Server provides a turnkey solution for connecting non-TCP/IP networks to the Internet. Some of its features are outlined below.

♦ **Proxy service and protocol converter** provides a way to connect non-TCP/IP networks (that is, IPX networks) to other networks. Proxy Server and Remote Windows Sockets Service deliver Internet applications to your desktops via standard protocols. When a user makes an Internet request using a Web, Gopher, or FTP service, Proxy Server establishes a TCP/IP connection to the site on behalf of the service. It then accepts only responses back from the Internet that are from the site where the requests were made. Packets that do not originate from an internal user request are discarded.

♦ **Encryption** allows users to transmit secure information over the Internet, using protocols that provide encryption—such as Secure Sockets Layer (SSL) and Private Communication Technology (PCT) protocols.

♦ **Firewall capability** includes options for setting up secure firewalls to block and filter network traffic. Administrators can grant or deny outbound access by user, service, port, or IP domain. Access to specific sites can be blocked.

Proxy Server acts as a secure gateway between the internal network and the Internet. Domain-name filtering provides a way to control which Internet resources internal network users can access. A list is created of the domains that users can access or of the domains that users cannot access. Once implemented, the policies affect all users connecting to Internet resources through Proxy Server. User-level permissions allow network administrators to control which users have access to Internet applications by setting user- and group-level permissions for the World Wide Web, Gopher, and FTP. The user-level control is fully integrated with the Windows NT domains and username accounts.

Web content is filtered and replicated by the proxy server, which also caches frequently accessed Web pages and documents. The most popular Web pages are automatically updated. Caching helps conserve network bandwidth by providing the accessed Web pages directly from the cache itself for all internal users who need them. Caching can cut nearly in half the time it takes for a user's information request to be filled. Network administrators can control the cached data—including allocating how much disk space should be used for caching and storing cached information—as well as setting Time out and Refresh intervals. Caching is particularly useful for small businesses that have slower links to the Internet and whose clients access the same Internet resources.

Proxy Server works on a Windows NT multihomed system, which is a computer with two network interface cards installed. One is attached to the local network, and the other is attached to the Internet.

♦   The network card attached to the local network uses Remote Procedure Calls (RPCs) to transmit Internet requests and responses over the network.

♦   The local network can run TCP/IP, IPX/SPX, NetBEUI, and other transport protocols.

♦   The Internet-connected network card must run the TCP/IP protocol.

♦   Proxy Server acts as a policy manager and protocol translator between the internal and external network.

When an internal network client needs to make a request to an Internet server, Proxy Server gets into gear. As shown in Figure 19-1, client browsers redirect their Windows Socket requests to Proxy Server using in-house protocols. Proxy Server then transmits those requests on the Internet using Windows Sockets over TCP/IP. This mechanism offers advanced security features, such as per-user rights policy control and Windows NT security integration. The client can be running Windows NT Workstation, Windows 95, Windows for Workgroups, or Windows version 3.1.

More About Proxy Services

A proxy server allows one computer to communicate with another computer by acting on behalf of that computer. This arrangement provides security for internal systems, and the proxy server itself becomes a centrally managed system where security policies can be implemented.

The Microsoft Proxy Server is basically a security gateway. It connects two different networks and monitors and manages the traffic between those networks in a way that is designed to protect internal resources from unauthorized use.

The system that runs the proxy services must include two network interface cards as shown in Figure 19-2. TCP/IP must be used on the Internet-connected network. The internal network can run TCP/IP, IPX, or NetBEUI protocols. You must disable routing between the two network cards to prevent traffic from one network from reaching the other network. You also need to disable services and selected ports on the Internet connection. Proxy Server then manages all traffic flow between the networks.

NOTE: The Microsoft Proxy Server is fully compatible with the CERN proxy protocol, which has become the industry standard for providing proxy services. The server will accept proxy requests from any browser that is compatible with the CERN proxy protocols. Compatible browsers include the Microsoft Internet Explorer and Netscape Navigator. The advantage of this arrangement is that the proxy server does not need any special components to support Web clients. All client-side proxy support must be built into Web browsers.

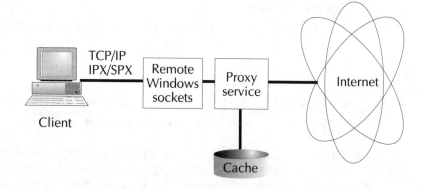

Proxy Server
architecture
Figure 19-1.

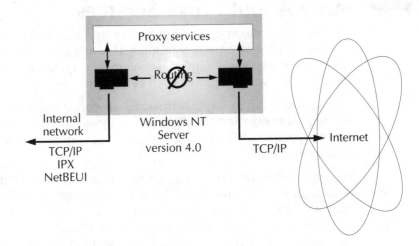

All communication between the client and the server is done with the HTTP protocol. HTTP provides the request and response command protocol that clients and servers use to ask for information, fulfill requests, accept responses, and provide acknowledgments.

When a proxy server stands between a client and a target server, as shown in Figure 19-3, the HTTP request and response protocol is altered slightly.

1. The Web client makes a request to a specific Web server on the Internet as normal.

2. Proxy Server checks the standing between the client and the target. The Web server receives the request and checks to see if the client is authorized to make this type of access.

3. Proxy Server checks to see if the user can make the request to the specified domain.

4. Proxy Server checks its cache to see if the requested document is in the cache. If so, it returns it to the client.

5. If the document is not in the cache, Proxy Server requests it from the target Web server.

6. The target Web server returns the document to Proxy Server.

7. Proxy Server returns the document to the client.

Microsoft's Proxy Server is an application-level proxy service that has knowledge of the protocols used by applications. Because of this, it can provide high-level services such as authentication, filtering, caching, and protocol conversion.

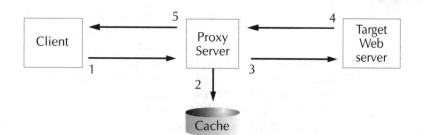

Fulfilling
proxy requests
Figure 19-3.

Proxy Server Setup and Configuration

This section is not intended to provide every detail you need to set up and
run the Proxy Server. Rather, it is designed to provide you with an overview
of how to configure the services to fit your needs so that you can begin
planning the installation.

Setting up Proxy Server requires that you install a computer system that
can run the Windows NT Server version 4.0 operating system. Microsoft
recommends that for performance reasons you install the server as a member
server in a domain, not as a primary or backup domain controller, although
the latter options will work. You will need to install two network interface
cards in the server.

NOTE: If you just want to use the caching features of the Proxy Server,
you can get by with installing just one network interface card. This option is
appropriate on trusted internal networks.

Make sure that the TCP/IP protocols are installed by accessing the Network
utility from the Control Panel. You bind TCP/IP to the network interface
card that is connected to the Internet. Do not bind other protocols, such as
IPX/SPX and NetBEUI to this network card. However, you can bind either
TCP/IP or IPX/SPX to the internal network adapter.

Once the protocols are installed, you must disable routing between the two
network interface cards. Doing this is critical if both internal and external
networks are running TCP/IP. It prevents unwanted traffic on the external
network from crossing over into your internal network. You disable routing
by opening the TCP/IP Routing page, which you can access from the
Network dialog box on the Control Panel.

Disabling the Routing option is critical. If some malicious users were to
enable it, the door to your internal network will be wide open. There is one
key in the Registry called

`HKEY_LOCAL_MACHINE/System/Control_Set001/Services/Tcpip/Parameters/IPEnableRouter`

This key controls whether the router is enabled or disabled. If an intruder manages to gain access to this setting, he can enable routing and open the floodgates. By default, only Administrators and System have the ability to change this option. Enter the Registry to view the settings and confirm that no other users or groups can change it (Appendix F provides information on working in the Registry and setting security options for keys). Another security precaution is to disable the right in the User Manager that allows any administrative user to log on to the server from the network. Doing this will prevent intruders from attacking the administrative accounts.

Here are some other precautions:

♦ Use only NTFS volumes.

♦ Disable as many unnecessary services as possible in the Services utility of the Control Panel.

♦ Since the system is connected to the Internet, you'll want to make sure that the Guest account is disabled and that the Everyone group does not have more than Read permissions in any directory, unless specifically required. If this system is providing proxy services for only authorized users, you may be able to revoke all permissions for the Everyone group in all directories.

♦ To allow only designated users to access Proxy Server, remove the Everyone group from the "Access this computer from network" right in the User Manager, then create a new global group called something like "Internet users," add users to the group, and grant it the "Access this computer from network" right.

♦ Check the membership of the Administrators group and remove unnecessary users. You may need to set the Proxy Server up in its own domain to implement the exact policies you need in this respect, then set up a trusting relationship with another domain that has the accounts of users that can access this server.

♦ Make sure that auditing is enabled, as outlined in Chapter 10.

♦ Unbind SMB services (Server, Workstation, and NetBIOS) from the network interface card connected to the Internet.

This last option prevents potentially dangerous hacker activities associated with these protocols. An example dialog box is pictured in Figure 19-4. Notice that bindings for the Server service are visible and that WINS Client (TCP/IP) is bound to two network interface adapters. Click the adapter that is connected to the Internet and click the Disable button. Since it is

Disabling
bindings
on Internet-
connected
adapters
Figure 19-4.

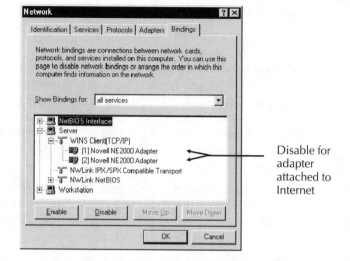

Disable for
adapter
attached to
Internet

not recommended that the Proxy Server be used for any type of file services,
you may want to unbind these services on the internal network card as well.
Internal or external users will still be able to access HTTP (Web) services on
the Proxy Server if you choose to set it up that way.

You also need to disable ports on the Internet-connected interface. Open
Networks on the Control Panel, then choose the TCP/IP protocols on the
Protocols page. Click the Advanced button, then mark Enable Security and
click the Configure button. In the Adapter field, choose the adapter that is
connected to the Internet, then in each of the columns, click the Permit
Only option. Now click the Add button in each column and add the port
number for the service you want to allow. This will be port 80 (the HTTP
service), but you can add other ports as well. Refer to Appendix G for port
numbers. After setting ports, you'll need to restart the server.

Running Setup

Once the preceding options are taken care of, you log on as an
administrative user, then run the Setup program that comes with the Proxy
Server software. You then choose the folder where you want to install Proxy
Server and answer questions about which components to install, the type of
clients you want to support, and the location of the cache drives.

You're also asked to define the IP addresses of your *internal* networks that
can access Proxy Server. Proxy Server uses these to determine which clients
can access the external network and to determine if a client is attempting
unauthorized access. The IP addresses are entered as pairs that represent a
range of IP addresses. You don't need to enter each client's IP address

individually. These address pairs are stored in the Local Address Table (LAT), which is a text file called IASLAT.TXT in the C:\IAS\CLIENT directory.

The LAT gets downloaded to clients who set up to use the service. A remote Windows Sockets client who needs to access an IP address can look in this table to determine whether the address being requested is on the internal or external network. If it is on the external network, then the request is sent to Proxy Server for handling. Note that if a client attempts to access the Internet through the Proxy Server and that client is not one of the registered addresses, access will be denied because Proxy Server will consider the client a security threat.

You should not enter any external (Internet) IP addresses in the LAT. Proxy Server would identify these addresses as internal computers, opening the possibility of a security breach. External clients working at the designated computers could access the internal network.

After configuring the IP addresses, you set up client options for the Proxy Server. A Client Access dialog box appears, in which you specify how the client Setup programs will configure clients to connect to the Proxy Server. You can also set an access control option that specifies either that all internal clients will be able to use the Remote Windows Socket service or that only those clients who have been assigned permissions for specific protocols in the Internet Service Manager will be able to use the Remote Windows Socket service.

Once you set these options, the proxy server installation completes and you can set all further configuration options by using the Internet Service Manager, as described next.

Configuring the Proxy Server

You use the Internet Service Manager to configure the Proxy Server. Choose Programs on the Start menu, then Proxy Server, and finally Internet Service Manager. The dialog box in Figure 19-5 appears. Notice in this case that the FTP, Gopher, and Web services supplied with Windows NT 4.0 have already been installed on the server and are listed in the dialog box.

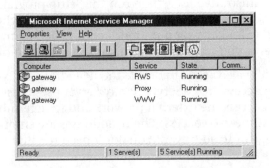

The Internet
Service
Manager
Figure 19-5.

19

Each service is listed under the computer heading. To manage a service, simply double-click it in the dialog box. A properties sheet then appears to help you configure the service.

If you double-click the Proxy service, you can set the following options:

♦ **Service** Enter comments in the field provided for such. "Current Session" button lets you view a list of users who have sent recent requests to the proxy server.

♦ **Permissions** Grant or deny access to the services. See "Proxy Server Permissions" next.

♦ **Caching** Specify the settings for the Proxy Server cache. See "Proxy Server Caching" next.

♦ **Logging** Set options for logging Internet transactions to text files or to ODBC/SQL-compliant databases.

♦ **Filters** Grant or deny access to Internet sites on the basis of IP addresses.

Client Authentication

Proxy Server operates like the Internet Information Server when it comes to client authentication and user access. In fact, you configure authentication by double-clicking the WWW service, as pictured in Figure 19-5. A dialog box similar to the following appears; here you can set the logon authentication options discussed in this section.

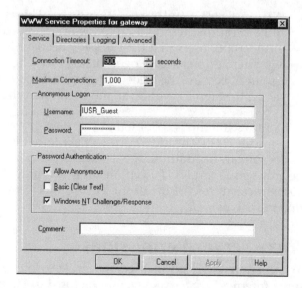

Proxy Server uses the Windows NT user account logon and authentication, along with access controls that allow users to access resources if their accounts have appropriate permissions. Users can be authenticated by the server and allowed to access indirectly (through the proxy service) resources on internal servers. Anonymous user access is also allowed in cases where general public access will be allowed. An anonymous user does not need to provide a username and password to access information.

All access to resources in the Windows NT environment is performed by a particular service that impersonates the user. Even anonymous users access resources by logging in to an account, although all anonymous users log in to a single account that normally does not require a password. You use anonymous logons for public access to services, but keep in mind that, because they do not supply their usernames, individual users who log on as anonymous users can't be tracked.

If you require users to log on in order to access a service, the server will request credentials from clients before giving them access to the service. There are two ways that this is done:

♦ **Basic Authentication** This authentication method displays a Logon dialog box and requires the user to enter a username and password when accessing a restricted resource. If a user has not been authenticated by an Internal Windows NT server, her request to the Proxy Server will not have appropriate credentials, and a Logon dialog box will pop up on the user's workstation.

♦ **Windows NT Challenge/Response** This is the same logon authentication method used to log on to any Windows NT Server. With this method, users that have already been authenticated by a Windows NT system do not see a Logon dialog box when connecting with other resources, because the credentials they entered at logon are automatically passed through to the server and used for authentication.

Both of these methods require that the Web browser support the "proxy-authenticate" HTTP header. Microsoft's Internet Explorer 3.0 supports this header format. In addition, the Challenge-Response method requires that the browser support HTTP Keep-Alives, which provides a way to keep the user "authenticated" for the life of the TCP connection. Internet Explorer 3.0 supports this as well.

Proxy Server Permissions

To set permissions for the Proxy Server, you double-click the Proxy service in the Internet Service Manager, as pictured in Figure 19-5, then click the Permissions tab to display the following dialog box. In this dialog box, you choose a service (WWW, FTP, Gopher, and so on) in the Right field, then click the Add button to select the users or groups that can access the designated service on the Internet. When you click the Add button, a standard user account dialog box appears in which you can choose users and groups in the current domain or some other domain that will be allowed to use the service.

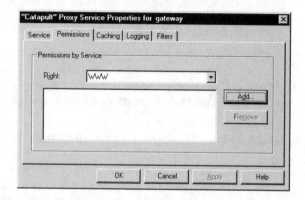

Proxy Server Caching

If you click the Caching tab, the following dialog box appears:

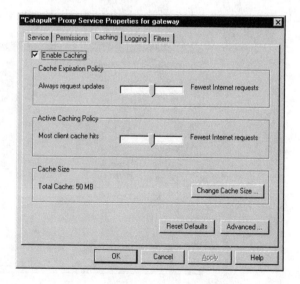

This is where you configure the proxy cache. Make sure the Enable Caching button is checked, then set the caching options as follows. The disk cache stores a copy of each object accessed by clients on your network. If another person needs the same object, it is retrieved from the cache, assuming it is not outdated. Your system may need a large cache, depending on access patterns and usage.

♦ **Cache Expiration Policy** This option sets the "freshness" of objects in the cache, which is a measure of how long a local copy of an object in the cache is used before a new copy is retrieved from the Internet. Move the slider to set this option as appropriate. You will need to experiment to find a setting that is appropriate for your site.

♦ **Active Caching Policy** This setting determines how often the cache manager updates objects in the cache on its own. If the slider is closer to **Most client cache hits**, then the cache is frequently updated. If it is closer to **Fewest Internet requests**, then the cache manager makes fewer updates.

♦ **Cache Size** This option determines the size of the cache.

The Advanced button displays the Advanced Cache Options dialog box, which is where you can specify which objects will be cached by protocol (WWW, FTP, or Gopher), specify the maximum object size to be kept in the cache, set server protection options, and set filtering options.

Proxy Server Filtering

Click the Filters tab and the following dialog box appears:

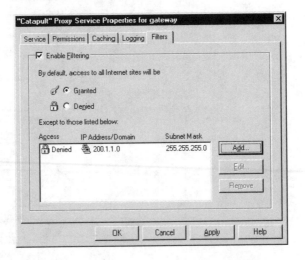

Here you can enable filtering and set the type of filtering you want to use. You can either grant access to all Internet sites or deny access to all Internet sites and then fill the exceptions box. For example, you click Granted to grant access to all Internet sites, then fill out the exceptions list with the names or IP addresses of the sites you don't want users to visit. In the exception list, you specify the IP address of a single site, a range of IP addresses (such as those owned by some organization), or domain names.

To create exceptions, click the Add button. The following dialog box appears. You click either Single Computer, Group of Computers, or Domain, then fill out the IP Address field or Domain field. Note that the domain name can be a specific computer name or a domain name that indicates multiple computers.

19

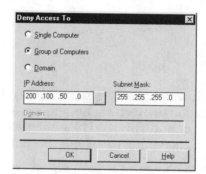

Remote Windows Sockets (RWS) Service

Windows Sockets is an application programming interface (API) that programmers use to build applications that communicate with one another over networks. Specifically, Sockets is an interprocess communication (IPC) mechanism that clients and servers use to create connections for the exchange of data. All of the parameters for initiating a connection, sending and receiving data, and closing a connection are defined within Windows Sockets. Many applications have been built with this service.

Remote Windows Sockets extends this interface by allowing Windows Sockets-compatible applications running on an internal network to use a gateway computer (e.g., Proxy Server) and make requests to the Internet. Basically, the applications think they are connected to the Internet, when in fact they are communicating with the gateway.

One of the most interesting aspects of this relationship is that the client can use the IPX/SPX protocol to communicate to the gateway, or the connection can be standard TCP/IP. With IPX/SPX support, organizations do not need to convert the protocol of their internal network. Only applications that are written to use Windows Sockets over TCP/IP can be remoted in this way. As shown in Figure 19-6, clients running IPX/SPX can connect with an internal Web server that is running Proxy Server or with a Proxy Server that is connected to the Internet.

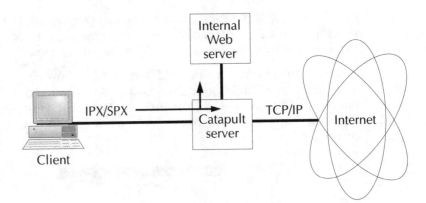

Remote
Windows
Sockets
services
Figure 19-6.

Remote Windows Sockets also supports Windows NT Challenge/Response authentication between clients and servers, whether the client application supports it or not. This level of authentication provides a high level of security by encrypting passwords for transport across the network.

Proxy Server contains the RWS service, which receives requests from clients and passes them to the proxy service. The RWS service allows the caching features of the proxy service to be used for HTTP, FTP, and Gopher resources.

To set up RWS software components on the client computer, run the SETUP command located in the IASCLNT directory, as mentioned earlier. The Internet browser used on the client's computer is configured to use the Proxy Server.

Recall that the Local Address Table (LAT) defines the IP addresses that are part of the private internal network. You create it when you set up Proxy Server, and it is stored as a file called IASLAT.TXT in the C:\IAS\CLIENT directory. When a client computer is set up for RWS, this table is downloaded to the client and the client uses the LAT to determine whether IP addresses are on the inside network or on the Internet. If the addresses are on the Internet, all requests go to Proxy Server.

RWS Configuration

If you look at Figure 19-5, you will notice that the RWS service is listed in the Internet Service Manager. You double-click the service to configure its properties. A dialog box similar to this one appears:

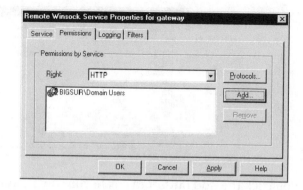

There are four options:

♦ **Service** Add a comment or remark about the server.

♦ **Permissions** Set permissions to use services, as described next.

♦ **Logging** Set logging options and the location of where log information will be stored.

♦ **Filters** Set filtering options to restrict access to Internet sites for all RWS clients that access the server. This is basically the same as the filtering options discussed earlier under "Proxy Server Filtering."

If you click the Permissions tab, you can configure the available protocols and their assigned port numbers. You can also allow selected users and groups to access the Internet using those protocols. You can set the inbound and outbound connection privileges for users and domains by protocol and by port number.

The first thing you do in this dialog box is select a service such as HTTP in the Right field, then click the Add button to specify the users and groups that can use the service. A standard list of user accounts appears for the domain, and you can choose any users or groups. You can also select users and groups from other trusted domains. Follow this same procedure for other allowed services. If you need to edit or configure a service, click the Protocols button. A dialog box similar to the following appears; here you can pick a service and click the Edit button to change its parameters.

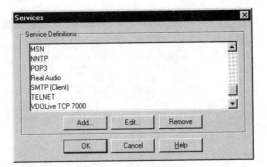

You click the Add button to create your own service. The options you can change include names, port numbers, packet type (TCP or UDP), direction (inbound or outbound), and other features.

Configuring Clients

One of the last things to do is set up and configure clients to use the Proxy Server to request and receive objects from the Internet. In Windows 95, for example, you open the Internet utility on the Control Panel and click the Connection tab. You then enable "Connect through a proxy server" and click the Settings button to open a dialog box similar to the following:

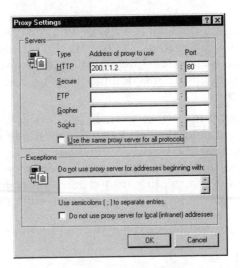

In the Servers field, enter the address of the proxy to use along with a port number. In the Exceptions field, enter the name of computers, domains, and ports through which client applications can request objects without going through the Proxy service (that is, computers that provide services on the inside network).

19

To configure Remote Windows Sockets clients, go to the client computer and then connect to the shared directory on the server called IASCLNT. Run Setup in this directory. The setup program will automatically configure the client computer to use the RWS service. If the client's Web browser is the Microsoft Internet Explorer or Netscape Navigator for Windows NT or Windows 95, the client Setup also attempts to configure the browser to use the Proxy service. You can make the client setup program configure the client to use only the RWS service, preventing it from configuring browsers to use the Proxy service.

The Proxy Server documentation provides more information on configuring clients. In particular, you'll find information on configuring Macintosh clients, UNIX clients, RealAudio (streaming audio) clients, and VDOLive (streaming video) clients.

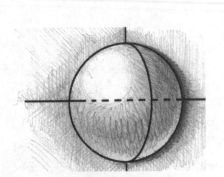

CHAPTER 20

Securing the Microsoft Internet Information Server

The World Wide Web is built on top of the Internet and uses the TCP/IP protocols to transport information between Web clients and Web servers. Web servers are not just for the Internet. Web servers also provide a new and unique way to make information available to internal network (*intranet*) users. Windows NT includes the Microsoft Internet Information Server, so your startup costs for implementing Web-based intranet or Internet servers are minimal.

Web browsers provide a unique tool for accessing information on any network, whether it is an internal intranet or the Internet. They remove the mystery of the Internet and eliminate the need for users to understand arcane commands. Most people begin accessing resources the first time they use a browser. Little training is necessary, and most browsers are free. Because of this, it is worth your while to consider building your own internal networks using Web technologies.

This chapter discusses security issues for the Microsoft Internet Information Server. If you plan to set up a Web server for internal or external access, this chapter will help you maintain security for the server.

NOTE: This chapter touches on security issues for Microsoft Web clients and servers only. It does not discuss other vendors' Web products, nor does it explore the incredibly vast issue of security on the Web. For more information on Web security issues in general, check **www.ncsa.com** and **www.gocsi.com**.

Web Protocols and Standards

The underlying protocol for Web servers is Hypertext Transfer Protocol (HTTP). HTTP supports hyperlinks in documents. When a client running a Web browser types a server name (or IP address) in the Address field of a browser, the browser locates the address on the network (either an internal intranet or the Internet, depending on the connection), and a connection is made to the designated Web server.

Web pages contain hyperlinks, which reference other information. When you click a hyperlink, you jump to another part of the same page, a new page at the same Web site, or to another Web site. You might also execute a program, display a picture, or download a file.

All of this hyperlinking is the work of the Hypertext Markup Language (HTML), which works in concert with HTTP. HTTP is the command and control protocol that sets up communication between a client and a server and passes commands between the two systems. HTML, on the other hand, is the document formatting language.

As shown in Figure 20-1, the client makes a request to the Web server, and the Web server sends HTML information back to the client. The client's Web browser properly formats and displays the HTML information from the server.

The HTTP protocol sets up the connection between the client and the server, and in many cases that connection must be secure. For example, assume your company sets up an Internet Web server to provide sensitive

20

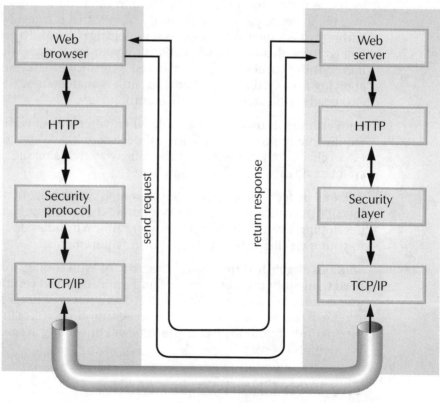

Web
client-server
architecture
Figure 20-1.

Intranet or Internet

documents to its mobile work force. These documents should not be accessible to anyone else (since the site is connected to the Internet, anyone could attempt to access them). To prevent unauthorized access, you set up private directories and require logon authentication. You can also do the following:

♦ Secure the TCP/IP channel between the client and the server by encrypting all the data that is transmitted.

♦ Use certificates (digital IDs) to prove the authenticity of the Web client.

♦ Use Windows NT logon authentication to verify a user's access to her account and use access controls (NTFS permissions) to restrict access to folders on the server.

Channel encryption and certificates are optional features that are handled by the security protocol layer as pictured in Figure 20-1. To prove authenticity over the Internet, you need a *personal certificate* that is issued by a certification authority (CA), such as Verisign (**www.verisign.com**). To get this certificate, you go through a process of establishing your credentials with the CA, and, if everything checks out, you are issued a certificate. This process is similar to applying for a credit card, where the bank is analogous to the CA. Servers also need certificates to prove their authenticity.

The certificate is used automatically when you connect with Web sites that require you to prove your identity. If necessary, the Web site can contact the CA to check your credentials in the same way that a retailer checks your credit card when you make a purchase.

These same techniques can be implemented on internal networks by installing certificate services on Windows NT Server computers. Microsoft is developing a certificate server that you can use in-house to issue certificates to your own clients based on your own requirements.

So we've established the need for security of Web connections and the need to identify users by means of authentication and certificates. Once a user is authenticated and allowed to access a server, what techniques can you use to control access? As you'll see, controlling access in the Microsoft Internet Information Server is the same as controlling access on any Windows NT server.

The Web Client-Server Model

Keep in mind that Web services provide a new and unique way to provide information to people on your internal network as well as on the Internet. With the secure channel and authentication features of Microsoft's Internet

Explorer (and other browsers), you can establish secure connections between clients and servers on your network with little trouble.

Many organizations are making the transition to the Web client-server model because of its unique way of providing information to users. You can quickly set up a Web site and allow users on existing TCP/IP networks to access that site with the browsers they probably already have. You can then set up servers to provide much of the information that users have accessed with special applications. For example, Microsoft SQL Server data can be accessed by filling out query forms in HTML format. In other words, users access the database server with their Web browser. The basic technique is as follows:

20

1. A user connects with a Web server.
2. The Web server sends a database query form to the user's Web browser.
3. The user fills out the form and submits it back to the Web server.
4. The Web server takes the information off the form, repackages it, and submits it to a back-end database server.
5. The database server runs a query with the provided information and returns the results to the Web server.
6. The Web server builds a new Web page on the spot and inserts the query results on the page, then sends the page back to the client.

The point of all this is that Web services are becoming a bigger part of both intranet and the Internet. The graphic nature of Web pages makes them attractive, and the hypertext capabilities make them a much more interesting and useful way to disseminate information. Tools are available to make Web pages much more exciting and dynamic. For internal users, all of this translates into an interface that is easy to use and learn and that is consistent across many platforms. When you access systems with a Web browser, you rarely know or care about the type of server you are accessing. In this sense, Web browsers have become universal clients.

There is a trend to use this technology everywhere. In fact, the next releases of Windows 95 and Windows NT will use Web browser technology as the standard interface. Users will access information on their own computer or anywhere on internal networks or the Internet in the same way.

More About HTTP

This section takes a quick look at the HTTP protocol and how the security components fit in. HTTP controls the connection of a Web browser to a Web server and the exchange of information between the two systems. It is a fast and efficient communication protocol that controls many different operations that take place between client and server. HTTP uses the Transmission Control Protocol (TCP) to transport all of its control and data messages from one computer to another.

The link process starts when you type the address of a Web site in your Web browser (or click a button). First, the IP address for this Web site is needed, so a lookup is performed at a DNS (Domain Name System) server that knows about the name and its associated address. The corresponding address is returned to your Web browser, which then makes a direct connection to the Web server.

Web servers may provide any of the following to Web clients:

♦ The version of HTTP in use

♦ Status information about the request, such as whether the information was found

♦ The MIME (Multipurpose Internet Mail Extensions) type, which defines the media format (text, sound, pictures, video, and so on)

♦ An HTML-coded document is sent

To connect with a Web site, you type the URL (Universal Resource Locator) for the site into the Address field of a Web browser. Here is an example of the URL that retrieves a document called INFO.HTM from a Web site called **www.bigsur.com**.

www.bigsur.com/public/info.htm

When you type this request, the Web browser first gets the IP address of **www.bigsur.com** from a DNS server, then it connects with the target server. The server responds to the client and the tail end of the URL (PUBLIC/INFO.HTM) is processed. In this case, the INFO.HTM file in the PUBLIC directory has been requested, so the Web server transfers the HTML-coded document to your Web browser. Your Web browser then displays the HTML information.

♦ Alternatively, a Web server might have a directory for private documents. Only authorized users are granted permissions in the directory. When you attempt to connect with the directory, a Logon dialog box appears, where you must enter a username and password. If your credentials are authentic and your account is allowed to access the directory, one of two things may occur. Either a default Web page for the directory appears, or, if the directory does not have a default page, a list of files in the directory appears.

NOTE: If you are accessing a Web server on an internal network, you can type the NetBIOS name of the server you want to connect with in the Address field of the Web browser. If NetBIOS naming is not used, just type the IP address of the Web server.

Web Server Directory Structures

A typical Web server uses directories to store information and operates like any file server, except that the HTTP protocol is used to make requests for files. In most cases, those files are HTML documents, but, as you'll see, Web users can use HTTP to request just about any type of information on a Web server.

20

The Microsoft Internet Information Server sets up a directory that branches from your *systemroot*\System32 directory called INETSRV. Branching from this are several directories that contain the server files, some sample HTML files, and the WWWROOT directory. When users connect to your Web server, they are automatically placed in the WWWROOT directory, and the DEFAULT.HTM file in that directory is automatically sent to and displayed on the user's Web browser.

This strategy of displaying a default document is the standard operating procedure for most Web servers, although you can alter the operation. The default document in the WWWROOT directory is basically the *home page* for the Web site. From it, users navigate to other pages on the site. To create a home page for your site, use an HTML coding language and save the file in the WWWROOT directory with the name DEFAULT.HTM.

By placing hyperlink buttons on your home page, you can let users link to any other directory and display the default document that exists in those directories. So the directory structure reflects the hyperlinked structure of your Web pages in many cases, although you can put all your hyperlinked documents in a single directory. Refer to my companion book in this series, *The Windows NT Web Server Handbook* (Osborne/McGraw-Hill, 1996) for more information on this topic.

Two things can happen when users browse directories on the Internet Information Server (assuming a feature is set that allows *directory browsing*). If a directory has a file called DEFAULT.HTM, that document is displayed on the client's Web browser. If the file doesn't exist, a list of files in the directory appears, as shown in Figure 20-2. Each filename in the list appears as a hyperlink. If you click one of these hyperlinked filenames, the file opens. You can also right-click a file to see the context menu (shown in the figure), then choose one of the options listed. For example, you can choose

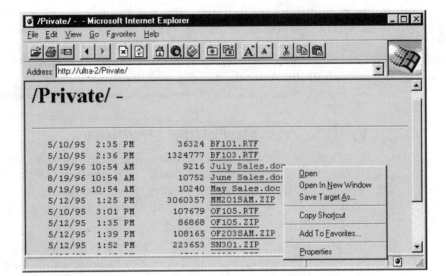

File listings
appear when
directory
browsing is
enabled
Figure 20-2.

Save Target As to save the file on your own system. In this respect, Web servers act like file servers, dishing up documents to Web clients.

When the server is installed, sample files are installed that describe how to use the server and how to take advantage of its advanced features. You can go to any client workstation on your server (or the Web server itself), start a Web browser, and type the name of the server in the Address field. The sample HTML files will appear to instruct you on the use of the Web server and to describe some of its more important features.

NOTE: After you have looked over the files, delete them to prevent possible security problems. They are located in the Sample folder and also include the DEFAULT.HTM file in the WWWROOT folder. You replace this file with a new DEFAULT.HTM file that represents the new home page for your Web server.

Setup and Management

Microsoft Internet Information Server can be set up in a matter of minutes. It loads as a service and runs in the background once installed. In fact, after running the setup procedure, you can start a browser on your own network and access the sample Web documents immediately.

Most of your involvement with the server will be in planning the connections to your intranet or to the Internet, deciding on the structure and content of the Web server, and planning security, which includes figuring out who can access the server and what level of access they will have. Some of the tools and techniques for managing the server are covered in the following sections.

Physical Configuration

In most cases, you'll connect your Web server to the Internet as a stand-alone system. Your primary concern is then to prevent Internet hackers from attacking the server itself and accessing unauthorized information or corrupting the system.

20

In other cases, you might have the Web server connected to an internal network on the outside of a firewall or even have a small LAN connected to the Web server attaching for other servers or for attaching the workstations of content developers. These configurations were discussed in Chapter 18.

One of the first things to do is disable the bindings for Server, Workstation, and NetBIOS on the network interface card that is connected to the Internet, as described in Chapters 10 and 18. You can do this in the Network utility of the Control Panel by accessing the TCP/IP protocol Bindings options. Once these bindings are removed, Internet users won't be able to access your system by using standard Windows file services. You can also disable all ports except HTTP port 80 in the Network utility.

It is recommended that you disable the Guest account on any Internet connected systems (use only the IUSR_*computername* account for anonymous logon) and make sure that the Everyone group does not have excess permissions in sensitive directories. Also keep in mind that by default the Everyone group gets automatic access to any new directories you create, so you should check permissions after creating new directories.

Refer to Chapters 18 and 19 for more information on building firewalls and enabling proxy services if other networks are connected to the server.

The Server Manager

The Server Manager is a Windows-based graphical management tool you use to configure the server and its security options. You use it to manage Web services, FTP services, and Gopher services. It is installed automatically on the Web server itself, but you can copy the files to any Windows NT system and manage Internet Information Servers on the network. To start the utility, choose Service Manager from the Start/Programs menu. You then double-click the server you want to manage and choose one of the property sheets shown in Figures 20-3 through 20-6. The options on these property sheets are discussed throughout this chapter.

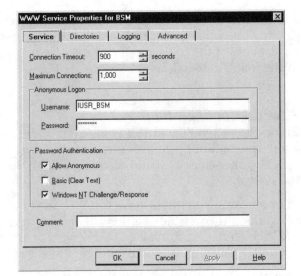

The Service
property sheet
Figure 20-3.

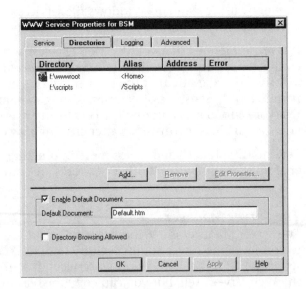

The
Directories
property sheet
Figure 20-4.

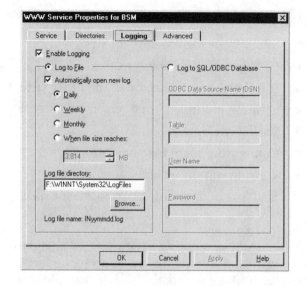

The Logging
property sheet
Figure 20-5.

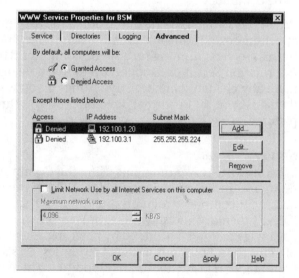

The Advanced
property sheet
Figure 20-6.

20

With the property sheet, you manage the following tasks:

♦ Establishing logon requirements

♦ Configuring access permissions

♦ Specifying home directories and other virtual directories

♦ Creating multiple virtual servers on a single computer

♦ Setting encryption options

♦ Configuring event logging options

♦ Viewing current sessions

♦ Enabling or disabling server access for specific IP addresses

Virtual Servers

Although Web servers are traditionally linked to a single domain name, the Microsoft Internet Information Server lets you configure several domain names on the same computer. For example, a single server could support domains such as **marketing.bigsur.com**, **sales.bigsur.com**, and **support.bigsur.com**. This is possible because the Windows NT Server will support multiple network interface cards and/or multiple IP addresses for the same computer.

When users attach to one of the domains, they may think that they are attaching to an individual server, when in fact they are attaching to "virtual servers" running on a single computer. The Microsoft Internet Information Server can support up to five domains by default, but you can manually change some Registry settings if you want to support more domains. You set up virtual directories on the Directories property sheet pictured in Figure 20-4.

Server Programs

You can write server programs using the Common Gateway Interface (CGI) or Microsoft's Internet Server API (ISAPI). Of the two, ISAPI is your best bet because it compiles programs into libraries that get loaded into the Internet Server's memory and stay there, thus improving performance. Another advantage of ISAPI is achieved by pluggable filters, which allow preprocessing of requests and post-processing of responses. This feature permits site-specific handling of HTTP requests and responses. There were some security breaches using CGI in the first version of the Internet Information Server, which are discussed later.

Once you've written programs and scripts, you place them in the appropriate directory on the server. The Internet Information Server creates a virtual directory called \SCRIPTS for this purpose. This directory has *Execute* permission, so users can run programs. If the program interacts with other files, the Internet anonymous user account (or whatever account people will use to access your server) must have the right permissions to use those files.

Keep in mind that you are allowing remote users to run programs on the Internet Server. These programs might have a bug or hole that some hacker could exploit to break into your system. To prevent someone from uploading a virus or other destructive program and running it, never grant Write and Execute permissions on any directory that is accessible by Web users except in rare cases, like trusted users who have been fully authenticated.

20

Database Integration

The Microsoft Internet Information Server integrates with Microsoft's SQL Server database system or other database systems, so content providers and businesses can provide information that is located in structured storage or use the input of users to update and/or access information in databases.

The Internet Server provides access to databases through a component called the Internet Database Connector (IDC), which is part of the Internet Server API. The Internet Connector uses ODBC (Open Database Connectivity) to gain access to databases. Because ODBC provides a layer of connectivity between back-end databases and front-end clients, it is used to provide connections to a variety of back-end database systems.

Other Tools and Techniques

The Windows NT Server and the Microsoft Internet Information Server have some additional features, including the following:

♦ *Bandwidth throttling* provides a way to limit the amount of information that can be sent from the server at any one time so other requests can be serviced with a fair share of time.

♦ You can set up several Internet Information Servers on their own network that is isolated from your internal network but connected to the Internet. All of these servers can then be managed with the Internet Service Manager running from a Windows NT Workstation.

♦ The server creates logs that contain information about user activity. You can view logs to see what has been accessed and when. Server logs must initially be configured.

♦ The Windows NT Performance Monitor utility can perform real-time measurements of your Web server and provide statistical information that you can use to troubleshoot the system, track usage, or justify the need to upgrade equipment.

Anonymous Logon and Subscription Services

When a user connects to the Internet Information Server, all access to resources on the server is handled by the Internet services running on that computer, either World Wide Web services, Gopher services, or FTP services. More specifically, the server "impersonates" the client so that users never access objects directly. This is true for all user access to a Windows NT system. For example, a Web user makes a request to the HTTP service, which presents the credentials of the user (username/password) to the security system for comparison to the access list of the resource being accessed.

Most Web servers on the Internet allow anyone to access information without prior logon. However, some sites (The *Wall Street Journal* site, for instance) require subscription accounts; you must register to get a password before you can access certain information. Note the following:

♦ Servers that let you log on without typing a password provide what is called *anonymous logon*. All anonymous users access the server under the same account (similar to the Guest account), which makes it difficult for administrators to know who is accessing the server.

♦ Logon access requires users to supply a username and password to gain access to restricted resources. Typically, a Web site will have some anonymous access but require logon when users attempt to access restricted areas. Some servers require logon right at the "front door."

This last case is usually called a *subscription service* because it requires users to register with the server before access is granted. The usual procedure is to have users fill out a registration form and submit it for approval. The approval process may be automated, or it may require a manager's approval, depending on the type of service. Security requirements may vary. For example, in some cases the information in the directory is not sensitive—you only want users to identify themselves. Perhaps you are building a mailing list. In this type of situation, you are not too concerned about protecting the contents of the private directory, nor are you concerned about whether the user's password is encrypted or sent as clear text.

If your private directories contain sensitive information, you'll need strong security. You'll want to establish the authenticity of users and make sure that their passwords are not compromised during transmission. To do this, you can use the advanced security features of the Internet Information Server to specify logons using the Microsoft Windows NT Challenge/Response protocol. This protocol encrypts all passwords and sets up secure sessions. However, to use it, clients must be running a compatible browser, such as the Microsoft Internet Explorer, that can negotiate the Challenge/Response with the server.

Assume that a Web client accesses a Web site that presents a home page with the following buttons:

♦ Click Here For Free Information
♦ Registered Users Click Here
♦ Register

The Web site has the following directory structure, with the lock on the Private directory indicating that only registered users with accounts on the server can access the directory after being authenticated.

20

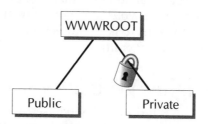

Users register by clicking the Register button, filling out a form, and submitting it back to the server. An automatic or manual process is used to create an account for the user and to grant the account permissions in the Private directory. Permissions are granted in the usual way with the User Manager utility.

Here's what happens when a visitor accesses this hypothetical site:

♦ When a user types the basic URL (**www.bigsur.com**), the home page for the site appears. In this case, the Web server returns the file \WWWROOT\DEFAULT.HTM to the user.

♦ If the user clicks the Click Here For Free Information button, the default page in the PUBLIC directory appears and the URL becomes **www.bigsur.com/public/.** The Web server returns the file \WWWROOT\PUBLIC\DEFAULT.HTM to the user.

♦ If the user clicks the Registered Users Click Here button, the following Logon dialog box appears:

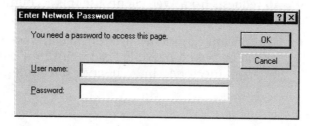

The visitor then types his or her username and password to access the PRIVATE directory. The default page for the directory appears and the URL becomes **www.bigsur.com/private/**. The Web server returns the file \WWWROOT\PRIVATE\DEFAULT.HTM to the user. This option assumes that the user has access rights in the PRIVATE directory and types an authentic username and password.

You can require users to log on to a directory that is reserved for company employees, content designers, or business partners who access the directory from the Internet or over an internal network and do more than just read documents. These people may need additional rights to change the content in the directory or add information of their own and will probably already have accounts on your server or network domain. All you need to do is grant them permissions to access directories. This is done with the Windows NT Server User Manager utility.

Managing Web Server User Accounts

You use the Windows NT Server security features in combination with the directory access controls in the Microsoft Internet Information Server to control how Web users access your server. Techniques for implementing these features are discussed in this section.

More About the Anonymous User Account

When you install the Microsoft Internet Information Server, a special anonymous Guest account is created with the name IUSR_*computername,* where *computername* is the name of the server (I refer to this account as the *anonymous user account*). This account is given the right to log on locally, so when someone accesses the Web server without providing any sort of logon credentials, they are granted access to the server as if they are logging on locally (at the console). The account is a member of the Guests local group and the Domain Users group.

The anonymous user account does not require users to enter a username or password, which makes it easy for users to access your server—and you won't know who is accessing the server. Note the following:

♦ All requests from Web clients use this account if you allow only anonymous logons.

♦ The account cannot delete or change files on NTFS file systems by default because it has only Read rights (or Execute rights in script and program directories) in Web server directories.

◆ Because the account has limited rights, users cannot download files to the server or execute files except in designated directories.

◆ On domain controllers, this account is added to the domain database.

◆ Other Web servers at your site will have similar anonymous accounts, but you can create a single anonymous account for the domain if necessary, then update the Directories property sheet (shown in Figure 20-4) so that the Anonymous Logon Username field has the new name.

How Anonymous Users Access Directories

20

An important concept is that any user accessing Web services can access only directories that are specified on the Directories property sheet of the Internet Service Manager, as pictured in Figure 20-4, or that are subdirectories of directories specified on this sheet. To create a new directory, you first create it in the file system, grant user accounts permission to the directory, then add the directory to the Directories property sheet as a directory that Web users can access. This prevents Web users from accessing every directory on the server.

After a directory is created and added to the Directories property sheet, there are three conditions when anonymous users can access a designated directory:

◆ If the Everyone group has at least Read or Execute rights in the directory

◆ If the IUSR_*computername* account has been specifically granted at least Read or Execute rights in the directory

◆ If the Guests group (which IUSR_*computername* is a member of) has been specifically granted at least Read or Execute rights in the directory

If you create a directory and you only want anonymous users to access the directory, remove the Everyone and Guests groups from the permissions list and add only the IUSR_*computername* account.

If Everyone and/or the IUSR_*computername* account do not have permissions to access a directory, then anonymous users cannot access the directory. Removing these two groups is how you restrict a directory to anonymous Web users and require logon access, as described next.

Requiring User Account Logon

If you want to restrict access to a directory to only users who have accounts on the server and require those users to log on when they access the Web server, follow the steps outlined here:

1. Restrict anonymous user access to directories by removing the Everyone, Guests, and IUSR_*computername* accounts from the permission list for the directory.

2. Add the specific user or group that you want to access the directory and assign the appropriate access rights by making a selection in the Type of Access field.

3. In the Internet Service Manager, add the directory to the Directories property sheet if it is not a subdirectory of a directory that is already specified.

4. Enable Basic or Challenge/Response on the Service dialog box. These options are discussed later.

Logon Controls

There are three levels of access for the Web server, which we'll now examine. You select these on the Service property sheet in the Internet Service Manager as pictured in Figure 20-3.

Allow Anonymous   This is the anonymous user option that allows Web users to log on to the IUSR_*computername* account. When this option is enabled (the default), users can access directories in which Everyone, the Guests group, and/or the IUSR_*computername* accounts have access. If Allow Anonymous is checked and the Basic and Windows NT Challenge/Response check boxes are both cleared, only anonymous users can log on. If you disable this option, you must enable Basic or Windows NT Challenge/Response (then all users must log on by providing a username and password, and those users must have appropriate user accounts on the Web server before any user can log on).

Basic (Clear Text)   The Basic option requires users to enter a username and password to access a secure folder. This is useful if you want to set up a "subscription" service that requires users to log on with a password once they have been "registered" with the service, as discussed earlier. This option sends passwords in scrambled clear text, a code that's easy for any hacker to break. The password could be compromised, and if it is the same password that users use to log in to more secure accounts, a hacker who captures the password could gain unauthorized access to those accounts. Use this option with care. However, if you require logon for users who access non-sensitive information, then perhaps you require passwords only as a "formality" and encryption is not essential.

Windows NT Challenge/Response   This option assumes that users have already been authenticated by some other Windows NT computer (or compatible computer). When this option is set, the header information in the user's HTTP requests, which contains the user's credentials (username and password), is used to log the user in to the restricted directory. This option is mostly used if the Web server is connected to an internal intranet and users on the network have already been logged in, although it can also be used over the Internet. The Windows NT Challenge/Response protocol uses an encryption technique that prevents passwords from being transmitted across the network in the clear. However, at the time of this writing, this type of encryption is supported only by Microsoft Internet Explorer browsers.

20

When the Web server receives a client request that contains credentials, the anonymous logon user account is bypassed and the credentials are used by the service to log the user on.

Directory Access Controls

After you add a new directory to your server for Web users to access, you add it to the Directories property sheet, pictured in Figure 20-4, so you can set special options. Note that you don't need to add a directory to this list if it is the subdirectory of a directory that is already listed, but if you want to set the special options described here, then add it to the list. Click the new directory in the list and then click the Edit Properties button. The dialog box in Figure 20-7 appears. Not all the features of the Directory Properties dialog box are described here, only those concerned with security. For a full description, refer to the help feature.

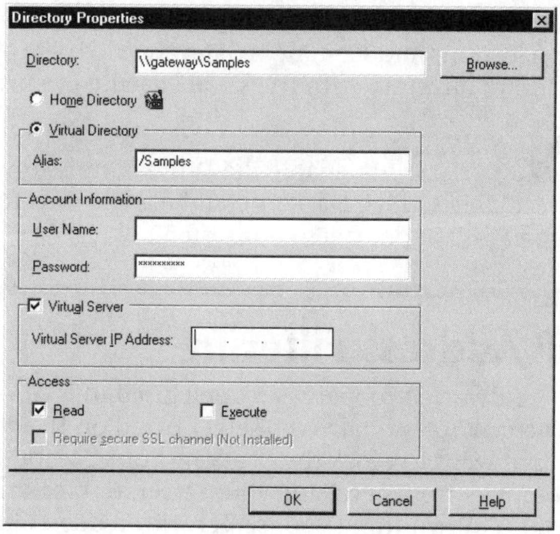

Changing
Directory
properties

Figure 20-7.

There are three types of access that you can specify for directory permissions (Read, Execute, and Require Secure SSL Channel), as shown in the Directory Properties dialog box and described next.

Read   With the Read setting, users can view the files in the directory but cannot change the files or add files of their own. This is the most secure option. You enable the Read option on publishing directories and disable it on directories that contain programs, so clients can't download your programs.

Execute   With the Execute setting, users can start applications or scripts in the directory. A client request could execute a CGI application or an ISAPI application by typing the filename of the application in the URL. You can also use the Web File Extension Mapping feature, which allows your executables and DLLs to be stored somewhere other than the Web publishing tree. Web File Extension Mapping is used to locate a file on the local Web server or another Web server. Refer to the Microsoft Internet Information Server help system for information on the mapping features.

Require Secure SSL Channel   When Secure Sockets Layer is installed, the Require Secure SSL Channel option is available and allows for the private transmission of information in the directory to the client. When this option is enabled, a secure channel with encryption is used between the client and the server. SSL is discussed in the following section.

When you install the Microsoft Internet Information Server a directory called \SCRIPTS is created. This directory has the Execute permission (and not the Read permission) and branches from the root directory of the installation drive. You should store all of your Internet Server API (ISAPI) applications and Common Gateway (CGI) scripts in this directory, or create another directory with the same Execute permission for storing scripts.

 NOTE: Do not enable the Write permission on directories that hold executable scripts. Hackers could use the directory to upload and run a program that damages your system.

IP Address Filtering

The Advanced property sheet pictured in Figure 20-6 is where you specify who can access your Web server based on IP addresses. For example, you might want to block the IP address of a competitor to prevent people in that company from accessing your server, or block the IP address of someone who is overrunning your server with requests in a denial-of-service attack.

There are two models for specifying IP addresses—either Granted Access or Denied Access. You must specify one of the models, then add IP addresses to the exception list box.

- ♦ **Granted Access** Allows all hosts access to the Web server, except for the IP addresses that are added to the Lower Exception list box.
- ♦ **Denied Access** Denies all hosts access to the Web server, except for the IP addresses that are added to the Lower Exception list box.
- ♦ **Add button** Click this button to add IP addresses to the exception list.
- ♦ **Limit Network Use by all Internet Services on This Computer** Lets you control the amount of traffic that the Web server generates. Enabling this option prevents one server from taking up too much of the bandwidth on a shared connection.

Restricting access by IP address is not a foolproof security measure. A hacker or someone else who you want to keep out of your system can simply move to a computer with a different IP address or change his or her IP address. It is, however, an effective way to block known users on your own internal network or users who are flooding your network with unnecessary or intrusive requests.

Client-Server Channel Security

Microsoft Web clients and servers support the Secure Sockets Layer (SSL) and the Private Communication Technology (PCT) protocols for securing a communication channel. SSL is an older standard, while PCT is a more efficient and secure upgrade to the SSL protocol. The Microsoft Internet Security Framework (see Chapter 21) supports SSL versions 2.0 and 3.0 and PCT version 1.0, as well as a new security protocol called Transport Layer Security (TLS). TLS incorporates both SSL and PCT into a single standard that supports both certificates and password-based authentication.

NOTE: Only the Microsoft Internet Explorer 3.0 supports all of the protocols discussed here. Earlier versions of the Internet Explorer support only SSL.

The security protocols are layered between the TCP/IP protocol and the HTTP services. Both the client and server must negotiate the level of security they want to use, and once a session is established, encryption is used to encode all data sent between a client and server. You typically enable SSL or

PCT on specific directories of your Web site, rather than on the entire Web site, although you can do the latter to achieve a high level of security. Usually, it is not necessary to encrypt the home page or public directories, only private directories with sensitive information.

SSL and PCT provide these levels of protection:

♦ Encryption assures that the data cannot be read by anyone other than the client and server who have negotiated a secure channel.

♦ Data integrity assures that the data being transferred has not been altered.

♦ Authentication is implemented to assure the client that data is being sent to the correct server and that the server is secure.

♦ If you use Basic authentication (which normally sends passwords in clear text), SSL will improve its security level by encrypting the password at the client before it is transmitted.

To fully implement these levels of security, you must obtain a digital certificate from a certification authority. Here are the steps involved in obtaining a digital certificate:

1. Generate a key pair file and a request file.
2. Request a certificate from a certification authority, such as Verisign (**www.verisign.com**).
3. Install the certificate on your server.
4. Activate PCT/SSL security on a specific directory of your Web server.

The complete instructions for this process can be found in Chapter 5 of the Internet Server users manual. The basic steps include using a utility called KEYGEN located in the INETSRV\SERVER directory to create two files called KEYPAIR.KEY and REQUEST.REQ. These are the files you send to the certification authority. The utility requires information such as the Fully Distinguished Name for your server, which includes the Web site name, country designation, locality and other information outlined in the manual.

Once you generate the files, you prepare a letter that identifies the Webmaster at your organization and that states the formal name of the organization, along with the names of other people to contact in the organization. This letter and the keys get sent to the certification authority. For more information on the contents of the letter and the information you need to gather, contact a certification authority such as Verisign (**www.verisgn.com**).

After applying for a certificate with a certification authority, you will receive a signed certificate that is basically a text file with a long string of coded letters. Copy the information to a text-only file by using a utility such as Notepad. Give the file a name like SSLCODE.TXT.

Type a SETKEY command similar to the following, assuming you used the name SSLCODE.TXT. Replace *password* with a suitable password and *ip_address* with the IP address of a particular server that this certificate should be applied to:

> SETKEY *password* KEYPAIR.KEY SSLCODE.TXT *ip_address*

20

If you don't specify an IP address, the same certificate will be applied to all virtual servers created on the system.

CAUTION: Once you've performed this step, save the key file KEYPAIR.KEY to a floppy disk and remove it from the server. Store the disk in a safe place. The information it contains is extremely confidential and private to your organization. If someone gets hold of the information, you will need to obtain a new key.

Now you are ready to enable security for the directories on your Web server. Open the Service properties sheet (pictured in Figure 20-3) and then enable the Windows NT Challenge/Response option. On the Directories property sheet, double-click a directory that will require secure connections. In the Directories properties sheet, click the Require Secure SSL Channel option. At this point, any PCT/SSL client that connects with the directory will get a secure channel connection.

Microsoft Internet Explorer 3.0

Microsoft Internet Explorer 3.0 is Microsoft's most secure Web browser to date. It supports SSL versions 2.0 and 3.0, as well as the PCT standard. It also allows servers to identify and authenticate clients using public key certificates. Internet Information Server 2.0 (included with Windows NT 4.0) supports this public key authentication strategy. These security protocols and standards allow users to set up private communications with others that prevent electronic eavesdropping and to connect with sites on the Internet and be assured that the site is legitimate and not a masquerade. With this type of secure communications, Internet users can safely purchase items with their credit cards and without worrying that someone might intercept private information.

Another advantage of these security protocols is user authentication. By implementing secure channel capabilities and certificate-based authentication in its Web browsers and servers, Microsoft is extending the single-server logon concept available on Windows NT internal networks to clients who connect with servers over the Internet. These features are implemented as part of the Microsoft Security Framework, which is discussed in Chapter 21.

Internet Explorer version 3.0 uses 128-bit encryption, which provides a much higher level of security than previous versions of the Web browser. Microsoft claims that "it is virtually impossible for users to listen in on Internet traffic encrypted with 128-bit security."

Internet Explorer's personal certificate feature will automatically verify a user's identity when visiting sites that require user logon. Microsoft calls it the equivalent of "flashing your badge." Credentials are exchanged in the background so you don't need to get directly involved with the security validations every time you connect with a secure Web site. Web users can also store the certificates obtained at Web sites for future use.

You can obtain Personal certificates to use with the Internet Explorer or any other Web browser from Verisign and other certification authorities. The company has a free "class 1" digital ID that provides e-mail authentication. It also has a "class 2" digital ID for personal identity authentication.

CHAPTER 21

Internet Commerce
Security Issues

The Internet provides incredible opportunities to make yourself or your company known to a whole world of people you could not reach before. With it, you can tell the world about your products and services. You may have already decided to establish a presence on the Web. Here are some of the advantages of doing so:

◆ You can advertise products while reducing the cost of paper-based advertising.

◆ You can also expand your market to a global scale and use new procurement methods and business-to-business electronic transaction techniques to improve how you do business in general.

◆ You can provide better support by giving customers instant access to information about your products.

Small businesses can create effective Web sites for a low price and compete with large companies that have big advertising budgets. Large businesses can quickly respond to changing markets. Of course, doing business over the Internet can be risky, but new security techniques can make financial transactions safe and reliable. Encryption and financial exchange mechanisms can make buying on the Internet as easy as purchasing with a credit card at a retail store.

Almost everything is in place to do business over the Internet. All that is required is trust that there are adequate mechanisms to keep information safe and secure. This chapter will help you decide whether that is the case.

Where to Get Internet Business Information

There are many organizations that can help you get your business started on the Internet or that provide information about commerce on the Internet. You can search at AltaVista (**www.altavista.digital.com**) or Yahoo! (**www.yahoo.com**) on topics such as "electronic commerce" or "Internet business." Also check out Microsoft's Small Business Resource site at **www.microsoft.com/smallbiz**.

One of the best places to find information about doing business on the Internet is at Commerce Net (**www.commerce.net**). The goal of Commerce Net is to make electronic commerce a reality. Backed by sponsors such as Apple Computer, Bank of America, Dunn & Bradstreet, IBM, Intel, Pacific Bell, and Wells Fargo, Commerce Net was started in 1994 as a place where businesses with similar needs could pool their resources. From Commerce Net you can order Internet business starter kits that help you build and maintain Web sites.

Commerce Net focuses on connectivity, data transfer, secure transactions, payment services, marketing, collaboration techniques and tools, computer-aided logistics support, public policy, electronic directories and catalogs, Internet EDI (Electronic Data Interchange), and network services. Commerce Net also works extensively on security issues and financial transaction techniques, particularly transaction security features in Web browsers.

If you need more information about security, contact RSA Data Security, Inc. at **www.rsa.com**. RSA's technologies are the global de facto standard for public key encryption and digital signatures and are part of existing and proposed standards for the Internet and business and financial networks around the world. The company develops and markets platform-independent software-developer kits and end-user products; it also provides comprehensive consulting services in the cryptographic sciences.

21

Internet Security Issues

Security is a primary concern on the Web, and there are many works in progress aimed at protecting financial transactions. Most security solutions focus on encryption to secure private communication. The use of protocol analyzers by technicians to monitor network traffic has made managers aware that their data transmissions are not secure. Anyone with such a device can view selected data streams on the network. International networks, public and private e-mail systems, and radio communications are growing at a rate that requires a greater need for security. Fortunately, advances in processor design are making encryption fast and easy to implement.

Perhaps the best introduction to the problems of security on the Internet can be found in "Frequently Asked Questions About Internet Security," a document written by John Harrington and Cary Griffin and available at the Commerce Net site:

> In the "real" world, where information is exchanged in physical form, there is a great deal of security infrastructure, built up over literally thousands of years, that we take for granted.

> The postal service is a good example. For a nominal fee, you are able to send a message anywhere in the world. If you want that message to be private, you enclose it within an envelope. Tampering or changing the message would require breaking the seal on the envelope and committing a Federal crime. If you wish to make sure that your message was received, you ask for a return receipt. To make sure that the person who received

the message was the one you intended him or her to be, you might check his or her signature. He or she might check yours.

Now imagine that someone has just constructed a brand-new postal service from scratch. The service operates at blinding speed, sorting and forwarding messages through various postal clearinghouses in seconds instead of days. But the new service has some drawbacks. Anyone can be a postmaster, and there is nothing to prevent a postmaster from making copies of the mail as it passes through his clearinghouse. Messages are written on postcards, and instead of signatures and return receipts, all message identification is written in identical block letters: "This message is from John at IBM." So the postcard-sorters can't help but see entire messages; there is little to prevent a phony message from being swapped out for a genuine one; there is no guarantee that the persons on either end of the message exchange are the people on the address; and there is no means of verifying that a message was received.

Such a postal service exists today, and it's known as the Internet. By design, the Internet allows wiretapping, and it's estimated that 20 percent of the message traffic sent via the Internet is copied and stored somewhere (by someone other than sender and receiver) for later reference. Most messages are sent as plain block text so an intercepted message can be read by different software platforms.

On the Internet, people other than the recipient can look at and duplicate your mail, or change the content of messages. To transact business, companies must have the means to conduct safe, private, and reliable transactions. To get to that level, the four cornerstones of secure electronic transactions must be present:

♦   The ability to prevent unauthorized monitoring of data transmissions

♦   A way to prevent the content of messages from being altered after they are sent and/or a way to prove such alteration occurred

♦   The ability to determine whether a transmission is from an authentic source or from someone or something masquerading as that source

♦   A way to prevent a sender from denying (repudiating) that they sent a message (such as a buy order) or that they received and read a message

Public key cryptography and digital signature technology are the means by which companies are securing transactions over the Internet. A *key* is an alphanumeric password that is used with an encryption algorithm to encrypt information. Once a message is encrypted, the key must be used to decrypt the information.

Cryptographic Techniques

Cryptographic systems provide a way to transmit information across an untrusted communication system in a scrambled and hidden form to prevent people from reading the information. Cryptography provides confidentiality and can also provide proof that a transmission has or has not been viewed or altered. However, the encryption system itself must be reliable. How can you be sure that the encryption method is unbreakable? How do you protect the key and give it to other people without compromising security?

Consider the process of sending confidential data. You would use a key to encrypt the message and send it, but you also need to get the key to all recipients so they can decrypt the message. How do you do that without compromising security? You can't send the key with the message.

One method is to send keys in advance. But can you be sure that keys have not been intercepted by unauthorized people? You could send keys through other channels, like an express delivery service, but this is not always a timely solution, and the key still could be compromised on the way. Also, this method is impractical if you're sending a one-time message to someone you don't know.

21

There are two cryptographic key techniques: private key and public key encryption. Private key encryption methods are called *symmetric ciphers*, and public key methods are called *asymmetric ciphers*.

The Private Key Scheme   In a private key scheme, information is encrypted with a key that both the sender and receiver hold privately. The security of this system relies on both parties being able to exchange keys without compromise. Private key encryption is also the technique used to secure information stored on disk. You encrypt data files with a key that you hold yourself and never need to exchange.

 NOTE: Encryption can be used against you. Someone with access to your system might encrypt the data on your drive and sell you the key for a ransom.

The Public Key Scheme   The public key system consists of two separate but related keys: a public key and a private key. Everyone gets his or her own set of keys. You give your public key to other people or place it on a special security server that other people can access. Security servers might be within your own organization, or you can use certification authority services, such as Commerce Net. If someone wants to send you a message, he or she encrypts the message with your public key. Upon receipt of the message, you decrypt it with your private key.

The public key scheme is a simple and elegant solution for exchanging messages over the Internet. It solves the problem of passing keys to other parties who need to decrypt your messages. In fact, it allows any user to encrypt a message and send it to any other person without any prior exchange or agreement. It is not even necessary that either party know the other, be part of the same organization, or be connected to the same network. All that is required is that both parties have access to a common server that manages public key security. Certification authorities (such as Commerce Net) are required to guarantee the authenticity of public keys. You register your own keys with such an authority.

 NOTE: Appendix B explores the public key systems and cryptography in general.

Digital Signatures and Message Integrity

In many cases, the person who receives your message will have no doubt that the message is from you and will have no reason to question the validity of its contents. However, electronic business transactions must assure authenticity and integrity. Suppose you are a stockbroker and you receive an order from a client to buy 10,000 shares of Ajax Typewriter Company. How can you be sure that this message is authentic? What if you place the order, the stock drops, and then the buyer tries to deny that she ever sent the order in the first place? Did the message get altered in transmission by some unscrupulous person? These are issues of authentication and integrity that can be solved with the public key system.

Digital signatures provide a way of verifying a document originated from the person who sent the document and that the document has not been altered since leaving the sender. The basic steps for "signing" documents with digital signatures are

1. Joe creates a special encrypted "token" from information in the message itself, encrypts the message and token with his *private* key, and then sends the message to Sue.

2. Sue uses Joe's *public* key to decrypt the message and then creates a similar token using Joe's public key to decrypt information in the message.

3. Sue compares the token she created with the token sent by Joe. If they match, the message is considered authentic.

Of course, this is all handled electronically and in the background in most cases. Vendors are building security-enabled applications that handle these tasks automatically. Microsoft's Cryptographic APIs (or CryptoAPI) provide the tools for such applications, as discussed later. You'll find a more complete discussion of digital signatures and other techniques for authentication and integrity in Appendix B.

Certification Authorities

The authenticity of public keys is an issue as well. If you are transacting business, how can you be sure that the server you are communicating with is an authentic server for the company you think you are doing business with? Are you willing to submit your credit card number to an Internet business system? There have been cases where ATMs located in malls were fakes. These machines actually gave customers cash and returned their credit card, but the machines also collected personal identification numbers for fraudulent use at a later time. The moral of this is to use only ATMs located at trusted buildings, such as your bank.

Similarly, you will probably want to perform Internet business transactions only at trusted sites, or sites that have been certified as authentic by a certification authority (CA). Commerce Net and VeriSign are CAs. CAs issue public key certificates that establish the authenticity of any person, organization, or merchant on the Internet. People and businesses who want this certification must meet certain requirements, in the same way that credit card holders have been authorized by a bank to purchase goods with the card. A CA basically guarantees that people and companies on the Internet are authentic and reliable.

Certificates are the equivalent of "digital credentials" issued by the CA to organizations that have passed their requirements for certification. Some of the requirements for sign-up and ongoing certification are outlined here:

♦ The applicant must submit documents to prove that it actually owns and operates the servers it wishes to certify and that it is authorized to do so by various state and local authorities.

♦ The applicant must submit a list of authorized representatives for the company, including the Webmasters. Any changes to this list must be submitted to the CA as they occur.

♦ The applicant must take measures to ensure that the private key it is issued is not compromised in any way. These measures include building firewalls and other systems to keep hackers out.

The U.S. Postal Service is providing CA services. It uses public key encryption and related technologies to develop a public key certification authority and a set of associated trusted third-party services, which it calls the *postal electronic commerce services* (Postal ECS). When Postal ECS is deployed, it will provide a basis for electronic assurance within and among government agencies, and between government agencies and their constituents. The Postal Service has developed the following services:

♦ Issue public key certificates and store them in a public directory

♦ Provide for the "sealing" of selected documents or other electronic objects and associating them with a digital signature and a trusted time and date stamp

♦ Provide services for public key certificate publication and revocation

♦ Provide for encryption of confidential information moving between the user environment and the Postal ECS management system

♦ Provide near real-time access to certificates and their status

Users can retrieve a certificate from the Postal Service and use its public key to authenticate a digital signature generated by the complementary private key.

Electronic Cash

One of the problems with the Internet has been the difficulty of implementing simple cash transactions. Online services such as CompuServe, America Online, and The Microsoft Network have been successful at providing convenient cash-exchange systems, because these services authenticate you at sign-on and handle all the transaction processing. Since you are doing all your business transactions within the confines of the online service, the transactions are usually safe and reliable. The online service handles some or all of the billing for online merchants. Charges for goods may appear on your monthly statement from the service provider, or on your credit card bill.

On the Internet, there is no central service or authority that can provide these services. That's where the concept of electronic or digital cash comes into play. What exactly is electronic cash? To get an idea, just visit the following sites:

♦ CyberCash (**www.cybercash.com**)

♦ DigiCash (**www.digicash.com**)

♦ First Virtual Holdings (**www.fv.com**)

These organizations basically make and distribute their own money, like electronic IOUs, over the Internet. It's almost like "play money" that you can use like real money while you're on the Internet. You "buy" some digital cash (*cyberbucks*) from one of the above companies using your credit card, then you visit sites that honor the cyberbucks. When you use electronic money, you keep it in an electronic Wallet.

CyberCash is a good example of a system that enables electronic commerce by providing a safe, convenient, immediate, and secure payment service for the Internet. Consumers use normal browsers to shop at Web merchant sites. CyberCash transactions move between three separate software programs: the electronic Wallet program that resides on the consumer's PC, one that operates as part of the merchant server, and one that operates within the CyberCash servers. The merchant and consumer software is free.

A consumer selects items to buy, and the merchant presents him or her with an invoice and a request for payment. The consumer can then have the *CyberCash Wallet* pay for the purchase by simply clicking the Pay button. From there, the appropriate transfer of funds is accomplished through encrypted messages exchanged between the merchant server, the consumer, and the CyberCash server as well as the conventional credit card networks.

21

First Virtual's Internet Payment System operates with ordinary e-mail. You use a VirtualPIN (an alias for your credit card) to make purchases, and your credit card number is never transmitted over the Internet. Every purchase is confirmed by a return e-mail.

To become a buyer using First Virtual's system, you must have an Internet e-mail address and a valid Visa or MasterCard. You also must complete an application and receive your VirtualPIN. Your credit card is registered with First Virtual over the telephone, not over the Internet.

To buy, you give a seller your VirtualPIN instead of a credit card number. First Virtual will then send you an e-mail to confirm the purchase, and you reply to the e-mail with a "yes" to confirm the sale or a "no" to cancel it. If you confirm the sale, your credit card is charged by First Virtual completely off the Internet. Obviously, you don't give out your VirtualPIN at any site. That is where certification authorities come into the picture. They can verify that the site where you plan to give out your VirtualPIN is authentic.

Micropayments

Electronic transactions are so easy and inexpensive that selling things that cost mere pennies or even less than a cent is worthwhile, as long as you can sell a lot of them. Charging very small amounts of money for information as services is called *micropayments*.

The first place you will see micropayments are sites that provide information and documents. When you visit a site that provides information you need, you may be automatically charged to access that information. A message such as "accessing this information will deduct 25 cents from your wallet" may pop up.

Managing Copyrights

One of the problems with selling information is that the recipient can simply copy it for other people with no kickback to the publisher. IBM has developed the Cryptolope technology as a way to secure payment while managing copyrights. A Cryptolope is a secure, digital "container" that charges the user for the right to view the information within. The contents are normally encrypted, but a key to decrypt the information is made available once a payment is made to the provider. The Cryptolope object can only be opened within a special Cryptolope-enabled browser and can only be copied as an encrypted object. Therefore, no one can open the object and copy the opened contents to another user.

Microsoft Merchant Services

To alleviate some of the difficulties of building and operating an electronic retail site, Microsoft has developed Merchant Services. Merchant Services includes a set of technologies for building and operating an electronic retailing system. It provides consistent software formats and interoperability so merchants can integrate their services with suppliers, and it provides a secure shopping experience for customers. Merchant services are closely tied to the Microsoft Internet Information Server.

One of the primary goals of Merchant Services is to let merchants quickly create their own online store operation and focus on merchandising rather than on developing their own in-house solutions. Merchant Services includes well-defined interfaces so third-party developers can extend its features. Microsoft is working with standards organizations such as the Association of Retail Technology Standards, the World Wide Web Consortium, and the Internet Engineering Task Force, to promote and extend standards for electronic retailing.

The core product provides all the components required to set up an online store, including:

- Shopping user interface
- Order capture system
- Processing and routing software
- Merchandising tools

An online store consists of a collection of HTML pages. Merchants can use tools such as Microsoft Internet Assistant, FrontPage, and Internet Studio to develop content. In addition, Merchant Services includes templates for designing HTML pages and icons to put on those pages. To manage online stores, Microsoft has developed a "workbench" of tools for tracking orders, managing returns, analyzing customer behavior, and managing virtual shelf space and layout.

The Internet Shopper

The *Internet Shopper* is the most important part of Microsoft Merchant Services. This application runs on the customers' computers and lets them purchase from merchants who are running Merchant Services. Customers can receive Internet Shopper at no charge by simply downloading it from any merchant site.

The Internet Shopper provides customers with a consistent shopping experience from one online service to the next. The Internet Shopper is designed to mimic a real shopping experience. As online shoppers browse for things to buy, they can put items in a *shopping basket*. When they are ready to buy, they authorize payment from their *Wallet*, which holds credit information. Customers enter credit card information once, when they first use their card. The information is password-protected, so the next time they use a service, they enter only their password to authorize payments.

Here are just a few of the more interesting aspects of Internet Shopper:

♦ It stores credit card information on the local system in a secure way and encrypts order information before transmitting it.

♦ It calculates shipping, handling, sales tax, and totals online, and credit information is authenticated at the same time.

♦ An address book stores shipping and billing addresses so customers don't need to do a lot of retyping.

♦ Customers can place items in a shopping basket and defer purchases until later. This lets customers shop over a period of time and, for example, choose the best Christmas gifts from selections they have made at many different online stores.

♦ Internet Shopper stores a history of online shopping for later reference. Customer-tracking numbers are also maintained for this purpose.

Server-Side Components of Merchant Services

The server components of Merchant Services handle order processing, financial transactions, and the creation of Web pages from information pulled from product databases. An online store consists of a collection of HTML pages that customers browse through when connected to the store. This browsing is designed to mimic walking around a real store with a shopping basket.

When a customer adds an item to a shopping basket, the server returns a description of the item to the customer. The customer makes a request, which goes to the Microsoft Internet Information Server. The Internet Information Server gets information about the product from an online database and combines that information with information about the merchant and the customer. This collected information is then sent back to the Internet Shopper on the customer's computer.

When a customer wants to purchase an item, the *order catcher* and *order pump* get involved. First, the Internet Shopper produces an encrypted Description of Goods/Payment Instruction (DOG/PI) and sends it to the server. The order catcher captures this information and returns a tracking number to the customer. The order pump decrypts the order and saves it in an ODBC-compliant database, such as an SQL Server, or a legacy system, such as an IBM host.

Merchant Services incorporates the Secure Electronic Transactions (SET), which is a joint security specification defined by Microsoft, IBM, Netscape, Visa, MasterCard, and American Express. A public/private key pair is used to encrypt data, and private keys are stored in a secure location on the server. Public keys can be read by anyone, and they must be digitally signed by a trusted third-party certification authority, such as a credit card company or a financial institution.

Microsoft is extending Merchant Services to accommodate a variety of retail and business-to-business transactions. The goal is to make Internet shopping as natural as real shopping, while providing customers with the assurance that their transactions are handled in a safe and secure way. At the same time, Merchant Services makes it easy for merchants to "set up shop" on the Internet.

Microsoft Internet Security Framework

The Microsoft Internet Security Framework is a set of public key and password-based security technologies for exchanging security information across public networks, controlling access from outside networks to inside networks, and engaging in electronic commerce across the Internet. This section briefly explains the Security Framework. For more detailed information, visit Microsoft's Web site at **www.microsoft.com.**

The Microsoft Internet Security Framework is built on the Cryptographic API (or CryptoAPI), which is discussed in the next section. The following higher-level security services and mechanisms rest on top of the CryptoAPI.

- ◆ Secure channels for private communications using SSL (versions 2.0 and 3.0) and PCT
- ◆ Certificate-based authentication
- ◆ Authenticode technology for ensuring that downloaded code has not been tampered with and has a known publisher
- ◆ The SET protocol for secure credit card transactions
- ◆ The certificate server for issuing and revoking certificates
- ◆ The Microsoft Wallet for storing personal security information such as keys, certificates, and credit card information
- ◆ The Personal Information Exchange (PFX) for moving personal security information between computers and platforms
- ◆ Password-based authentication
- ◆ Access control using either passwords or certificates
- ◆ Distributed authentication technology based on passwords, including integration with Internet protocols

21

This last technology allows pass-through authentication with password protection, distributed authorization, and integration with the security features of the Windows NT operating system. The Microsoft Internet Security Framework is a platform that consists of the latest security technologies. It is a framework for secure online communications and electronic commerce. Issues of identity, authentication, and authorization are addressed using public key and password-based technologies. Table 21-1 summarizes the technologies and delivery mechanisms that make this possible.

Microsoft's implementations of the Wallet, client authentication, distributed authentication, secure channel protocols, CryptoAPI, Authenticode, and SET will all be made available, via Microsoft Internet Explorer, on Windows NT, Windows 95, Windows 3.*x*, Macintosh, and UNIX platforms. Also, Microsoft is working with Metrowerks to develop Authenticode technology for the Macintosh.

The CryptoAPI

The CryptoAPI is the foundation of the Microsoft Internet Security Framework. It provides developers with system-level access to common

Requirement	Technology	Function
Secure exchange of information	CryptoAPI 1.0	Base cryptographic services
	CryptoAPI 2.0	Certificate management
	SSL 2.0/3.0 and PCT 1.0	Secure channel
	Client authentication	Secure channel
	Microsoft Wallet and Personal Information Exchange (PFX)	Secure storage
	Authenticode	Shrink-wrap for the Internet
Access control	Certificate server	Issues, manages, and revokes certificates; supports customizable policies
	Pass-through authentication and distributed access Technologies for secure information exchange	Integrates Shared-Secrets Security with Internet protocols
Secure transactions	SET Technologies for access control	Secure credit card transactions

Microsoft
Internet
Security
Framework
technologies
Table 21-1.

cryptographic and certificate functions without the need to become experts in the underlying implementation. Developers can use whatever cryptographic algorithm, strength of encryption, or certificate format they need. Figure 21-1 illustrates the architecture of the CryptoAPI.

The following are components of the CryptoAPI architecture:

Cryptographic Service Providers (CSPs)   These are optional software modules, such as the RSA implementation Microsoft supplies, or hardware devices, such as the BBN SafeKeyper.

Cryptographic Primitives   These allow developers to select cryptographic service providers, create and store public keys, encrypt and decrypt data, digitally sign their programs, and verify the signatures of others.

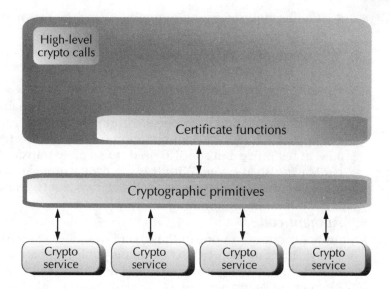

21

Certificate Functions These include functions for generating requests to create certificates, functions for storing and retrieving certificates, and functions for parsing certificates.

High-level Cryptographic Calls These encapsulate a number of the cryptographic primitives into single calls. Developers will, for example, be able to encrypt and decrypt data, sign code, and verify signatures using single functions, rather than a series of them.

High-Level Security Services

This section describes some of the higher-level security services that take advantage of the CryptoAPI. These services include protocols for private communications, authentication, security in business transactions, electronic cash management, password-based authentication, and access controls.

The Wallet

The Wallet is the electronic cash component that has the following features:

♦ Resides on the user's computer or another hardware device such as a smartcard.

♦ Stores personal security information such as private keys, credit card numbers, and certificates.

♦ Can be moved from place to place using the Personal Information Exchange (PFX) protocol.

♦ Access is controlled by policies.

Personal Information Exchange

The Personal Information Exchange (PFX) protocol enables users to transfer sensitive information from one environment or platform to another. For example, a user may have information such as certificates and keys stored on a PC in her office, but she also needs to securely transfer this information to her Macintosh at home. With this protocol, a user can securely export personal information from one computer system to another.

Authenticode

Authenticode solves one of the larger questions facing the software industry today: How can users trust code that is published on the Internet? It provides a way to sign code so users know that programs obtained from the Internet are legitimate, just as shrink wrap and sealed boxes imply that off-the-shelf packaged software is authentic. Authenticode provides

♦ Authenticity, so you know who published the code

♦ Integrity, so you know that code hasn't been tampered with since it was published

♦ A legitimate and safe way to exchange programs over the Internet

The basic procedure for signing code is for a publisher to get a certificate from a certification authority. The publisher then encrypts its certificates into the code with its private key to create a unique digital signature. The code can then be verified using functions that validate the digital signature, as discussed in Appendix B. The functions indicate whether the code is valid or whether it is possibly fake or has been tampered with.

Secure Channel Services

People who use Web browsers to connect with Internet Web servers often need secure connections to ensure privacy, especially if they are engaged in business transactions or looking at sensitive information. A secure channel service can provide this level of security. Secure Sockets Layer (SSL) is a protocol that provides channel security. With SSL, the client and the server use a handshaking technique to agree on the level of security they want to use during a session. Authentication takes place over a security channel, and all information transmitted during the sessions is encrypted. Early versions of SSL are not considered strong enough for the transmission of sensitive information.

Another standard for electronic security is Secure Hypertext Transfer Protocol (S-HTTP), an applications-level protocol that can, for example, secure specific parts of documents. It is useful in workflow and document routing applications where documents must be signed and verified using digital signatures.

The Microsoft Internet Security Framework includes support for SSL versions 2.0 and 3.0 and Personal Communications Technology (PCT) version 1.0 and will include support for the Transport Layer Security Protocol (TLS), which is being considered by IETF. This protocol will provide a single standard encompassing both SSL and PCT.

PCT 1.0 is similar to Secure Sockets Layer (SSL) 2.0, but offers enhancements in the areas of authentication and protocol efficiency. By separating authentication from encryption, PCT allows applications to use authentication that is stronger than the 40-bit key limit for encryption allowed by the U.S. government for export. Microsoft's implementation of PCT is backward-compatible with SSL.

21

SSL version 3.0 provides authentication for the client or server so that either one can require authentication of the other. With authentication, users can verify the identity of servers, and servers can verify the identity of clients. A certificate authority is required.

Client Authentication

Clients and servers that communicate over the Internet need a way to identify and *authenticate* one another. The Microsoft Internet Security Framework supports authenticating clients in a secure channel session, either with passwords, or with public key certificates, as discussed here:

Certificate-based Authentication   Certificate users who have public keys are mapped to a Windows NT-based group or user account. Windows NT access controls are assigned to the user or group. This technique uses familiar tools for authenticating users outside of the network.

Password-based Authentication   Password-based security provides both network-level and application-level security that integrates with Internet protocols and Windows security. This security technology provides distributed, scalable authentication, authorization, and billing services to Internet servers (and their respective clients) that are directly accessible to end users of Internet services.

Payment Protocols

In order for merchants to automatically and safely collect and process payments from Internet clients, a secure protocol is required that must be supported by all the major credit card companies and software developers. The Secure Electronic Transaction (SET) protocol is being developed by Microsoft, IBM, Netscape, GTE, Visa, and MasterCard for this purpose.

NOTE: Until SET standards are more clearly defined, Microsoft recommends using SSL and PCT secure channel protocols to protect Internet transactions. However, keep in mind that this method provides no authentication.

SET is designed to secure credit card transactions by authenticating cardholders, merchants, and banks and by preserving the confidentiality of payment data. SET requires digital signatures to verify that the customer, the merchant, and the bank are legitimate. It also uses multiparty messages that allow information to be encrypted directly to banks. This feature prevents credit card numbers from ending up in the wrong hands. In addition, it requires integration into the credit card processing system, which is currently underway. Figure 21-2 illustrates how the SET system works.

There will be a negotiation layer on top of SET and other payment protocols. The definition of this layer is the task of the Joint Electronic Payment Initiative project (JEPI), of which Microsoft is a member.

The JEPI project explores the technology required to provide a negotiation layer over multiple payment methods, protocols, and transports. Examples of payment methods include credit cards, debit cards, electronic cash, and checks. Payment protocols (for example, SET) define the message format and sequence required to complete the payment transaction. Payment transports are the mechanisms for message transmission and include, for example, TCP/IP, SSL, and S-HTTP.

Additional Information

For information about Microsoft Internet Security Framework and other Microsoft technologies, refer to the following Microsoft Web sites:

www.microsoft.com/devonly

www.microsoft.com/intdev/security

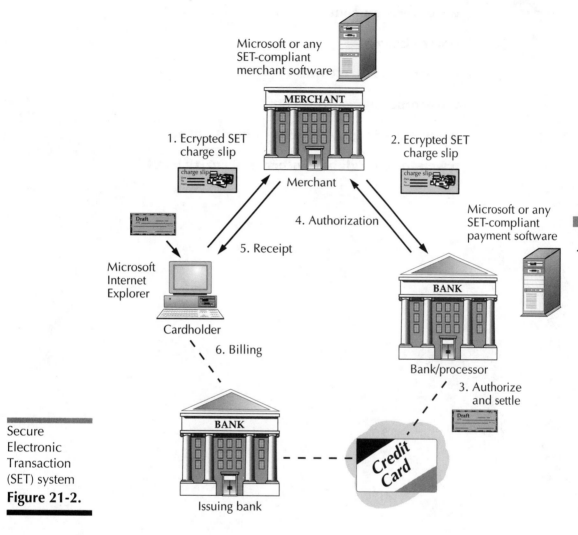

Microsoft or any
SET-compliant
merchant software

MERCHANT

1. Ecrypted SET
charge slip

2. Ecrypted SET
charge slip

charge slip

charge slip

Merchant

Microsoft or any
SET-compliant
payment software

4. Authorization

21

5. Receipt

Draft

Microsoft
Internet
Explorer

Cardholder

BANK

6. Billing

Bank/processor

3. Authorize
and settle

Draft

Secure
Electronic
Transaction
(SET) system
Figure 21-2.

BANK

Issuing bank

Credit
Card

The following Web sites provide general information on Internet security
and electronic commerce:

www.netscape.com

www.rsa.com

www.cylink.com

www.verisign.com

www.visa.com

www.mastercard.com

www.americanexpress.com

www.alw.nih.gov/Security/security.html

lcweb.loc.gov/global/internet/security.html

PART 5

Appendixes

APPENDIX A

Windows NT Security
and Logon

The Windows NT security model is designed to meet both national and international security criteria. In the United States it is the C2-level criteria as defined by the U.S. Department of Defense's *Trusted Computer System Evaluation Criteria* document (DOD 5200.28-STD - December 1985). This document is commonly referred to as the *Orange Book*. The C2-level is one level in a range of seven for DOD computer system security. The following are important C2 requirements:

♦   Each user must be identified and authenticated using a unique logon name and password, and all the user's activities must be tracked using this identification.

♦   Resources must have owners who can control access to those resources.

♦   Objects must be protected so that other processes do not randomly use them. This protection applies to memory locations, files, and other objects.

♦   All security-related events must be audited and the auditing data must be restricted to all but authorized users.

♦   The system must protect itself from external interference or tampering, such as modifications to the running system or to system files stored on disk.

Note that the Orange Book criteria are for a stand-alone system (a node on a network) and that the National Computer Security Center is evaluating the Windows NT operating system for networking functions.

The Windows NT Server C2 implementation is entirely software-based and does not require additional hardware. Other operating systems require hardware components that intercept and route all file and server requests for security. Windows NT Server and Windows NT Workstation were designed from the ground up to be C2 secure. Some of Windows NT Server features are so secure (identification and authentication, and the ability to separate a user from his/her functions) that they meet higher-level B2 security requirements.

Additional security features in Windows NT Server include:

♦   Administrator control of access rights to resources, including files, folders, servers, printers, and applications

♦   User account management and account lock outs

♦   User ownership of resources and the ability to define access to those resources

♦ Password expirations, password complexity rules, and system-level encryption of passwords to prevent unauthorized discovery of a user's password through wire "sniffing"

These password features are a primary focus of this appendix. The logon process is one of the most important security considerations in any operating system. Gaining valid account passwords is the biggest goal of most hackers. Protecting those passwords is what Windows NT is best at.

Windows NT Security Model

The security model for Windows NT is discussed in Chapter 5. The security subsystem consists of the following components:

♦ *Logon processes*, which are provided by Winlogon. These processes provide the initial interactive logon and display the Logon dialog box.

♦ *Local Security Authority* (LSA), which ensures that the user has permission to access the system. It generates access tokens, manages the local security policy, and provides interactive user authentication services. Auditing is also handled by this component.

♦ *Security Account Manager* (SAM), which maintains the user accounts database and validates users for LSA.

♦ *Security Reference Monitor* (SRM), which is the Kernel level process that checks access permissions and enforces access validations and audit policies defined by LSA.

During the logon sequence, the Local Security Authority works in concert with the Security Accounts Manager (SAM) on the local computer or for the domain or trusted domain to authenticate the user's name and password.

Another component that I'll discuss in this appendix is Netlogon, which handles the logon between a client computer and a server.

Logon and Authentication

First, let's discuss where you are likely to get confused when trying to understand the Windows NT logon procedure. Microsoft's documentation must be read very carefully because their terminology makes it easy to assume a certain understanding of the process. Hopefully, the information presented here is a little more understandable. This is a complex topic because there are many variables.

A

NOTE: For the most part, this discussion describes logon procedures for Windows NT Server and Windows NT Workstation computers. There is some variation in the background procedure when you log on to Windows 95 and Windows for Workgroups computers.

Types of Logon and Authentication

Be aware that there are two types of logon: *interactive* and *remote*. Interactive logon is what happens when you first log on to a computer. A process verifies that you are who you say you are based on the credentials (i.e., username and password) you typed in the Logon dialog box. Once validated, your credentials are kept on hand because they might be required again for a remote logon authentication.

NOTE: In the next paragraph, the local computer is the computer you are working at (i.e., the one you logged on to) and the remote computer is a computer in the local domain or a trusted domain with a shared resource like a folder or printer that you want to access.

A remote logon occurs when you attempt to access some shared resources like a folder or printer after you logged on using the interactive logon process. Remote logon is really a process of "reverifying" that you are an authentic user. When the remote computer is satisfied that you are authentic, it returns a user ID that you can use for any future requests for service. These steps are described later in this appendix.

Now, assume you attempt to access a computer in another domain, which cannot authenticate you. The remote computer must send your credentials to a domain controller in its domain and that domain controller asks a domain controller in your domain to authenticate you. This process is like getting cash from a foreign bank. The bank will check with your bank to verify that you are a customer and that you have funds.

Local and Domain Logon

It is important to understand where the user account database is stored that allows users to log on to a computer or network. The database is either stored on a local computer (i.e., the computer you are physically sitting at when you log on), or on a domain controller. Once again, the following discussion assumes you are logging on at a Windows NT computer rather than a Windows 95 computer, and that you are using domain networking rather than workgroup networking.

When you log on, you can choose to log on to an account on the local computer, log on to an account on the local domain, or log on to an account on some remote domain. The latter is usually called "logging on to a trusted domain." Ideally, all these accounts should be the same, but that is often not the case if different networks have been joined together.

If you log on to the local computer, your credentials are verified against a user account database stored on that computer. A problem occurs if you then try to access a resource on the network, because you might need to log on again and have your credentials verified against the user account database on a domain controller. This is really just an inconvenience.

This gets more confusing (I'm not trying to confuse you, just make you aware of the potential variations). Assume you log on to the workstation, then try to open a shared resource on a server. Also assume that you have an account on the local computer and an account in the domain with the same name but a different password. In this case, your original username and password are passed through to the server, but an "Access is denied" message appears because the passwords are different. While the passwords could be synchronized, it is better to have one account on the domain controller and always log on to the domain, rather than have separate accounts on different machines.

A

The same also applies if your network consists of multiple domains. Assume that you need to access resources in other domains. One way to accomplish this is to have a separate user account in each domain, then log in to each account when you need to access the domain. However, this can cause confusion and problems. It is better to have one account in one domain, then set up a trust relationship that allows your account to access resources in a trusting domain. Then you can log on once with one password.

NOTE: A service called Netlogon handles network logons. To access another computer using this service, your computer must be running the Workstation service, and you must have the "Access This Computer from Network" right on the target server.

Logon Sequence Details

When you press CTRL-ALT-DEL at a Windows NT computer, the Logon dialog box appears with the Username, Password, and Domain text entry fields.

What you put in the Domain field will make a big difference to what happens during the logon process, as pictured in Figure A-1.

The user's logon information can be authenticated in a user account database on the local computer, on the home domain controller, or on a domain controller in a trusted domain. To reiterate:

1. If the user types a local Windows NT Workstation name to log on locally, the local user account database is used to validate the user.

2. If the user types a home domain name, the SAM on a home domain controller validates the user in its user account database.

3. If the user types a remote domain name to log on to another trusted domain, the logon request is *passed through* to a domain controller on the trusted domain, where the user can be authenticated.

The steps in the initial logon process are to take the credentials (username, password, domain name) you typed in the Logon dialog box and authenticate you. The security system on the computer (remember, it's

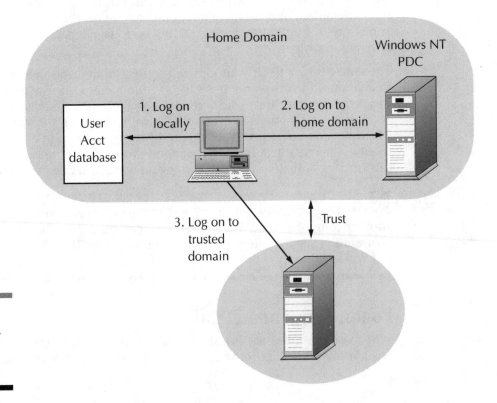

Types of logon in the Windows NT environment

Figure A-1.

called the Local Security Authority) calls up an *authentication package* (technically, the MSV1_0, discussed later under "Authentication Procedure"). The authentication package checks your credentials in the user account database by interacting with the Security Accounts Manager (SAM). If you specified a domain logon, this last step takes place over the network at a domain controller.

If your credentials are authentic, they are cached for later use and an *access token* is created to identify you for all subsequent requests for resources. The access token contains your *security identifier* (SID), group IDs, and user rights.

As described in Chapter 5 under "Discretionary Access Controls," the security system determines the access to a resource by matching the user's requested access with the access permissions stored in the ACL for the resource. The user ID determines which access token is used to compare against the ACL for the resource. If a match is found and the user (or group containing the user) has not been specifically denied access, then the requested access is granted.

Remote Logon and Access

A

When a user needs to access a resource on a remote server, the server must authenticate the user or have some other computer authenticate the user for it. This process that a computer uses to authenticate a remote user is pictured in Figure A-2. The components that are used for this authentication process are pictured in Figure A-3.

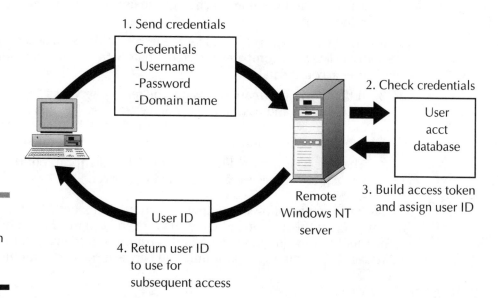

1. Send credentials

Credentials
-Username
-Password
-Domain name

2. Check credentials

User acct database

3. Build access token and assign user ID

Remote Windows NT server

User ID

4. Return user ID to use for subsequent access

The remote logon and authentication process

Figure A-2.

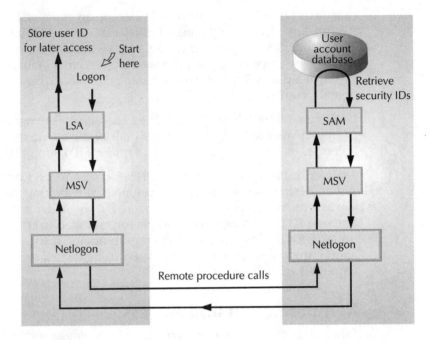

The
components
used for
remote
authentication
Figure A-3.

The remote logon process assumes the user has already logged on to a local Windows NT Workstation computer.

1. The credentials that are cached in the user's computer are passed to the remote server.

2. On the remote server, the LSA requests that the SAM authenticate the user. The SAM compares the credentials with user information in the user account database.

3. If the logon information is valid, the remote server's LSA builds an access token and passes it to the Server service. The Server service then creates a user ID for the client; this user ID will be used to identify all subsequent communication between the client and the server.

4. The user ID is returned to the client so the client can put the ID in any subsequent requests that it sends to the server.

The Server service allows a computer to entertain requests from a client computer on the network. The user ID is referenced in all requests made by the client to the remote server, and it is packaged into every SMB (Server Message Block) message communicated between the two computers. SMB is the application-level file sharing protocol used by Windows computers. In the Windows graphical user interface, SMB setup commands are initiated when you select remote resources in the Network Neighborhood. At the DOS level, SMB commands are executed with the NET command. SMB messages are embedded in transport-level network protocols like NetBEUI or TCP/IP.

Looking at the session setup process in more detail, assume that a Windows NT client executes the following command:

NET USE *x*: *servername**sharename*

where *x* is a drive letter to map, *servername* is the name of the server to use, and *sharename* is the name of a shared folder on that server. The NET USE command initiates a Session Setup SMB that contains the username, password, and logon domain name for the user. The following may occur:

♦   If the specified domain is the same as the home domain, then the logon process pictured in Figure A-4 takes place.

♦   If the user specifies a different domain that is trusted, the server will do pass-through authentication and send the user's logon request information to a domain controller in the trusted domain. In this case, a logon process similar to that pictured in Figure A-4 is performed. However, there are some slight differences. If the account is found in the local database and it is a *local account*, then the Guest account must also be enabled, otherwise the logon fails. If the account is a *global account*, the specified password must match. If an account is not found, Guest permissions are tested on the user's home domain controller (not the domain controller remote to the user). If Guest is enabled, the user gets the same guest privileges in the remote domain.

♦   Another logon scenario is that the domain specified by the user is unknown. In other words, the user's local domain controller did not recognize the domain specified by the user as a trusted domain. In this case, the user's account is checked in the local user account database following the procedures pictured in Figure A-4.

♦   Still another scenario is similar to the preceding one, except that the user does not specify any domain (the Domain field in the Logon box is left blank). In this case, the server treats the logon as a local network logon following the procedure pictured in Figure A-4. However, if an account is not found in the local user account database, then the server asks servers in each of the domains that it trusts if they have an account for the user. The first trusted server to reply is sent a request to perform pass-through authentication for the client. In addition, the Guest account must be enabled for local accounts, and a global account requires a password.

A

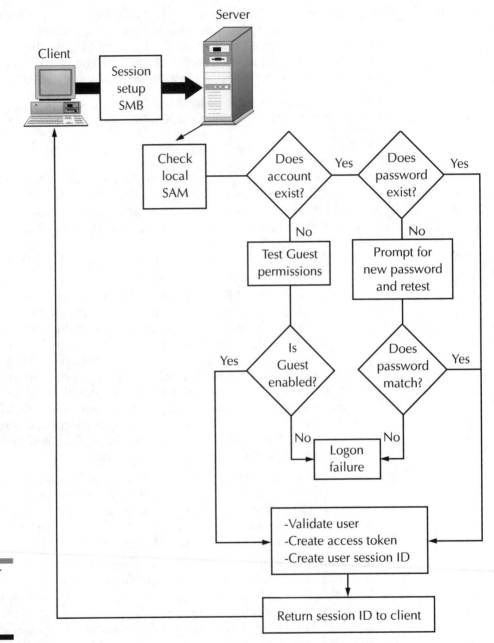

Flowchart for
the logon
process
Figure A-4.

Password Security and Authentication Procedures

The Security Accounts Manager (SAM) stores information about users in the user account database. The actual database is part of the Registry and is stored in the *systemroot*\System32\CONFIG directory. The information in these files is stored in a highly encrypted form to prevent attacks. In addition, when a user logs on, the passwords typed in the Logon dialog box are encrypted before they are transmitted across the line to prevent eavesdroppers from capturing an easily discernible password. The encryption schemes and authentication processes are discussed here.

The encrypted password sent from the client is received by the LSA and sent to the SAM for validation. The SAM compares the encrypted user password with the encrypted password in the user account database. The real password is never exposed in this process. In fact, the password is sent in a double-encrypted form, as described later, which virtually ensures that no one can crack it.

The SAM Database

The SAM database may store two passwords for each user if a LAN Manager server is present on the network. One of those passwords is a LAN Manager-compatible password and one is a Windows NT password:

LAN Manager Password   This password is compatible with passwords used by the LAN Manager. It is based on the standard OEM character set, is not case sensitive, and can be up to 14 characters long.

Windows NT Password   This password is based on the Unicode character set, is case sensitive, and can be up to 128 characters long.

Now for the encryption part. Each password is double-encrypted in the SAM database. The first encryption is a one-way function (OWF) version of the clear text password. This password is then encrypted again to make it even more obscure. One-way encrypted passwords are generally considered non-decryptable. The trick to validating a client is to compare his encrypted password with the encrypted password in the SAM database. You don't need to decrypt (to expose the original passwords) in order to make this validation.

In fact, the SAM database is never decrypted. Not even the SAM itself can decrypt passwords in the database. This prevents someone from writing a

A

program that uses SAM APIs to read encrypted passwords out of the database. Such a program could be used to stage a *dictionary attack* on the SAM database. A dictionary attack is where you encrypt an entire dictionary and compare the encrypted dictionary to the database to see if any patterns match.

Authentication Procedure

When a user attempts to log on to a server, the LSA handles user authentication by calling the *MSV1_0 authentication package*. The MSV packages can log a user on to the local machine (assuming Windows NT), to the home domain, or to another trusted domain. These types of logons were discussed previously under "Remote Logon and Access;" now, however, we look at the actual authentication process. Note in this discussion that passwords are encrypted to either a LAN Manager OWF or a Windows NT OWF, depending on the local environment.

When users are logging on to the machine that can directly authenticate them, the clear text password typed at the keyboard is converted into a LAN Manager OWF password and/or Windows NT OWF password. This OWF password is then compared to the OWF password that is stored in the local SAM database.

If the user is logging on to a server in the domain, a different procedure is used to challenge the user and hide the password as it traverses the network. This is pictured in Figure A-5.

1. The user attempts to log on.
2. The server issues a 16-byte challenge (or "nonce").
3. The nonce is encrypted with the user's password, which has already been encrypted as a one-way function (OWF) password. This double-encryption further protects the password from snooping.
4. This information is returned to the server as a response.
5. In a separate process, the server gets a copy of the nonce that was sent to the user and the user's OWF password from the SAM database. It then encrypts these two items using a process similar to what took place at the client's workstation in step 3.
6. The server compares its calculated Challenge-Response with the Challenge-Response received from the client.

If the two compare, the user is authenticated and his associated account security IDs (SIDs) are retrieved, along with the SIDs of global groups the user belongs to.

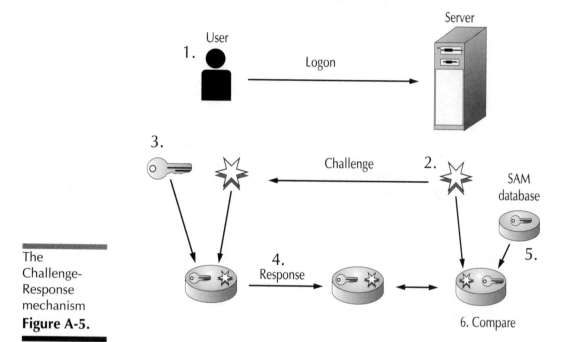

The
Challenge-
Response
mechanism
Figure A-5.

A

When a user is successfully validated on a system, a new process is created in which the user can run the Program Manager or the Explorer shell (in Windows NT 4.0). The user's token is attached to the process, just as it is attached to every other process that the user runs. If the user opens a file or accesses a network resource, the token is given to the file system that manages that resource. For example, if the file system is NTFS, it can compare the security IDs in the token with the security IDs in the Access control list for the file that the user wants to open. If there are appropriate matches between the lists, the user is granted access.

CAUTION: All of these logon procedures go a long way to ensure that the user is valid, but once the user is logged on, information is sent in the clear between clients and servers. You must use encryption to protect data transmissions. For remote users, the PPTP protocol discussed in Chapter 14 is a good idea. Also, any TCP/IP user sessions can be hijacked after authentication. See "Sniffing the Network" in Chapter 17.

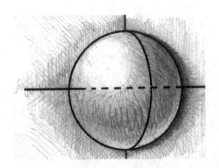

APPENDIX B

Cryptography and Private Communication

Encryption is the transformation of data into an unreadable form using a key value. The key is then a decoder that can be used to decrypt the data. Encryption is commonly used to protect information stored on disk that is potentially vulnerable to data thieves or to protect data transmission over insecure communication channels. Here's a roundup of where and how cryptography is often used. I list these examples so you can differentiate between encryption of local information, such as files on a disk, and encryption of information that is transmitted.

♦ Passwords that are transmitted during a logon

♦ Password files stored on the disk of a logon server (used to validate a password sent by a user)

♦ Boot records and file tables (to hide disk partitions and file locations, as described under "PC/DACS for Windows 95" in Chapter 12)

♦ Sensitive files stored on disk that are vulnerable to theft

♦ Communication sessions

♦ Digital envelopes to hide and protect the contents of e-mail

♦ Digital signatures for authenticating messages and business transactions

♦ Certification services for validating users on public networks

Cryptography hides data from prying eyes. That's the bottom line. The process involves *encryption* (hiding data) and *decryption* (unhiding data). These processes depend on two important things: the *key* and an *algorithm* (encryption/decryption mechanism).

To take a very simplistic example, assume you encrypt a message by converting every letter to a letter that is five characters away from it in the alphabet. So the letter A becomes F, for example. In this case, the *algorithm* is the process of switching characters such as A to F and the *key* is 5. You could change the key to 4 or 6 or some other number and still use the same algorithm. The text you encrypt is called the *input* and the encrypted text is called the *output*.

The key allows someone with the same encryption algorithm to decrypt the message. But in some cases, decryption is not necessary. For example, when you log on to a Windows NT computer, your encrypted password is compared with an encrypted form of the password that is already stored in a password file on the logon server. It is the encrypted values that are compared, so no decryption takes place.

Cryptographic algorithms are what people like Ron Rivest of RSA Data Security create (and what make them famous). The stronger the algorithm, the longer it will stand up to attack and protect the data that is encrypted.

As you'll see, schemes developed just a few years ago are not holding up to crackers who break keys using networks of computers.

As outlined in the previous list, encryption is used to hide both information that is stored and information that is transmitted. This is where the discussion diverges. Cryptographic techniques for local information storage are discussed later in this Appendix under "Cryptographic Techniques." The next section discusses how cryptography is used in transaction environments and combined with various techniques to provide secure communications, privacy, authentication, and verification of public networks.

 NOTE: This appendix makes frequent reference to a very informative paper called "*Frequently Asked Questions About Today's Cryptography*." The paper is available at RSA Laboratory's Web site at **www.rsa.com**. This paper is an encyclopedic work that should provide you with just about everything you need to know about cryptography.

Securing Private Communications

Assume two people want to exchange private messages over an insecure system like the Internet. They choose an encryption method that will make the messages unreadable to any person who happens to capture the transmissions. The sender encrypts the message using an encryption key. The receiver must have this key to decrypt the message. Now, the basic problem: How does the sender get the key to the receiver so she can decrypt the message? One method is to just call the person on the phone, but what if the phone line is tapped? If you work on top-secret projects or have information that competitors want, line taps are a big concern. Another method is to send the key in a separate e-mail message or via courier, but what if that message is intercepted along the way? It happens.

Traditionally, both the sender and receiver have already agreed on a key and have established some trust. For example, before leaving port, the captain of a submarine gets a decoder book that will unscramble encrypted radio messages from home port. This is *symmetric cryptography* (both parties know the same secret key). It is often referred to as just *secret key cryptography*. DES (Digital Encrypt Standard) is the usual encryption method and is described later under "Cryptographic Techniques."

But it is not always the case that both parties in a message exchange know and/or trust each other and have exchanged any keys in advance. For example, to ensure safe credit card purchases at your Web site, you will need to use encryption and exchange keys, and that needs to be done in a safe way with people you've never done business with.

To resolve these problems, Whitfield Diffie and Martin Hellman developed *asymmetric public key* cryptography in the mid-1970s. Basically, anybody who wants to encrypt and send messages to someone else generates a pair of security keys. One key is kept private and the other is put in a public place. If someone wants to send you a private message, they obtain your public key, encrypt the message with it, then send you the message. Only your private key can decrypt the message. Someone who intercepts the message cannot decrypt it with the generally available public key.

Figure B-1 illustrates public-key cryptography in action. Sue and Joe want to exchange secure messages. Both Sue and Joe are on the same company network and so have easy access to a security server where they can store their public keys.

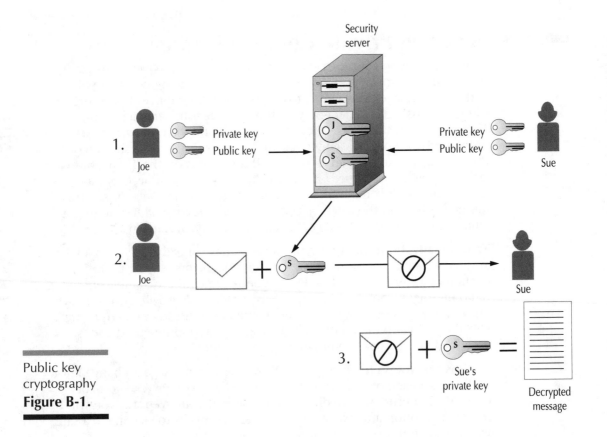

Public key
cryptography
Figure B-1.

1. Sue and Joe, and everybody else in the company, generate a set of keys and place the public version of that key on a security server.

2. When Joe wants to send a secure message to Sue, he obtains Sue's public key from the security server, encrypts the message with it, and sends it to Sue.

3. Sue receives the message and decrypts it with her private key.

The public key scheme solves the problem of passing keys to other parties who need to decrypt your messages. In fact, it allows any person to encrypt a message and send it to another person without any prior exchange or agreement. It is not even necessary that the parties know each other, be part of the same organization, or be connected to the same network. All that is required is that both parties have a way to exchange public keys.

This is where *key management* comes into the picture. Key management is all about making public keys available for general use. If someone wants to send you a message, he needs to get a copy of your public key. On a private network, he might get it in a shared directory on a key management server that holds keys for everyone in the organization. On the Internet, *certification authorities* (CAs) like VeriSign (**www.verisign.com**), Commerce Net (**www.commerce.net**), and even the U.S. Postal Service (**www.usps.gov**) provide key management. An important role of the CA is to guarantee to other people that your public key is authentic, just as the banking system verifies credit cards.

In general, public key cryptography is convenient. In addition, it can provide some interesting solutions to problems of authentication and electronic commerce, in which people buy and sell using electronic money.

B

Keep in mind that public key cryptography is suited for open environments where people need to exchange private information without it being compromised. However, the other encryption scheme—secret key cryptography (direct encryption with a single key)—is a better choice for personal/local encryption, such as hiding passwords, encrypting information stored on disk, and transmitting information to a branch office over a pre-existing secure channel.

Secret key cryptography is suited for environments where keys can be exchanged safely and easily. For example, to set up a secure channel to a branch office, you purchase two encrypting routers, program them with the same encryption keys, then install one of the routers at the branch office by delivering it there yourself. In another example, you give a coworker the key required to access encrypted data on disk. Secret key cryptography is the obvious choice in a single-user environment where you want to encrypt files on your own computer.

Digital Envelopes

In practice, public key cryptography is combined with a secret key cryptography system, such as DES, to create *digital envelopes*. A digital envelope provides a way to encrypt a secret key in a message so you can send the key with the message to another person. Here's how a digital envelope is created:

1. Joe want to send a message to Sue, so he encrypts the message with DES (secret key) using an appropriate key.

2. Joe then encrypts the DES key with Sue's public key. The combination of the DES-encrypted message and the public key encrypted DES key form a digital envelope.

3. Joe sends the digital envelope to Sue, who decrypts the DES key with her own private key and then uses the DES key to decrypt the message contents.

This technique combines public key cryptography with secret key cryptography to give you the best of both worlds. You get the secure exchange capabilities of public key systems and the speed advantages of secret key systems.

Digital Signatures and Message Integrity

Another aspect of public keys is their ability to verify messages. If you're a stockbroker and you receive a message from a client to buy 1,000 shares of Microsoft, you probably want some verification that the message is valid and a way to ensure that the sender cannot disavow knowledge of the message. This is where *digital signatures* and *digital timestamps* come into play. A digital signature "binds" a document (such as a purchase order) with a key owned by the person who is placing the order. The encrypted message is unique to that user and can be used to prove that the message actually came from the user. A digital timestamp "binds" the time to a document to verify when it was created. Digital signatures and timestamps are critical to doing business over computer communication systems.

NOTE: The following examples may lead you to believe that signing and verification are done manually. In fact, software designers are building programs that make all of these procedures fairly automatic. Microsoft's CryptoAPI, discussed later in this appendix and in Chapter 21, provides all the functions needed to build security-enabled applications.

Business transactions require integrity for three reasons:

- So the sender cannot deny having sent a message and the recipient cannot deny having received it
- So the sender can be assured that the recipient receives the message exactly as sent, without any alterations
- So the recipient can be assured that the message has not been changed by someone else

Digital signatures provide a way of verifying that documents originate from the person who sent the document and that the document has not been altered since leaving the sender. Let's look at the steps involved if Joe wants to send a digitally signed message to Sue:

1. Joe's computer performs a computation that produces a digital signature that is unique for the message he is sending. Technically, a *hash function* (described later) is used to create a *message digest,* which serves as a "digital fingerprint" of the message.

2. Joe then uses his private key to encrypt the message digest, thus creating a *digital signature.* The fact that Joe uses his private key is significant. Doing this allows Sue to use Joe's public key to unlock the message digest.

3. The digital signature is attached to the message, and Joe sends the message to Sue. For privacy, he can encrypt the entire package.

4. Upon receipt of the message, Sue decrypts the digital signature with Joe's public key to recover the message digest. Sue then hashes the message she received to produce her own message digest and compares it to the message digest from Joe.

If there is any difference in the message digests, the authenticity of the message is questionable. It may have been altered in transit, for example. Once Sue has validated Joe's message, she can create a digitally signed confirmation message using the same techniques and send that to Joe.

The confirmation receipt is a critical part of the message exchange, especially if a transaction is taking place. It contains Joe's original digital signature plus Sue's digital signature. Joe can verify Sue's digital signature in the message by using her public key and verify his own digital signature in the receipt with his private key. Fortunately, most of this is handled automatically by software applications. If Joe does not receive a receipt from Sue, he can assume the message exchange was unsuccessful or compromised and abort any transactions that might be taking place.

B

NOTE: Digital time stamps can be added to time-sensitive messages by a trusted digital time-stamping service (DTS). Such services are available from Bellcore and others.

The RSA Public Key Cryptosystem

The ability of public key schemes to provide both message encryption and digital signatures is a boon to communication over digital networks. The strength of the encryption becomes the defining factor for ensuring privacy. The size of the key ensures that encrypted information will be secure for a long time.

If you're a real crypto-head, you might be wondering how the public and the private keys are generated in the RSA Cryptosystem. First, the RSA system is based on taking two large prime numbers and multiplying them to produce a key. From this, it follows that factoring is the process of attempting to crack the key by discovering the original prime numbers. Recall that a factor is one of two or more quantities that divide a given quantity without a remainder (that is, 2 and 3 are factors of 6).

The RSA paper *Frequently Asked Questions About Today's Cryptography* describes RSA public key cryptography as follows:

> Take two large primes, p and q, and find their product $n = pq$; n is called the modulus. Choose a number, e, less than n and relatively prime to $(p-1)(q-1)$, which means that e and $(p-1)(q-1)$ have no common factors except 1. Find another number, d, such that $(ed - 1)$ is divisible by $(p-1)(q-1)$. The values e and d are called the public and private exponents, respectively. The public key is the pair (n,e); the private key is (n,d). The factors p and q may be kept with the private key, or destroyed. It is difficult (presumably) to obtain the private key d from the public key (n,e). If one could factor n into p and q, however, then one could obtain the private key d. Thus the security of RSA is related to the assumption that factoring is difficult. An easy factoring method or some other feasible attack would "break" RSA.

Note the third to the last sentence, "If one could factor n into p and q, however, then one could obtain the private key d." *Factoring* is the process of breaking the keys, as discussed later.

The size of the key depends on the security requirements, with larger keys requiring more processing time. Some work done by A.M. Odlyzko in 1995* showed that a 512-bit RSA key could be factored for less than $1,000,000 with eight months of effort by 1997. According to the RSA paper:

*"The Future of Integer Factorization," *CryptoBytes*, May 12, 1995

It is believed that 512-bit keys no longer provide sufficient security with the advent of new factoring algorithms and distributed computing. Such keys should not be used after 1997 or 1998. The RSA Laboratories recommended key sizes are now 768 bits for personal use, 1,024 bits for corporate use, and 2,048 bits for extremely valuable keys like the key pair of a certifying authority...A 768-bit key is expected to be secure until at least the year 2004.

Individual user keys should expire after a period of two years to maintain a level of security. When the keys expire, the user should generate new keys that are five digits longer than the old keys to accommodate advances in key-cracking algorithms. RSA also notes that "Although the security of any individual key is still strong, with some factoring (cracking) methods there is always a small chance that the attacker may get lucky and factor some key quickly."

Factoring and Other Attacks

A cryptanalyst is a person who analyzes and attacks a cipher. In most cases, attacks require time, money, and coordination of resources. While teenagers might have a lot of time on their hands, it is unlikely that they will have the equipment or resources to break any of the current encryption schemes. On the other hand, foreign governments might have such resources. The typical dollar amount quoted for such attacks is more than $1,000,000. Still, the threat exists.

Note the following from the RSA paper:

B

All practical public key cryptosystems are based on functions that are believed to be one-way, but no function has been proven to be so. This means that it is theoretically possible that an algorithm will be discovered that can compute the inverse function easily without a trap door (key). This development would render any cryptosystem based on that one-way function insecure and useless. On the other hand, further research in theoretical computer science may result in concrete lower bounds on the difficulty of inverting certain functions, and this would be a landmark event with significant positive ramifications for cryptography.

Factoring is the technique that cryptanalysts use to split the modulus into the original integers that were multiplied together to obtain it. Prime factorization requires splitting an integer into factors that are prime numbers. The strength of the public key system relies on the fact that multiplying two prime integers together is easy, but factoring the product is difficult (at least to date). Factoring an RSA modulus would allow an attacker to figure out the private key and decrypt messages and forge signatures. Because factoring large numbers takes more time than factoring small numbers, the size of the modulus determines how resistant to attack it is. RSA notes that "there remains a possibility that a quick and easy factoring method might be discovered, although factoring researchers consider this possibility remote."

Factoring has become easier because of more powerful computer hardware and because better factoring algorithms have been developed. At the same time, improvements in hardware actually make RSA more secure. Users can simply choose much larger keys (without degrading performance) that make factoring even more difficult. RSA notes that the key sizes used today may not be appropriate in the future if you want to protect today's information from future attacks. This is an important consideration if you are archiving information for long-term storage.

Cryptographic Techniques

The preceding sections described the ways that encryption is put to use on public networks—but what are the methods for actually encrypting data? This section will describe some of these methods, including the ones that apply to the Windows NT environment, but there is no way to cover all the possible encryption and security techniques in this book. Entire books are written on the subject. The RSA paper referred to throughout this appendix is a 200-page synopsis!

One-Way Functions (OWFs) and Trap Doors

One of the basic encryption techniques is a *one-way function* (OWF). For performance and security reasons, this function is easy to perform in one direction—that is, to encrypt—but difficult to perform in the other direction—that is, to decrypt. The terminology for describing these processes is *forward function* (encrypt) and *inverse function* (decrypt).

The forward encryption process is usually easy and may take only a few seconds, but the reverse decryption process is difficult and may take years, depending on the algorithm used to decrypt the message and the size of the key. Windows NT uses the OWF to encrypt passwords because the process is speedy but difficult to break. As mentioned earlier, there is no need to ever decrypt the password once it is encrypted because all comparisons are done on the encrypted form. The difficulty of running OWF in the opposite direction significantly stalls any would-be crackers from discovering the password by reversing the encryption.

A trap door one-way function is a one-way function where the decryption is easy because a key (the trap door) has been generated for that purpose. The RSA public key cryptosystems are based on trap door one-way functions:

♦ The public key provides the forward encryption mechanism. It can be used to make messages private or to validate digital signatures.

♦ The private key provides a reverse trap door function. It can be used to unlock private messages and to create digital signatures.

Ciphers and Hash Algorithms

Secret key cryptography is the process of encrypting data by using a single key, as opposed to the dual key (public/private key) methods used in public key cryptography. There are block and stream ciphers as well as hash functions.

Block Cipher   A block cipher is a transformation of plain text into ciphertext using a secret key. The ciphertext can be decrypted by using the secret key to apply the reverse transformation. The plain text is transformed in blocks of 64 bits in size (thus the name). An iterated block cipher consists of several rounds in which the original plain text is transformed using subkeys. The subkeys are derived from the original user-supplied secret key. Increasing the number of rounds improves security.

Stream Cipher   A stream cipher works at the bit level rather than on blocks of data and is generally much faster than a block cipher. Most importantly, applying the same key to the same text two different times will result in different ciphertext. In contrast, a block cipher will produce the same ciphertext when the same key is used.

B

Data compression can be used with encryption to some advantage because it removes redundant character strings in data. The compressed file has a uniform distribution of characters that impedes some cracking techniques. Note that compression must be done before the data is encrypted, not after.

Data Encryption Standard (DES)

DES is the official encryption standard of the U.S. government. It is a block cipher symmetric cryptosystem originally developed at IBM. Since its introduction, DES has been scrutinized extensively. It is widely used throughout the world. It is also often used in single-user environments for encrypting files on disk. Microsoft uses DES for message encryption in Microsoft Exchange and to provide encrypted authentication for logons to Windows NT servers.

DES has a 64-bit block size and uses a 56-bit key to encrypt data. The original design specified a hardware implementation. It has been shown to be very difficult to crack. Brute force methods were used to do an exhaustive search of the key space, but this type of approach is usually impractical for most crackers. Triple-encryption DES is available that is far more secure than plain DES.

To use DES safely, you should change your keys often. In addition, if a DES key must be exchanged with someone, use public key encryption methods in which you encrypt the DES key with the recipient's public key and the recipient decrypts the key with her private key.

When using DES to encrypt files on hard disks, it is often impractical to change the DES keys often. There is also the possibility of forgetting keys used to encrypt files after a long period of time. To solve this problem, create a list of DES keys that are used to encrypt files, then encrypt the list with a master DES key.

DES Alternatives

There are a number of alternative cipher algorithms that have been designed to possibly replace DES. In some cases, algorithms were found to be prone to attack. Some of the more encouraging ciphers are described here.

IDEA (International Data Encryption Algorithm)   This is a 64-bit block cipher with a 128-bit key that uses eight rounds of computation. It is designed for both software and hardware implementations and its speed in software is similar to DES. A principal design goal was to guard against specific types of attacks that were previously staged against DES. IDEA is generally considered secure.

SAFER (Secure And Fast Encryption Routine)   This is a non-proprietary block cipher developed in 1993 for Cylink Corporation. It implements a 64-bit block size, key sizes up to 64-bits, and up to ten rounds of computation. The cipher is designed to work in smartcards with limited processing power.

Blowfish   This is a 64-bit cipher with variable length keys of up to 4,448 bits. The key is used to generate several subkey arrays. The cipher was designed for 32-bit machines, but some attacks were successfully staged against it, although it is still considered secure because the types of attacks used were impractical for most anyone to perform.

Skipjack   This algorithm is part of the U.S. government's Capstone project and it is the encryption algorithm contained in the Clipper chip. It was designed by the National Security Agency. Skipjack uses an 80-bit key and

32 rounds of computation, whereas DES uses a 56-bit key and 16 rounds. Note that Skipjack is available in hardware only from government-authorized manufacturers, and its details are classified.

Ron Rivest of RSA Data Security created the following algorithms as drop-in replacements for DES. They all have a variable key size, allowing adjustments of security levels when necessary. All three algorithms are faster than DES in software. Most importantly, RC2 and RC4 have the advantage of special U.S. Government status whereby export approval is simplified and expedited if the key size is limited to 40 bits. RC2 and RC4 have been widely used by developers who want to export their products; DES is almost never approved for export.

RC2   This is a block cipher (64 bits) that is about two to three times faster than DES in software. The algorithm is confidential and proprietary to RSA Data Security. RC2 can be used in the same modes as DES. As mentioned, the export approval process is easier for RC2, but to qualify, RC2 (and RC4) must limit key sizes to 40 bits (56 bits is allowed for foreign subsidiaries and overseas offices of United States companies). An additional string (40 to 88 bits long) called a *salt* can be used to thwart attackers who try to precompute a large look-up table of possible encryptions. The salt is appended to the encryption key, and this lengthened key is used to encrypt the message; the salt is then sent, unencrypted, with the message.

RC4   This is a stream cipher with variable key size and byte-oriented operations. The algorithm is confidential and proprietary to RSA Data Security, although it has been scrutinized under conditions of non-disclosure by independent analysts and is considered secure.

B

RC5   This is a fast block cipher that allows custom parameters so you can vary the level of security and the efficiency of the cipher. You can vary the block size (32, 64, or 128), key size (from 0 bits to 2,048 bits), and the number of rounds used during encryption (from 0 to 255). According to RSA, the security of RC5 is provided by the heavy use of data-dependent rotations and the mixture of different operations. In particular, the use of data-dependent rotations helps defeat differential and linear cryptanalysis.

Hash Algorithm

A hash function is used to create a message digest that can be used for digital signature applications. As described earlier under "Digital Signatures and Message Integrity," you hash a message to produce the digest, then encrypt the digest with your private key. When the recipient receives the message, he hashes the message as well and compares the resulting digest with the decrypted digest you sent. If the digests match, the message is considered valid and unaltered.

Ron Rivest created three hash functions that are widely used: MD2, MD4, and MD5. All three algorithms take a message of arbitrary length and produce a 128-bit message digest.

MD2   This algorithm was developed in 1989 and was optimized for 8-bit machines (MD4 and MD5 were aimed at 32-bit machines). The message is first padded (null characters are added) so that its length in bytes is divisible by 16. A 16-byte checksum is then appended to the message, and the hash value is computed on this resulting message.

MD4   This algorithm was developed in 1990. The message is padded to ensure that its length in bits plus 448 is divisible by 512. A 64-bit binary representation of the original length of the message is then concatenated to the message. Three rounds of processing are used to create the hash. According to RSA, "Attacks on versions of MD4 with either the first or the last rounds missing were developed very quickly" and "Collisions for the full version of MD4 can be found in under a minute on a typical PC. Clearly, MD4 should now be considered broken."

MD5   This algorithm was developed in 1991. It is a more secure version of MD4 that consists of four distinct rounds.

The Microsoft CryptoAPI

Microsoft has developed the Cryptographic Application Program Interface (CryptoAPI) to make it easier for developers to create applications that contain encryption and digital signature functions while providing protection for the user's sensitive private key data. The CryptoAPI consists of modules called cryptographic service providers (CSPs). Each module performs some cryptographic services that developers can tap into. One CSP, the *Microsoft RSA Base Provider,* is bundled with the operating system.

The CryptoAPIs make it easy to implement security features in tasks and applications such as the following:

♦ Creation of key container for default user, along with a signature public/private key pair and a key exchange public/private key pair

♦ Applications that encrypt and decrypt files

♦ Applications that encrypt, sign, and verify messages and files

The Microsoft CryptoAPI is available for Microsoft's Internet Explorer, Windows NT 4.0, and Windows 95. Third-party vendors are using CryptoAPI to develop applications that use Windows NT as a platform for electronic commerce. The API can also be used to write token-based authentication and security applications and to provide an enterprise-wide public key infrastructure for encryption and digital signature services. In general, the CryptoAPIs will make cryptography more readily available on a worldwide scale. Refer to Chapter 21 for more information.

B

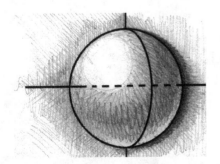

APPENDIX C

Viruses, Trojan Horses, and Other Threats

A *virus* is a computer program that infects other programs with copies of itself. It clones itself from disk to disk or from one system to the next over computer networks. A virus executes and does its damage when the program it has infected executes. Only code that executes can be infected with viruses. Previously, only executable files were at risk, but new viruses attack macros in programs like Microsoft Word and do their damage when the macro is executed.

The damage caused by viruses may be harmless, such as displaying a happy birthday message for the creator on the appropriate day. Perhaps the creator only wanted to know how far his virus could spread. Alternatively, the virus may do considerable damage by destroying boot records, file tables, and valuable data on disk. Virus prevention measures must be put into place before virus infections, otherwise your data is at risk.

This appendix provides general information about viruses and other destructive programs, and it provides specific information about virus attacks in the Windows NT environment. To maintain a protective stance against these threats, you must stay in contact with the organizations and vendors outlined in this section. Notice that only two antivirus software vendors are listed. Although others exist, I believe that you should consider using antivirus software from only the most popular and well-financed companies. Antivirus software must be updated constantly—in fact, almost daily. Symantec and McAfee have proven that they can maintain this effort.

National Computer Security Association (NCSA)   This organization of experts provides information about computer security. You'll find the latest information about viruses and how to manage the virus threat. Contact NCSA at their Web site (**www.ncsa.com**). You'll find topics such as "Virus Help," "Security Alerts," and "Virus Studies."

Computer Security Institute (CSI)   CSI is another organization that provides information about computer security, viruses, and other threats. Its Web site includes important late-breaking news about viruses. CSI posts papers and provides ongoing seminars related to security. Point your Web browser at **www.csi.com**.

Symantec Corporation   Symantec is the maker of the popular Norton Antivirus software. You can contact them directly at (800)-441-7234 or contact their Web site at **www.symantec.com**.

McAfee   This company has become the leader in virus detection and control. Their software can protect desktop systems, servers, and systems connected to the World Wide Web. Contact McAfee at (408)-988-3832 or go to **www.mcafee.com**. The company's NetShield for Windows NT Server is described later in this appendix.

Viruses and Other Threats

Now let's examine just a few of the virus classifications outlined by organizations such as NCSA and CSI.

Boot Sector Virus   This type of virus infects the master boot record of a computer by overwriting the original boot code and replacing it with infected boot code. A boot virus is spread to the hard disk when the system is booted with an infected floppy disk.

File-infecting Virus   This virus infects files on disk—usually executable files with the extension COM, EXE, or OVL. Operating system files are also targeted. Differences in file size usually indicate an infection. In some cases, the original program is often replaced with an infected program.

Polymorphic Virus   This type of virus changes its appearance to avoid detection by antivirus software. The virus encrypts itself with a special algorithm that changes every time an infection occurs. To find polymorphic viruses, antivirus software must use special scanning techniques.

Stealth Virus   This is a virus that attempts to hide itself from the operating system and antivirus software. Stealth viruses stay in memory to intercept attempts to use the operating system and hide changes made to file sizes. These viruses must be detected while they are in memory.

Multipart Virus   This type of virus infects boot sectors as well as executable files. Multipart viruses are a real problem because they use stealth and polymorphism to prevent detection.

Macro Virus   This is the newest breed of virus. Macro viruses are executable programs that attach themselves to documents created in Microsoft Word and Excel. When an unsuspecting user receives the document and executes a macro, the virus executes and does its damage.

The Microsoft Word macro virus, which has the official name *Winword.concept*, reproduces itself by traveling with documents that have auto-executing macros. These macros are written in Microsoft WordBasic. At the time of this writing, *Winword.concept* was the most reported virus on record. The reason for this is that more and more people access documents on the Internet that are viewed by Microsoft Word. It is a simple matter to set Word as the viewer for all files with the DOC extension. A solution to this problem is to use Word Viewer rather than the full working version of Word when viewing Internet documents. Word Viewer is available free from Microsoft's web site (**www.microsoft.com**).

Table C-1 outlines actual viruses and the damage that they can do to your system. This table was created as part of an NCSA and Dataquest study done in 1996. Note that the Encountered column shows the percent of respondents with more than 300 PCs who were hit at least once by the specified virus.

Virus name	Encountered	What it infects	Damages
Stoned	48%	Partitions, memory, floppy disk booting	Run-time, booting, file links
Jerusalem	37%	Memory, system files	Run-time, program files
Joshi (stealth)	6%	Memory, hard disk and floppy disk booting, partitions	Booting, run-time, data files
Cascade (self-encrypting)	5%	Memory, system files	Run-time, partition
4096 (stealth)	4%	Memory, system files	Run-time, data files, file links, partition
Sunday	4%	Memory, system files	Run-time, partition
Yankee Doodle	3%	Memory, system files	No damage, but plays a tune at 5 o'clock
Ping Pong	2%	Memory, hard disk and floppy disk booting	Run-time, booting
Dark Avenger	2%	Memory, system files	Run-time, file links, partition
Brain (Pakistani)	1%	Memory, floppy disks only	Booting

Well-Known Viruses, as Outlined by NCSA/Dataquest Study (Source: NCSA)
Table C-1.

Other Threats

Besides viruses, your systems are also vulnerable to other types of destructive programs that are not classified as viruses. These include *worms*, *Trojan Horses*, and *logic bombs*.

Worm   A worm is often mistaken for a virus. It is a single destructive program on a single system often planted by someone who has direct access to the system. Worms do not replicate themselves like viruses.

Trojan Horse   This is a program that may appear to be another program. An unsuspecting user who executes the program unleashes its destructive potential. A virus might be unleashed that starts to infect other files on the system or on other network computers. In some cases, a Trojan Horse is not destructive. Instead, it collects information, such as logon passwords, or copies sensitive files to another system on a network without the host user knowing what is happening. Once again, a Trojan Horse does not replicate itself in the same way as a virus, but is usually planted by someone who has access to a system.

A Trojan Horse program is especially dangerous because you often don't even know that it is running. You might continue working on your computer even while the program ships your files to another location. For example, assume you obtain a hypothetical program named DISKINFO from a coworker. The program may in fact provide you with disk information, but at the same time, it might also capture vital information and ship it to your coworker using electronic mail.

In early 1996, a Trojan Horse virus that masqueraded as the popular PKZIP file compression utility appeared on the Internet. Unsuspecting users who downloaded the phony file assumed they were getting an upgrade, but instead had their hard drives completely erased. The Trojan Horse is a downloadable file called PKZIP300.ZIP. The real PKZIP at the time the Trojan Horse appeared was version 2.04.

Logic Bomb   A logic bomb is basically a Trojan Horse with a timing device. It goes off at a certain time and does its damage, which might be to destroy data on a local hard drive or to release a virus. A disgruntled employee may create a bomb to go off after he has left the company. The creator may also hold an organization hostage, only turning the bomb off after a ransom has been paid. In some cases, the creator of a logic bomb is protecting her own interest. For example, a programmer may plant a bomb that disables a program she has created for a company if that company does not pay for the program.

How Infections Occur

A system becomes contaminated with a virus through file system activity. A contaminated file is either copied from a disk or downloaded from an online service, bulletin board, or the Internet. Employees may bring viruses into an organization on their portable computers or disks that they have brought from home.

When files are contaminated, they may increase in size, so it is relatively easy for a virus detection program to report such problems. However, so-called *stealth viruses* are able to spoof the pre-infected file size of a document so it appears that nothing has changed. Worse, *active stealth viruses* can actually fight back against virus detection programs by disabling their detection functions.

Still worse is the *polymorphic* or *mutation* virus, which changes its unique features upon replication. Virus detection programs rely on these unique features to quickly locate "known" viruses.

In almost all cases, it is easy to avoid viruses if one is careful to never copy files from unknown or untrusted sources. That is a particularly difficult strategy to maintain, however.

The Internet and World Wide Web have created a whole new way to spread viruses. It is now possible to execute programs while browsing the Web without actually copying a file to your system's disk. Java and Microsoft ActiveX modules are copied from a Web server to a client's memory space and executed. Although a number of precautions have been taken to prevent contamination or destruction, recent examples have shown that the systems are not completely safe.

Trojan Horse programs and worms are typically installed by people inside the company with specific intentions to capture data or do some damage to a system. The best protection is to lock up systems and carefully monitor the activities of employees, especially people who might be leaving the company or who are suspected of being malicious for some reason.

Detection and Prevention

A virus is often hard to detect. It may wait on your system before it executes. If you are vigilant, you may notice an increase in the size of files that are infected or notice unusual activity, such as an increase in system crashes, programs that don't work in the normal way, or files that are suddenly inaccessible.

You could monitor your system for telltale signs of virus activity, such as increased file sizes, changes in file timestamps, unusual disk activity, or an abrupt decrease in disk space. A better way is to install virus detection software that does this for you automatically.

Even after detecting and cleaning up a virus infection, there is still a good chance that the virus is lurking somewhere in your organization, ready to reinfect systems. If the virus is detectable, you need to check all workstations for its existence. You might need to check all floppy disks and other data sources for infections and in some cases, destroy floppy disks.

It may be necessary to reformat hard drives to remove some viruses. Before formatting, back up all the non-executable files to a preferred backup medium. Restore programs only from original disks, then restore the data files.

Virus Control Policies

Protecting your systems against virus attacks requires user training. Users must be aware of how viruses are spread and should avoid downloading files from online services, bulletin boards, and the Internet. If files are downloaded, they must be checked. Here are some general policies:

♦ Create education programs and post regular bulletins about virus problems.

♦ Never transfer files from unknown or untrusted sources unless an antivirus utility is available to scan the files.

♦ Set up "quarantine computers" that are isolated from other computers. Test new programs or open unknown documents on this system.

♦ Lock down computers to prevent malicious people from infecting systems or installing Trojan Horse programs.

♦ Use the Windows NT operating system because of its secure logon and authentication.

♦ Do not use dual-boot partitions. A virus in one partition may infect the other. These issues are discussed later under "Viruses in the Windows NT Environment."

Administrators should keep up with the latest virus information by reading weekly computer journals or joining organizations like the NCSA. Check the NCSA and CSI Web sites on a regular basis to get late-breaking news about new viruses.

Virus Detection Programs

There are a number of virus protection programs for desktop computers and for networks. As mentioned, use only programs from reputable vendors that have the resources to constantly track new viruses and provide you with upgrades that can detect and remove them. Virus detection software will scan disks, looking for files that have changed since the last virus detection scan.

Virus detectors will also attempt to detect known viruses that have infected files. A detection method is also used to detect known viruses in memory by checking their memory locations. On workstations, interrupts can be monitored to detect and stop system calls that may indicate virus activity. Another technique is to look for unique identifiers that indicate a virus. These methods are called *signature scanning*. In order for an antivirus program to detect the latest viruses, it must be periodically updated with the latest identifiers by the vendor. The downside is that signature scanning is only as good as the most recent signature file.

Some programs run as resident programs, continuously checking for viruses. These programs provide good protection, but may also slow your system down. A user might prefer to check for viruses as the need arises, such as before or after copying files from unknown sources or during and after an online session. To counteract these viruses, virus detection software must dynamically update its ability to detect virus signatures that constantly change.

McAfee NetShield

The NetShield program from McAfee provides an antivirus solution for network servers. It is available for both NetWare and Windows NT. The software is designed to minimize and manage the virus threat within networks without jeopardizing server operation. The Windows NT version is a 32-bit service that captures viruses in real-time as they are written to or read from the server, and can scan stored files either immediately or at scheduled intervals. The software has the following features:

♦ Predefined actions upon virus detection, such as logging, deletion, and isolation

♦ Notification of support personnel when a virus incident occurs by using e-mail, pagers, or network broadcasts

♦ Works in multiserver environments

♦ Uses Windows NT remote management services, such as server-to-client remote task distribution, scan launch, scan monitoring, and central event reporting

♦ Auto-update feature for immediate or scheduled updating via central shared directory or FTP

For additional information and pricing, contact McAfee at the phone number or Web site listed earlier in this appendix.

Viruses in the Windows NT Environment

The information in this section is adapted from "Understanding Virus Behavior in the Windows NT Environment," a white paper produced by Symantec, makers of the Norton antivirus software. It is designed to give you a "quick read." For the full paper, connect with the Symantec Web site at **www.symantec.com**. Note that a similar paper exists at the Alternative Computer Technology site (**www.icubed.com/virus/documents.html**).

For the purposes of this discussion, viruses are classed as follows:

♦ Master Boot Record (MBR) and boot record viruses on floppy disks and hard drives

♦ DOS and Windows 3.1 viruses in Windows NT DOS sessions

♦ Viruses that execute directly in Windows NT environment

Master Boot Record and Boot Record Viruses

In the Windows NT environment, all low-level disk access is handled by NT-specific software drivers and not the computer's ROM BIOS disk drivers. This is good because the NT drivers provide an effective defense against virus infection. However, when a system boots, the BIOS drivers are used for a very short period. A virus present in the MBR can become memory-resident or can trigger some activity such as altering data during the boot-up process. MBR viruses are obtained by booting off an infected floppy disk or by cross-infection from a DOS or Windows 95 partition.

Typically, the virus passes control to the system MBR, which in turn passes control to the Windows NT boot record. The rest of the Windows NT operating system loads, including protected-mode disk drivers, and the system is switched into protected mode. After NT boots, the protected-mode drivers protect the system, since the BIOS disk drivers and any viruses that hooked into them are no longer used.

Still, all components of the operating system that are read from disk before the protected-mode drivers are loaded have the potential of becoming corrupted and allowing the virus to do further damage during subsequent boots. A virus like *One-half* can make data unavailable to Windows NT by encrypting data during boot-up. The *Monkey* virus hides the partition table during booting so that Windows NT cannot identify the logical drives on the system.

Note that Windows NT does not have a DOS compatibility mode, which would allow disk requests to be sent to BIOS disk drivers that might be infected. Once Windows NT boots, MBR viruses cannot infect other floppy disks.

Boot record viruses are obtained in the same way as MBR viruses: while booting a system with an infected floppy disk, or by having an infected DOS or Windows 95 partition on the system that is booted at some point. A boot record virus relocates the original boot record to a new location in the partition and then replaces the original boot record with a viral boot record. On the FAT file system, Windows NT may overwrite the relocated boot record and the system crashes or cannot access an infected drive. On an NTFS volume, Windows NT crashes if the virus manages to corrupt part of the boot-strap program and prevent Windows NT from loading.

Installing Windows NT on existing DOS or Windows 95 FAT-based partitions is a problem if the original boot records have been infected. What sometimes happens is that the person installing this type of system creates a "dual-boot" environment in which DOS/Windows 95 can be selected during the boot-up process. When DOS/Windows 95 is subsequently booted, the virus may contaminate the system. Note also that Windows NT-specific virus detection programs may not detect this virus because it lives on the other partitions.

 CAUTION: Never install a Windows NT Server on a system where dual-booting is enabled. Not only do you stand the chance of virus infection, but someone could boot with the other partition and use utilities to low-level scan the NTFS partition, as described in Chapter 9.

DOS and Windows 3.1 Viruses in Windows NT DOS Sessions

If you start the Command Prompt in Windows NT or directly execute a DOS program or Windows 3.1 program, viruses that operate in those environments can corrupt data within the confines of the session (that is, the virus cannot spread to other DOS boxes). Virus infection is possible in these sessions because Windows NT faithfully emulates all the functionality of DOS, allowing viruses to intercept system services.

Direct-action file viruses will use the standard DOS system services, which are emulated in the Windows NT DOS session, to corrupt the system. *Memory-resident file viruses* will stay memory-resident and infect any programs accessed or executed within the session if the user has Write access to the programs. If the command shell (CMD.EXE and NDOS.COM) itself is infected, then every DOS session that is started will launch the memory-resident virus into the memory space of the session. An antivirus program must scan memory for every DOS session that is loaded.

In all cases, you must properly configure permissions in the Windows NT file system to prevent viruses from attacking programs and files. Access controls such as Write and Execute must be set properly to prevent a virus from changing a program or executing a program that has been inappropriately copied to the system. Viruses that attempt to directly change a disk using direct access are stopped by Windows NT.

Viruses That Execute in Windows NT Environments

A *macro virus* is a virus that takes advantage of macro routines available in applications such as Microsoft Word for Windows. The *Winword.concept* virus executes when a user opens a file that has been infected with the virus. A macro virus is spread through electronic mail and publicly accessible files. Since Word for Windows runs on most Windows systems, including Windows NT, macro viruses are a potential source of virus infection. However, the file access controls in Windows NT, when used correctly, can reduce the amount of damage caused by the virus.

Native Windows NT viruses are less common for a number of reasons. The Symantec paper states that teenagers are responsible for many viruses and that it is unlikely that they will have a Windows NT platform on which to test viruses. Then again, all it takes is one well-funded person to create and spread such a virus. Another reason stated in the paper is that executable file formats are more complex in Windows NT than in other environments. In contrast, standard DOS system service calls are relatively easy to work with, allowing virus writers with little knowledge of the operating system to create DOS-based viruses. Windows 3.1 viruses were prevalent because the operating system uses the same DOS system service calls. Therefore, someone running an old Windows 3.1 program on Windows NT or Windows 95 is susceptible to attack.

Windows NT and Windows 95 do not use DOS system service calls in 32-bit mode, so applications written specifically for these environments avoid viruses of this type. Because of this, virus writers must have a good understanding of the Windows 32-bit API to create viruses for these environments. As more documentation on these environments becomes available, more viruses will no doubt appear.

Norton AntiVirus Scanner for Windows NT

The Norton AntiVirus Scanner protects Windows NT systems against boot record viruses and file viruses. It can be scheduled to automatically run periodic scans that detect and destroy virus infections on NTFS and FAT file systems. The software can detect and eliminate every common virus or class of virus and their activities. It can also detect and remove polymorphic viruses, which, as mentioned, are viruses that mutate in order to hide themselves.

Symantec provides an update facility so you can get the latest virus definition files. Information on new viruses and updated virus definition files are available from Symantec's Antivirus Research Center via a bulletin board system or a subscription service.

APPENDIX D

Security Evaluation Packages

One of the main problems with networks is lax security standards. When defensive walls are down, intruders will attempt unauthorized access to your systems. In many cases, passwords are weak and easy to guess, or accounts exist that don't even require a password. In other cases, utilities and tools are available on servers or networks that can be used to circumvent security.

A number of vendors have developed software that can detect security holes in advance. Some of these systems are designed specifically for Windows NT, while others are designed to detect security holes in systems connected to the Internet. First, I will describe the tools available in the Windows NT Resource Kit. Then I will describe the Kane Security Analyst (KSA), an elaborate utility that analyzes security risks in relation to common security practices. Another package is Somarsoft DumpACL, a much simpler program that helps you evaluate permissions, audit settings, the file system, the Registry, and other security features for Windows NT. DumpACL is available for free evaluation at the Somarsoft Web site and is much less expensive than the more ambitious KSA product. Finally, I will mention the Internet Scanner, a package that simulates an attack on a network from the Internet, which is covered in Chapter 17.

Microsoft Windows NT Resource Kit Utilities

The Microsoft Windows NT Resource Kit provides a number of utilities that can help you evaluate the security of your Windows NT installations. The resource kit is available in bookstores everywhere.

♦ The Windows NT C2 Configuration Manager, C2CONFIG.EXE, can be used to compare the current security configuration on your Windows NT Workstation with the C2-level security requirements of the federal government's National Computer Security Center, and then to configure the workstation to conform up to that C2 level.

♦ Crystal Reports Event Log Viewer is a full-feature report writer that allows you to view, sort/filter/group, save, and print Windows NT Event Logs from one or more computers in a variety of formats.

An Expert System: Kane Security Analyst

Intrusion Detection System's KSA is designed to help busy, time-strapped network administrators monitor a wide range of computer and network activities. The product uses artificial intelligence and statistics to compare users' activities against historical user profiles. User profiles are drawn from samplings of everyday computer use. These profiles can leave a distinctive signature that can help trace unusual activities. User profiles are analyzed for significant discrepancies. According to Robert Kane, president of Intrusion Detection, Inc.,

> The essence of intrusion detection are statistical algorithms applied to the data to see if any particular behavior is significantly anomalous. Over time each profile is modified and expanded on a regular basis. Any deviations from historical use could suggest security violations including compromised user IDs, abuse of privileged users, one user masquerading as another user and password cracking attempts. The computer abuse that intrusion detection can identify goes on and on.

One of the reasons for analysis software is that operating systems like Windows NT can produce mounds of auditing data that is hard to sort through. At the same time, audit records may not provide enough information to detect masquerading users and abuses to systems from inside your own company. Another important factor is timeliness. If it takes you all day to sift through audit records, you may miss your opportunity to catch a hacker. According to Kane, "auditing demands too much from human memory." Most likely, audit records will pile up while administrators deal with more pressing problems. In fact, intruders take advantage of this tendency.

As networks continue to grow, the network administrator becomes increasingly strapped for time and resources. Unknown and unsecured entry points grow. Monitoring programs are the solution. The Kane Security Analyst (KSA) is an enterprise-wide network security assessment tool for Windows NT. It produces security reports that LAN administrators, corporate security officers, and auditors can use to evaluate the security of their networks. KSA uses a built-in expert knowledge base to compare the security attributes of the LAN with a set of security industry "best practices," established through years of expert security consulting.

 NOTE: You can get more information about KSA at **www.intrusion.com**, or by calling (212) 348-8900.

D

KSA assesses the overall security status of six areas—password strength, access control, user account restrictions, system monitoring, data integrity, and data confidentiality—by looking specifically at these features:

♦ Registry security settings

♦ Trust relationships

♦ Domain security

♦ Audit policies

- Excessive rights, user rights
- ACL directory permissions
- Event Logs
- Shares
- RPCs
- UPS status

Other important features include interactive Registry assessment, ACL maps, and the Kane File Rights for NTFS volumes. The Kane File Rights is an interactive tool included with the KSA that allows users to investigate rights and privileges associated with various users, groups, and directories. This is an important feature, since it would take a great deal of time to investigate every user ID manually.

KSA can also be used to test and discover how security breaches might take place, so that administrators can plug holes before they become a problem. The utility will also identify and deactivate unused accounts.

Figure D-1 shows the opening menu for KSA. When you start the utility, you can choose to search for other Windows NT Servers that KSA will include in its analysis. The buttons at the bottom are numbered in the order that you click them to use the product for a typical system analysis. First, you set security standards, which are the baselines for comparing security. KSA includes default security standards that are based on best practices determined by Intrusion Detection. You can alter these settings to tighten security on your own network.

Next, you click the Run Security Audit button. The software goes through the analysis process and, when done, produces a report card that provides some percentage figures about how compliant you are with security standards. You then see a list of *top risks* for your domain. A typical Top Risk page might list items such as "Account lockout is not turned on," "A machine appears to have passwords scripted in clear text," and "Auditing is not enabled for this domain."

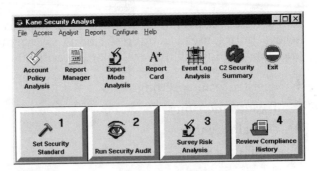

Kane Security
Analyst
Figure D-1.

After viewing this information, you can return to the main menu and click the Security Risk Analysis button. This displays a dialog box similar to this one:

Here you can select the audit mode, the server to run the audit on, and several run options. For example, you can run the audit on all the computers in the domain and scan for logon violations.

When the report is complete, a dialog box similar to the following appears:

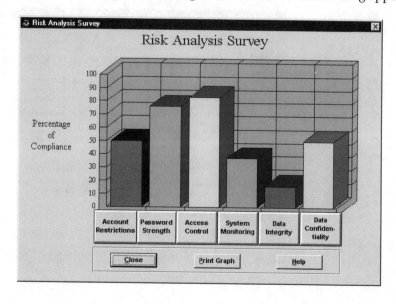

D

Here you see a quick graphical analysis of the survey results. You can then click any of the buttons under the graph to see more detailed information. For example, the following illustration shows detailed results for Access Control:

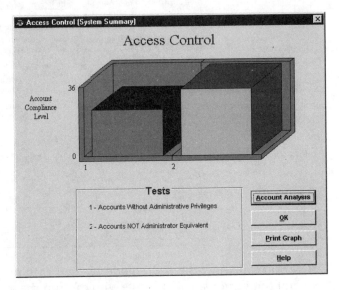

Notice the Account Analysis button. If you click this button, you see a dialog box similar to the following:

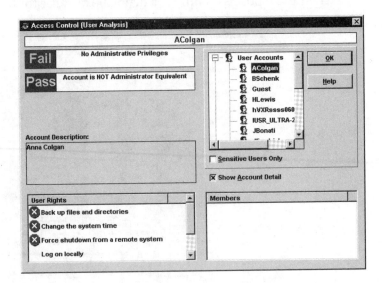

From this dialog box, you can pick a specific user to get detailed information about the user's rights on the system. Information is available from the options on the Risk Analysis Survey window, which are outlined here:

- ◆ **Account Restrictions** View information about user accountability and control, such as account restrictions, station restrictions, and time restrictions.

- ◆ **Password Strength** View information about password controls that can help you assess whether they are easy to guess.

- ◆ **Access Control** View information about rights and how users can access the system (the previous illustrations show this option).

- ◆ **System Monitoring** Lets you monitor repeated attempts to bypass protection systems and monitor how privileged users are accessing the system. This information can help you assess the damage from successful, unauthorized access and review patterns of access.

- ◆ **Data Integrity** Check the status of the underlying systems that ensure data integrity, such as settings for the uninterruptible power supply and station shutdown options.

- ◆ **Data Confidentiality** Check features that enhance confidentiality of data, such as whether the root directory of the system is on an NTFS drive.

Somarsoft DumpACL

Somarsoft DumpACL is a utility for dumping various security information from Windows NT systems. You can obtain information about the utility and a trial version by contacting the Somarsoft Web site at **www.somarsoft.com**.

Specific capabilities of the program include:

- ◆ Dumps permissions for file system, Registry, shares, printers.
- ◆ Dumps user/group information.
- ◆ Dumps policies, rights, trusts, and other security information.
- ◆ Data can be saved in a file or copied to the clipboard for importing into a spreadsheet or database.
- ◆ Reporting by exception to reduce size of report (for example, file permissions report shows only files whose permissions differ from permissions of parent directory).
- ◆ Can answer queries such as "show all files for which *useraccount* (where *useraccount* is an account you specify) has Write or Delete access in

D

all shared directories on all servers," making it easy to spot holes in system security.

♦ Dumps information for local systems or remote computers on a network.

♦ Can be run from command line for background report generation.

DumpACL provides extensive reporting, as outlined in the following sections. You can create reports of file system permissions, users, and user rights.

File System Permissions Report   Here is an example of the permissions report for the file system:

```
┌─┬─────────────────── Somarsoft DumpAcl - \\AMAX (local) ──────────┬─┬─┐
│─│                                                                  │▼│▲│
├─┴──────────────────────────────────────────────────────────────┴─┴─┤
│ File   Edit   Search   Report   View   Help                         │
├─────────────────────────────────────────────────────────────────────┤
│ Path (exception dirs and files)  Account      Own Dir      File    │ │
│ C:\ROOT\DIR1\                    SOMAR\user1   o  all       all    │▲│
│ C:\ROOT\DIR1\                    SOMAR\frankr     RWXD      RWXD   │ │
│                                                                     │ │
│ C:\ROOT\DIR1\FILE3.TXT           SOMAR\frankr              all    │ │
│ C:\ROOT\DIR1\FILE3.TXT           SOMAR\user1   o                  │ │
│                                                                     │ │
│ C:\ROOT\DIR2\                    SOMAR\user1   o  WX              │ │
│ C:\ROOT\DIR2\                    SOMAR\frankr     all       all    │ │
│                                                                     │ │
│ C:\ROOT\DIR2\*.*                 Everyone                  RWXD   │ │
│ C:\ROOT\DIR2\*.*                 SOMAR\frankr              all    │ │
│ C:\ROOT\DIR2\*.*                 SOMAR\user1   o                  │▼│
├─────────────────────────────────────────────────────────────┬──────┤
│ Processed 16203 files in 876 directories                     │00001 │
└──────────────────────────────────────────────────────────────┴──────┘
```

There are similar reports for the Registry, shares, and printers. There are also reports that show file system permissions for a single shared directory or for all shared directories on a computer.

The "dump all shared directories" report makes it possible to quickly determine all the files that a remote user could possibly access on a file server (that is, those that could be accessed because they are shared) and then, by using filtering, determine which of those files the user has permission to access. It is also possible to combine multiples of these "all shared directories" reports to determine all the files on the network to which a user has access. For example:

♦ All files in the C:\ROOT\DIR1 directory have the same permissions as the directory itself, except for the FILE3.TXT file. Since reporting by exception is enabled, only this exception file is shown, and not any of the other files.

♦ All files in the C:\ROOT\DIR2 directory have the same permission, but this permission is different from that of the directory itself. Since reporting by exception is enabled, only a single item for all the files in the directory is shown (that is, "*.*").

♦ Full reporting by exception is enabled. This produces the most compact report. There are other reporting options, as shown here:

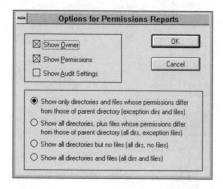

Filtering Filtering allows formulating requests such as "show all files for which account *XXX* has Write or Delete access, in all shared directories on all servers." The filter dialog box for the file system permissions report is shown here:

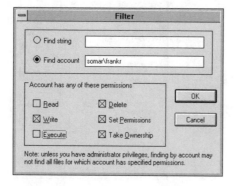

The reports can be made much more concise by the use of filters.

Users Report

User information can be dumped in either table or column format. The table format, shown here, is the best format for exporting to a database or spreadsheet:

D

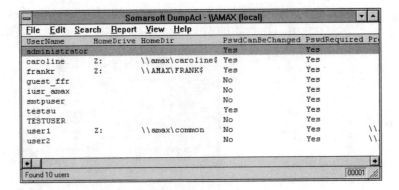

The column format is sometimes easier to read interactively.

The following dialog box shows the various fields that can be displayed. There is a similar report and dialog box for groups.

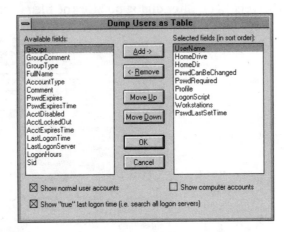

Policies Report

The policies report shows a variety of system policies and miscellaneous security information that isn't shown on any of the other reports. Only a portion of this report is shown in the following screen shot:

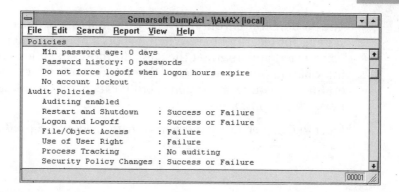

User Rights Report

This report dumps all rights and the accounts to which those rights have been granted. Both the internal name of the right and the description shown in User Manager are displayed:

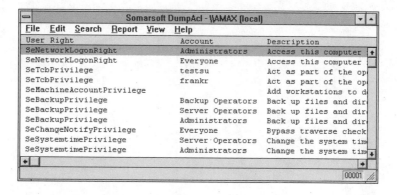

Internet Scanner from Internet Security Systems

Internet Security Systems (**www.iss.net**) is a program that can help managers experience the hacker attack from the other side of the firewall. Internet Scanner is an "attack simulator" that automatically scans each networked machine, searching for weaknesses and misconfigurations. Unlike the other products mentioned in this appendix, Internet Scanner works over a variety of platforms and is designed to look specifically for holes that Internet hackers commonly take advantage of. At the time of this writing, a Windows NT version was in the works.

D

The product learns your network, then makes scheduled rounds to scour systems for security holes. When it spots a hole, Internet Scanner can send you an alert and interpret the data, diagnose the holes, and present information on how to correct them. Internet Scanner primarily spots holes on Internet-connected systems, but it can also spot holes on internal TCP/IP networks, or "intranets."

Refer to Chapter 17 for more information about ISS products.

APPENDIX E

Steps for Evaluating NT Security

What do you do when you face the task of evaluating the security of a Windows NT system? One approach is to obtain a package such as the Kane Security Analyst (KSA) discussed in Appendix D. Another approach is to manually evaluate the security of a system. Although this can be a daunting task, you will find it a little easier if you follow the steps provided here.

This discussion provides quick steps for analyzing the security of a server. For more specific details about security auditing, refer to the Microsoft Press publication "Windows NT 3.5, Guidelines for Security, Audit, and Control," a joint research project by Citibank N.A., Coopers & Lebrand, The Institute of Internal Auditors, and Microsoft Corporation (1994). The discussion in this appendix is based upon security checks performed by the Kane Security Analyst and does not follow the same strategy outlined in the Microsoft Press book, nor does it go against those strategies. You should reference the information in this appendix and the book just described to build your own security auditing strategy, or get a copy of KSA.

NOTE: The descriptions for accessing the user interface in this appendix relate to the Windows NT 4.0 GUI.

Check C2 Compliance

C2 compliance relates to stand-alone system security, rather than network security, but it can help you evaluate the strength of a system. Technically, a C2-compliant workstation cannot be hooked into a network; if you are creating these settings on a server you can never be C2-compliant. However, the following settings can serve as the basis for building a very secure system even if they don't necessarily apply to a network server.

- The system should not dual boot. Windows NT should be the only operating system installed.

- The OS/2 and POSIX subsystems should not be installed.

- All drives on the system must be formatted for the NT File System, not the FAT file system. To check drive status in Windows NT 4.0, right-click on the drive and choose Properties.

- The Security Log should not overwrite old events. To check this, open the Event Viewer and choose Log Settings from the Log menu. The option called "Do Not Overwrite Events (Clear Log Manually)" should be enabled.

♦ Do not allow blank passwords. To check this, open the User Manager for Domains and choose Account from the Policies menu and disable Permit Blank Passwords in the Minimum Password Length field. This will require that you choose the "At Least *x* Characters" field and specify a value for *x*.

♦ Disable the Guest account. In the User Manager, double-click on the Guest account and put a check mark on the item called "Account Disabled."

Standard Evaluation

The steps in this section outline the security settings you check for standard evaluation of a Windows NT system. Many of the settings are checked in the User Manager. Keep in mind that these recommendations may or may not be appropriate for your environment.

One of the first things to check are the logon policies and restrictions—the "welcome mat" into the Windows NT Server. Are your users educated about password safety and appropriate use of the system? Do users read and sign a security policy?

You should post legal notices in Logon dialog boxes to indicate that only authorized users may access the system and that all activities may be monitored. Refer to Chapter 6 for details about setting these options.

T IP: Run the batch file presented under "The NET Commands" in Chapter 10 to produce an automatic security analysis report.

Account Policies and Restrictions

Account policies and restrictions determine how password and logon policies are enforced for the entire domain. Keep in mind that each domain has its own policies. Open the User Manager and choose Account from the Policies menu. If you want to check a different trusting domain, choose Select Domain on the user menu. When the Account Policy dialog box appears, evaluate and choose the following settings under Password Restrictions based on your password policies.

♦ **Maximum Password Age** Password should expire in *x* number of days.

♦ **Minimum Password Length** Password should be greater than eight characters.

E

♦ **Minimum Password Age** Set to allow changes in *x* number of days.

♦ **Password Uniqueness** Set to Remember *x* Passwords.

Enable the Account Lockout option to prevent unauthorized users from attempting to access the system by guessing passwords. For optimum security, never run the server with this option disabled. Set the following options as appropriate:

♦ **Lockout after *x* bad logon attempts** Set *x* to 4.

♦ **Reset Count After *x* minutes** Set to approximately 20 minutes to avoid unnecessary lockouts.

♦ **Lockout Duration field** Set according to your logon policies. If forever is set, an administrator must restore the account.

♦ **Forcibly disconnect remote users from server when logon hours expire** Set this option to prevent after-hours activities or disconnect systems that were left on unintentionally.

♦ **User must log on in order to change password** Set this option to prevent users whose passwords have expired from logging on. The administrator must change the password.

User Accounts

After setting the domain account policies, check the status of each user account and group in the User Manager. This can be a tedious process if you have hundreds of accounts, so consider using the utilities discussed in Appendix D.

Double-click on each account if you are checking manually. This opens the New User properties dialog box:

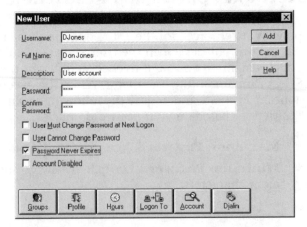

As you can see, this box displays password information and has buttons for checking group membership and other options. Check these options as follows:

♦ Look for old user accounts of employees who have left the company and remove the accounts if appropriate.

♦ Check the password options. Should the user be able to change the password? Does the password never expire? Is this account disabled? If it is disabled, has the user left the company? If so, consider removing the account.

♦ Click the Groups button to determine which groups the user belongs to. Is membership in these groups appropriate for the user? What rights and permissions does the user obtain from the groups? What access does the group have to other domains?

♦ Click the Profile button in the New User properties dialog box to check the location of the user's home directory. If you remove the account, also remove the specified directory. Does the user have a profile, and if so, is it mandatory? Are System Policies required? Refer to Chapter 12.

♦ Click the Hours button to evaluate the times that the user can access the network. Make sure no one can log on after hours if that is your policy.

♦ Click the Logon To button to evaluate which computers the user can log on to. Make sure that no one can log on from a computer in an unsupervised area.

♦ Click the Account button to set an account expiration date if necessary. All temporary accounts or administrator "test" accounts should expire automatically.

♦ Click the Dialin button to evaluate dial-in capabilities. If users can dial in, enable Call Back options to a specified telephone number in the dialog box for added security.

Groups

The membership of groups should be carefully evaluated. A group that is granted permissions to sensitive files might contain users that should not have that access. Open each group listed in the User Manager and inspect its members. A dialog box similar to the following appears:

E

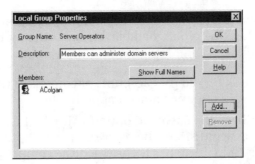

♦ Are any of the accounts in a group inactive? If so, consider removing the accounts.

♦ Carefully evaluate the members of management groups such as Administrators, Server Operators, Account Operators, Backup Operators, and Print Operators. Remove all unnecessary accounts.

♦ Make sure that all administrative users have two accounts: one for administrative tasks and one for regular use. Administrators should only use their administrative accounts when absolutely necessary.

♦ Evaluate each global group membership and the resources that the group has access to. Does the group have access in other domains?

♦ What folders and files do groups have permission to access? This can be difficult to evaluate. Use a program like Somarsoft DumpACL as discussed in Appendix D to help you with this task.

♦ Do local groups hold global groups from other domains? Check the membership of these global groups and make sure that no users have unnecessary access to resources in the current domain.

The Administrator Account and Administrators Group

The Administrator account and Administrators group have unlimited rights on the system. Therefore, you need to carefully evaluate the membership of the Administrators group and take care of some other housekeeping related to the Administrator account:

♦ If you are taking over the management of an existing system, you should change the Administrator account name and password immediately. You do not know who might have a password that would give them access to the account.

♦ The Administrator account is often the target of attacks because of its well-known name. You should rename the Administrator account to an obscure name and create a "decoy" account called "Administrator" with no permissions. Intruders will attempt to break in to this decoy account instead of the real account.

♦ Enable failed logons in the auditing system to detect attempts to log on to any account, including Administrator.

♦ Look for unnecessary accounts that have Administrator status. Perhaps an intruder has created such an account as a backdoor into the system.

♦ Review the membership of the Administrators group and the Domain Admins group. Remove all unnecessary users from this group.

♦ If you have a large network that consists of multiple administrators, interview these administrators on a regular basis to evaluate their activities and need for Administrator status.

♦ To protect against the loss of the Administrator, create a "backdoor" Administrator account with an obscure name and a three-part password. Give three people one part of this password. In the event that Administrator access is required, all three must be present to access the Administrator account.

The Administrators group has "Access this computer from network" right, which you can block to prevent account hijacking or unauthorized activities. Without this right, administrators must log on at the computer itself in a controlled environment to do any administrative tasks. You will also need to remove the right from the Everyone group then add back in accounts that are allowed to log on from network.

When a Windows NT Workstation computer is added to a domain, the Domain Admins group is added to the workstation's Administrators group. This gives any member of the Domain Admins group access to the workstation computer as well. Determine whether this is appropriate. You may need to remove the Domain Admins group at the workstation and add only a specific Administrator account.

The Guest Account and Everyone Group

Evaluate the need for the Guest account. Most administrators agree that it should be disabled, although removing it will require that everyone log on, even users that access public directories. In some organizations, people who don't normally work with computers might need to occasionally access a system to obtain some information. For example, factory floor workers might want to look up pension plan information on a kiosk system in the break room. Consider creating a separate domain for these public services where the Guest account is enabled. Alternatively, use a Web server for this type of system.

Note the following:

E

♦ Users who log on as guests can access any shared folder that the Everyone group has access to (i.e., if the Everyone group has Read permissions to the Private folder, guests can access it with Read permissions).

♦ You don't know who Guest users are and there is no accountability because all guests log in to the same account.

♦ Always disable the Guest account on networks that are connected to untrusted networks such as the Internet. It provides too many opportunities for break-ins.

NOTE: If you have Microsoft Internet Information Server software installed, a special Guest account called IUSR_*computername* exists with the rights to log on locally. Remove this account if you don't want the general public to access your Web server. Users must then have an account to access the Web server.

User Rights

In the User Manager for Domains, check the rights that users and groups have on the system. Choose User Rights from the Policies menu to display the User Rights Policy dialog box. Initially, the box shows the basic rights. To evaluate all rights, click the Show Advanced User Rights option. Here are some considerations for basic rights:

♦ **Access this computer from the network** By default, only the Administrators and the Everyone group have this right. Remove the Everyone group (why would you want everyone to access this server from the network if you are interested in security?), then add specific groups as appropriate. For example, create a new group called "Network Users" with this right, then add users who should have network access.

♦ **Backup files and directories** User's with this right can potentially carry any files off-site. Carefully evaluate which users and groups have this right. Also evaluate the **Restore files and directories** right.

♦ **Log on locally** For servers, only administrators should have this right. No regular user ever needs to logon directly to the server itself. By default, the administrative groups (Administrators, Server Manager, etc.) have this right. Make sure that any user who is a member of these groups has a separate management account.

♦ **Manage auditing and security logs** Only the Administrators group should have this right.

♦ **Take ownership of files or other objects** Only the Administrators group should have this right.

Scan all the advanced rights to make sure that a user has not been granted rights inappropriately. Some rights should only be assigned to the System account. A rogue administrator might manage to grant himself inappropriate rights and gain extended privileges on the system.

Files, Folders, Permissions and Shares

This discussion assumes that you are only using NTFS volumes on your servers. Do not use FAT volumes in secure installations.

To check permissions on folders and other resources, you must go to each resource individually to review which users and groups have permissions. This can be a bewildering task, so for large systems obtain a copy of the Somarsoft DumpACL utility discussed in Appendix D.

To open the Permissions dialog box for a folder or file, right-click it and choose Properties, then click either the Sharing or the Security tab. The Sharing options show who has access to the folder over the network. The Security tab has the Permission and Auditing buttons so you can check local permissions or set auditing options. The Directory Permissions dialog box is pictured here:

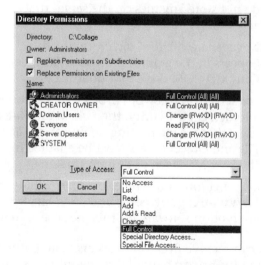

Start your evaluation with the most sensitive and critical folders if you are doing this procedure manually or performing a periodic checkup. Take care to do the following:

E

♦ Check each folder and/or file to determine which local users and groups have access and whether that access is appropriate.

♦ Check all shared folders and the share permissions on those folders to determine which network users and groups have access and whether that access is appropriate.

♦ Program files and data files should be kept in separate folders to make management and permission setting easier. Also, if users can copy files into a data folder, remove the Execute permission on the folder to prevent someone from copying and executing a virus or Trojan Horse program.

♦ Separate public files from private files so you can apply different permission sets.

♦ If users or groups have access to a folder, should they have the same access to every file in the folder? To every subdirectory? Check the sensitivity of files and attached subdirectories to evaluate whether inherited permissions are appropriate.

♦ Keep in mind that the Everyone group gets Full access by default for all new folders you create. To prevent this, change the Everyone group's permission for a folder, then any new subdirectories you create will get the new permission settings.

♦ If the server is connected to an untrusted network such as the Internet, do not store any files on the server that are sensitive and for in-house access only.

♦ Never share the root directory of a drive or one of the drive icons that appears in the graphical display. An exception would be sharing a Read Only CD-ROM drive for public access.

♦ For sensitive, password protected directories, enable Auditing. Right-click a folder, click Security, then click Auditing and enable Failure to track users that are attempting unauthorized access a folder or file. Note that File and Object access must be enabled from the Audit Policies menu in the User Manager, as described later.

♦ Use encryption wherever possible to hide and protect files. Mergent (**www.mergent.com**) and RSA Data Systems (**www.rsa.com**) provide encryption software for this purpose, as described in Chapter 12.

You can remove Everyone's access to an entire folder tree by going to the root of the drive, changing the permissions, and propagating those permissions to subdirectories. Do not do this for the *systemroot* folder (usually C:\WINNT). You must manually update Everyone's right there.

Virus and Trojan Horse Controls

Viruses are a particularly serious problem in the network environment because the client computer can become infected, transferring the virus to server systems. Other users may come into contact with infected files at the server. Evaluate and set the following options:

♦ Program directories should have permissions set to Read and Execute (not Write) to prevent a virus from being written into a directory where it can be executed. To install programs, tempararily set Write on, then remove it.

♦ Install new software on a separate, quarantined system for a test period, then install the software on working systems once you have determined that it is safe to run.

♦ Public file sharing directories should have the least permissions possible, i.e., Read Only, to prevent virus infections.

♦ If a user needs to put files on your server, create a "drop box" directory that has only the Write permission. Check all new files placed in this directory with a virus scanner.

♦ Implement backup policies and other protective measures.

♦ Educate and train users.

Auditing and Event Logs

Check the status of audit settings by choosing Audit on the Policies menu in the User Manager for Domains. A dialog box similar to the following appears:

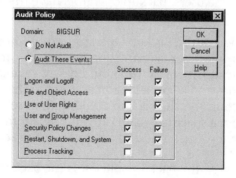

The settings in this box reflect the minimum settings that are appropriate for auditing in most environments. Keep in mind that auditing too many events can affect a system's performance.

E

Protect auditing and security logs from other administrators who might change or delete them. You can grant only the Administrators group the ability to access the logs. To restrict access to only one user (the "auditor"), remove all users except the auditor from the Administrators group. This means all of your other administrators should be members of a management group that does not have the "Manage auditing and security log" right.

Check for failed logons in the Event Viewer. You can enable security auditing for logon attempts, file and object access, use of user rights, account management, security policy changes, restart and shutdown, and process tracking.

Fault Tolerance, Backup, and UPS

Fault-tolerant systems duplicate various hardware components and process to guard against failures. Evaluate all fault-tolerant systems for proper installation and operation. Use the Disk Administrator utility (on the Start|Programs menu) to check disk systems and use the UPS utility (on the Control Panel) to check the status of uninterruptible power supplies.

♦   In Disk Manager, make sure disk mirroring or duplexing is taking place to protect against failed drives or hardware components.

♦   Check to make sure an uninterruptible power supply (UPS) is installed and configured properly. The UPS will protect data on a server that fails from a power loss. To check the UPS, open the UPS utility on the Control Panel.

Backup policies and procedures are essential. In your evaluation, determine which users belong to the Backup Operators group. Carefully evaluate if you trust these users. Backup operators have the ability to access all areas of the system to back up and restore files.

Members of the Backup Operators group should have special logon accounts (not regular user accounts) on which you can set logon restrictions. If Joe is the backup operator, he should have a regular logon account for his personal activities and a special logon account for backing up the system. Set restrictions on the backup account, then set restrictions that force Joe to log on from a specific system only during appropriate hours. Change, with frequency, the name and password of the account to guard against hijacking.

♦   Review the backup policies. Is the backup schedule appropriate? Are files safely transported to secure backup locations? How might backup compromise the confidentiality of files?

♦   View the Event Log to audit backup activities.

APPENDIX F

Registry Security
Issues

The Registry is a unified database that stores configuration data for the operating systems. The information is stored in a hierarchical form. In most cases, you change the Registry indirectly by using a utility on the Control Panel, or when you run various applications. That is the most appropriate way to make Registry changes. In some cases, you can modify the Registry with the Registry Editor. Microsoft warns that modifying the Registry directly with the Registry Editor may lead to problems if you make the wrong changes. You should make changes only by following explicit instructions provided by reliable sources.

You can start the Registry Editor at a Windows NT computer by typing **REGEDT32** in the Run dialog box. The so-called *hives* for the local computer automatically open. These are the hierarchical structures that contain information about local users, computers, and other configuration information. Items in the Registry's hierarchical structure are called *keys*, and keys can have subkeys. Keys hold information such as executable code, text strings, and numeric values. The Registry is analogous to the .INI files used in Windows 3.1 but is much more flexible and powerful in its functionality.

NOTE: This appendix concentrates on security issues for the Registry. For more information about hives, Registry contents, and how to use the Registry Editor, be sure to refer to online help.

The hierarchical structure of the Registry is similar to the hierarchical structure of a file system with its folders and subfolders, except that the Registry has keys and subkeys. In the same way that each folder and subfolder can have its own access permissions, each key in the Registry has access controls. Users need some access to the Registry when running programs.

An administrator has full rights in the Registry and may perform operations like the following:

♦ Repairing a damaged hive on a remote computer

♦ Viewing and editing hives that include profile information for users

♦ Creating custom settings in the Registry for management and security purposes

You can access a remote computer's Registry from the Registry Editor, a feature that allows a unique level of management control but also presents potential security problems, as discussed later. Remote management is useful for examining and changing the configuration of client and server systems throughout your network. Remote management requires that the Server service on the remote computer be running. Appropriate permissions are also required. Note that Windows NT 4.0 does not allow remote computers to fully access its Registry, but for management purposes you can enable remote editing by changing permissions on the system, as discussed later.

The ability to modify the Registry depends on access privileges, which are similar to the access privileges required to run most utilities on the Control Panel. In other words, you must be an administrator to set most of the options. However, some options in the Registry have privileges that allow the Everyone group to make changes. This is necessary so the user can run applications or perform other tasks. At the same time, this is where security holes develop if you are not careful.

Registry Security and Protection

The Registry must be protected from tampering by unauthorized users and from accidents. You can back up the Registry to ensure its recoverability, as described later. This section describes Registry protection via permissions and rights. Some basic things you can do to keep the Registry safe are:

♦ Make sure that unauthorized users do not access the folder holding the Registry files.

♦ Never allow unauthorized users to log on as members of the Administrators group.

♦ Remove REGEDT32.EXE from workstations, or use permissions to limit its use.

♦ Use only NTFS volumes. The Registry is vulnerable if FAT volumes are in use.

The actual files for the Registry are stored in the *systemroot*\System32\CONFIG directory. This is the directory that you need to protect, as well as the files in the directory. Each hive in the Registry is related to a hive file and a .LOG file in the directory. These files are listed in the following table.

Registry Hive	Filenames
HKEY_LOCAL_MACHINE\SAM	SAM and SAM.LOG
HKEY_LOCAL_MACHINE\SECURITY	SECURITY and SECURITY.LOG
HKEY_LOCAL_MACHINE\SOFTWARE	SOFTWARE and SOFTWARE.LOG
HKEY_LOCAL_MACHINE\SYSTEM	SYSTEM and SYSTEM.ALT

F

Registry Hive	Filenames
HKEY_CURRENT_USER	*USER###* and *USER###.*LOG or *ADMIN###* and *ADMIN###.*LOG
HKEY_USERS\DEFAULT	DEFAULT and DEFAULT.LOG

In addition to these hive files, there are hive files for user profiles, which can be stored in other locations, as described in Chapter 12. Recall that each user on a Windows NT system is assigned a user profile, which can be set up on a local or remote computer. This profile contains the user's preferences and settings for the desktop, environment variables, and other items. Administrators can use the User Profile Editor to move user profiles to other computers and the User Manager to assign mandatory or individual profiles to users. To edit profiles offline or to manage user profiles on remote computers, you use the Registry Editor.

Because the user profile hives might not be in the same protected directory as the other hive files, you need to use file permissions to protect the files from tampering. For maximum protection, make sure the files are stored on an NTFS volume.

Changing Key Permissions

This section explains how to change the permission on Registry keys to limit access to those keys. In most cases, changing permissions on specific keys of the Registry is an action you take in very rare situations. You should use extreme caution in doing this. For example, assigning No Access permission to keys that operating system utilities or applications must access in order to run will cause the utility or application to fail. The Administrators group and the System should always have full access to any key you want to change permissions on. This will ensure that the system can restart and that an administrator can repair the Registry key. You should also audit failures after changing permissions, as described later.

To assign permissions and ownership of keys in the Registry Editor, follow the steps outlined here:

1. Back up the Registry key as described earlier.
2. Select the key, then choose Permissions from the Security menu.

   The following dialog box appears:

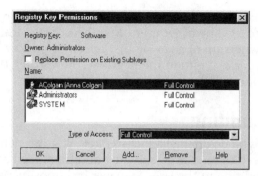

You set options in this dialog box in the same way you set permissions for files. The types of access are described shortly.

3. Select a user to remove and click Remove (or click Add to add a new user). To set permissions, click a user and choose a permission in the Type of Access field.

4. Click OK when done.

5. Next, test the changes as described in the next section to make sure they work for normal use.

Here is a description of the permissions that are allowed for keys in the Registry.

♦ **Read**   User can read the key's contents, but any changes are not saved.

♦ **Full Control**   User can access, edit, or take ownership of the selected key.

♦ **Special Access**   User can be granted the custom access and edit rights for the selected key, as described here:

Query Value   Right to read a value entry from a Registry key

Set Value   Right to set value entries in a Registry key

Create Subkey   Right to create subkeys on a selected Registry key

Enumerate Subkeys   Right to identify the subkeys of a Registry key

Notify   Right to audit notification events from a key in the Registry

Create Link   Right to create a symbolic link in a particular key

Delete   Right to delete the selected key

Write DAC   Right to gain access to a key for the purpose of writing to the key a discretionary ACL

Write Owner   Right to gain access to a key for the purpose of taking ownership of it

F

Another option is to take ownership of a key to protect it from being accessed by other users. Members of the Administrators group can take ownership of a key by first selecting the key, then choosing Owner from the Security menu in the Registry Editor. Click the Take Ownership button to complete the operation.

Auditing

If you do change a Registry key, you can determine whether applications need to have access to it by auditing failed access attempts. You enable auditing in the User Manager by choosing Audit from the Policies menu and then enabling the Failure option for File and Object Access. According to Microsoft, after changing permissions, you should "test the system extensively through a variety of activities while logged on using different user and administrative accounts."

To audit Registry activities, you first turn on auditing by choosing Audit in the Policies menu of the User Manager. Set the Failure option for File and Object Access as the primary option, then set other options as appropriate. You can audit the success of events, but doing so is often not necessary and results in an overworked server.

You can audit specific Registry keys to track changes made by users or applications or to test keys that you have added. In the Registry Editor, choose a key to audit, then choose Auditing from the Security menu. A dialog box similar to the following appears:

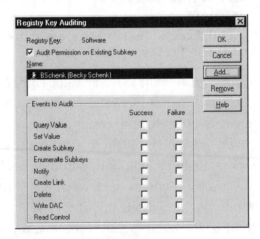

Click the Add button to add a user, then set the Success or Failure options in the lower field. These options are described here:

♦   **Query Value**   Open a key with Query Value access

- ◆ **Set Value**   Open a key with Set Value access
- ◆ **Create Subkey**   Open a key with Create Subkey access
- ◆ **Enumerate Subkeys**   Open a key with Enumerate Subkeys access (that is, events that try to find the subkeys of a key)
- ◆ **Notify**   Open a key with Notify access
- ◆ **Create Link**   Open a key with Create Link access
- ◆ **Delete**   Delete the key
- ◆ **Write DAC**   Determine who has access to the key
- ◆ **Read Control**   Find the owner of a key

TIP: To view audited events, run the Event Viewer, select the computer whose events you want to view, and choose Security in the Log menu to view the security events.

Backing Up and Restoring Keys

A Save Key command exists on the Registry menu for the Registry Editor. You use this key to save the information in a particular portion of the Registry as a file on disk for backup purposes. You don't use this option to save changes to the Registry because changes are saved automatically. The Save Key command requires that you have Backup privileges. To return a saved hive to the system, you use the Restore command. This command requires Restore privileges. Members of the Administrators group have both of these privileges.

The SAM or SECURITY subtrees cannot be restored because Windows NT always has part of these subtrees open. You typically use the RESTORE command to restore user profiles on damaged systems, assuming that you previously saved them to disk.

The following tools are on the Microsoft Windows NT Resource Kit. You can use them to help administer the Registry. Refer to the resource kit for more information.

REGBACK.EXE   Creates backups of Registry files

REGENTRY.HLP   Documents Windows NT Registry entries

REGINI.EXE   Makes Registry changes by script

F

High-Security Registry Settings

Microsoft makes the following recommendations for changing the Registry in a high-security installation to protect certain keys. The standard settings are designed to balance a reasonable level of security with each access to the Registry. In a high-level security environment, you want to strengthen the security on the following keys so that the Everyone group is allowed only QueryValue, Enumerate Subkeys, Notify, and Read Control accesses.

In the HKEY_LOCAL_MACHINE in the Local Machine dialog box:

> \Software\Microsoft\RPC (and its subkeys)
> \Software\Microsoft\Windows NT\CurrentVersion

In the HKEY_CLASSES_ROOT in the Local Machine dialog box:

> \HKEY_CLASSES_ROOT (and all subkeys)

Under the \Software\Microsoft\Windows NT\CurrentVersion\ subtree:

> Profile List
> AeDebug
> Compatibility
> Drivers
> Embedding
> Fonts
> FontSubstitutes
> GRE_Initialize
> MCI
> FontSubstitutes
> GRE_Initialize
> MCI
> MCI Extensions
> Port (and all subkeys)
> WOW (and all subkeys)
> Windows3.1MigrationStatus (and all subkeys)

Additional Registry Security Information

The following information was prepared by Frank Ramos of Somarsoft, maker of the DumpACL utility described in Appendix D. You can obtain more information by visiting Frank's site at **www.somarsoft.com**. Readers should note that Windows NT Server version 4.0 no longer allows remote users to access the Registry with full access, although it is possible to allow that. The following information provides some useful insight into the operation of the Registry and how a hacker might attack it.

Lax Registry Permissions, By Frank Ramos, Somarsoft

NT installs by default with Everyone given Write access to much of the registry. To see just how much, use the Somarsoft DumpACL program. This is a major problem because the Registry on any machine running NT, both servers and workstations, can be accessed remotely using the Registry Editor. So a user running on some workstation can modify the Registry on any server or workstation on which this user has an account (normally this means all servers), or on which the Guest account is enabled.

Since the Registry is similar to a file system, the obvious solution is either to stop sharing the Registry or else set Registry permissions securely. Unfortunately, there is no way to stop sharing the Registry currently. The best way to set permissions securely is to remove the permission for Everyone at the root of the HKEY_LOCAL_MACHINE hive. Do NOT propagate this change to lower-level keys in the hive. This will prevent anyone other than a member of the local Administrators group from remotely connecting to the Registry.

Unfortunately, this modification to the default Registry permissions may break some programs. Often, the only users who log on to a server locally are members of the local Administrators group and the only services running on the server are members of either the local Administrators group, or are running under the System account. In this case, there should be no problems. Problems can occur if some users who log on locally or some services are not members of the local Administrators group or running under the System account. You have to test on your system to determine the impacts of changing Registry permissions.

The change is easy to undo, and is one of the most important things you can do to secure an NT machine, so you should at least try it.

If you do not change permissions to prevent remote access, then you are opening your machine to all kinds of mischief. For example, a malicious user might change a few Registry entries so that various services begin functioning strangely, but not so strangely that it is obvious what has happened. The problems are not reproducible at other sites and the system administrator feels like a fool. If logging is enabled, the system administrator might eventually track the problem to the user who made the changes, but in reality, most system administrators will just reinstall NT. The user might wait a few months, then make the changes again. So the system administrator comes to the conclusion that NT needs reinstallation every few months to keep things running properly.

It is also possible for a user to make the changes while logged on using another user's account (the other user stepped out of the room without locking their workstation, or they wrote their password down in a notebook and the malicious user found it, etc., etc.). In this case, even if the system administrator traces the changes using the Registry Audit Logs, they won't find the real culprit.

Or how about this? Suppose the malicious user has an account and Write access to some directory on a server. For example, the user's home directory. The user then creates a Trojan Horse program which does the following:

1. Starts another program, whose path is the first command line parameter. The remaining command line parameters are passed unchanged to the other program. This way the user notices nothing suspicious happening.

2. Gives the user Administrator privileges, if possible. It will be possible if the account under which the program is executing is an Administrator. If not possible, then exit.

3. (optional) Sends a mail message to the user informing them of success.

4. Performs some registry cleanup to erase all traces of itself.

The user then replaces some appropriate executable file path in the Registry with the path of the Trojan Horse program, followed by the original path as the first parameter.

A previous version of this white paper listed

    HKEY_LOCAL_MACHINE\SOFTWARE\CLASSES\txtfile\shell
    \open\command

as an appropriate Registry value to change. This hole was detected during the C2 evaluation process (according to Alva Nims of the Aerospace Corporation) and now the NT 3.51 resource kit recommends making this tree Read Only:

    HKEY_LOCAL_MACHINE\SOFTWARE\CLASSES

The resource kit also shows how to close most of the other holes of this sort. But there is still the PathName value under the key:

HKEY_LOCAL_MACHINE\SOFTWARE\Microsoft\RasMan \CurrentVersion

And if this key doesn't exist on your system, then just use Somarsoft DumpACL and Somarsoft DumpReg together to find some other key which Everyone can write and which has an .EXE file as one of its values.

When the Trojan Horse program executes, it will start the original program, give Administrator privileges to the malicious user, notify the malicious user via an e-mail message or whatever, and then erase all traces of itself. The user can then do whatever they want to the server, including taking steps to erase all traces of the attack. There is little you can do to stop such an attack by someone who has an account on your network.

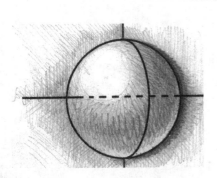

APPENDIX G

Ports in the TCP/IP Environment

The following table* describes assignments for well-known ports in the TCP/IP internetwork protocol.

Decimal	Keyword	Description and Microsoft Networking Alias
0/tcp, udp		Reserved
1/tcp, udp	tcpmux	TCP Port Service Multiplexer
2/tcp, udp	compressnet	Management Utility
3/tcp, udp	compressnet	Compression Process
4/tcp, udp		Unassigned
5/tcp, udp	rje	Remote Job Entry
6/tcp, udp		Unassigned
7/tcp, udp	echo	Echo
8/tcp, udp		Unassigned
9/tcp, udp	discard	Discard; alias=sink null
10/tcp, udp		Unassigned
11/udp	systat	Active Users; alias=users
12/tcp, udp		Unassigned
13/tcp, udp	daytime	Daytime
14/tcp, udp		Unassigned
15/tcp, udp		Unassigned [was netstat]
16/tcp, udp		Unassigned
17/tcp, udp	qotd	Quote of the Day; alias=quote
18/tcp, udp	msp	Message Send Protocol
19/tcp, udp	chargen	Character Generator; alias=ttytst source

*Table source: Microsoft Technet, 1996.

Decimal	Keyword	Description and Microsoft Networking Alias
20/tcp, udp	ftp-data	File Transfer [Default Data]
21/tcp, udp	ftp	File Transfer [Control]
22/tcp, udp		Unassigned
23/tcp, udp	telnet	Telnet
24/tcp, udp		Any private mail system
25/tcp, udp	smtp	Simple Mail Transfer Protocol; alias=mail
26/tcp, udp		Unassigned
27/tcp, udp	nsw-fe	NSW User System FE
28/tcp, udp		Unassigned
29/tcp, udp	msg-icp	MSG ICP
30/tcp, udp		Unassigned
31/tcp, udp	msg-auth	MSG Authentication
32/tcp, udp		Unassigned
33/tcp, udp	dsp	Display Support Protocol
34/tcp, udp		Unassigned
35/tcp, udp		Any private printer server
36/tcp, udp		Unassigned
37/tcp, udp	time	Time; alias=timserver
38/tcp, udp		Unassigned
39/tcp, udp	rlp	Resource Location Protocol; alias=resource
40/tcp, udp		Unassigned
41/tcp, udp	graphics	Graphics
42/tcp, udp	nameserver	Host Name Server; alias=nameserver

Decimal	Keyword	Description and Microsoft Networking Alias
43/tcp, udp	nicname	Who Is; alias=nicname
44/tcp, udp	mpm-flags	MPM FLAGS Protocol
45/tcp, udp	mpm	Message Processing Module
46/tcp, udp	mpm-snd	MPM [default send]
47/tcp, udp	ni-ftp	NI FTP
48/tcp, udp		Unassigned
49/tcp, udp	login	Login Host Protocol
50/tcp, udp	re-mail-ck	Remote Mail Checking Protocol
51/tcp, udp	la-maint	IMP Logical Address Maintenance
52/tcp, udp	xns-time	XNS Time Protocol
53/tcp, udp	domain	Domain Name Server; alias=nameserver, dns
54/tcp, udp	xns-ch	XNS Clearinghouse
55/tcp, udp	isi-gl	ISI Graphics Language
56/tcp, udp	xns-auth	XNS Authentication
57/tcp, udp		Any private terminal access
58/tcp, udp	xns-mail	XNS Mail
59/tcp, udp		Any private file service
60/tcp, udp		Unassigned
61/tcp, udp	ni-mail	NI MAIL
62/tcp, udp	acas	ACA Services
63/tcp, udp	via-ftp	VIA Systems-FTP
64/tcp, udp	covia	Communications Integrator (CI)
65/tcp, udp	tacacs-ds	TACACS-Database Service

Decimal	Keyword	Description and Microsoft Networking Alias
66/tcp, udp	sql*net	Oracle SQL*NET
67/tcp, udp	bootpc	DHCP/BOOTP Protocol Server
68/tcp, udp	bootpc	DHCP/BOOTP Protocol Server
69/tcp, udp	tftp	Trivial File Transfer
70/tcp, udp	gopher	Gopher
71/tcp, udp	netrjs-1	Remote Job Service
72/tcp, udp	netrjs-2	Remote Job Service
73/tcp, udp	netrjs-3	Remote Job Service
74/tcp, udp	netrjs-4	Remote Job Service
75/udp		Any private dial out service
76/tcp, udp		Unassigned
77/tcp, udp		Any private RJE service; alias=netrjs
78/tcp, udp	vettcp	Vettcp
79/tcp, udp	finger	Finger
80/tcp, udp	www	World Wide Web HTTP
81/tcp, udp	hosts2-ns	HOSTS2 Name Server
82/tcp, udp	xfer	XFER Utility
83/tcp, udp	mit-ml-dev	MIT ML Device
84/tcp, udp	ctf	Common Trace Facility
85/tcp, udp	mit-ml-dev	MIT ML Device
86/tcp, udp	mfcobol	Micro Focus Cobol
87/tcp, udp		Any private terminal link; alias=ttylink
88/tcp, udp	kerberos	Kerberos
89/tcp, udp	su-mit-tg	SU/MIT Telnet Gateway

Decimal	Keyword	Description and Microsoft Networking Alias
90/tcp, udp		Default WINS name server destination port
91/tcp, udp	mit-dov	MIT Dover Spooler
92/tcp, udp	npp	Network Printing Protocol
93/tcp, udp	dcp	Device Control Protocol
94/tcp, udp	objcall	Tivoli Object Dispatcher
95/tcp, udp	supdup	SUPDUP
96/tcp, udp	dixie	DIXIE Protocol Specification
97/tcp, udp	swift-rvf	Swift Remote Virtual File Protocol
98/tcp, udp	tacnews	TAC News
99/tcp, udp	metagram	Metagram Relay
100/tcp	newacct	[unauthorized use]
101/tcp, udp	hostname	NIC Host Name Server; alias=hostname
102/tcp, udp	iso-tsap	ISO-TSAP
103/tcp, udp	gppitnp	Genesis Point-to-Point Trans Net; alias=webster
104/tcp, udp	acr-nema	ACR-NEMA Digital Imag. & Comm. 300
105/tcp, udp	csnet-ns	Mailbox Name Nameserver
106/tcp, udp	3com-tsmux	3COM-TSMUX
107/tcp, udp	rtelnet	Remote Telnet Service
108/tcp, udp	snagas	SNA Gateway Access Server
109/tcp, udp	pop2	Post Office Protocol - Version 2; alias=postoffice

Decimal	Keyword	Description and Microsoft Networking Alias
110/tcp, udp	pop3	Post Office Protocol - Version 3; alias=postoffice
111/tcp, udp	sunrpc	SUN Remote Procedure Call
112/tcp, udp	mcidas	McIDAS Data Transmission Protocol
113/tcp, udp	auth	Authentication Service; alias=authentication
114/tcp, udp	audionews	Audio News Multicast
115/tcp, udp	sftp	Simple File Transfer Protocol
116/tcp, udp	ansanotify	ANSA REX Notify
117/tcp, udp	uucp-path	UUCP Path Service
118/tcp, udp	sqlserv	SQL Services
119/tcp, udp	nntp	Network News Transfer Protocol; alias=usenet
120/tcp, udp	cfdptkt	CFDPTKT
121/tcp, udp	erpc	Encore Expedited Remote Pro.Call
122/tcp, udp	smakynet	SMAKYNET
123/tcp, udp	ntp	Network Time Protocol; alias=ntpd ntp
124/tcp, udp	ansatrader	ANSA REX Trader
125/tcp, udp	locus-map	Locus PC-Interface Net Map Server
126/tcp, udp	unitary	Unisys Unitary Login
127/tcp, udp	locus-con	Locus PC-Interface Conn Server
128/tcp, udp	gss-xlicen	GSS X License Verification

G

Decimal	Keyword	Description and Microsoft Networking Alias
129/tcp, udp	pwdgen	Password Generator Protocol
130/tcp, udp	cisco-fna	Cisco FNATIVE
131/tcp, udp	cisco-tna	Cisco TNATIVE
132/tcp, udp	cisco-sys	Cisco SYSMAINT
133/tcp, udp	statsrv	Statistics Service
134/tcp, udp	ingres-net	INGRES-NET Service
135/tcp, udp	loc-srv	Location Service
136/tcp, udp	profile	PROFILE Naming System
137/tcp, udp	netbios-ns	NetBIOS Name Service
138/tcp, udp	netbios-dgm	NetBIOS Datagram Service
139/tcp, udp	netbios-ssn	NetBIOS Session Service
140/tcp, udp	emfis-data	EMFIS Data Service
141/tcp, udp	emfis-cntl	EMFIS Control Service
142/tcp, udp	bl-idm	Britton-Lee IDM
143/tcp, udp	imap2	Interim Mail Access Protocol v2
144/tcp, udp	news	NewS; alias=news
145/tcp, udp	uaac	UAAC Protocol
146/tcp, udp	iso-tp0	ISO-IP0
147/tcp, udp	iso-ip	ISO-IP
148/tcp, udp	cronus	CRONUS-SUPPORT
149/tcp, udp	aed-512	AED 512 Emulation Service
150/tcp, udp	sql-net	SQL-NET
151/tcp, udp	hems	HEMS

G

Decimal	Keyword	Description and Microsoft Networking Alias
152/tcp, udp	bftp	Background File Transfer Program
153/tcp, udp	sgmp	SGMP; alias=sgmp
154/tcp, udp	netsc-prod	NETSC
155/tcp, udp	netsc-dev	NETSC
156/tcp, udp	sqlsrv	SQL Service
157/tcp, udp	knet-cmp	KNET/VM Command/Message Protocol
158/tcp, udp	pcmail-srv	PCMail Server; alias=repository
159/tcp, udp	nss-routing	NSS-Routing
160/tcp, udp	sgmp-traps	SGMP-TRAPS
161/tcp, udp	snmp	SNMP; alias=snmp
162/tcp, udp	snmptrap	SNMPTRAP
163/tcp, udp	cmip-man	CMIP/TCP Manager
164/tcp, udp	cmip-agent	CMIP/TCP Agent
165/tcp, udp	xns-courier	Xerox
166/tcp, udp	s-net	Sirius Systems
167/tcp, udp	namp	NAMP
168/tcp, udp	rsvd	RSVD
169/tcp, udp	send	SEND
170/tcp, udp	print-srv	Network PostScript
171/tcp, udp	multiplex	Network Innovations Multiplex
172/tcp, udp	cl/1	Network Innovations CL/1
173/tcp, udp	xyplex-mux	Xyplex
174/tcp, udp	mailq	MAILQ

Decimal	Keyword	Description and Microsoft Networking Alias
175/tcp, udp	vmnet	VMNET
176/tcp, udp	genrad-mux	GENRAD-MUX
177/tcp, udp	xdmcp	X Display Manager Control Protocol
178/tcp, udp	nextstep	NextStep Window Server
179/tcp, udp	bgp	Border Gateway Protocol
180/tcp, udp	ris	Intergraph
181/tcp, udp	unify	Unify
182/tcp, udp	audit	Unisys Audit SITP
183/tcp, udp	ocbinder	OCBinder
184/tcp, udp	ocserver	OCServer
185/tcp, udp	remote-kis	Remote-KIS
186/tcp, udp	kis	KIS Protocol
187/tcp, udp	aci	Application Communication Interface
188/tcp, udp	mumps	Plus Five's MUMPS
189/tcp, udp	qft	Queued File Transport
190/tcp, udp	gacp	Gateway Access Control Protocol
191/tcp, udp	prospero	Prospero
192/tcp, udp	osu-nms	OSU Network Monitoring System
193/tcp, udp	srmp	Spider Remote Monitoring Protocol
194/tcp, udp	irc	Internet Relay Chat Protocol

Decimal	Keyword	Description and Microsoft Networking Alias
195/tcp, udp	dn6-nlm-aud	DNSIX Network Level Module Audit
196/tcp, udp	dn6-smm-red	DNSIX Session Mgt Module Audit Redir
197/tcp, udp	dls	Directory Location Service
198/tcp, udp	dls-mon	Directory Location Service Monitor
199/tcp, udp	smux	SMUX
200/tcp, udp	src	IBM System Resource Controller
201/tcp, udp	at-rtmp	AppleTalk Routing Maintenance
202/tcp, udp	at-nbp	AppleTalk Name Binding
203/tcp, udp	at-3	AppleTalk Unused
204/tcp, udp	at-echo	AppleTalk Echo
205/tcp, udp	at-5	AppleTalk Unused
206/tcp, udp	at-zis	AppleTalk Zone Information
207/tcp, udp	at-7	AppleTalk Unused
208/tcp, udp	at-8	AppleTalk Unused
209/tcp, udp	tam	Trivial Authenticated Mail Protocol
210/tcp, udp	z39.50	ANSI Z39.50
211/tcp, udp	914c/g	Texas Instruments 914C/G Terminal
212/tcp, udp	anet	ATEXSSTR
213/tcp, udp	ipx	IPX
214/tcp, udp	vmpwscs	VM PWSCS

Decimal	Keyword	Description and Microsoft Networking Alias
215/tcp, udp	softpc	Insignia Solutions
216/tcp, udp	atls	Access Technology License Server
217/tcp, udp	dbase	dBASE UNIX
218/tcp, udp	mpp	Netix Message Posting Protocol
219/tcp, udp	uarps	Unisys ARPs
220/tcp, udp	imap3	Interactive Mail Access Protocol v3
221/tcp, udp	fln-spx	Berkeley rlogind with SPX auth
222/tcp, udp	fsh-spx	Berkeley rshd with SPX auth
223/tcp, udp	cdc	Certificate Distribution Center
224-241		Reserved
243/tcp, udp	sur-meas	Survey Measurement
245/tcp, udp	link	LINK
246/tcp, udp	dsp3270	Display Systems Protocol
247-255		Reserved
345/tcp, udp	pawserv	Perf Analysis Workbench
346/tcp, udp	zserv	Zebra server
347/tcp, udp	fatserv	Fatmen Server
371/tcp, udp	clearcase	Clearcase
372/tcp, udp	ulistserv	UNIX Listserv
373/tcp, udp	legent-1	Legent Corporation
374/tcp, udp	legent-2	Legent Corporation

Decimal	Keyword	Description and Microsoft Networking Alias
512/tcp	exec	Remote process execution; authentication performed using passwords and UNIX login names
512/udp	biff	Used by mail system to notify users of new mail received; currently receives messages only from processes on the same computer; alias=comsat
513/tcp	login	Remote login like telnet; automatic authentication performed based on privileged port numbers and distributed databases that identify "authentication domains"
513/udp	who	Maintains databases showing who's logged in to machines on a local net and the load average of the machine; alias=whod
514/tcp	cmd	Like exec, but automatic authentication is performed as for login server
514/udp	syslog	
515/tcp, udp	printer	Spooler; alias=spooler

Decimal	Keyword	Description and Microsoft Networking Alias
517/tcp, udp	talk	Like tenex link, but across
518/tcp, udp	ntalk	
519/tcp, udp	utime	Unixtime
520/tcp	efs	Extended file name server
520/udp	router	Local routing process (on site); uses variant of Xerox NS routing information protocol; alias=router routed
525/tcp, udp	timed	Timeserver
526/tcp, udp	tempo	Newdate
530/tcp, udp	courier	RPC
531/tcp	conference	Chat
531/udp	rvd-control	MIT disk
532/tcp, udp	netnews	Readnews
533/tcp, udp	netwall	For emergency broadcasts
540/tcp, udp	uucp	Uucpd
543/tcp, udp	klogin	
544/tcp, udp	kshell	Krcmd; alias=cmd
550/tcp, udp	new-rwho	New-who
555/tcp, udp	dsf	
556/tcp, udp	remotefs	Rfs server; alias=rfs_server rfs
560/tcp, udp	rmonitor	Rmonitor
561/tcp, udp	monitor	
562/tcp, udp	chshell	Chcmd
564/tcp, udp	9pfs	Plan 9 file service

G

Decimal	Keyword	Description and Microsoft Networking Alias
565/tcp, udp	whoami	Whoami
570/tcp, udp	meter	Demon
571/tcp, udp	meter	Udemon
600/tcp, udp	ipcserver	Sun IPC server
607/tcp, udp	nqs	Nqs
666/tcp, udp	mdqs	
704/tcp, udp	elcsd	Errlog copy/server daemon
740/tcp, udp	netcp	NETscout Control Protocol
741/tcp, udp	netgw	NetGW
742/tcp, udp	netrcs	Network-based Rev. Cont. Sys.
744/tcp, udp	flexlm	Flexible License Manager
747/tcp, udp	fujitsu-dev	Fujitsu Device Control
748/tcp, udp	ris-cm	Russell Info Sci Calendar Manager
749/tcp, udp	kerberos-adm	Kerberos administration
750/tcp	rfile	Kerberos authentication; alias=kdc
750/udp	loadav	
751/tcp, udp	pump	Kerberos authentication
752/tcp, udp	qrh	Kerberos password server
753/tcp, udp	rrh	Kerberos userreg server
754/tcp, udp	tell	Send; Kerberos slave propagation
758/tcp, udp	nlogin	

Decimal	Keyword	Description and Microsoft Networking Alias
759/tcp, udp	con	
760/tcp, udp	ns	
761/tcp, udp	rxe	
762/tcp, udp	quotad	
763/tcp, udp	cycleserv	
764/tcp, udp	omserv	
765/tcp, udp	webster	
767/tcp, udp	phonebook	Phone
769/tcp, udp	vid	
770/tcp, udp	cadlock	
771/tcp, udp	rtip	
772/tcp, udp	cycleserv2	
773/tcp	submit	
773/udp	notify	
774/tcp	rpasswd	
774/udp	acmaint_dbd	
775/tcp	entomb	
775/udp	acmaint_transd	
776/tcp, udp	wpages	
780/tcp, udp	wpgs	
781/tcp, udp	hp-collector	HP performance data collector
782/tcp, udp	hp-managed-node	HP performance data managed node
783/tcp, udp	hp-alarm-mgr	HP performance data alarm manager
800/tcp, udp	mdbs_daemon	
801/tcp, udp	device	

Decimal	Keyword	Description and Microsoft Networking Alias
888/tcp	erlogin	Login and environment passing
996/tcp, udp	xtreelic	XTREE License Server
997/tcp, udp	maitrd	
998/tcp	busboy	
998/udp	puparp	
999/tcp	garcon	
999/udp	applix	Applix ac
999/tcp, udp	puprouter	
1000/tcp	cadlock	
1000/udp	ock	

G

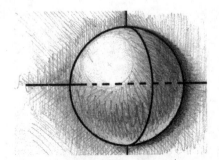

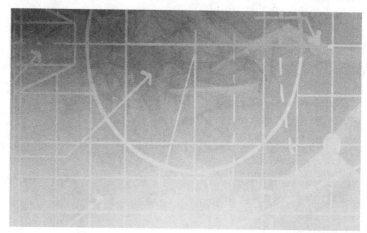

Index

D

E

F

I

Z